W9-AJQ-629

# WELCOME TO LONDON

History and tradition greet you at every turn in London; it's also one of the coolest, most modern cities in the world. If London contained only landmarks such as Westminster Abbey and Buckingham Palace, it would still rank as one of the world's great destinations, but Britain's capital is much more. People come to glimpse the royals and stop by hot galleries; to take in theater and trendy shops; to sample tea and scones or cutting-edge cuisine. When you need a break from the action, pop into a pub, relax in a park—or take a walk and make London your own.

## TOP REASONS TO GO

★ **Architectural Icons:** The Tower of London and Big Ben are quintessential London.

★ **Art Museums:** From the National Gallery to the Tate Modern, a visual feast awaits.

★ **Top Theater:** Whether it's Shakespeare or avant-garde drama, the play's the thing.

★ **City of Villages:** Unique neighborhoods from Mayfair to the East End invite discovery.

★ **Shopping:** Fun markets, famous flagship department stores, chic boutiques.

★ **Parks and Squares:** Distinctive green spaces large and small are civilized retreats.

# Fodor's LONDON

**Publisher:** Amanda D'Acierno, *Senior Vice President*

**Design:** Tina Malaney, *Associate Art Director*; Erica Cuoco, *Production Designer*

**Photography:** Jennifer Arnow, *Senior Photo Editor*; Mary Robnett, *Photo Researcher*

**Maps:** Rebecca Baer, *Senior Map Editor*; David Lindroth, Mark Stroud (Moon Street Cartography), *Cartographers*

**Production:** Angela L. McLean, *Senior Production Manager*

**Sales:** Jacqueline Lebow, *Sales Director*

**Marketing & Publicity:** Heather Dalton, *Marketing Director*; Katherine Punia, *Publicity Director*

**Business & Operations:** Susan Livingston, *Senior Vice President, Strategic Business Planning*; Sue Daulton, *Vice President, Operations*

**Fodors.com:** Megan Bell, *Executive Director, Revenue & Business Development*; Yasmin Marinaro, *Senior Director, Marketing & Partnerships*

Copyright © 2017 by Fodor's Travel, a division of Penguin Random House LLC

**Writers:** Jo Caird, Kate Hughes, Jack Jewers, James O'Neill, Ellin Stein, Alex Wijeratna

**Editors:** Amanda Sadlowski (lead editor), Penny Phenix, Kristan Schiller

**Production Editor:** Elyse Rozelle

32nd edition

ISBN 978-1-101-87995-5

ISSN 0149-631X

## SPECIAL SALES

This book is available at special discounts for bulk purchases for sales promotions or premiums. For more information, e-mail specialmarkets@penguinrandomhouse.com.

PRINTED IN THE UNITED STATES OF AMERICA

10 9 8 7 6 5 4 3 2 1

# Fodor's

# LONDON

# CONTENTS

# CONTENTS

## MAPS

# ABOUT THIS GUIDE

## Fodor's Ratings

Everything in this guide is worth doing—we don't cover what isn't—but exceptional sights, hotels, and restaurants are recognized with additional accolades. **Fodor's**Choice★ indicates our top recommendations, and **Best Bets** call attention to notable hotels and restaurants in various categories. Care to nominate a new place? Visit Fodors.com/contact-us.

## Trip Costs

We list prices wherever possible to help you budget well. Hotel and restaurant price categories from $ to $$$$ are noted alongside each recommendation. For hotels, we include the lowest cost of a standard double room in high season. For restaurants, we cite the average price of a main course at dinner or, if dinner isn't served, at lunch. For attractions, we always list adult admission fees; discounts are usually available for children, students, and senior citizens.

## Hotels

Our local writers vet every hotel to recommend the best overnights in each price category, from budget to expensive. Unless otherwise specified, you can expect private bath, phone, and TV in your room. For expanded hotel reviews visit Fodors.com.

| Top Picks | Hotels & |
| --- | --- |
| ★ **Fodor's**Choice | **Restaurants** |
| | ⊞ Hotel |
| **Listings** | ↵ Number of |
| ⊠ Address | rooms |
| ⊠ Branch address | ℞◎ Meal plans |
| ☎ Telephone | ✕ Restaurant |
| 🖷 Fax | ⌕ Reservations |
| ⊕ Website | 🏛 Dress code |
| ✍ E-mail | ⊟ No credit cards |
| 🎫 Admission fee | $ Price |
| ☉ Open/closed times | **Other** |
| Ⓜ Subway | ⇨ See also |
| ✛ Directions or Map coordinates | ☞ Take note |
| | 🏌 Golf facilities |

## Restaurants

Unless we state otherwise, restaurants are open for lunch and dinner daily. We mention dress code only when there's a specific requirement and reservations only when they're essential or not accepted.

## Credit Cards

The hotels and restaurants in this guide typically accept credit cards. If not, we'll say so.

# EUGENE FODOR

Hungarian-born Eugene Fodor (1905–91) began his travel career as an interpreter on a French cruise ship. The experience inspired him to write *On the Continent* (1936), the first guidebook to receive annual updates and discuss a country's way of life as well as its sights. Fodor later joined the U.S. Army and worked for the OSS in World War II. After the war, he kept up his intelligence work while expanding his guidebook series. During the Cold War, many guides were written by fellow agents who understood the value of insider information. Today's guides continue Fodor's legacy by providing travelers with timely coverage, insider tips, and cultural context.

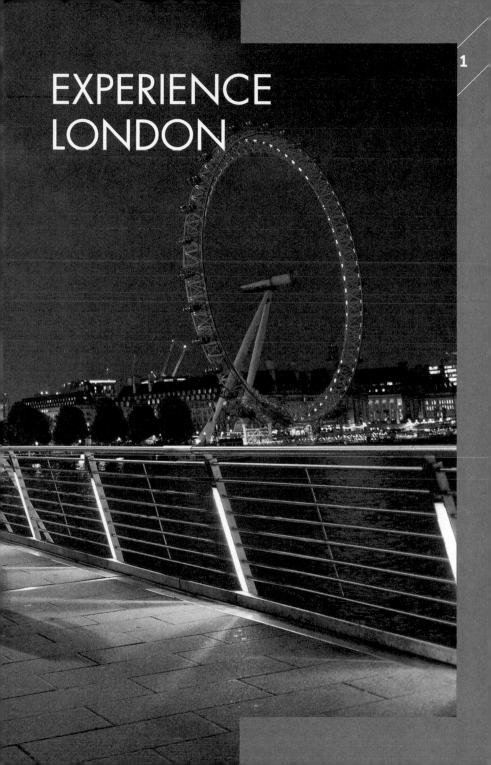

# EXPERIENCE LONDON

# LONDON TODAY

Welcome to London—variously described by great poets and statesmen as "modern Babylon," "Unreal City," "enormous Babel," and ". . . the City of the free." Indeed, majestic London's always been a city in flux, and these days it's hard to turn a corner without stumbling into some work-in-progress crater so vast you can only imagine what was there before. This latest wave of development was turbocharged as the city became a safe haven during the global economic crisis. New neighborhoods continually rise up and burst to the fore—a visit to Shoreditch at the eastern edge of The City, for example, should provide you with your quotient of London hipness. The creative fervor that swirls through London like a fog shows up in DIY galleries, miniboutiques, pop-up restaurants, nighttime street-food markets, and slick hipster hotels.

Discovery takes a bit of work, however. Modern-day London still largely reflects its medieval layout, a willfully difficult tangle of streets and alleys. Even Londoners get lost in their own city. But London's bewildering street pattern will be a plus for the visitor who wants to experience its indefinable historic atmosphere. London is a walker's city and will repay every moment you spend exploring on foot.

Although many images are seared on your consciousness before you arrive—the guards at Buckingham Palace, big red doubledecker buses, Big Ben, and the River Thames—tide or time does not stand still in this ancient and yet gloriously modern city. Instead, "London, the buskin'd stage . . . The heart, the centre of the living world!" is in permanent revolution, and evolves, organically, mysteriously, historically through time.

## New Architecture

London has loosened its collar and showcases some spectacular new architecture, with the Shard providing a pyramid-shape beacon for the city. With the exceptions of Canary Wharf, the former Swiss Re HQ ("the Gherkin"), the Lloyd's of London building, and the London Eye, London's skyline has traditionally been low-key, with little of the sky-scraping swagger of, say, Shanghai or Manhattan. But a spectacular crop of soaring new office towers with wonderful monikers—the Quill, the Shard, the Pinnacle, the Cheese Grater, the Nutmeg, and the Walkie-Talkie—is revitalizing the city skyline. With an astonishing 263 new skyscrapers being built or planned, opinions are split. Not everyone loves Renzo Piano's jagged pointy Shard and its 95-floor cloud-piercing "Vertical City" at London Bridge, which has stunning viewing galleries on the 68th, 69th, and 72nd floors. However, once you whiz up and visit it, your take on the wonderful immensity of London is transformed forever.

## Immigration

The nationalities keep coming, and London now holds the crown as one of *the* most cosmopolitan cities on Earth. White Britons are in the minority for the first time (according to the latest census), representing 45% of London's population of 8.2 million, while Asians make up 18%, black Londoners 13%, European "White Others" 13%, and mixed-race residents at 5%. But London's always been a city of immigrants—from the 10th century, the city had Cymric Brythons, Belgae and Gauls, East Saxons, and Mercians, Danes, Swedes, and Norwegians, plus Jutes, Franks, and Angles.

## Arts and Culture

Have you picked up a free copy of the daily London *Evening Standard* newspaper at a Tube stop lately? They're stuffed with a smorgasbord of world-class shows, plays, performances, readings, recitals, concerts, fashion follies, lectures, talks, tastings, cabarets, auctions, and blockbuster art exhibitions. Whether it's wacky contemporary art and religious Old Masters paintings at the Frieze London art fair in Regents Park or a nighttime street food truck jam in a derelict car park in Shoreditch, London is one of the most happening places on the planet.

## Public Transportation

You'll notice that the public transport's gotten more frequent and more reliable. While London's traffic often seems more chaotic than New York City's, the Congestion Charge, an £11.50-per-day fee imposed on vehicles entering central London during the day, has reduced both traffic and pollution. Mercifully, the Underground now runs 24 hours a day on weekends on six key "Night Tube" lines, and massive tunneling continues apace on London's flagship, high-speed Cross Rail underground railway line, which includes new interchanges at Paddington, Tottenham Court Road, and Farringdon stations, slated to open in 2018. Meanwhile, don't miss London's bike-sharing program, Santander Cycles, of Boris Bikes, as it's known locally (named after flamboyant former London mayor Boris Johnson). With 10,245 bikes available at 718 docking stations, you'll find (after paying £2 for a 24-hour pass) that the first half hour's free, and each additional 30 minutes is £2.

## New Upgrades and Exhibits

We really shouldn't begrudge it, but some of London's top cultural attractions seem to be caught in a post–Cold War upgrade arms race and are investing heavily in new galleries, exhibits, restorations, expansions, and assorted shiny new bells and whistles. Look, then, for the major £50 million major upgrade of the National Theatre, which includes a series of scrubbed-up Brutalist public spaces, or enjoy the recently sprung-to-life Granary Square at King's Cross, where 1,080 choreographed water jets are the buzzy area's answer to an Italian piazza. Tate Modern has added a quirky brick pyramid to its front, but it's really the cash-rich private art galleries like the U.S.-based Gagosian in Mayfair or Damien Hirst's massive red-brick Newport Street Gallery in Vauxhall that are now setting the pace.

# WHAT'S WHERE

*The following numbers refer to chapters.*

**2 Westminster, St James's, and Royal London.** This is the place to embrace your inner tourist. Snap pictures of the mounted Horse Guards, watch kids clambering onto the monumental bronze lions in Trafalgar Square, and visit stacks of world-class art in the fantastic national galleries. Brave the crowds to peruse historic Westminster Abbey and its ancient narrative in stone.

**3 Mayfair and Marylebone.** You may not have the wallet for London's most prestigious shops, but remember window-shopping in Mayfair is free. Meanwhile, chic boutiques in Marylebone are a refreshing change from gaudy Oxford Street a few blocks south.

**4 Soho and Covent Garden.** More sophisticated than seedy these days, the heart of London puts Theatreland, strip joints, Chinatown, burger boîtes, and the trendiest of film studios side by side. Hold tight through the hectic hordes in Leicester Square. Covent Garden's historic piazza is one of the most raffishly enjoyable parts of the city.

**5 Bloomsbury and Holborn.** Once the bluestocking and intellectual center of London, elegant 17th- and 18th-century Bloomsbury is now also a mixed business district. The British Museum has enough amazing objets d'art and artifacts to keep you busy for a month; the Law Courts, the University of London, and quaint Lamb's Conduit Street are worth a gander. Clerkenwell, meanwhile, is a hotbed of history and culinary invention.

**6 The City.** London's Wall Street might be the oldest part of the capital, but thanks to new skyscrapers and a sleek Millennium Bridge, it also looks like the newest. History fans won't be short-changed, however: head for St. Paul's Cathedral, Tower Bridge, and the Tower of London.

**7 East London.** Once famed for the noxious 19th-century slums immortalized by Charles Dickens and Jack the Ripper, today the area is a fulcrum of London's contemporary art scene and a trendy party zone. For spit-and-sawdust sensations of market London on the weekend, dive headfirst into the eclectic wares at Spitalfields, Brick Lane (popular for Bangladeshi curry houses and 24-hour Jewish bagel bakeries), and Columbia Road's much-loved early-morning flower market.

# WHAT'S WHERE

**8 South of the Thames.**
The Southbank Centre—
including the National
Theatre and Royal Festival
Hall, the Haywood Gallery,
the Purcell Room and Queen
Elizabeth Hall, plus nearby
Shakespeare's Globe and
Tate Modern—showcases the
capital's crowning artistic
glories. Or put it all in aerial
perspective from the 72nd
floor of the Shard.

**9 Kensington, Chelsea,
Knightsbridge, and Belgravia.** Although the many
boutiques of King's Road have
lost much of their heady '60s
swagger, the free museums
are as awe-inspiring as ever.
Kensington High Street is
slightly more affordable
than King's Road; otherwise,
flash your cash at London's
snazziest department stores,
Harrods and Harvey Nichols.

**10 Notting Hill and
Bayswater.** North of
Kensington, around Portobello
Road, Notting Hill Gate is a
trendsetting couple of square
miles of multiethnic finds,
photographers' galleries,
bookshops, fashionable
boutiques, and hip restaurants.
Nearby, Bayswater mixes
eclectic ethnic fashions,
organic fresh food shops, and
gaudy Chinese restaurants.

**11 Regent's Park and
Hampstead.** Surrounded
by elegant "terraces"—in
truth, mansions as big
as palaces—designed by
19th-century architect John
Nash, Regent's Park is a
Regency extravaganza. The
nearby hilltop villages of
Hampstead and Primrose Hill
attract starry residents like
Kate Moss and Jude Law.

**12 Greenwich.** The Royal
Observatory, Sir Christopher
Wren's architecture, the Old
Royal Naval College, *Cutty
Sark,* and the Prime Meridian
all add up to one of the
best Thames-side excursions
beyond the cut-and-thrust of
central London.

**13 The Thames Upstream.**
As an idyllic retreat from the
city, stroll around London's
historic gardens and enjoy
the stately homes of Kew,
Richmond, and Putney. Better
yet, take a gentle river cruise
and end up at the famous
Hampton Court Maze.

# LONDON PLANNER

### When to Go

The heaviest tourist season runs April–September, with another peak around Christmas. Late spring is the time to see the Royal Parks and gardens at their freshest; fall brings autumnal beauty and fewer people. Summer gives the best chance of good weather, although the crowds are intense. Winter can be dismal—it's dark by 5—but all the theaters, concerts, and exhibitions go full-speed ahead, and Christmas lights bring a major touch of festive magic. Weather-wise, winter is cold and wet with occasional light snow and spring is colorful and fair. June through August can range from a total washout to a long hot summer and anything in between. Autumn ranges from warm to cool to mild. It's impossible to forecast London weather but you can be certain that it will not be what you expect.

### When Not to Go

The October "half-term," when schools in the capital take a break for a week or two, results in most attractions being overrun by children. The start of August can be a very busy time, and hot weather makes Tube travel a sweltering and sweaty nightmare. Air-conditioning is far from the norm in London, even in hotels; although it rarely tops 90°F, it can feel much hotter. And festive shopping in central London just before Christmas borders on the insane.

### Getting Around

London is, above all, a walker's city, and will repay every moment you spend exploring on foot. But if you're in a rush, there are other options. By far the easiest and most practical way to get around is on the Underground, known as the Tube. Trains run daily from early morning past midnight during the week and 24 hours on weekends on six key lines. Frequent all-cash-free buses crisscross London and often have their own lanes, which only buses and black taxis can use. They are a great way to see London, but navigation can be more complicated than the Tube's; scan the route posted at the bus stop and check the number and destination on the front of the bus, and ask the bus conductor if in doubt.

Put a deposit on an Oyster card for £5, which will allow you to use London's transport—including bus, Tube, tram, DLR, London Overground, and most National Rail services in London—at a lower cost than using paper tickets. The plastic card can be topped up as often as you want, and your £5 deposit will be reimbursed when you hand the card back. Alternatively, buy a Travelcard pass (from £12 per day in the central Zones 1 and 2), which offers unlimited use of the Tube, buses, and the commuter rail. Check ⊕ *www.tfl.gov.uk* for details on ongoing Tube renovations.

⇨ *For further details on transport around London, see Travel Smart.*

### Addresses

Central London and its surrounding districts are divided into 32 boroughs (33, counting The City of London). More useful for navigating, however, are the subdivisions of London into postal districts. Throughout the guide we've given the abbreviated postal code for most listings. The first one or two letters give the location: N means north, NW means northwest, and so on. Don't expect the numbering to be logical, however. (You won't, for example, find W2 next to W3.) The general rule is that the lower numbers, such as W1 or SW1, are closest to the city center.

| WHAT IT COSTS | | |
| --- | --- | --- |
| | IN LONDON | IN NEW YORK |
| Pair of theater tickets | £40–£100 | $70–$240 |
| Museum admission | Usually free; sometimes £4–£17 | Usually $8–$35; rarely free |
| Fast-food value meal | £7 | $8 |
| Tall latte | £3.90 | $4 |
| Pint of beer in a pub | £4.10 and up | $7 and up |
| 1-mile taxi ride before tip | £8.50 | $7 |
| Subway ride within city center | Up to £8.80 without Oyster or Travelcard | $2.75 |

### London Hours

The usual shop hours are Monday–Saturday 9–6 and Sunday 11–5. Around Oxford Street, Kensington High Street, and Knightsbridge, hours are 9:30–6, with late-night hours (until 7:30 or 8) on Wednesday or Thursday.

Many businesses are closed on Sunday and national ("bank") holidays, except in the center, where most open 10–4. Banks are open weekdays 9:30–4:30; offices are generally open 9–6.

The major national museums and galleries are open daily, mainly 10–6, and often they're open late one night a week.

### Street Smarts

London is generally a safe and friendly place, but like any large city it's wise to take a few precautions. Make sure your possessions are properly insured before you travel, and don't carry all your valuables around with you. Carry as much cash as you'll need that day, and leave the rest in your hotel safe. Don't use ATM machines after dark, avoid isolated or poorly lighted spots, and try not to travel around on your own late at night. Keep bags zipped up and close to you in the Tube, on buses, and at pubs and other crowded places. Never leave bags unattended in any public place—it may be stolen or seen as a security threat. Finally, use black cabs and don't get into a minicab on your own.

### Saving Money

There's no getting around it: London can be as expensive as—or even *more* expensive than—New York, Paris, or any other large global city. So it's best to accept this fact in advance and factor it into your vacation planning, tailoring outings and trips to your interests—and your budget.

Often, booking in advance, harnessing cut-price and low-season deals, and taking advantage of Internet specials for flights and hotel rooms can cut down on costs. London is also great at offering things for free (particularly the museums), and the quality of the culture, entertainment, relaxation, and general fun to be had in the city means that if you target your spending wisely, you'll go home penny-pinched but deeply satisfied.

# LONDON TOP ATTRACTIONS

## Westminster Abbey
**(A)** The front towers of this soaring early–English Gothic abbey stand around the tombs of British monarchs and the great men and women who built Britain. The Abbey plays a preeminent role in the spiritual life of the nation, from the coronation of 38 sovereigns to royal weddings and state funerals.

## Buckingham Palace
**(B)** Not the largest or prettiest royal residence, the palace at the heart of London is nonetheless a must-see. The opulence of the 19 State Rooms open to the public are jaw-dropping, and don't overlook the collection of Old Master paintings and gilded state carriages at the Queen's Gallery.

## Tower of London
**(C)** The 900-year-old Tower is London at its historic, gory best. Every brick tells a grisly story, and the axe blows and personal fortunes that have risen and fallen within this 20-towered mini-city provide an inexhaustible supply of intrigue.

## St. Paul's Cathedral
**(D)** Sir Christopher Wren's neoclassical masterpiece never fails to take one's breath away. Climb the enormous 360-foot dome, one of the world's finest and largest, to experience the acoustics of the Whispering Gallery, and higher still to the Golden Gallery for far-reaching panoramas across London.

## British Museum
**(E)** The oldest public museum in the world has been wowing visitors to London since 1753. Its unrivaled 8-million-strong collection spans all recorded history, including the 4th-century BC Egyptian mummies, the Elgin Marbles, the Rosetta Stone, and the Anglo-Saxon warrior treasures of Sutton Hoo.

## Shakespeare's Globe

**(F)** You can catch a Shakespeare play any evening in London. But standing in the open-air "pit" or yard with the "groundlings" on a floor of sawdust watching King Lear in a scrupulously re-created English oak version of the original Tudor theater for which Shakespeare wrote is a genuine thrill.

## Tate Modern

**(G)** The world's most visited modern art gallery, Tate Modern is a hip and massively successful feature of London's artistic landscape. Passing wry judgment on the latest exhibit inside the giant Turbine Hall at this former Bankside Power Station is a civic duty among art-loving Londoners.

## Royal Parks

**(H)** A whopping 25% of London is parkland, so it is mighty hard to choose between St. James's Park (those fairy-tale views), Kensington Gardens (the beloved *Peter Pan* statue), Hyde Park (pedalos on the Serpentine Lido), and Regent's Park's fragrant rose gardens.

## Hampton Court Palace

**(I)** Henry VIII's palace has a majestic Tudor-turreted charm, augmented by Sir Christopher Wren's touch, and a picturesque Thames side location, all of which make for a great day out. Not even dour Lord Protector of the Realm Oliver Cromwell, who moved here in 1653, could resist its charms.

## National Gallery

**(J)** There are enough world-class paintings—from Da Vinci to Valázquez—at this collection of 2,300 works to have the most indifferent art enthusiast drool with delight. Note the raised front entrance and its great photo op: Big Ben and Nelson's Column framed by Trafalgar Square.

# LONDON'S ROYAL LEGACY

### The Rocky Monarchy

From medieval castles and keeps, to royal parks, palaces, pageants, ceremonies and processions, London has had a tumultuous and sometimes bloody royal history, which can still be glimpsed or encountered at practically every turn. London has been the royal capital of England since 1066, when William the Conqueror began the tradition of royal coronations at Westminster Abbey. Every reigning monarch since then—including Richard I (the "Coeur de Lion") in 1189, to the current Queen Elizabeth II in 1953—has been crowned at the Abbey, and many of England's illustrious (and sometimes downright notorious) kings and queens have left a legacy or their majestic mark on the city. Many of the finest places have royal associations: William I subjugated London with the imposing Tower of London; Henry VIII hunted deer at Hampton Court; Elizabeth I enjoyed bear baiting in Southwark; and Charles I was publicly executed on Whitehall. Tyrannical but weak monarchs like King John (1199–1216) granted the City of London more powers under Magna Carta, while the first "Parliament" sat at the royal Palace of Westminster in 1240 under Henry III. The Tudors, however, rarely brooked dissent: Elizabeth I's half-sister, "Bloody" Mary I (1553–58), burned heretic Protestant bishops at the stake, and traitors were hung, drawn, and quartered, with their heads stuck on pikes on London Bridge.

### A Cultural Renaissance

From 1558 to 1601, peace under Elizabeth I ("the Virgin Queen") led to a cultural renaissance and the great flowering of English theater, poetry, letters, and drama, centered on Shakespeare's Globe and the open-air playhouses of Southwark. Charles I was later captured by the formidable Puritan Oliver Cromwell during the English Civil War, and beheaded on a freezing day outside Banqueting House in 1649. Although the Interregnum lasted only 16 years (outlawing simple pleasures, such as dancing and theater), the Restoration of Charles II in 1660 and subsequent monarchs including the Dutch Protestant William III and Mary II—who moved into Kensington Palace, now the current home of the Duke and Duchess of Cambridge—and the House of Hanover's four Georgian kings and later Queen Victoria saw London grow and transform into a teeming metropolis.

### The Down-to-Earth Duke and Duchess

These days you might spot the glamorous Duke and Duchess of Cambridge walking with their kids in Kensington Gardens, or elegantly stepping out onto the red carpet at a royal gala performance in the West End. Besides the color, pageantry, and marching bands of the Changing the Guard ceremony at Buckingham Palace, there's also a rich calendar of royal ceremonies. The Ceremony of the Keys to lock up the Tower of London has taken place at 9:53 pm each night for more than 700 years, and you can see the Queen take the Royal Salute from the Household Division at the annual Trooping the Colour march from Horse Guards Parade to St. James's Park. The Queen is also drawn by four horses in the dazzling Irish State Coach from Buckingham Palace to the Palace of Westminster in a huge royal procession for the State Opening of Parliament each autumn, and you can see her pay homage to the war dead at the Cenotaph on Remembrance Sunday.

1

# SPORTS IN LONDON

Sport in the capital is best watched rather than participated in. If you're lucky enough to score a ticket for a Premier League football match, you'll experience a seething mass of mockery, jeering, and chanting. Tennis, horse racing, and cricket impinge on Londoners' horizons at crucial times of the year, too, but you're unlikely to see grown men crying at the outcome of the Wimbledon Men's Final.

## Rowing

**The Boat Race.** Join more than a quarter of a million merry devotees along the banks of the River Thames between Putney and Mortlake for a glimpse of the annual Oxford and Cambridge University Boat Race, held on the last Saturday of March or the first Saturday of April. Sink a few pints and soak up the tweed cap and-Barbour-clad Thames-side atmosphere as these heavyweight eight-man university crews clash oars and tussle head-to-head for supremacy. First raced in 1829, the 4-mile route is a picturesque stretch between Putney and Chiswick Bridges. The equally exciting women's eight Boat Race is also held the same day. ⊠ *Putney Bridge, Putney* ⊕ *www.theboatraces.org.*

## Cricket

At its best, cricket can be a slow build of smoldering tension and unexpected high-wire excitement. At its worst, it can be too slow and uneventful for the casual observer, as five-day games crawl toward a draw or as rain stops play. But try to visit Lord's—the home of cricket—on match days, just to hear the *thwack* of leather on willow and to see the English aristocracy and upper middle classes on full display.

**Lord's.** Lord's Cricket Ground, home of the venerable 1787 Marylebone Cricket Club (MCC), has been hallowed cricketing turf since 1814, and MCC rules codified the game. Tickets for major Test matches are hard to come by: obtain an application form online and enter the ballot (lottery) to purchase them. ⊠ *Marylebone Cricket Club, Lord's Cricket Ground, St. John's Wood Rd., St. John's Wood* ☎ *020/7432–1000* ⊕ *www.lords.org* Ⓜ *St. John's Wood.*

## Football

London's top teams—Chelsea, Tottenham Hotspur, Arsenal, and West Ham—are top-class and the first three often progress in the Europe-wide Champions League. It's unlikely you'll get tickets for anything except the least popular Premier League games during the August–May season, despite the high ticket prices—£42 for a walk-up match-day seat at Chelsea, and £124 for the most expensive tickets at Arsenal.

## Tennis

**Wimbledon Lawn Tennis Championships.** The All England Club's Wimbledon Lawn Tennis Championships are famous for Centre Court, rain, strawberries and cream, and a nostalgic old-school insistence on players wearing white. Thankfully, the rain has been banished on Centre Court by the retractable roof, but whether you can get tickets for Centre Court all comes down to the luck of the draw—there's a ballot system for advance purchase. (See website for details.) ⊠ *The All England Lawn Tennis Club, Church Rd.* ☎ *020/8944–1066 for general inquires* ⊕ *www.wimbledon.com.*

# FREE AND CHEAP

The exchange rate may vary, but there is one conversion that will never change: £0 = $0. Here are our picks for the top free (and cheap) things to do in London.

### Concerts

St. Martin-in-the-Fields, St. Stephen Walbrook, St. Olaves in the City, and St. James's Church Piccadilly host free lunchtime concerts and recitals, as does St. Giles-in-the-Fields on Friday and St. George, Bloomsbury, on Sunday afternoon. There are also regular organ recitals at Westminster Abbey.

Of the music colleges, the Royal Academy of Music, the Royal College of Music, the Guildhall, Trinity College, and the Royal Opera House offer free recitals. For contemporary ears, there's free jazz and classical music on an exquisite 1897 Bechstein on the first Sunday of the month at the Dysart Petersham restaurant (☎ 0208/940–8005) in Richmond and live jazz at the Lamb & Flag (✉ 33 Rose St. ☎ 0207/497–9504) in Covent Garden, from 8 pm one Sunday a month. For free blues Sunday–Thursday or before 8:30 pm on Friday and Saturday, head to the Ain't Nothin But . . . honky-tonk blues bar in Soho (20 Kingly St. ☎ 020/7287–0514).

### Film, Theater and Opera

If all seats have been sold, the National Theatre sells unobstructed-view £5 standing-room tickets on the day of performances at their Olivier and Lyttleton theaters. Standing-room tickets run £10–£15 at the Royal Opera House, and 44 tickets are available in person from the box office from 10 am on the day of most performances. Under 30 or a full-time student? Becoming an "Access all Arias" member of the English National Opera is free, and allows you to buy £10–£30 tickets. There are 700 £5 standing-room tickets available for every performance at the historical replica of Shakespeare's Globe theater, as well as £10 standing-room tickets for evocative candle-lit plays and concerts at the adjacent indoor Sam Wanamaker Playhouse. At Sloane Square, the Royal Court Theatre has four standing-room tickets for 10 pence each at the Jerwood Theatre Downstairs, available an hour before performances; otherwise all tickets at both theaters there are £10 on Monday.

### Sightseeing on the Cheap

Prop yourself on the top deck of a red double-decker bus for a fantastically free sightseeing tour through the most scenic parts of the city. Routes 9 and 15 also operate Heritage routes on the traditional 1930s Routemaster buses. With all buses now cashless, you can instead use your Oyster card or buy tickets from machines at the bus stops for the following routes:

**Bus 11:** King's Road, Sloane Square, Victoria Station, Westminster Abbey, Houses of Parliament and Big Ben, Whitehall, Trafalgar Square, the Strand, the Royal Courts of Justice, Fleet Street, and St. Paul's Cathedral.

**Bus 19:** Sloane Square, Knightsbridge, Hyde Park Corner, Green Park, Piccadilly Circus, Shaftsbury Avenue, Bloomsbury, Sadler's Wells Theatre and The Angel, Islington.

**Bus 88:** Oxford Circus, Conduit Street, Piccadilly Circus, Haymarket, Trafalgar Square, Whitehall, Horse Guards Parade, Westminster Station, Westminster Abbey, Horseferry Road, and Tate Britain.

# THE ARTS FOR FREE

## Classical Music and Jazz

The Barbican, the Royal National Theatre, and the Royal Opera House often have free music in their public foyers or in dedicated spaces. On the South Bank, free festivals and take place alongside the river.

Many of London's music colleges give free concerts several times a week. The Royal Academy of Music and the Royal College of Music have free recitals. St. Martin-in-the-Fields has free lunchtime concerts, as does St. James's Piccadilly. Westminster Abbey and St. Paul's in Covent Garden also have frequent free music. For the BBC Proms, hundreds of same-day standing-room tickets are available at £5.

## Contemporary Music

Brixton's three-floor Dogstar pub has a great selection of DJs, often playing for free on weekday evenings. Blues bar Ain't Nothing But . . . in Soho has live music most nights, often without a cover charge, and pubs such as the Monarch and the Hawley Arms near Camden Market offer the chance to see tomorrow's indie stars today. East London establishment Stories hosts free acoustic acts, while Cecil Sharp House in Camden, the home of folk, has tickets for as little as £3. There's no cover charge at Piāno Kensington, where talented pianists delight often raucous crowds.

## Drama, Dance, and Performance Arts

Look out for occasional festivals where innovative performances take place on the South Bank. Check the newspapers and *Time Out* for upcoming performances.

Book ahead or turn up at the box office on a performance day for £5–£12.50 tickets to see ballet rehearsals and full performances of shows like *Romeo and Juliet* by **The Royal Ballet** at **The Royal Opera House.** The cheapest **English National Ballet** tickets

for gigs like the *Nutcracker* at the **London Coliseum** are £14, and there's always at least 100 £12 tickets for every dance show and performance at the contemporary powerhouse **Sadler's Wells** dance theater program (including shows at the **Peacock Theatre, Roundhouse,** and **Lilian Baylis Studio.**)

## Museums and Galleries

Most of the city's museums and galleries do not charge admission. The monthly *Galleries* magazine, available at galleries themselves or online at ⊕ *www.galleries.co.uk*, has listings for all private galleries in the capital.

## Park Life

London's royal parks come to life in the spring and summer with a wide-ranging program (⊕ *www.royalparks.org.uk* for details, or call *020/3061–2000*). There are several summer festivals in London parks, some with major pop stars, like British Summer Time in Hyde Park (⊕ *www.bsthydepark.com*; day tickets around £90) and the more indie Field Day in Victoria Park (⊕ *www.fielddayfestivals.com*; day tickets around £40, weekend tickets around £85). Notable contemporary art fairs are October's Frieze London in Regent's Park (⊕ *www.friezelondon.com*; around £40) and the Affordable Art Fair in Battersea Park and Hampstead Heath in spring (⊕ *www.affordableartfair.com*; weekdays £12, weekends £15).

## Radio and Television

With so much broadcast material recorded in front of live London audiences, there are often great opportunities to watch a free quiz show, current affairs debate, comedy, drama, or live BBC symphony (⊕ *www.bbc.co.uk/showsandtours/shows*).

# LONDON MUSEUMS

London's museums are one of the capital's crown jewels, and many have free entry.

## Major Galleries

Giddy art lovers will target the big four—the **National Gallery**, the **National Portrait Gallery, Tate Britain,** and **Tate Modern.** The National Gallery has more than 2,300 masterpieces dating 1250–1900, and wows with once-in-a-generation blockbuster shows like *Goya: The Portraits,* while the world's largest collection of portraits is next door at the National Portrait Gallery which captures greats from Henry VIII to Elizabeth I. Tate Britain takes you on a chronological walk through 500 years of British art and Tate Modern showcases contemporary art and installations.

## Academies and Galleries

Must-visits include the 1768 **Royal Academy of Arts** for its sell-out exhibitions on artists like Monet and the diminutive **Courtauld Institute** at Somerset House, which has a classy capsule collection from the early medieval period to the postimpressionists. The **Queen's Gallery** at Buckingham Palace showcases the Royal Collection and hosts blockbusters on world-class greats like Leonardo da Vinci. The historic and brilliant **Dulwich Picture Gallery** exhibits exquisite European Old Masters from 1600 to the 1700s and the **Guildhall Art Gallery** has awesome Pre-Raphaelites.

## House Museums

London's historic house museums are treats within treats: the art and the house itself. One of the finest is the private **Wallace Collection** at the majestic damask-filled 1788 Hertford House on Manchester Square in Marylebone, which hosts a 5,500-strong collection of European Old Masters and fine French decorative arts. Other historic humdingers with grand Old Masters and sumptuous antique-strewn interiors include **Apsley House, Kenwood House,** and **Leighton House** in Holland Park.

## Contemporary Art

With London now a top-two global art hub, you'll find many excellent contemporary art galleries. The **Serpentine Gallery** in Hyde Park may be small but packs a mean modern art punch, with its summer exhibition a major cultural highlight. The **Hayward Gallery** at the Southbank Centre concentrates on bleeding-edge exhibitions—from early photographer Jacques Henri Lartigue to Tracy Emin—while the **Whitechapel Gallery** kindles the smoldering East London art scene. Flush private galleries like the **Saatchi Gallery, Hauser & Wirth, Gagosian, Newport Street Gallery, Herald Street,** and **Maureen Paley** push a mix of up-and-comers and unknowns.

## Major Museums

The **British Museum** was the world's first national public museum in 1753 and still captivates with its vast collection of artifacts from the Rosetta Stone to Ramesses the Great. A 105-foot Diplodocus greets you at the **Natural History Museum** with its trove of 70 million artifacts spanning 4½ billion years while the **Science Museum** has a collection of 300,000 items showcased in 12 galleries. The **V&A Museum** is stuffed with magnificent jewelry and design exhibits. At St. Pancras, the permanent exhibition at the **British Library** has manuscripts like Magna Carta, a Gutenberg Bible, and Shakespeare's First Folio from 1623.

## British History

The **Museum of London** explores London since way before Roman times while the **Museum of London Docklands** tells the 2,000-year story of the port of London and captivates with a diorama on the

1666 Great Fire of London. The **Royal Observatory** in Greenwich tells of Britain's role in the story of navigation and astronomy, and is the home of the Prime Meridian while the **National Maritime Museum** charts British naval ascendancy and shows star exhibits like Admiral Lord Nelson's battle-scarred navy blue uniform worn at the Battle of Trafalgar. The **National Army Museum, IWM London,** and **Household Cavalry Museum** venerate Britain's military history, while the **Royal Air Force Museum** houses Spitfires and a Lancaster bomber. You'll find all the clocks have stopped at 4:58 pm at the **Churchill War Rooms,** which preserves the bunkered World War II Cabinet War Rooms, and you can operate a "dead man's handle" on a 1930s Underground train at the **London Transport Museum. Shakespeare's Globe** and its indoor candlelit **Sam Wanamaker Playhouse** theaters are enthralling replicas of the Elizabethan originals.

## Royal Palaces

London's a royal wonderland, with palaces doubling down as de facto museums. You can get into **Buckingham Palace** August 1–late September and tour 19 impossibly grand State Rooms, including the Queen's Throne Room. **Kensington Palace** is home to the Duke and Duchess of Cambridge and you can glide through former King William III and Queen Mary II's closet and oak-paneled Eating Room. The Tudor turrets, tapestries, and historic kitchens fascinate all comers at **Hampton Court Palace,** as do the sparkling 23,587-gem Crown Jewels regalia at the Royal Palace and Fortress at the **Tower of London.** Pocket-size **Kew Palace** and **Eltham Palace** are two other prize royal retreats.

## Best for Kids

Kids adore the gory Black Death scenes and gruesome Jack the Ripper scenes at the **London Dungeon** and are always intrigued by the waxwork models of celebs at **Madame Tussauds.** The eclectic **Horniman Museum** has 350,000 quirky objects amassed by a Victorian tea trader and there are scientific, medical, and surgical specimens galore at the **Wellcome Collection,** the **Royal Institution,** and **Hunterian Museum.** The **London Fire Brigade Museum,** tiny **Pollock's Toy Museum Trust,** and the **Guards Museum** on Birdcage Walk all cater brilliantly to the whims of kids of all ages.

## One-Man Shows

London is fab at preserving the homes of illustrious native sons and daughters, with the best including the **Charles Dickens Museum, Florence Nightingale Museum, Freud Museum, Handel House Museum,** plus artist William **Hogarth's House** and essayist Thomas **Carlyle's House** on Cheyne Row. Candlelit tours at **Dennis Severs' House** in Spitalfields chart the tale of a 17th-century French Huguenot silk merchants' family, and the **Sir John Soane's Museum** is crammed with a magpie collection of antiquities from the namesake neoclassical architect and collector.

# LONDON WITH KIDS

## Education Without Yawns

**Kew Gardens.** Kew Gardens is great for young ones, with activities, the "climbers and creepers" play zone, a treetops Sky Walk, zip wires, scramble slides, and children's trails; it's free for kids.

**The London Dungeon.** It's gore galore at this museum that plunges you into the blood-soaked depths of London history, with tales from a gruesome Jack the Ripper pub, Sweeney Todd barbers, and Mrs. Lovett's pie shop.

**London Zoo.** Disappear into the animal kingdom among the enclosures, complete with sessions for kids about all kinds of bugs and spiders in this popular animal retreat in Regent's Park.

**Natural History Museum.** It doesn't get more awe-inspiring than bloodsucking bats, a cabinet of hummingbirds, simulated Kobe earthquakes, and a life-size blue whale. Just make sure you know your dodo from your diplodocus.

**Science Museum.** Special effects, virtual space voyages, 800 interactive exhibits, puzzles, and mysteries from the world of science can keep kids effortlessly amused all day.

**Tower of London.** Perfect for playing prince and princess in front of the Crown Jewels, but not so perfect for imagining what becomes of the fairy tale—watch your royal necks.

## Performances

**Covent Garden street performers.** You can't beat the open-air gaggle of jugglers, fire-eaters, unicyclists, mime artists, and human statues tantalizing crowds at Covent Garden piazza.

**Regent's Park Open-Air Theatre.** Welcome to the land of fairy dust and magic. Don't miss an evening performance under the stars of *A Midsummer Night's Dream* in high summer.

## Activities

**Ride the London Eye.** Europe's biggest observation wheel looks like a giant fairground ride, and you can see across what seems like half of London from the top.

**Pose with a Queen's Horse Guard.** There's always an erect soldier in uniform standing watch by the entrance to Horse Guards on the Trafalgar Square end of Whitehall. They don't mind posing for pictures, but they're not allowed to smile.

**Ice-skating at Somerset House.** Send your kids whizzing, arms whirling, across ice mid-November–January at this spotlighted ice rink at this former royal palace.

**Night at the Natural History Museum.** Find out what the dinosaurs really do when the lights go out at the monthly Dino Snores sleepover (minimum of one adult and five kids per group).

**Pedalo on the Serpentine.** Pack a picnic and take a blue pedalo out into the middle of Hyde Park's famed Serpentine lake; settle back and tuck in to lunch.

**Lose the kids at Hampton Court Maze.** The topiary might be more than 300 years old, but the quest to reach the middle of Hampton Court's world-famous trapezoid-shape yew hedge maze remains as challenging as ever.

**West End musicals.** Foot-stompingly good West End musicals and shows like *Les Misérables, Billy Elliot, Matilda, Mamma Mia!, The Lion King Oliver!, Grease,* and *The Phantom of the Opera* will mesmerize the over-seven crowd.

# GREAT ITINERARIES

The sheer amount of what London offers, along with its constantly evolving culture, means you can easily live a lifetime here and still not see it all. But if you're like most visitors and only visiting for a short time, you can still get a taste of London life. In one day, you can get to the heart of the city's history and feel the force of its river setting. With five days, you can knock off many of the main attractions, and have a deeper sense of the seen and unseen majesty of this global metropolis.

## LONDON IN 1 DAY

Do a giant best-of loop of the city by open top boat and bus through six key districts, with a stop at the thousand-year-old Tower of London and fun in Soho at the end. Start early, with the first ride of the London Eye at 10 am; you'll have the rest of the day to explore at whatever pace you wish, but be sure to get to Buckingham Palace before the sun sets and you miss out on some great photo opportunities.

On your morning ride on the **London Eye**, you'll be able to get a bird's eye view of the city. Then launch from the Eye's namesake pier for a swivel-eyed Thames cruise past four bridges and Traitor's Gate before landing in front of the iconic **Tower of London.**

Once inside the Tower, take in the Crown Jewels and gory history on a Yeoman Warder's tour, before jumping on a double-decker bus over **Tower Bridge,** past Monument, the Embankment, Park Lane, Oxford, Piccadilly Circuses and stopping at **Trafalgar Square,** where you can a glimpse of Big Ben and the Houses of Parliament here, and stop for lunch at one of the atmospheric pubs. Then take a walk over to **Westminster Abbey,** where a self-guided tour will take

you through centuries of British history within one awe-inspiring building (note that the Abbey closes early on Saturday). Then take another short walk through **St. James's Park** to **Buckingham Palace;** you'll have missed the daily Changing of the Guards, but that means the palace grounds will be less crowded, with more photo ops. End the day by meandering over to the hip Soho neighborhood, where foodies will find many eclectic restaurants for dinner and party-goers will find the city's best nightlife.

## LONDON IN 5 DAYS

In five days you can check off most of London's cultural and sightseeing highlights, and weave in enough time for some world-class shopping and people-watching. Iconic photo ops abound with stops at places like Big Ben, Buckingham Palace, and the London Eye. For a shorter stay, mix and match from this list.

### Day 1: Buckingham Palace, Trafalgar Square, and the National Portrait Gallery

Start Day 1 with coffee in a Dickensian alleyway just north of **St. James's Palace,** before being first into the 19 impossibly grand State Rooms at **Buckingham Palace.** Afterwards, join the crowds outside the palace to watch a sea of bearskin Foot Guards perform the **Changing of the Guard** ceremony, held 11:30 am most days. Some Palace tickets include tours of the **Queen's Gallery,** which showcases top art from the Royal Collection. Then take a stroll through **St. James's Park** before lunch at a historic Pall Mall pub. It's a short stroll to the **National Gallery** at **Trafalgar Square.** Hit its quieter Sainsbury Wing, pick up an audio guide, and hunt down a few choice Renaissance masterpieces. Enjoy portraits of Tudor monarchs at the **National Portrait Gallery** next door, before browsing the antiquarian booksellers off Charring Cross Road and dim sum in **Chinatown.**

### Day 2: Westminster Abbey, Houses of Parliament, and the East End

Devote the early morning of Day 2 to a 90-minute verger-led tour of **Westminster Abbey** and get the skinny on this world famous resting place of Britain's monarchs. Then investigate the **Houses of Parliament.** If in session, you can attend debate in the Public Galleries. If in recess, the **Peers' Dining Room** is occasionally open to the public for lunch; otherwise have a ploughman's lunch at an historic politicos pub. Take pics of **Big Ben** and walk up Whitehall to the gates of **No 10. Downing Street,** the Prime Minister's residence. For a complete change of tune, take the Tube over to the gritty yet hip East End and Indian-influenced Brick Lane, where you can stroll along the art galleries and have a classic English curry for dinner.

### Day 3: The South Bank

Day 3 is all the South Bank and its unique culture. Start with a ride on the **London Eye** for eye-popping city panoramas. Take a nice long walk along the Thames, popping into any galleries or shops that catch your eye. Eventually meander along to **Tate Modern** for a modern art fix, stopping for lunch nearby. Then enjoy a Shakespeare hit with tours of the replica Elizabethan **Shakespeare's Globe.** Wiggle along for killer venison burgers and foodie stall heaven at **Borough Market** before backtracking over the pedestrian **Millennium Bridge** for a stunning approach to **St. Paul"s Cathedral.** Hopefully you'll catch Choral Evensong there at 5 pm, then wend east

towards Bow Lane alleyway for a customary City pub fish 'n' chips dinner.

### Day 4: The British Museum and Soho

On Day 4, start early at the **British Museum** and leave a few hours to explore hits like the Egyptian mummies, the Rosetta Stone, and the 7th-century Anglo-Saxon Sutton Hoo treasures. Afterwards, Tube it to restaurant-mad **Soho** where you can stop for lunch at any of the trendy eateries, before browsing **Carnaby Street** and the surrounding indie boutiques. Cut across Regent Street via the gentlemen's tailors of **Savile Row** and head south for **Fortnum & Mason** and the old world outfitters on Jermyn Street. Work back through the twinkly Regency red-carpet **Burlington Arcade** and pop into the **Royal Academy** before taking Afternoon Tea at a cozy wood-paneled and open-fire Mayfair hotel.

### Day 5: Kensington's Museums, Piccadilly, and the West End

Finally on Day 5, start with a one-hour tour of the **V&A Museum** of art and design, whose collection ranges from Persian rugs to Tudor chalices. Once out, mill about for a mid-morning crêpe on pedestrianized Exhibition Road near the South Kensington Tube, then chose either all things science at the **Science Museum,** or the *T. rex* dinosaur trail at the **Natural History Museum.** Then stroll up Knightsbridge to **Harrod's** Food Hall, where you can drool and people-watch to your heart's content. Either duck in for the ace fashion at **Harvey Nichols** or double decker it to **The Ritz** at Green Park. Enjoy the lights at **Piccadilly Circus** and **Leicester Square** before having a pretheater dinner and then seeing a West End play.

# BEST TOURS IN LONDON

With its crooked medieval streets, layers of history, and atmospheric buildings, London is a true walking city often best explored on a guided tour. Tours are a great way to investigate out-of-the-way, hidden, historic, and secret districts; to get an insider's eye on where locals like to eat, drink, and be merry; and to learn all the juicy and infamous aspects of London's history, inhabitants, and architecture.

## Boat Tours

**City Cruises.** In nice weather, an open top-deck ride from Westminster, the London Eye, or Tower Piers to the ancient royal romping ground of Greenwich along the Thames River is one of the best ways to get acquainted with the city. You'll pass sights like Tower Bridge, the Tower of London, and St. Paul's Cathedral, all with a chirpy Cockney running commentary. Lunch, Afternoon Tea, and nighttime cruises are also available. ⊠ *Cherry Garden Pier, Cherry Garden St.* ☎ *020/740–0400* ⊕ *www.citycruises.com* ✉ *From £9.75.*

**London Duck Tours.** Hop aboard one of the garish yellow open-side vintage trucks (originally used during World War II), and get ready to sputter past a stack of sights including 10 Downing and Westminster Abbey. Once at the MI6 building, you'll take like a duck to water and gently chunter up the Thames to the Houses of Parliament. Other tours focus on James Bond and the D-Day Landings. ⊠ *55 York Rd.* ☎ *020/7928–3132* ⊕ *www. londonducktours.co.uk* ✉ *From £24.*

**RIB Experience.** Make like James Bond in an exhilarating special forces–style inflatable speedboat as you whiz past the MI6 building, Shakespeare's Globe, and Tower Bridge on a high-speed 50-minute round trip to Canary Wharf. There are also 20-minute rollercoaster blasts to the O2

Arena in Greenwich and 75-minute round trips from Tower Pier to the Thames Barrier. ⊠ *Embankment Pier* ☎ *020/3613– 2354* ⊕ *www.thamesribexperience.com* ✉ *From £24.50.*

## Bus Tours

**Golden Tours.** Various hop-on, hop-off open-top double-decker tours with this company take in the main sites on four key loops. With 60 drop-off points and two-day passes, they also offer discount tickets to attractions like the Tower of London and the London Dungeon, as well as nighttime tours and free Thames boat trips. ⊠ *London* ☎ *0800/210–0520* ⊕ *www.goldentours.com* ✉ *From £24.75.*

**The Original London Sightseeing Tour.** Like its double-decker competitors, the Original London Sightseeing Tour offer various hop-on, hop-off open-top tours of the city, but its most popular feature is its 48-hour pass that includes loops of the main historic sites, the City, Westminster, and the museum districts. They also throw in free tickets for a Thames boat cruise, plus Jack the Ripper, Changing of the Guard, and Rock 'n' Roll walking tours. ⊠ *London* ☎ *020/8877–1722* ⊕ *www.theoriginaltour.com* ✉ *From £26.*

## Walking Tours

**Context Travel.** This company takes a high-brow approach to their small-group walks program, providing PhD- and MA-level scholars, authors, architects, and historians to lead walks of no more than six people. Lasting up to three hours, walks include the evolution of London theater to Charles Dickens and Victorian London. ⊕ *www.contexttravel.com* ✉ *From £75.*

**London Food Lovers.** Combine walking and eating (but not at the same time) on these fabulous multistop trails, featuring restaurants and local food history. There's a ten-stop half-day Soho International Food tour, as well as shorter five-stop tours focusing on pizza, burgers and beer, and one called the "Jack the Ripper Happy Hour" tour, focusing on bagels and locally brewed craft beers. ☎ *07404 /802–703* ⊕ *www.londonfoodlovers.com* ✉ *From £40.*

**London Walks.** With London's oldest established walking tours, there's no need to book ahead; instead, just turn up at the meeting point and pay £10 for a first-rate, two-hour walk with themes like secret London, literary London, Harry Potter film locations, haunted London, and more. Top crime historian Donal Rumbelow often leads the 7:30 pm Jack the Ripper walk in Whitechapel. ☎ *020/7624–3978* ⊕ *www.walks.com* ✉ *From £10.*

**Love London.** Travel journalist and former BBC *Travel Show* broadcaster Sophie Campbell specializes in super-long London walks. Full day walks include Old Church Chelsea (by the river) to St. Michael's Highgate (high on a north London hill); or Hampton Court Palace to Richmond Palace via the noble palazzi of the non-tidal Thames. Half-day hikes include a forensic examination of journalism and the law in the City. ☎ *020/7498–6589* ⊕ *www.love-london.com* ✉ *From £200.*

## Speciality Tours

**Brit Movie Tours.** See the exterior of Grantham House and the spot where Branson first confesses his love for Lady Sybil on this insiders' central London tour of Downton Abbey filming locations. Tours focusing on James Bond, *Sherlock,* and Harry Potter filming locations, among many others, are also available. ☎ *0844/2471–007* ⊕ *www. britmovietours.com* ✉ *From £74.*

## Free Tours

**City Tours.** The City of London City Guides offer a small program of top-quality daily walks, including an insider tour of Guildhall, Mansion House, the Bank of England, and Royal Exchange, plus others focusing on topics like the city's gardens and famed architect Sir Christopher Wren's churches. ☎ *020/7606–3030* ⊕ *www.cityoflondonguides.com* ✉ *Free.*

**Sandemans New Europe London.** It almost seems too good to be true: Sandemans offers an excellent free, three-hour Royal London walking tour daily, which winds from Buckingham Palace to Big Ben. Led by wisecracking actors, poets, and art historians, other paid walks include a boozy five-stop pub crawl and a spooky East End's Dark Secrets tours. ⊕ *www. newlondon-tours.com* ✉ *Free.*

# AFTERNOON TEA

### An Age-Old Tradition
So what is Afternoon Tea, exactly? Well, it is real loose-leaf tea—Earl Grey, English Breakfast, Ceylon, Darjeeling, or Assam—brewed in a fine bone china or porcelain pot and served with elegant cups and saucers, milk or lemon, and silver spoons, taken between noon and 6 pm. For the full monty there should be elegant finger foods on a three-tier silver cake stand: crustless cucumber finger sandwiches on the bottom; scones with Devonshire clotted cream and strawberry jam in the middle; and rich English fruitcake, shortbread, pâtisseries, macarons, and dainty fancies on top.

Teagoers dress smartly, and conversation by tradition should naturally avoid politics and religion. Here are some top places in town to head:

### Classic Choices
Hands down, **The Savoy** on the Strand offers one of the most beautiful settings for Afternoon Tea. The Thames Foyer, a symphony of grays and golds centered on a winter garden wrought-iron gazebo, is just the place for the house pianist to accompany you as you enjoy 74 rare house teas along with finger sandwiches, homemade scones, and pastries.

Setting the standard in its English Tea Room for some of London's best-known traditional teas, **Brown's Hotel**, at 33 Albermarle Street in Mayfair offers Afternoon Tea for £47.50 in an Agatha Christie-esque wood-paneled salon or, if you wish to splurge, Champagne Afternoon Tea for £57.

If you seek timeless chic, the art deco dining room at the **The Delaunay** grand café at the Aldwych remains a deeply fashionable hangout. The silver service teas here—light Cream Tea is £10.75, Viennese Tea is £23.75, and Champagne Tea £33.50—come with wheat-free poppyseed *gugelhupf* cakes and are among the best in town.

### Something Different
Add spice to your tea time by trying a popular Moroccan-style Afternoon Tea (£22 or £32) at the souk-chic tea room at **Momo** off Regent Street, where you'll enjoy sweet mint tea plus scones with fig jam, Maghrebian pastries, Moroccan chicken wraps, and honey-and-nut-rich Berber-style crêpes.

Alternatively, you can munch Coronation chicken wraps and look out onto the immaculate lawns amid mini potted orange trees at **The Orangery** at Prince William and Kate's London pad, Kensington Palace, inside resplendent Kensington Gardens. Afternoon Tea is £26, and a suitably Royal Afternoon Tea (with a glass of Laurent-Perrier NV) is £36.

Covent Garden's grand French brasserie **Balthazar** has a fabulous fashion-focused English Afternoon Tea, curated by fêted fashion designer Matthew Williamson. From cucumber-and-pea purée sandwiches to Yuzu éclairs and raspberry and hibiscus babas, everything has a ultra creative twist.

### An Edwardian Escape
For some true gilt-edged grandeur, few can compete with Afternoon Tea at **The Ritz** on Piccadilly. It's served in the stunning Palm Court, replete with linen-draped tables, Louis XIV chaise longues, chandeliers, resplendent bouquets, and musical accompaniment; it's a true taste of Edwardian London in the 21st century. Afternoon Tea is £50, and celebration Champagne Tea is £77. There are five sittings from 11:30 am; be sure to book 3 months ahead and wear a jacket and tie.

# WESTMINSTER, ST. JAMES'S, AND ROYAL LONDON

# GETTING ORIENTED

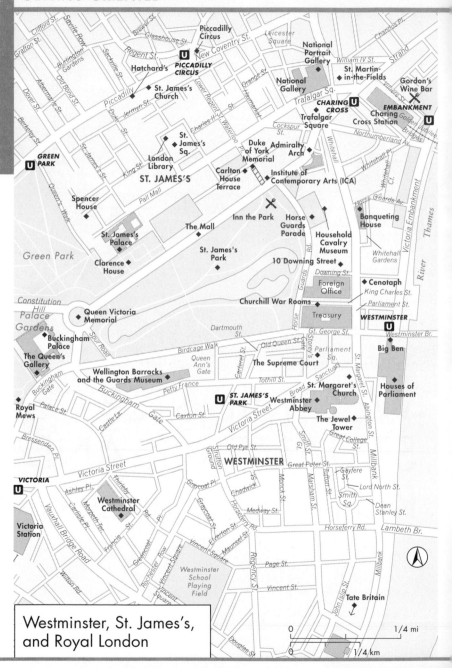

## Westminster, St. James's, and Royal London

## TOP REASONS TO GO

**Glorious Westminster Abbey:** This Gothic church was not only the site of William and Kate's marriage but also has seen 38 coronations, starting with William the Conqueror in 1066.

**Calling on Buckingham Palace:** Even if you miss the palace's summer opening, keep pace with the marching soldiers as they enact the time-honored Changing the Guard.

**Masterpieces Theater:** Leonardo, Raphael, Van Eyck, Rembrandt, and many other artistic greats are shown off in the gorgeous rooms at the National Gallery.

**Discover the preserved Churchill War Rooms:** Listen to Churchill's radio addresses to the British people as you explore this cavernous underground wartime hideout.

**Hear Big Ben's chimes:** As the Eiffel Tower is to Paris, so is Big Ben to London—just follow your ears from Trafalgar Square to catch sight of the 320-foot-high Clock Tower.

## FEELING PECKISH?

**Gordon's Wine Bar.** Gordon's is the oldest wine bar in the city (est. 1890). Head to the back room, windowless and still lighted entirely by candles; it's been used as a wine cellar for 800 years. Soak up some excellent wine with a cheese board or a sharing plate of hot or cold nibbles. ⊠ *47 Villiers St., Trafalgar Sq.* ☎ *020/7930–1408* ⊕ *www.gordonswinebar. com* Ⓜ *Embankment, Charing Cross.*

**Inn the Park.** Great food, drink, and location: what more could you want? Come at lunch for delicious homemade soups, salads and light mains, or in the evening for a classic bistro-style menu. ⊠ *St. James's Park, St. James's* ☎ *020/7451–9999* ⊕ *www.innthepark.com* ☉ *No dinner weekends* Ⓜ *St. James's Park.*

### GETTING THERE

Trafalgar Square is in the center of the action. Take the Tube to Embankment (Northern, Bakerloo, District, and Circle lines) and walk north until you cross the Strand, or exit to Northumberland Avenue at Charing Cross (Bakerloo and Northern lines). Buses are another great option, as almost all roads lead to Trafalgar Square.

Two Tube stations are right in the heart of St. James's: Piccadilly Circus (Piccadilly or Bakerloo lines) and Green Park (Piccadilly, Victoria, or Jubilee lines).

### MAKING THE MOST OF YOUR TIME

For royal pageantry, begin with Buckingham Palace, Westminster Abbey, and the Guards Museum, followed by the Houses of Parliament and Big Ben. For art, the National Gallery, Tate Britain, and the Queen's Gallery top anyone's list.

### NEAREST PUBLIC RESTROOMS

Paid restrooms (£1.50) are across the street from Westminster Abbey at the bottom of Victoria Street. Banqueting House and the Queen's Gallery have elegant restrooms.

Sightseeing
★★★★★
Nightlife
★★
Dining
★★★
Lodging
★
Shopping
★★

This is postcard London at its best. Crammed with historic churches, grand state buildings, and some of the world's best art collections, Royal London and Westminster unite politics and high culture. (Oh, and the Queen lives here, too.) The places you'll want to explore are grouped into four distinct areas—Trafalgar Square, Whitehall, St. James's, and Buckingham Palace—each nudging a corner of triangular St. James's Park. There is as much history in these few acres as in many whole cities, so pace yourself— this is concentrated sightseeing.

# WESTMINSTER

Updated by
Jack Jewers

Home to London's most photogenic pigeons, **Trafalgar Square** is not only the official center of the district known as **Westminster,** nominally a separate city but in fact the official center of London. What will bring you here are the two magnificent museums on the northern edge of the square, the **National Gallery** and the **National Portrait Gallery.** From the square, two boulevards lead to the seats of different eras of governance. The avenue called **Whitehall** drops south to the neo-Gothic **Houses of Parliament,** where members of both (Commons and Lords) hold debates and vote on pending legislation. Just opposite, **Westminster Abbey** is a monument to the nation's history and for centuries the scene of daily worship, coronations, and royal weddings. Poets, political leaders, and 17 monarchs are buried in this world-famous, 13th-century Gothic building. Sandwiched between the two is the **Jewel Tower,** the only surviving part of the medieval Palace of Westminster (a name still given to Parliament and its environs). Halfway down Whitehall, **10 Downing Street** is both the residence and the office of the prime minister. One of the most celebrated occupants, Winston Churchill, is commemorated in the **Churchill War Rooms,** his underground wartime headquarters off Whitehall. Just down the road is the **Cenotaph,** built for the dead of World War I and since then a focal point for the annual remembrance of others lost in war.

**The Mall,** a wide, elegant avenue beyond the stone curtain of **Admiralty Arch,** heads southwest from Trafalgar Square toward the **Queen Victoria Memorial** and **Buckingham Palace,** the sovereign's official residence. The building is open to the public only in summer, but you can see much of the royal art collection in the **Queen's Gallery** and spectacular ceremonial coaches in the **Royal Mews,** both open all year. Farther south toward Pimlico, **Tate Britain** focuses on prominent British artists from 1500 to today.

This area can be considered "Royal London" partly because it is neatly bounded by the triangle of streets that make up the route that Queen Elizabeth II usually takes when processing from Buckingham Palace to Westminster Abbey or to the Houses of Parliament on state occasions, and also because it contains so much of British history going back a thousand years.

The main drawback to sightseeing here is that half the world is doing it at the same time. So, for a large part of the year a lot of Royal London is floodlit at night (when there's more elbow room), adding to the theatricality of the experience.

## TOP ATTRACTIONS

FAMILY

Fodor'sChoice

★

**Churchill War Rooms.** It was from this small warren of underground rooms—beneath the vast government buildings of the Treasury—that Winston Churchill and his team directed troops in World War II. Designed to be bombproof, the whole complex has been preserved almost exactly as it was when the last light was turned off at the end of the war. Every clock shows almost 5 pm, and the furniture, fittings, and paraphernalia of a busy, round-the-clock war office are in situ, down to the colored map pins.

During air raids, the leading government ministers met here, and the Cabinet Room is still arranged as if a meeting were about to convene. In the Map Room, the Allied campaign is charted on wall-to-wall maps with a rash of pinholes showing the movements of convoys. In the hub of the room, a bank of differently colored phones known as the "Beauty Chorus" linked the War Rooms to control rooms around the nation. The Prime Minister's Room holds the desk from which Churchill made his morale-boosting broadcasts; the Telephone Room (a converted broom cupboard) has his hotline to FDR. You can also see the restored rooms that the PM used for dining and sleeping. Telephonists (switchboard operators) and clerks who worked 16-hour shifts slept in lesser quarters in unenviable conditions.

A great addition to the War Rooms is the Churchill Museum, a tribute to the great wartime leader himself. ⊠ *Clive Steps, King Charles St., Westminster* ☎ *020/7930–6961* ⊕ *www.iwm.org.uk/visits/churchill-war-rooms* ✎ *£18* ⊗ *Daily 9:30–6; last admission 5* Ⓜ *Westminster.*

## A BRIEF HISTORY OF WESTMINSTER

The Romans may have shaped The City, but England's royals created Westminster. Indeed, it's still technically a separate city—notice it reads "City of Westminster" on street signs, not "City of London"—although any formal divide between the two vanished centuries ago, along with the open countryside that once lay between them. Edward the Confessor started the first Palace of Westminster in the 11th century; in 1050, he also founded Westminster Abbey, where every British monarch since then has been crowned.

The district became the focus of political power in England after the construction of Whitehall Palace in the 16th century; a vast and opulent building, it was the official residence of the monarch until it burned down in 1698. It survives both as the name of Westminster's most important road, and as a term still used in Britain to refer to the seat of government in general. The first Parliament building was part of the same complex; it, too, was nearly destroyed by the Gunpowder Plot of 1605 (still commemorated annually on November 5, Guy Fawkes Day) and eventually succumbed to fire in 1834. The Westminster we see today took shape during the Georgian and Victorian periods, as Britain reached the zenith of its imperial power. Grand architecture sprang up, and Buckingham Palace became the principal royal residence in 1837, when Victoria acceded to the throne. Trafalgar Square and Nelson's Column were built in 1843, to commemorate Britain's most famous naval victory, and the Houses of Parliament were rebuilt in 1858 in the trendy neo-Gothic style of the time. The illustrious Clarence House, built in 1825 for the Duke of Clarence (later William IV), is now the home of Prince Charles and Camilla, Duchess of Cornwall.

**Downing Street.** Were it not for the wrought-iron gates and armed guards that block the entrance, you'd probably miss this otherwise unassuming Georgian side street off Whitehall—but this is the location of the famous **No. 10,** London's modest equivalent of the White House. The Georgian entrance to the mid-17th-century mansion is deceptive; it's actually a huge complex of discreetly linked buildings. Since 1732 it has been the official home and office of the prime minister—the last private resident was the magnificently named Mr. Chicken. The current prime minister actually lives in the private apartments above No. 11, because those in No. 10 are too small to house a family. (No. 11 is traditionally the residence of the Chancellor of the Exchequer, the head of the Treasury.) There are no public tours, but the famous black front door to No. 10 is clearly visible from Whitehall. Just south of Downing Street, in the middle of Whitehall, is the **Cenotaph,** a stark white monolith built to commemorate the 1918 armistice. On Remembrance Day (the Sunday nearest November 11) it's strewn with red poppy wreaths to honor the dead of both world wars and all British and Commonwealth soldiers killed in action since; the first wreath is always laid by the Queen. A hundred yards farther, toward Parliament, is the **Monument to the Women of World War II.** The prominent black marble sculpture uses a string of empty uniforms to symbolise the vital service of women in then-traditionally male jobs during the war, as well as in front line roles, as medics and auxiliary officers. ⊠ *Whitehall* ⊕ *www.number10. gov.uk* Ⓜ *Westminster.*

QUICK BITES

**Notes Music and Coffee.** Next door to the London Coliseum (home of the English National Opera), this hip café serves some of the best sandwiches, salads, and coffee in the neighborhood. Keep an eye out for their popular jazz nights. ⊠ *31 St. Martin's La., Westminster* ☎ *020/7240–0424* ⊕ *www. notes-uk.co.uk* Ⓜ *Charing Cross.*

FAMILY **Horse Guards Parade.** Once the tiltyard for jousting tournaments, Horse Guards Parade is best known for the annual Trooping the Colour ceremony, in which the Queen takes the salute on her official birthday tribute, on the second Saturday in June. (Though it's called a birthday it's actually the anniversary of her coronation—her real birthday is April 21.) It's a must-see if you're around, with marching bands and throngs of onlookers. Throughout the rest of the year, the changing of two mounted sentries known as the **Queen's Life Guard** at the Whitehall facade of Horse Guards provides what may be London's most popular photo opportunity. The ceremony takes place daily from April to July, and on alternate days from August to March (usually odd numbered days, but check the monthly schedule at www.householddivision.org. uk/changing-the-guard-calendar). It starts at 11 am at St. James' Palace, where the guard begins its march to Buckingham Palace, and the new guards take up their posts in a ceremony at 11:30. (It's sometimes cancelled in bad weather). At 4 pm daily is the dismounting ceremony, aka the 4 O'Clock Parade, during which sentries are posted and horses are returned to their stables. It began in 1894, when Queen Victoria discovered the guards on duty drinking and gambling. As a punishment she decreed that the regiment should be inspected every day at 4 pm for the next 100 years. ⊠ *Whitehall* ☎ *020/7930–4832* ⊕ *www. royalcollection.org.uk* ✄ *Free* Ⓜ *Westminster.*

Fodor's Choice ★ **Houses of Parliament.** The Palace of Westminster, as the complex is called, was first established on this site by Edward the Confessor in the 11th century. William II started building a new palace in 1087, and this became the seat of English power. Fire destroyed most of the palace in 1834, and the current complex dates largely from the mid-19th century. The best view is from the opposite (south) bank of the Thames, across Lambeth Bridge. It is most dramatic at night when lighted green and gold.

The **Visitors' Galleries** of the House of Commons provide a view of democracy in action when the benches are filled by opposing MPs (members of Parliament). Debates are formal but raucous, especially during the **Prime Minister's Questions** (PMQs), when any MP can put a question to the nation's leader. Tickets to PMQs are free but highly sought after, so the only way for non-U.K. citizens to gain access is by lining up on the day and hoping for returns or no-shows. The action starts at 1 pm every Wednesday when Parliament is sitting, and the whole shebang is broadcast live on television. For non-PMQ debates,

Embassies and High Commissions have a quota of tickets available to their citizens, which can help you avoid long lines. The easiest time to get into the Commons is during an evening session—Parliament is still sitting if the top of the Clock Tower is illuminated. There are also Visitors Galleries for the House of Lords. The Clock Tower—renamed **Elizabeth Tower** in 2012, in honor of the Queen's Diamond Jubilee—was completed in 1858, and contains the 13-ton bell known as **Big Ben.** At the southwest end of the main Parliament building is the 323-foot-high Victoria Tower.

Public tours of Parliament cost £25 and must be booked in advance online or by phone. They are available daily for most of the year, but sell out six months in advance. Other tours, including afternoon tea on the Pavillion Terrace, overlooking the Thames, are also available for £59. ✉ *St. Stephen's Entrance, St. Margaret St., Westminster* ☎ *020/7219–4272 for info and tours, 0161/425–8677 for public tours (from overseas), 0207/219–4114 for public tours* ⊕ *www.parliament.uk/visiting* 🎫 *Free; tours £25 (must be booked ahead)* ⊙ *Tour times and Visitor's Gallery hrs vary* Ⓜ *Westminster.*

**The Jewel Tower.** Overshadowed by the big-ticket attractions of Parliament to one side and Westminster Abbey to the other, this is the only significant portion of the Palace of Westminster complex to have survived intact from medieval times. Built in the 1360s to contain treasures belonging to Edward III, it once formed part of the palace's defensive walls—hence the fortresslike appearance. Check out the original ribbed stone ceiling on the ground floor; look up to see the carved stone images of men and beasts. The Jewel Tower was later used as a records office for the House of Lords, but hasn't served any official function since the rest of the old palace was destroyed by fire in 1834 and the ancient documents were moved to the greater safety of the Tower of London. Today it contains an exhibition on the history of Parliament. ✉ *Abingdon St., Westminster* ☎ *020/7222–2219* ⊕ *www.english-heritage.org.uk/visit/places/jewel-tower* 🎫 *£4.20* ⊙ *Mar.–Oct., daily 10–5; Nov.–Feb., weekends 10–4; last admission 30 mins before closing* Ⓜ *Westminster.*

FAMILY  
Fodor's Choice  
★

**National Gallery.** Anyone with even a passing interest in art will want to put this near the top of their to-do lists while visiting London, for it is truly one of the world's great art museums. More than 2,300 masterpieces are on show here, including works by Michelangelo, Leonardo, Turner, Monet, Van Gogh, Picasso, and more. Enter through the grand portico overlooking the north side of Trafalgar Square to delve headlong into the highlights of the collection, although the Sainsbury Wing (the modern building immediately to the left), which focuses mainly on medieval art, is invariably less crowded. You could easily spend all day discovering what the National Gallery has to offer, but among the best-known highlights are: in Room 4, *The Ambassadors* by Hans Holbein (1497–1543), a portrait of two wealthy visitors from France, surrounded by objects laden with enough symbolism to fill a book—including, most beguilingly, a giant skull at the base, which only takes shape when viewed from an angle; in Room 56, the *Arnolfini Portrait* by Van Eyck (1390–1441), in which a solemn couple holds hands, the fish-eye mirror behind them mysteriously illuminating what can't be seen from the front view; in Room 57, *The Virgin and the Rocks* by Leonardo da Vinci (1452–1519), a magnificent sculpted altarpiece from 1480; in Room 34, *Rain, Steam and Speed: The Great Western Railway* by J.M.W. Turner (1775–1851), which seems, in its mad whirl of rain, steam and mist, to embody the mystical dynamism of the steam age (spot the fleeing hare); in Room 32, *The Supper at Emmaus* by Caravaggio (1573–1610), in which a freshly resurrected Christ blesses bread in an astonishingly domestic vision from the master of chiaroscuro; and, perhaps more famous than any of them, the *Sunflowers* by Van Gogh (1853–90), in Room 45. Special exhibitions, of which there are several every year, tend to be major events. Generally they're ticketed, so booking is advisable if it's a big name (the Rembrandt exhibition in 2015 sold more than a quarter of a million tickets, for instance). The permanent collection, however, is always free. Also free are weekday lunchtime lectures, or Ten Minute Talks, which illuminate the story behind a key work of art. Daily hour-long free guided tours start at the Sainsbury Wing weekdays at 11:30 and 2:30 (Friday also at 7 pm) and on weekends at 11:30, 2:30, and 4. ⊠ *Trafalgar Sq., Westminster* ☎ *020/7747–2885* ⊕ *www.nationalgallery.org.uk* ⊠ *Free; charge for special exhibitions; audio guide £4* ☉ *Sat.–Thurs. 10–6, Fri. 10–9* Ⓜ *Charing Cross, Embankment, Leicester Sq.*

FAMILY

Fodor's Choice

★

**National Portrait Gallery.** The National Portrait Gallery was founded in 1856 with a single aim: to gather together portraits of famous (and infamous) Britons throughout history. More than 150 years and 160,000 portraits later, it is an essential stop for all history and literature buffs. If you visit with kids, ask at the desk about the excellent Family Trails, which make exploring the galleries with children much more fun. Galleries are arranged clearly and chronologically, from Tudor times to contemporary Britain. A Holbein miniature of Henry VIII is among the most famous images in the Tudor Gallery, although the enormous portrait of Elizabeth I—bejeweled and literally astride the world in a powerful display of imperial intent—may be the most impressive. The huge permanent collections include portraits of Shakespeare, the Brontë sisters, and Jane Austen. Look for the four Andy Warhol *Queen Elizabeth II* silkscreens from 1985 and Maggi Hambling's surreal self-portrait. Contemporary portraits range from the iconic (*Julian with T-shirt*—an LCD screen on a continuous loop—by Julian Opie) to the extreme (Marc Quinn's *Self*, a realization of the artist's head done in frozen blood). Temporary exhibitions can be explored on the first three floors, particularly in the Wolfson and Porter galleries on the ground floor. ∎**TIP→** On the top floor, the Portrait Restaurant has one of the best views in London—a panoramic vista of Nelson's Column and the backdrop along Whitehall to the Houses of Parliament. ⊠ *St. Martin's Pl., Westminster* ☎ *020/7306–0055, 020/7312–2463 for info* ⊕ *www. npg.org.uk* ⊠ *Free; charge for special exhibitions; audiovisual guide £3; family audio guides £6 for 5 people, £4 for 2 people* ☉ *Sat.–Wed. 10–6, Thurs. and Fri. 10–9; last admission 10 mins before closing* Ⓜ *Charing Cross, Leicester Sq.*

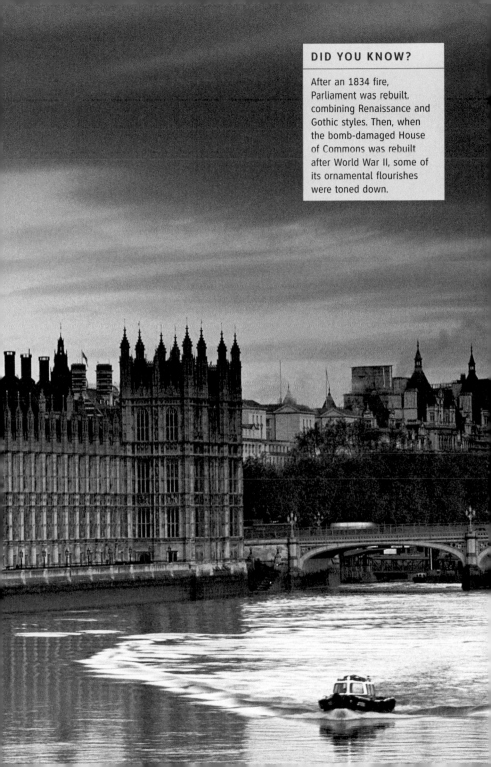

FAMILY **St. Martin-in-the-Fields.** One of London's best-loved and most welcoming of churches is more than just a place of worship. Named after St. Martin of Tours, known for the help he gave to beggars, this parish has long been a welcome sight for the homeless, who have been given soup and shelter at the church since 1914. The church is also a haven for music lovers; the internationally known Academy of St. Martin-in-the-Fields was founded here, and a popular program of concerts continues today. (Although the interior is a wonderful setting for a recital, beware the hard wooden benches!) The crypt is a hive of activity, with a popular café and shop. Here you can also make your own life-size souvenir knight, lady, or monarch from replica tomb brasses, with metallic waxes, paper, and instructions (prices start at £4.50). ⊠ *Trafalgar Sq., Westminster* ☎ *020/7766–1100* ⊕ *www.smitf.org* ☞ *Free; concerts free–£30* ☉ *All day for worship. Sightseeing: Mon., Tues., and Fri. 8:30–1 and 2–6, Wed. 8:30–1:15 and 2–5, Thurs. 8:30–1 and 2–6, Sat. 9:30–6, Sun. 3:30–5* Ⓜ *Charing Cross, Leicester Sq.*

> ## ST. MARTIN'S CONCERTS
>
> Classical concerts (some by candlelight) are held Thursday–Saturday (and some Tuesdays) at 7:30 pm with evening jazz concerts in the crypt every Wednesday at 8 pm. Tickets are available from the box office in the crypt. Free (donation suggested £3.50) lunchtime concerts take place Monday, Tuesday, and Friday 1–2 pm.

**QUICK BITES**

The atmospheric **St. Martin's Café in the Crypt,** with its magnificent high-arched brick vault and gravestone floor, has a superb setting at the heart of London. It serves full English and continental breakfasts, sandwiches, salads, snacks, afternoon tea, and wine. Lunch and dinner options include vegetarian meals.

FAMILY
**Fodor's**Choice
★

**Tate Britain.** First opened in 1897, and funded by the sugar magnate Sir Henry Tate, this stately neoclassical institution may not be as ambitious as its South Bank sibling, Tate Modern, but its bright galleries lure only a fraction of the Modern's overwhelming crowds and are a great place to explore British art from 1500 to the present. The museum includes the Linbury Galleries on the lower floors, which stage temporary exhibitions, and a permanent collection on the upper floors. And what a collection it is—with classic works by John Constable, Thomas Gainsborough, David Wilkie, Francis Bacon, Duncan Grant, Barbara Hepworth, and Ben Nicholson, and an outstanding display from J.M.W. Turner in the Clore Gallery, including many later vaporous and light-infused works such as *Sunrise with Sea Monsters.* Sumptuous Pre-Raphaelite pieces are a major draw, while the Contemporary British Art galleries bring you face to face with Damien Hirst's *Away from the Flock* and other recent conceptions. The Tate Britain also hosts the annual Turner Prize exhibition, with its accompanying furor over the state of contemporary art, from about October to January each year. There's a good little café, and the excellent Rex Whistler Restaurant has been something of an institution since it first opened in 1927. It's

The Tate Britain showcases British art from the last 500 years, including contemporary works.

open daily for lunch, and for dinner on semiregular **Late at Tate** Friday evening events, when the gallery is open late for talks or performances; check the website for details.

■**TIP→** Craving more art? Head down the river on the Tate Boat (£7.50 one-way) to the Tate Modern; it runs between the two museums every 40 minutes. A Family River Roamer ticket (£36 for two adults and two children) permits a day's travel, with stops including the London Eye and the Tower of London. You get a discount of roughly a third if you have a Travelcard. ⊠ *Millbank, Westminster* ☎ *020/7887–8888* ⊕ *www.tate. org.uk/britain* 🎫 *Free; charge for special exhibitions* ⊗ *Daily 10–6; last ticket sold and special exhibitions close at 5:15* Ⓜ *Pimlico.*

Fodor's Choice  **Trafalgar Square.** This is officially the center of London: a plaque on
★  the corner of the Strand and Charing Cross Road marks the spot from which distances on U.K. signposts are measured. (London's *actual* geographic center, as measured in 2015, is a rather dull bench on the Victoria Embankment.) Medieval kings once kept their aviaries of hawks and falcons here; today the humbler gray pigeons flock en masse to the open spaces around the ornate fountains (feeding them is banned). The square was designed in 1830 by John Nash, who envisaged a new public space with striking views of the Thames, the Houses of Parliament, and Buckingham Palace. Of those, only Parliament is still clearly visible from the square, but it remains a magnet for open-air concerts, political demonstrations, and national celebrations, such as New Year's Eve. Dominating the square is 170-foot **Nelson's Column**, erected as a monument to the great admiral in 1848. Note that the lampposts on

the south side, heading down Whitehall, are topped with ships—they all face Portsmouth, home of the British navy. The column is flanked on either side by enormous bronze lions. Climbing them is a very popular photo op, but be extremely careful, as there are no guardrails and it's a long fall onto concrete if you slip. Four plinths border the square; three contain militaristic statues, but one was left empty—it's now used for contemporary art installations, often with a wry and controversial edge. Surprisingly enough, given that this was a square built to honor British military victories, the lawn at the north side, by the National Gallery, contains a statue of George Washington—a gift from the state of Virginia in 1921. At the southern point of the square is the **equestrian statue of Charles I.** After the Civil War and the king's execution, Oliver Cromwell, the antiroyalist leader, commissioned a brazier, John Rivett, to melt the statue down. The story goes that Rivett instead merely buried it in his garden. He made a fortune peddling knickknacks wrought, he claimed, from its metal, only to produce the statue miraculously unscathed after the restoration of the monarchy—and then made another fortune reselling it. In 1667 Charles II had it placed where it stands today, near the spot where his father was executed in 1649. Each year, on January 30, the day of the king's death, the Royal Stuart Society lays a wreath at the foot of the statue. ⊠ *Westminster* Ⓜ *Charing Cross.*

**Fodor's Choice** ★ **Westminster Abbey.** Steeped in millennia of rich and often bloody history, Westminster Abbey is one of England's most iconic buildings. An abbey has stood here since the 7th century, although the current building mostly dates to the 1240s. It has hosted 38 coronations—beginning in 1066 with William the Conqueror—and no fewer than 16 royal weddings, the latest being that of Prince William and Kate Middleton in 2011. But be warned: there's only one way around the abbey, and it gets very crowded, so you'll need to be alert to catch the highlights. Enter via the North Door; as you walk east toward the apse, you'll see the **Coronation Chair** at the foot of the Henry VII Chapel. It's been used for nearly every coronation since Edward I's in 1301, right up to Queen Elizabeth II's in 1952. Farther along, the exquisite confection of the Henry VII's **Lady Chapel** is topped by a magnificent fan-vaulted ceiling. The tomb of Henry VII lies behind the altar. Elizabeth I is buried above her sister "Bloody" Mary I in the tomb just to the north, while her arch enemy, Mary Queen of Scots, rests in the tomb to the south. Continue through the South Ambulatory to the **Chapel of St. Edward the Confessor,** which contains the shrine to the pre-Norman king, who reigned from 1042 to 1066. Because of its great age, you must join the vergers' tours to be admitted to the chapel (£3; book at the admission desk), or attend Holy Communion within the shrine on Tuesday at 8 am. To the left, you'll find **Poets' Corner.** Geoffrey Chaucer was the first poet to be buried here in 1400, and other statues and memorials include those to William Shakespeare, D. H. Lawrence, T. S. Eliot, and Oscar Wilde. The medieval **Chapter House** is adorned with 14th-century frescoes and a magnificent 13th-century tiled floor, one of the finest in the country. Near the entrance is Britain's oldest door, dating from the 1050s. Continue back to the nave of the abbey. If you walk toward the West Entrance, you'll see a plaque to Franklin D. Roosevelt—one of

One of London's most iconic sites, Westminster Abbey contains more than 600 monuments and memorials, and serves as the final resting place of some of England's most famous citizens.

the Abbey's very few tributes to a foreigner. The poppy-wreathed **Grave of the Unknown Warrior** commemorates soldiers who lost their lives in both world wars. Exact hours for the various parts of the abbey are frustratingly long and complicated, and can change daily, so it's important to check before setting out, particularly if you're visiting early or late in the day, or off-season. The full schedule is posted online daily (or you can call). Certain areas of the abbey are completely inaccessible to wheelchair users; however, you will get free entry for yourself and one other. ⊠ *Broad Sanctuary, Westminster* ☎ *020/7222–5152* ⊕ *www. westminster-abbey.org* ⊡ *£20; audio tour free* ☉ *Abbey: Mon., Tues., Thurs., and Fri. 9:30–4:30, Wed. 9:30–7, Sat. 9:30–2:30; last admission 1 hr before closing; Sun. for worship only. Cloisters daily 8–6. College Garden: Apr.–Sept., Tues.–Thurs. 10–6; Oct.–Mar., Tues.–Thurs. 10–4. Chapter House daily 10:30–4. Verger tours: Apr.–Sept., weekdays at 10, 10:30, 11, 2, and 2:30, Sat. at 10, 10:30, and 11; Oct.–Mar., weekdays at 10:30, 11, 2, and 2:30, Sat. at 10:30 and 11. Hrs do vary, so always call ahead* Ⓜ *Westminster, St. James's Park.*

## WORTH NOTING

**Admiralty Arch.** This stately gateway is an impressive counterpoint to Buckingham Palace, at the opposite end of the Mall (rhymes with "shall"). On the southwest corner of Trafalgar Square, the arch, named after the adjacent Royal Navy headquarters, was designed by Sir Aston Webb and completed in 1912 as a memorial to Queen Victoria. Actually comprising five arches—two for pedestrians, two for traffic, and the central arch which is only opened for state occasions—it was a government building until 2012, and has even served as an alternative residence for the Prime Minister while Downing Street was under renovation. It is now expected to become a luxury hotel. Look out for the bronze nose grafted onto the inside wall of the right-hand traffic arch (when facing the Mall); it was placed there in secret by a mischievous artist in 1997 and has been allowed to remain. ☒ *The Mall, Cockspur St., and Trafalgar Sq., Westminster* Ⓜ *Charing Cross.*

### WORD OF MOUTH

"I went on a daytime guided tour [of Buckingham Palace] last month. The small numbers on the tour means you get time to stand and look round each room thoroughly, rather than being herded through. There are no ropes, so you can get right up to the paintings and furniture. You also get the drama of standing in front of the beautiful mirrored and gilded doors as they are pushed open to reveal yet another over-the-top room."

—anicecupoftea

**Banqueting House.** James I commissioned Inigo Jones, one of England's great architects, to undertake a grand building on the site of the original Tudor Palace of Whitehall, which was (according to one foreign visitor) "ill-built, and nothing but a heap of houses." Jones's Banqueting House, finished in 1622 and the first building in England to be completed in the neoclassical style, bears all the hallmarks of the Palladian sophistication and purity which so influenced Jones during his time in Italy. James's son, Charles I, enhanced the interior by employing the Flemish painter Peter Paul Rubens to glorify his father and himself (naturally) in a series of vibrant painted ceiling panels called *The Apotheosis of James I.* As it turned out, these allegorical paintings, depicting a wise monarch being received into heaven, were the last thing Charles saw before he stepped through the open first-floor window onto the scaffold, which had been erected directly outside for his execution by Cromwell's Parliamentarians in 1649. Twenty years later, his son, Charles II, would celebrate the restoration of the monarchy in the exact same place. ☒ *Whitehall, Westminster* ☎ *084/4482–7777* ⊕ *www.hrp. org.uk/BanquetingHouse* 🎟 *£6.60* ◷ *Daily 10–5; last admission 45 mins before closing. May close at short notice for events; call ahead* Ⓜ *Charing Cross, Embankment, Westminster.*

**Carlton House Terrace.** Architect John Nash designed Carlton House, a glorious example of the Regency style, under the patronage of the Prince Regent (later George IV), who ruled in place of George III while the "mad king" was considered too unstable to rule. Carlton House was considered a most extravagant building for its time; it was demolished after the prince's accession to the throne in 1820. In its place Nash built Carlton House Terrace—no less imposing, with white-stucco facades and massive Corinthian columns. Carlton Terrace was a smart address, home to several of the 19th century's greatest luminaries—including two prime ministers, William Gladstone (1856) and Lord Palmerston (1857–75). Today Carlton House Terrace houses the Royal Society (No. 6–9), Britain's most prestigious society of scientific minds; still active today, its previous members have included Isaac Newton and Charles Darwin. ⊠ *The Mall, St. James's* Ⓜ *Charing Cross.*

FAMILY **Household Cavalry Museum.** Hang around Horse Guards for even a short time and you'll see a member of the Household Cavalry on guard, or trotting past on horseback, resplendent in a bright crimson uniform with polished brass armor. Made up of soldiers from the British Army's most senior regiments, the Life Guards and the Blues and Royals, membership is considered a great honor; they act as the Queen's official bodyguards and play a key role in state occasions. (It is they who perform the daily Changing the Guard ceremony at 11 am, 10 am on Sunday.) Housed in the cavalry's original 17th-century stables, the museum has displays of uniforms and weapons going back to 1661 as well as interactive exhibits on the regiments' current operational roles. In the tack room you can handle saddles and bridles, and try on a trooper's uniform, including a distinctive brass helmet with horsehair plume. You can also observe the working horses being tended to in their stable block behind a glass wall. ⊠ *Horse Guards Parade, Whitehall* ☎ *020/7930–3070* ⊕ *www.householdcavalrymuseum.co.uk* ⊡ *£7* ⊘ *Apr.–Oct., daily 10–6; Nov.–Mar., daily 10–5; last admission 45 mins before closing* Ⓜ *Charing Cross, Westminster.*

**St. Margaret's Church.** Dwarfed by its neighbor, Westminster Abbey, St. Margaret's was founded in the 11th century and rebuilt between 1488 and 1523. It's the unofficial parish church of the House of Commons— Winston Churchill tied the knot here in 1908, and since 1681, a pew off the south aisle has been set aside for the Speaker of the House (look for the carved portcullis). Samuel Pepys, Geoffrey Chaucer, and John Milton worshipped here. The stained glass in the north windows is classically Victorian, facing abstract glass from John Piper in the south. These were to replace the originals, which were ruined in World War II. ⊠ *St. Margaret's St., Parliament Sq., Westminster* ☎ *020/7654–4840* ⊕ *www.westminster-abbey.org/st-margarets* ⊡ *Free* ⊘ *Weekdays 9:30– 3:30, Sat. 9:30–1:30, Sun. 2–4:30 (entry via east door). May close on short notice for services; call ahead* Ⓜ *Westminster.*

**The Supreme Court.** The highest court of appeal in the United Kingdom is a surprisingly young institution, only having heard its first cases in 2009. Visitors are welcome to drop by and look at the three courtrooms, housed in the carefully restored Middlesex Guildhall, including the impressive Court Room 1, with its magnificent carved wood ceiling. The Court's art collection, on permanent display, includes portraits by Thomas Gainsborough and Joshua Reynolds. Guided tours are available on Friday (book ahead). There is a café downstairs. ⊠ *Parliament Sq., Westminster* ☎ *020/7960–1500* ⊕ *www.supremecourt.uk* ⊡ *Free; guided tour £5, audio guide £1* ⊘ *Weekdays 9:30–4:30; guided tours most Fri. at 11, 2, and 3* Ⓜ *Westminster (take Exit 6 for Whitehall west).*

FAMILY **Wellington Barracks and the Guards Museum.** These are the headquarters of the Guards Division, the Queen's five regiments of elite foot guards (Grenadier, Coldstream, Scots, Irish, and Welsh), who protect the sovereign and, dressed in tunics of gold-purled scarlet and tall bearskin caps, patrol her palaces. Guardsmen alternate these ceremonial postings with serving in current conflicts, for which they wear more practical uniforms. If you want to learn more about the guards, visit the **Guards Museum,** which has displays on all aspects of a guardsman's life in conflicts dating back to 1642; the entrance is next to the Guards Chapel. Next door is the **Guards Toy Soldier Centre,** a great place for a souvenir. ✉ *Birdcage Walk, Westminster* ☎ *020/7414–3428* ⊕ *www.theguardsmuseum.com* 🎫 *£6* ⊗ *Daily 10–4; last admission at 3:30* Ⓜ *St. James's Park, Green Park.*

**Westminster Cathedral.** Tucked away on traffic-clogged Victoria Street lies this remarkable neo-Byzantine gem, seat of the Archbishop of Westminster, head of the Roman Catholic Church in England and Wales. Faced with building a church with Westminster Abbey as a neighbor, architect John Francis Bentley looked to the east for inspiration, to the basilicas of St. Mark's in Venice and the Hagia Sofia in Istanbul. The asymmetrical redbrick edifice, dating to 1903, is banded with stripes of Portland stone and abutted by a 273-foot-high bell tower (the bell is nicknamed "Big Edward") at the northwest corner, ascendable by elevator for sterling views. The interior remains incomplete, but the unfinished overhead brickwork of the ceiling lends the church a dark, brooding intensity. Several side chapels, such as the Chapel of the Blessed Sacrament and the Holy Souls Chapel, are beautifully finished in glittering mosaics. The Lady Chapel—dedicated to the Virgin Mary—is also sumptuously decorated. Look out for the Stations of the Cross, done here by Eric Gill, and the striking baldachin—the enormous stone canopy standing over the altar with a giant cross suspended in front of it. The nave, the widest in the country, is constructed in green marble, which also has a Byzantine connection—it was cut from the same place as the marble used in the Hagia Sofia, and was almost confiscated by warring Turks as it traveled west. All told, more than 200 different types of marble can be found within the cathedral's interior. There's a café in the crypt. ✉ *Ashley Pl., off Victoria St., Westminster* ☎ *020/7798–9055* ⊕ *www.westminstercathedral.org.uk* 🎫 *Bell Tower and viewing gallery £5, Treasures of the Cathedral exhibition £5; combination ticket £8* ⊗ *Cathedral weekdays 8–7, weekends 10–1; Bell Tower and Treasures of the Cathedral exhibition weekdays 9:30–5, weekends 9:30–6* Ⓜ *Victoria.*

# ST. JAMES'S

As a fitting coda to all of Westminster's pomp and circumstance, St. James's—packed with old-money galleries, restaurants, and gentlemen's clubs that embody the history and privilege of traditional London—is found to the south of Piccadilly and north of the Mall.

When Whitehall Palace burned down in 1698, all of London turned its attention to St. James's Palace, the new royal residence. In the 18th and 19th centuries, the area around the palace became the place to live, and many of the estates surrounding the palace disappeared in a building frenzy, as mansions were built and streets laid out. Most of the homes here are privately owned and therefore closed to visitors, but there are some treasure houses that you can explore (such as Spencer House), as well as many fancy shops that have catered to the great and good for centuries.

**2**

## ROYALTY WATCHING

You've seen Big Ben, the Tower, and Westminster Abbey. But somehow you feel something is missing: a close encounter with Britain's most famous attraction—Her actual Maj, Elizabeth II. The Queen and the Royal Family attend hundreds of functions a year, and if you want to know what they are doing on any given date, turn to the Court Circular, printed in the major London dailies, or check out the Royal Family website (⊕ www.royal.gov.uk) for the latest events on the Royal Diary. Trooping the Colour is usually held on the second Saturday in June, to celebrate the Queen's official birthday. This spectacular parade begins when she leaves Buckingham Palace in her carriage and rides down the Mall to arrive at Horse Guards Parade at 11 exactly. To watch, just line up along the Mall with your binoculars.

Another time you can catch the Queen in all her regalia is when she and the Duke of Edinburgh ride in state to open the Houses of Parliament. The famous black and gilt-trimmed Irish State Coach travels from Buckingham Palace on a clear day, it's to be hoped, for this ceremony takes place in late October or early November. The Gold State Coach, an icon of fairy-tale glamour, is used for coronations and jubilees only.

But perhaps the most relaxed, least formal time to see the Queen is during Royal Ascot, held at the racetrack near Windsor Castle—a short train ride out of London—usually during the third week of June (Tuesday–Friday). The Queen and members of the Royal Family are driven down the track to the Royal Box in an open carriage, giving spectators a chance to see them. After several races, the famously horse-loving Queen invariably walks down to the paddock, greeting racegoers as she proceeds. If you meet her, the official etiquette is to first make a short bow or curtsy, and then to address her first as "Your Majesty," and then "Ma'am" (to rhyme with "ham," not "farm") thereafter.

Today, St. James's remains a rather masculine enclave, containing most of the capital's celebrated gentlemen's clubs (especially the classic Atheneum), long-established men's outfitters and clothiers, and some interesting art galleries and antiques shops. In one corner is St. James's Park, framed on its western side by the biggest monument in the area: Buckingham Palace, official residence of the Queen. The smaller St. James's Palace is where much of the office work for the House of Windsor gets done; nearby is Clarence House, London home of Prince Charles and his wife, Camilla.

## TOP ATTRACTIONS

Fodor's Choice ★ **Buckingham Palace.** If Buckingham Palace were open year-round, it would be by far the most visited tourist attraction in Britain; as it is, the Queen's main residence, home to every British monarch since Victoria in 1837, opens its doors to the public only in August and September. The Queen is almost never there at the time—traditionally she heads off to Scotland for a couple of months every summer, where she takes up residence at Balmoral Castle. (Here's a quick way to tell if the Queen's at home: if she's in residence, the Royal Standard flies above the palace; if not, it's the more famous red, white, and blue Union Jack.) The tour covers the palace's 19 State Rooms, with their fabulous gilt moldings and walls adorned with old masters. The **Grand Hall,** followed by the **Grand Staircase** and **Guard Room,**

are visions in marble and gold leaf, filled with massive, twinkling chandeliers. Don't miss the theatrical **Throne Room,** with the original 1953 coronation throne, or the sword in the Ballroom, used by the Queen to bestow knighthoods and other honors with a touch on the recipient's shoulders. Royal portraits line the **State Dining Room,** and the **Blue Drawing Room** is dazzling in its splendor. The bow-shape **Music Room** features lapis lazuli columns between arched floor-to-ceiling windows, and the alabaster-and-gold plasterwork of the **White Drawing Room** is a dramatic statement of wealth and power. Admission is by timed-entry ticket every 15 minutes throughout the day. Allow up to two hours for your visit. Those with impaired mobility should contact the Palace in advance, as they may have to enter a different way (it's no bad thing, as you are sometimes taken via the front instead; practise your wave to the crowds on the Mall). **Changing the Guard** remains one of London's best free shows and culminates in front of the palace. Marching to live military bands, the old guard proceed up the Mall from St. James's Palace to Buckingham Palace. Shortly afterward, the new guard approach from Wellington Barracks. Then within the forecourt, the captains of the old and new guards symbolically transfer the keys to the palace. Get there early for the best view. ⊠ *Buckingham Palace Rd., St. James's* ☎ *020/7766–7300* ⊕ *www.royalcollection.org.uk/visit* 🖅 *£21.50 (£30.50 including garden highlights tour); joint ticket with Queen's Gallery and Royal Mews £37* ◷ *Aug., daily 9:15–7:45 (last admission at 5:15); Sept., daily 9:15–6:45 (last admission at 4:15). Hrs subject to change; check website* Ⓜ *Victoria, St. James's Park, Green Park.*

**The Mall.** This stately, 115-foot-wide processional route sweeping from Admiralty Arch to the Queen Victoria Memorial at Buckingham Palace is an updated 1904 version of a promenade laid out around 1660 for the game of *paille-maille* (a type of croquet crossed with golf), which also gave the parallel road Pall Mall its name. (That's why Mall is pronounced to rhyme with "pal," not "ball.") The tarmac is colored red to represent a ceremonial red carpet. During state visits, several times a year, the Mall is traditionally bedecked with the flag of the visiting nation, alongside the Union Jack. The **Duke of York Memorial** up the steps toward Carlton House Terrace is a towering column dedicated to George III's second son, who was further immortalized in the English nursery rhyme "The Grand Old Duke of York." Be sure to stroll along the Mall on Sunday when the road is closed to traffic, or catch the bands and troops of the Household Division on their way from St. James's

A classic photo op: cavalry from the Queen's Life Guard at Buckingham Palace

Palace to Buckingham Palace for the Changing the Guard. ✉ *St. James's* Ⓜ *Charing Cross, Green Park.*

**Piccadilly Circus.** The origins of the name "Piccadilly" relate to a humble 17th-century tailor from the Strand named Robert Baker who sold picadils—stiff ruffled collars all the rage in courtly circles—and built a house with the proceeds. Snobs dubbed his new-money mansion Piccadilly Hall, and the name stuck. Pride of place in the circus—a circular junction until the construction of Shaftesbury Avenue in 1886—belongs to the statue universally referred to as Eros, dating to 1893. (Although even most Londoners don't know that it is, in reality, a representation of Eros's brother Anteros, the Greek God of requited love.) The other instantly recognizable feature of Piccadilly Circus is the enormous bank of lit-up billboards on the north side; if you're passing at night, frame them behind the Tube entrance sign on the corner of Regent Street for an unforgettable photograph. ✉ *St. James's* Ⓜ *Piccadilly Circus.*

**The Queen's Gallery.** Technically speaking, the sovereign doesn't "own" the rare and exquisite works of art in the Royal Collection: she merely holds them in trust for the nation—and what a collection it is! Only a selection is on view at any one time, presented in themed exhibitions. Let the excellent (free) audio guide take you through the elegant galleries filled with some of the world's greatest artworks.

A rough time line of the major royal collectors starts with Charles I (who also commissioned Rubens to paint the Banqueting House ceiling). An avid art enthusiast, Charles established the basis of the Royal Collection, purchasing works by Raphael, Titian, Caravaggio, and

Dürer. During the Civil War and in the aftermath of Charles's execution, many masterpieces were sold abroad and subsequently repatriated by Charles II. George III, who bought Buckingham House, scooped up a notable collection of Venetian (including Canaletto), Renaissance (Bellini and Raphael), and Dutch (Vermeer) art, and a large number of baroque drawings, in addition to patronizing English contemporary artists such as Gainsborough and Beechey. The Prince Regent, later George IV, had a particularly good eye for Rembrandt, equestrian works by Stubbs, and lavish portraits by Lawrence. Queen Victoria had a penchant for Landseer animals and landscapes, and Frith's contemporary scenes. Later, Edward VII indulged Queen Alexandra's love of Fabergé, and

> ## THE GUARDMEN'S BEARSKINS
>
> While on duty, guardsmen take their job very, very seriously. They don't speak, don't acknowledge anyone (even those tourists trying in vain to make them laugh—and yes, they will behave like soldiers if you go too far), don't even swat away troublesome flies from their noses. And they're certainly not allowed to keel over under the weight of their enormous hats. Called "bearskins" (and still made, highly controversially, from the pelts of Canadian black bears), the headdresses were first worn by the French Imperial Guard defeated in the Battle of Waterloo in 1815.

many royal tours around the empire produced gifts of gorgeous caliber, such as the Cullinan diamond from South Africa and an emerald-studded belt from India. ⊠ *Buckingham Palace, Buckingham Palace Rd., St. James's* ☎ *020/7766–7301* ⊕ *www.royalcollection.org.uk* ⊠ *£10; joint ticket with Royal Mews and Buckingham Palace £37* ⊙ *Jan.–July and late Sept.–Dec., daily 10–5:30; Aug–late Sept., daily 09:30–5:30; last admission 1 hr 15 mins before closing* Ⓜ *Victoria, St. James's Park, Green Park.*

FAMILY **Royal Mews.** Fairy-tale gold-and-glass coaches and sleek Rolls-Royce state cars emanate from the Royal Mews, next door to the Queen's Gallery. Designed by John Nash, the Mews serves as the headquarters for Her Majesty's travel department (so beware of closures for state visits), complete with the Queen's own special breed of horses, ridden by wigged postilions decked in red-and-gold regalia. Between the stables and the riding school arena are exhibits of polished saddlery and riding tack. The highlight of the Mews is the splendid Gold State Coach, a piece of art on wheels, with its sculpted tritons and sea gods. There are activities for children, and free guided tours are available April–October (daily at 10:15, then hourly 11–4). ⊠ *Buckingham Palace, Buckingham Palace Rd., St. James's* ☎ *020/7766–7302* ⊕ *www.royalcollection.org. uk* ⊠ *£9.30; joint ticket with Queen's Gallery and Buckingham Palace £37* ⊙ *Late Mar.–Oct., daily 10–5; Nov., Feb., and early–mid-Mar., Mon.–Sat. 10–4; last admission 45 mins before closing* Ⓜ *Victoria, St. James's Park.*

**St. James's Palace.** Commissioned by Henry VIII, this Tudor brick palace was the residence of kings and queens for more than 300 years; indeed, while all monarchs have actually lived at Buckingham Palace

Gentlemen's shops in St. James's specialize in high-quality, handmade goods.

since Queen Victoria's day, it is still the *official* residence of the Sovereign. (This is why foreign ambassadors are received by the "Court of St. James.") Today it contains various royal apartments and offices, including the working office of Prince Charles. The palace is not open to the public, but the surprisingly low-key Tudor exterior is well worth the short detour from the Mall to see. Friary Court out front is a splendid setting for Trooping the Colour, part of the Queen's official birthday celebrations. Everyone loves to take a snapshot of the scarlet-coated guardsman standing sentry outside the imposing Tudor gateway. Note that the Changing the Guard ceremony at St. James's Palace occurs only on days when the guard at Buckingham Palace is changed. If you're approaching from St. James Street, take a quick peek at the delightfully old-looking **Berry Bros. & Rudd** wine store at No. 3, near the back entrance to the palace; it's been trading here continuously since 1698. ✉ *Friary Ct., St. James's* ⊕ *www.royal.gov.uk* Ⓜ *Green Park.*

FAMILY
Fodor's Choice
★

**St. James's Park.** There is a story that, many years ago, a royal once enquired of a courtier how much it would cost to close St. James's Park to the public. "Only your crown, ma'am" came the reply. Bordered by three palaces—Buckingham, St. James', and the governmental complex of the Palace of Westminster—this is one of London's loveliest public parks. It's also the oldest; the former marshland was acquired by Henry VIII in 1532 as royal deer-hunting grounds. Later, James I drained the land and installed an aviary, which gave Birdcage Walk its name, and a zoo (complete with crocodiles, camels, and an elephant). When Charles II returned from exile in France, where he had been hugely impressed by the splendor of the gardens at the Palace of Versailles, he transformed the park into formal gardens, with avenues, fruit orchards, and a canal. Lawns were grazed by goats, sheep, and deer, and in the 18th century the park became a different kind of hunting ground, for wealthy lotharios looking to pick up nighttime escorts. A century later, John Nash redesigned the landscape in a more naturalistic, romantic style, and if you gaze down the lake toward Buckingham Palace, you could easily believe yourself to be on a country estate.

> **PHOTO OP**
>
> The best place for a photo opportunity alongside one of the Queen's guardsmen is at St. James's Palace, or try to keep up alongside them during the morning Changing the Guard. They leave St. James's at about 10:50 am for Buckingham Palace. Failing that, shuffle up to the mounted horse guards on the Whitehall side, there until 4 pm.

A large population of waterfowl—including pelicans, geese, ducks, and swans (which belong to the Queen)—breed on and around Duck Island at the east end of the lake. From April to September, the deck chairs (charge levied) come out, crammed with office workers at midday, eating lunch while being serenaded by music from the bandstands. One of the best times to stroll the leafy walkways is after dark, with Westminster Abbey and the Houses of Parliament rising above the floodlit lake. The popular Inn the Park restaurant is a wood-and-glass pavilion with a turf roof that blends in beautifully with the surrounding landscape; it's an excellent stopping place for a meal or a snack on a nice day. ⊠ *The Mall or Horse Guards approach or Birdcage Walk, St. James's* ⊕ *www.royalparks.org. uk* ⊙ *Daily 5 am–midnight* Ⓜ *St. James's Park, Westminster.*

## WORTH NOTING

**Clarence House.** The London home of the Queen Mother for nearly 50 years until her death in 2002, Clarence House is now the residence of Charles, the Prince of Wales; his wife, Camilla, the Duchess of Cornwall; and Prince Harry. The Regency mansion was built in 1825 by John Nash for the Duke of Clarence (later to become William IV) who considered next-door St. James's Palace to be too cramped for his liking, although postwar renovation work means that little remains of Nash's original. Since then it has remained a royal home for princesses, dukes, and duchesses, including the present monarch, Queen Elizabeth II, as a newlywed before her coronation. The rooms have been sensitively preserved to reflect the Queen Mother's taste, with the addition of many works of art from the Royal Collection, including works by Winterhalter, Augustus John, and Sickert. Clarence House is usually open only for the month of August, and tickets must be booked in advance. ⊠ *St. James's Palace, The Mall, St. James's* ☎ *020/7766–7300* ⊕ *www. royalcollection.org.uk* ⊠ *£10* ⊙ *Aug., weekdays 10–4:30, weekends 10–5:30; last admission 1 hr before closing* Ⓜ *Green Park.*

**Institute of Contemporary Arts (ICA).** You would never suspect that behind the stately white stucco facade in the heart of Establishment London is to be found that champion of the avant-garde, the ICA. Since 1947, the ICA has been pushing boundaries in visual arts, performance, theater, dance, and music. There are two movie theaters, a performance theater, three galleries, a high-brow bookstore, a reading room, a café, and a bar. You have to become a day member to enter, but at just £1, to cover all art exhibitions and other facilities, it's hardly a stretch. ⊠ *The Mall, St. James's* ☎ *020/7930–3647* ⊕ *www.ica.org.uk* ✉ *Entry £1; movies £3–£11; performances and exhibitions vary (most are free)* ⊙ *Galleries Tues.–Sun. 11–11; exhibitions Tues., Wed., and Fri.–Sun. 11–6, Thurs. 11–9* Ⓜ *Charing Cross, Piccadilly Circus.*

■ QUICK
BITES

**ICA Café Bar.** Overlooking The Mall, this café and bar offers a tasty, reasonably priced lunch and dinner menu, with coffees and snacks available throughout the day. Like the venue itself, it's open 11–11. ⊠ *The Mall, St. James's* ☎ *020/7930–8619* ⊕ *www.ica.org.uk* ⊙ *Closed Mon.*

**Spencer House.** Ancestral abode of the Spencers—Princess Diana's family—this is perhaps the finest extant example of an elegant 18th-century London townhouse. Reflecting his passion for the Grand Tour and classical antiquities, the first Earl Spencer commissioned architect John Vardy to adapt designs from ancient Rome for a magnificent private palace. Vardy was responsible for the exteriors, including the gorgeous west-facing Palladian facade, its pediment adorned with classical statues, and the ground-floor interiors, notably the lavish Palm Room, with its spectacular screen of columns covered in gilded carvings that resemble gold palm trees. The lavish style was meant not only to attest to Spencer's power and wealth but also to celebrate his marriage, a love match then rare in aristocratic circles (the palms are a symbol of marital fertility). Midway through construction—the house was built between 1756 and 1766—Spencer changed architects and hired James "Athenian" Stuart, whose designs were based on a classical Greek aesthetic, to decorate the gilded State Rooms on the first floor. These include the Painted Room, the first completely neoclassical room in Europe. Since the 1940s, the house has been leased by the Spencers to a succession of wealthy residents. Entry is by tour only, strictly limited to 20. Tickets are sold from 10 am, on the day only, first-come, first-served. ■TIP→ Note that children under ten are not allowed inside. ⊠ *27 St. James's Pl., St. James's* ☎ *020/7499–8620 for recorded info, 020/7514–1958 for tour reservations* ⊕ *www.spencerhouse.co.uk* ✉ *£12* ⊙ *Sept.–Dec. and Feb.–July, Sun. 10:30–5:45; last tour 1 hr before closing* Ⓜ *Green Park.*

**St. James's Church.** Bombed by the German Luftwaffe in 1940 and not restored until 1954, this was one of the last of Sir Christopher Wren's London churches—and his favorite. Completed in 1684, it contains one of the finest works by the master carver Grinling Gibbons (1648–1721): an ornate limewood *reredos* (the screen behind the altar). The church is a lively place, with all manner of lectures and concerts (some are free). A café occupies a fine location right alongside the church, while a small, sedate garden is tucked away at the rear. The market out front is full of surprises; come Tuesday for antiques, Wednesday–Saturday for arts and crafts. ✉ *197 Piccadilly, St. James's* ☎ *020/7734–4511, 020/7381–0441 for concert program and tickets* ⊕ *www.sjp.org.uk* ✉ *Free* ☉ *Daily 9–6, but hrs vary; call ahead* Ⓜ *Piccadilly Circus, Green Park.*

**St. James's Square.** One of London's oldest squares, St. James's was first laid out in 1670. It soon became the capital's most fashionable address; by 1720, it was home to 14 dukes and earls. These days you're more likely to find it populated with office workers eating their lunches under the shade of its leafy old trees on a warm summer's day, but it still has some prestigious residents. Most famous among them is the **London Library** at No. 14, one of the several 18th-century residences spared by World War II bombs. Founded by Thomas Carlyle, it contains a million or so volumes, making it the world's largest independent lending library, and is also considered the best private humanities library in the land. Nonmembers can take an evening tour of the library, although reservations must be made in advance. ✉ *St. James's* Ⓜ *Piccadilly Circus.*

# MAYFAIR AND MARYLEBONE

# GETTING ORIENTED

Mayfair and Marylebone

## TOP REASONS TO GO

**At home with the Duke of Wellington:** The Iron Duke's Apsley House is filled with splendid salons lined with grand old master paintings.

**Get a passion for fashion:** There's great shopping aplenty on Bond and Mount streets, where the likes of McQueen and McCartney will keep your credit card occupied, but don't forget stylish, gigantic Selfridges.

**London's most charming shopping arcade:** Built for Lord Cavendish in 1819, the beautiful Burlington Arcade is right out of a Victorian daguerreotype.

**The Wallace Collection:** Savor room after room of magnificent furniture, porcelain, silver, and top old master paintings, in the former residence of the marquesses of Hertford.

**Dress to impress at Claridge's:** Afternoon tea at this sumptuous art deco gem is the perfect end to a shopping spree in Mayfair.

## FEELING PECKISH?

**Crussh.** This successful chain serves up delicious juices and smoothies, as well as sandwiches, soups, and wraps. Decamp to nearby Green Park, where—if you're lucky—you can grab one of the deck chairs. ✉ *1 Curzon St., Mayfair* ☎ *020/7629–2554* ⊕ *www.crussh.com* ☽ *Closed weekends* Ⓜ *Green Park.*

**Richoux.** This has been an affordable refuge from busy Piccadilly for more than a century. Simple but well-executed French bistro food is served all day, as well as scrumptious afternoon tea. ✉ *172 Piccadilly, Mayfair* ☎ *020/7493–2204* ⊕ *www.richoux.co.uk* Ⓜ *Green Park, Piccadilly Circus.*

**Truc Vert.** Just south of Oxford Street, this rustic French café-deli is open for breakfast, lunch, and dinner, with a menu that changes daily. ✉ *42 N. Audley St., Mayfair* ☎ *020/7491–9988* ⊕ *www.trucvert.co.uk* Ⓜ *Bond St.*

## GETTING THERE

Three Tube stations on the Central line are handy for reaching these neighborhoods: Marble Arch, Bond Street (also on the Jubilee line), and Oxford Circus (also on the Victoria and Bakerloo lines).

You can also take the Piccadilly or Bakerloo line to the Piccadilly Circus Tube station, the Piccadilly line to the Hyde Park Corner station, or the Piccadilly, Victoria, or Jubilee line to the Green Park station.

The best buses are the C2, which takes in Green Park, Berkeley Square, and New Bond Street, and the 9—London's oldest existing bus route—which runs along Piccadilly.

## MAKING THE MOST OF YOUR TIME

Set aside at least a day to experience Mayfair and Marylebone. Leave enough time for shopping and also to wander casually through the streets and squares.

The only areas to avoid are the Tube stations at rush hour, and Oxford Street if you don't like crowds. At all costs, stay away from Oxford Circus around 5 pm, when the commuter rush can, at times, resemble an East African wildebeest migration—but without the charm.

The area becomes quiet at night, so plan to party elsewhere.

**3**

Sightseeing
★★★★
Nightlife
★
Dining
★★★★
Lodging
★★★★
Shopping
★★★★

Mayfair forms the core of London's West End, the city's most stylish central area. This neighborhood oozes class and old-school style. The sense of being in one of the world's most wealthy and powerful cities is palpable as you wander along its grand and graceful streets. Scoot across the district's one exception to all this elegance—Oxford Street—and you'll discover the pleasant thoroughfares of Marylebone, the most central of London's many "villages."

# MAYFAIR

Updated by
James O'Neill

Ultraritzy Mayfair, lined with beautiful 18th-century mansions (along with Edwardian apartment buildings made of deep-red brick), is the address of choice for many of London's wealthiest residents—note the number of Rolls-Royces, Bentleys, and Jaguars on the streets. Even the delivery vans all seem to bear some royal coat of arms, advertising that they've been purveyors of fine goodies for as long as anyone can remember.

The district can't claim to be stuffed with must-sees, but that is part of its appeal. There is no shortage of history and gorgeous architecture; the streets here are custom-built for window-shopping, expansive strolling, and getting a peek into the lifestyles of London's rich and famous, past and present. Mayfair is primarily residential, so its homes are off-limits except for one satisfyingly grand example: **Apsley House,** the Duke of Wellington's home, built by Robert Adam in 1771, and once known as No. 1, London; the nearby **Wellington Arch** also commemorates the great hero.

Despite being bordered by four of the busiest streets in London—the busy budget-shopping mecca Oxford Street (to the north), the major traffic artery Park Lane (to the west), and the bustling Regent Street and Piccadilly (to the east and south, respectively)—Mayfair itself is remarkably traffic-free and a delight to explore. Starting at **Selfridges,**

Each June for the past 240 years, the iconic Royal Academy of Arts has put on its Summer Exhibition, a huge draw for art-loving visitors and Londoners alike.

on Oxford Street, a southward stroll will take you through quiet streets lined with Georgian townhouses (the area was largely developed in the 17th and 18th centuries). From there, with a bit of artful navigating, you can reach four pleasant patches of green: **Grosvenor Square, Berkeley Square, Hanover Square**, with its splendid **St. George's Church** where Handel worshipped, and the quiet **St. George's Gardens**, bounded by a maze of streets and mews. Some of London's most exclusive shopping destinations are here, including **Mount Street, Bruton Street, Savile Row**, and the **Burlington Arcade**. The **Royal Academy of Arts** is at the southern fringe of Mayfair on Piccadilly, beyond which begins more sedate St. James's.

## TOP ATTRACTIONS

**Apsley House.** Apsley House was built by Robert Adam in the 1770s and was bought by the Duke of Wellington two years after his famous victory over Napoléon at the Battle of Waterloo in 1815. Long known simply as No. 1, London, on account of its being the first mansion at the old tollgate from Knightsbridge village, the Duke's old regency abode is looking hale and hearty after a major refurbishment. Victory over the French made Wellington the greatest soldier and statesman in the land. The so-called Iron Duke lived here from 1817 until his death in 1852, and, although the 7th Duke of Wellington gave the house to the nation, the family retained some residential rights. Opposite the house, and now marooned in a roundabout in the middle of the constant Hyde Park traffic, is the **Wellington Arch**, designed by Decimus Burton and unveiled in 1828, although Burton's original plan to have a sculpture of the Angel of Peace descending upon a chariot of war at the arch's pinnacle wasn't realized until 1912. As you'd expect, the mansion has many uniforms and weapons on display, but it also houses a celebrated art collection, the bulk of which was once owned by Joseph Bonaparte, onetime King of Spain and younger brother of Napoléon. With works by Brueghel, Van Dyck,

> **A BRIEF HISTORY**
>
> The name Mayfair derives from the 15-day May fair that was once held in the charming warren of narrow streets known as Shepherd Market. But in the 18th century, the residents of this now-fashionable neighborhood felt the fair was lowering the tone and so put a stop to it.

and Rubens, as well as the Spanish masters Velázquez and Murillo (note the former's famous portrait of Pope Innocent X), the collection also includes a Goya portrait of the duke himself on horseback. An 11-foot-tall statue of a nude (fig-leafed) Napoléon looms over you as you approach the grand central staircase. The statue was taken from the Louvre and given as a gift to Wellington from the grateful British government in 1816. ⊠ *149 Piccadilly, Hyde Park Corner, Mayfair* ☎ *0370/333–1181* ⊕ *www.english-heritage.org.uk* ⊡ *£8.30; joint ticket with Wellington Arch £10* ⊙ *Apr.–Oct., Wed.–Sun. and bank holiday Mon. 11–5; Nov.–Feb., weekends 10–4* ⌕ *Every Wed. in Oct. there are Twilight Tours 6–9 pm (£12); advance reservation advised* Ⓜ *Hyde Park Corner.*

**Bond Street.** This world-class shopping haunt is divided into northern "New" (1710) and southern "Old" (1690) halves. You can spot the juncture by a bronzed bench on which Franklin D. Roosevelt sits companionably next to Winston Churchill. At No. 35, on New Bond Street, you'll find **Sotheby's**, the world-famous auction house, as well as upscale retailers like Asprey's, Burberry, Louis Vuitton, Georg Jensen, and Church's. You'll find even more opportunities to flirt with financial ruin on Old Bond Street, with flagship boutiques of top-end designers like Chanel, Gucci, and Yves Saint Laurent; an array of fine jewelers including Tiffany; and art dealers Colnaghi, Spink Leger, and Agnew's. **Cork Street,** which parallels the top half of Old Bond Street, is where many top dealers in contemporary art have their galleries. ⊠ *Mayfair* ⊕ *www.bondstreet.co.uk* Ⓜ *Bond St., Green Park.*

**Fodor's Choice** **Burlington Arcade.** With ceilings and lights now restored to how they ★ would have looked when it was built in 1819, Burlington Arcade is the finest of Mayfair's enchanting covered shopping alleys. Originally built for Lord Cavendish, it was meant to stop the hoi polloi from flinging garbage into his garden at next-door Burlington House. Top-hatted watchmen called beadles—the world's smallest private police force—still patrol, preserving decorum by preventing you from singing, running, or carrying an open umbrella. The arcade is also the main link between the Royal Academy of Arts and its extended galleries at 6 Burlington Gardens. ⊠ *Piccadilly, Mayfair* ☎ *020/7493–1764* ⊕ *www.burlington-arcade.co.uk* ⊙ *Mon.–Sat. 9–7:30, Sun. 11–6* Ⓜ *Green Park, Piccadilly Circus.*

Marble Arch was originally a gateway to Buckingham Palace before it was moved to the corner of Hyde Park.

QUICK BITES

Several of London's most fabled and stylish hotels are in Mayfair. Even if you're not staying at one, sample the high life by popping into their glamorous bars for a cocktail or some afternoon tea. **Claridge's Bar** takes its cue from art deco, as do the intimate **Rivoli Bar** (at the Ritz) and the **Connaught Bar** ; the bar at **Brown's Hotel** is modernist.

**Marble Arch.** John Nash's 1827 arch, moved here from Buckingham Palace in 1851, stands amid the traffic whirlpool where Bayswater Road segues into Oxford Street, at the top of Park Lane. The arch actually contains three small chambers, which served as a police station until the mid-20th century. Search the sidewalk on the traffic island opposite the movie theater for the stone plaque recalling the Tyburn Tree, an elaborately designed gallows that stood here for 400 years, until 1783. The condemned would be conveyed here in their finest clothes from Newgate Prison in The City, and were expected to affect a casual indifference or face a merciless heckling from the crowds. Towering across the grass from the arch toward Tyburn Way is *Horse at Water,* a vast patina-green statue of a horse's head by sculptor Nic Fiddian. Cross over (or under) to the northeastern corner of Hyde Park for Speakers' Corner, a parcel of land long-dedicated to the principle of free speech. On Sunday, people of all views—or none at all—come to pontificate, listen, and debate about everything under the sun. ⊠ *Park La., Mayfair* Ⓜ *Marble Arch.*

**Fodor's**Choice ★ **Royal Academy of Arts.** Burlington House was built in 1664, with later Palladian additions for the 3rd Earl of Burlington in 1720. The piazza in front dates from 1873, when the Renaissance-style buildings around the courtyard were designed by Banks and Barry to house a gaggle of noble scientific societies, including the Royal Society of Chemistry and the Royal Astronomical Society.

The house itself is home to the Royal Academy of Arts. Re-development works are well on course to ensure the Royal Academy—still one of the capital's premier public galleries—will celebrate its 250th anniversary in 2018 in fine style. The statue of the academy's first president, Sir Joshua Reynolds, palette in hand, stands prominently in the piazza. Free tours show off part of the collection and the excellent temporary exhibitions. Every June–August, the RA puts on its Summer Exhibition, a huge and eclectic collection of art by living Royal Academicians and many other contemporary artists. ⊠ *Burlington House, Piccadilly, Mayfair* ☎ *020/7300–8000, 020/7300–5839 for lectures and family programs* ⊕ *www.royalacademy.org.uk* ✉ *£10–£16* ⊙ *Sat.–Thurs. 10–6, Fri. 10–10; tours Tues.–Sun. at noon* Ⓜ *Piccadilly Circus, Green Park.*

### ROYALTY IN AISLE 9

Shoppers and historians alike will enjoy **Fortnum & Mason** at 181 Piccadilly. This old-fashioned fine-foods store, built in 1788, seems stuck in another century, with ornate murals decorating the walls, glass cabinets, and brass fixtures casting a dazzling glow all around. The store is especially famous for its loose-leaf tea and luxury picnic hampers (a tempting purchase, given that St. James's Square is just a stone's throw away). Fortnum & Mason sent hams to the Duke of Wellington's army and baskets of treats to Florence Nightingale in the Crimea. (It also happens to be the Queen's grocery store.)

**QUICK BITES**

**The RA Grand Café.** With its walls covered in Gilbert Spencer murals, the Royal Academy's café is almost as beautiful as the art hanging in the galleries. The accent is on variety, with hearty dishes like fish pie, cold cuts, and upscale salads and sandwiches. It's open daily 10:30–5:30. ⊠ *Burlington House, Piccadilly, Mayfair* ☎ *020/7300–5608* ⊕ *www.royalacademy. org.uk* Ⓜ *Piccadilly Circus, Green Park.*

**Wellington Arch.** Opposite the Duke of Wellington's mansion, Apsley House, this majestic stone arch surveys the traffic rushing around Hyde Park Corner. Designed by Decimus Burton and completed in 1828, it was created as a grand entrance to the west side of London and echoes the design of that other landmark gate, Marble Arch. Both were triumphal arches commemorating Britain's victory against France in the Napoleonic Wars. Atop the building, the Angel of Peace descends on the *quadriga,* or four-horse chariot of war. Inside the arch, three floors of permanent and temporary exhibits reveal the monument's history. From the balconies at the top of the arch you can peek into the Queen's back garden at across-the-road Buckingham Palace. ⊠ *Hyde Park Corner, Mayfair* ☎ *020/7930–2726* ⊕ *www.english-heritage.org.uk* ✉ *£4.30* ⊙ *May–Oct., daily 10–6; Nov.–Apr., daily 10–4; platform sometimes closes for exhibition load-in* Ⓜ *Hyde Park Corner.*

Regent Street, home to Liberty department store and Hamleys toy shop, decorated for the holidays

## WORTH NOTING

**Grosvenor Square.** Pronounced "*Grove*-na," this leafy square was laid out in 1725–31 and is as desirable an address today as it was then. Americans have certainly always thought so—from John Adams, the second president, who as ambassador lived at No. 38, to Dwight D. Eisenhower, whose wartime headquarters was at No. 20. The entire west side of the square has long been home to the U.S. Embassy, which is relocating south of the river during 2016, and a British memorial to Franklin D. Roosevelt still stands in the center. There is also a classically styled memorial to those who died in New York on September 11, 2001. Grosvenor Chapel, completed in 1730 and used by Eisenhower's men during World War II, stands a couple of blocks south of the square on South Audley Street, with the entrance to pretty **St. George's Gardens** to its left. ✉ *Mayfair* Ⓜ *Bond St.*

**Handel and Hendrix in London.** This newly renamed museum celebrates the lives of not one, but two, musical geniuses: classical composer George Frederick Handel and rock guitar legend Jimi Hendrix. Comprising two adjoining buildings, the bulk of the museum centers on the life and works of Handel who lived at No. 25 for more than 30 years until his death in 1759. In rooms decorated in fine Georgian style, you can linger over original manuscripts and gaze at portraits. Some of the composer's most famous pieces were created here, including the *Messiah* and *Music for the Royal Fireworks*. Fast-forward 200 years or so, and the apartment on the upper floors of No. 23 housed one of rock's great innovators, Jimi Hendrix, for a short but creative period in the late 1960s.

221B Baker Street and "Holmes" himself

Formerly the museum's administrative offices, Hendrix's apartment has now been lovingly restored to its late 1960s heyday and is open to the public. ⊠ *23–25 Brook St., entrance in Lancashire Court, Mayfair* ☎ *020/7495–1685* ⊕ *www.handelhendrix.org* ✉ *£7.50 for each exhibition; £10 combined ticket for both. Visits must be booked in advance* ⊙ *Mon.–Sat. 11–6, Sun. noon–6; last admission at 5* Ⓜ *Bond St.*

# MARYLEBONE

A favorite of newspaper style sections everywhere, Marylebone High Street forms the heart of Marylebone Village (pronounced "Marr-le-bone"), a vibrant, upscale neighborhood that encompasses the squares and streets around High Street and nearby Marylebone Lane. The district took its name from a church dedicated to St. Mary and the bourne (another word for "stream") that ran through the original village. Nowadays, it's hard to believe you're just a few blocks north of gaudy Oxford Street as you wander in and out of Marylebone's small shops and boutiques, the best of which include Cadenheads Whisky Shop and Tasting Room (26 Chiltern Street); La Fromagerie (2–6 Moxon Street), an excellent cheese shop; Daunt Books (Nos. 83–84 Marylebone High Street), a superlative travel bookshop; the "Cabbages and Frocks" market (Saturday 11–5) on the grounds of the St. Marylebone Parish Church, purveying specialty foods and vintage clothing; and a large farmers' and artisanal-food market (Sunday 10–2) in a parking lot on Cramer Street, just behind High Street. But some memorable sights await, too, including the best remnant of ancien régime France in London, the fabled Wallace Collection. The best Tube stop for the area is Bond Street.

## TOP ATTRACTIONS

**Sherlock Holmes Museum.** Outside Baker Street station, by the Marylebone Road exit, is a 9-foot-high bronze statue of Arthur Conan Doyle's celebrated detective, who "lived" around the corner at number 221B Baker Street—now a museum to all things Sherlock. Inside, Mrs. Hudson, Holmes's housekeeper, guides you into a series of Victorian rooms where the great man lived, worked, and played the violin. It's all carried off with such genuine enthusiasm and attention to detail that you could be forgiven for thinking that Mr. Holmes actually *did* exist. ⊠ *221B Baker St., Regent's Park* ☎ *020/7224–3688* ⊕ *www.sherlock-holmes. co.uk* ⊇ *£15* ⊗ *Daily 9:30–6* Ⓜ *Baker St.*

FAMILY

**Fodor's** Choice

★

**Wallace Collection.** With its Great Gallery stunningly refurbished, there's even more reason to visit this exquisite gem of an art gallery—although housing one of the world's finest collections of old master paintings is reason enough. This glorious collection and the 18th-century mansion in which it's located were bequeathed to the nation by the widow of Sir Richard Wallace (1818–90). Wallace's father, the 4th Marquess of Hertford, took a house in Paris after the French Revolution and set about snapping up paintings by what were then dangerously unpopular artists, for a song. Frans Hals's *Laughing Cavalier* is probably the most famous painting here, or perhaps Jean-Honoré Fragonard's *The Swing*. The full list of painters in the collection reads like a "who's who" of classical European art—from Rubens, Rembrandt, and Van Dyck to Canaletto, Titian, and Velázquez. English works include paintings by Gainsborough and Turner. There are also fine collections of furniture, porcelain, Renaissance gold, and *majolica* (15th- and 16th-century Italian tin-glazed pottery). With craft activities, hands-on sessions, the "Little Draw" drawing workshops, as well as the chance to try on a suit of armor in the "Arms and Armour" collection, there's plenty to keep kids occupied, too. The conditions of the bequest mean that no part of the collection can leave the building; this is the only place in the world you'll ever be able to see these works. ⊠ *Hertford House, Manchester Sq., Marylebone* ☎ *020/7563–9500* ⊕ *www.wallacecollection.org* ⊇ *Free* ⊗ *Daily 10–5* Ⓜ *Bond St.*

QUICK
BITES

**Wallace Restaurant.** Bringing the outside in, this café and restaurant is in the Wallace Collection's glass-roofed courtyard. It's open (daily 10–4:30) for breakfast, lunch, and afternoon tea, and for dinner on Friday and Saturday evenings (last seating is at 9:30 pm). The menu includes lamb rump, pan-roasted lemon sole, and other tasty offerings. If you don't want to strain your budget too much, you can just linger over coffee in the gorgeous surroundings. ⊠ *The Wallace Collection, Hertford House, Manchester Sq., Marylebone* ☎ *020/7563–9505.*

## WORTH NOTING

FAMILY **Madame Tussauds.** One of London's busiest tourist attractions, this is nothing less (and nothing more) than the world's most famous exhibition of lifelike waxwork models of celebrities. Madame T. learned her craft while making death masks of French Revolution victims, and in 1835 she set up her first show of the famous ones near this spot. Top billing still goes to the murderers in the Chamber of Horrors, who stare glassy-eyed at visitors—one from an electric chair, one sitting next to the tin bath where he dissolved several wives in quicklime. ■TIP➔ **Beat the crowds by booking timed-entry tickets in advance. You can also buy nondated, "priority access" tickets via the website (at a premium).** ⊠ *Marylebone Rd., Regent's Park* ☎ *0870/400–3000 for timed-entry tickets* ⊕ *www.madametussauds.com* ✉ *£23–£66 according to time; call or check website. Combination ticket with London Eye, London Dungeon, and London Aquarium £39–£55* ⊙ *Early Apr. and mid-July–Aug., daily 9–7; Sept.–Mar. and mid-Apr.–mid-July, weekdays 9–5:30, weekends 9–6* Ⓜ *Baker St.*

FAMILY **Ripley's Believe It Or Not!** Inspired by the legendary American traveler/cartoonist/curator Robert Ripley, this museum has six floors of the weird, the wacky, and the downright bizarre (life-size knitted Ferrari, anyone?) to delight even the most tired and jaded among us. Nothing is too unusual or outlandish to take its place among the 700-plus authentic artifacts. From dinosaur eggs to a sculpture of the Beatles made from chewing gum (yes, chewing gum!), there is so much to see, with interactive exhibits aplenty. ⊠ *The London Pavilion, 1 Piccadilly Circus, Mayfair* ☎ *020/3238–0022* ⊕ *www.ripleyslondon.com* ✉ *£20–£26.95 (book in advance for best prices)* ⊙ *Daily 9:30 am–midnight; last admission at 10:30 pm* Ⓜ *Piccadilly Circus (Exit 4 to Coventry St.).*

# SOHO AND
# COVENT GARDEN

# GETTING ORIENTED

## GETTING THERE

Almost all Tube lines cross the Covent Garden and Soho areas, so it's easy to hop off for dinner or a show in one of the hippest parts of London. For Soho, take any train to Piccadilly Circus, Leicester Square, Oxford Circus, or Tottenham Court Road. For Covent Garden, get off at Covent Garden station on the Piccadilly line. (It may be easier to exit the Tube at Leicester Square or Holborn and walk.) Thirty buses connect to the Covent Garden area from all over London; check out the area's website (⊕ *www.coventgarden.uk.com*).

## TOP REASONS TO GO

**Find tomorrow's look in the Newburgh Quarter:** Head to this adorable warren of cobblestone streets for stylish boutiques, edgy stores, and young indie upstarts.

**Indulge yourself in gourmet country:** London has fallen in love with its chefs, and Soho is home to many of the most talked-about restaurants in town.

**Covent Garden Piazza:** Eliza Doolittle's former backyard has been taken over by fun boutiques and by street performers who play to the crowds at night.

**Royal Opera House:** Even if you're not going to the opera or ballet, take in the beautiful architecture and sense of history.

**See a West End hit in Theatreland:** Shaftesbury Avenue is the heart of London's theater district, where more than 40 West End theaters pull in the crowds with a mix of extravagant musicals, Shakespeare, and new plays.

# Soho and Covent Garden

4

## MAKING THE MOST OF YOUR TIME

You can comfortably tour all the sights around Soho and Covent Garden in a day. Visit the small but perfect Courtauld Gallery in the morning, leaving plenty of time to watch street entertainment or shop at the stalls around Covent Garden Piazza or in the fashion boutiques of Soho in the afternoon. Save some energy for a night on the town in Soho.

## FEELING PECKISH?

The coffee shops on Covent Garden Piazza can be overpriced and mediocre. Head north for Seven Dials or west for Soho when the munchies strike.

**Canela.** Bright and casual by day, intimate and atmospheric by night, this is a great spot for refueling mid-shopping trip, grabbing a bite before a show (think filling dishes like pork stew or salted cod, plus charcuterie and sandwiches) or lingering over a glass of reasonably priced Portuguese wine. ⊠ *33 Earlham St., Covent Garden* ☎ *020/7240–6926* ⊕ *www.canelacafe.com* Ⓜ *Covent Garden, Leicester Sq.*

**Flat White.** It was this compact little coffee bar that kicked off London's passion for Antipodean-style coffee, and the place is still going strong today. The beverages are second to none, and they serve tasty sandwiches and cakes too. ⊠ *17 Berwick St., Soho* ☎ *020/ 7734–0370* ⊕ *www.flatwhitesoho. co.uk* Ⓜ *Tottenham Court Rd., Leicester Sq.*

## GAY LONDON

Old Compton Street in Soho is the epicenter of London's affluent, stylish gay scene. There are some fun nightclubs in the area, with crowds forming in Soho Square, south of Oxford Street. Some of the more well-known clubs and bars in the area include Friendly Society, Ku Bar, the Yard, and the Shadow Lounge.

Sightseeing
★★★

Nightlife
★★★★★

Dining
★★★★

Lodging
★★

Shopping
★★★

A red-light district no more, today's Soho is more stylish than seedy and offers some of London's best bars, live music venues, restaurants, and theaters. By day, this hotbed of media production reverts to the business side of its late-night scene. If Soho is all about showbiz, neighboring Covent Garden is devoted to culture. Both districts offer an abundance of narrow streets packed with one-of-a-kind shops and lots of antique character.

# SOHO

Updated by
Jo Caird

Soho, which, along with Covent Garden, is loosely known as "the West End," has long been known as the entertainment and arts quarter of London's center. Bordered to the north by Oxford Street, Regent Street to the west, and Chinatown and Leicester Square to the south, the narrow streets of Soho are unabashedly devoted to pleasure. Wardour Street bisects the neighborhood, with lots of interesting boutiques and some of London's best-value restaurants to the west (especially around Foubert's Place and on Brewer and Lexington streets). Most nightlife lies to the east—including the gay clubs of Old Compton Street—and beyond that is the city's densest collection of theaters, on Shaftesbury Avenue. London's compact Chinatown is wedged between Soho and Leicester Square. A bit of erudition surfaces to the east of the square on Charing Cross Road, famous for its secondhand bookshops, and on tiny Cecil Court, a pedestrianized passage lined with small antiquarian booksellers.

## TOP ATTRACTIONS

Fodor'sChoice
★

**Newburgh Quarter.** Want to see the hip style of today's London? Find it one block east of Carnaby Street—where the look of the '60s "Swinging London" was born—in an adorable warren of cobblestone streets now lined with specialty boutiques, edgy stores, and young indie upstarts. A

### DID YOU KNOW

Covent Garden really was a convent garden for 300 years before it was Britain's first planned public square with a fruit and vegetable market. The greengrocers are gone, but the 1830 market building and the courtyard still teem with shoppers.

## A BRIEF HISTORY

Almost as soon as a 17th-century housing development covered what had been a royal park and hunting ground, Soho earned a reputation for entertainment, bohemianism, and cosmopolitan liberality. When the authorities adopted a zero-tolerance policy towards soliciting in 1991 (the most recent of several attempts to end Soho's sex trade), they cracked down on an old neighborhood tradition that still resurfaces from time to time.

Successive waves of refugees— French Huguenots in the 1680s, followed by Germans, Russians, Poles, Greeks, Italians, and Chinese— settled and brought their national cuisines with them. So when dining out became fashionable after World War I, Soho was the natural place for restaurants to flourish (as they continue to do today).

Among the luminaries who have made their home here are landscape painter John Constable; Casanova; Canaletto, the great painter of Venice; the poet William Blake; and Karl Marx. In the 1950s and '60s, Soho was London's artists' quarter and the place to find the top jazz clubs and art galleries.

The outlines of present-day Covent Garden took shape in the 1630s, when Inigo Jones turned what had been agricultural land into Britain's first planned public square. After the Great Fire of 1666, it became the site of England's largest fruit-and-vegetable market (the flower market arrived in the 19th century). The district's many theaters and taverns gave the area a somewhat dubious reputation, and after the produce market relocated in 1973, the surviving buildings were scheduled for demolition. A local campaign saved them, and the restored market opened in 1980.

check of the ingredients reveals one part '60s London, one part Futuristic Fetishism, one part Dickensian charm, and one part British street swagger. The Nouveau Boho look best flourishes in shops like Peckham Rye, a tiny boutique crowded with rockers and fashion plates who adore its grunge–meets– *Brideshead Revisited* vibe. Quality independent coffee shops abound—take a break at Department of Coffee and Social Affairs, where you can also browse for home coffee-making equipment. ⊠ *Newburgh St., Foubert's Pl., Ganton St., and Carnaby St., Soho* ⊕ *www.carnaby.co.uk.*

# COVENT GARDEN

To the east of Charing Cross Road lies Covent Garden, the famous marketplace turned shopping mall. Although boutiques and haute fashion shops line the surrounding streets, many Londoners come to Covent Garden for its two outposts of culture: the **Royal Opera House** and the **Donmar Warehouse,** one of London's best and most innovative theaters. The area becomes more sedate just to the north, at the end of Wellington Street, where semicircular Aldwych is lined with grand buildings, and from there the Strand leads to the huge, stately piazza of **Somerset**

You can't miss the buskers performing in the streets of Soho and Covent Garden.

**House,** a vibrant center of contemporary arts and home to the many masterpieces on view at the **Courtauld Gallery.** You'll get a sense of old-fashioned London just behind the Strand, where small lanes are little changed since the 18th century. On the way to the verdant **Embankment Gardens** bordering the Thames, you may pass the **Adam Houses,** the remnants of a grand 18th-century riverside housing development, and the **Benjamin Franklin House,** where the noted statesman lived in the years leading up to the American Revolution.

Covent Garden joins Soho as an arts-and-entertainment center in the city, popularly referred to as "the West End." The neighborhood centers on the Piazza, site of the original Covent Garden market. High Holborn to the north, Kingsway to the east, and the Strand to the south form its other boundaries.

## TOP ATTRACTIONS

Fodor's Choice ★ **The Courtauld Gallery.** One of London's most beloved art collections, the Courtauld is to your right as you pass through the archway into the grounds of the beautifully restored, grand 18th-century neoclassical **Somerset House.** Founded in 1931 by the textile magnate Samuel Courtauld to house his remarkable private collection, this is one of the world's finest Impressionist and post-Impressionist galleries, with artists ranging from Bonnard to Van Gogh. A déjà-vu moment with Cézanne, Degas, Seurat, or Monet awaits on every wall (Manet's *Bar at the Folies-Bergère* and a study for *Le Déjeuner sur L'Herbe* are two of the stars). Botticelli, Bruegel, Tiepolo, and Rubens are also represented, thanks to the exquisite bequest of Count Antoine Seilern's Princes Gate collection. German Renaissance paintings, bequeathed in 1947, include the colorful and sensual *Adam and Eve* by Lucas Cranach the Elder. The second floor has a more provocative, experimental feel, with masterpieces such as Modigliani's iconic *Female Nude*. Don't miss the little café downstairs, a perfect place for a spot of tea. ⊠ *Somerset House, Strand, Covent Garden* ☎ *020/7848–2526* ⊕ *www.courtauld.ac.uk* 💷 *£7; additional charge for special exhibits* ☉ *Daily 10–6; last admission at 5:30* Ⓜ *Temple, Covent Garden.*

**Covent Garden Piazza.** Once home to London's main flower market,

> ## ICE-SKATING
>
> It's hard to beat the skating experience at Somerset House, where November–January a rink is set up in the grand courtyard of this central London palace. Check the website for current prices; its popularity is enormous, and if you can't get a ticket, other atmospheric venues such as Hampton Court, the Tower of London, the London Eye, and the Natural History Museum are following Somerset House's lead in having temporary winter rinks. ☎ *0844/847–1520* ⊕ *www. somersethouse.org.uk/ice-rink.*

where *My Fair Lady's* Eliza Doolittle peddled her blooms, the square around which Covent Garden pivots is known as the Piazza. In the center, the fine old market building now houses stalls and shops selling expensive clothing, plus several restaurants and cafés, and knickknack stores that are good for gifts. One particular gem is Benjamin Pollock's Toyshop at No. 44 in the market. Established in the 1880s, it sells delightful toy theaters. The superior **Apple Market** has good crafts stalls on most days, too. On the south side of the Piazza, the indoor **Jubilee Market,** with its stalls of clothing, army-surplus gear, and more crafts and knickknacks, feels a bit like a flea market. In summer it may seem that everyone in the huge crowds around you in the Piazza is a fellow tourist, but there's still plenty of office life in the area. Londoners who shop here tend to head for Neal Street and the area to the north of Covent Garden Tube station, rather than the market itself. In the Piazza, street performers—from global musicians to jugglers and mimes—play to the crowds, as they have done since the first English Punch and Judy Show, staged here in the 17th century. ⊠ *Covent Garden* ⊕ *www. coventgardenlondonuk.com* Ⓜ *Covent Garden.*

FAMILY **London Transport Museum.** Housed in the old flower market at the southeast corner of Covent Garden, this stimulating museum is filled with impressive vehicle, poster, and photograph collections. As you watch the crowds drive a Tube-train simulation and gawk at the steam locomotives and horse-drawn trams (and the piles of detritus that remained behind), it's unclear who's enjoying it more: children or adults. Best of all, the kid-friendly museum (under 18 admitted free) has a multilevel approach to education, including information for the youngest visitor and the most advanced transit aficionado alike. Food and drink are available at the Upper Deck café, and the shop has lots of good options for gift-buying. ■**TIP→ Tickets are valid for unlimited entry for 12 months.** ⊠ *Covent Garden Piazza, Covent Garden* ☎ *020/7379–6344*

⊕ *www.ltmuseum.co.uk*    🎫 *£16*
⊙ *Sat.–Thurs. 10–6, Fri. 11–6; last admission 45 mins before closing* Ⓜ *Covent Garden, Leicester Sq.*

FAMILY

**Fodor's Choice**

★

**Somerset House.** In recent years this huge complex—the work of Sir William Chambers (1723–96), and built during the reign of George III to house offices of the Navy—has been transformed from dusty government offices to one of the capital's most buzzing centers of culture and the arts, often hosting several interesting exhibitions at one time. The cobblestone Italianate courtyard, where Admiral Nelson used to walk, makes a great setting for 55 playful fountains and is transformed into a romantic ice rink in winter; the grand space is the venue for music and outdoor movie screenings in summer. The **Courtauld Gallery** occupies most of the north building, facing the busy Strand. Across the courtyard are the Embankment Galleries, with a vibrant calendar of design, fashion, architecture, and photography exhibitions. The East Wing has another fine exhibition space, and events are sometimes also held in the atmospherically gloomy cellars below the Fountain Court. Tom's Kitchen offers gourmet dining, and Fernandez & Wells is a great spot for a more informal meal or snack. In summer eating and drinking spills out onto the large terrace next to the Thames. ⊠ *Strand, Covent Garden* ☎ *020/7845–4600* ⊕ *www.somersethouse.org.uk* 🎫 *Embankment Galleries price varies, Courtauld Gallery £7, other areas free* ⊙ *Galleries daily 10–6 (last admission at 5:15); courtyard and river terrace daily 8 am–11 pm* Ⓜ *Charing Cross, Waterloo, Blackfriars.*

**CHEAP TICKETS**

One landmark certainly worth a visit by theatergoers is the **Society of London Theatre ticket kiosk (TKTS)**, on the south side of Leicester Square, which sells half-price tickets for many same-day performances. It's open Monday–Saturday 10–7, and Sunday 11–4:30. The kiosk also sells advance tickets for many shows. Watch out for illegal ticket touts (scalpers), who target tourists around the square.

## WORTH NOTING

**The Adam Houses.** Only a few structures remain of what was once a regal riverfront row of houses on a 3-acre site, but such is their quality that they are worth a detour from the Strand. The work of 18th-century Scottish architects and interior designers (John, Robert, James, and William Adam, known collectively as the Adam brothers), the original development was damaged in the 19th century during the building of the Embankment, and mostly demolished in 1936 to be replaced by an art deco tower. The original houses still standing are protected, and give a glimpse of their former grandeur. Numbers 1–4 Robert Street and 7 and 10 Adam Street are the best. ⊠ *Robert St. and Adam St., off The Strand, Covent Garden* Ⓜ *Charing Cross, Embankment.*

**Benjamin Franklin House.** This architecturally significant 1730 house is the only surviving residence of American statesman, scientist, writer, and inventor Benjamin Franklin, who lived and worked here for 16 years preceding the American Revolution. The restored Georgian townhouse

Leicester Square is home to many movie theaters and a half-price theater ticket booth.

has been left unfurnished, the better to show off the original features: 18th-century paneling, stoves, beams, bricks, and windows. Visitors are led around the house by the costumed character of Polly Hewson, the daughter of Franklin's landlady, who interacts with engaging video projections and recorded voices. On Monday you can take a guided tour focusing on the architectural details of the building, and a walking tour of the surrounding area lasting up to 90 minutes sets off from the house every Wednesday morning at 10:30. ⊠ *36 Craven St., Covent Garden* ☎ *020/7925–1405 for booking* ⊕ *www.benjaminfranklinhouse. org* ⊠ *Historical Experience £7; architectural tour £3.50; walking tour £5 (reservations recommended)* ⊗ *Historical Experience Wed.–Sun. at noon, 1, 2, 3:15, and 4:15; architectural tour Mon. at noon, 1, 2, 3:15, and 4:15* Ⓜ *Charing Cross, Embankment.*

**Leicester Square.** Looking at the neon of the major movie houses, the fast-food outlets, and the disco entrances, you'd never guess that this square (pronounced "Lester") was a model of formality and refinement when it was first laid out around 1630. By the 19th century, the square was already bustling and disreputable, and although it's not a threatening place, you should still be on your guard, especially at night—any space so full of people is bound to attract pickpockets, and Leicester Square certainly does. Although there's a bit of residual glamour (red-carpet film premiers) Londoners generally tend to avoid the place, though it's worth a visit for its hustle and bustle, its mime artists, and the pleasant modern fountain at its center. Also in the middle is a statue of a sulking Shakespeare, perhaps remembering the days when the movie houses were live theaters—burlesque houses, but live all the same. On the northeast corner, in Leicester Place, stands the church of **Notre Dame de France**, with a wonderful mural by Jean Cocteau in one of its side chapels. For more in the way of atmosphere, head north and west from here, through Chinatown and the narrow streets of Soho. ⊠ *Covent Garden* Ⓜ *Leicester Sq.*

**St. Paul's Church.** If you want to commune with the spirits of Vivien Leigh, Noël Coward, Edith Evans, or Charlie Chaplin, this might be just the place. Memorials to them and many other theater greats are found in this 1633 work of the renowned Inigo Jones, who, as the King's Surveyor of Works, designed the whole of Covent Garden Piazza. St. Paul's Church has been known as "the actors' church" since the Restoration, thanks to the neighboring theater district and St. Paul's prominent parishioners. (Well-known actors often read the lessons at services, and the church still hosts concerts and small-scale productions.) Fittingly, the opening scene of Shaw's *Pygmalion* takes place under its Tuscan portico (you might know it better from the movie version of the musical *My Fair Lady,* starring Audrey Hepburn). The western end of the Piazza is a prime pitch for street entertainers, but if they're not to your liking, you can repair to the serenity of the garden entered from King or Bedford streets. Charming open-air theater performances of Shakespeare plays and other works are staged there in the summertime. ⊠ *Bedford St., Covent Garden* ☎ *020/7836–5221* ⊕ *www.actorschurch.org* ☉ *Mon.–Thurs. 8:30–5, Sat. hrs vary, Sun. 9–1* Ⓜ *Covent Garden.*

**Theatre Royal, Drury Lane.** This is London's best-known auditorium—popularly known simply as Drury Lane—and almost its largest. Since World War II, it's forte has been musicals (from *My Fair Lady* and *South Pacific* to *Miss Saigon* and *Shrek*), although David Garrick, who managed the theater from 1747 to 1776, made its name by reviving the works of the by-then-obscure William Shakespeare. Drury Lane enjoys all the romantic accessories of a London theater: a history of fires (it burned down three times), riots (in 1737, when a posse of footmen demanded free admission), attempted regicides (George II in 1716 and his grandson George III in 1800), and even sightings of the most famous phantom of Theaterland, the Man in Grey (in the Circle during matinees). Seventy-five-minute dramatized tours, led by actors, are available. ⊠ *Catherine St., Covent Garden* ☎ *0844/412–4660 for box office, 0871/297–0777 for tour bookings* ⊕ *www.reallyuseful.com* 🎫 *Tours £10.50* ☉ *Tours daily; hrs vary* Ⓜ *Covent Garden.*

# BLOOMSBURY
# AND HOLBORN

# GETTING ORIENTED

Bloomsbury and Holborn

## TOP REASONS TO GO

**Take a tour of "Mankind's Attic":** From the Rosetta Stone to the Elgin Marbles, the British Museum is the golden hoard of booty amassed over centuries by the British Empire.

**Stroll through the Inns of Court:** The quiet courts, leafy gardens, and magnificent halls that make up the heart of Holborn are the closest thing to the spirit of Oxford in London.

**Time travel at Sir John Soane's Museum:** Quirky and fascinating, the former home of the celebrated 19th-century architect is a treasure trove of antiquities and oddities.

**View rare treasures at the British Library:** In keeping with Bloomsbury's literary traditions, this repository holds the Magna Carta, a Gutenberg Bible, and Shakespeare's First Folio.

**Pay your respects to Charles Dickens:** The former residence of the *Oliver Twist* author is now a fascinating museum.

## FEELING PECKISH?

**The Betjeman Arms.** Inside St. Pancras International's renovated Victorian station, this pub is the perfect place to grab a pint and some pub fare. ⊠ *Pancras Rd., Unit 53, King's Cross* ☎ *020/7923–5440* Ⓜ *King's Cross St. Pancras.*

**The Hare and Tortoise Dumpling & Noodle Bar.** This café serves scrumptious Asian fast food in huge portions at reasonable prices. ⊠ *11–13 Brunswick Shopping Centre, Brunswick Sq., Bloomsbury* ☎ *020/7278–9799* ⊕ *www. hareandtortoise.co.uk/bloomsbury* Ⓜ *Russell Sq.*

**Truckles of Pied Bull Yard.** The main attraction of this wine bar and café is the Georgian courtyard, where you can relax within a stone's throw of the British Museum. ⊠ *Off Bury Pl., Bloomsbury* ☎ *020/7404–5338* ⊕ *www.davy.co.uk/truckles* ⊙ *Closed weekends.*

## GETTING THERE

The Russell Square Tube stop on the Piccadilly line leaves you right at the corner of Russell Square.

The best Tube stops for the Inns of Court are Holborn on the Central and Piccadilly lines or Chancery Lane on the Central line.

Tottenham Court Road on the Northern and Central lines is best for the British Museum.

Once you're in Bloomsbury, you can easily get around on foot.

## MAKING THE MOST OF YOUR TIME

If you plan to visit the Inns of Court as well as the British Museum, and you'd like to get a feel for the neighborhood, devote an entire day to this literary and legal enclave.

An alternative scenario is to set aside a separate day for a visit to the British Museum, which can easily consume as many hours as you have to spare.

It's a pleasure to wander through the leafy squares at your leisure, examining historic Blue Plaques or relaxing at a streetside café. The students in the neighborhood add a bit of street life.

**5**

Sightseeing
★★★
Nightlife
★★
Dining
★★
Lodging
★★★★
Shopping
★★

With the British Library, the British Museum, and countless colleges of the University of London among its residents, Bloomsbury might appear all bookish and cerebral—but fear not, it's much more than that. There's a youthfulness about its buzzing thoroughfares, and this vitality extends from down-by-the-Thames Holborn—once Dickens territory, now the heartbeat of legal London—way up to revamped King's Cross and classy Islington to the north, and cool Clerkenwell out east.

## BLOOMSBURY

Updated by
James O'Neill

Fundamental to the region's spirit of open expression and scholarly debate is the legacy of the Bloomsbury Group, an elite corps of artists and writers who lived in this neighborhood during the first part of the 20th century. **Gordon Square** was at one point home to Virginia Woolf, John Maynard Keynes (both at No. 46), and Lytton Strachey (at No. 51). But perhaps the best-known square in Bloomsbury is the large, centrally located **Russell Square,** with its handsome gardens. Scattered around the **University of London** campus are Woburn Square, Torrington Square, and Tavistock Square. The **British Library,** with its vast treasures, is a few blocks north, across busy Euston Road.

Bloomsbury is bordered by Tottenham Court Road on the west, Euston Road on the north, Woburn Place (which becomes Southampton Row) on the east, and New Oxford Street on the south.

The area from Somerset House on the Strand, all the way up Kingsway to the Euston Road, is known as London's **Museum Mile** for the myriad historic houses and museums that dot the area. The **Charles Dickens Museum,** in the house where the author wrote *Oliver Twist*, pays homage to the master, and artists' studios and design shops share space near the majestic **British Museum.** And guaranteed to raise a smile from the most blasé and footsore tourist is **Sir John Soane's Museum,** where the colorful collection reflects the eclectic interests of the namesake founder.

Bloomsbury's liveliness extends north to the exciting redevelopment of King's Cross—once the ugly sister of *all* ugly sisters, now fast becoming a cultural and culinary destination in its own right. Newly polished King's Cross merges seamlessly into upscale Islington, with its bustling streets and elegant squares. Due south of Islington, and east of Bloomsbury, don't miss out on the charms of easygoing, fashionable Clerkenwell.

## TOP ATTRACTIONS

FAMILY **British Library.** With a collection totalling more than 150 million items, plus 3 million new additions every year, the British Library is a world-class repository of knowledge. Its greatest treasures are on view to the general public: the Magna Carta, the Codex Sinaiticus (an ancient bible containing the oldest complete copy of the New Testament), Jane Austen's writings, and Shakespeare's First Folio. Musical manuscripts by G.F. Handel as well as the Beatles are on display in the Sir John Ritblat Gallery. ⊠ *96 Euston Rd., Bloomsbury* ☎ *0330/333–1144* ⊕ *www. bl.uk* ☒ *Free, donations appreciated; charge for special exhibitions* ⊙ *Mon. 9:30–6, Tues.–Thurs. 9:30–8, Fri. 9:30–6, Sat. 9:30–5, Sun. and public holidays 11–5 (last admission is 1 hr before closing)* Ⓜ *Euston, Euston Sq., King's Cross St. Pancras.*

### KING'S CROSS STATION

Sick of living in the shadow of its sumptuously renovated next-door neighbor, St. Pancras station, King's Cross—and the area behind it—has undergone a major makeover of its own, with bars, restaurants, shops, cultural venues, and a stunning fountain display for all to enjoy. It's also a place dear to Harry Potter fans everywhere, because it was from the imaginary platform 9¾ that our hero boarded the *Hogwarts Express* (the station has helpfully put up a sign for platform 9¾ if you want to take a picture there).

FAMILY **British Museum.** One of the world's great repositories of human civiliza-
Fodor'sChoice tion, the British Museum is the premier visitor attraction in the whole
★ of the United Kingdom—and there are no prizes for guessing why. It is hard to overstate the scale and importance of the treasures on display (which are but a fraction of the 8 million items in the museum's catalog). Within yards of each other you'll find the **Rosetta Stone,** whose inscriptions were key to deciphering hieroglyphics (Room 4); the controversial but exquisite **Elgin Marbles** (aka the Parthenon Sculptures ) that once stood on the Acropolis in Athens (Room 18); and stunning fragments and friezes from the **Mausoleum of Halikarnassos** (aka one of the Seven Wonders of the Ancient World; Room 21). And that's just the ground floor!

Established in 1753 and initially based on the library and "cabinet of curiosities" of the Royal Physician Sir Hans Sloane, the collection grew exponentially over the following decades, partly due to bequests and acquisitions, and partly as a result of the burgeoning British Empire where priceless valuables were often plundered and shipped back home to Blighty. Whatever their provenance, there's no doubting the sheer majesty of what's on display.

The rear entrance to the museum in Montague Place may be less busy, but nothing quite beats the main Great Russell Street entrance, which shows off the neoclassical architecture of the exterior in all its pomp and grandeur. Highlights of the ground floor galleries (apart from those cited above) include the colossal **Statue of Ramesses II,** dating to circa 1270 BC and weighing in at just over 7 tons (Room 4), and the fascinating **Living and Dying** displays in Room 24, which explore how humanity has dealt with the harsh realities of life over the centuries.

Upstairs are some of the most popular galleries. Rooms 62–63 are where the **Egyptian mummies** live. Farther along is the glittering 4th-century **Mildenhall Treasure** and the equally splendid 8th-century Anglo-Saxon **Sutton Hoo Treasure** with magnificent helmets and jewelry aplenty (Room 41). Next along is the **Lindow Man,** a ritually slain chap from the 1st century who lay perfectly pickled in a Cheshire bog until he was unearthed by archaeologists in 1984.

Leave time for exploring the glass-covered **Great Court** designed by celebrated architect Norman Foster at the turn of the present millennium—it has become a focal point of the museum. Likewise, don't miss the revered circular **Reading Room** where Karl Marx wrote *Das Kapital* under the room's beautiful blue-and-gold papier-mache dome. If pushed for time, consider one of the excellent museum tours. **Eye-opener** tours (free; 30–40 minutes) focus on 15 individual galleries each day, while the 90-minute **Highlights Tour** covers all the major exhibits plus a few lesser-known ones, and begins at 11:30 am and 2 pm on Friday and weekends (£12; book online or at the information desk in the Great Court). Alternatively, **Multimedia Guides** can be rented from the information desk for £5. ⊠ *Great Russell St., Bloomsbury* ☎ *020/7323–8299* ⊕ *www.britishmuseum.org* 🖅 *Free; donations encouraged* ⊙ *Galleries Sat.–Thurs. 10–5:30, Fri. 10–8:30; Great Court Sat.–Thurs. 9–6, Fri. 9–8:30* Ⓜ *Russell Sq., Holborn, Tottenham Court Rd.*

**Charles Dickens Museum.** This is one of the few London houses Charles Dickens (1812–70) inhabited that is still standing, and it's the place where the master wrote *Oliver Twist* and *Nicholas Nickleby* and finished *The Pickwick Papers.* The house looks exactly as it would have in Dickens's day, complete with first editions, letters, and a tall clerk's desk (Dickens wrote standing up). The museum also houses a shop and café. ⊠ *48 Doughty St., Bloomsbury* ☎ *020/7405–2127* ⊕ *www.dickensmuseum. com* 🖅 *£8* ⊙ *Daily 10–5 (last admission at 4)* Ⓜ *Chancery La., Russell Sq.*

**Lamb's Conduit Street.** If you think Bloomsbury is about all things intellectual, then think again. Lamb's Conduit Street, a pedestrian-only street of gorgeous Georgian townhouses nestled to the east of Russell Square, is building a reputation as one of the capital's most charming—and fashionable—shopping thoroughfares. Avail yourself of what the boutiques have to offer, from fashion to ceramics, books to jewelry, fine art to flowers; there's even an excellent run-by-locals food cooperative called the People's Supermarket. Alternatively, you could just window-shop

your way down to **The Lamb,** a Victorian-era pub whose patrons have included Ted Hughes, Sylvia Plath, and Mr. Dickens himself. ⊠ *Bloomsbury* Ⓜ *Russell Sq.*

**Fodor's Choice**
★ **Sir John Soane's Museum.** Sir John (1753–1837), architect of the Bank of England, bequeathed his eccentric house to the nation on one condition: that nothing be changed. It's a house full of surprises. In the Picture Room, two of Hogarth's famous *Rake's Progress* paintings swing away to reveal secret gallery recesses where you can find works by Canaletto and Turner. Everywhere, mirrors play tricks with light and space, and split-level floors worthy of a fairground funhouse disorient you. Restoration work has opened up Soane's private apartments to the public, but they can only be viewed as part of a first-come, first-served tour (Tuesday–Saturday at 1 and 2 pm). ⊠ *13 Lincoln's Inn Fields, Bloomsbury* ☎ *020/7405–2107* ⊕ *www.soane.org* ✆ *Free; guided tours £10* ☉ *Tues.–Sat. 10–5 (last entry at 4:30); also 6–9 on 1st Tues. of month. See website for tour times* Ⓜ *Holborn.*

## WORTH NOTING

**▌OFF THE BEATEN PATH**

**London Canal Museum.** This quirky little museum, dedicated to the rise and fall of London's once-extensive canal network, is based in the former warehouse of ice-cream maker Carlo Gatti (hence it also partly features the ice-cream trade as well as London's canals). Children enjoy the activity zone and learning about Henrietta, the museum's horse. Outside, on the Battlebridge Basin, float the painted narrowboats of modern canal dwellers—a stone's throw from the hustle and bustle of the King's Cross redevelopment. You can walk to the museum along the towpath from Camden Lock; download a free audio tour from the museum's website to accompany the route. ⊠ *12–13 New Wharf Rd., King's Cross* ☎ *020/7713–0836* ⊕ *www.canalmuseum.org.uk* ✆ *£4* ☉ *Tues.–Sun. and bank holiday Mon. 10–4:30 (until 7:30 on 1st Thurs. of month); last admission 30 mins before closing* ☉ *Closed Dec. 23–Jan. 1* Ⓜ *King's Cross.*

**Petrie Museum.** If you don't get your fill of Egyptian artifacts at the British Museum, you can see more in the neighboring Petrie Museum, located on the first floor of the DMS Watson library. The museum houses an outstanding collection of Egyptian and Sudanese archaeological objects, including jewelry, toys, and some of the world's oldest garments. ⊠ *Malet Pl., Bloomsbury* ☎ *020/7679–2884* ⊕ *www.ucl. ac.uk/museums/petrie* ✆ *Free, donations appreciated* ☉ *Tues.–Sat. 1–5* Ⓜ *Euston Sq., Goodge St.*

**University College London.** Founded in 1826 the college is set in a classical edifice designed by the architect of the National Gallery, William Wilkins. Committed to providing higher education without religious exclusion, in 1878 it also became the first British University to accept women on an equal footing with men. The college has within its portals the **Slade School of Fine Art,** which did for many of Britain's artists what the nearby Royal Academy of Dramatic Art (on Gower Street) did for actors. The South Cloisters contain one of London's weirder treasures: the skeleton of one of the university's founders, Jeremy Bentham, who bequeathed himself to the college. ⊠ *Malet Pl., Bloomsbury* Ⓜ *Euston Sq., Goodge St.*

**Wellcome Collection.** If you fancy something quirky, sample this collection by U.S. pharmaceutical millionaire and philanthropist Henry Wellcome (1853–1936). Styled as "the free destination for the incurably curious," this museum explores the connections between medicine, life and art (some exhibits may not be suitable for younger children). Comprising an estimated 1 million items, the collection includes Napoleon's toothbrush, Horatio Nelson's razor, and Charles Darwin's walking stick. There are also anatomical models, Peruvian mummies, and Japanese sex aids as well as two permanent exhibitions to inspire debate, Medicine Man and Medicine Now. Watch out for original art works in the lobby by Picasso (just above the entrance when you come in) and Anthony Gormley. ⊠ *183 Euston Rd., Bloomsbury* ☎ *020/7611-2222* ⊕ *www.wellcomecollection.org* ✉ *Free* ☉ *Tues., Wed., Fri., and Sat. 10–6, Thurs. 10–10, Sun. 11–6; open until 10 pm 1st Fri. of the month (except Aug. and Jan.)* Ⓜ *Euston Sq., Euston.*

# HOLBORN

Southeast of Bloomsbury and west of The City, Holborn may appear to be little more than a buffer zone between the two—but although it may lack the panache of its neighbors, don't underestimate this varied slice of the capital. Home to legal London and the impressive Inns of Court, this is also Charles Dickens territory, with the Old Curiosity Shop snug within its borders and the Dickens museum close by. Add to that its fair share of churches and quirky places of interest, and you'll soon discover that Holborn can be a rewarding place to while away an hour or three. Holborn's massive Gothic-style **Royal Courts of Justice** ramble all the way to the Strand, and the **Inns of Court**—Gray's Inn, Lincoln's Inn, Middle Temple, and Inner Temple—are where most British trial lawyers have offices to this day. Geographically, Holborn's borders are probably best defined as: west, Kingsway; north, Theobald's Road; east, Gray's Inn Road; south, where the Strand becomes Fleet Street.

## WORTH NOTING

**Gray's Inn.** Although the least architecturally interesting of the four Inns of Court and the one most heavily damaged by German bombs in the 1940s, Gray's still has romantic associations. In 1594 Shakespeare's *Comedy of Errors* was performed for the first time in the hall, which was restored after World War II and has a fine Elizabethan screen of carved oak. You must make advance arrangements to view the hall, but the secluded and spacious gardens, first planted by Francis Bacon in 1597, are open to the public. The four Inns of the Court—Gray's Inn, Lincoln's Inn, Middle Temple, and Inner Temple—are where most British trial lawyers have offices to this day. In the 14th century, the inns were lodging houses where barristers lived so that people would know how to easily find them (hence, the label "inn"). ⊠ *Gray's Inn Rd.,*

*Holborn* ☎ *020/7458–7800* ⊕ *www.graysinn.org.uk* ✉ *Free* ☉ *Week-days noon–2:30* Ⓜ *Holborn, Chancery La.*

**Lincoln's Inn.** There's plenty to see at one of the oldest, best preserved, and most attractive of the Inns of Court—from the Chancery Lane Tudor brick gatehouse to the wide-open, tree-lined, atmospheric Lincoln's Inn Fields and the 15th-century chapel remodeled by Inigo Jones in 1620. The chapel and the gardens are open to the public, but to see more you must reserve a place on one of the official tours. But be warned: they tend to prefer group bookings of 15 or more, so it's best to check the website or call for details (and note that there are no tours on weekends or in August). ✉ *Chancery La., Holborn* ☎ *020/7405–1393* ⊕ *www. lincolnsinn.org.uk* ✉ *Free* ☉ *Gardens weekdays 7–7; chapel weekdays 9–5* Ⓜ *Chancery La.*

**Royal Courts of Justice.** Here is the vast Victorian Gothic pile of 35 million bricks containing the nation's principal law courts, with 1,000-odd rooms running off 3½ miles of corridors. This is where the most important civil law cases—that's everything from divorce to fraud, with libel in between—are heard. You can sit in the viewing gallery to watch any trial you like, for a live version of Court TV; the more dramatic criminal cases are heard at the Old Bailey. Other sights are the 238-foot-long main hall and the compact exhibition of judges' robes. Guided tours must be booked in advance. ✉ *The Strand, Holborn* ☎ *020/7947–6000, 07789/751–248 for tour reservations* ⊕ *www.justice.gov.uk (search for Royal Courts of Justice in A–Z option)* ✉ *Free, tours £12* ☉ *Weekdays 10–4:30* Ⓜ *Temple, Holborn, Chancery La.*

**Temple Church.** As featured in *The Da Vinci Code*, this church was built by the Knights Templar in the late 12th century. The Red Knights held their secret initiation rites in the crypt here. Having started poor, holy, and dedicated to the protection of pilgrims, they grew rich from showers of royal gifts until, in the 14th century, they were stripped of their wealth, charged with blasphemy and sodomy, and thrown into the Tower. So it goes. ✉ *King's Bench Walk, The Temple, Holborn* ☎ *020/7353–3470* ⊕ *www.templechurch.com* ✉ *£5* ☉ *Generally week-days 10–2 (check website)* Ⓜ *Temple.*

# ISLINGTON

Islington is one of the most fashionable of London's villagelike neighborhoods. Upper Street, with its high-street stores, independent boutiques, and myriad restaurants and bars, is where most of the action takes place. But wander off the main drag and you'll discover elegant residential streets and squares, as well as bustling charming markets. You'll also find a handful of top-flight Off West End theaters and music venues in the area, including the Almeida, the hugely atmospheric Union Chapel, and—down on Islington's border with Clerkenwell—the renowned contemporary dance venue, Sadler's Wells.

**Camden Passage.** A pretty pedestrian thoroughfare just off Upper Street, Camden Passage is famous for its many antiques shops selling everything from vintage furniture to period jewelry to timeless timepieces. In recent years, a sprinkling of independent boutiques, delis, and cafés has given the passage an eclectic, vibrant feel. Check out the antiques market held on Wednesday and Saturday mornings. ⊠ *Islington* ⊕ *www. camdenpassageislington.co.uk* Ⓜ *The Angel.*

**Chapel Market.** Chapel Market is what Islington used to be: an unpretentious, working-class enclave. There's a lively food market that runs for half the length of the street every day except Monday—just listening to the stallholders advertising their wares can be entertainment enough. Although trendy eateries are beginning to pop up here and there, it is still home to London's oldest eel, pie, and mash shop, Manze's, with its marble tables and tiled interior largely untouched since its establishment in 1902. ⊠ *Chapel Market, Islington* Ⓜ *The Angel.*

# KING'S CROSS

**5**

What a difference a decade makes! Until recently, King's Cross was a byword for sleaze and street crime, but after a multibillion-pound redevelopment—actually, make that transformation—it's become a lively new urban quarter. On what was once postindustrial wasteland and railroad yards, the 67-acre site is now home to bars, restaurants, street-food vendors, and shops. What's more, with the capital's premier art college, the University of the Arts in London, having relocated to Granary Square, alongside a raft of cultural venues, this former urban black spot now has a certain air of artistic credibility about it, too. If all that weren't enough, by courtesy of the Regent's Canal, this bustling quarter even has the occasional splendid oasis of calm as well.

FAMILY  **Camley Street Natural Park.** These 2 acres of splendid calm are bang in the middle of the King's Cross hustle and bustle. This urban nature reserve, just across the road from the concrete and glass of the Eurostar terminal, provides a habitat for birds, butterflies, bats, and a wide variety of plant and pond life. It's a delightful gem that's popular with schoolchildren and office workers on lunch break, but chances are you could have the whole place pretty much to yourself. ⊠ *12 Camley St., King's Cross* ☎ *020/7833–2311* ⊕ *www.wildlondon.org.uk/reserves/ camley-street-natural-park* ⊠ *Free* ☉ *Late Mar.–late Oct., daily 10–5; late Oct.–late Mar., daily 10–4* Ⓜ *King's Cross St. Pancras.*

**Granary Square.** The heart of the new King's Cross, Granary Square is London's liveliest open space. Pride of place is given to the ever-changing 1,000-strong fountain display, which is even more spectacular by night when lights accompany the choreography. The immense, six-story granary building—designed in 1852 to store wheat for London's bakers—has been renovated to house the University of the Arts in London (parts of which are open to the public), as well as a selection of excellent eateries. The square's south-facing steps double as an amphitheater for site-specific arts events; at times, the steps themselves *become* the installation—such as when they're covered with carved pumpkins at Halloween or a blanket of flowers in spring. ⊠ *King's Cross* Ⓜ *King's Cross St. Pancras.*

# CLERKENWELL

Once home to medieval religious orders such as the Knights of the Hospitallers of St. John of Jerusalem, Clerkenwell later became an epicenter of the industrial revolution in the capital and, subsequently, of political radicalism (a young Joseph Stalin is said to have met a young Vladimir Lenin at the Crown Tavern pub in Clerkenwell Green). The monks are long gone—so, too, the communists—and the neighborhood's warehouses and factory floors are now home to cutting-edge design agencies, new media start-ups, and übertrendy apartments. With its fashionable boutiques, bars, and restaurants, Clerkenwell can be a pleasant place to while away a few hours. Like its neighbor immediately to the east, the City of London, this area can be quite deserted on weekends.

**Exmouth Market.** A charming pedestrianized thoroughfare where trendy clothing stores, bookshops, jewelers, gift shops—even a tattoo parlor—all jostle for space with Exmouth Market's excellent cafés and restaurants, many of which offer outdoor seating. At its southern end is the 19th-century Church of Our Most Holy Redeemer, the only Italian basilica–style church in London. There's a vibrant food market on weekdays serving gourmet street food. ✉ *Exmouth St., Clerkenwell* ⊕ *www.exmouth.london* Ⓜ *Farringdon, The Angel.*

**Museum of the Order of St. John.** This fascinating museum tells the story of the Knights Hospitallers of St. John, from the Order's 11th-century Crusader origins in Jerusalem to its present-day incarnation as the St. John Ambulance service. The museum is spread across two adjacent sites: the arched St. John's Gatehouse, which dates back to 1504, and the Priory Church with its atmospheric Norman crypt. An excellent interactive display explores the Order's past, both as a military force and a religious institution, which cared for sick pilgrims, and the eclectic variety of objects on display reflects that colorful history: from antique medicinal jars and medical equipment to pieces of armor worn by the Knights when they defended Malta from the Ottomans in the 16th century, as well as a bronze cannon given by Henry VIII before he dissolved the Order altogether a few years later. ✉ *St. John's Gate, St. John's La., Clerkenwell* ☎ *020/7324–4005* ⊕ *www.museumstjohn.org.uk* ✇ *Free, guided tours £5 (suggested donation)* ☉ *July–Sept., daily 10–5; Oct.–June, Mon.–Sat. 10–5; guided tours Tues., Fri., and Sat. at 11 and 2:30 (see website for details)* Ⓜ *Farringdon.*

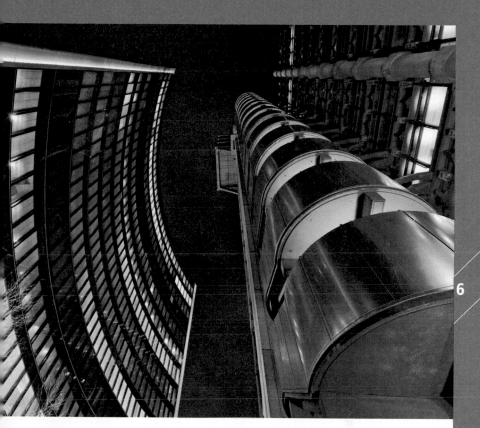

# THE CITY

# GETTING ORIENTED

The City

## GETTING THERE

The City area is well served by a concentrated selection of Tube stations—St. Paul's and Bank are on the Central line, and Mansion House, Cannon Street, and Monument are on the District and Circle lines. Liverpool Street and Aldgate border The City's eastern edge, while Chancery Lane and Farringdon lie to the west. Barbican and Moorgate provide easy access to the theaters and galleries of the Barbican, and Blackfriars, to the south, leads to Ludgate Circus and Fleet Street.

## TOP REASONS TO GO

**St. Paul's Cathedral, the "Symbolic Heart of London":** Now increasingly crowded by skyscrapers, St. Paul's still manages to dominate the skyline. Once inside, you'll see the beauty of this 17th-century masterpiece of Sir Christopher Wren.

**Linger on the Millennium Bridge:** Hurtle across centuries with this promenade between Tate Modern and St. Paul's—and get a great river view, too.

**Treachery and treasures at the Tower:** This mini city of melodramatic towers is bursting at the seams with history, pageantry, and the stunning Crown Jewels (bring sunglasses).

**Channel history at the Museum of London:** A Roman leather bikini and Queen Victoria's crinoline gowns; Selfridges's art deco elevators and a diorama of the Great Fire (sound effects! flickering flames!): this gem of a museum's got it all.

**6**

## MAKING THE MOST OF YOUR TIME

The "Square Mile" is as compact as the nickname suggests, with little distance between points of interest, making an afternoon stroll a rewarding experience. For full immersion in the Tower of London, however, set aside half a day, especially if seeing the Crown Jewels is a priority. Allow an hour minimum each for the Museum of London, St. Paul's Cathedral, and Tower Bridge. On weekends, without the scurrying suits, The City is nearly deserted, making it hard to find lunch—and yet this is when the major attractions are at their busiest.

## A GOOD WALK

Crossing the Millennium Bridge from Tate Modern to St. Paul's is one of the finest walks in London—with the river to either side and Christopher Wren's iconic dome towering at one end. Dubbed the "blade of light," the shiny aluminum-and-steel bridge was the result of a collaboration between architect Norman Foster and sculptor Anthony Caro

## FEELING PECKISH?

**The Old Bank of England.** This grand pub next to the Royal Courts of Justice on Fleet Street serves hearty pub food. Try one of the tasty pies, as long as you're not bothered by the plaque at the door informing you that this was once the site of a barbershop owned by one Mr. Sweeney Todd. ✉ *194 Fleet St., The City* ☎ *020/7430–2255* ⊕ *www.oldbankofengland.co.uk* Ⓜ *Temple.*

**White Mulberries.** This friendly coffee shop at St. Katharine Docks serves an outstanding cup of joe, along with tasty cakes and light bites. ✉ *D3 Ivory House, St. Katharine Docks, The City* ☎ *07507/572600* ⊕ *www.whitemulberries.com* Ⓜ *Tower Hill; Tower Gateway (DLR).*

**Ye Olde Cheshire Cheese.** This wonderfully higgledy-piggledy, multilevel inn on Fleet Street was built in 1667, but the basement bar is centuries older, lending credence to its claim as London's oldest pub. The list of famous people who've imbibed here is like a "who's who" of London history. ✉ *145 Fleet St., The City* ☎ *020/7353–6170* Ⓜ *St. Paul's.*

Sightseeing
★★★★★
Nightlife
★
Dining
★★★
Lodging
★
Shopping
★★★

The City is the capital's fast-beating financial heart, with a powerful architectural triumvirate at its epicenter: the Bank of England, the Royal Exchange, and Mansion House. The "Square Mile" also has historic currency as the place where London began. St. Paul's Cathedral has been looking after Londoners' souls for hundreds of years, and the Tower of London—a royal fortress, prison, and jewel house surrounded by a moat—has occasionally taken care of their heads.

Updated by
Jack Jewers

The City is a dizzying juxtaposition of the old and the new. You'll find yourself immersed in historic London if you begin your explorations on **Fleet Street,** the site of England's first printing press and the undisputed seat of British journalism until the 1980s. Nestled behind Fleet Street is **Dr. Johnson's House,** former home of the author of *A Dictionary of the English Language*, who claimed that "when a man is tired of London, he is tired of life." The nearby church of **St. Bride's,** recognizable by its tiered-wedding-cake steeple, is a Sir Christopher Wren gem and still the church for journalists, while eastward rises the iconic **St. Paul's Cathedral,** also designed by Wren and largely considered the architect's masterpiece. You'll encounter more of traditional London at the **Central Criminal Court** (nicknamed The Old Bailey, and home to London's most sensational criminal trials) and the 800-year-old **Smithfield Market,** whose Victorian halls are the site of a daily early-morning meat market. Nearby are the ancient church of **St. Bartholomew the Great** and **St. Bartholomew Hospital,** both begun in 1123; the **Guildhall,** the site of the only Roman amphitheater in London; the church of **St. Mary-le-Bow;** and the maze of charmingly old-fashioned, narrow streets around **Bow Lane.**

You can put all this history into context at the **Museum of London,** where archaeological displays include a portion of the original **Roman Wall** that ringed The City.

Just beyond rises the modern **Barbican Centre,** a concrete complex of arts venues and apartments that was controversial at the time it was built in the early 1980s, but now has become an indispensable part of the London landscape. A plethora of bold new structures now rise above The City, not all of which are popular; outlandish designs such as **20 Fenchurch Street** and the **Swiss Re Tower** (nicknamed "the Walkie Talkie" and "the Gherkin" respectively) are almost as contentious today as the Barbican was 30 years ago. But all this adds to the appeal of this living, constantly developing part of London, and whenever you return—in years or merely months—The City will literally never be the same as when you saw it last.

The **Monument,** near the banks of the Thames, was built to commemorate the Great Fire of London of 1666. From here, the river leads to one of London's most absorbing and bloody attractions, the **Tower of London. Tower Bridge** is a suitably giddying finale to an exploration of this fascinating part of London.

## TOP ATTRACTIONS

FAMILY   **Monument.** Commemorating the "dreadful visitation" of the Great Fire of London, in 1666, this huge stone column stands both 202 feet tall and exactly 202 feet from Farrier's baking house in Pudding Lane, where the fire started. (Note the gilded orb of fire at the column's pinnacle.) It was designed by Sir Christopher Wren and Dr. Robert Hooke, who were asked to erect it "on or as neere unto the place where the said Fire soe unhappily began as conveniently may be." The view of The City from the viewing platform at the top is spectacular, but if climbing the 311 steps seems too arduous, you can watch a live view relayed on a screen at the entrance. ✉ *Monument St., The City* ☎ *020/7626–2717* ⊕ *www.themonument.info* 💷 *£4, combined ticket with Tower Bridge £10.50* ⊙ *Apr.–Sept., daily 9:30–6; Oct.–Mar., daily 9:30–5:30; last admission 30 mins before closing* Ⓜ *Monument.*

FAMILY   **Museum of London.** If there's one place to absorb the history of London, Fodor's Choice   from 450,000 BC to the present day, it's here. There are 7,000 objects ★   to wonder at in all, including Oliver Cromwell's death mask, Queen Victoria's crinoline gowns, Selfridges's art deco elevators, and an original door from the infamous Newgate Prison. The collection devoted to Roman London contains some extraordinary gems, including an astonishingly well-preserved floor mosaic uncovered just a few streets away. (Appropriately enough the museum itself shelters a section of the 2nd- to 4th-century London wall, which you can view through a window.) Permanent displays highlight prehistoric, medieval, and Tudor London. The Galleries of Modern London are equally enthralling: experience "Expanding City," "People's City," and "World City," each gallery dealing with a section of London's history from 1666 to the 21st century. Innovative interactive displays abound, and there's also a fine schedule of temporary exhibitions. New collections are being added all the time, most notably some extraordinary Bronze Age and Roman artifacts uncovered during the building of the Crossrail underground railway from the early to mid-2010s. Check the website for details

**6**

## A BRIEF HISTORY

Although there is evidence of Celtic habitation on the north bank of the Thames, in many ways London begins with the Romans, who established the settlement of Londinium in AD 47 as an outpost of the Empire (before those pesky Celts, led by Queen Boudicca, returned and burned it to the ground 17 years later). The Saxons came and stayed for a while, as did the Vikings, and by the time the Normans turned up in the 11th century and declared it the capital of England, London was already established as the most important city in the realm. William the Conqueror began building the palace that was to become the Tower of London, which by Tudor times was known as the world's most forbidding prison, and where two of Henry VIII's six wives were

executed. During the Middle Ages, powerful guilds that nurtured commerce took root in the capital, followed by the foundation of great trading companies, such as the Honourable East India Company, which started up in 1600.

London's history has often been one of disaster and renewal. The Great Fire of 1666 spared only a few of the cramped, labyrinthine streets where the Great Plague had delivered such devastation the previous year. Yet the gutted wastelands ushered in an era of architectural renaissance, led by Sir Christopher Wren. Further punishment would come during the Blitz of World War II, when German bombers destroyed many buildings— but again London rebounded. As it likely always will.

about the fantastic **Street Museum** app, which allows you to hold up your phone in many London streets and be shown pictures of how things looked in the past. ✉ *London Wall, The City* ☎ *020/7001–9844* ⊕ *www.museumoflondon.org.uk* ✉ *Free* ⊙ *Daily 10–6; last admission at 5:30, galleries start to close at 5:40* Ⓜ *Barbican, St. Paul's.*

**Fodor'sChoice**  **St. Paul's Cathedral.** For centuries this has been one of London's most
★  iconic buildings, and it remains a breathtaking structure, inside and out. Sir Christopher Wren's masterpiece, was started in 1675 and took 35 years to build. It was actually Wren's third design; the Trophy Room has his 20-foot "Great Model" of design No. 2, rejected for being too "Italian" (in other words, Catholic). Indeed, it's thanks only to Wren's spectacular architectural off-roading that the iconic dome of St. Paul's exists at all, given that the approved plans featured a steeple instead. In the crypt is Wren's famous and succinct epitaph, which his son composed and had set into the pavement: "*Lector, si monumentum requiris, circumspice*" ("Reader, if you seek his monument, look around you").

Up 163 spiral steps is the Whispering Gallery, with its incredible acoustic phenomenon: you whisper something to the wall on one side, and a second later it transmits clearly to the other side, 107 feet away. Ascend to the Stone Gallery, which encircles the base of the dome. Farther up (280 feet from ground level) is the small Golden Gallery, the dome's highest point. From both these galleries (if you have a head for heights) you can walk outside for a spectacular panorama of London. The remains of the poet John Donne, who was Dean of St. Paul's for

Walking over the Millennium Bridge takes you to St. Paul's Cathedral, the Sir Christopher Wren–designed masterpiece considered the spiritual heart of England.

his final 10 years (he died in 1631), are in the south choir aisle. The vivacious choir-stall carvings nearby are the work of Grinling Gibbons, as are those on the great organ, which Wren designed. Behind the high altar is the American Memorial Chapel, dedicated to the 28,000 GIs stationed in the United Kingdom who lost their lives in World War II. Among the famous figures whose remains lie in the Crypt are the Duke of Wellington; and, Admiral Lord Nelson.

Free, 20-minute introductory talks happen all day. Free 90-minute guided tours take place Monday–Saturday at 10, 11, 1, and 2; reserve a place at the welcome desk as you arrive. A tour of the Triforium (upper galleries) can be taken on Tuesday and Friday at 2, but you have to book at least two working days in advance; call or see the website for details. ■TIP➔ Save £2.50 per ticket and get fast-track entry by booking online. ⊠ *St. Paul's Churchyard, The City* ☎ *020/7246–8350, 020/7246–8357 for Triforium tours* ⊕ *www.stpauls.co.uk* ✉ *£18; general tours £3, Triforium tours £8* ⊗ *Mon.–Sat. 8:30–4:30 (last ticket sold at 4), Sun. services only* Ⓜ *St. Paul's.*

FAMILY
Fodor'sChoice
★

**Tower Bridge.** Despite its medieval, fairy-tale appearance, Britain's most iconic bridge was actually built at the tail end of the Victorian age, first opening to traffic in 1894. Constructed of steel, then clothed in Portland stone, the Horace Jones masterpiece was built in the Gothic style that was highly popular at the time (and it nicely complements the Tower of London, next door). The bridge is famous for its enormous bascules—the 1,200-ton "arms" that open to allow large ships to glide beneath. This still happens a few times per month (the website lists upcoming times), but when river traffic was dense, the bascules were raised about five times a day.

The **Tower Bridge Exhibition** is a family-friendly tour where you can discover how the bridge actually works before heading out onto the walkways for wonderful city views. First, take in the romance of the panoramas from the east and west walkways between those grand turrets. On the east are the modern superstructures of the Docklands, and on the west is the Tower of London, St. Paul's, the Monument, and the misshapen steel-and-glass egg that is Greater London Assembly's City Hall (memorably described as "a glass testicle" by Ken Livingstone, mayor from 2000 to 2008). Then it's back down to explore the Victorian engine rooms and discover the inner workings, which you learn about through films and hands-on displays. ⊠ *Tower Bridge Rd., The City* ☎ *020/7403–3761* ⊕ *www.towerbridge.org.uk* ☛ *£9* ☼ *Apr.–Sept., daily 10–5:30; Oct.–Mar., daily 9:30–5; last admission 30 mins before closing* Ⓜ *Tower Hill.*

FAMILY
Fodor's Choice
★

**Tower of London.** Nowhere else does London's history come to life so vividly as it does in this mini city of 20 towers, the intimate details of lords and dukes and princes and sovereigns etched in its walls (literally, in some places), and quite a few buckets of royal blood spilled on its stones. Thousands of unfortunate souls spent their last days here, from its heyday in the medieval period, until it fell out of use in the early 19th century (although its last actual prisoner was Hitler's deputy, Rudlof Hess, in 1941). A person was mighty privileged to be beheaded in the peace and seclusion of **Tower Green** instead of before the mob at Tower Hill. In fact, only seven people were ever so honored, among them Anne Boleyn and Catherine Howard—wives two and five of Henry VIII's six—and the nine-day queen, Lady Jane Grey, age 16. In prime position stands the oldest part of the Tower and the most conspicuous of its buildings, the **White Tower.** William the Conqueror began the central keep in 1078 and Henry III (1207–72) had it whitewashed (hence the name). Inside you'll find the **Armouries,** a splendid collection of arms and armor. Across the moat, to the right, is **Traitors' Gate,** where the most famous prisoners could be brought in by boat (all the better to shame and humiliate them).

Opposite is the **Bloody Tower,** so called because it was the scene of perhaps the most notorious murders in English history: that of the infant Edward V and his brother, the "little princes in the Tower." (Spoiler: their uncle did it, becoming King Richard III in the process). The most famous exhibit is, of course, the **Crown Jewels** in the Waterloo Barracks. Not only are these crowns, staffs, and orbs encrusted with heavy-duty gems, they are invested with the authority of monarchical power in England, dating back to the 1300s. Free tours of the Tower depart every half hour or so (until mid-afternoon) from the main entrance. They are conducted by the Yeoman Warders, better known as Beefeaters, dressed in resplendent navy-and-red Tudor outfits (scarlet-and-gold on special occasions). Beefeaters have been guarding the Tower since Henry VII appointed them in 1485. ■TIP➔ Avoid lines by buying a ticket in advance online, by phone, or from the automatic kiosks on Tower Hill. For free tickets to the 700-year-old Ceremony of the Keys (locking of main gates, nightly between 9:30 and 10), write several months in advance; check the tower website for details. Also, check for winter twilight tours of the Tower on selected evenings. ✉ *Tower Hill, The City* ☏ *020/3166–6000* ⊕ *www.hrp.org.uk* ✉ *£24.50* ☉ *Mar.– Oct., Tues.–Sat. 9–5:30, Sun. and Mon. 10–5:30; Nov.–Feb., Tues.–Sat. 9–4:30, Sun. and Mon. 10–4:30. Last admission 30 mins before closing. Last tour at 2:30 in winter, at 3:30 in summer* Ⓜ *Tower Hill.*

## WORTH NOTING

**Bank of England.** The United Kingdom's main bank has been central to the British economy since 1694. Known for the past couple of centuries as "the Old Lady of Threadneedle Street," after the name appeared in a caption to a political cartoon (which can be seen in the museum), the bank manages the national debt and foreign exchange reserves, issues banknotes, sets interest rates, looks after England's gold, and regulates the country's banking system. Sir John Soane designed the neoclassical hulk in 1788, wrapping it in windowless walls, which are all that survive of his original building. The bank's history is traced in the surprisingly varied Bank of England Museum (the entrance is around the corner on Bartholomew Lane). In addition to the bank's original Royal Charter, there's a lively program of special exhibitions, plus interactive displays (try your hand at controlling inflation!). Still, most visitors make a beeline for the solid gold bar that can be stroked and held in the central trading hall—before you get any ideas, there's security everywhere. ✉ *Threadneedle St., The City* ☏ *020/7601–4878* ⊕ *www.bankofengland.co.uk* ✉ *Free* ☉ *Weekdays 10–5; last admission at 4:45* Ⓜ *Bank, Monument.*

**Dr. Johnson's House.** Built in 1700, this elegant Georgian residence, with its paneled rooms and period furniture, is where Samuel Johnson lived between 1748 and 1759. The Great Bear (as he was affectionately known) compiled *A Dictionary of the English Language* in the attic as his health deteriorated. Two early editions are on view, among other mementos of Johnson and his friend, diarist, and later, his biographer, James Boswell. After soaking up the atmosphere, repair around the corner in Wine Office Court to the famed **Ye Olde Cheshire Cheese** pub, once Johnson and Boswell's favorite watering hole. ✉ *17 Gough Sq., The City* ☏ *020/7353–3745* ⊕ *www.drjohnsonshouse.org* ✉ *£4.75* ☉ *May–Sept., Mon.–Sat. 11–5:30; Oct.–Apr., Mon.–Sat. 11–5* Ⓜ *Holborn, Chancery La., Temple.*

**Guildhall.** The Corporation of London, which oversees The City, has ceremonially elected and installed its Lord Mayor here for the last 800 years. The Guildhall was built in 1411, and though it failed to avoid the conflagrations of either 1666 or 1940, its core survived. The Great Hall is a psychedelic patchwork of coats of arms and banners of the City Livery Companies, which inherited the mantle of the medieval trade guilds. Tradesmen couldn't even run a shop without kowtowing to these prototypical unions, and their grand banqueting halls, the plushest private dining venues in The City, are testimony to the wealth they amassed. Inside the hall, Gog and Magog, the pair of mythical giants

6

A testament to the long and often grisly history of the city, the Tower of London was the setting of some of history's most famous imprisonments and executions.

who founded ancient Albion (the earliest known name for Britain) and the city of New Troy, on which London was said to have been built, glower down from their west gallery grandstand. The hall was also the site of famous trials, including that of Lady Jane Grey in 1553, before her execution at the Tower of London. To the right of Guildhall Yard is the **Guildhall Art Gallery,** which includes portraits of the great and the good, cityscapes, famous battles, and a slightly cloying pre-Raphaelite section. The construction of the gallery in the 1980s led to the exciting discovery of London's only **Roman Amphitheater,** which had lain underneath Guildhall Yard undisturbed for more than 1,800 years. It was excavated and now visitors can walk among the remains, although most of the relics are now at the Museum of London. ✉ *Aldermanbury, The City* ☎ *020/7606–3030, 020/7332–3700 for gallery* ⊕ *www. cityoflondon.gov.uk* ✉ *Free (fee for some gallery exhibitions)* ⊗ *Hall: Mon.–Sat. 10–4:30 (also Sun. 10–4:30 1st weekend in May–last weekend in Sept.). Gallery and amphitheatre: Mon.–Sat. 10–5, Sun. noon–4. Last admission 30 mins before closing. Sometimes closed for events; call ahead* Ⓜ *St. Paul's, Moorgate, Bank, Mansion House.*

**The Old Bailey.** England and Wales don't allow cameras in courtrooms, so the only way to see a trial in action is to show up. The most high-profile ones usually happen here, at any of the 16 public courtrooms of the **Central Criminal Court** (universally known as "the Old Bailey," a reference to the fact that it sits atop a section of the old London wall, or "bailey" in Medieval English). Oscar Wilde stood trial here for "gross indecency" (homosexuality) in 1895, but far darker souls than his have passed through these doors, including the nation's most notorious murderers, fraudsters, gangsters, and traitors. The day's proceedings are posted outside; there are security restrictions and children under 14 are not allowed. Restrained dress is expected (no sleeveless T-shirts or shorts for men, no low-cut tops or miniskirts for women) the Old Bailey was originally part of Newgate Prison, England's most feared jail after the Tower, in use

### SUMMER FESTIVAL

Every year, for four weeks in June and July, the **City of London Festival** (⊕ www.colf.org) features numerous walks, dances, and street art, and you can see concerts that are held in buildings not usually open to the public.

from the 12th century all the way to 1902; the present building dates to 1907. Note the 12-foot gilded statue of Justice perched on top; she's not, as usually depicted, wearing a blindfold—her female form was thought by the Edwardians to imply virtue and impartiality enough. ⊠ *Newgate St., The City* ☎ *020/7248–3277* ⊕ *www.cityoflondon.gov.uk* ⌨ *Free* ☉ *Public galleries weekdays 9:55–12:40 and 1:55–3:40* ☞ *Line forms at Newgate St. entrance or in Warwick St. Passage* Ⓜ *St. Paul's.*

**St. Bartholomew the Great.** This is one of London's oldest churches. Construction on the church and the hospital nearby was begun in 1123 by Henry I's favorite courtier, Rahere, who, surviving malaria, dedicated his life to serving the saint who had visited him in his fevered dreams. With the dissolution of the monasteries—by which Henry VIII violently dismantled the Catholic Church in England—most of the building was torn down; the Romanesque choir loft is all that survives from the 12th century. In more recent times, this ancient church has become a bit of a movie star, having appeared in *The Other Boleyn Girl, Four Weddings and a Funeral,* and *Shakespeare in Love,* to name a few. ⊠ *Cloth Fair, West Smithfield, The City* ☎ *020/7606–5171* ⊕ *www.greatstbarts.com* ⌨ *£4 (free for prayer), photography £1* ☉ *Mid-Feb.–mid-Nov., weekdays 8:30–5, Sat. 10:30–4, Sun. 8:30–8; mid-Nov.–mid-Feb., weekdays 8:30–4, Sat. 10:30–4, Sun. 8:30–8* Ⓜ *Barbican, Farringdon.*

**St. Bride's.** According to legend, the distinctively tiered steeple of this Sir Christopher Wren–designed church gave rise to the shape of the traditional wedding cake. One early couple inspired to marry here were the parents of Virginia Dare, the first European child born in colonial America in 1587. As St. Paul's (in Covent Garden) is the actors' church, so St. Bride's belongs to journalists, many of whom have been buried or memorialized here. By 1664 the crypts were so crowded that diarist Samuel Pepys, who was baptized here, had to bribe the gravedigger to "justle together" some bodies to make room for his deceased brother. Now the crypts house a museum of the church's rich history, and a bit of Roman sidewalk. Ninety-minute guided tours are held on Tuesday afternoons (no need to book). ⊠ *Fleet St., The City* ☎ *020/7427–0133* ⊕ *www.stbrides.com* ⌨ *Free, guided tours £6* ☉ *Weekdays 8–6, Sat. hrs vary (call to confirm), Sun. 10–6:30; tours Tues. at 3* Ⓜ *St. Paul's, Blackfriars.*

**6**

**St. Mary-le-Bow.** Various versions of this church have stood on the site since the 11th century. In 1284 a local goldsmith took refuge here after committing a murder, only to be killed inside by enraged relatives of his victim. The church was abandoned for a time afterward, but was rebuilt as its current form by Sir Christopher Wren after the Great Fire. This 1673 incarnation has a tall steeple (in The City, only St. Bride's is taller) and one of the most famous sets of bells in England. Technically, a Londoner must be born within the sound of the "Bow Bells" to be a true Cockney; the origin of that idea may have been the curfew rung on the bells during the 14th century. The Bow takes its name from the bow-shaped arches in the Norman crypt. The church was rebuilt again after severe bomb damage in World War II. The garden contains a statue of local boy Captain John Smith, who founded Virginia in 1606 and was later captured by Native Americans. Opening times can be a little unpredictable, so it's wise to call ahead. Classical music concerts are held here regularly; check the website for listings. ⊠ *Cheapside, The City* ☎ *020/7248–5139* ⊕ *www.stmarylebow.co.uk* ⊠ *Free* ⊗ *Mon.– Wed. 7:30–6, Thurs. 7:30–6:30, Fri. 7–4* Ⓜ *Mansion House, St. Paul's.*

**QUICK BITES**

**Café Below.** In St. Mary-le-Bow's Norman crypt, this café is packed with City workers weekdays 7:30–2:30 for a menu covering breakfasts, scrumptious light lunches, and delicious cakes. It's also open for dinner Wednesday, Thursday, and Friday. ⊠ *Cheapside, The City* ☎ *020/7329–0789* ⊕ *www.cafebelow.co.uk* Ⓜ *Mansion House, St Paul's.*

# EAST LONDON

# GETTING ORIENTED

East London

## TOP REASONS TO GO

**Dennis Severs' House by candlelight:** The atmospheric set-pieces in this Georgian townhouse use visuals, sounds, and aromas to evoke the lives of its fictional previous inhabitants.

**Eat artisanal at Broadway Market:** Check out more than 100 food stalls here on Saturday, offering everything from cheeses to oysters.

**Immerse yourself in London's hottest art scene:** Edgy galleries mix with large collections.

**Trace the footsteps of Jack the Ripper:** Track Britain's most infamous serial killer through streets that were part of a major slum area in Victorian times.

**Peek into the lives of Londoners at the Geffrye Museum of the Home:** This former almshouse showcases middle-class domestic interiors over the centuries.

## SAFETY

Around Shoreditch, Spitalfields, and Brick Lane, streets are largely safe during daylight hours. Be cautious on the rougher streets of Whitechapel, Bethnal Green, and Hackney at night.

## FEELING PECKISH?

**Beagle.** A great spot (with terrace) for weekend brunch after a morning's shopping. Beagle also serves lunch and dinner, including venison, oysters, and house-smoked salmon. ⊠ *397–400 Geffrye St., Hoxton* ☎ *020/7613–2967* ⊕ *www.beaglelondon.co.uk* Ⓜ *Overground: Hoxton.*

**E5 Bakehouse.** This bakery, which supplies bread to many of East London's top eateries, has a friendly café on site, where you can sample some of the tastiest toasted sandwiches in London. ⊠ *Mentmore Terr., Arch 395, Dalston* ☎ *020/8986–9600* ⊕ *www.e5bakehouse.com* ⊗ *No dinner* Ⓜ *Overground: London Fields.*

## GETTING THERE

The London Overground, with stops at Shoreditch High Street, Hoxton, Whitechapel, Dalston Junction, Dalston Kingsland, London Fields, and Hackney Central, is the easiest way to reach East London. Alternatively, the best Tube stations to use are Old Street on the Northern line, Bethnal Green on the Central line, and Liverpool Street on the Metropolitan and Circle lines.

## MAKING THE MOST OF YOUR TIME

To experience East London at its most lively, visit on the weekend. Spitalfields Market bustles all weekend, while Brick Lane and Columbia Road are best on a Sunday morning and Broadway Market on Saturday. If you're planning to explore East London's art galleries, pick up a free map at the Whitechapel Art Gallery. As for the area's booming nightlife scene, there's no time limit: you'll find people partying Wednesday–Sunday.

## GUIDED TOURS

The two-hour **Jack the Ripper Walk** (⊕ *www.london premierwalkingtours.co.uk*), departs from Tower Hill Tube station daily at 7:30 pm, plus Saturday at 3. **Street Art London** (⊕ *www.streetartlondon. co.uk*) offers two- and four-hour walking tours of East London's street art on Tuesday and Thursday at 10 am and weekends at 11 am.

7

Sightseeing
★★★

Nightlife
★★★★★

Dining
★★★★

Lodging
★★★

Shopping
★★★★

Made famous by Dickens and infamous by Jack the Ripper, East London is one of London's most enduringly evocative neighborhoods, rich in popular history, architectural gems, and artists' studios. Since the early 1990s, hip gallerists, designers, and new-media entrepreneurs have colonized its handsome Georgian buildings and converted industrial lofts. Today, this collection of neighborhoods lays claim to being the city's most trendsetting area.

Updated by
Jo Caird

The British equivalent of parts of Brooklyn, East London is a patchwork of districts encompassing struggling artists, multicultural enclaves, upscale professionals, and the digerati, occasionally teetering, like its New York equivalent, on the edge of self-parody. The vast area ranges from gentrified districts like Spitalfields, where bankers and successful artists live in desirable renovated townhouses, to parts of Hackney, where seemingly derelict, graffiti-covered industrial buildings are hives of exciting creative activity. It remains a little rough around the edges, so stick to busier streets at night.

At the start of the new millennium, Hoxton, an enclave of Shoreditch, became the glossy hub of London's buzzing contemporary art scene, which accelerated the gentrification process. Some artists, such as Tracey Emin and Gilbert & George, long-term residents of Spitalfields' handsome Georgian terraces—and successful enough to still afford the area—have remained.

One such residence, **Dennis Severs' House,** was transformed two decades ago by the eponymous American artist into a unique "living house museum" that evokes how past generations of a fictional Huguenot family might have lived there. Not far away, **Spitalfields Market** offers an ever-changing selection of crafts and funky clothes stalls under a glass roof in what was once a Victorian produce market. Across from the market, **Christ Church, Spitalfields,** Nicholas Hawkmoor's masterpiece, soars above Fournier Street.

## DID YOU KNOW?

The Columbia Road Flower Market opens at 8 am on Sunday. Arrive early to see the photogenic market at its best and to find the freshest selection. The road is lined with funky shops selling antiques, vintage clothing, horticultural accessories, and more.

## EAST END STREET SMARTS

Brick Lane and the narrow streets running off it offer a paradigm of East London's development. Its population has moved in waves: communities seeking refuge, others moving out in an upwardly mobile direction.

**Brick Lane** has seen the manufacture of bricks (during the 16th century), beer, and bagels, but nowadays it's primarily known as the heart of Banglatown—Bangladeshis make up one-third of the population in this London borough, and you'll see that the names of the surrounding streets are written in Bengali—where you find many kebab and curry houses along with shops selling DVDs, colorful saris, and stacks of sticky sweets. On Sunday morning, cars aren't allowed on the upper section of the street. Shops and cafés are open, and several stalls are set up, creating a companion market to the one on nearby **Petticoat Lane.**

**Fournier Street** contains fine examples of the neighborhood's characteristic Georgian terraced houses, many of them built by the richest of the early-18th-century Huguenot silk weavers (note the enlarged windows on the upper floors to maximize light for the intricate work). Most of those along the north side of Fournier Street have been restored, but some still contain textile sweatshops—only now the workers are Bengali.

**Wilkes Street,** with more 1720s Huguenot houses, is north of Christ Church, Spitalfields, and neighboring **Princelet Street** was once important to East London's Jewish community. Where No. 6 stands now, the first of several thriving Yiddish theaters opened in 1886. **Elder Street,** just off Folgate, is another gem of original 18th-century houses. On the south and east side of Spitalfields Market are yet more time-warp streets that are worth a wander, such as **Gun Street,** where artist Mark Gertler (1891–1939) was born, at No. 16.

In the last decade, streets around the Old Street roundabout (as well as converted warehouses in Hackney and Dalston) have flourished with start-ups, with attendant stylish boutiques (especially on Redchurch Street), destination restaurants, and hipster bars as part of a government initiative to attract IT-oriented businesses to the neighborhood. Old and new Shoreditch meet on **Brick Lane,** the heart of the Bangladeshi community, lined with innumerable curry houses and glittering sari shops, plus vintage-clothing emporia. Here you'll also find the **Old Truman Brewery,** an East London landmark converted into a warren of street fashion and pop-up galleries. On Sunday, the Columbia Road Flower Market to the north of Brick Lane becomes a colorful, fragrant oasis of greenery.

As property prices have climbed, up-and-coming artists have sought more affordable studio spaces in former industrial buildings eastward toward Whitechapel and Bethnal Green, where there are also some notable galleries. Here you'll find the **V&A Museum of Childhood,** a delight for children of all ages, and—a design connoisseur's favorite—the

**Geffrye Museum,** a collection of domestic interiors through the ages that occupies a row of early-18th-century almshouses.

Probably the best start to an East London tour is via the London Overground, getting off at Shoreditch High Street Station. Immediately northwest of the station, on the west side of Shoreditch High Street, is the heart of the neighborhood that aspires to be the U.K. equivalent to Silicon Valley. To the northeast is Shoreditch's boutique, gallery, and restaurant zone. The subneighborhood of Hoxton is located just above Shoreditch, north of the Old Street roundabout. To the southeast of the station are the handsome Georgian streets of Spitalfields. Bethnal Green is due east, past busy Brick Lane. Whitechapel, formerly Jack the Ripper's patch, is to the south of Spitalfields. All of these neighborhoods are within what is traditionally referred to as the "East End," although East London extends farther to the north and east.

## TOP ATTRACTIONS

Fodor'sChoice ★ **Broadway Market.** This parade of shops in hipster-centric Hackney (north of Regent's Canal) is worth visiting for the specialty bookshops, independent boutiques, organic cafés, neighborhood restaurants, and even a traditional (but now rare) pie-and-mash shop. But wait for Saturday (9–5), when it really comes into its own with a farmers' market and more than 100 street-food and produce stalls rivaling those of south London's famed Borough Market. Artisanal breads, cheeses, chocolates, organic meats, fruit and vegetables, oysters, smoked salmon, and international food offerings: this is foodie heaven. There are also stalls selling vintage clothes, crafts, jewelry, and more, which also spill over into the schoolyard at the top of the street. ⊠ *Hackney* ☎ *0787/246–3409* ⊕ *www.broadwaymarket.co.uk* Ⓜ *London Fields.*

Fodor'sChoice ★ **Christ Church, Spitalfields.** This is the 1729 masterpiece of Sir Christopher Wren's associate Nicholas Hawksmoor, one of his six London churches and an example of English baroque at its finest. It was commissioned as part of Parliament's 1711 "Fifty New Churches" Act, passed in response to the influx of immigrants with the idea of providing for the religious needs of the "godless thousands"—and to help ensure they joined the Church of England, as opposed to such nonconformist denominations as the Protestant Huguenots. (It must have worked; you can still see gravestones with epitaphs in French in the crypt.) As the local silk industry declined, the church fell into disrepair, and by 1958 the structure was crumbling, with the looming prospect of demolition. But after 25 years—longer than it took to build the church—and a huge local fund-raising effort, the structure was meticulously restored and is a joy to behold, from the colonnaded Doric portico and tall spire to its soaring, heavily ornamented plaster ceiling. Its excellent acoustics make is a superb concert venue. Tours that take you "backstage" to the many hidden rooms and passages, from the tower to the vaults, are offered by appointment. ⊠ *Commercial St., Spitalfields* ☎ *020/7377–6793* ⊕ *www. ccspitalfields.org* 🖾 *Free, tours £6* ☉ *Weekdays 10–4 (may be closed for event; call ahead), Sun. 1–4* Ⓜ *Overground: Shoreditch High St.*

7

# The East End Art Scene

Banksy, the Bristol-based artist and provocateur who has maintained his anonymity despite works that now command six figures, is widely credited with making Londoners see street art as more than vandalism. He first came to public attention in the East End in the late '80s, and the area continues to attract new talent from around the globe today. Unfortunately, much of Banksy's early work has been lost, either from being covered over by local councils and building owners, defaced by other graffiti artists, or removed by profiteers. As of this writing, murals remain at Rivington Street near Old Street (in the garden of Cargo bar and nightclub), and Stoke Newington Church Street. **Shoreditch Street Art Tours** (⊕ www. shoreditchstreetarttours.co.uk) offers a knowledgeable, insider view on the ever-changing scene, taking you through the history of street art and graffiti in this area and highlighting the best of Banksy's successors. Take the Saturday tour to avoid the noise of weekday traffic.

Today, East London is a global hotbed of contemporary art, but its avant-garde roots go way back. **Shoreditch's** cheap industrial units and Georgian–Victorian terraced streets have attracted artists since the 1960s, when op-art pioneer Bridget Riley established a service to find affordable studio space for her contemporaries. In the early '90s it gained new notoriety when Young British Artists Sarah Lucas and Tracey Emin began selling their own and their friends' work in The Shop, joining Maureen Paley's influential Bethnal Green gallery, and the long-established Whitechapel Art Gallery, where many leading abstract expressionists and pop artists had their first U.K. shows. **Hoxton** truly became a destination for well-heeled collectors when Jay Jopling, the most important modern-art dealer in town, set up his White Cube gallery in 2000 (it's now in Bermondsey, with a second location at Mason's Yard in Westminster), followed by Kate MacGarry's gallery in 2002.

Priced out by the area's fashionability, the emerging artists themselves have relocated farther off the beaten path to edgier neighborhoods such as **Hackney**, with several trendsetting galleries found clustered around **Cambridge Heath Road** and **Vyner Street**.

**Fodor's Choice** ★ **Dennis Severs' House.** The remarkable interiors of this extraordinary time machine of a house are the creation of Dennis Severs (1948–99), a performer-designer-scholar from Escondido, California, who dedicated his life to restoring this Georgian terraced house. More than that, he created "still-life dramas" using sight, sound, and smell to evoke the world of a fictitious family of Huguenot silk weavers, the Jervises, who might have inhabited the house between 1728 and 1914. Each of the 10 rooms has a distinctive, compelling atmosphere that encourages visitors to become lost in another time, deploying evocative design details like rose-laden Victorian wallpaper, Jacobean paneling, Georgian wing-back chairs, baroque carved ornaments, rich "Catholic" wall colors downstairs, and more sedate "Protestant" shades upstairs. The Silent Night candlelight tour offered each Monday and Wednesday evening, a stroll

On Sunday, additional clothing and craft stalls surround Spitalfields covered market.

through the rooms with no talking allowed, is the most theatrical and memorable way to experience the house. The Exclusive Silent Night visits, which conclude with champagne or mulled wine by the fire and a chat with the curators, are available one night per month (more frequently, near the Christmas holiday), and private group visits can also be arranged. ⊠ *18 Folgate St., Shoreditch* ☎ *020/7247–4013* ⊕ *www. dennissevershouse.co.uk* 🎫 *£10 Sun. and Mon., £15 Mon. and Wed. evenings* ⊙ *Sun. noon–4, Mon. noon–2 and 5–9, Wed. 5–9; last admission 45 mins before daytime tours, 1 hr before evening tours; reservations essential* Ⓜ *Overground: Shoreditch High St.*

**Fodor'sChoice**
★  **Geffrye Museum of the Home.** In contrast to the West End's grand aristocratic townhouses, this charming museum is devoted to the life of the city's middle class over the years. Originally a row of almshouses built in 1714 by Sir Robert Geffrye, a former Lord Mayor of London, it contains a series of 11 period rooms that re-create everyday domestic interiors from the Elizabethan period through the 1950s to the present day. One of the almshouses has been restored to its original condition, offering a glimpse into how the poor and the dependent elderly lived in previous centuries (to visit the almshouse you must go as part of a tour). Outside, a series of period gardens charts the evolution of the town garden over the past 400 years, and next to them is a walled herb garden. The museum's extension wing houses the 20th-century galleries, a lovely café overlooking the gardens, and a shop. ⊠ *136 Kingsland Rd., Hoxton* ☎ *020/7739–9893* ⊕ *www.geffrye-museum.org.uk* 🎫 *Free (charge for special exhibitions), almshouse £4* ⊙ *Tues.–Sun. and bank*

*holiday Mon. 10–5; tours hourly 11–4 on certain days (check website); gardens Tues.–Sun. Apr.–Nov.* Ⓜ *Overground: Hoxton.*

FAMILY **Old Spitalfields Market.** An impressive piece of architecture in itself, this large restored Victorian market hall (covered by a glass canopy) is part bazaar and part food court. The main market days are Thursday–Sunday, with a notable antiques market on Thursday and a fashion and art market on Friday. On every first and third Friday and every second Saturday, there's a record fair, and a vintage fair sets up here every third Saturday of the month. Markets on other days sell goods that include handmade clothes, toys, hats, and jewelry. While some of the quality is pedestrian, you can also find interesting clothes, accessories, and leather goods by new designers. Late-night shopping, dining, and nightlife events take place every first Thursday. ✉ *16 Horner Sq., Spitalfields* ☎ *020/7375–2963* ⊕ *www.oldspitalfieldsmarket.com* 🖘 *Free* ⊙ *Shops daily 10–6; market stalls weekdays 10–5, Sat. 11–5, Sun. 9–5* Ⓜ *Liverpool St.*

FAMILY **V&A Museum of Childhood.** A treat for children of all ages, this East
**Fodor's**Choice London outpost of the Victoria & Albert Museum—in an iron, glass,
★ and brown-brick building transported here from South Kensington in 1868—houses one of the world's biggest toy collections. One highlight (among many) is the large Dolls' Houses collection—a bit like a miniature Geffrye Museum, with interiors from 1673 up to the present. You'll find everything from board games and puzzles to teddy bears and train sets. The collection is organized into galleries: Moving Toys, which includes everything from rocking horses to Xboxes; Creativity, which encompasses dolls, puppets, chemistry sets, play kitchens, construction toys, and musical instruments; and Childhood, with areas devoted to babies, an exhibit of children's clothes from the mid-1600s to the present, and toys inspired by adult pursuits, such as toy soldiers, toy guns, and toy hospitals. Don't miss the magnificent 18th-century commedia dell'arte puppet theater, thought to have been made in Venice. There are special activities for the under-fives. The shop has replica toys that make great presents. ✉ *Cambridge Heath Rd., Bethnal Green* ☎ *020/8983–5200* ⊕ *www.museumofchildhood.org.uk* 🖘 *Free* ⊙ *Daily 10–5:45* Ⓜ *Bethnal Green.*

**Fodor's**Choice **Whitechapel Art Gallery.** Founded in 1901, this internationally renowned
★ gallery mounts exhibitions that rediscover overlooked masters and showcase tomorrow's legends. Painter and leading exponent of abstract expressionism Jackson Pollock was exhibited here in the 1950s as was pop artist Robert Rauschenberg in the 1960s; the 1970s saw a young David Hockney's first solo show. The exhibitions continue to be on the cutting edge of contemporary art. The gallery also hosts talks, film screenings, workshops, and other events; tours of local galleries take place on the first Thursday of every month. Pick up a free East London art map to help you plan your visit to the area. ✉ *77–82 Whitechapel High St., Whitechapel* ☎ *020/7522–7888* ⊕ *www.whitechapelgallery. org* 🖘 *Free (charge for some special exhibits)* ⊙ *Tues., Wed., and Fri.– Sun. 11–6, Thurs. 11–9* Ⓜ *Aldgate East.*

# WORTH NOTING

**Columbia Road Flower Market.** On Sunday morning this largely built-up area is transformed into a riot of color and scent with the arrival of the flower sellers. There's everything from bedding plants to banana trees, including herbs, cut flowers, and bouquets at very reasonable prices. The vendors' patter is part of the fun. Columbia Road itself is lined with some 60 independent shops, so you can pick up some art, antiques, handcrafted jewelry, or, of course, garden accessories to go with your greenery. To avoid the crowds, get here the earlier the better. ⊠ *Columbia Rd., Hackney* ⊕ *www.columbiaroad.info* ✆ *Sun. 8–3* Ⓜ *Old St., Northern Line.*

**Maureen Paley Gallery.** Inspired by the DIY punk aesthetic and the funky galleries of New York's Lower East Side, Maureen Paley started putting on exhibitions in her East End home back in 1984, when it was virtually the only gallery in the area. Since then, this American artist and gallerist has shown such respected contemporary artists as Gillian Wearing, Helen Chadwick, Jenny Holzer, Peter Fischli, and Wolfgang Tillmans and, today, is considered the doyenne of East End gallerists. The gallery has been in its current home, a converted warehouse in Bethnal Green, since 1999. ⊠ *21 Herald St., Bethnal Green* ☎ *020/7729–4112* ⊕ *www.maureenpaley.com* ✆ *Wed.–Sun. 11–6* Ⓜ *Bethnal Green.*

FAMILY **Old Truman Brewery.** The last East End brewery still standing—a handsome example of Georgian and 19th-century industrial architecture, and in late Victorian times the largest brewery in the world—has been transformed into a cavernous hipster mall housing galleries, record shops, fashion-forward boutiques, bars, clubs, and restaurants, along with an array of international street-food vendors. The retailers are at street level with offices and studios on the upper floors. Events include fashion shows for both new and established designers, excellent sample sales, art installations, and, on weekends, a food hall and a vintage clothes fair. Truman's Brewery itself shut down in 1989, but has risen from the ashes in recent years. Its location out in Hackney Wick is open for brewery tours (Thursday at 6:30 and Saturday at 2). ⊠ *91 Brick La., Spitalfields* ☎ *0207/770–6000* ⊕ *www.trumanbrewery.com* Ⓜ *Overground: Shoreditch High St.*

**Royal London Hospital Museum.** Located in the crypt of a Victorian church, the Royal London Hospital Museum uses exhibits of historic medical equipment, surgical instruments, and archives to document the history of this East London institution from its foundation in 1740 to the present day. Highlights include a forensic medicine section with documentation and original materials connected to the Jack the Ripper murders and the RLH surgeon who helped investigate them. There are also artifacts and documents relating to Joseph Merrick (aka "the Elephant Man") who spent his final years in the hospital, and a set of dentures worn by George Washington. Opening hours are subject to change on short notice, so call ahead. ⊠ *St. Augustine with St. Philip's Church, Newark St., Whitechapel* ☎ *020/7377–7608* ⊕ *www.bartshealth.nhs.uk/rlhmuseum* 🎫 *Free* ✆ *Tues.–Fri. 10–4:30.*

7

FAMILY   **Spitalfields City Farm.** An oasis of rural calm in an urban landscape, this little community farm raises a variety of animals, including some rare breeds, to help educate city kids about life in the country. A tiny farm shop sells freshly laid eggs, along with organic seasonal produce. Gardening sessions take place on Tuesday (10–2) and Wednesday (11–2). ✉ *Buxton St., Spitalfields* ☎ *020/7247–8762* ⊕ *www. spitalfieldscityfarm.org* 🎟 *Free* ⊗ *Tues.–Sun. 10–4* Ⓜ *Overground: Shoreditch High St.*

FAMILY   **Sutton House.** Built by a courtier to King Henry VIII, this Tudor mansion has since been home to merchants, Huguenot silk weavers, and, in the 1980s, a group of arty squatters. The house dates back to 1535, when Hackney was a village on the outskirts of London surrounded by fields. Later, in 1751, it was split into two self-contained houses. Its oak-paneled rooms, tranquil courtyard, and adorable café are an unexpected treat in an area that's yet to entirely shake off its grit. Visit at the weekend for guided tours of the house, or on the first Thursday of the month for an evening tour by candlelight. ✉ *2–4 Homerton High St., Hackney* ☎ *020/8986–2264* ⊕ *www.nationaltrust.org.uk/sutton-house* 🎟 *£5.50* ⊗ *Sept.–July, Wed.–Sun. noon–5; Aug., daily noon–5* Ⓜ *Overground: Hackney Central.*

**The Ten Bells.** Although the number of bells in its name has varied between 8 and 12, depending on how many bells were used by neighboring Christ Church, Spitalfields, this pub retains its authentic mid-Victorian interior and original tiles, including a frieze depicting the area's weaving tradition on the north wall and particularly fine floral tiling on two others. Legend has it the Ripper's third victim, Annie Chapman, had a drink here before meeting her gory end—the pub is depicted in Alan Moore's acclaimed graphic novel *From Hell.* ✉ *84 Commercial St., Spitalfields* ☎ *07530/492986* ⊕ *www.tenbells.com* Ⓜ *Overground: Shoreditch High St.*

# 8

# SOUTH OF
# THE THAMES

# GETTING ORIENTED

## South of the Thames

| GETTING THERE | TOP REASONS TO GO |
|---|---|
| For the South Bank, use Embankment on the District, Circle, Northern, and Bakerloo lines and walk across the Golden Jubilee Bridges; or Waterloo on the Northern, Jubilee, and Bakerloo lines, from where it's a 10-minute walk.<br><br>London Bridge on the Northern and Jubilee lines is five minutes from Borough Market and Southwark Cathedral. The station also serves Bermondsey Street, although, confusingly, the next stop on the Jubilee line is called Bermondsey. Brixton has its own stop on the Victoria line. | **Join the "groundlings" at Shakespeare's Globe:** See one of Shakespeare's plays in this historically accurate replica of the Elizabethan theater where they were first performed.<br><br>**View a new master at Tate Modern:** One of the world's great collections of post-1900 modern art, the centerpiece of this Tate branch is the huge renovated electric turbine hall, now an exhibition space used for large installations.<br><br>**Get bloodthirsty at the London Dungeon:** Did you ever wonder what a disembowelment looks like? That's just one of the gory tableaux on view in this lively, somewhat jokey, history-themed Grand Guignol. You'll be amazed at how many children adore this place.<br><br>**Take in a Waterloo sunset on Waterloo Bridge:** This is one of London's most romantic views, with St. Paul's to the east and the Houses of Parliament to the west. |

## MAKING THE MOST OF YOUR TIME

Don't attempt to visit the area south of the Thames in one go. Tate Modern alone deserves a whole afternoon, especially if you want to do justice to both the temporary exhibitions and the permanent collection. The Globe requires about two hours for the exhibition theater tour and two to three hours for a performance. Finish with drinks at the Oxo Tower or one of the Shard's restaurants, with their spectacular views. You can return across the river to central London via Southwark on the Jubilee line from Tate Modern, although it's a good walk to the station. Crossing the Millennium Bridge for St. Paul's on the Central line or the Golden Jubilee Bridge to Embankment station offer longer but more scenic alternatives.

### FEELING PECKISH?

**Konditor & Cook.** Known for their exquisite cakes and pastries, this chain of patisseries offers daily specials such as paella or vegetarian moussaka. This branch has a Brownie Bar on Saturday. ⊠ *10 Stoney St., Borough* ☎ *020/7633–3300* ⊕ *www.konditorandcook.com* ⊗ *Closed Sun. No dinner* Ⓜ *London Bridge.*

**Pieminister.** In the shopping enclave of Gabriel's Wharf, you'll find this branch of Pieminister, which began life in Borough Market. Have a meat pie made with ethically farmed ingredients like chicken and tarragon. ⊠ *Gabriel's Wharf, 56 Upper Ground, South Bank* ☎ *020/7928–5755* ⊕ *www. pieminister.co.uk* ⊗ *No dinner.* Ⓜ *Waterloo.*

Sightseeing
★★★★★
Nightlife
★★★★
Dining
★★★
Lodging
★
Shopping
★★

This area is one of London's leading destinations, with attractions including the IWM London, the Southbank Centre (Europe's largest arts center), and the heavenly Borough Market. Most are clustered around the Southbank and in Bankside and Southwark, but the surrounding neighborhoods of Bermondsey and Lambeth are rising rapidly, with galleries, shops, and restaurants proliferating. And the formerly drab Nine Elms area (near Vauxhall) is in the process of being totally transformed, with luxury highrises and shops proliferating in anticipation of the huge new U.S. embassy that will open there in 2017.

Updated by
Ellin Stein

A borough of the City of London since 1327, Southwark first became well known for its inns (the pilgrims in Chaucer's *A Canterbury Tale* set off from one), theaters, prisons, tanneries, and brothels, as well as entertainments such as cockfighting. For four centuries, this was a sort of border town outside the city walls (and jurisdiction) where Londoners went to let their hair down and behave badly. Originally, you were just as likely to see a few bouts of bearbaiting at the Globe as you were Shakespeare's most recent work. But now that south London encompasses a world-class museum, high-caliber art, music, film, and theater venues, as well as an aquarium, a historic warship, two popular food markets, and greatly improved transportation links, this region has become one of the leading destinations in England.

Today, you can walk the **Thames Path** along the river from the London Eye all the way to Greenwich. The segment beside the South Bank is alive with skateboarders, secondhand-book stalls, and street entertainers. At one end the **London Eye,** a 21st-century landmark that became an instant favorite with both Londoners and out-of-towners, rises next to the **London Aquarium** and the **Southbank Centre,** home to the **Royal Festival Hall,** the **Hayward Gallery,** the **BFI Southbank,** and the **National Theatre.**

The restaurant at Tate Modern has some of the best views in London. Here you can see St. Paul's Cathedral in the distance.

Farther east you'll come to a reconstruction of Sir Francis Drake's 16th-century ship the *Golden Hinde;* **Butler's Wharf,** where some notable restaurants occupy what were once shadowy Dickensian docklands; **The Shard,** the tallest building in the EU, which offers spectacular views over the city; and, next to **Tower Bridge,** the massive headlight-shape **City Hall.** Nearby Bermondsey Street (from "Beormund's Eye," as it was known in Saxon times) is home to the bright yellow Fashion Museum, the White Cube Gallery, and lots of trendy shops, restaurants, and cafés. Meanwhile, younger visitors will enjoy the **London Dungeon** and **HMS** *Belfast,* a decommissioned Royal Navy cruiser, while food lovers should make a straight line to London's oldest food market, **Borough Market,** where the independent stallholders sell farm-fresh produce, artisanal bread and cheese, and specialty fish and meat.

Even from the Shard's lofty viewing platform 1,016 feet up, the area south of the Thames still isn't one of London's most beautiful, but you'll be able to see how this patchwork of neighborhoods fits together. The heart is the South Bank, which extends east from the London Eye to Blackfriars Bridge, with the river to the north and Waterloo station to the south. From Blackfriars Bridge east to London Bridge is Bankside, where you'll find the Globe and Tate Modern. Moving east from London Bridge is Borough, with its cobbled streets and former factories now turned into expensive lofts. Next, southeast of Borough, is buzzy, urban Bermondsey, while leafy Dulwich, with its renowned gallery and charming period streets, is quite a distance to the south. Returning up the river to the west of the South Bank is Lambeth and then Vauxhall, with the imposing IWM London (formerly the Imperial

War Museum), a thriving gay scene, and scary through-traffic routes. It's a rapidly changing district, thanks to a regeneration spearheaded by the construction of the new U.S. Embassy in adjacent Nine Elms and a slew of upscale riverside residential developments. South of here is Brixton, long the heartland of London's Afro-Caribbean community—with a lively club scene—and now attracting young families priced out of nearby Clapham.

## TOP ATTRACTIONS

FAMILY

Fodor'sChoice

★

**Dulwich Picture Gallery.** Famed for its regal old master painting collection, the Dulwich (pronounced "Dull-ich") Picture Gallery, designed by Sir John Soane, was the world's first purpose-built art museum when it opened in 1811 (the recent extension was designed by Rick Mather). The permanent collection includes landmark works by Rembrandt, Van Dyck, Rubens, Poussin, and Gainsborough, and the museum also hosts three or so major temporary exhibitions each year. Check the website for its schedule of family activities; there's a lovely café here, too. While you're in the area, take a short wander and you'll find a handful of cute clothing and crafts stores and the well-manicured Dulwich Park, which has lakeside walks and a fine display of rhododendrons in late May. Development in Dulwich Village is tightly controlled, so it feels a bit like a time capsule, with old-fashioned street signs and handsome 18th-century houses on the main street. ⊠ *Gallery Rd., Dulwich* 🕾 *020/8693–5254* ⊕ *www.dulwichpicturegallery.org.uk* 🖾 *£5 (temporary exhibitions may be extra), guided tours free* ☉ *Tues.–Sun. and bank holiday Mon. 10–5; last entry at 4:30. Tours weekends at 3* ☉ *Closed Mon.* Ⓜ *Brixton station, then Bus P4. National Rail: West Dulwich from Victoria or North Dulwich from London Bridge.*

**Fashion and Textile Museum.** The bright yellow and pink museum (it's hard to miss) designed by Mexican architect Ricardo Legorreta features changing exhibitions devoted to developments in fashion design, textiles, and jewelry from the end of World War II to the present. Founded by designer Zandra Rhodes, and now owned by Newham College, the FTM is a favorite with fashionistas. There are weekday fashion-based workshops and lectures on aspects of fashion history; the excellent gift shop sells books on fashion and one-of-a-kind pieces by local designers. After your visit, check out the many trendy restaurants, cafés, and boutiques that have bloomed on Bermondsey Street. ⊠ *83 Bermondsey St., Bermondsey* 🕾 *020/7407–8664* ⊕ *www.ftmlondon.org* 🖾 *£9* ☉ *Tues., Wed., Fri., and Sat. 11–6, Thurs. 11–8, Sun. 11–5; last admission 45 mins before closing* Ⓜ *London Bridge.*

**Gabriel's Wharf.** This is a cluster of small shops specializing in jewelry, art, clothing, and ceramics by designer-manufacturers, with an adjoining cluster of informal restaurants and cafés, most with outdoor seating. A project of the Coin Street Community Builders, a social enterprise group, it bustles with activity. The same group converted the nearby **Oxo Tower Wharf,** an art deco warehouse with three levels of designer studios that also serve as retail outlets. The Oxo Tower Restaurant, Bar and Brasserie, a pricey restaurant operated by the swish department store Harvey Nichols, occupies the top floor, and you can see the same spectacular views from an adjacent free public viewing area (open daily). ⊠ *56 Upper Ground, South Bank* ☎ *020/7021–1600* ⊕ *www. coinstreet.org* ⧠ *Free* ☉ *Shops and studios Tues.–Sun. 11–6* Ⓜ *Black-friars, Waterloo.*

FAMILY **Golden Hinde II.** This is a full-size reconstruction of the little galleon in which the famed Elizabethan explorer Sir Francis Drake circumnavigated the globe in 1577–80. Launched in 1973, the exact replica made one full and one partial round-the-world voyage, calling in at ports—many along the Pacific and Atlantic coasts of the United States—to do duty as a maritime museum. Now berthed at the St. Mary Overie Dock, the ship continues its educational purpose, complete with a "crew" in period costumes and three decks of artifacts. Call for information on guided tours. ⊠ *1 Pickfords Wharf, Clink St., Bankside* ☎ *020/7403–0123* ⊕ *www.goldenhinde.com* ⧠ *£6; 1-hr guided tour £7* ☉ *Daily 10–5:30* Ⓜ *London Bridge.*

FAMILY **London Dungeon.** Saved by a keen sense of its own borderline ridiculousness, this gory attraction is more funny than frightening, with tableaux depicting the bloody demise of famous figures alongside the torture, murder, and ritual slaughter of lesser-known victims, all to a sound track of screaming, wailing, and agonized moaning. There are lively dramatizations about the Great Plague, Henry VIII, (the fictional) Sweeney Todd, and (the real) Jack the Ripper, to name a few, with costumed characters leaping out of the gloom to bring the information to life and add to the fear and fun. Perhaps most shocking are the crowds of children baying to get in: most kids absolutely love this place, although those with more a sensitive disposition may find it too frightening (that goes for adults as well). Be sure to get the souvenir booklet to impress all your friends back home. Expect long lines on weekends and during school holidays. Savings are possible through online booking. ⊠ *Riverside Bldg., County Hall, Westminster Bridge Rd., South Bank* ☎ *0870/423–2240* ⊕ *www.thedungeons.com* ⧠ *From £18.95* ☉ *Mon., Tues., Wed., and Fri. 10–6:30, Thurs. 11–6:30, weekends 10–7:30; last entry 90 mins before closing. Hrs may vary; phone or check website to confirm* Ⓜ *Waterloo.*

FAMILY
Fodor's Choice
★
**London Eye.** To mark the start of the new millennium, architects David Marks and Julia Barfield devised an instant icon that allows Londoners and visitors alike to see the city from a completely new perspective. The giant Ferris wheel was the largest cantilevered observation wheel ever built at the time, and one of the city's tallest structures. The 25-minute slow-motion ride inside one of the enclosed passenger capsules is so smooth you'd hardly know you were suspended over the Thames. On a clear day you can see up to 25 miles, with a bird's-eye view of London's most famous landmarks as you circle 360 degrees. If you're looking for a special place to celebrate, champagne and canapés can be arranged ahead of time. ■ TIP➔ Buy your ticket online to avoid the long lines and get a 10% discount. For an extra £9, you can save even more time with a Fast Track flight (check in 15 minutes before your "departure." You can buy a combination ticket for the Eye and other London attractions (check online for details) and board the London Eye River Cruise here

8

Built at the site of the original theater where Shakespeare's plays were performed, the modern-day Globe is a painstaking reconstruction of an open-air theater.

for a 40-minute sightseeing voyage on the Thames. In December, there's a scenic ice rink just below the wheel. ⊠ *Jubilee Gardens, South Bank* 🕿 *0871/781–3000* ⊕ *www.londoneye.com* ✉ *From £19.35; cruise from £11.83 (bookable online only)* ⊗ *Hrs vary; see website. Closed Jan.* ⊗ *Closed Jan. 7–14* Ⓜ *Waterloo.*

FAMILY

Fodor's Choice

★

**Shakespeare's Globe.** This spectacular theater is a replica of Shakespeare's open-roof, wood-and-thatch Globe Playhouse (built in 1599 and burned down in 1613), where most of the Bard's greatest works premiered. American actor and director Sam Wanamaker worked ceaselessly for several decades to raise funds for the theater's reconstruction 200 yards from its original site, using authentic materials and techniques, a dream that was realized in 1997. "Groundlings" (patrons with £5 standing-only tickets) are not allowed to sit during the performance. Fortunately, you can reserve an actual seat on any one of the theater's three levels, but you will want to rent a cushion for £1 (or bring your own) to soften the backless wooden benches. The show must go on, rain or shine, warm or chilly, so come prepared for anything. Umbrellas are banned, but you can bring a raincoat or buy a cheap Globe rain poncho, which doubles as a great souvenir. In the winter months, the Sam Wanamaker Playhouse, a 350-seat re-creation of an indoor Jacobean theater lighted by candles, offers plays and concerts in a less exposed though still atmospheric setting.

**Shakespeare's Globe Exhibition,** a museum under the theater (the entry is adjacent), provides background material on Shakespeare's life, the London in which he lived, the original Elizabethan Globe, and the construction of the modern version. Admission to the museum also includes a 30-minute tour of the theater (tours leave every half hour 9:30–5, mornings only during the performance season). On matinee days in summer (there are no winter matinees), tours of the archaeological remains of the nearby Rose Theatre, the oldest theatre in Bankside, may be offered instead. There are also tours of the Wanamaker every half-hour between 1 and 5, depending on the performance schedule. On days when no tours are available, the Exhibition has reduced price admission (check the website). ☒ *21 New Globe Walk, Bankside* ☏ *020/7902–1400 for general info, 020/7401–9919 for box office* ⊕ *www.shakespearesglobe.com* ☒ *Exhibition and Globe Theatre tour £15 (£2 off with valid performance ticket); Globe performances £5–£43, Wanamaker performances £10–£62* ☉ *Exhibition daily 9–5:30. Globe mid-Apr.–mid-Oct., Wanamaker mid-Oct.–mid-Apr; call or check website for performance schedules* Ⓜ *London Bridge; Mansion House, then cross Southwark Bridge.*

**Fodor's Choice**
★

**Southbank Centre.** The public has never really warmed to the Southbank Centre's hulking concrete buildings (beloved by architecture aficionados), products of the Brutalist style popular when the Centre was built in the 1950s and '60s, but all the same they flock to the concerts, recitals, festivals, and exhibitions held here at Europe's largest arts center. The **Royal Festival Hall** is truly a People's Palace, with seats for 2,900 and a schedule that ranges from major symphony orchestras to pop stars (catch the annual summer Meltdown Festival, where artists like Patti Smith or David Byrne put together a personal selection of concerts by favorite performers). The smaller **Queen Elizabeth Hall** is more strictly classically oriented. It contains the smaller **Purcell Room,** which hosts lectures and chamber performances. For art, head to the **Hayward Gallery,** which hosts shows on top contemporary artists such as Anthony Gormley and Cy Twombly. (The terrace here has some restaurants worth a visit.) Not officially part of the Southbank Centre but moments away on the east side of Waterloo Bridge, the **National Theatre** is home to some of the best productions in London (several, such as *War Horse,* have become movies) at prices well below those in the West End. You can hear leading actors, directors, and writers discuss their work at the National Theatre's Platforms, a series of inexpensive early evening and afternoon talks. Meanwhile, film buffs will appreciate the **BFI Southbank** (formerly the National Film Theatre), which has a schedule that true cinema connoisseurs will relish. The Centre's riverside street level has a terrific assortment of restaurants and bars. The BFI's Benugo bar and the Wahaca restaurant at Queen Elizabeth Hall are particularly attractive. Note that the Hayward Gallery, Purcell Room, and Queen Elizabeth Hall have been closed for renovations but are due to open in late 2017. ☒ *Belvedere Rd., South Bank* ☏ *020/7960–4200* ⊕ *www.southbankcentre.co.uk* ☒ *Varies; check website* ☉ *Hrs vary by venue; check website* Ⓜ *Waterloo, Embankment.*

**Fodor's Choice**
★

**Tate Modern.** This spectacular renovation of a mid-20th-century power station is one of the most-visited museums of modern art in the world. Its great permanent collection, which starts in 1900 and ranges from modernist masters like Matisse to the most cutting-edge contemporary artists, is arranged thematically—Energy and Process, Making Traces,

8

Pop Art and Modern Art, Structure and Clarity. Its blockbuster temporary exhibitions showcase the work of individual artists like Gaugin, Rauschenberg, and O'Keeffe.

The vast **Turbine Hall** is a dramatic entrance point used to showcase big, audacious installations that tend to generate a lot of publicity. Past highlights include Olafur Eliasson's massive glowing sun, Ai Weiwei's porcelain "sunflower seeds," and Carsten Holler's huge metal slides.

A new 10-story addition is opening in the summer of 2016. On the ground floor, The Tanks is a gallery devoted to performance, moving image, soundscapes, and installations, while at the top is a roof terrace offering spectacular views of the London skyline. In between are spaces offering more room for large-scale installations, for art from outside Europe and North America, and for digital and interactive projects.

Not to be missed in the original building is the collection of Rothko murals, originally created for the Four Seasons restaurant in New York, and displays devoted to Gerhard Richter (both on Level 2) and works by the video pioneer Nam June Paik (Level 4). Levels 2 and 3 include temporary exhibitions, for which there's a charge, and ever-changing video installations are scattered throughout the building

Head to the Restaurant on Level 6 or the Espresso Bar on Level 3 for stunning vistas of the Thames. The view of St. Paul's from the Espresso Bar's balcony is one of the best in London.

You can join free 45-minute guided tours, each covering a different gallery: Pop Art and Modern Art at 11, Making Traces at noon, Structure and Clarity at 2, and Energy and Process at 3. Private "Tate Tours for Two" can be booked online (£120–£140) with afternoon tea for an additional £25 or a champagne dinner or lunch for an additional £100. If you plan to visit Tate Britain, too, take advantage of the Tate to Tate Boat, which takes visitors back and forth between the two Tates every 40 minutes. ⊠ *Bankside, Bankside* ☏ *020/7887–8888* ⊕ *www.tate.org. uk/modern* ✆ *Free (charge for special exhibitions)* ⊗ *Daily 10–6; last admission 45 mins before closing* Ⓜ *Southwark, Mansion House, St. Paul's.*

## WORTH NOTING

**Florence Nightingale Museum.** Compact, highly visual, and engaging, this museum on the grounds of St. Thomas's hospital is dedicated to Florence Nightingale, who founded the first school of nursing and played a major role in establishing modern standards of health care. Exhibits are divided into three areas: one is devoted to Nightingale's Victorian childhood, the others to her work tending soldiers during the Crimean War (1854–56) and her subsequent health-care reforms. The museum incorporates Nightingale's own books and famous lamp as well as interactive displays of medical instruments and medicinal herbs. There is a free half-hour tour on Wednesday at 3:30. ⊠ *2 Lambeth Palace Rd., Lambeth* ☏ *020/7620–0374* ⊕ *www.florence-nightingale.co.uk* ✆ *£7.50* ⊗ *Daily 10–5; last admission at 4:30* Ⓜ *Waterloo.*

FAMILY **HMS *Belfast*.** At 613½ feet, this large light cruiser is one of the last remaining big-gun armored warships from World War II, in which it played an important role in protecting the Arctic convoys and supporting the D-Day landings in Normandy; the ship later saw action during the Korean War.

This floating museum has been moored in the Thames as a maritime branch of **IWM London** since 1971. A tour of all nine decks—including the admiral's quarters, mess decks, bakery, punishment cells, operations room, engine room, and more—gives a vivid picture of life on board the ship, while the riveting interactive gun-turret experience puts you in the middle of a World War II naval battle. ⊠ *The Queen's Walk, Borough* ☎ *020/7940–6300* ⊕ *www.iwm.org.uk* 🎫 *£14.50* ⊗ *Mar.–Oct., daily 10–6; Nov.–Feb., daily 10–5; last admission 1 hr before closing* Ⓜ *London Bridge.*

**OFF THE BEATEN PATH**

**Horniman Museum.** Set amid 16 acres of gardens, this eclectic museum is considered something of a well-kept secret by the residents of south London—perhaps because of its out-of-the-way location. You can explore world cultures, natural history, and a fine collection of musical instruments (including a giant tuba) here. The emphasis is on fun and a wide range of activities, including London's oldest nature trail. Recent additions include an African Worlds section, an Animal Walk that features domesticated creatures such as sheep, chickens, and alpacas, and an aquarium stocked with endangered species. There's also a café and shop. It's a 15-minute bus ride from here to the Dulwich Picture Gallery; Bus P4, heading toward Brixton, takes you from door to door. ⊠ *100 London Rd., Forest Hill, London* ☎ *020/8699–1872* ⊕ *www.horniman. ac.uk* 🎫 *Free (small charge for temporary exhibitions and aquarium)* ⊗ *Museum daily 10:30–5:30; gardens Mon.–Sat. 7:15 am–sunset, Sun. 8 am–sunset (website has exact closing times); Animal Walk daily 12:30–4; Nature Trail daily 9–4 (may be closed in bad weather; call ahead)* Ⓜ *National Rail: Forest Hill from London Bridge or Victoria.*

FAMILY
**Fodor's**Choice
★

**IWM London.** Despite its name, the cultural venue formerly known as the Imperial War Museum (one of five IWM branches around the country) does not glorify either Empire or bloodshed but emphasizes understanding through conveying the impact of 20th- and 21st-century warfare on citizens and soldiers alike. After a major renovation, a dramatic six-story atrium at the main entrance encloses an impressive amount of hardware—including a Battle of Britain Spitfire, a German V2 rocket, tanks, guns, and submarines—along with accompanying interactive material and a café. The First World War galleries explore the wartime experience on both the home and fighting fronts, with the most comprehensive collection on the subject in the world—some 1,300 objects ranging from uniforms, equipment, and weapons to letters and diaries. Three permanent exhibitions in the Second World War galleries shed light on that conflict: an extensive and haunting Holocaust exhibition; *A Family In Wartime*, which documents the story of one London

Designed by renowned architect Renzo Piano, The Shard punctures the London skyline with its record-breaking height and spectacular modernity.

family living through the Blitz; and *Turning Points 1934–1945,* which relates key moments in the conflict to objects on display. *Peace and Security 1945–2015* looks at more contemporary hostilities, including the Cold War, Iraq, Afghanistan, and Kosovo. Other galleries are devoted to works relating to conflicts from World War I to the present day by painters, poets, documentary filmmakers, and photographers. James Bond fans won't want to miss the intriguing Secret War Gallery, which charts the work of secret agents. ⊠ *Lambeth Rd., South Bank* ☎ *020/7416–5000* ⊕ *www.iwm.org.uk* ✉ *Free (charge for special exhibitions)* ⊗ *Daily 10–6; last admission at 5:30* Ⓜ *Lambeth North.*

**Newport Street Gallery.** Putting the seal on Vauxhall's status as an up-and-coming neighborhood, business-savvy artist Damien Hirst opened this gallery in 2015. Following in the footsteps of his former patron Charles Saatchi, he bought the cavernous space (a former Victorian scenery-painting workshop) to house a rotating selection from his large private collection of contemporary art that includes works by Francis Bacon, Banksy, Picasso, Jeff Koons, Richard Hamilton, and Tracey Emin, to name just a few. There's also a shop selling artists' books, limited edition prints, and sculptures, as well as a restaurant, Pharmacy 2, a reincarnation of Hirst's fashionable millennium-era Notting Hill watering hole. ⊠ *Newport St., London* ☎ *020/3141–9320* ⊕ *www.newportstreetgallery.com* ✉ *Free* ⊗ *Tues.–Sun. 10–6* Ⓜ *Vauxhall, Lambeth North.*

FAMILY **Sea Life London Aquarium.** The curved, colonnaded, neoclassical former County Hall that once housed London's municipal government is now home to a superb three-level aquarium where you can walk above sharks and stingrays and view more than 500 other aquatic species, both common and rare. There are also hands-on displays. It's not the biggest aquarium you've ever seen, but the educational exhibits are particularly well arranged, with 14 zones for different oceans, water environments, and climates, ranging from a stunning coral reef to the Antarctic to a rain forest. Regular feeding times and free talks are offered throughout the day. There are also special "experiences" that include behind-the-scenes tours, snorkeling with sharks, or sea turtle feeding at an extra charge. ■TIP➔ **Admission is by time slot, but for an additional £3 you can purchase flexible priority-entry tickets that also avoid the long lines.** ✉ *County Hall, Westminster Bridge Rd., South Bank* ☎ *0871/663–1678* ⊕ *www.visitsealife.com* 💲 *From £23.50 (up to 15% discount for online booking)* ☉ *Daily 10–7; last admission 1 hr before closing* Ⓜ *Westminster, Waterloo.*

**Southwark Cathedral.** Pronounced "Suth-uck," this is the oldest Gothic church in London, parts of it dating back to the 12th century. It remains off the beaten track, despite being the site of some remarkable memorials and a concert program that offers regular organ recitals at lunchtime on Monday (except in August and December) and classical music at 3:15 on Tuesday (except in December), with frequent additional musical events on Saturday evenings. Originally the priory church of St. Mary Overie (as in "over the water," on the South Bank), it became a palace church under Henry VIII and was only promoted to cathedral status in 1905. Look for the vivid 15th-century roof bosses (small ornamental wood carvings), the gaudily renovated 1408 tomb of John Gower, Richard II's poet laureate and a friend of Chaucer's, and for the Harvard Chapel, where John Harvard, a local butcher's son who went on to found the American university, was baptized. Another notable buried here (between the choir stalls) is Edmond Shakespeare, brother of William. The Refectory serves full English breakfasts, light lunches, and teas, as well as summer barbecues (weekdays 9–6, weekends 10–6). ✉ *London Bridge, Bankside* ☎ *020/7367–6700* ⊕ *cathedral.southwark.anglican.org* 💲 *Free (suggested donation £4)* ☉ *Daily 10–5* Ⓜ *London Bridge.*

**The View from the Shard.** At 800 feet, this 2013 addition to the London skyline currently offers the highest vantage point in Western Europe. Designed by the noted architect Renzo Piano, it has attracted both admiration and disdain. While the building itself is generally highly regarded, many felt it would have been better sited in Canary Wharf (or perhaps Dubai), as it spoils views of St. Paul's Cathedral from traditional vantage points such as Hampstead's Parliament Hill. No matter how you feel about the building, there's no denying that it offers a spectacular 360-degree view over London (extending 40 miles on a clear day) from viewing platforms on floors 68, 69, and 72—almost twice as high as any other viewpoint in the city. Digital telescopes provide information about 200 points of interest. There's a weather guarantee that lets you return on a more clement day if visibility is seriously impeded, and various themed events like wine tastings or silent discos are offered at an extra charge. If you find the price as eye-wateringly high as the viewing platforms, there's a less dramatic but still very impressive (and free) view from the lobby of the Shangri-La hotel on the 35th floor, or, in the evenings, the hotel's chic Gong bar on the 52nd floor (over-18s only). ✉ *32 London Bridge St., Borough* ☎ *0344/499–7222* ⊕ *www.theviewfromtheshard.com* ✉ *From £25.95* ⊗ *Apr.–Oct., daily 10–10 (last entry at 9:30); Nov.–Mar., Sun.–Wed. 10–7 (last entry at 6), Thurs.–Sat. 10–10 (last entry at 9:30); admission by timed-entry ticket only. May be closed for special events* Ⓜ *London Bridge.*

# KENSINGTON, CHELSEA, KNIGHTSBRIDGE, AND BELGRAVIA

# GETTING ORIENTED

## Kensington, Chelsea, Knightsbridge, and Belgravia

## GETTING THERE

Several Tube stations are nearby: Sloane Square and High Street Kensington on the District and Circle lines; Knightsbridge and Hyde Park Corner on the Piccadilly line; Earl's Court, South Kensington, and Gloucester Road on the District, Circle, and Piccadilly lines; Holland Park on the Central line; Ladbroke Grove on the Hammersmith and City line; and Victoria on the District, Circle, and Victoria lines.

## SAFETY

This is one of London's safest districts, but beware of pickpockets in shopping areas.

## TOP REASONS TO GO

**Treasure hunt at the V&A Museum:** The Victoria & Albert is the world's best decorative arts museum. Artists have been sketching in the Sculpture Court since Victorian times.

**Attract a dinosaur's attention at the Natural History Museum:** Watch children catch on that the museum's animatronic *T. rex* has noticed *them*—and is licking its rather large chops.

**Glimpse royal domestic life at Kensington Palace:** Visit the public areas and gardens of this royal family commune that has housed Queen Victoria, Princess Diana, and (currently) the Duke and Duchess of Cambridge (William and Kate).

## MAKING THE MOST OF YOUR TIME

You could fill three or four days in this borough: a shopping stroll along the length of King's Road can easily take half a day. Give yourself a half day, at least, for the Victoria & Albert Museum and a half day for either the Science or Natural History Museum.

## A GRAZER'S PARADISE

**Duke of York Square Farmers' Market.** West London's answer to Borough Market, this Saturday open-air market is in a pedestrian-only plaza off Duke of York Square, a chic shopping precinct. It hosts 40 stalls purveying artisanal and locally produced products from more than 150 small producers. Like Borough Market, this is a grazer's paradise, giving you the chance to sample fresh oysters and cooked sausages as well as yummy hot snacks from countries ranging from Brazil to Thailand. ⊠ *Duke of York Sq., Chelsea* ☎ *020/7823–5577* ⊕ *www.dukeofyorksquare.com* ⊙ *Sat. 10–4* Ⓜ *Sloane Sq.*

## FEELING PECKISH?

**Stick and Bowl.** This hole-in-the-wall restaurant, a neighborhood favorite for more than 20 years, is an amazing bargain for this pricey part of town, serving good basic Chinese food at reasonable prices. Standouts on the extensive menu include roast duck, BBQ pork, and crispy pork in noodle soup. It's not fancy, but service is fast. ⊠ *31 Kensington High St., Kensington* ☎ *020/7937–2778* ⊟ *No credit cards* Ⓜ *High St. Kensington.*

## NEAREST PUBLIC RESTROOMS

Most public restrooms have been replaced by futuristic "autoloos": booths on street corners that cost £1. If you're not brave enough to try them, head to the restrooms at department stores Peter Jones or Harvey Nichols. Or ask for the "loo" in a pub, but be prepared for "sorry" if you're not a customer.

**9**

Sightseeing
★★★★
Nightlife
★★
Dining
★★★★
Lodging
★★★★
Shopping
★★★★★

The Royal Borough of Kensington & Chelsea (or K&C, as the locals call it) is where you'll find London at its richest, and not just in the moneyed sense. South Kensington offers a concentration of great museums near Cromwell Road, with historic Kensington Palace nearby in Kensington Gardens. Once-raffish Chelsea, where the Pre-Raphaelites painted and Mick Jagger partied, is now a thoroughly respectable home for the discreetly wealthy, while flashier Knightsbridge has become a haven for international plutocrats, with shopping to match their tastes.

# KENSINGTON

Updated by
Ellin Stein

Kensington comprises the area along the southern edge of Hyde Park from Exhibition Road (where the big museum complex is) and the area to the west of the park bordered by leafy Holland Park Avenue on the north and traffic-heavy Cromwell Road on the south. This more westerly zone includes the satellite neighborhood of Holland Park, with its serenely grand villas and charming park, as well as local shopping mecca Kensington High Street and the antiques shops on Kensington Church Street.

Kensington's first royal connection was created when King William III, fed up with the dampness arising from the Thames, bought a country place there in 1689 and converted it into **Kensington Palace.** Queen Victoria's consort, Prince Albert, added the jewel in the borough's crown when he turned the profits of the Great Exhibition of 1851 into South Kensington's metropolis of museums: the **Victoria & Albert Museum (V&A),** the **Science Museum,** and the **Natural History Museum.** Posthumous tributes to the prince in the area include the **Royal Albert Hall,** with bas-reliefs that make it resemble a giant, redbrick Wedgwood teapot, and the lavish **Albert Memorial.**

Turn into Derry Street or Young Street and enter **Kensington Square,** one of the most complete 17th-century residential squares in London. The house at **18 Stafford Terrace,** one of London's most gorgeously decorated from the Victorian era—its lavish use of Islamic tiles, inlaid mosaics, gilded ceilings, and marble columns make for an Arabian Nights fantasy—is nearby as well.

## TOP ATTRACTIONS

**Design Museum.** Reopening in late 2016 in its new home—the former Commonwealth Institute, a modernist landmark—this was the first museum in the United Kingdom to place everyday contemporary objects in a social and cultural context and to consider their role in the history of design. Furniture, digital technology, and domestic products from the museum's permanent collection are on display. Temporary exhibitions focus on leading individual designers, such as Charles and Ray Eames, Isamu Noguchi, Terence Conran, or Christian Louboutin, or on themes such as Sport and Design. There's also a design library and archive, two shops, a café, and a restaurant. ⊠ *224–238 Kensington High St., London* ⊕ *www.designmuseum.org* ✉ *Free (charge for temporary exhibitions)* ⊙ *Daily 10–5:45; last admission at 5:15* Ⓜ *High Street Kensington.*

**18 Stafford Terrace.** The home of *Punch* cartoonist Edward Linley Sambourne in the 1870s is filled with delightful Victorian and Edwardian antiques, fabrics, and paintings (as well as several samples of Linley Sambourne's work for *Punch*) and is one of the most charming extant 19th-century London houses. The Italianate house was the scene for society parties when Anne Messel was in residence in the 1940s. This being Kensington, there's inevitably a royal connection: Messel's son, Antony Armstrong-Jones, was married to the late Princess Margaret, and their son has preserved the connection by taking the title Viscount Linley. Admission in the morning is by reservation on a 75-minute guided tour only (Saturday morning tours are given by costumed actors), but in the afternoon you are free to wander at will. ⊠ *18 Stafford Terr., Kensington* ☎ *0207/602–3316* ⊕ *www.rbkc.gov.uk/ linleysambournehouse* ✉ *£7 (£10 with guided tour)* ⊙ *Mid-Sept.–mid-June, Wed. and weekends 2–5:30 for open access; guided tours Wed. and weekends at 10:15 and 11:30 (booking closes 1 hr before tour)* Ⓜ *High Street Kensington.*

FAMILY **Kensington Palace.** This is a rare chance to get a glimpse into the more domestic and personal side of Royal life. Neither as imposing as Buckingham Palace nor as charming as Hampton Court, Kensington Palace is something of a Royal Family commune, with various close relatives of the Queen occupying large apartments in the private part of the palace. Bought in 1689 by Queen Mary and King William III, it was converted into a palace by Sir Christopher Wren and Nicholas Hawksmoor, and royals have been in residence ever since. Princess Diana lived here with her sons after her divorce, and this is where Prince William now lives with his wife, Catherine, Duchess of Cambridge, their young son, George, and daughter, Charlotte.

The State Apartments are open to the public. One permanent exhibition, *Victoria Revealed,* is devoted to the private life of Queen Victoria, who was born and grew up here. The Queen's State Apartments are given over to William and Mary and the Glorious Revolution. The lavish King's State Apartments, originally built for George I, have a semipermanent exhibit that explores the world of the Georgian Court through the story of George II and his politically active queen, Caroline. There is also a changing temporary exhibition. Through late 2016, this will be *Fashion Rules,* a collection of gowns worn by Princess Margaret, Princess Diana, and Queen Elizabeth, which in 2017 will be replaced by another fashion-related exhibition.

Look for the King's Staircase, with its panoramic trompe-l'oeil painting, and the King's Gallery, with royal artworks surrounded by rich red damask walls, intricate gilding, and a beautiful painted ceiling. Outside, the grounds are almost as lovely as the palace itself, and are a fine location for a picnic on one of the benches—or head for the delightful café (busy during peak hours) in the Orangery, near the Sunken Garden, where you can indulge in a formal afternoon tea.

If you also plan to visit the Tower of London, Hampton Court Palace, Banqueting House, or Kew Palace, become a member of Historic Royal Palaces. It costs $75 per person, or $135 for a family, and gives you free entry to all five sites for a year. ⊠ *The Broad Walk, Kensington Gardens, Kensington* ☎ *0844/482–7799 for advance booking, 0844/482–7777 for info, 0203/166–6000 from outside U.K.* ⊕ *www. hrp.org.uk* ⤴ *£17.50 Mar.–Oct £16.50 Nov.–Feb.* ۞ *Mar.–Sept., daily 10–6; Oct.–Feb., daily 10–5; la admission 1 hr before closing* ↪ *The palace has a wheelchair-accessible elevator, and Kensington Gardens has electric buggies for mobility-impaired visitors* Ⓜ *Queensway, High Street Kensington.*

FAMILY
Fodor's Choice
★

**Natural History Museum.** Originally built to house the British Museum's natural history collection and bolstered by samples provided by Britain's great 19th-century explorers and scientists—notably Charles Darwin— this is one of the world's preeminent museums of natural history and earth sciences. The terracotta facade of this enormous Victorian cathedral of science (which featured prominently in the movie *Paddington*) is embellished with relief panels depicting living creatures to the left of the entrance and extinct ones to the right (although some species have subsequently changed categories). Most are represented inside the museum, which contains more than 70 million different specimens. Only a small percentage is on public display, but you could still spend a day here and not come close to seeing everything.

As of early 2017, the skeleton of a giant blue whale will dominate the vaulted, cathedral-like entrance hall. Meanwhile, similarly huge dino bones can be found in the **Dinosaur Gallery** (Gallery 21), along with fossils and some extremely long teeth. You'll also come face-to-face with velociraptors and a giant animatronic *T. rex* that's programmed to sense when human prey is near and "respond" in character. When he does, you can hear the shrieks of fear and delight all the way across the room. Kids love it. ■**TIP**➔ If you have under-sevens with you, check out

Ice-skaters outside the Natural History Museum in South Kensington

the museum's free "Explorer Backpacks," containing a range of activity materials to keep the little ones amused.

An escalator takes you into a giant globe in the **Earth Galleries**, where there's a choice of levels to explore. Don't leave without checking out the earthquake simulation in the **Volcanoes and Earthquake Gallery**. The **Darwin Centre** houses some of the millions of items the museum itself doesn't have room to display, including "Archie," a 28-foot giant squid. If you want to see Archie and some of the other thousands of specimens on the shelves, you'll need to book one of the low-cost behind-the-scenes Spirit Collection tours (around £5). These half-hour tours take place at 10:40, 11:40, and 12:40, with a longer 50-minute tour at 1:30, and can be booked on the same day (space is limited, so come early). The Centre's **Cocoon Experience** is a 45-minute tour, during which you can see specimens from plant and insect collections previously in storage, and "Nature Live" is a program of free, informal talks given by scientists, covering a wildly eclectic range of subjects, usually at 2:30 (and at 12:30 on weekends) in the David Attenborough Studio.

The museum has an outdoor ice-skating rink October–January, and a popular Christmas fair. ⊠ *Cromwell Rd., South Kensington* ☎ *0207/942–5000* ⊕ *www.nhm.ac.uk* ✉ *Free (some fees for special exhibitions)* ⊙ *Daily 10–5:50; last admission at 5:30* Ⓜ *South Kensington.*

FAMILY
Fodor's Choice
★

**Science Museum.** With attractions ranging from painlessly educational exhibits, like the new interactive gallery where kids can perform their own hands-on scientific experiments, to a sublime exhibition on science in the 18th century, the Science Museum brings the subject alive for

9

visitors of all ages. One of the three great South Kensington museums, it stands next to the Natural History Museum in a more modern, plainer building. Highlights include the Launch Pad gallery, which demonstrates basic laws of physics; *Puffing Billy*, the oldest steam locomotive in the world; and the actual Apollo 10 capsule. The six floors are devoted to subjects as diverse as the history of flight, space exploration, jet flight simulators, the large Hadron collider, 3-D printing, and (opening early 2017) the history of robots over the last 400 years. The **Information Age** gallery, devoted to communication networks including telegraph, television, mobile phones, and the Internet, was opened in 2014 by Queen Elizabeth, who marked the occasion by sending her first tweet. Overshadowed by a three-story blue-glass wall, the **Wellcome Wing** is an annex to the rear of the museum, devoted to contemporary science and technology. It contains a 450-seat IMAX theater and the Legend of Apollo—an advanced motion simulator that combines seat vibration with other technical gizmos to re-create the experience of a moon landing. If you're a family of at least five, you might be able to get a place on one of the popular Science Night sleepovers by booking well in advance. Aimed at kids seven years old, these nighttime science workshops offer the chance to camp out in one of the galleries, and include a free IMAX show the next morning; check the website for details. ⊠ *Exhibition Rd., South Kensington* ☎ *0870/870–4868* ⊕ *www. sciencemuseum.org.uk* ☒ *Free (charge for special exhibitions, IMAX, and simulator rides)* ☉ *Daily 10–6; last admission at 5:15* Ⓜ *South Kensington.*

FAMILY  **Victoria & Albert Museum.** Known to all as the V&A, this huge museum is
Fodor's Choice  devoted to the applied arts of all disciplines, all periods, and all nation-
★  alities. First opened as the South Kensington Museum in 1857, it was renamed in 1899 in honor of Queen Victoria's late husband and has since grown to become one of the country's best-loved cultural institutions, with high-profile temporary exhibitions alongside its stunning permanent collections.

Many collections at the V&A are presented not by period but by category—textiles, sculpture, jewelry, and so on (it's a tricky building to navigate, so be sure to use the free map). Nowhere is the benefit of the categorization more apparent than in the **Fashion Gallery** (Room 40), where formal 18th-century court dresses are displayed alongside the haute couture styles of contemporary designers. The Fashion Gallery has become known for high-profile temporary exhibitions devoted to icons such as David Bowie and Alexander McQueen.

The **British Galleries** (Rooms 52–58 and 118–125), devoted to art and design from 1500 to 1900, are full of beautiful diversions—among them the Great Bed of Ware (immortalized in Shakespeare's *Twelfth Night*). Here, a series of actual rooms have been painstakingly reconstructed piece by piece. These include an ornate music room and the Henrietta St. Room, a breathtakingly serene parlor dating to 1722.

The **Asian Galleries** (Rooms 44–47) are full of treasures, but among the most striking items on display is a remarkable collection of ornate samurai armor in the **Japanese Gallery** (Room 44). There are also galleries devoted to China, Korea, and the Islamic Middle East. More recent installations include the Ceramics gallery and the Medieval and Renaissance galleries, which have the largest collection of works from the period outside of Italy. The Europe Gallery (Rooms 1–7), opened after an extensive refurbishment, brings together more than 1,100 objects from 1600 to 1815. And after extensive renovations, an enhanced entrance off Exhibition Road offering access through a new public courtyard, as well as new underground galleries, is expected to open in spring 2017.

As a whirlwind introduction, you could take a free one-hour tour (at 10:30, 11:30, 12:30, 1:30, or 3:30). There is also a free tour devoted just to the British Galleries at 2:30 and a one-hour tour of the Theatre and Performance collections (including costumes from *The Lion King*) at 2. Occasional public lectures during the week are delivered by visiting bigwigs from the art and fashion worlds. There are free lectures throughout the week given by museum staff, who give an additional Introductory tour of the collection on Friday night at 7. ■**TIP→ Whatever time you visit, the spectacular sculpture hall will be filled with artists, both amateur and professional, sketching the myriad artworks on display there. Don't be shy; bring a pad and join in.** ✉ *Cromwell Rd., South Kensington* ☎ *020/7942–2000* ⊕ *www.vam.ac.uk* 🎫 *Free (charge for some special exhibitions, from £5)* ⏱ *Sat.–Thurs. 10–5:45, Fri. 10–10 (partial gallery closures after 6)* Ⓜ *South Kensington.*

# CHELSEA

Chelsea was settled before the Domesday Book was compiled and already fashionable when two of Henry VIII's wives lived there. On the banks of the Thames are the vast grounds of the **Royal Hospital,** designed by Christopher Wren. A walk along the riverside embankment will take you to **Cheyne Walk,** a lovely street dating back to the 18th century. Several of its more notable residents—from J. M. W. Turner and Henry James to Laurence Olivier and Keith Richards—are commemorated by blue plaques on their former houses.

The **Albert Bridge,** a sherbet-color Victorian confection of a suspension bridge, provides one of London's great romantic views, especially at night. Leave time to explore the tiny Georgian lanes of pastel-color houses that veer off King's Road to the north—especially **Jubilee Place** and **Burnsall Street,** leading to the hidden "village square" of **Chelsea Green.** On Saturday there's an excellent farmers' market up from the Saatchi Gallery selling artisanal cheese and chocolates, local oysters, and organic meats, plus stalls serving international food.

Residential Chelsea extends along the river from the Chelsea Bridge west to the Battersea Bridge and north as far as the Old Brompton Road.

9

# TOP ATTRACTIONS

**Royal Hospital Chelsea.** Charles II founded this residence for elderly and infirm soldiers in 1682 to reward the troops who had fought for him in the civil wars of 1642–46 and 1648. A creation of three of England's greatest architects—Wren, Vanbrugh, and Hawksmoor—this small enclave of brick and Portland stone set in manicured gardens (which you can visit) surrounds the Figure Court (the figure being a 1682 gilded bronze statue of Charles II dressed as a Roman general), the Great Hall (dining room), and a chapel. The beautiful Wren-designed chapel and the Great Hall, where you can see Antonio Verrio's vast oil painting of Charles on horseback, are open to the public at certain times during the day. There is a small museum devoted to the history of the resident "Chelsea Pensioners," but the real attraction, along with the building, is the pensioners themselves. Recognizable by their traditional scarlet frock coats with gold buttons, medals, and tricorne hats, they are all actual veterans, who wear the uniform, and the history it represents, with a great deal of pride. Individuals can visit the grounds, chapel, courts, and museum for free, or for £10 you can go on a 90-minute guided tour for groups of 10 or more (must be booked a month in advance) led by one of the pensioners. ⊠ *Royal Hospital Rd., Chelsea* ☎ *020/7881–5298* ⊕ *www.chelsea-pensioners.co.uk* *Free, guided tour (for groups of 10 or more) £10* ☉ *Grounds and chapel Mon.–Sat. 10–4:30; Great Hall Mon.–Sat. 10–noon and 2–4:30; museum weekdays 10–4, Sat. 10–4:30. Closed holidays and for special events* Ⓜ *Sloane Sq.*

**RHS Chelsea Flower Show.** Run by the Royal Horticultural Society, the Chelsea Flower Show, the year's highlight for thousands of garden-obsessed Brits, is held every May (usually the third week). The huge showcase for garden design and plants takes up all of the Royal Hospital's large grounds, and the surrounding streets throng with visitors. ⊠ *Chelsea* ☎ *0844/338–0338 for tickets, 0203/176–5800 from outside U.K.* ⊕ *www.rhs.org.uk* *£33–£61 (discounts for RHS members)* ☉ *Tues.–Fri. 8–8, Sat. 8–5:30.*

**Saatchi Gallery.** Charles Saatchi, who made his fortune in advertising, is one of Britain's canniest collectors of contemporary art, credited with popularizing the Young British Artists movement through his championing of early works by the likes of Damien Hirst and Tracey Emin. The museum's home is at the former Duke of York's HQ, just off King's Road. Built in 1803, its grand period exterior belies its imaginatively restored modern interior, which was transformed into 15 exhibition spaces of varying size and shape. Unlike Tate Modern, there is no permanent collection other than ongoing site-specific installations: at any one time, galleries are devoted to between one and three exhibitions that normally run for up to six months. There's also an excellent café, which is open late. ⊠ *Duke of York's HQ Bldg., King's Rd., Chelsea* ☎ *020/7811–3070* ⊕ *www.saatchigallery.com* *Free* ☉ *Daily 10–6; last entry at 5:30* Ⓜ *Sloane Sq.*

World-famous Harrods has been luring shoppers with its classic wares since 1834.

# KNIGHTSBRIDGE

There's no getting away from it. With two world-famous department stores, **Harrods** and **Harvey Nichols**, a few hundred yards apart and surrounded by numerous boutiques selling the biggest names in international luxury and expensive jewelry, London's wealthiest enclave—not many other neighborhoods are plagued with street racers in Maseratis—will appeal most to those who enjoy conspicuous consumption.

Nearby Sloane Street is lined with top-end designer boutiques such as Prada, Dior, and Tods. If it all starts to become a bit generic (expensive generic), **Beauchamp Place** (pronounced "Beecham") is lined with equally luxe one-off boutiques, which tend to be more distinctive and less global.

Posh Knightsbridge is located to the east of Kensington, bordered by Hyde Park on the north and Pont Street just past Harrods on the south.

## WORTH NOTING

**Brompton Oratory** (*London Oratory*). This is a late product of the mid-19th-century English Roman Catholic revival led by John Henry Cardinal Newman (1801–90), who established the oratory in the 1840s and whose statue you see outside. Architect Herbert Gribble, a previously unknown 29-year-old, won the competition to design the place, an honor that you may conclude went to his head when you see the vast, incredibly ornate interior. It's punctuated by treasures far older than the church itself, like the giant Carrara marble *Twelve Apostles* in the nave, sculpted by Giuseppe Mazzuoli in the 1680s for Siena's cathedral. The Oratory is known for the quality of its organs and choir, with exceptional music being an integral part of services here. ⊠ *Brompton Rd., Knightsbridge* ☎ *0207/808–0900* ⊕ *www.bromptonoratory.com* ✉ *Free* ⊙ *6:30 am–8 pm* Ⓜ *South Kensington.*

# BELGRAVIA

Steps away from the roaring traffic of Hyde Park Corner is quiet, fashionable Belgravia, one of the most impressive set pieces of 19th-century urban planning, which lies just to the east of Kensington and Chelsea. Street after street is lined with grand, cream-color stucco terraces, once aristocrats' townhouses and most still part of the Grosvenor estate owned by the Duke of Westminster. Many buildings are leased to embassies or organizations, but a remarkable number around **Lowndes Square, Eaton Place,** and **Eaton Square** remain in the hands of private owners, whether old money or new oligarchs who put their security guards in the attached mews houses. Some people consider the area near **Elizabeth Street** to be southern Belgravia, others call it Pimlico-Victoria. Either way, you'll find small, unique stores here specializing in baked goods, wine, gifts, and stationery.

## TOP ATTRACTIONS

**Belgrave Square.** This is the heart of Belgravia, once the preferred address for the gentry's London town houses, though now mostly occupied by organizations, embassies, and the international rich. The Square and the streets leading off it share a remarkably consistent elegant architectural style thanks to all being part of a Regency redevelopment scheme commissioned by the Duke of Westminster and designed by Thomas Cubitt with George Basevi. The grand, cream-color stucco terraced houses were snapped up by aristocrats and politicians due to their proximity to Buckingham Palace just around the corner, and still command record prices on the rare occasions when they come onto the market. The private garden in the center is open to the public once a year (⊕ *www. opensquares.org*). Walk down Belgrave Place toward Eaton Place and you pass two of Belgravia's most beautiful mews: Eaton Mews North and Eccleston Mews, both fronted by grand rusticated entrances right out of a 19th-century engraving. Traffic can really whip around Belgrave Square, so be careful. ⊠ *Belgravia* Ⓜ *Hyde Park Corner.*

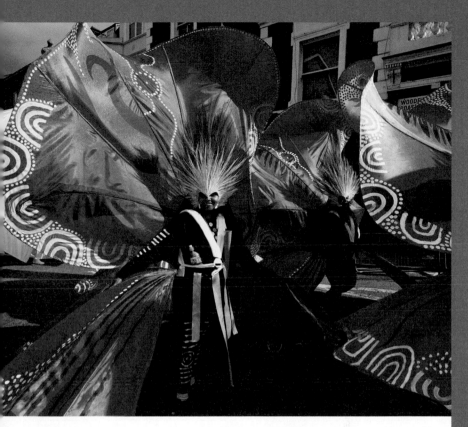

# NOTTING HILL
# AND BAYSWATER

# GETTING ORIENTED

## GETTING THERE

For Portobello Market and environs, the best Tube stops are Ladbroke Grove and Westbourne Park (Hammersmith and City lines); ask for directions when you emerge. The Notting Hill Gate stop on the District, Circle, and Central lines enables you to walk the length of Portobello Road while going slightly downhill.

## A GOOD WALK

To spot Notting Hill's grandest houses, stroll over to Lansdowne Road, Lansdowne Crescent, and Lansdowne Square—two blocks west of Kensington Park Road.

## TOP REASONS TO GO

**Unearth a bargain on Portobello Road:** The early bird can catch considerably more than the worm; go before 10 am on Saturday to hook the good stuff at London's world-famous antiques market, or come during the week for a leisurely browse.

**Refresh in Hyde Park:** Explore one of London's largest green spaces by walking, cycling ("Boris bikes" are available at several sites), skating with the Friday Night Skate, or rowing on the Serpentine, the tranquil lake that snakes through the park.

**Take in contemporary art at the Serpentine Galleries:** Expand your cultural horizons at one of London's foremost showcases for modern art, or just have a bite at the café in the extension to the Serpentine Sackler Gallery, designed by famed architect Zaha Hadid and a work of art in itself.

# Notting Hill and Bayswater

## MAKING THE MOST OF YOUR TIME

Saturday is the most exciting day for shopping, eating, and drinking here.

The market gets crowded by noon in summer, so come early if you are serious about shopping.

Head south from the north end of Portobello Road, using the parks to take a break on the way.

On Sunday, the Hyde Park and Kensington Gardens railings along Bayswater Road are lined with artists displaying their work, which may slow your progress.

Well-heeled locals are often out on Sunday with friends in the pubs or with kids in the parks.

## SAFETY

At night, avoid straying from the main streets north of Westbourne Park Road toward Ladbroke Grove's high-rise estates (projects) and the surrounding areas.

## FEELING PECKISH?

**The Prince Bonaparte.** It's had an art deco makeover, but one thing hasn't changed: the high standard of its modern British food and a fine selection of artisanal ales and carefully chosen wines. A stone's throw from Portobello Market, it's the perfect place for a drink or a bite to eat. ⌧ *80 Chepstow Rd., Bayswater* ☎ *020/7313–9491* ⊕ *www. theprincebonapartew2.co.uk* ⊙ *Mon.–Sat. noon–11, Sun. noon–10:30* Ⓜ *Notting Hill Gate, Royal Oak.*

**The Tabernacle.** The Victorian Gothic interior of this bar, café, and arts center combo hosts intimate music gigs (some by big names like Adele), literary events with the likes of Tales of The City's Armistead Maupin, and 15-minute talks with speakers such as historian Niall Ferguson. The food is Caribbean-influenced, and the atmosphere, especially in the outdoor courtyard, is relaxed. ⌧ *34–35 Powis Sq., Notting Hill* ☎ *020/7221–9700* ⊕ *www.tabernaclew11.com* ⊙ *Closed Sun.* Ⓜ *Notting Hill Gate.*

**10**

Sightseeing
★★

Nightlife
★★★

Dining
★★★

Lodging
★★★

Shopping
★★★★

The center of London's West Indian community from the 1950s through the '70s, Notting Hill these days is the address of choice for the well-heeled, be they bankers, rock stars, media and advertising types, or rich hippies. Teeming with trendy restaurants, cool bars, and buzzing street markets, the area is also studded with some of London's most handsome historic residences, crescents, and terraces. Every weekend, the hordes descend on Portobello Road to go bargain-hunting at one of the world's great antiques markets. Holland Park, to the west, has even grander villas, while Bayswater (to the east) has excellent world-cuisine restaurants.

## NOTTING HILL

Updated by
James O'Neill

Notting Hill as we know it emerged in the 1840s when the wealthy Ladbroke family developed a small suburb to the west of London. Before then, the area had the far less glamorous name of "the Potteries and the Piggeries," after the two industries it was best known for: ceramics and pig farming.

During the 1980s, Notting Hill transformed from a lively but down-at-heel and sometimes dangerous West Indian enclave to a supertrendy fashionable neighborhood. The area's Caribbean legacy persists, however, not least in the form of the annual Notting Hill Carnival in late August. The new millennium saw Notting Hill's fame go global thanks to the hit romcom of the same name, though the movie itself was criticized by locals for downplaying the area's cultural diversity. For the Notting Hill of the silver screen, head for fashionable **Westbourne Grove** and **Ledbury Road,** lined with eclectic independent boutiques offering

The Wellington Arch Monument proudly welcomes visitors to Hyde Park, one of London's largest royal parks.

highly desirable designer goods for the home and family, as well as contemporary art—prices and taste levels are high.

For less rarefied shopping, try **Portobello Road**; the famous Saturday antiques market and shops are at the southern end. Due south of Holland Park Avenue (the westerly continuation of Notting Hill Gate), and southwest of Ladbroke Grove, lies the handsome Holland Park neighborhood, where you'll find quiet streets filled with gorgeous stucco villas.

## TOP ATTRACTIONS

FAMILY **Holland Park.** Formerly the grounds of an aristocrat's house and open to the public only since 1952, Holland Park is an often-overlooked gem and possibly London's most romantic park. The northern "Wilderness" end offers woodland walks among native and exotic trees first planted in the early 18th century. Foxes, rabbits, and hedgehogs are among the residents. The central part of the park is given over to the manicured lawns—still stalked by raucous peacocks—one would expect at a stately home, although Holland House itself, originally built by James I's chancellor and later the site of a 19th-century salon frequented by Byron, Dickens, and Disraeli, was largely destroyed by German incendiary bombs in 1940. The east wing was reconstructed and has been incorporated into a youth hostel, while the remains of the front terrace provide an atmospheric backdrop for the open-air performances of the April–September **Holland Park Opera Festival** (☎ 0300/999–1000 box office, ⊕ www.operahollandpark.com). The glass walled Garden Ballroom (every home should have one) is now the **Orangery**, which hosts art exhibitions and other public events, as does the **Ice House,** while an adjoining former granary has become the upscale Belvedere restaurant. In spring and summer the air is fragrant with aromas from a rose garden, great banks of rhododendrons, and an azalea walk. Garden enthusiasts will also not want to miss the tranquil, traditional **Kyoto Garden,** a legacy of London's 1991 Japan Festival. The southern part of the park is given over to sport and play: cricket and football (soccer) pitches; a golf practice area; tennis courts; a well-supervised children's Adventure Playground; and a giant outdoor chess set. ⊠ *Ilchester Pl., Holland Park* ⊕ *www.rbkc.gov.uk (under Leisure and Culture)* ☉ *Daily 7:30–30 min before dusk* Ⓜ *Holland Park, High Street Kensington.*

FAMILY
Fodor'sChoice
★

**Hyde Park.** Along with the smaller St. James's and Green parks to the east, the 350-acre Hyde Park started as Henry VIII's hunting grounds. Along its south side runs Rotten Row, once Henry's royal path to the hunt—the name is a corruption of *Route du Roi* (route of the king). It's still used by the Household Cavalry, who live at the Hyde Park Barracks—a high-rise and a low, ugly red block, now up for sale—to the left. You can see the Guardsmen in full regalia leaving on horseback for guard duty at Buckingham Palace at about 10:30 (or come at noon when they return). Hyde Park is wonderful for strolling, cycling, or just relaxing by the Serpentine, the long body of water near its southern border. On the south side, by the 1930s **Serpentine Lido,** is the site of the **Diana Princess of Wales Memorial Fountain,** which opened in 2003 and is a good spot to refuel at a café. On Sunday, close to Marble Arch you'll find the uniquely British tribute to free speech, Speakers' Corner. Though not what it was in the days before people could use the Internet to vent their spleen, it still offers a unique assortment of passionate, if occasionally irrational, advocates literally getting up on soapboxes. ⊠ *Hyde Park* ☏ *030/0061–2000* ⊕ *www.royalparks.org.uk* ⊡ *Free* ☉ *Daily 5 am–midnight* Ⓜ *Hyde Park Corner, Knightsbridge, Lancaster Gate, Marble Arch.*

FAMILY
Fodor'sChoice
★

**Kensington Gardens.** Laid out in 1689 by William III, who commissioned Sir Christopher Wren to build Kensington Palace, the gardens are a formal counterpart to neighboring Hyde Park. Just to the north of the palace itself is the Dutch-style **Sunken Garden.** Nearby, the 1912 bronze statue *Peter Pan* commemorates the boy in J. M. Barrie's story who lived on an island in the Serpentine and who never grew up. Kids will enjoy the magical **Diana Princess of Wales Memorial Playground,** whose design was also inspired by Barrie's book. The **Elfin Oak** is a 900-year-old tree trunk that was carved with scores of tiny elves, fairies, and other fanciful creations in the 1920s. The **Italian Gardens** (1860) comprise several ornamental ponds and fountains, while the **Round Pond** attracts model-boat enthusiasts. ⊠ *Kensington* ☏ *030/0061–2000* ⊕ *www.royalparks.org.uk* ⊡ *Free* ☉ *Daily 6 am–dusk* Ⓜ *High Street Kensington, Lancaster Gate, Queensway, South Kensington.*

Fodor'sChoice
★

**Leighton House Museum.** Leading Victorian artist Frederic (Lord) Leighton lived and worked in this building on the edge of Holland Park, spending 30 years (and quite a bit of money) transforming it into an opulent "private palace of art" infused with an orientalist aesthetic sensibility. The interior is a sumptuous Arabian Nights fantasy, with walls lined in peacock blue tiles designed by Leighton's friend, the ceramic artist William de Morgan, and beautiful mosaic wall panels and floors, marble pillars, and gilded ceilings. The centerpiece is the Arab Hall, its marble walls adorned with even more intricate murals made from 16th- and 17th-century ceramic tiles imported from Syria, Turkey, and Iran, surmounted by a domed ceiling covered in gold leaf with a gold mosaic frieze running underneath. You can also visit Leighton's studio, with its huge north window and dome; the house is filled with paintings, several of his own along with works by other Pre-Raphaelites. ⊠ *12 Holland Park Rd., Holland Park* ☎ *020/7602–3316 weekdays, 020/7471–9160 weekends* ⊕ *www.rbkc.gov.uk (under Leisure and Culture)* ⊡ *£7* ⊙ *Wed.–Mon. 10–5:30* Ⓜ *Holland Park, South Kensington.*

**Portobello Road.** Looking for a 19th-century snuff spoon? Perhaps a Georgian salt cellar? What about a 1960s-era minidress? Then head to Portobello Road's famous Saturday market—and arrive at about 9 am to avoid the giant crowds. Stretching almost 2 miles from Notting Hill, the market is made up of four sections, each with a different emphasis: antiques, fresh produce, household goods, and a flea market. The antiques stalls are packed in between Chepstow Villas and Westbourne Grove, where you'll also find almost 100 antiques shops plus indoor markets, which are open on weekdays, when shopping is much less hectic. Where the road levels off, around Elgin Crescent, youth culture and a vibrant neighborhood life kicks in, with a variety of interesting small stores and food stalls interspersed with a fruit-and-vegetable market. On Friday and Saturday the section between Talbot Road and the Westway elevated highway becomes one of London's best flea markets, specializing in discounted new household goods, while north of the Westway you'll find secondhand household goods and bric-a-brac. Scattered throughout, but especially under the Westway, are vendors selling a mishmash of designer, vintage, and secondhand clothing, together with jewelry, custom T-shirts, and assorted junk. There's a Trinidad-style Carnival centered on Portobello Road on the late August bank-holiday weekend, a tribute to the area's past as a center of the West Indian community. ⊠ *Notting Hill* ⊕ *www.portobelloroad.co.uk* Ⓜ *Notting Hill Gate, Ladbroke Grove.*

**10**

**Serpentine Galleries.** Taking its name from the lake that curves its way through Hyde Park, the Serpentine Gallery, housed in a modest redbrick building in Kensington Gardens, is one of London's foremost showcases for contemporary art. Just about everyone who's anyone has exhibited here: Louise Bourgeois, Jeff Koons, Marina Abramovic, and Gerhard Richter, to name a few. A permanent work on the gallery's grounds, consisting of eight benches and a carved stone circle, commemorates its former patron, Princess Diana. The Serpentine Sackler Gallery, a second exhibition space that's in a small Georgian gunpowder storeroom just over the water, has a dramatic extension designed by Zaha Hadid as well as a stylish restaurant. If you're in town between May and September, check out the annual Serpentine Pavilion, where each year a leading architect is given free rein to create a temporary pavilion of their choosing—always with imaginative results. Past designers have included Frank Gehry, Daniel Liebeskind, and Jean Nouvel. ⊠ *Kensington*

*Gardens, Kensington* ☎ *0207/402–6075* ⊕ *www.serpentinegalleries. org* ✉ *Free* ⊙ *Tues.–Sun. and bank holiday Mon. 10–6* Ⓜ *Lancaster Gate, Knightsbridge, South Kensington.*

## WORTH NOTING

**Graffik.** Not everyone thinks graffiti can be a bonus to the urban landscape, but those who do should head for this leading gallery of contemporary street art. The big name here is Banksy, but there are works for sale by several other artists in the same vein such as Trust.iCON and CODE FC, who are more concerned with social commentary than tagging. This is one gallery experience that really appeals to young people, especially if the visit coincides with one of Graffik's two-hour weekend workshops. ✉ *284 Portobello Rd., Notting Hill* ☎ *020/8354–3592* ⊕ *www.graffikgallery.com* ✉ *Free* ⊙ *Tues.–Sun. 11–6:30* Ⓜ *Notting Hill Gate, Ladbroke Grove.*

**Museum of Brands, Packaging and Advertising.** Now expanded and relocated, this fascinating museum specializes in branded toys, clothes, games, and domestic goods, and explores how advertising has come to infiltrate our lives. Curios from the 1800s to the present day include World War II–era toilet paper (brand name: Nasti toilet roll) that has Adolf Hitler's face on every sheet. ✉ *111–117 Lancaster Rd., Notting Hill* ☎ *020/7908–0880* ⊕ *www.museumofbrands.com* ✉ *£7.50* ⊙ *Tues.–Sat. 10–6, Sun. 11–5; last entry 45 mins before closing. Closed during Notting Hill Carnival* Ⓜ *Ladbroke Grove.*

# BAYSWATER

East of Notting Hill Gate Tube station, Notting Hill turns into Bayswater, characterized by wide streets lined with imposing white stucco terraced houses. Traditionally given over to cheap B&Bs, many are being converted back to private homes as the area continues to gentrify. The eastern end of Westbourne Grove and the streets around it are known for their excellent restaurants, particularly Chinese, Lebanese, and Greek. On **Queensway**, Bayswater's main street, **Whiteleys**, originally a huge department store built in 1912, has been converted into a shopping center containing a luxury movie theater, restaurants (try Le Café Anglais for a swanky evening out), a bowling alley, and, of course, shops.

Nearby **Paddington station** is as well known for its association with the world's most famous marmalade fan, Paddington Bear, as it is for being one of London's most handsome rail terminals.

# REGENT'S PARK
# AND HAMPSTEAD

# GETTING ORIENTED

## Regent's Park and Hampstead

Kenwood House

Highgate Cemetery

Waterlow Park

Hampstead Heath

Ladies Bathing Pond

Mixed Bathing Pond

2 Willow Rd.

Parliament Hill

Burgh House and Hampstead Museum

Ginger and White

Fenton House

**HAMPSTEAD**

Christchurch Hill

Hampstead Heath Rail

Gospel Oak Rail

**HAMPSTEAD** U

St. John's-at-Hampstead

Keats House

North London Line

Finchley Road & Frognal Rail

Freud Museum London

Kentish Town Rail

**PRIMROSE HILL**

**CHALK FARM**

Marine Ices

**SWISS COTTAGE** U

Primrose Hill

Regent's Park Rd.

Cecil Sharp House

**CAMDEN TOWN** U

**CAMDEN TOWN**

Jewish Museum

**ST. JOHNS WOOD** U

**ST. JOHN'S WOOD**

ZSL London Zoo

The Hub

*Regent's Park*

Cumberland Terrace

Lord's Cricket Ground & Museum

Regent's Park Open-Air Theatre

York Bridge

**MARYLEBONE** U

**BAKER STREET** U

**REGENT'S PARK** U

**GREAT PORTLAND STREET**

RIBA

0    1/4 mi

0    1/4 km

## TOP REASONS TO GO

**Ramble across Hampstead Heath:** Londoners adore the Heath for bringing a bit of countryside to the city.

**Go romantic at Keats House:** Visit the rooms where one of England's greatest poets wrote some of his greatest works inspired by his love for the girl-next door, Fanny Brawne.

**Get sporty in Regent's Park:** Cycle past Nash's grand neoclassical stucco terraces or walk up Primrose Hill for a great view over the city.

**Gracious living at Kenwood:** See one of Britain's best art collections at this 18th-century gentleman's estate largely designed by Robert Adam.

**Meet the penguins at the London Zoo:** A VIP ticket will let you get up close and personal with the penguins.

## SAFETY

Avoid Hampstead Heath, Primrose Hill, and Regent's Park at night unless there's an event; all are perfectly safe during the day. Also to be avoided after dark: the canal towpath in Primrose Hill and Camden.

## FEELING PECKISH?

**Ginger and White.** Family-friendly and thoroughly modern, Ginger and White is a delightful fusion of continental-style café and traditional British "caff"—all bound up with a sophisticated Hampstead vibe. ⊠ *4A–5A Perrins Ct., Hampstead* ☎ *020/7431–9098* ⊕ *www.gingerandwhite.com* ⊗ *No dinner* Ⓜ *Hampstead.*

**Marine Ices.** Near the Camden Lock market, this place has some of London's best ice cream. ⊠ *Old Dairy Mews, 61 Chalk Farm Rd., Camden Town* ☎ *020/7428–9990* ⊕ *www.marineices.co.uk* ⊗ *Daily 11–10* Ⓜ *Chalk Farm.*

## GETTING THERE

To get to Hampstead by Tube, take the Northern line (the Edgware branch) to Hampstead or Golders Green station, or take the London Overground to Hampstead Heath station. The south side of Hampstead Heath can also be reached by the London Overground Gospel Oak station. To get to Regent's Park, take the Bakerloo line to Regent's Park Tube station or, for Primrose Hill, the Chalk Farm stop on the Northern line. Little Venice is reachable by the Warwick Avenue stop on the Bakerloo line and St. John's Wood has its own stop on the Jubilee Line.

## MAKING THE MOST OF YOUR TIME

Regent's Park, Primrose Hill, and Hampstead can be covered in a day. Spend the morning in Hampstead, with a brief foray onto the Heath, then head south to Regent's Park in the afternoon so that you're closer to central London come nightfall, if that is where your hotel is located. (You'll also be heading downhill instead of up.) You can always return to Hampstead another day for a long walk across the Heath or to head west to Little Venice's canals.

Sightseeing
★★★★
Nightlife
★★★
Dining
★★
Lodging
★★
Shopping
★★★

Regent's Park, Primrose Hill, Belsize Park, and Hampstead are four of London's prettiest and most civilized neighborhoods. The city becomes noticeably calmer and greener as you head uphill from Marylebone Road through Regent's Park to the refreshing greenery of Primrose Hill and the handsome Georgian houses and Regency villas of Hampstead. To the west, the less bucolic but equally elegant St. John's Wood and Little Venice also provide a taste of moneyed London.

Updated by
Ellin Stein

Leaving the park at the London Zoo, walk up adjoining **Primrose Hill** for one of the most picturesque views of London. Long a magnet for the creative (though these days within reach of only the most well-heeled creatives), this is the kind of neighborhood where the local library's screening of *The Madness of King George* is introduced by its writer, longtime resident Alan Bennett. Peel off from the Hill to explore Regent's Park Road and its attractive independent shops and cafés, as well as the surrounding streets with their pastel Victorian villas.

Alternatively, continue hugging the Hill heading north along Primrose Hill Road. This will take you to Belsize Park, itself a celebrity hot spot (Tim Burton and Hugh Laurie have houses here) with a mixture of Victorian, Arts and Crafts, and art deco buildings. Turn right onto England's Lane, another street full of independent shops and nice cafés, then left onto Haverstock Hill and head farther uphill. At the corner of Pond Street you will see two enormous Victorian Gothic buildings: one, St. Stephen's Church, is now a community arts center. The other, AIR Studios, founded by the Beatles' producer, Sir George Martin, is where scores for movies, including *Iron Man 3, Les Misérables,* and *Brave,* have been recorded.

Turn right onto Pond Street and go downhill past the unlovely Royal Free hospital to South End Green and the entrance to **Hampstead Heath.** Or go straight to stay on Rosslyn Hill and then Hampstead High Street, the neighborhood's main drag. Turn left onto Church Row, with its unspoiled early Georgian terraced houses leading to **St.**

John's-at-Hampstead, where the painter John Constable is buried. To the north of Hampstead Heath is Highgate, another upscale north London "village" with a large concentration of Georgian and early Victorian buildings, particularly around The Grove (home to Kate Moss, George Michael, and Sting).

To reach **Little Venice,** go to the west entrance of Regent's Park by the gold-domed London Central Mosque and then north past **Lord's Cricket Ground** to the St. John's Wood Tube stop. Turn left onto Grove End Road, which will bring you to the famous Abbey Road crosswalk featured on the Beatles' album of the same name. Head southwest for Little Venice, known as the Belgravia of north London due to its stucco terraces (found on streets such as Randolph Avenue, Clifton Avenue, and Randolph Road) that are very similar to the other neighborhood's. The "Venice" comes from its proximity to a picturesque stretch of the Grand Union Canal along Blomfield Road, where highly decorative houseboats are moored. If you happen to be here on the second Sunday in May, you'll be able to see houseboats from all over London's canals gather here in Paddington Basin for the Blessing of the Boats.

# REGENT'S PARK

Commissioned by his patron the Prince Regent (later George IV) to create a master plan for this part of London, formerly a royal hunting ground, London's great urban planner and architect John Nash laid out the plans for the 410-acre Regent's Park in 1812. Bordered by grand neoclassical terraces, the park holds many attractions, including the London Zoo and the summer display of more than 400 varieties of rose in Queen Mary's Gardens.

## TOP ATTRACTIONS

FAMILY
Fodor'sChoice
★
**Primrose Hill.** More conventionally parklike than Hampstead Heath, the rolling lawns of Primrose Hill, the northerly extension of Regent's Park which rises to 256 feet, provide outstanding views over the city to the southeast, encompassing Canary Wharf and the London Eye. Filled with families and picnickers in nice weather, it has featured in books—it was here that Pongo engaged in "twilight barking" in *The Hundred and One Dalmatians,* and the Martians set up an encampment in H.G. Wells's *The War of The Worlds.* It's also been mentioned in songs by Blur, Madness, and Paul McCartney, among others, and served as a location for films including *Bridget Jones: The Edge of Reason* and *Paddington Bear.* ✉ *Regent's Park Rd., Regent's Park* ☎ *0300/061–2300* ⊕ *www.royalparks.org.uk* ✉ *Free* Ⓜ *Chalk Farm.*

FAMILY
Fodor'sChoice
★
**Regent's Park.** One of London's principal charms is to find the formal, cultivated serenity of Regent's Park—more country-house grounds than municipal amenity—just on the edge of the intensely urban West End, a world away from the traffic-clogged surrounding roads. The 395-acre park, with the largest outdoor sports area in central London, draws the athletically inclined from around the city.

At the center of the park, **Queen Mary's Gardens**, created in the 1930s, are a fragrant 17-acre circle containing some 30,000 individual specimens and more than 400 varieties of roses. Unsurprisingly, it's a favorite spot for weddings. Just to the east of the Gardens is the **Regent's Park Open-Air Theatre** and the **Boating Lake**, which you can explore by renting a pedalo (paddleboat) or rowboat. Heading east from the rose gardens along Chester Road past the **Broad Walk** will bring you to Nash's iconic white stucco **Cumberland Terrace**, with its central Ionic columns surmounted by a triangular Wedgwood-blue pediment. At the north end of the Broad Walk you'll find the **London Zoo**, while to the northwest of the central circle is **The Hub** (☏ *0300/061–2323*), a state-of-the-art community sports center that has changing rooms, exercise classes, and a café with 360-degree views of the surrounding sports fields, used for soccer, rugby, cricket, field hockey, and softball contests. There are also tennis courts toward the park's southeast (Baker Street) entrance, and the park is a favorite north–south route for cyclists.

If watching all this activity works up an appetite, in addition to the Hub's own café there's the Regent's Bar & Kitchen outside the rose garden that serves salads, sandwiches, and wood-fired pizzas (8 am–9 pm), the Smokehouse near the zoo that specializes in BBQ, burgers, and summer salads, the Boatyard Cafe by the boating lake, the Tennis Centre Cafe by the courts, an espresso bar with wraps and cakes, and a kiosk by the children's playground that serves sandwiches and snacks. ■ **TIP→** Regent's Park also hosts two annual events: the prestigious Frieze Art Fair, and the Taste of London, a foodie-oriented extravaganza. ✉ *Chester Rd., Regent's Park* ☏ *0300/061–2300* ⊕ *www.royalparks. org.uk* 🎟 *Free* Ⓜ *Baker St., Regent's Park, Great Portland St.*

FAMILY
Fodor's Choice
★

**ZSL London Zoo.** With an emphasis on education, wildlife conservation, and the breeding of endangered species, London Zoo offers visitors the chance to see tigers, gorillas, meerkats, and more in something resembling a natural environment rather than a cage. Operated by the nonprofit Zoological Society of London, the zoo was begun with the royal animals collection, moved here from the Tower of London in 1828; the zoo itself did not open to the public until 1847. A recent modernization program has seen the introduction of several big attractions. The huge B.U.G.S. pavilion (Biodiversity Underpinning Global Survival) is a self-sustaining, contained ecosystem for 140 less-cuddly species, including invertebrates such as spiders and millipedes, plus some reptiles and fish. At Gorilla Kingdom, a walk-through re-creation of the habitat of the Western Lowland Gorilla, you can watch the four residents at close range. Rainforest Life is an indoor tropical rain forest (complete with humidity) inhabited by the likes of armadillos, monkeys, and sloths. A special nighttime section offers glimpses of nocturnal creatures like slow lorises and bats. The Animal Adventures Children's Zoo allows kids to get up close to animals including mongooses and llamas, as well as to feed and groom sheep and goats. Two of the most popular attractions are Penguin Beach, especially at feeding time (1:30) and Meerkat Manor, where you can see the sociable animals keeping watch over their own sandy territory. The new Land of The Lions exhibit provides a habitat for a pride of the endangered Asiatic big cats, while another new exhibit offers the chance to get up close and personal with 15 ring-tailed lemurs. If you're feeling flush, try to nab one of the six daily "Meet the Penguins" VIP tickets (2 pm) that offer a 20-minute guided close encounter with the locals (£45 weekdays, £60 weekends); there are similar VIP encounters with giraffes, lions, owls, meerkats, kangaroos, and aardvarks. Other zoo highlights include Butterfly Paradise; the Blackburn Pavilion, with its hundreds of tropical bird species and Tiger Territory, an enclosure for five beautiful endangered Sumatran tigers (including three cubs born at the zoo). Sunset Safari evenings, offering premium Guided Safari Tours and (limited) alcohol availability are held on Friday (6–10 pm) June 5–July 17. Check the website or the information board out front for free events, including creature close encounters and "ask the keeper" sessions. ⊠ *Outer Circle, Regent's Park* ☎ *0844/225–1826* ⊕ *www.zsl. org* ⌷ *From £22.50* ⊘ *Mar.–early Sept., daily 10–6; early Sept.–Oct., daily 10–5:30; Nov.–Feb., daily 10–4; last admission 1 hr before closing* Ⓜ *Camden Town, then Bus 274.*

## WORTH NOTING

**Cecil Sharp House.** The home of the English Folk Dance and Song Society, this soaring building from 1930 hosts concerts by artists ranging from Mumford & Sons and Laura Marling to the Ukulele Orchestra of Great Britain, as well as family barn dances and *céilidhs* (Irish barn dances). Meet the locals at drop-in classes to learn a variety of dance styles, such as morris, baroque, Irish step dancing, zydeco, and the tango. There are also temporary exhibitions on British folk arts, a café and bar, and an outstanding specialist library with an extensive collection of recordings, manuscripts, sheet music, and images relating to British folk song, dances, and local cultures in general. ⊠ *2 Regent's Park Rd., Primrose Hill* ☎ *020/7485–2206* ⊕ *www.cecilsharphouse.org* ⌷ *Free, classes from £4* ⊘ *Library Tues.–Fri. 9:30–5:30, 1st and 3rd Sat. of each month (except Aug.) 10–4; call or check website for evening concerts and classes* Ⓜ *Chalk Farm, Camden Town.*

**Jewish Museum.** This fascinating museum tells the story of the Jewish people in Britain from 1066 to today, including the period between the 13th and 17th century when Judaism was outlawed in England. Using a combination of art, religious artifacts, photographs, manuscripts, and interactive displays, its exhibits include a re-creation of a Jewish East End street from the Victorian era and another documenting the 10,000 Jewish refugee children who came to Britain, although without their parents, as part of the Kindertransport organized as World War II loomed. There are also temporary themed exhibitions, such as Jews in Football or the life of Amy Winehouse. There's a free overview of the collection on the ground floor, including a medieval *mikveh* (ritual bath) excavated a few miles from here in 2001. ⊠ *Raymond Burton House, 129–131 Albert St., Camden Town* ☎ *020/7284–7384* ⊕ *www.jewishmuseum.org.uk* ⌷ *£7.50* ⊘ *Sun.–Thurs. 10–5, Fri. 10–2; last admission 30 mins before closing. Closed on major Jewish holidays* Ⓜ *Camden Town.*

**Lord's Cricket Ground & Museum.** The spiritual home of this most English of games—and the headquarters of the MCC (Marylebone Cricket Club)—opens its "behind the scenes" areas to visitors during a 100-minute tour. Highlights include the beautiful Long Room, a VIP viewing area where portraits of cricketing greats are on display (you can also book a traditional Afternoon Tea here for £44); the players' dressing rooms; and the world's oldest sporting museum, where cricket's 400-year progress from gentlemanly village-green game to worldwide sport is charted via memorabilia, equipment, trophies, and footage of memorable performances. Don't miss the prize exhibit: the urn known as the Ashes—allegedly the remains of a cricket bail (part of the wicket assembly) presented to the English captain in 1883 by a group of Australian women, a jokey allusion to a newspaper's satirical obituary for the death of English cricket published after a resounding defeat. It's been a symbol of the two nations' long-running rivalry ever since. They still play for possession of the Ashes—an official (as opposed to joke) trophy only since 1998—every two years. A Waterford crystal version changes hands these days, although the winners still hold a replica of the original urn aloft. There is no separate nontour admittance to the museum, except for match ticket holders. Tours are not available during major matches but are offered during smaller "county" matches. ⊠ *St. John's Wood Rd., St. John's Wood* ☎ *020/7616–8595* ⊕ *www.lords. org* ⌦ *Tour £18; museum £3 with county match ticket, free with major match ticket* ⏱ *Tours on the hr: Apr.–Oct., nonmatch days daily 10–3, match days daily at 9 and 11–3; Jan.–Mar., daily 11– 2; Nov.–Dec., daily 10–2* Ⓜ *St. John's Wood.*

**Regent's Park Open-Air Theatre.** Works by Shakespeare have been performed here every summer since 1932, with casts including luminaries such as Vivien Leigh, Dame Judi Dench, and Damien Lewis. Today the theater also mounts productions of classic plays, musicals, and shows for family audiences among its four annual productions. *A Midsummer Night's Dream* is the one to catch, if it's on—never has that enchanted Greek wood been better evoked, especially when enhanced by genuine birdsong and a rising moon. There's a covered restaurant for pretheater dining, as well as a patio restaurant, an informal café, and, of course, a bar. You can also order picnic hampers in advance. The park can get chilly, so bring a blanket. Performances proceed rain or shine (umbrellas aren't allowed) with refunds only in case of a very heavy downpour. ⊠ *Inner Circle, Regent's Park* ☎ *0844/826–4242 for tickets, 0844/375–3460 for inquiries* ⊕ *www.openairtheatre.org* ⌦ *£25–£65* ⏱ *May–mid-Sept., evening performances at 7:45, matinees at 2:15* Ⓜ *Baker St., Regent's Park.*

# HAMPSTEAD

Even an impoverished Romantic poet like John Keats could afford **Hampstead.** In 1818 he moved to what is now **Keats House,** a pretty Regency residence where he spent two years and wrote several of his most famous works. Hampstead's bohemian days are long gone, although a few distinguished artists and musicians, plus television stars, still live here. Artisanal food shops and boutiques for the skinny of frame and fat of wallet cluster along Rosslyn Hill, while high-street chains start to proliferate the closer you get to Hampstead Tube station. Be sure to leave the beaten path to explore the numerous narrow charming roads, like Flask Walk, Well Walk, and New End Road. Also hidden among Hampstead's winding streets are **Fenton House,** a Georgian townhouse with a lovely walled garden, and Burgh House, the oldest house (1704) in the village and a repository of local history. On the way to Highgate you'll find **Kenwood House,** an 18th-century mansion that was designed by Robert Adam and is noted for its remarkable art collection and grounds.

Hampstead's crowning glory, however, is **Hampstead Heath** (known locally as "The Heath"), 791 acres of parkland, swimming ponds, and some of Europe's oldest oaks. It's also home to one of London's highest vantage points (321 feet), Parliament Hill.

## TOP ATTRACTIONS

FAMILY **Hampstead Heath.** For generations, Londoners have headed to Hampstead Heath to escape the dirt and noise of the city, and this unique 791-acre expanse of *rus in urbe* ("country in the city") is home to a variety of wildlife and habitat: grassy meadows, woodland, scrub, wetlands, and some of Europe's most venerable oaks. Be aware that, aside from the southern slope of Parliament Hill and Golders Hill Park, it is more like countryside than a park, with signs and amenities in short supply. Pick up a map at Kenwood House, or the **Education Centre** near the Lido off Gordon House Road, where you can also get details about the history of the Heath and its flora and fauna. An excellent alfresco café near the Athletics Field serves Italian food.

Fodor's Choice
★

Coming onto the Heath from the South End Green entrance, walk east past a well-equipped children's adventure **Playground** and **Paddling Pool,** turn left, and head to the top of **Parliament Hill.** At 321 feet above sea level, it's one of the highest points in London. You'll find a stunning panorama over the city. On clear days you can see all the way to the South Downs, the hills beyond southern London.

If you keep heading east from the playground instead, you'll come to the **Lido,** an Olympic-size outdoor unheated swimming pool that gets packed on all-too-rare hot summer days. More swimming options are available at the Hampstead ponds, which have been refreshing Londoners for generations. You'll find the "Mens" and "Ladies" ponds to the northeast of Parliament Hill, with a "Mixed" pond closer to South End Green. A £2 donation is requested.

■ TIP→ Golders Hill Park offers a good café, tennis courts, a duck pond, a croquet lawn, and a walled flower garden, plus a Butterfly House (May–September) and a small zoo with inhabitants including lemurs, coatis, and rare birds. ⊠ *Hampstead* ☎ *020/7482–7073 for Super* ⊕ *www.cityoflondon.gov.uk/hampstead* ☏ *Free* Ⓜ *Overground: Hampstead Heath for south of Heath or Gospel Oak for Lido; Hampstead for east of Heath; Golders Green, then Bus 210 or 268 to Whitestone Pond for north and west of Heath.*

**11**

**Highgate Cemetery.** Highgate is not the oldest cemetery in London, but it is probably the best known, both for its roster of famous "inhabitants" and the quality of its funerary architecture. After it was consecrated in 1839, Victorians came from miles around to appreciate the ornate headstones, the impressive tombs, and the view. Such was its popularity that 19 acres on the other side of the road were acquired in 1850, and this additional East Cemetery contains what may be the most visited grave: that of Karl Marx (1818–83), only one of several notables interred here—George Eliot is another. At the summit is the **Circle of Lebanon,** a ring of vaults built around an ancient cypress tree, a legacy of the 17th-century gardens that formerly occupied the site. Leading from the circle is the **Egyptian Avenue,** a subterranean stone tunnel lined with catacombs, itself approached by a dramatic colonnade that screens the main cemetery from the road. Both sides are impressive, with a grand (locked) iron gate leading to a sweeping courtyard built for the approach of horses and carriages. By the 1970s the cemetery had become unkempt and neglected until a group of volunteers, the Friends of Highgate Cemetery, undertook the huge upkeep. Tours are conducted by the Friends, who will show you the most interesting graves among the numerous statues and memorials once hidden by overgrowth. The West side can only be seen during a one-hour tour, which you must prebook for weekdays but not weekends; tours of the East side on Saturday are first come, first served. You're expected to dress respectfully, so skip the shorts and the baseball cap; children under eight are not admitted and neither are dogs, tripods, or video cameras. ⊠ *Swains La., Highgate* ☎ *020/8340–1834* ⊕ *www.highgatecemetery. org* ⊠ *East Cemetery £4, tours £8; West Cemetery tours £12, includes admission to East Cemetery. No credit cards* ⊙ *East: Mar.–Oct., weekdays 10–5, weekends and holidays 11–5; Nov.–Feb., weekdays 10–4, weekends 11–4. Last admission 30 mins before closing; hrs vary, call ahead. West: tours Mar.–Nov., weekdays at 1:45, weekends every ½ hr 11–3* Ⓜ *Archway, then Bus 210, 271, or 143 to Waterlow Park; Belsize Park, then Bus C11 to Brookfield Park.*

**Keats House.** It was while living in this house between 1818 and 1820 that the major Romantic poet John Keats (1795–1821) fell in love with girl-next-door Fanny Brawne and wrote some of his best-loved poems. (Soon after, ill health forced him to move to Rome, where he died the following year.) After a major refurbishment to make the rooms more consistent with their original Regency style, the house now displays all sorts of Keats-related material, including portraits, letters, many of the poet's original manuscripts and books, the engagement ring he gave to Fanny, and items of her clothing. A pretty garden contains the plum tree under which Keats supposedly composed *Ode to a Nightingale.* There are frequent guided tours and special events featuring local literary luminaries. The ticket gives you entry for a full year, so you can come back as often as you like. Picnics can be taken onto the grounds during the summer. ⊠ *10 Keats Grove, Hampstead* ☎ *020/7332–3868* ⊕ *www.cityoflondon. gov.uk/things-to-do/keats-house/Pages/default.aspx* ⊠ *£5.50* ⊙ *Mar.–Oct., Tues.–Sun. 1–5; Nov.–Feb., Fri.–Sun. 1–5 (last admission at 4:30). Free 30-min tour at 3* Ⓜ *Overground: Hampstead Heath.*

The fabled cover of the Beatles' album *Abbey Road,* with the world's most famous traffic crossing

**Fodor's Choice** ★    **Kenwood House.** This largely Palladian villa offers an escape to a gracious country house with a magnificent collection of Old Masters and beautiful grounds, all within a short Tube ride from Central London. It was originally built in 1616 and later expanded, first by Robert Adam starting in 1767 and later by George Saunders in 1795. Adam refaced most of the exterior and added the splendid library, which, with its vaulted ceiling and Corinthian columns, is the highlight of the house's design. A major renovation restored four rooms to reflect Adam's intentions as closely as possible, incorporating the furniture he designed for them and his original color schemes. Kenwood is also home to the **Iveagh Bequest,** a world-class collection of some 60 paintings that includes masterworks like Rembrandt's *Portrait of the Artist* and Vermeer's *The Guitar Player,* along with major works by Reynolds, Van Dyck, Hals, Gainsborough, and Turner. The grounds, designed by Humphrey Repton and bordered by Hampstead Heath, are equally elegant and serene, with lawns sloping down to a little lake crossed by a trompe-l'oeil bridge. All in all, the perfect home for an 18th-century gentleman. In summer, the grounds host a series of popular and classical concerts, culminating in fireworks on the last night. The Brew House café, occupying part of the old coach house, has outdoor tables in the courtyard and a terraced garden. The exteriors for the 2014 movie *Belle,* the story of Kenwood House's 18th-century resident Lord Mansfield and his family, were shot here. ⊠ *Hampstead La., Highgate* ☎ *0870/333–1181* ⊕ *www.english-heritage.org.uk* ☜ *Free* ⊙ *House daily 10–5, gardens daily 8–dusk* Ⓜ *Golders Green or Archway, then Bus 210. Overground: Gospel Oak.*

## A TRIP TO ABBEY ROAD

11

The black-and-white crosswalk (known as a "zebra crossing") near the Abbey Road Studios at No. 3 is a place of pilgrimage for Beatles' fans from around the world, many of them teenagers born long after the band split up. They converge here to re-create the cover of the Beatles' 1969 *Abbey Road* album, posing on the crossing despite the onrushing traffic. ■ TIP➜ Be careful if you're going to attempt this: Abbey Road is a busy intersection. The studio is where the Beatles recorded their entire output, from "Love Me Do"

onward. One of the best ways to explore landmarks in the Beatles' story is to take one of the excellent walking tours offered by **Original London Walks** (☎ *020/7624–3978* ⊕ *www.walks.com*). Try **The Beatles In-My-Life Walk** (Saturday and Tuesday at 11:20 am outside Marylebone Underground) or **The Beatles Magical Mystery Tour** (Wednesday at 2 pm, February–November, and Thursday and Sunday at 11 am, year-round, at Underground Exit 3, Tottenham Court Road).

## WORTH NOTING

**Burgh House and Hampstead Museum.** One of Hampstead's oldest buildings, Burgh House was built in 1704 to take advantage of the natural spa waters of the then-fashionable Hampstead Wells. A private house until World War II, it was saved from dereliction in the 1970s by local residents, who have maintained it ever since. The building is a fine example of the genteel elegance common to the Queen Anne period, with redbrick box frontage, oak-paneled rooms, and a terraced garden that was originally designed by Gertrude Jekyll. Today the house contains a small but diverting museum on the history of the area, and also hosts regular talks, concerts, and recitals. The secluded garden courtyard of the café is a lovely spot for lunch, tea, or glass of wine on a summer's afternoon. Call ahead if you're visiting on a weekend, however, as the house is often rented out as a wedding venue on Saturday. ⊠ *New End Sq., Hampstead* ☎ *020/7431–0144* ⊕ *www.burghhouse. org.uk* ⊐ *Free* ☉ *Wed.–Fri. and Sun. noon–5* Ⓜ *Hampstead.*

**Fenton House.** This handsome 16th-century merchant's home, Hampstead's oldest surviving house, has fine displays of porcelain, Georgian furniture, and 17th-century needlework. The 2-acre walled garden, with its rose plantings and apple orchard, has been virtually unchanged for 300 years. International musicians give recitals on the important collection of early keyboard instruments throughout the week; check the website for details. ⊠ *Hampstead Grove, Hampstead* ☎ *020/7435–3471* ⊕ *www.nationaltrust.org.uk* ⊐ *£6.50; £9 combination ticket, includes 2 Willow Rd.* ☉ *Mar.–Oct., Wed.–Sun. 11–5; Dec., weekends 11–4. Last admission 30 mins before closing* Ⓜ *Hampstead.*

**Freud Museum London.** The father of psychoanalysis lived here with his family for a year, between his escape from Nazi persecution in his native Vienna in 1938 and his death in 1939. His daughter Anna (herself a pioneer of child psychoanalysis) remained in the house until her own death in 1982, bequeathing it as a museum to honor her father.

The centerpiece is Freud's unchanged study, containing his remarkable collection of antiquities and his library. Also on display is the family's Biedermeier furniture—and, of course, the couch. As well, there are lectures, study groups, and themed exhibitions, in addition to a psychoanalysis-related archive and research library. Looking for a unique souvenir for the person who has everything? The gift shop here sells "Freudian Slippers." ⊠ *20 Maresfield Gardens, Swiss Cottage* ☎ *020/7435–2002* ⊕ *www.freud.org.uk* ⊠ *£7* ⊙ *Wed.–Sun. noon–5* Ⓜ *Swiss Cottage, Finchley Rd.*

**St. John's-at-Hampstead.** There has been a church here since 1312, but the current building—consecrated in 1747 and later extended in 1877—is a fine example of neoclassical serenity, enhanced by Ionic columns and vaulting arches. The church stands at the end of Church Row, a narrow street lined with flat-fronted brick Georgian houses that gives you a sense of what Hampstead was like when it truly was a rural village as opposed to a traffic-clogged North London neighborhood. Many local notables are buried in the picturesque churchyard, including painter John Constable (some of whose most famous works depict the Heath), John Harrison (the inventor of the marine chronometer discussed in the book *Longitude*), members of the artistic Du Maurier family, Jane Austen's aunt, and comedy god Peter Cook. ⊠ *Church Row, Hampstead* ☎ *020/7794–5808* ⊕ *www.hampsteadparishchurch.org.uk* ⊠ *Free* Ⓜ *Hampstead.*

**2 Willow Road.** Among the many artists and intellectuals fleeing Nazi persecution who settled in the area was noted architect Erno Goldfinger, who built this outstanding modernist home opposite Hampstead Heath in 1939 as his family residence. (His plans drew the ire of several local residents, including novelist Ian Fleming, who supposedly borrowed his neighbor's name for a Bond villain as a result.) As well as design touches and building techniques that were groundbreaking at the time, the unique house, a place of pilgrimage for 20th-century architecture enthusiasts, also contains Goldfinger's impressive collection of modern art and self-designed innovative furniture. Before 2 pm admission is by first-come, first-served hourly tour only, but you can visit independently after 3. ⊠ *2 Willow Rd., Hampstead* ☎ *020/7435–6166* ⊕ *www. nationaltrust.org.uk/2-willow-road* ⊠ *£6; £9 combination ticket with Fenton House* ⊙ *Mar.–Oct., Wed.–Sun. 11–2 (guided tour only) and 3–5 (last admission at 4:30)* Ⓜ *Overground: Hampstead Heath.*

# GREENWICH

# GETTING ORIENTED

Museum of
London Docklands

Up the O2

Firepower
Royal
Artillery
Museum

Eltham Palace

Greenwich

River Thames

Crane St.

Eastney St.

Old Woolwich Rd.

Park Row

Greenwich Pier

Greenwich Foot
Tunnel

TO WOOLWICH

Cutty
Sark

DLR:
Cutty Sark

Greenwich Church St.

College App.

Discover
Greenwich

Trinity
College

Painted
Hall

Old
Royal Naval
College

Trafalgar Rd.

Trafalgar
Tavern

Feathers Pl.

Park Row

Park Vista

Seamen's
Hospital

Greenwich
Market

Romney Rd.

National
Maritime
Museum

Queen's
House

Nelson Rd.

King William Walk

Stockwell St.

Greenwich High Rd.

Burney St.

Greenwich
Park

Clock Tower
Antiques
Market

Gloucester
Circus

Pavillion Café

Royal
Observatory

Greenwich Meridian Line

Royal Hill

King George St.

Croom's Hill

The Avenue

Greenwich

0                                1/8 mile

0                    1/8 kilometer

Ranger's House
and the Wernher Collection

## TOP REASONS TO GO

**Stand astride the Greenwich Meridian Line:** At the Royal Observatory—where the world's time is set—you can be in the eastern and western hemispheres simultaneously.

**See the Queen's House, an architectural masterwork:** Sir Inigo Jones's 17th-century building was the first in England to embrace the styles of the Italian Renaissance.

**Discover Britain's seafaring past at the National Maritime Museum:** See how Britannia ruled the waves and helped shape the modern world.

**Step aboard the *Cutty Sark*:** Take a stroll along the deck of the last surviving 19th-century tea clipper, now shipshape after years of renovation.

## FEELING PECKISH?

**The Pavilion Café.** Healthy snacks and lunches are served at this excellent café next to the Royal Observatory. Homemade soups and sandwiches are good for a quick refuel, or try one of the delicious stone-baked pizzas for something more substantial. Check out the fancy weathervane on the roof, depicting Lord Nelson looking through his telescope. ⊠ *Charlton Way, Greenwich* ☎ *020/8858-9695* ⊕ *www.royalparks.org.uk.*

**Trafalgar Tavern.** With its excellent vista of the Thames, there is no more handsomely situated pub in Greenwich than the Trafalgar Tavern. Featured in Charles Dickens's *Our Mutual Friend*, it's still as grand a place as it ever was to have a pint and a quick, tasty meal. ⊠ *Park Row, Greenwich* ☎ *020/8858-2909* ⊕ *www.trafalgartavern.co.uk.*

## GETTING THERE

12

Docklands Light Railway (DLR) is a zippy way to get to Cutty Sark station from Canary Wharf and Bank Tube stations in The City. Or take the DLR to Island Gardens and walk the old Victorian Foot Tunnel under the river. (Sitting at the front of a train can be disconcerting, as you watch the controls in the fully automated driver's cab move about as if a ghost were at the helm.) The best way to arrive, however—time and weather permitting—is like a sea captain of old: by water (although it takes an hour from central London ⇨ *For more on cruising the Thames, see Chapter 13*).

## MAKING THE MOST OF YOUR TIME

Set apart from the rest of London, Greenwich is worth a day to itself—those who love maritime history will want to spend two—in order to make the most of walks in the rolling parklands and to immerse yourself in the richness of Greenwich's history, science, and architecture. The boat trip takes about an hour from Westminster Pier (next to Big Ben) or 25 minutes from the Tower of London, so factor in enough time for the round trip.

## NEAREST PUBLIC RESTROOMS

Duck into Discover Greenwich, where the loo is free.

Sightseeing
★★★★

Nightlife
★

Dining
★★

Lodging
★

Shopping
★★★

About 8 miles downstream (meaning seaward, to the east) from central London, Greenwich is a small borough that looms large across the world. Once the seat of British naval power, it is not only home to the Old Royal Observatory, which measures time for our entire planet, but also the Greenwich Meridian, which divides the world into two—you can stand astride it with one foot in either hemisphere.

Updated by
Jack Jewers

Bear in mind that the journey to Greenwich is an event in itself. In a rush, you can take the driverless DLR train, but many opt for arriving by boat along the Thames. This way, you glide past famous sights on the London skyline—there's a guaranteed spine chill on passing the Tower—and ever-changing docklands, and there's usually a chirpy Cock-er-ney navigator enlivening the journey with fun commentary.

A visit to Greenwich feels like a trip to a rather elegant seaside town—albeit one with more than its fair share of historic sites. The grandiose **Old Royal Naval Hospital,** designed by Sir Christopher Wren, was originally a home for veteran sailors. Today it's a popular visitor attraction, with a more glamorous second life as one of the most widely used movie locations in Britain.

Greenwich was originally home to one of England's finest Tudor palaces, and the birthplace of Henry VIII, Elizabeth I, and Mary I. Inigo Jones built what is considered the first "classical" building in England in 1616: the **Queen's House,** which now houses a collection of fine art. Britain was the world's preeminent naval power for more than 500 years, and the excellent **National Maritime Museum** details that history in an engaging way. Its prize exhibits include the coat worn by Admiral Lord Nelson (1758–1805) in his final battle—bullet hole and all. The 19th-century tea clipper *Cutty Sark* was nearly destroyed by fire in 2007 but reopened in 2012 after a painstaking restoration. Now it's more pristine than ever and has an impressive visitor center.

**Greenwich Park,** London's oldest royal park, is still home to fallow red deer, just as it has been since they were first introduced here for hunting by Henry VIII. The **Ranger's House** now houses a private art collection, next door to a beautifully manicured rose garden. Above it all is the **Royal Observatory,** where you can be in two hemispheres at once by standing along the **Greenwich Meridian Line,** before seeing a high-tech planctarium show.

Toward north Greenwich, the hopelessly ambitious Millennium Dome has been successfully reborn as the O2 and now hosts major concerts and stand-up comedy gigs. More adventurous visitors can also go **Up the O2** on a climbing expedition across the massive domed surface. Meanwhile, those who prefer excursions of a gentler kind may prefer to journey a couple of miles south of the borough, farther out into London's southern suburbs, to the shamefully underappreciated **Eltham Palace,** once a favorite of Henry VIII. Parts of the mansion were transformed into an art deco masterpiece in the 1930s.

**12**

## TOP ATTRACTIONS

**Fodor's Choice**   *Cutty Sark.* This sleek, romantic clipper was built in 1869, one among a
★   vast fleet of tall-masted wooden ships that plied the oceanic highways of the 19th century, trading in exotic commodities—in this case, tea. *Cutty Sark* (named after a racy witch in a Robert Burns poem) was the fastest in the fleet, sailing the London–China route in 1871 in only 107 days. The clipper has been preserved in dry dock as a museum ship since the 1950s, but was severely damaged in a devastating fire in 2007. Yet up from the ashes, as the song goes, grow the roses of success: after a major restoration project, the visitor facilities are now better than ever. Not only can you tour the ship in its entirety, but the glittering visitor center (which the ship now rests directly above, in an enormous gold mount) allows you to view the hull from below. There's plenty to see here, and the cramped quarters form a fantastic time capsule to walk around in—this boat was never too comfortable for the 28-strong crew (as you'll see). Don't forget to take in the amusing collection of figureheads. ⊠ *King William Walk, Greenwich* ☎ *020/8858–4422* ⊕ *www. rmg.co.uk/cuttysark* ⊠ *£14; £19 combination ticket, includes Royal Observatory attractions* ☉ *Daily 10–5; last admission at 4* Ⓜ *DLR: Cutty Sark.*

**Discover Greenwich.** Intended as a kind of anchor point for Greenwich's big three attractions—the Old Royal Naval College, *Cutty Sark,* and the National Maritime Museum—this excellent, state-of-the-art visitor center includes interactive exhibitions on the history of Greenwich, plus an assortment of local treasures and artifacts. Most intriguing among them is a 17th-century "witch bottle," once used to ward off evil spirits. High-tech scans have revealed it to contain a mixture of human hair, fingernails, and urine. ⊠ *Pepys Bldg., King William Walk, Greenwich* ☎ *020/8269–4799* ⊕ *www.ornc.org/visit/attractions/discovergreenwich-visitor-centre* ⊠ *Free* ☉ *Daily 10–5* Ⓜ *DLR: Greenwich.*

**Fodor's Choice**   **Eltham Palace.** Once a favorite getaway for Henry VIII (who liked to
★   spend Christmas here), Eltham Palace has been drastically remodeled twice in its lifetime: once during the 15th and 16th centuries, and again during the 1930s, when a grand mansion was annexed onto the Tudor

## DID YOU KNOW?

Once sailors could determine their distance from the Greenwich meridian (longitude), maritime navigation was greatly improved. Look for the brass line marking the two hemispheres throughout the cobblestone streets.

great hall by the superwealthy Coulthard family. Today it's an extraordinary combination of late medieval grandeur and art deco masterpiece, laced with an eccentric whimsy—the Coulthards even built an entire room to be the personal quarters of their beloved pet lemur. The house and its extensive gardens were fully restored when the palace finally entered public ownership in the late 1990s. A 2015 renovation opened up previously unseen rooms, including the Map Room, where the Coulthards planned their round-the-world adventures, and a reconstruction of a lavish 1930s walk-in wardrobe, complete with genuine dresses from the time period. ⊠ *Court Rd., Eltham* ☎ *020/8294–2548* ⊕ *www.english-heritage.org.uk/elthampalace* 🎫 *£13* ⊙ *Apr.–Oct., Sun.–Wed. 10–5; Nov.–Mar., Sun. 10–4; late Feb. and late Oct., daily 10–4* Ⓜ *Eltham.*

**Greenwich Market.** Established as a fruit-and-vegetable market in 1700, the covered market now offers around 120 mixed stalls of art and crafts on Wednesday, Saturday, and Sunday, and antiques and collectibles on Tuesday, Thursday, and Friday. You can get food to go on each market day, although the offerings are usually best on weekends. Shopping for handicrafts is a pleasure here, as in most cases you're buying directly from the artist. ⊠ *College Approach, Greenwich* ☎ *020/8269–5096* ⊕ *www.greenwichmarketlondon.com* ⊙ *Tues.– Sun. 10–5:30* Ⓜ *DLR: Cutty Sark.*

**Museum of London Docklands.** This wonderful old warehouse building, on a quaint cobbled quayside near the tower of Canary Wharf, is worth a visit in its own right. With uneven wood floors, beams, and pillars, the museum used to be a storehouse for coffee, tea, sugar, and rum from the West Indies, hence the name: West India Quay. The fascinating story of the old port and the river is told using films, together with interactive displays and reconstructions. Excellent permanent exhibitions include *City and River,* which chronicles the explosion of trade and industry that, by the mid-19th century, had transformed this district into the world's most important port. *Sailortown* is an effective reconstruction of the Wapping district in Victorian times, complete with period shops, a pub, spooky alleys, and costumed guides. Young kids can hunt for treasure and let off some steam in the soft play area in the Mudlark's Gallery. Special events happen year-round; check the museum's website for details. ⊠ *No. 1 Warehouse, West India Quay, Canary Wharf* ☎ *020/7001–9844* ⊕ *www.museumoflondon.org.uk/docklands* 🎫 *Free* ⊙ *Daily 10–6; last admission 20 mins before closing* Ⓜ *Canary Wharf. DLR: West India Quay.*

**Fodor's Choice**
★

**National Maritime Museum.** From the time of Henry VIII until the 1940s, Britain was the world's preeminent naval power, and the collections here trace half a millennia of that seafaring history. The story is as much about trade as it is warfare: *Atlantic: Slavery, Trade and Empire* gallery explores how trade in goods (and people) irrevocably changed the world, while *Traders: The East India Company and Asia* focuses on how the epoque-defining company shaped trade with Asia for 250 years. One gallery is devoted to Admiral Lord Nelson, Britain's most famous naval commander, and among the exhibits is the uniform he was wearing, complete with bloodstains, when he died at the Battle of Trafalgar

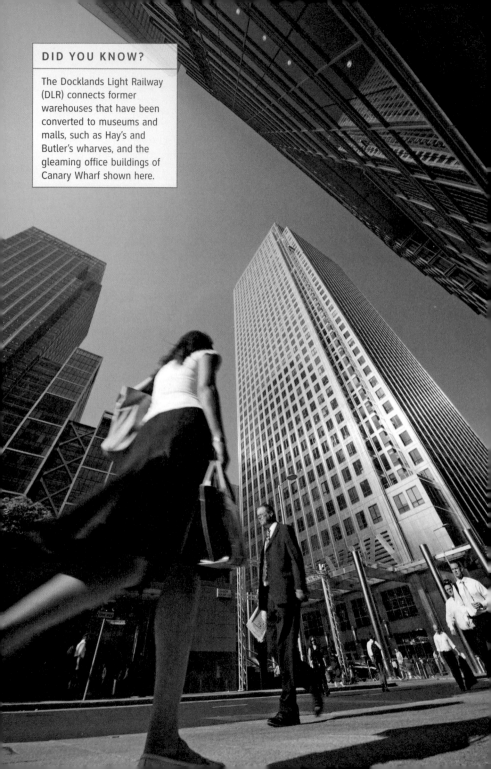

in 1805. Temporary exhibitions here are usually fascinating—those in recent years have included personal accounts of the First World War at sea. Borrow a tablet computer from the front desk and take it to the giant map of the world in the courtyard at the center of the museum; here, a high-tech, interactive app opens up hidden stories and games as you walk between continents. The adjacent **Queen's House** is home to the museum's art collection, the largest collection of maritime art in the world, including works by William Hogarth, Canaletto, and Joshua Reynolds. Permission for its construction was granted by Queen Anne only on condition that the river vista from the house be preserved, and there are few more majestic views in London than Inigo Jones's awe-inspiring symmetry. ⊠ *Romney Rd., Greenwich* ☎ *020/8858–4422* ⊕ *www.rmg.co.uk/national-maritime-museum* 🎫 *Free* ☉ *Daily 10–5; last admission at 4:30* Ⓜ *DLR: Greenwich.*

**GREENWICH FOOT TUNNEL**

In a brilliant piece of foresight in 1849, Greenwich Hospital bought Island Gardens, on the other side of the Thames, to guard against industrial sprawl and to preserve one of the most beautiful views in London. Take the stone spiral steps down into Greenwich Foot Tunnel and head under the Thames (enjoying the magnificently creepy echo) to Island Gardens, at the southern tip of the Isle of Dogs. Then look back over the river for a magnificent vista: the Old Royal Naval College and Queen's House in all their glory, framed by the verdant green borders of the park.

**Fodor'sChoice**
★ **Old Royal Naval College.** Begun by Sir Christopher Wren in 1694 as a rest home for ancient mariners, the college became a school in 1873. It's still used for classes by the University of Greenwich and the Trinity College of Music, although you're more likely to recognize it as a film location—recent blockbusters to have made use of its elegant interiors include *Skyfall, Les Misérables,* and *The King's Speech.* Architecturally, you'll notice how the structures part to reveal the **Queen's House** across the central lawns. Behind the college are two more buildings you can visit. The **Painted Hall,** the college's dining hall, which derives its name from the baroque murals of William and Mary (reigned jointly 1689–95; William alone 1695–1702) and assorted allegorical figures. James Thornhill's frescoes, depicting scenes of naval grandeur with a suitably pro-British note, were painstakingly completed 1708–12 and 1718–26, and were good enough to earn him a knighthood. In the opposite building stands the **College Chapel,** which was rebuilt after a fire in 1779 in an altogether more restrained, neo-Grecian style. Free guided tours are held at 1:30 and 3 on weekdays, and at 11, 12:30, 1:30, and 3 on weekends; they depart from the Discover Greenwich Visitor Center. Check the website for an outstanding program of special events, including talks, tours, and concerts—many of them free. ⊠ *King William Walk, Greenwich* ☎ *020/8269–4747* ⊕ *www.ornc.org* 🎫 *Free* ☉ *Painted Hall and chapel daily 10–5, grounds daily 8–11* Ⓜ *DLR: Greenwich.*

Without a central support, the Tulip Stair spirals up to the Great Hall of Queen's House.

**Royal Observatory.** Greenwich is on the prime meridian at 0° longitude, and the ultimate standard for time around the world has been set here at the Royal Observatory since 1884, when Britain was the world's maritime superpower. The observatory is actually split into two sites, a short walk apart: one devoted to astronomy, the other to the study of time. The enchanting **Peter Harrison Planetarium** is London's only planetarium, its bronze-clad turret glinting in the sun. Shows on black holes and how to interpret the night sky are enthralling and enlightening. Even better for kids are the high-technology rooms of the **Astronomy Centre,** where space exploration is brought to life through cutting-edge interactive programs and fascinating exhibits—including the chance to touch a 4½-billion-year-old meteorite.

Across the way is **Flamsteed House,** designed by Sir Christopher Wren in 1675 for John Flamsteed, the first Royal Astronomer. The Time Ball atop Flamsteed House is one of the world's earliest public time signals. Each day at 12:55, it rises halfway up its mast. At 12:58 it rises all the way to the top, and at 1 exactly, the ball falls. A climb to the top of the house also reveals a **28-inch telescope,** built in 1893 and now housed inside an onion-shape fiberglass dome. It doesn't compare with the range of modern optical telescopes, but it's still the largest in the United Kingdom. Regular viewing evenings reveal startlingly detailed views of the lunar surface. In the **Time Galleries,** linger over the superb workmanship of John Harrison (1693–1776), whose famous **Maritime Clocks** won him the Longitude Prize for solving the problem of accurate timekeeping at sea, paving the way for modern navigation. Outside, a brass line laid among the cobblestones marks the meridian. As darkness falls, a green laser shoots out, following exactly the path of the meridian line. The hill that is home to the observatory gives fantastic views across London, topped off with £1-a-slot telescopes to scour the skyline. ⊠ *Romney Rd.* ☏ *020/8858–4422* ⊕ *www. rmg.co.uk/royal-observatory* 🖃 *Astronomy Centre free, Flamsteed House and Meridian Line courtyard £9.50, planetarium shows £7.50; combined "Astro Ticket" £12.50; combined ticket with Cutty Sark £19* ⊘ *Daily 10–5 (May–Aug., Meridian courtyard until 6); last entry 30 mins before closing; last planetarium show at 4:15. Planetarium closed 1st Tues. of every month except Aug. and during Easter* Ⓜ *DLR: Greenwich.*

> **FUN FACT**
>
> Hang out beneath the lightning-cracked Elizabeth Oak in Greenwich Park and you'll be following in illustrious footsteps—Elizabeth I is supposed to have played in its branches as a girl.

12

## WORTH NOTING

**Clock Tower Antiques Market.** The weekend Clock Tower Antiques Market on Greenwich High Road has vintage shopping, and browsing among the "small collectibles" makes for a good half-hour diversion. ⊠ *166 Greenwich High Rd., Greenwich* ☏ *020/7237–2001* ⊕ *www. clocktowermarket.co.uk* ⊘ *Weekends and bank holiday Mon. 10–5* Ⓜ *Greenwich Rail.*

FAMILY  **Firepower Royal Artillery Museum.** Adjacent to the old Royal Dockyard at Woolwich is a brilliant exhibition, the Firepower Royal Artillery Museum. Housed in the old Royal Arsenal leading down to the river shore, the museum's setting provides an evocative sense of the Thames and its lingering effect on the capital's history. Inside, the **Field of Fire** experience is a powerful recreation of what it was actually like to be in the thick of the London Blitz and the D-Day Landings, complete with giant projections of archive film on all sides, live smoke effects, and a floor that quakes in time to the roar of exploding bombs. The **Gunnery Hall** exhibition contains a vast array of artillery, armored vehicles, and assorted firepower (some bearing the scars of battle) from more than a century's worth of conflict. During school holidays, there are plenty of activities for kids, such as learning the basic skills of a field medic or "battle wound" face painting. ⊠ *Royal Arsenal, Woolwich* ☏ *020/8855–7755* ⊕ *www.firepower.org.uk* 🖃 *£5.50* ⊘ *Tues.–Sat. 10–5; last admission at 4* Ⓜ *DLR: Woolwich Arsenal.*

**Ranger's House and the Wernher Collection.** This handsome, early-18th-century villa, which was the Greenwich Park ranger's official residence during the 19th century, is hung with Stuart and Jacobean portraits, but the most interesting diversion is the Wernher Collection, which contains more than 700 pieces of art that were amassed by the diamond millionaire Julius Wernher (1850–1912) and were once housed in his fabulous stately house, Luton Hoo, in Bedfordshire. The collection ranges from Old and Dutch Master paintings to Renaissance jewelry and assorted pieces of decorative art and curios from the medieval period onward. Entry is by guided tour only and space is limited, so it's a good idea to book ahead on Sunday. The Ranger's House is just under a mile's walk from the DLR station at Greenwich, or you can catch a bus there from Greenwich or Deptford DLR. ✉ *Blackheath, Chesterfield Walk, Greenwich Park, Greenwich* ☎ *020/8853–0035* ⊕ *www.english-heritage.org.uk* ▭ *£7.20* ◷ *Apr.–Sept., Sun.–Wed. guided tours only, usually at 11:30 and 2:30; call ahead* Ⓜ *DLR: Deptford Bridge, then Bus 53; or Greenwich, then Bus 386.*

**Fodor's Choice** **Up at the O2.** Certainly one of the most unique ways to see London, this thrilling urban expedition takes you on a journey across the giant dome ★ of the O2 arena. After a short briefing, you're dressed in safety gear and taken in small groups across a steep walkway, running all the way to the summit and down the other side. The high point (literally) is a viewing platform, 161 feet aboveground, with magnificent views of the city. On a clear day you can see for 15 miles (that's as far as Waltham Abbey to the north and Sevenoaks to the south). Climbs at sunset and twilight are also available. It's quite an experience, but unsurprisingly there are restrictions: you have to be at least 10 years old, taller than 4 feet, have a waist measurement that's less than 49 inches, weigh less than 286 pounds, and pregnant women can't make the climb at all. Wheelchairs can be accommodated on a few tours. Advanced booking is essential. ✉ *Peninsula Sq., London* ☎ *020/463–2000* ⊕ *www.theo2.co.uk/do-more-at-the-o2/up-at-the-o2* ▭ *From £28* ◷ *Tours: summer, daily 10–10; winter, daily 10–6* Ⓜ *North Greenwich.*

# THE THAMES
# UPSTREAM

# GETTING ORIENTED

## The Thames Upstream

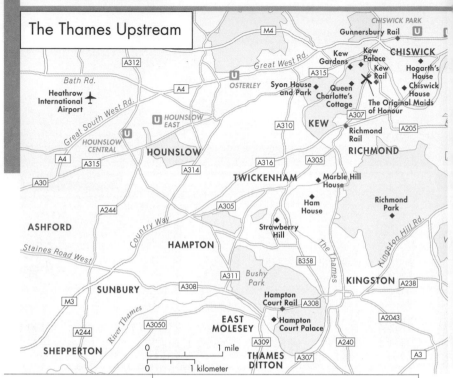

## A GOOD WALK

From Chiswick House, follow Burlington Lane and take a left onto Hogarth Lane—which, in reality, is anything but a lane—to reach Hogarth's House. Chiswick's Church Street (reached by a rather unappealing underpass from Hogarth's House) is the nearest thing to a sleepy country village street you're likely to find in London. Follow it down to the Thames and turn left at the bottom to reach the 18th-century riverfront houses of Chiswick Mall, referred to by locals as "Millionaire's Row." There are several pretty riverside pubs near Hammersmith Bridge.

## MAKING THE MOST OF YOUR TIME

Hampton Court Palace requires half a day to experience its magic, although you could make do with a few hours for the other attractions. Because of the distance between sights, it's best to focus on one sight, add in some others within the area, then a riverside walk and a pint at a pub.

## FEELING PECKISH?

**The Original Maids of Honour.** This most traditional of Old English tearooms is named for a kind of jam tart invented near here in Tudor times. Legend has it that Henry VIII loved them so much he had the recipe kept under armed guard. This place has specialized in the authentic royal recipe for more than 120 years now, and still bakes the Maids by hand on the premises. Full afternoon tea is served daily 2:30–6, and lunch (mainly pies, quiches, sandwiches) in two sittings, at 12:30 and 1:45. ✉ *288 Kew Rd., Kew* ☎ *020/8940–2752* ⊕ *www.theoriginalmaidsofhonour.co.uk* ⊘ *No dinner.*

**13**

## TOP REASONS TO GO

**Explore Hampton Court Palace:** Go ghost hunting or just admire the beautiful Tudor architecture at Henry VIII's beloved home, then lose yourself in the maze as night begins to fall.

**Go "Goth" at Strawberry Hill:** The 19th-century birthplace of connoisseur Horace Walpole's "Gothick" style, this mock-castle is a joyous riot of color and invention.

**Escape to magical Kew Gardens:** See the earth from above by visiting Kew's treetop walkway at the famous Royal Botanic Gardens.

**Pay your respects to Father Thames:** Enjoy a pint from the creaking balcony of a centuries-old riverside pub as you watch the boats row by on the loveliest stretch of England's greatest river.

## NEAREST PUBLIC RESTROOMS

Richmond Park, Kew Gardens, and all the stately homes have public restrooms.

## GETTING THERE

The District line is your best Tube option, stopping at Turnham Green (in the heart of Chiswick but a walk from the houses), Gunnersbury (for Syon Park), Kew Gardens, and Richmond. For Hampton Court, overland train is quickest: South West trains run from Waterloo twice an hour, with roughly half requiring a change at Surbiton. There are also regular, direct trains from Waterloo to Chiswick station (best for Chiswick House), Kew Bridge, Richmond (for Ham House), and St. Margaret's (best for Marble Hill House). London Overground trains also stop at Gunnersbury, Kew Gardens, and Richmond.

A pleasant way to go is by river. Boats depart from Westminster Pier, by Big Ben, for Kew (1½ hours), Richmond (2 hours), and Hampton Court (3 hours). The trip is worth taking if you make it an integral part of your day, and know that it gets breezy. Round-trip tickets run £18–£23. For more details contact **Transport For London** (☎ 0843/222–1234 ⊕ www.tfl.gov.uk).

Sightseeing
★★★★
Nightlife
★★
Dining
★★★
Lodging
★★
Shopping
★★

The upper stretch of the Thames links a string of fashionable districts—Chiswick, Kew, Richmond, and Putney—with winding old streets, horticultural delights, cozy riverside pubs, and Henry VIII's Hampton Court Palace. The neighborhoods along the way are as proud of their villagey feel as of their stately history, witnessed by such handsome estates as Strawberry Hill and Syon House. After the sensory overload of the West End, it's easy to forget you're in a capital city at all.

# CHISWICK

Updated by
Jack Jewers

On the banks of the Thames just west of central London, far enough out to escape the crush and crowds you're just getting used to, Chiswick is a low-key, upscale district, content with its run of restaurants, stylish shops, and film-star residents. No doubt its most famous son wouldn't approve of all the conspicuous wealth, though; Chiswick was home to one of Britain's best-loved painters, William Hogarth, who tore the fabric of the 18th-century nation to shreds with his slew of satirical engravings. **Hogarth's House** has been restored to its former glory. Incongruously stranded among Chiswick's row houses are a number of fine 18th-century buildings, which are now some of the most desirable suburban houses in London. By far the grandest of all is **Chiswick House,** a unique Palladian-style mansion born from the 3rd earl of Burlington's love of classical and Renaissance architecture—a radical style at the time.

## TOP ATTRACTIONS

**Fodor's Choice**
★

**Chiswick House.** Completed in 1729 by the 3rd earl of Burlington (also known for Burlington House—home of the Royal Academy—and Burlington Arcade on Piccadilly), this extraordinary Palladian mansion was envisaged as a kind of temple to the arts. Burlington was fascinated

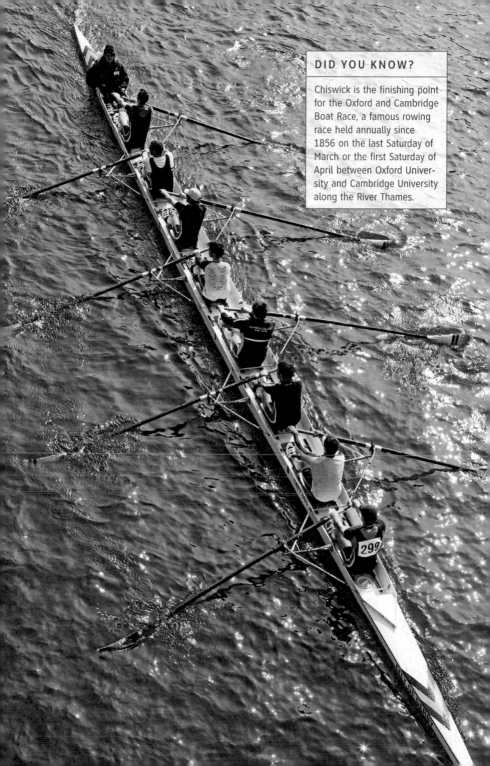

by the architecture he saw in Italy while on the Grand Tour as a young man. When his country home was destroyed by fire in 1725, he seized the chance to rebuild it in homage to those classical and Renaissance styles. The building is loosely modeled on the Villa Capra near Vicenza, while the colonnaded frontage is a partial replica of the Pantheon in Rome (which also inspired the domed roof—you can see it from the inside in the Upper Tribune).

The sumptuous interiors were the work of William Kent (1685–1748), and it's easy to see how they made such a profound impact at the time; the astonishing Blue Velvet Room, with its gilded decoration and intricate painted ceiling, is an extraordinary achievement, as are the gilded domed apses that punctuate the Gallery (an homage to the Temple of Venus and Roma from the Fora Romana in Rome). Such ideas were so radical in England at the time that wealthy patrons clamored to have Kent design everything from gardens to party frocks.

The rambling grounds are one of the hidden gems of West London. Italianate in style (of course), they are filled with classical temples, statues, and obelisks. Also on the grounds are a café and a children's play area. ⊠ *Burlington La., Chiswick* ☎ *020/8995–0508* ⊕ *www.chgt. org.uk* ▦ *£6.30, grounds free* ⊗ *Grounds daily 7 am–dusk. House: Mar.–Oct., Sun.–Wed. and bank holiday Mon. 10–6* Ⓜ *Turnham Green, Chiswick. National Rail: Chiswick.*

**Hogarth's House.** The satirist and painter William Hogarth (1697–1764), little-known in the rest of the world, is hugely famous in Britain. His witty, acerbic engravings, which railed against the harsh injustices of the time, may be called the visual equivalent of the satires of Jonathan Swift and were no less influential in their time. Unfortunately his beloved house has had an appalling streak of bad luck; as if the decision, in the 1960s, to route one of the nation's busiest highways outside the front gates wasn't ignoble enough, it was closed after not one, but two, devastating fires in the early 2000s. Now fully restored, the rooms contain absorbing exhibitions, featuring many of Hogarth's 18th-century prints, together with replica furniture of the period, Look out for the 300-year-old mulberry tree in the garden; Hogarth and his wife used its fruit to bake pies for destitute children. The original copies of some of Hogarth's most famous works can be seen elsewhere in the city: *The Rake's Progress* at Sir John Soane's Museum; *Marriage à la Mode* at the National Gallery; and *Gin Lane* at the British Museum. His tomb is in the cemetery of St. Nicholas's church on nearby Chiswick Mall. ⊠ *Hogarth La., Great West Rd. (A4), Chiswick* ☎ *020/8994–6757* ⊕ *www. hounslow.info/arts/hogarthshouse* ▦ *Free* ⊗ *Tues.–Sun. and bank holiday Mon. noon–5* Ⓜ *Turnham Green. National Rail: Chiswick.*

---

### HOGARTH HEAVEN

**Fosters Bookshop.** A great place to buy Hogarth prints is at Fosters Bookshop, based in Chiswick's oldest shop building. The shop has its original Georgian frontage, creaking floorboards, and a glorious number of original Victorian novels and essays. ⊠ *183 Chiswick High Rd., Chiswick* ☎ *020/8995–2768* ⊕ *www. fostersbookshop.co.uk* ⊗ *Tues.– Sat. 10:30–5:30.*

Some of the loveliest pubs in London sit beside the Thames at Chiswick, dotted along the northern bank of the river as far as Hammersmith Mall— the last remaining fragment of what was once a pretty old village, now all but replaced by urban sprawl.

**Blue Anchor.** This cozy 18th-century watering hole on the Thames overlooks Hammersmith Bridge, a High Victorian, wrought-iron suspension bridge designed by Sir Joseph Bazalgette in 1887. The rowing memorabilia on the walls hints at the Blue Anchor's importance on the day of the annual Oxford-versus-Cambridge university boat race, when it's an unofficial meeting point for fans and race officials. The pub also serves light meals. ✉ *13 Lower Mall, Hammersmith* ☎ *020/8748–5774* ⊕ *www. blueanchorlondon.com* Ⓜ *Hammersmith.*

**City Barge.** One of the few pubs in this upscale quarter of Chiswick that retains a proper, old-school feel (enhanced by renovation) the City Barge overlooks a tiny island in the middle of the Thames. Stop for some excellent pub food at lunchtime (it's not-too-gentrified modern British), or just enjoy a pint and watch the river flow by. ✉ *27 Strand-on-the-Green, Chiswick* ☎ *020/8994–2148* ⊕ *www.metropolitanpubcompany.com/our-pubs/ the-city-barge* Ⓜ *Gunnersbury. National Rail: Kew Bridge.*

**Dove Inn.** Retaining the charm of its 300-plus-year heritage, the Dove has a tranquil little terrace that's perfect for watching the river flow by. Check out the Lilliputian room immediately on the right as you enter— it's in the *Guinness Book of World Records* for being the smallest bar in the world. ✉ *19 Upper Mall, Hammersmith* ☎ *020/8748–9474* ⊕ *www. dovehammersmith.co.uk* Ⓜ *Ravenscourt Park, Hammersmith.*

# KEW

A mile or so beyond Chiswick is Kew, a leafy suburb with little to see other than its two big attractions: the lovely **Kew Palace** and the **Royal Botanic Gardens**—anchored in the landscape for several miles around by a towering, mock-Chinese pagoda.

## TOP ATTRACTIONS

FAMILY

Fodor's Choice ★

**Kew Gardens.** Enter the Royal Botanic Gardens, as Kew Gardens are officially known, and you are enveloped by blazes of color, extraordinary blooms, hidden trails, and lovely old follies. Beautiful though it all is, Kew's charms are secondary to its true purpose as a major center for serious research. Academics are hard at work on more than 300 scientific projects across as many acres, analyzing everything from the cacti of eastern Brazil to the yams of Madagascar. First opened to the public in 1840, Kew has been supported by royalty and nurtured by landscapers, botanists, and architects since the 1720s. Today the gardens, now a UNESCO World Heritage Site, hold more than 30,000 species of plants, from every corner of the globe.

Architect Sir William Chambers built a series of temples and follies, of which the crazy 10-story **Pagoda**, visible for miles around, is the star. The Princess of Wales conservatory houses 10 climate zones, and the Rhizotron and Xstrata Treetop Walkway takes you 59 feet up into the air. Two great 19th-century greenhouses—the **Palm House** and the **Temperate House**—are filled with exotic blooms, and many of the plants have been there since the final glass panel was fixed into place. Unfortunately the enormous Temperate House is closed for maintenance until 2018, so until then you won't be able to gawk at the largest greenhouse plant in the world, a Chilean wine palm planted in 1846 (and so big that you have to climb the spiral staircase to the roof to get a proper view of it).

To get around the gardens, the Kew Explorer bus (£4.50) runs on a 40-minute, hop-on, hop-off route, starting at the Victoria Gate, every hour 11–3. Free guided tours, run by volunteers, are given daily at 11 and 1:30, plus special seasonally themed tours at noon. Discovery Tours (£5), fully accessible for visitors in wheelchairs, are also available with advance booking, as are bus tours specifically for groups of visitors with limited mobility; usually run Tuesday, Wednesday, and Thursday, they are priced at £30 per bus. ⊠ *Kew Rd. at Lichfield Rd., for Victoria Gate entrance, Kew* ☎ *020/8332–5655* ⊕ *www.kew.org* ✑ *£16.50* ⊗ *Mid-Feb.–Mar., daily 10:30–5:30; Apr.–Aug., weekdays 10:30–6:30, weekends and bank holiday Mon. 10:30–7:30; Sept.–late Oct., daily 10:30–6; late Oct.–mid-Feb., daily 10:30–4:15. Last admission to park, greenhouses, galleries, and treetop walkway 30 mins before closing* Ⓜ *Kew Gardens. National Rail: Kew Gardens, Kew Bridge.*

**Fodor's** Choice
★
**Kew Palace and Queen Charlotte's Cottage.** The elegant redbrick exterior of the smallest of Britain's royal palaces seems almost humble when compared with the grandeur of, say, Buckingham or Kensington palaces. Yet inside is a fascinating glimpse into life at the uppermost end of society from the 17th to 19th century. This is actually the third of several palaces that stood here; once known as Dutch House, it was one of the havens to which George III retired when insanity forced him to withdraw from public life. Queen Charlotte had an *orné* (a rustic-style cottage retreat) added in the late 18th century. In a marvelously regal flight of fancy, she kept kangaroos in the paddock outside. The main house and gardens are maintained in the 18th-century style. Entry to the palace itself is free, but it lies within the grounds of Kew Gardens, and you must buy a ticket to that to get here. ⊠ *Kew Gardens, Kew Rd. at Lichfield Rd., Kew* ☎ *0844/482–7777 in U.K., 020/3166–6000* ⊕ *www. hrp.org.uk* ✑ *Free with entry to Kew Gardens* ⊗ *Palace: Apr.–Sept., daily 10:30–5:30 (last admission at 5). Queen Charlotte's Cottage: late Mar.–Sept., weekends and bank holiday Mon. 10–4* Ⓜ *Kew Gardens.*

# RICHMOND

Named after the (long-vanished) palace Henry VII started here in 1500, Richmond is still a welcoming suburb with a small-town feel, marred only by choking levels of traffic. Duck away from the main streets to find many handsome Georgian and Victorian houses, antiques shops, a Victorian theater, a grand stately home—and, best of all, the largest of London's royal parks.

## TOP ATTRACTIONS

**13**

**Ham House.** To the west of Richmond Park, overlooking the Thames and nearly opposite the memorably named Eel Pie Island, Ham House was built in 1610 and remodeled 50 years later. It's one of the most complete examples in Europe of a lavish 17th-century house, and as such you can get a clear sense of how the English aristocracy really lived during that period (in short: comfortably). The beautiful formal gardens, with their distinctive spherical and conical topiary, have become an influential source for other palaces and grand villas seeking to restore their gardens to how they were in their heyday. The original decorations in the Great Hall, Round Gallery, and Great Staircase have been replicated, and all the furniture and fittings are on permanent loan from the Victoria & Albert Museum. A tranquil and scenic way to reach the house is on foot, which takes about 30 minutes, along the eastern riverbank south from Richmond Bridge. ✉ *Ham St., Richmond* ☎ *020/8940–1950* ⊕ *www. nationaltrust.org.uk/hamhouse* ▤ *£11 house, gardens, and outbuildings; £4.50 gardens and servants' quarters only* ☼ *House daily 10–4, gardens daily 11–5* Ⓜ *Richmond, then Bus 65 or 371.*

FAMILY
Fodor's Choice
★

**Hampton Court Palace.** The beloved seat of Henry VIII's court, sprawled elegantly beside the languid waters of the Thames, Hampton Court is steeped in more history than virtually any other royal building in England. The Tudor mansion, begun in 1514 by Cardinal Wolsey to curry favor with the young Henry, actually conceals a larger 17th-century baroque building, which was partly designed by Sir Christopher Wren. The earliest dwellings on this site belonged to a religious order founded in the 11th century and were expanded over the years by its many subsequent residents, until George II moved the royal household closer to London in the early 18th century. After entering through the magnificent Tudor courtyard, start with a look through the **State Apartments,** decorated in the Tudor style, and on to the wood-beamed magnificence of Henry's Great Hall, before taking in the strikingly azure ceiling of the **Chapel Royal.** Watch out for the ghost of Henry VIII's doomed fifth wife, Catherine Howard, who lost her head yet is said to scream her way along the **Haunted Gallery.** (Believe it or not, what is certainly true is that the corridor is prone to sudden drops in temperature—and no one quite knows why.) Latter-day masters of the palace, the joint rulers William and Mary (reigned 1689–1702), were responsible for the beautiful **King's and Queen's Apartments** and the elaborate baroque of the Georgian Rooms.

Hampton Court Palace, the seat of Henry VIII's court, is a prime example of a Tudor mansion, and features the oldest hedge maze in the world.

Well-handled reconstructions of Tudor life take place all year, from live appearances by "Henry VIII" to cook-historians preparing authentic Tudor feasts in the 15th-century **Henry's Kitchens.** (Dishes on offer in the adjacent café include a few of these traditional recipes.) The highlight of the formal grounds is undoubtedly the famous maze (the oldest hedge maze in the world), its half-mile of pathways among clipped hedgerows still fiendish to negotiate. There's a trick, but we won't give it away here: it's much more fun just to go and lose yourself. Meanwhile, the **Lower Orangery Exotic Garden** shows off thousands of exotic species that William and Mary, avid plant collectors, gathered from around the globe. Family tickets offer savings—two adults and up to three children are covered for £43.80 (£40.80 if you book online). Family ghost tours (£14 per person) are given on evenings throughout the year. Not only are they entertainingly spooky, but they're a great opportunity to see the older parts of the palace without the crowds. Scarier, adults-only versions cost £27.50 and last two hours. Tours can sell out several weeks in advance, particularly in holiday seasons, so book well in advance. ⊠ *Hampton Court Rd., East Molesley* ☎ *0844/482–7799 for tickets, 0844/482–7777 info (24 hrs), 020/3166–6000 from outside U.K.* ⊕ *www.hrp.org.uk/ hamptoncourtpalace* 🖼 *£19.30 palace, maze, and gardens; £4.50 maze only; £6.20 gardens only* ☉ *Late Mar.–late Oct., daily 10–6; late Oct.– late Mar., daily 10–4:30; last admission 1 hr before closing, last entry to maze 45 mins before closing. Formal Gardens daily: 10–6 summer, 10–5:30 winter. Informal Gardens: summer, daily 7–8; winter, daily 7–6* Ⓜ *Richmond, then Bus R68. National Rail: Hampton Court, 35 mins from Waterloo (most trains require change at Surbiton).*

**Marble Hill House.** This handsome Palladian mansion is set on 66 acres of parkland on the northern bank of the Thames, almost opposite Ham House. It was built in the 1720s by George II for his mistress, the "exceedingly respectable and respected" Henrietta Howard. Later the house was occupied by Mrs. Fitzherbert, who was secretly married to the Prince Regent (later George IV) in 1785. The house was restored in 1901 and opened to the public two years later, looking very much like it did in Georgian times, with extravagant gilded rooms in which Mrs. Howard entertained the literary superstars of the age, including Pope, Gay, and Swift. A ferry service from Ham House operates during the summer; access on foot is a half-hour walk south along the west bank of the Thames from Richmond Bridge. Note that entry is by guided tour only, run by English Heritage and volunteers from a local history group. ⊠ *Richmond Rd., Twickenham* ☎ *037/0333–1181* ⊕ *www. english-heritage.org.uk/marblehillhouse* ⧉ *£6.20* ☉ *House (by guided tour only): Apr.–Oct., Sat. at 10:30 and noon, Sun. and bank holiday Mon. at 10:30, noon, 2:15, and 3:30. Park: Apr.–Oct., daily 10–5; Nov.–Mar., daily 10–4* Ⓜ *Richmond. National Rail: St. Margaret's.*

FAMILY **Richmond Park.** This enormous park was enclosed in 1637 for use as a royal hunting ground—like practically all other London parks. Unlike the others, however, Richmond Park still has wild red and fallow deer roaming its 2,360 acres (three times the size of New York's Central Park) of grassland and heath. Its ancient oaks are among the last remnants of the vast, wild forests that once encroached on London in medieval times. The Isabella Plantation (near the Ham Gate entrance) is an enchanting and colorful woodland garden, first laid out in 1831. There's a splendid, protected view of St. Paul's Cathedral from King Henry VIII's Mound, the highest point in the park; find it, and you have a piece of magic in your sights. The park is also home to White Lodge, a 1727 hunting lodge that now houses the Royal Ballet School. ⊠ *Richmond* ☎ *030/0061-2200* ⊕ *www.royalparks.org.uk* ⧉ *Free* ☉ *Apr.–Oct., daily 7–dusk; Nov.–Mar., daily 7:30–dusk* Ⓜ *Richmond, then Bus 371 or 65.*

QUICK BITES

**White Cross.** Overlooking the Thames so closely that the waters almost lap at the door in high tide, the White Cross is a popular spot that serves traditional, hearty, and crowd-pleasing snacks and meals. ⊠ *Water La., Richmond* ☎ 020/8940-6844 ⊕ www.youngs.co.uk Ⓜ Richmond.

Fodor's Choice ★ **Strawberry Hill.** From the outside, this rococo mishmash of towers, crenellations, and white stucco is dazzling in its faux-medieval splendor. Its architect and owner, Sir Horace Walpole (1717–97) knew a thing or two about imaginative flights of fancy; the flamboyant son of the first British prime minister, Robert Walpole, he all but single-handedly invented the Gothic novel with *The Castle of Otranto* (1764). Once you pass through Strawberry Hill's forbidding exterior, you'll experience explosion of color and light, for Walpole boldly decided to take elements from the exteriors of Gothic cathedrals and move them inside. The detail is extraordinary, from the cavernous entrance hall with its vast Gothic trompe-l'oeil, to the Great Parlour with its Renaissance stained glass, to the Gallery, where extraordinary fan vaulting is a replica of the vaults found in Henry VIII's chapel at Westminster Abbey. Neglected for years, Strawberry Hill reopened in 2011 after a stunningly successful £9 million restoration. The gardens have also been meticulously returned to their original 18th-century design, right down to a white marble loveseat sculpted into the shape of a shell. You can book a tour of the house at twilight for £20, which includes a glass of prosecco. Opening days can vary, so call ahead to check times. ⊠ *268 Waldegrave Rd., Twickenham* ☎ *020/8744–1241* ⊕ *www.strawberryhillhouse.org. uk* ⌾ *£12* ⊘ *Sat.–Wed. 1:40–4; timed entry, every 20 mins—see website for details. Garden: early Jan.–mid-Dec., daily 10–6* Ⓜ *Richmond, then Bus 33. National Rail: Strawberry Hill.*

FAMILY

Fodor's Choice

★

**Syon House and Park.** The residence of the Duke and Duchess of Northumberland, this is one of England's most lavish stately homes. Set in a 55-acre park landscaped by the great gardener "Capability" Brown (1716–83), the core of the house is Tudor—it was one of the last stopping places for Henry VIII's fifth wife, Catherine Howard, and the extremely short-lived monarch, Lady Jane Grey ("Queen for a day" as the saying goes, although it was actually 13) before they were sent to the Tower. It was remodeled in the Georgian style in 1761 by famed decorator Robert Adam. He had just returned from studying the sights of classical antiquity in Italy and created two rooms sumptuous enough to wow any Grand Tourist: the entryway is an amazing study in black and white, pairing neoclassical marbles with antique bronzes, and the Ante-Room contains 12 enormous verd-antique columns surmounted by statues of gold—and this was just a waiting room for the duke's servants and retainers. The Red Drawing Room is covered with crimson Spitalfields silk, and the Long Gallery is one of Adam's noblest creations. On certain Sundays and bank holidays in the summer you can take a miniature steam-train ride in the grounds. ⊠ *Syon Park, Brentford* ☎ *020/8560–0882* ⊕ *www.syonpark.co.uk* ⌾ *£12, £7 gardens and conservatory only* ⊘ *House: mid-Mar.–Oct., Wed., Thurs., Sun., and bank holiday Mon. 11–5. Gardens: mid-Mar.–Oct., daily 10:30–5. Also certain dates in Dec. (call or check online). Last admission 1 hr before closing* Ⓜ *Gunnersbury, then Bus 237 or 267 to Brentlea.*

**Thames River.** The twists and turns of the Thames through the heart of the capital make it London's best thoroughfare and most compelling viewing point. Every palace, church, theater, wharf, museum, and pub along the bank has a tale to tell, and traveling on or alongside the river is one of the best ways to soak up views of the city. Frequent daily tourist-boat services are at their height April–October. In most cases you can turn up at a pier, and the next departure won't be far away; however, it never hurts to book ahead if you can. The trip between Westminster Pier and the Tower of London takes about 30 minutes, as does the trip between the Tower and Greenwich. A full round trip can take several hours. Ask about flexible fares and hop-on, hop-off options at the various piers.

# WHERE TO EAT

# EAT LIKE A LOCAL

A handful of foods are forever associated with London: think fish-and-chips, full English breakfasts, and Indian curry. All these and other innovations are permanently on locals' lips, not to mention their Twitter feeds and Instagram accounts.

## GASTROPUBS

Londoners still love heading to their local gastropub for a rowdy combo of unpretentious Brit-focused dishes and draught beer, cask ales, and cheap wines served in soaring Victorian pubs or ornate gin palaces. Ever since food started being served in The Eagle pub in Farringdon in 1991, the homegrown, foodie-led gastropub revolution has swept London. From George Orwell's historic old haunt, the Newman Arms in Fitzrovia, to The Harwood Arms in Fulham or The Marksman in Hackney, ducking into a bristling gastropub is a surefire way of dining out like a true-grit Londoner.

## CURRY

As a one-time global port and seat of the British Empire, London has enjoyed Indian cuisine for over four hundred years and opened its first dedicated Indian curry house for Colonial returnees (the Hindostanee Coffee House in Marylebone) in 1809. Originally linked to Sylheti Bengali "lascar" seamen and boiler stokers, and later an exotic cuisine championed by Queen Victoria, London's love affair with spicy curry has burgeoned since the Edwardian era. Nowadays, the capital's curry hounds can be found along the gaudy Bengali-focused Brick Lane in the East End. There are also several dashingly decked-out locations of the Dishoom curry emporium.

## CHINESE

Endless waves of Londoners and tourists alike throng the lantern-strewn grid of Georgian streets centered on Chinatown's pulsating Gerrard Street. Breaking out from Hong Kong Cantonese to embrace a wider spread of Sichuan, Hunan, Tawainese, and Malaysian offerings, Londoners tend to hit old favorites like the Wardour Street Four Seasons for roast Peking duck, the Joy Luck Restaurant for Lanzhou noodles, Beijing Dumpling for hand-made dim sum, Ba Shan for Hunanese steamed fish and chilies, and Rasa Sayang for spicy Malay chicken curries.

## FISH-AND-CHIPS

With a focus on crisp batter, juicy cod or haddock, and thick crispy chips, locals seek out low-key traditional fish-and-chip shops and old-school Formica-topped "chippies" for their insatiable fix. Old stagers like The Golden Hind in Marylebone, The Fryer's Delight in Holborn, and The Rock & Sole Plaice in Covent Garden have their nostalgic charms, while a fresh batch of newbies like the Golden Union in Soho, Poppies Fish & Chips in Spitalfields, and Kurbisher & Malt in Clerkenwell tweak around with beer batters, double-cooked chips, homemade tartar sauce, and sustainably sourced fish.

## ENGLISH BREAKFAST

A full English breakfast at one of the city's many workmen's cafés is every Londoner's favorite guilty pleasure. While there are endless varieties, a typical English breakfast consists of fried, poached, or scrambled eggs, streaky bacon, sausages, baked beans, white toast, fried mushrooms, grilled tomatoes, black pudding, chips, fried bread, brown sauce, and scorching mugs of tea.

## NIGHT MARKETS

A recent development to the London food scene, night street-food markets have begun popping up in hipster zones like Shoreditch and Dalston. Housed in edgy DIY indoor/outdoor venues, thousands of London's young foodie fanatics blitz their way through the mini-festivals to try some of the best food trucks, stalls, and stands around. With kooky tunes, ample brews, and raw bench seating, it's impossible not to have a blast flipping from cheap Korean burritos to Folkestone crab buns to a pimped-up Devil Burger with green chili sauce and double jalapeños.

14

Updated
by Alex
Wijeratna

British food hasn't always had the best reputation, but nowhere in the country is that reputation being completely stomped on more than in London. The city has zoomed up the global gastro charts, and can now seriously mix it with the world's top culinary heavyweights. No other city—barring New York—has the immense range of global cuisines that London has to offer. Standards have rocketed at all price points and it seems like the London restaurant scene might be in the most robust health it's ever been in.

A bottom-up local foodie revolution and a top-down cascade of the city's wealth has juiced things up fabulously. Feel like eating the most-tender Kagoshima wagyu beef on planet Earth? It can be yours for £140 at CUT at 45 Park Lane. Want to try old English gastronomy from the time of Henry VIII with an ultramodern twist? Ashley Palmer-Watts is your man at Dinner by Heston Blumenthal. Do you only eat Sri Lankan *hoppers*? No worries, we've got just the thing: try Hoppers in Soho to get a taste of the south Indian pancake, for £3.50 a pop. Can't stand any more snobby culinary nonsense? The low-key British wild game is so good at The Harwood Arms in Fulham that they've earned London's first gastropub-based Michelin star.

To appreciate how far London has risen in the culinary game, just look back to the days of Somerset Maugham, who was once justified in warning, "To eat well in England you should have breakfast three times a day." Change was slow after World War II, when it was understood that the British ate to live, while the French lived to eat. When people thought of British cuisine, fish and chips—a greasy grab and gulp dish that tasted best wrapped in yesterday's newspaper—first came to mind. Then there was always shepherd's pie, ubiquitously found in smoke-filled pubs, though not made, according to *Sweeney Todd*, "with real shepherd in it."

These days, standards are miles higher and shepherd's pie has been largely replaced by the city's unofficial dish, Indian curry. London's restaurant revolution is built on its extraordinary ethnic diversity, and you'll find the quality of other global cuisines has grown immeasurably in recent years, with London becoming known for its Chinese, Japanese, Indian, Thai, Spanish, Italian, French, Peruvian, and North African restaurants. Thankfully, pride in the best of British food—local, seasonal, wild, and foraged—is enjoying a renaissance. And you, too, will be smitten: you'll be spending an average 24% of your travel budget on eating out, but it'll be worth every penny.

# PLANNING

**14**

### EATING OUT STRATEGY

Where should you eat? With thousands of London eateries competing for your attention, it may seem like a daunting question. But fret not: our expert writers and editors have done most of the legwork. The selections here represent the best this city has to offer—from haute cuisine to humble pub food. *Search "Best Bets" for top recommendations by price, cuisine, and experience. Or find a review quickly in the neighborhood listings.*

### RESERVATIONS

Plan ahead if you're determined to snag a sought-after reservation. Some renowned restaurants like Chiltern Firehouse, Palomar, or Duck & Waffle are booked weeks or even months in advance. It's always a good idea to book as far ahead as you can and reconfirm when you arrive in London. Note that some top restaurants also now take credit card details and charge a penalty fee if you're a no-show. *In the reviews, we mention reservations only when they're essential or not accepted.*

### DINING TOURS

FAMILY

Fodor's Choice

★

**London Food Lovers Food + Wine Tours.** London's now a *top* global foodie city, and the London Food Lovers walking tour of Soho is a fascinating way to explore the capital's gastro delights. The half-day walk kicks off with Hawaiian blueberry pancakes at Kua'Aina burger joint off Carnaby Street and takes in offbeat stops for truffle pumpkin ravioli at Soho's Lina Stores Italian delicatessen, a hot chocolate tasting at SAID artisanal Roman chocolatiers, and a sit-down lunch of beer-battered cod and chips and Indian pale ale in quaint Soho boozer The Dog and Duck. Participants pick up tasty cultural and historical tidbits along the way. Supertimed and synchronized throughout, you'll stop in Chinatown to sample steamed prawn dim sum at Leong's Legends, and celeb spot amid the clink of china for afternoon tea at the Maison Bertaux vintage French patisserie and tearoom. The tour ends with a gooey dessert and wine pairing in the Dickensian underground vaults of the 1890 Gordon's Wine Bar. ⊠ *258A Pentonville Rd., Islington* ☎ *802703* ⊕ *www.londonfoodlovers.com* ⌨ *£70* Ⓜ *Angel.*

REGENT'S PARK

HAMPSTEAD
bustling neighborhood eateries

CLERKENWELL
gastro-heaven

NOTTING HILL
trendy cafés and buzzing bars

BLOOMSBURY
hip student-filled spots

MARYLEBONE
slick cafes and ethnic fare

FITZROVIA
stylish small-plates restos

THE CITY
expense account dining

BAYSWATER
best ethnic eats

OXFORD CIRCUS

COVENT GARDEN
avoid the tourist traps

MAYFAIR
chic hotel restaurants

ST JAMES'S
top-notch cuisine for big spenders

SOUTH BANK
new foodie destination

HYDE PARK

KNIGHTSBRIDGE
up-market food halls

Green Park

St. James's Park

WESTMINSTER

KENSINGTON
posh neighborhood eats

BELGRAVIA

River Thames

LAMBETH

VICTORIA

CHELSEA
see-and-be-seen scene

Albany Rd.
Euston Rd.
Gray's Inn Rd.
Clerkenwell Rd.
Marylebone Rd.
Albany St.
Gt. Portland St.
Portland Pl.
Tottenham Court Rd.
Holborn
Kingsway
Fleet St.
Baker St.
Wigmore St.
New Oxford St.
Charing Cross Rd.
Aldwych
Strand
Oxford St.
Bayswater Rd.
New Bond St.
Regent St.
Shaftesbury Ave.
Victoria Embankment
Waterloo Br.
Stamford St.
Pall Mall
Whitehall
Waterloo Rd.
Piccadilly
The Mall
Westminster Br.
Westminster Bridge Rd.
Knightsbridge
Constitution Hill
Birdcage Walk
Sloane St.
Victoria St.
Horseferry Rd.
Lambeth Palace Rd.
Lambeth Br.
Lambeth Rd.
Kennington Rd.
Buckingham Palace Rd.
Wilton Rd.
Vauxhall Br. Rd.
Millbank
Albert Embankment
King's Rd.
Pimlico Rd.
Kennington Park Rd.

0    1/2 mile
0    1/2 km

## WHAT TO WEAR

When in England's style capital, do as the natives do: dress up to eat out. Whatever your style, dial it up a notch and have some fun while you're at it. Pull out the clothes you've been saving for a special occasion and get a little glamorous. As unfair as it seems, the way you look can influence how you're treated—and where you're seated. Generally speaking, jeans and a button-down shirt will suffice at most table-service restaurants in the budget to moderate range. Moving up from there, many pricier restaurants require jackets, and some (like the Ritz) insist on ties. Shorts, sweatpants, baseball caps, and sports jerseys are rarely appropriate. *Note that in reviews we mention dress only when men are required to wear a jacket, or a jacket and tie.*

## TIPPING AND TAXES

Do not tip bar staff in pubs and bars, although you can always offer to buy them a drink. In restaurants, tip 12.5% of the check for full meals if service is not already included; tip a small token if you're just having coffee or tea. If paying by credit card, double-check that a tip has not already been included in the bill.

## CHILDREN

Unless your children behave impeccably, it's best to avoid the haute-cuisine establishments, although increasingly many top places like the Wolseley and Fischer's are surprisingly child-friendly. London's many burger and rib joints, pizzerias, and Italian restaurants are popular with kids. Other family-friendly establishments include chains like Bill's, Côte, Byron, and Wagamama.

## HOURS

In London you can find breakfast all day, but it's generally served 7 am–noon. Lunch is noon–3, and brunch 11–4. Afternoon tea, often a meal in itself, is taken 1–6, and dinner is typically eaten 7–11, although it can be taken earlier. Many ethnic restaurants, especially Indian, serve food until midnight. Sunday is a proper lunch day, and some restaurants are open for lunch only. Over the Christmas period, London has a reputation for shutting down, but a growing number of hotels and other brave bastions are prepared to feed all visitors.

## PRICES

London is a very pricey city by global standards. A modest meal for two can easily cost £40, and the £100-a-head meal is not unknown. Damage-control strategies include making lunch your main meal (the top places have bargain midday menus), going for early- or late-evening deals, or sharing an à la carte entrée and ordering a second appetizer instead. Seek out fixed-price menus, and watch for hidden extras on the check, that is, bread, vegetables, or a cover charged separately.

| WHAT IT COSTS | | | | |
|---|---|---|---|---|
| | $ | $$ | $$$ | $$$$ |
| Restaurants | Under £16 | £16–£23 | £24–£31 | Over £31 |

Prices in the reviews are the average cost of a main course at dinner or, if dinner is not served, at lunch. Note: If a restaurant offers only prix-fixe (set-price) meals, it has been given the price category that reflects the full prix-fixe price.

# RESTAURANT REVIEWS

*Listed alphabetically within neighborhoods. Use the coordinate (⊕ 1:B2) at the end of each listing to locate a property on the Where to Eat and Stay in London atlas at the end of this chapter.*

## WESTMINSTER, ST. JAMES'S, AND ROYAL LONDON

### ST. JAMES'S

St. James's—home to Buckingham Palace and Clarence House, where Prince Charles and Camilla live—has a magnificent olde-world, royal feel. Appropriately, most of the restaurants here are fit for a future king. This is where you'll find London's top-end restaurants—dining experiences that are geared toward a well-heeled, deep-pocketed clientele. Mere mortals should make reservations well in advance to dine at any of these restaurants for dinner (or reserve a table for the earlier or later parts of the evening, when demand is lower). Keep in mind that no-shows mean last-minute tables often crop up, and lunch here can be a great money-saving strategy.

**$$$** ✕ **Le Caprice.** Celebville grande dame Le Caprice commands the deep-
MODERN est loyalty of any restaurant in London. Why? Because it gets prac-
EUROPEAN tically everything right—*every* time. It's the 35-odd-year celebrity history—think Liz Taylor, Joan Collins, and Lady Di—the sparkling monochrome decor, the giddy David Bailey '60s black-and-white pics, charming Bolivian-born Jesus Adorno as the veteran maître d', the pitch-perfect service, and the long-standing menu that sits somewhere between Euro peasant and trendy fashion plate. Sit at the raised counter or at a coveted corner table and enjoy calves' liver with crispy pancetta, slip soles with Amalfi lemon butter, and the signature Scandinavian iced berries with a swirl of hot white chocolate sauce. Note the weekend live jazz sessions. $ *Average main: £25* ⊠ *Arlington House, 20 Arlington St., St. James's* ☎ *020/7629–2239* ⊕ *www.le-caprice.co.uk* ⊲ *Reservations essential* Ⓜ *Green Park* ⊕ *5:A1.*

**$$$$** ✕ **The Ritz Restaurant.** The most flamboyant dining room at the Ritz
BRITISH would moisten the eye of Marie Antoinette with its sumptuous belle époque–inspired trompe-l'oeil frescoes, baroque gilt garland chandeliers, silk drapery, and towering marble columns. Charming liveried waiters glide across the carpeted salon, and gentlemen are expected to wear a jacket and tie. Sit at the late Baroness Thatcher's favorite seat overlooking Green Park (Table 1) and enjoy unreconstructed "Palace-style" British haute cuisine. Bresse chicken with black Périgord truffle

stuffed under its skin is carved tableside and served with *sauce suprême* (a French white sauce). Top-dollar set menus (£95) might captivate with exquisite turbot with cep, or Anjou pigeon with *pomme Anna* (layers of sliced potatoes in butter), and don't miss the *crêpes Suzette* (pancakes with caramalized sugar, orange zest, and Grand Marnier liqueur), which are flambéed tableside by the maître d'. $ *Average main: £39* ⊠ *The Ritz London, 150 Piccadilly, St. James's* ☎ *020/7300–2370 for reservations only* ⊕ *www.theritzlondon.com* ⪻ *Reservations essential* ⌂ *Jacket and tie* Ⓜ *Green Park* ✛ *5:A1.*

$$$$   ✕ **Wiltons.** Wannabe aristocrats and European princes-in-exile blow the
BRITISH   family bank at this old-fashioned bastion of English fine dining on Jermyn Street (the place first opened on the Haymarket as a shellfish stall in 1742). Male diners are requested to wear long-sleeved shirts at this linen-draped time capsule, an often snooty ode to all things English. Posh patrons tend to order a dozen Beau Brummell oysters, followed by grilled Dover sole or fabulous native game, such as roast partridge or grouse. There is also soft herring roe on toast, plus desserts like sherry trifle. The wine selection tilts heavily toward Bordeaux, and the service would put Jeeves to shame. $ *Average main: £34* ⊠ *55 Jermyn St., St. James's* ☎ *020/7629–9955* ⊕ *www.wiltons.co.uk* ☯ *Closed Sun. and bank holidays. No lunch Sat.* ⪻ *Reservations essential* ⌂ *Jacket required* Ⓜ *Green Park* ✛ *5:A1.*

$$   ✕ **The Wolseley.** A glitzy procession of stars come for the spectacle, swish
AUSTRIAN   service, and soaring elegance at this bustling Viennese-style grand café
FAMILY   on Piccadilly. Framed with 1920s black lacquerware in a former Wolseley luxury-car showroom, this all-day brasserie begins its long decadent days with breakfast at 7 am and serves Dual Monarchy delights until midnight. Don't be shy about popping by (they welcome walk-ins) for dishes like Hungarian goulash, Austrian pork belly, chicken soup with dumplings, or breaded Wiener schnitzel. For dessert, go for luscious *Kaiserschmarren* (caramelized pancakes with stewed fruit and raisins) or Black Forest gâteaux, and don't forget to return to savor the Viennoiserie pastries at one of their classy afternoon teas. $ *Average main: £18* ⊠ *160 Piccadilly, St. James's* ☎ *020/7499–6996* ⊕ *www.thewolseley. com* ⪻ *Reservations essential* Ⓜ *Green Park* ✛ *5:A1.*

## MAYFAIR AND MARYLEBONE

If you're looking for something more wallet-friendly, head north to Marylebone, formerly dowdy but now prized for its überchic, villagelike feel. Here you'll find an array of low-key little cafés, boîtes, and tapas bars, Champagne-and-hot-dog joints, and the odd world-class sizzler, offering everything from Moroccan and Spanish to Thai and Japanese.

### MAYFAIR

$$$   ✕ **Cecconi's.** Spot an A-lister and wallow in the glamorous buzz at
MODERN ITALIAN   this upscale Italian brasserie wedged between Old Bond Street, Cork Street, and Savile Row, and across from the 1768 Royal Academy of Arts. The jet-setting and fine art world connoisseurs spill out onto pavement tables for breakfast, brunch, and *cicchetti* (Italian tapas), and return later in the day for something more substantial. The luxe

# BEST BETS FOR LONDON DINING

With so many restaurants to choose from, how to decide where to eat? Fodor's writers and editors have tramped around and selected their favorite restaurants by price, cuisine, and experience in the Best Bets lists below. Fodor's Choice properties represent the "best of the best" in every price category. You can also search by neighborhood for excellent eats—just peruse the following pages. Or find specific details about a restaurant in the full reviews, listed later in the chapter by neighborhood.

## Best by Cuisine

### BRITISH
The Harwood Arms, $$$
Hereford Road, $
Lyle's, $$
Newman Arms, $
St. John, $$

### CHINESE
HKK, $$$
Hunan, $$

### FRENCH
Brasserie Gustave, $$$
Casse-Croûte, $$
Hélène Darroze at the Connaught, $$$$
Koffmann's, $$$
Le Gavroche, $$$$

### ITALIAN
Bocca di Lupo, $$
Cecconi's, $$$
Oldroyd, $
Polpetto, $$

### JAPANESE
Yashin, $$$
Zuma, $$

### SEAFOOD
Bonnie Gull Seafood Shack, $$
J Sheekey, $$$
Scott's, $$$$
Sexy Fish, $$$
Sweetings, $$

## Fodor's Choice ★

BAO, $
Barrafina, $$$
Blacklock, $
Blanchette, $$
Burger & Lobster, $$
Casse-Croûte, $$
Chez Bruce, $$$
City Social, $$$
Dabbous, $$
The Delaunay, $$
Duck & Waffle, $
Fera at Claridge's, $$$$
Fischer's, $
Gymkhana, $$$
The Harwood Arms, $$$
Hedone, $$$
Hereford Road, $
Hoppers, $
The Ivy, $$
Kitty Fisher's, $$$
The Ledbury, $$$$

Le Gavroche, $$$$
Le Pont de la Tour, $$$
Little Social, $$
Lyle's, $$
Newman Arms, $
The Palomar, $
Rules, $$$
Sexy Fish, $$$
Social Eating House, $$$
Typing Room, $$

## Best by Price

### $

BAO
Blacklock
Blixen
Dishoom
Flat Iron
Hoppers
Newman Arms
The Riding House Café

### $$

Burger & Lobster
Casse-Croûte
The Ivy
Little Social
Lyle's
Polpetto
Portland
Typing Room

### $$$

Chez Bruce
City Social
Gymkhana
Le Pont de la Tour

### $$$$

The Ledbury
Le Gavroche
Scott's

14

## STEAK

The Colony Grill Room, $$$
CUT at 45 Park Lane, $$$$
Flat Iron, $
Goodman, $$$$
Kitty Fisher's, $$$

## Best by Experience

### BRASSERIE

Balthazar, $$
The Delaunay, $$
Fischer's, $
The Wolseley, $$

### BREAKFAST AND BRUNCH

Dean Street Townhouse, $$
The Delaunay, $$
Dishoom, $
Duck & Waffle, $
Fischer's, $
The Modern Pantry, $$
The Riding House Café, $
The Wolseley, $$

### BUSINESS DINING

City Social, $$$
The Colony Grill Room, $$$
The Delaunay, $$
Le Gavroche, $$$$
Scott's, $$$$

## CELEB SPOTTING

The Delaunay, $$
J Sheekey, $$$
Park Chinois, $$
Scott's, $$$$
Sexy Fish, $$$
34, $$$

### GASTROPUBS

Anchor & Hope, $$
Great Queen Street, $$
The Harwood Arms, $$$
Newman Arms, $

### GOOD FOR GROUPS

Blacklock, $
Burger & Lobster, $$
Dean Street Townhouse, $$
Dishoom, $
The Riding House Café, $

### HISTORIC

Maison Bertaux, $
Rules, $$$
Simpson's Tavern, $
Sweetings, $$
Wiltons, $$$$

### HOTEL DINING

Bar Boulud, $$
Berners Tavern, $$
Dinner by Heston Blumenthal, $$$$
Fera at Claridge's, $$$$
Hélène Darroze at the Connaught, $$$$

## HOT SPOTS

Gymkhana, $$$
The Ivy, $$
The Palomar, $
Park Chinois, $$
Sexy Fish, $$$

### LATE-NIGHT DINING

The Delaunay, $$
Duck & Waffle, $
J Sheekey, $$$
Park Chinois, $$
Sexy Fish, $$$

### LOCAL FAVORITES

Brasserie Gustave, $$$
Chez Bruce, $$$
The Harwood Arms, $$$
Hereford Road, $
Lemonia, $

### LUNCH PRIX-FIXE

Bar Boulud, $$
Galvin Bistrot de Luxe, $$$
Hereford Road, $
Le Gavroche, $$$$
Merchants Tavern, $$
Newman Arms, $

### PRETHEATER

Côte, $
Dean Street Townhouse, $$
Opera Tavern, $$
Social Eating House, $$$

## ROMANTIC

Clos Maggiore, $$$
The Delaunay, $$
J Sheekey, $$$
Scott's, $$$$
Sexy Fish, $$$

### WINE LISTS

Bocca di Lupo, $$
The Greenhouse, $$$$
Hibiscus, $$$$
The Ledbury, $$$$
Typing Room, $$

green-and-brown interior is a tony backdrop for classics like sea bream carpaccio, veal Milanese, and pappardelle with Chianti ragù, and don't forget the pick-me-up tiramisù. It's perfect for a pit stop during a West End shopping spree or after an art buying at the nearby Mayfair auction houses. $ *Average main: £26* ✉ *5A Burlington Gardens, Mayfair* ☎ *020/7434–1500* ⊕ *www.cecconis.co.uk* ⚓ *Reservations essential* Ⓜ *Green Park, Piccadilly Circus* ✛ *3:A6.*

**$$$**
AMERICAN

✗ **The Colony Grill Room.** Glide past the royal blue Armstrong Siddeley, through the foyer of the five-star Beaumont Hotel and into the art deco–inspired dining salon of the Colony Grill Room. Fans of 1920s New York cool will admire the John Mattos American-sporting-life mis en scène murals, burnished wood, blood-red leather banquettes, and vintage caricatures (from Clark Gable to Dorothy Parker), before choosing between claw-hammer throwbacks like mock turtle soup, chicken marengo, and Kenny's meat loaf (minced beef baked in a loaf pan). There's also rare breaded veal Pojarski, plus four types of Caesar salad, and American sandwiches from lobster rolls to hot dogs. The exemplary service is, naturally, from a gilded age. $ *Average main:* ✉ *The Beaumont, 8 Balderton St., Brown Hart Gardens, Mayfair* ☎ *020 /7499–9499* ⊕ *www.colonygrillroom.com* ⚓ *Reservations essential* Ⓜ *Marble Arch* ✛ *1:G4.*

**$$**
PERUVIAN

✗ **Coya.** London's most beautiful citizens come here to binge on the mesmerizing parade of top-end Peruvian dishes and sizzling char-grilled offerings, set in an Inca-inspired, dimly lit basement pisco party zone. London Fashion Weekers and models guzzle low- and low-carb marinated yellowfin tuna or sea bream and *ají amarillo* chili ceviches. There's also baby squid with rare Peruvian marigold or charred asparagus spears along with protein-packed *anticuchos* (marinated meat) grilled skewers—look for the special duck's heart or tiger prawns with *ají panca* red peppers. $ *Average main: £23* ✉ *118 Piccadilly, Mayfair* ☎ *020/7042–7118* ⊕ *www.coyarestaurant.com* ☾ *No dinner Mon.* ⚓ *Reservations essential* Ⓜ *Green Park, Hyde Park Corner* ✛ *1:H6.*

**$$$$**
STEAKHOUSE
FAMILY

✗ **CUT at 45 Park Lane.** Austrian-born star chef Wolfgang Puck amps up the stakes at this ultra-expensive steak emporium on Park Lane. Set against a luxe backdrop of Damien Hirst kaleidoscope paintings, globe lights, and a soundtrack of T'Pau and Bon Jovi, carnivores go crazy for the prime cuts from England, Australia, Japan, and the United States. Grilled over charcoal and hardwood, and finished under a 650°C broiler, there's awesome 35-day Creekstone filet mignon for £36, Black Angus New York sirloins for £54, and an 8 oz. ribeye of wagyu Kagoshima beef from Kyusyu in Japan for a top-whack £140. Add bone marrow, French fries, chimichurri, or creamed spinach with a fried egg on top for the whole nine yards. $ *Average main: £41* ✉ *45 Park La., Mayfair* ☎ *020/7439–4554 for reservations only* ⊕ *www. dorchestercollection.com* ⚓ *Reservations essential* Ⓜ *Marble Arch, Hyde Park Corner* ✛ *1:G5.*

**$$$$**
BRITISH
Fodor's Choice
★

✗ **Fera at Claridge's.** Top toque Simon Rogan—a local produce fanatic and Cumbrian field-to-fork farm owner—banishes table linen at this famed restaurant at Claridge's and guides diners on a madcap meander through his take on the best of wild, seasonal, and wickedly paired

Britain. Admire the art deco walnut, nickel, and olive green hues of the carpeted salon—centerpieced around a sandblasted Manzanita tree—before enjoying a blizzard of edible flowers, rare herbs, and shoots-strewn dishes served on hand-cast or -carved slates and plates. Jump on the signature Cumbrian Cartmel Valley smoked venison if it's available, or the aged hogget lamb with pickled tongue and turnips. Desserts range from a liquid-nitrogen meringue of Hereford strawberries with meadsweet to chocolate cream with rapeseed jam. ⑤ *Average main: £32* ✉ *Claridge's, 49 Brook St., Mayfair* ☎ *020/7107–8888 for reservations only* ⊕ *www.feraatclaridges.co.uk* ⟁ *Reservations essential* Ⓜ **Bond St.** ✢ *1:H4.*

**$$$$**
STEAKHOUSE

✗**Goodman.** This Manhattan-themed, Russian-owned, Mayfair-based swanky steakhouse, named after Chicago jazz legend Benny Goodman, has everyone in agreement: these truly are some of the best steaks in town. USDA-certified, 150-day corn-fed and on-site dry-aged Black Angus T-bones, ribeye, porterhouse, and New York sirloins compete for taste and tenderness with heavily marbled grass-fed prime cuts from Scotland and the Lake District. There's also token Russian sweet herring, lobster bisque, beef carpaccio, and Caesar salad, but everyone at this sultry dark-wood mecca seems to have only one big thing on their minds: the sizzling 250g–400g Josper char-grilled steaks, which come with lobster tails or pan-fried foie gras, truffle chips, and creamed spinach, plus Béarnaise, pepper, or Stilton sauce. ⑤ *Average main: £34* ✉ *24–26 Maddox St., Mayfair* ☎ *020/7499–3776* ⊕ *www. goodmanrestaurants.com* ⊘ *Closed Sun.* ⟁ *Reservations essential* Ⓜ *Oxford Circus, Piccadilly Circus* ✢ *3:A5.*

**$$$$**
FRENCH

✗**The Greenhouse.** Tucked away amid imposing redbrick Mayfair mansions and approached via a quiet tree-lined garden, this elegant ground-floor dining salon attracts wealthy new-media titans and aficionados of world-class French haute cuisine. Feast on complex dishes like Cornish crab on mint gelée with Granny Smith apple mousse or sumptuous sea bass with calamari, Sicilian prawns, and green "zebra" tomato sauce. The well-heeled crowd come for the smooth and attentive service, the soft lighting, the glassed-off private dining room, and the legendary 111-page wine list, which includes a 1929 Domaine de la Romanée-Conti from Burgundy and an 1870 Château Lafite-Rothschild 1er cru classé. ⑤ *Average main: £33* ✉ *27A Hay's Mews, Mayfair* ☎ *020/7499–3331* ⊕ *www.greenhouserestaurant.co.uk* ⊘ *Closed Sun. No lunch Sat.* ⟁ *Reservations essential* Ⓜ *Green Park* ✢ *1:H5.*

**$$$**
MODERN INDIAN
FAMILY
Fodor's Choice
★

✗**Gymkhana.** The last days of the Raj are invoked here at London's finest top-end curry emporium in Mayfair. Inspired by the Colonial-era Anglo-Indian gymkhana sporting clubs of yesteryear, you'll be charmed by the ceiling fans, rattan chairs, lacquered oak floors, and dark chocolate leather banquettes. Chuckle at the vintage Punch sketches and peruse the hunting trophies from the Maharajah of Jodhpur before exploring the exceptional menu. Choices include all-India delights such as golden pancakelike dosas with fennel-rich Chettinad ducky, Lucknowi scallops, and wild Muntjac deer biryani with pomegranate mint raita. There's also a famed suckling pig vindaloo and oodles of well-spiced game—like guinea fowl pepper fry—while the saffron pistachio

**14**

*kulfi falooda* (a sort of sundae) with wild basil seeds is surprisingly fine. ⑤ *Average main: £27* ✉ *42 Albemarle St., Mayfair* ☎ *020/3011–5900* ⊕ *www.gymkhanalondon.com* ⊘ *Closed Sun.* ⚖ *Reservations essential* Ⓜ *Green Park* ✛ *1:H5.*

$$$$
FRENCH

✕ **Hélène Darroze at the Connaught.** London's crème de la crème flock to French virtuoso Hélène Darroze's restaurant at the Connaught for her dazzling regional French haute cuisine, served up in a sexy Edwardian wood-paneled dining salon tricked out with geometric carpets and comfy high-back chairs. Taking inspiration from Les Landes in southwestern France, Darroze sallies forth with a procession of magnificent dishes, like Robert Dupérier foie gras with fig and port or Limousin sweetbreads with *girolles* (mushrooms) and Jerusalem artichokes. Spitroasted Racan pigeon comes gloriously pink and the Pyrenean lamb is served *en rognonade* (with its kidneys). To finish, choose the poached yellow peaches from Provence with gingerbread cream. ⑤ *Average main: £38* ✉ *The Connaught, Carlos Pl., Mayfair* ☎ *020/3147–7200 for reservations only* ⊕ *www.the-connaught.co.uk* ⊘ *Closed Sun. and Mon.* ⚖ *Reservations essential* �🎩 *Jacket required* Ⓜ *Green Park* ✛ *1:H5.*

$$$$
MODERN FRENCH

✕ **Hibiscus.** Burly two-star French chef/patron Claude Bosi bosses the scene at this understated Mayfair epicurean hide-out, with nouvelle Modern French dishes like carpaccio of hand-dived Isle of Skye scallops with blobs of truffle and pickled black radish, salted roast duck with winter *tardivo* (radicchio), or Cornish John Dory with Morteau sausage and girolles. The desserts are as complex as his mains, with an unlikely sounding but wickedly flavorful sweet cep tart standing out. The brilliant wine list features an ever-growing 30-odd selection of rare but top-rank biodynamic, organic, or heirloom-variety wines. Note that in the evening, the tasting menu is the only option available. ⑤ *Average main: £35* ✉ *29 Maddox St., Mayfair* ☎ *020/7629–2999* ⊕ *www.hibiscusrestaurant.co.uk* ⊘ *Closed Sun. and Mon. No lunch Tues. and Wed.* ⚖ *Reservations essential* Ⓜ *Oxford Circus, Piccadilly Circus* ✛ *3:A5.*

$$$
MODERN BRITISH
**Fodor's** Choice
★

✕ **Kitty Fisher's.** Named after an infamous Georgian-era courtesan, Kitty Fisher's is situated in a classy, dark, and creaky 18th century townhouse in Mayfair's Dickensian Shepherd Market. Come and let it seduce you with some of the finest modern wood grill and smokehouse fare around. The famous grilled 12-year-old Galician milk-cow sirloin is a singed and seared yet pink and oozing carved column of meat, accompanied by a heap of grilled onions, pickled walnuts, and barbecued Pink Fir potatoes with soft white Tunworth cheese. Look for the steak tartare with nasturtium or charred lamb cutlets with mint and parsley. It's a tiny space, with only 40 seats, and filled with vintage 18th-century prints, paintings and antique silver candelabras. ⑤ *Average main: £27* ✉ *10 Shepherd Market, Mayfair* ☎ *020/3302–1661* ⊕ *www.kittyfishers.com* ⊘ *Closed Sun. No lunch Sat.* ⚖ *Reservations essential* Ⓜ *Green Park* ✛ *1:H6.*

$$$
FRENCH

✕ **La Petite Maison.** With the legend "*Tous Célèbres Ici*" ("All Famous Here") boldly etched on the frosted glass front doors, the light-filled and delightful Petite Maison boasts an impressively well-sourced and balanced French Mediterranean, Ligurian, and Provençal menu. Try the figure-friendly broad bean and Pecorino salad, soft burrata cheese with sweet Datterini-tomato-and-basil spread, or aromatic baked turbot with artichokes, chorizo, five spices, and gloppy white wine sauce. Based on the Riviera style of the original Petite Maison in Nice, dishes come to the table as soon as they're ready, and the chirpy and informal waitstaff make for a convivial party vibe. $⟋ Average main: £28 ⊠ 53–54 Brook's Mews, Mayfair ☎ 020/7495–4774 ⊕ www.lpmlondon.co.uk ⌂ Reservations essential ⓂBond St., Oxford Circus ✢ 1:H4.

**$$$$**
**FRENCH**
**Fodor's Choice**
**★**

✕ **Le Gavroche.** Masterchef Michel Roux Jr. works the floor in the old-fashioned proprietorial way at this clubby Mayfair basement institution—established by his uncle and father in 1967—which many still rate as the best formal dining in London. Resplendent with magnificent silver domes and unpriced ladies' menus, Roux's mastery of classical French haute cuisine hypnotizes with signature dishes like foie gras with cinnamon-scented crispy duck pancake, soufflé Suissesse, roast venison with red wine jus, or saddle of rabbit with Parmesan cheese. Desserts like the chocolate omelet soufflé or upside-down apple tart are expertly accomplished. Notable three-course set lunches (£56) are the sanest way to experience such flummery—with half a bottle of wine, water, coffee, and petits fours thrown in. $⟋ Average main: £41 ⊠ 43 Upper Brook St., Mayfair ☎ 020/7408–0881 ⊕ www.le-gavroche.co.uk ⊗ Closed Sun. and Mon. ⌂ Reservations essential ⓜ Jacket required ⓂBond St, Marble Arch ✢ 1:G5.

**$$**
**MODERN FRENCH**
**Fodor's Choice**
**★**

✕ **Little Social.** A neon sign may caution "Silence, Logique, Securité, Prudence," but there's always a hubbub here at this below-the-radar French bistro hidden away in Mayfair. Ease into a Burgundy banquette booth and admire the elm tables, art deco lamps, and Michelin road maps in the narrow dining salon before diving into the artfully classic-with-a-twist menu. The crab salad appetizer comes on a round of tomato with miso dressing, while the braised Irish ox cheeks with roast bone marrow, carrots, and horseradish mash is a top-ranked comfort food of the highest order. There's also always aged the Scottish bacon cheeseburger, plus a side of unusual Québécois poutine—a messy bowl of fries piled high with cheese curds, gravy, chorizo, and jalapeños. $⟋ Average main: £23 ⊠ 5 Pollen St., Mayfair ☎ 020/7870–3730 ⊕ www.littlesocial.co.uk ⌂ Reservations essential ⓂOxford Circus, Piccadilly Circus ✢ 3:A4.

**$$**
**CHINESE**

✕ **Park Chinois.** This vast two-story, 300-seat opulent 1920s-style Chinese dining and dance fandango is inspired by the maximalist French rococo period—think golden candelabras, gleaming black floors, and sumptuous tassled chairs upholstered in pale blue floral fabrics. The first-floor dining room hosts a singer and a pianist, while the downstairs Club Chinois has a seven-piece swing band and vocalist. Equally classy are the Chinese dishes served on both floors, which range from Peking duck with caviar and double-boiled chicken soup to Kamchatka king crab and udon with pancetta and sea urchin. $⟋ Average main: £22 ⊠ 17 Berkeley St., Mayfair ☎ 020/7291–5118 ⊕ www.parkchinois.com ⌂ Reservations essential ⓂGreen Park ✢ 3:B6.

**$$$$**
**MODERN**
**EUROPEAN**

✕ **Pollen Street Social.** Gastro god Jason Atherton knocks the London dining scene for a loop at his smash-hit flagship touched down in a cute alleyway off Regent Street. Fans enjoy refined small and large dishes ranging from a full English breakfast appetizer (a miniature poached egg on tomato compote, with parsley-flecked bacon, morels, and croutons) to sublime Scottish ox cheek with 50-day Black Angus ribeye. Diners can opt to sit at the Dessert Bar to watch staff as they chop, squeeze, and slice to prepare an immaculate Eton Mess with wild strawberries and basil-ash meringue or sashimi-like pressed watermelon with basil sorbet. $ *Average main: £33* ✉ *8–10 Pollen St., Mayfair* ☎ *020/7290–7600* ⊕ *www.pollenstreetsocial.com* ⚓ *Reservations essential* Ⓜ *Oxford Circus, Piccadilly Circus* ✛ *3:A5.*

$ ✕**The Riding House Café.** Hipster-chic London diners flock to this NYC-style small plates and luxe burger brasserie behind Oxford Circus in Noho (North of Soho). Everything's appropriately salvaged, reclaimed, or bespoke, here so you'll find stuffed squirrel lampholders, birds, and other taxidermy dotted around, along with reclaimed blue leather theater seats at the bar and old snooker-table legs holding up your dining table. Opt for bargain £7 small plates of spicy crayfish tails with lemongrass, or superfood salads; then try the poached egg chorizo hash browns, 28-day hormone-free cheeseburger with chips, or the famed lobster lasagna. You'll also find neat all-day breakfasts, plus milk shakes, cocktails, and sundaes. Service is friendly. $ *Average main: £14* ✉ *43–51 Great Titchfield St., Noho* ☎ *020/7927–0840* ⊕ *www.ridinghousecafe.co.uk* ⚓ *Reservations essential* Ⓜ *Oxford Circus* ✛ *3:A2.*

BURGER
FAMILY

$ ✕**Sartoria.** Italian maestro Francesco Mazzei bestrides this plush and patterned Savile Row salon and welcomes giddy diners like the proud chef-patron that he is. Cop a whiff of Alba truffle as it's delicately sliced tableside over an extravagantly creamy spaghetti carbonara that sits snuggly beneath a soft-boiled egg. A platter of fritto misto includes monkfish, red mullet, and Mazzara shrimp bites, while desserts boast an unmissable parade of Mont Blanc, tiramisù, and Bergamot creams. $ *Average main: £16* ✉ *20 Savile Row, Mayfair* ☎ *0207/534–7000* ⊕ *www.sartoria-restaurant.co.uk* ☽ *Closed Sun.* Ⓜ *Oxford Circus* ✛ *3:A5.*

MODERN ITALIAN

$$$$ ✕**Scott's.** Doormen in bowlers greet visitors with a wee nod at this ever-fashionable seafood haven on Mount Street in Mayfair. Originally founded in 1851, and a former haunt of James Bond author Ian Fleming, these days you're more likely to see Bill Clinton in one corner and Kate Winslet in another, with plenty of other celebrities joshing around nearby. Scott's draws the wealthiest of London, who enjoy day-boat Lindisfarne oysters, salt-baked whole turbot, and scrummy shrimp burgers. Prices could make a Saudi sheikh blanch, but that's what you get for truly the hottest table in town. $ *Average main: £33* ✉ *20 Mount St., Mayfair* ☎ *020/7495–7309* ⊕ *www.scotts-restaurant.com* ⚓ *Reservations essential* Ⓜ *Green Park, Bond St* ✛ *1:H5.*

SEAFOOD

$$$ ✕**Sexy Fish.** Located in bougie Berkeley Square, this place is what its name suggests: both sexy (in terms of the clientele) and fish-focused (in terms of the cuisine and decor). Stuffed to the gills with ethereal Damien Hirst bronze mermaids and swooping Frank Gehry mobile fish lamps, the restaurant's menu features rare fish dishes like miso-glazed Chilean sea bass, giant Madgascan prawns, and slow-baked Alaskan king crab with shiso Béarnaise sauce. Desserts also stay on the piscine theme, with salted caramel and faux sour cherry "pebbles." Huge tanks light up the

SEAFOOD
Fodor'sChoice
★

Coral Reef Room, where resident DJs rock the bar until 2 am Thursday–Saturday. $ *Average main: £26* ✉ *Berkeley Sq. House, Berkeley Sq., Mayfair* ☎ *020/3764–2000* ⊕ *www.sexyfish.com* ⌘ *Reservations essential* Ⓜ *Green Park* ✛ *1:H5.*

$$$
INTERNATIONAL

✕ **34.** A Listers head straight for 34 in Mayfair, simply because all the other celebrities are here too. It must be the plush Edwardian- and art deco–inspired dining salon, the swank paintings and burnt-orange banquettes, the nightly live jazz, the neat fish, game, and steak-focused menu, the copious starched white table linens, and the smooth Upper Manhattan–style service. Appetizers like braised octopus with chorizo square off against chunkier delights from the Argentine *parrilla* (charcoal grill)—think 28-day Scottish Bridge of Allan ribeyes, USDA New York strips, and Australian wagyu sirloins. Top crowd pleasers include the meatball spaghetti and truffled lobster macaroni. $ *Average main: £28* ✉ *34 Grosvenor Sq., entrance on South Audley St., Mayfair* ☎ *020/3350–3434* ⊕ *www.34-restaurant.co.uk* ⌘ *Reservations essential* Ⓜ *Marble Arch* ✛ *1:G5.*

**14**

## MARYLEBONE

$$$
ECLECTIC

✕ **Chiltern Firehouse.** It can be quite tricky to get into the Chiltern Firehouse, but if you do snag a table, you're in for a treat. Set inside a sensationally converted 1888 redbrick fire station, this place sets the bar for glamour-chic dining. Sit at the raised open-kitchen counter and watch the chefs plate up, while taking in the buzzy buttermilk-hue decor that's part mid-'70s Parisian brasserie and part industrial heritage–chic splendor (including a firefighter's pole). Pick winners from a spanking menu—like slider-style crabmeat "donuts," charred octopus with cep mushrooms, or red prawns in almond milk—and get down to the serious business of major league celeb spotting. $ *Average main: £29* ✉ *Chiltern Firehouse, 1 Chiltern St.* ☎ *020/7073–7676 for reservations only* ⊕ *www.chilternfirehouse.com* ⌘ *Reservations essential* Ⓜ *Baker St., Bond St.* ✛ *1:G3.*

$
AUSTRIAN
FAMILY
Fodor's Choice
★

✕ **Fischer's.** It almost feels like Gustav Klimt or Sigmund Freud might doff their Homburg hats and shuffle into a dark leather banquette at this evocative early century–style Viennese neighborhood café. Savor the antique light fittings, distressed wallpaper, and gilt-edged paintings before diving into brotchen-chopped chicken livers with dill on rye bread or creamy käsespätzle egg dumplings with Gruyère and bacon. Be sure to try the Emmental and bacon-wrapped *Berner Würstel* sausages piled high with sauerkraut and mustard-swooshed potatoes. Expect top service from staff in natty *Tracht*-style Tyrolean green waistcoats and dark green ties. $ *Average main: £14* ✉ *50 Marylebone High St., Marylebone* ☎ *020/7466–5501* ⊕ *www.fischers.co.uk* ⌘ *Reservations essential* Ⓜ *Baker St., Bond St.* ✛ *1:H3.*

$$$
BRASSERIE

✕ **Galvin Bistrot de Luxe.** The Galvin brothers, Chris and Jeff, blaze a trail for the time-tested French *bistrot de luxe* formula on this fast-moving stretch of Baker Street. Seasoned fans return time and again for the impeccable food, smart service, and sparkling mahogany-paneled Parisian-style dining salon. There's no finer Dorset crab lasagna in town, and mains consistently punch above their weight: the calves' liver with Alsace bacon, classic stuffed pig's trotter, and Cumbrian shorthorn beef with Bordelaise sauce are all devilishly tasty. Monday through Saturday, £21.50 three-course set lunches and £23.50 dinners (6–7 and after 9) are top values, and look out for live Sunday afternoon jazz. ⑤ *Average main: £25* ✉ *66 Baker St., Marylebone* ☎ *020/7935–4007* ⊕ *www. galvinrestaurants.com* ⌖ *Reservations essential* Ⓜ *Baker St.* ✢ *1:G3.*

$ ✕ **The Golden Hind.** You'll land some of the best fish-and-chips in town
SEAFOOD at this great British chippy in a cheery retro 1914 art deco café. Gag-
FAMILY gles of satisfied tourists and Marylebone locals alike hunker down for homemade cod fishcakes, skate wings, feta cheese fritters, and breaded scampi tails, but it's the neatly prepared and decidedly nongreasy deep-fried or steamed battered cod, haddock, and plaice, the classic hand-cut Maris Piper chips, and the traditional mushy peas that are the big draw. It's also BYO (£1 corkage) and offers takeaway. ⑤ *Average main: £9* ✉ *73 Marylebone La., Marylebone* ☎ *020/7486–3644* ⊘ *Closed Sun. No lunch Sat.* ⌖ *Reservations not accepted* Ⓜ *Bond St.* ✢ *1:H3.*

$ ✕ **Tommi's Burger Joint.** "Be Nice or Leave" and "Sharing is Caring" are
BURGER a few choice aphorisms found on cardboard signs at this cult Icelandic-
FAMILY run burger boîte in Marylebone. The decor also includes overhead fairy lights, Han Solo stickers, and a surfing Chewbacca poster. Besides the organic beef patties from top butcher HG Walter, you'll find grilled cheese sandwiches and veggie burgers, plus a steak burger made with fillet, rump, and ribeye; all come in fist-size brioche buns with tomato, lettuce, onion, ketchup, mayo, and mustard, and then there's the estimable condiments bar. Everyone loves the edgy DIY vibe and the £10.90 burger, fries, and soda deal. ⑤ *Average main: £11* ✉ *30 Thayer St., Marylebone* ☎ *020/7224–3828* ⊕ *www.burgerjoint.co.uk* ⌖ *Reservations not accepted* Ⓜ *Bond St.* ✢ *1:H3.*

---

# SOHO AND COVENT GARDEN

Soho and Covent Garden are the city's historic playground and pleasure zone, an all-day, all-night jostling neon wonderland of glitz, glamour, grime, and greasepaint. This area is London's cultural heart, with old and new media companies, late-night dive bars, cabaret, street performers, West End musicals, and world-class theater, ballet, and opera houses. Rising rents have recently forced out many of Soho's seedier red-light businesses and ushered in more edgy, top-notch restaurants. Just follow your nose in Covent Garden and Theatreland to find copious options for pretheater dining.

## SOHO

$$ ✕ **Andrew Edmunds.** Candlelit at night, with a haunting Dickensian vibe,
MEDITERRANEAN Andrew Edmunds is a permanently packed old-school Soho dining institution—although it could be larger, less creaky underfoot, and its wooden church-pew seats more forgiving. Tucked away behind Carnaby Street in an 18th-century Soho townhouse, it's a cozy favorite whose keenly priced dishes draw on the tastes of Ireland, the Mediterranean, and Middle East. Harissa-spiced mackerel, woodcock on toast, seafood paella, and Herdwick lamb shanks with champ and broccoli are all hale and hearty. Desserts like warm treacle tart or bread-and-butter pudding offer few surprises, but the wine's superb and the prices reasonable.

$ *Average main: £17* ⊠ *46 Lexington St., Soho* ☎ *020/7437–5708* ⊕ *www.andrewedmunds.com* ⚱ *Reservations essential* Ⓜ *Oxford Circus, Piccadilly Circus* ✛ *3:C5.*

**$**
**TAIWANESE**
**Fodor's**Choice
**★**

✕ **BAO.** Lines form daily to secure a prized seat, perch, or stool at this small 30-seater from a team of Tawainese steamed bao bun specialists. The gloriously soft and plump milk-based white bao buns— skillfully stuffed with top Cornish braised pork, peanut powder, and fermented greens, plus fried chicken, crumbed daikon, or lamb shoulder with soy-pickled chilies and garlicky mayo—are the undisputed stars of this tightly-packed show. Start off with the silky scallops in yellow bean garlic sauce and finish with a fried bao bun stuffed with a ball of Horlicks ice cream. $ *Average main: £5* ⊠ *53 Lexington St., Soho* ⊕ *www.baolondon.com* ☽ *Closed Sun.* ⚱ *Reservations not accepted* Ⓜ *Tottenham Court Rd* ✛ *3:B5.*

**$**
**CAFÉ**

✕ **Bar Italia.** This legendary Italian coffee bar on Frith Street is Soho's unofficial beating heart and a 22-hours-a-day institution. Established in 1949 during the Italian coffee bar craze and still run by the founding Polledri family, today most regulars grab an espresso or frothy cappuccino made from the vintage Gaggia coffee machine, and wolf down a slice of pizza, bacon sandwich, or chocolate cake at one of the mirrored bar counters. The walls are plastered with photos of Italian opera singers, movie legends, and '50s world boxing champs, and it is *the* best spot in London to watch Italy play during the World Cup. $ *Average main: £6* ⊠ *22 Frith St., Soho* ☎ *020/7437–4520* ⊕ *www.baritaliasoho. co.uk* ⚱ *Reservations not accepted* Ⓜ *Leicester Sq.* ✛ *3:D5.*

**$**
**STEAKHOUSE**
**FAMILY**
**Fodor's**Choice
**★**

✕ **Blacklock.** This subterranean meatopia serves up £20 platters of delectable char-grilled grass-fed lamb, beef, and pork skinny chops and juice-soaked flatbread, all served on antique pearlware. Supplied by ace butchers Philip Warren from Launceston in Cornwall, Blacklock's killer chops are beautifully seasoned and seared on an open charcoal grill under vintage Blacklock irons from the Deep South. The all-in platter includes slinky starters of Peter's Yard crisp breads topped with egg and anchovy and punchy sides like barbecued baby gems or the 10-hour ash-roasted sweet potato. There's wine on tap and the no-choice dessert is a liberal portion of white chocolate cheesecake, served tableside. Note that they only take reservations for groups with more than six people. $ *Average main: £10* ⊠ *The Basement, 24 Great Windmill St., Soho* ☎ *020/3441–6996* ⊕ *www. theblacklock.com* Ⓜ *Piccadilly Circus* ✛ *3:C5.*

**$$**
**FRENCH**
**Fodor's**Choice
**★**

✕ **Blanchette.** French tapas may sound sacrilegious, but Blanchette hits the nail on the head at this rustic chic hipster headquarters where a jazzy soundtrack complements the charming candlelit, art nouveau–tiled interior. Visually feast on the flea-market bric-a-brac and order a few small plates to share. Tables are cramped, but the crispy frogs' legs and truffle saucisson are spot on, while the seasonal veg and zingy salads, like leek vinaigrette with wild mushrooms, are off the scale. Baked scallops come with a spunky Café de Paris sauce, and desserts like macerated fruits with white wine sabayon are a fitting Gallic finale. $ *Average main: £18* ⊠ *9 D'Arblay St., Soho* ☎ *020/7439–8100* ⊕ *www.blanchettesoho. co.uk* ⚱ *Reservations essential* Ⓜ *Tottenham Court Rd.* ✛ *3:C4.*

**14**

**$$** ✕ **Bocca di Lupo.** This redbrick-fronted place is always packed and the
ITALIAN   tables jammed too close together, but everyone still rolls up for la dolce
vita and chef Jacob Kenedy's wicked spread of rustic regional Ital-
ian fare. Located off Theatreland's Shaftesbury Avenue in Soho, the
always-popular family-run trattoria offers a magnificent menu featuring
peasant-based pastas, stews, roasts, and crudité from Lazio to Pied-
mont, Bologna to Trentino. Try the Calabrian orecchiette pasta with
'nduja pork sausage or the Sicilian lobster spaghetti touched off with
mussels and ginger. Limber up with an Aperol spritz before plung-
ing into the regional Italocentric wine list, which weaves from Super
Tuscans to rare Barolos. ⑤ *Average main: £20* ✉ *12 Archer St., Soho*
☎ *020/7734–2223* ⊕ *www.boccadilupo.com* ⌕ *Reservations essential*
Ⓜ *Piccadilly Circus* ✛ *3:C5.*

**$$** ✕ **Burger & Lobster.** At this busy, limited-choice burger-and-lobster zone
BURGER   in Soho, there are no reservations (apart from larger groups), no start-
FAMILY   ers, and no printed menu—the blackboard says it all: "Burger or lob-
**Fodor's**Choice   ster or lobster roll. All with chips & salad. £20." Of the three choices
★   available, the Nova Scotia lobster is the best value; it comes in a but-
ter-soaked brioche bun, with wasabi mayo sauce and a sturdy pot of
fries. Sweet halved lobsters are served with lemon butter, while the
Worcestershire sauce–seasoned burgers are a hunky-dory mix of Irish
grass-fed beef and corn-fed cuts from Nebraska, with streaky bacon
or Monterey Jack cheese on top. ⑤ *Average main: £20* ✉ *36 Dean St.,
Soho* ☎ *020/7432–4800* ⊕ *www.burgerandlobster.com* ⌕ *Reservations
not accepted* Ⓜ *Piccadilly Circus, Tottenham Court Rd.* ✛ *3:D5.*

**$$** ✕ **Dean Street Townhouse.** Everyone feels 10 times more glamorous at
BRITISH   this candlelit Soho media muster attached to the 39-room Georgian
FAMILY   hotel of the same name; *simpatico* lighting, dark oak floors, red leather
banquettes, raised bar seats, and crack service create a hip hangout
for London's coolest. No frills, no fuss: retro-British favorites include
ham-and-pea soup, old-school mince and potatoes, twice-baked smoked
haddock soufflé, fish fingers, and yummy sherry trifle. You'll also find
traditional fruit scones and buttered crumpets for afternoon tea, and
Welsh rarebit for high tea. ⑤ *Average main: £21* ✉ *69–71 Dean St.,
Soho* ☎ *020/7434–1775* ⊕ *www.deanstreettownhouse.com* ⌕ *Reserva-
tions essential* Ⓜ *Oxford Circus, Tottenham Court Rd.* ✛ *3:D5.*

**$** ✕ **Flat Iron.** Premium £10 Dexter steaks are the only mains on the printed
STEAKHOUSE   menu at this three-story hipster canteen on Beak Street in Soho, decked
FAMILY   out in exposed brick walls, enamel lights, and shared wooden tables.
The char-grilled shoulder cuts of grass-fed beef arrive sliced on wooden
blocks with watercress and mini meat cleavers. Sides include beef-drip-
ping chips, creamed spinach, and roasted eggplant with Parmesan, while
sauces include Béarnaise and French horseradish cream. Check Twitter
for daily specials like the 12-hour braised Hereford heifer steaks or a
Brazilian-style "Picanha" steak from grass-fed Galloway cows. ⑤ *Aver-
age main: £10* ✉ *17 Beak St., Soho* ⊕ *www.flatironsteak.co.uk* ⌕ *Reser-
vations not accepted* Ⓜ *Oxford Circus, Piccadilly Circus* ✛ *3:B5.*

$

SRI LANKAN

FAMILY

Fodor's Choice

★

✕ **Hoppers.** Londoners have gone mad for the cheap Sri Lankan fermented white rice and coconut milk-based steamed *hoppers* (pancakes) and griddled dosas at this highly spiced Soho haunt. The chefs here swirl the hopper batter in woklike *appachatti* pans to form the bowl-shape pancakes with a spongy center and crisp edges. Some have soft-cooked eggs in the middle, while others pair with wonderfully spiced curried meat, seafood, or a fenugreek-rich *kiri hoddy* vegetable broth. Three relishes—fresh coconut, caramelized onion, and chili and dried Maldives fish flakes—are also on hand. The delicious dosas come with coconut or curry-leaf chutney; look for the Ceylon spit chicken with coconut rotis and *watalappan* (steamed custard pudding). Ⓢ *Average main: £5* ✉ *49 Frith St., Soho* ☎ *020/3040–0887* ⊕ *www.hopperslondon.com* ⌕ *Reservations not accepted* Ⓜ *Tottenham Court Rd., Oxford Circus* ⊹ *3:D4.*

$

CAFÉ

FAMILY

✕ **Maison Bertaux.** Francophiles and romantics cherish this quirky, two-story 1871 French pâtisserie, vintage tea parlor, and occasional pop-up art space, where happily nothing seems to have changed since the 1940s. Colorful pastries, tarts, croissants, and sweet cakes are still well loved and baked on-site; you can choose from the chocolate and fruit éclairs, Saint-Honoré and Black Forest gâteaux, marzipan figs, and flaky almond croissants. Maison Bertaux also hosts a cheery retro afternoon tea service, which comes with tasty savories like Dijon slice or broccoli quiche. Ⓢ *Average main: £7* ✉ *28 Greek St., Soho* ☎ *020/7437–6007* ⊕ *www.maisonbertaux.com* ⊟ *No credit cards* ⌕ *Reservations not accepted* Ⓜ *Leicester Sq.* ⊹ *3:D5.*

$

MIDDLE EASTERN

Fodor's Choice

★

✕ **The Palomar.** It's Jerusalem meets Palestine meets Beirut meets a bonkers scenester vibe at this Arab-Israeli funky food party zone. Sit down at the 16-seat open-kitchen counter and down shots of *arak* while trading quips over the booming soundtrack with the Middle Eastern chefs, who offer a mélange of Levantine delights. Rip away at Yemeni Jewish challah-style *kubaneh* bread before digging into truffled Jerusalem polenta with a smoky mushroom ragù. Paprika-laced pork-belly tagine with Israeli couscous is a must, as is the Persian oxtail stew and Palestinian steak tartare. Look for the lavish Kurdish-style mussels inspired by the head chef's beloved grandmother. Ⓢ *Average main: £14* ✉ *34 Rupert St., Soho* ☎ *020/7439–8777* ⊕ *www.thepalomar.co.uk* ⌕ *Reservations essential* Ⓜ *Piccadilly Circus, Leicester Sq.* ⊹ *3:D6.*

$$

ITALIAN

FAMILY

✕ **Polpetto.** Smashing the ruff 'n' tumble Soho dining scene with its Venetian-style small plates, Polpetto is a feminine wonderland of white linen–covered hanging lamps, distressed Farrow & Ball duck-egg-blue plaster walls, a tintile ceiling, and glowing maple-wood tabletops and flooring. The regional and seasonal Italian ingredients do all the talking, from a dazzling creamy Puglian burrata with *agretti* (monk's beard) to simple crab and chili linguine. Besides favorites like pork and fennel meatballs or pistachio and polenta cake, you'll swoon over heartier dishes like beef-shank pappardelle with rich chicken-liver ragù. Note that reservations are only accepted for lunch. Ⓢ *Average main: £16* ✉ *11 Berwick St., Soho* ☎ *020/7439–8627* ⊕ *www.polpetto.co.uk* ⌕ *Reservations not accepted* Ⓜ *Tottenham Court Rd., Oxford Circus* ⊹ *3:C4.*

**14**

**$$$**  ✕ **Social Eating House.** At this lighthearted but brilliant French bistrono-
FRENCH  mie hangout, witty and pretty dishes like smoked duck's ham (made
FAMILY  from cured duck's breast) and Scotch-egg-and-chips are served along-
**Fodor's** Choice  side the unique "CLT," consisting of white crabmeat, lettuce, and roast
★  heritage tomato. The moodily lit bare-brick salon is tricked out with
dark parquet floors, antique mirrored ceilings, and red leather ban-
quettes. The first-floor speakeasy, the Blind Pig, is very hip, and the
£21 set lunch is seriously worth investigating. ⑤ *Average main: £25*
✉ *58 Poland St., Soho* ☎ *020/7993–3251* ⊕ *www.socialeatinghouse.
com* ⊗ *Closed Sun.* ⚐ *Reservations essential* Ⓜ *Oxford Circus, Tot-
tenham Court Rd.* ✛ *3:B4.*

**$**  ✕ **Spuntino.** Edison bulbs, bluegrass tunes, popcorn machine, and only
DINER  27 raised counter stools at this pewter-top bar and Lower East Side diner
make for one of the coolest spots in town. Naturally, there's no phone, no
reservations, and minimal signage, but that only adds to the speakeasy
vibe. Once seated, settle in with a Brooklyn Manhattan cocktail and then
dive into truffled egg toast before moving on to deep-fried grits, softshell
crab, or mini Yankee sliders (try the salt beef with dill). Don't overlook
the glorious mac 'n' cheese, and for dessert, go for a PB&J sandwich.
⑤ *Average main: £12* ✉ *61 Rupert St., Soho* ⊕ *www.spuntino.co.uk*
⚐ *Reservations not accepted* Ⓜ *Piccadilly Circus* ✛ *3:C5.*

**$$**  ✕ **10 Greek Street.** There may only be 28 table seats and nine coun-
MODERN  ter stools overlooking the open kitchen at this stripped-down Modern
EUROPEAN  European Soho humdinger, but the great food, cheap wine, good prices,
and excellent service more than make up for it. The only downside is
the evenings-only no-reservations policy, but most happily saunter off
for a drink at the local pub two doors down and wait to be called back
on their cell phones. Once seated, expect simple starters and mains like
butternut ravioli with sage, or scallops and chorizo. Gutsy meats like
Brecon lamb shank with mash or venison with potato galette are big
and bold, and swing with the seasons. ⑤ *Average main: £17* ✉ *10 Greek
St., Soho* ☎ *020/7734–4677* ⊕ *www.10greekstreet.com* ⊗ *Closed Sun.*
⚐ *Reservations not accepted* Ⓜ *Tottenham Court Rd.* ✛ *3:D4.*

## COVENT GARDEN

**$$**  ✕ **Balthazar.** Restaurateur Keith McNally recreates his famed New York
BRASSERIE  Parisian brasserie at this winning spot off Covent Garden's piazza. The
FAMILY  decor (distressed vintage mirrors, illuminated columns, pewter-top bar,
and mosaic floors) creates an enchanting backdrop to enjoy a clas-
sic all-day French brasserie menu of few surprises. Pick out flavor-
packed dishes like macaroni and Gruyère cheese, duck Shepherd's pie,
or ox cheek Bourguignonne, and linger over the all-French wine list,
which carries everything from a modest 2012 Colombier Chablis to a
grand 1971 Château Palmer Margaux (£540 a pop). ⑤ *Average main:
£21* ✉ *4–7 Russell St., Covent Garden* ☎ *020/3301–1155* ⊕ *www.
balthazarlondon.com* ⚐ *Reservations essential* Ⓜ *Covent Garden,
Charing Cross* ✛ *3:F5.*

**$$$**  ✕ **Barrafina.** London's top Spanish tapas bar is modeled after Cal Pep in
TAPAS  Barcelona, and similarly has only a few raised bar stools (29 in total) at
**Fodor's** Choice  the three-sided marble-top counter. It's no-reservations, but the tapas are
★  well worth the wait. Some of the brilliant small plates prepared in front of

you include giant Spanish red *carabineros* (scarlet prawns), black squid-ink risotto with cuttlefish, rare Galician *percebes* ("goose barnacles") crustaceans, and octopus with capers, plus classics like Spanish tortillas, spicy chorizo, and thin-sliced cured Montanera ham. There's a crack selection of Spanish reds, whites, sherries, and sparkling cavas, and leave room for desserts like the Catalan crème brûlée or the almond-based Santiago tart. Note that they don't seat parties larger than four. ⑤ *Average main: £26* ✉ *10 Adelaide St., Covent Garden* 🖥 ⊕ *www.barrafina.co.uk* ⌁ *Reservations not accepted* Ⓜ *Charing Cross, Leicester Sq.* ✛ *3:E6.*

**$$$**
FRENCH
FAMILY

✕ **Clos Maggiore.** Insist on a seat in the white blossom–filled sky-lit conservatory at this warm and seriously romantic Provençal country inn–style escape in the heart of Covent Garden. A bouquet's throw away from the Royal Opera House, service is decidedly Gallic and formal, while the warren of candlelit, oak-paneled rooms and open fires never fails to enchant. Meal deals and theater specials are a cute way in, where you'll be wooed by unapologetically old-fashioned and refined French cuisine, such as Loire Valley rabbit ballotine, poached wild turbot with herring-roe beurre blanc, or Charolais beef cheeks with fine French beans. ⑤ *Average main: £25* ✉ *33 King St., Covent Garden* 🖥 *020/7379–9696* ⊕ *www. closmaggiore.com* ⌁ *Reservations essential* Ⓜ *Covent Garden* ✛ *3:F5.*

**$**
BISTRO
FAMILY

✕ **Côte.** Where else can you find an amazing three-course French meal in Covent Garden for £13.65? The Côte brasserie chain—softly lighted and decked out in gray-and-white striped awnings and Parisian-style café tables—does the trick, and offers popular daily meal deals from noon until 7 pm. With four choices per course, you'll find all your classic French brasserie favorites: crêpes with mushrooms and Gruyère cheese, boeuf Bourguignonne, *moules marinières* (mussels with white wine), and iced berries and white chocolate sauce. Service is brisk and friendly, and if you're lucky enough to be attending a performance at the nearby Royal Opera House, this is perfect for a pretheater (or posttheater) meal. ⑤ *Average main: £12* ✉ *17–21 Tavistock St., Covent Garden* 🖥 *020/7379–9991* ⊕ *www.cote-restaurants.co.uk* ⌁ *Reservations essential* Ⓜ *Covent Garden* ✛ *3:G5.*

**$$**
MODERN BRITISH
FAMILY

✕ **Great Queen Street.** Expect a boisterous foodie crowd here at one of Covent Garden's leading gastropubs, which proudly serves hearty retro-British dishes. Unadulterated wine-fueled diners dive into nostalgic yesteryear offerings like pressed tongue, pickled herrings, pigs' cheeks, or smoked mackerel with rhubarb. You'll find stacks of other unpretentious vintage British fare, like brown crab on toast and rabbit livers, plus hunking carve-your-own roasts for the table—think seven-hour shoulder of lamb with dauphinoise potatoes. Salads and veggies follow the same theme, from sweet heritage carrots to forgotten Roseval potatoes. ⑤ *Average main: £17* ✉ *32 Great Queen St., Covent Garden* 🖥 *020/7242–0622* ⊕ *www.greatqueenstreetrestaurant.co.uk* ☽ *No dinner Sun.* ⌁ *Reservations essential* Ⓜ *Covent Garden, Holborn* ✛ *3:G4.*

**$$**
BRITISH
FAMILY
**Fodor's**Choice
★

✕ **The Ivy.** London's most famous celebrity haunt and West End landmark is still so popular it receives a thousand calls a day. Established in 1917, nowadays a mesmerizing mix of celebrities and out-of-towners dine on Thai-baked sea bass, calf's liver, potato gnocchi, and good ole English classics like Shepherd's pie. Perch at the central coral onyx

**14**

dining bar in pink mohair-backed raised seats, and enjoy the best free theater in town. $ *Average main: £21* ⊠ *1–5 West St., Covent Garden* ☎ *020/7836–4751* ⊕ *www.the-ivy.co.uk* ⚒ *Reservations essential* Ⓜ *Covent Garden* ✛ *3:E5.*

$$    ✕ **Ivy Market Grill.** Scrub up like Eliza Doolittle and perch at the pewter
BRITISH  bar sipping a dreamy My Fair Lady (with housemade gin and orange
FAMILY   blossom) at this Covent Garden laid-back little sister to the famed Ivy restaurant. Mottled green leather banquettes and dark timber tables are stunningly set off by late 19th-century brass lamps and chandeliers. If a "three martini lunch" isn't your thing, there's bargains galore on the all-day menu—from warm crispy duck salad and poached lobster cocktail to chicken Milanese and Shepherd's pie. For dessert, be sure to try the chocolate bombe, a chocolatey mush of milk foam, vanilla ice cream, and hot salted caramel sauce. $ *Average main: £16* ⊠ *1 Henrietta St., Covent Garden* ☎ *0203/3301–0200* ⊕ *www.theivymarketgrill. com* ⚒ *Reservations essential* Ⓜ *Covent Garden* ✛ *3:F5.*

$$$   ✕ **J Sheekey.** This classy 1896 side-alley seafood haven is a discreet
SEAFOOD  alternative to the more overtly celeb-central Scott's, 34, or The Ivy. Beautifully orchestrated by longtime maître d' John Andrews, Sheekey charms with warm wood panelling, vintage showbiz black-and-white portraits, and twinkly lava-rock bar tops. Opt for snappingly fresh Atlantic prawns, pickled Arctic herrings, scallop, shrimp, and salmon burgers or the famous Sheekey Fish Pie. Better still, sip Gaston Chiquet Champagne and down half a dozen briny Fine de Claire rock oysters at the antique mirrored oyster bar for the ultimate in true romance. $ *Average main: £26* ⊠ *28–35 St. Martin's Ct., Covent Garden* ☎ *020/7240–2565* ⊕ *www.j-sheekey.co.uk* ⚒ *Reservations essential* Ⓜ *Leicester Sq.* ✛ *3:E6.*

$$   ✕ **Opera Tavern.** Ibérico pig's head terrine or moreish foie gras and Man-
TAPAS  chego mini cheeseburgers are a few of the outstanding hybrid Spanish and Italian tapas found at the Opera Tavern in Covent Garden. After enjoying a snack of crispy pigs' ears or guindilla peppers, opt for a gentle flow of rich venison empanadas, Italian Scotch eggs, braised cuttlefish, wood pigeon with scamorza cheese, or char-grilled Venetian-style sardines. Veggies are their specialty—like stuffed courgette flower with goat cheese and honey—and desserts like dulce de leche panna cotta hit the spot. $ *Average main: £18* ⊠ *23 Catherine St., Covent Garden* ☎ *020/7836–3680* ⊕ *www.operatavern.co.uk* ⚒ *Reservations essential* Ⓜ *Covent Garden, Holborn* ✛ *3:G5.*

$$$         ✕ **Rules.** Opened in 1798, London's oldest restaurant is still London's
BRITISH       most beautiful. The main dining salons are a High Victorian won-
FAMILY        derland with lacquered yellow walls, etched-glass skylights, and every
Fodor's Choice  cranny covered with Regency oil paintings, antique clocks, and endless
★             prints and etchings. Little wonder Rules has fed everyone from Charles Dickens to Sir Laurence Olivier. Ask for a table in one of the skylight rooms, the bar area, or the Margaret Thatcher corner, then dig into classic British fare like jugged hare, steak-and-kidney pie, or roast beef and Yorkshire pudding. For a taste of the 18th century, choose game from the restaurant's High Pennines Lartington estate, including roast grouse, partridge, and snipe. $ *Average main: £28* ⊠ *35 Maiden La.,*

*Covent Garden* ☎ *020/7836–5314* ⊕ *www.rules.co.uk* ⚞ *Reservations essential* 🏛 *Jacket required* Ⓜ *Covent Garden* ✛ *3:F6.*

**$$$**
BRITISH
FAMILY
✕ **Savoy Grill.** You can feel the history in the room at this 1889 art deco hotel-dining powerhouse, which has hosted everyone from Oscar Wilde and Winston Churchill to Liz Taylor and Marilyn Monroe. Nowadays it caters to business barons, nostalgia lovers, and tourists who come for the Grill's famed tableside trolley, which might trundle up laden with hulking great roasts like beef Wellington, rack of pork, or saddle of lamb. Savoy signatures like omelet Arnold Bennett (with smoked haddock, double cream, and Parmesan) or baked egg cocotte with bacon, wild mushrooms, and red wine sauce excel, as do the timeless standbys like T-bone and Chateaubriand steaks. Ⓢ *Average main: £31* ✉ *The Savoy, 100 The Strand, Covent Garden* ☎ *020/7592–1600 for reservations only* ⊕ *www.gordonramsay.com/thesavoygrill* ⚞ *Reservations essential* Ⓜ *Charing Cross, Covent Garden* ✛ *3:G6.*

**14**

**$$$**
ITALIAN
✕ **Spring.** Australian chef Skye Gyngell worships the four seasons at this high-ceilinged and pillared dining salon in majestic Somerset House. A former Tudor royal palace and home to luminaries such as Elizabeth I and Catherine of Braganza, Gyngell offers his discerning crowd healthy produce-driven Italian dishes, from a tousled heap of Fern Verrow salad leaves to charred veal chop with anchovy courgettes. All bread, butter, yogurt, ice cream, cordials, bitters, vermouth, and tonics are made onsite. Ⓢ *Average main: £29* ✉ *Somerset House, Lancaster Pl., Covent Garden* ✛ *Turn right on entering courtyard at Someset House from Strand* ☎ *020/3011–0115* ⊕ *www.springrestaurant.co.uk* ☾ *No dinner Sun.* ⚞ *Reservations essential* Ⓜ *Holborn, Charring Cross* ✛ *3:G6.*

**$**
MEXICAN
FAMILY
✕ **Wahaca.** Crowds come for the fab-value Mexican street food at former MasterChef winner Thomasina Miers' brightly colored Covent Garden establishment. Concrete walls, shared wooden bench seating, and colorful murals make for a brisk and breezy basement setting, but it's the inexpensive, ethically and sustainably sourced Mexican market-style tacos, enchiladas, quesadillas, taquitos, and burritos that pull in the budget-conscious student and touristy crowds. A generous £21.95 spread for two hungry honchos to share will produce a feast of broad-bean quesadillas, pork pibil tacos, slaw, chicken tinga taquitos with green rice, black bean tostadas, and guacamole, but note that the Mexican music is often cranked up loud and the restaurant is invariably packed by 6:30 pm. Ⓢ *Average main: £7* ✉ *66 Chandos Pl., Covent Garden* ☎ *020/7240–1883* ⊕ *www.wahaca.co.uk* ⚞ *Reservations not accepted* Ⓜ *Covent Garden* ✛ *3:F6.*

## BLOOMSBURY, HOLBORN, AND FITZROVIA

The literary giants of the Bloomsbury set—from Virginia Woolf to E.M. Forster and Vanessa Bell—may be long gone but this bluestocking enclave (centered on the British Library and University of London) still excels at a cultured and pleasure-loving dining scene. Holborn, bordering Covent Garden, has some of those big, old-establishment hotel dining rooms, as well as a big, bright elegant shining star in The Delaunay on the Aldwych.

## BLOOMSBURY

$ ✕ **Dishoom.** Whirring ceiling fans, Indian film posters, and vintage Indian
MODERN INDIAN cola bottles create an evocative Bombay backdrop for this all-day Indian
FAMILY café at King's Cross. Modeled after the Persian-run Irani cafés of Victorian Bombay, try the hot naan bread with keema minced lamb and peas, or classic chili jam spiked and handkerchief-thin spicy charred chicken tikka roomali roti rolls. Drinks and tipples range from a Bollybellini to Limca lemonade or a mango-and-fennel-rich yogurt lassi. Reservations can be made only for groups larger than six people. $ *Average main: £7* ✉ *5 Stable St., King's Cross* ☎ *020/7420–9321* ⊕ *www.dishoom.com* ⚱ *Reservations not accepted* Ⓜ *King's Cross* ✛ *2:C1.*

$$ ✕ **Grain Store.** Located in a 1851 converted former grain warehouse,
MODERN FRENCH vegetables are the stars here, with earthy beetroot, artichoke, corn,
FAMILY quinoa, butternut squash, onions, potatoes, and shiitake mushrooms relegating proteins to the margins. In the kitchen-cum-dining room, the chef concocts veg-centric surprises like spiced mash, pickled cucumber, snowball turnips, and broad beans. You'll smirk at flourishes like the flowerpot of radishes that you roll in "olive soil" (dried black olives), and there's no denying the originality of the butternut squash ravioli or the brilliance of a humble vegetable "Scotch egg" with a tangle of fennel and aïoli. $ *Average main: £17* ✉ *Granary Sq., 1–3 Stable St., King's Cross* ☎ *020/7324–4466* ⊕ *www.grainstore.com* ☉ *No dinner Sun.* ⚱ *Reservations essential* Ⓜ *King's Cross, St. Pancras* ✛ *2:C1.*

## HOLBORN

$$ ✕ **The Delaunay.** It's all *fin de siècle* Vienna at this magnificent art
AUSTRIAN deco–style grand café on the Aldwych. Dishes on the majestic 60-item
FAMILY menu do the Austro-Hungarian Empire proud—think Wiener schnit-
Fodor'sChoice zels, Hungarian goulash, and *würstchen* (frankfurters and hot dogs),
★ served with sauerkraut and onions. There are other goodies like borscht and beef Stroganoff, kedgeree, and sour lamb-shank sauerbraten. Desserts delight, including an evocative three-peak Salzburg soufflé, while the innocuous Kinder ice cream coupe is a blowout, bursting with meringue, marshmallows, and whipped cream. $ *Average main: £20* ✉ *55 Aldwych, Holborn* ☎ *020/7499–8558* ⊕ *www.thedelaunay.com* ⚱ *Reservations essential* Ⓜ *Covent Garden, Holborn* ✛ *3:G4.*

## FITZROVIA

$$ ✕ **Berners Tavern.** All the cool cats swing by this grand brasserie at Ian
MODERN BRITISH Schrager's trendy London Edition Hotel. It's hard not to feel like a million dollars as you enter the dining salon crammed with 1835 stucco plasterwork, Grand Central Station–style bronze chandeliers, and 150-odd framed paintings. Start the day with a £16 full English breakfast (with herb sausage and Stornaway black pudding) and return for a light lunch of rock-shrimp roll or ironbark pumpkin risotto. Re-emerge refreshed for dinner, and swoon over the deep-fried duck egg, Cumbrian-ham-and-pea purée appetizer; then it's a toss-up between Creedy caver duck, Cornish cod, or Buccleuch Estate bavette. $ *Average main: £20* ✉ *The London Edition, 10 Berners St., Fitzrovia* ☎ *020/7908–7979* ⊕ *www.bernerstavern.com* ⚱ *Reservations essential* Ⓜ *Oxford Circus, Tottenham Court Rd.* ✛ *3:C3.*

**$$** ✕**Bonnie Gull Seafood Shack.** It almost feels like you're seaside here at
SEAFOOD    London's top seafood shack in Fitzrovia, where awesome fresh seafood
(from Shetland mussels to Brixham brill) takes diners on a tour of the
British Isles. Everything's bleached-out and weather-beaten at this tiny
42-seater, where you'll spot an old ship's bell and captain's hat, wall-
mounted rope *appliqué*, and a mini raw bar of iced Palourde clams and
Carlingford oysters stashed inside an antique sea chest. Start with Dorset
cockles or beer-battered queenie scallops with tartar sauce, and move
on to Selsey cod with Wye Valley asparagus or line-caught sea bass with
braised fennel. Desserts are Brit-focused with a twist (like Eton Mess with
basil jelly) and the staff are megafriendly. $ *Average main: £19* ✉ *21A
Foley St., Fitzrovia* ☎ *020/7436–0921* ⊕ *www.bonniegullseafoodshack.
com* ⚓ *Reservations essential* Ⓜ *Oxford Circus, Goodge St.* ✛ *3:B2.*

**$$** ✕**Dabbous.** Here at Dabbous, startlingly pure, inventive, and seasonally
MODERN    based new-wave dishes elicit excitement in the NYC industrial–chic set-
EUROPEAN    ting of exposed concrete and heavy metal screens and cages. Phenomenal
**Fodor's**Choice    flavors abound in ingredient-led dishes like a peas-and-mint appetizer
★    with frozen petit pois, mint oil, and edible violets, and a coddled hen's
egg with smoked butter and woodland mushrooms served in a rustic bowl
of hay. Palate-popping barbecued Romney Marsh lamb with lesser cala-
mint, halibut with coastal herbs (sea aster and oyster leaf), and chocolate
ganache with green basil moss are instant classics. $ *Average main: £23*
✉ *39 Whitfield St., Fitzrovia* ☎ *020/7323–1544* ⊕ *www.dabbous.co.uk*
☾ *Closed Sun.* ⚓ *Reservations essential* Ⓜ *Goodge St.* ✛ *3:C2.*

**$** ✕**Newman Arms.** Glimpse the future of British cuisine at this rickety
MODERN BRITISH    wood-paneled dining salon at the atmospheric 1730 Newman Arms pub
**Fodor's**Choice    in Fitzrovia. A one-time haunt of Dylan Thomas and George Orwell (it's
★    even mentioned in *1984*), the menu showcases the finest Cornish and
Devon-sourced meat, vegetables, and fresh fish with a rare instinctive
ease. Sashimi-thin slivers of mackerel happily vie with house-fermented
gherkins, while plump ducks' hearts pair off with baby beetroot and
outsized blackberries. Perfect turbot comes with charred whole baby
fennel plants seemingly pulled straight from the earth, and a block of
Old White pork belly mesmerizes with charred baby leeks, smoked
spelt, and a revelatory sauerkraut purée. $ *Average main: £14* ✉ *23
Rathbone St., Fitzrovia* ☎ *0020/3643–6285* ⊕ *www.newmanarmspub.
com* ⚓ *Reservations essential* Ⓜ *Goodge St* ✛ *3:C3.*

**$$** ✕**Portland.** Consistently brilliant modern fare in a low-key setting char-
MODERN    acterizes this restaurant on a quiet one-way street just north of Oxford
EUROPEAN    Circus. Marvel at the chef's brigade in the open kitchen before turn-
ing to a highly inventive seasonal produce–driven menu of exceptional
delights. The luscious Denham Estate deer is upstaged by a great glazed
heritage carrot with a dash of pickled elderberry sauce, while a rustic
game pithiver—heavy with whole mallard breasts, *duxelles* mushrooms,
black truffles, and game sauce—is a perennial smash. For dessert, you
might find an unlikely Jerusalem-artichoke ice cream accompanying
chocolate cake and hazel crémeux. Enjoy the thumping wine list, which
contains dozens of rare bottles. $ *Average main: £19* ✉ *113 Great Port-
land St., Fitzrovia* ☎ *020/7436–3261* ⊕ *www.portlandrestaurant.co.uk*
⚓ *Reservations essential* Ⓜ *Oxford Circus* ✛ *3:A2.*

**14**

## CLERKENWELL AND THE CITY

Historic and just beyond The City limits, chef-centric Clerkenwell is one of the most trendy and interesting quarters for London gastrodining, which sets it in marked contrast to the adjacent City, which caters overwhelmingly to business-focused dining. In Clerkenwell, the starchiness of The City fades into relaxed artiness: a fertile ground for avant-garde chefs and restaurants.

$ ✕ **Blixen.** Within a magnificent Kew Gardens–style tropical garden conservatory, you'll find this devilishly stylish all-day brasserie at Old Spitalfields Market. Housed in a former bank, Blixen offers evergreen European hits like squid, saffron, and chorizo or mushroom papardelle with semi-soft Taleggio cheese and hearty greens on its short but sweet (and inexpensive) menu. There's neat blueberry pancakes, potato rösti, or a raclette-rich croque madame for breakfast or brunch. Check out the small, nautically themed basement cocktail bar. $ *Average main: £13* ⊠ *65A Brushfield St., The City* ☎ *020/7101–0093* ⊕ *www.blixen. co.uk* Ⓜ *Liverpool St* ✛ *2:G2.*

BRASSERIE
FAMILY

$$$ ✕ **City Social.** A largely corporate crowd comes here for the Manhattanesque views of The City and the masterful and straightforward cuisine. Impressed diners look out on the majestic panoramas that take in buildings like the Gherkin and the Walkie Talkie. The Highland venison with braised red cabbage and smoked chestnuts is big, bold, and bloody, while a generous chunk of Isle of Gigha halibut with pancetta and sea kale is firm and meaty. The pistachio soufflé is a total winner, while service—like City Social itself—is stratospheric. $ *Average main: £24* ⊠ *Tower 42, 25 Old Broad St., The City* ☎ *020/7877–7703* ⊕ *www. citysociallondon.com* ◷ *Closed Sun.* ⚑ *Reservations essential* Ⓜ *Liverpool St.* ✛ *2:G2.*

MODERN BRITISH
**Fodor's**Choice
★

$ ✕ **Duck & Waffle.** Zoom up to the 40th floor of the Heron Tower and head straight for the cult signature dish of confit duck leg, Belgium waffle, fried duck egg, and grainy mustard maple syrup for a taste of awesomeness. Eclectic flourishes abound amid spectacular panoramas that take in the Tower of London, Tower Bridge, and the Gherkin. A wax-sealed paper bag contains spiced pigs ears, and the ox-cheek doughnuts with smoked paprika sugar are as big as tennis balls. Open 24/7 and often featuring live music, you might satisfy the munchies with a foie gras breakfast, served all day, with streaky bacon and homemade Nutella, an Elvis PB&J waffle with banana brûlée, or baked wild Cornish pollock meatballs with lobster cream. $ *Average main: £13* ⊠ *Heron Tower, 110 Bishopsgate, The City* ☎ *020/3640–7310* ⊕ *www. duckandwaffle.com* ⚑ *Reservations essential* Ⓜ *Liverpool St.* ✛ *2:G2.*

MODERN BRITISH
FAMILY
**Fodor's**Choice
★

$$$ ✕ **HKK.** World-class Peking duck—arguably the best in London—is the big thing at this Chinese trendsetter in The City. The Irish-sourced glazed Peking duck is marinated in five Chinese spices, cherrywood-roasted in a Beech oven, and carved ceremoniously by a specialist in the middle of the sleek dark-wood dining room. Diners can dab a caviar-topped dim sum trilogy with soy sauce (hope for the pan-fried Szechuan dumpling with Australian tiger prawns) while soups like truffled seafood with Osmanthus flower are rich and pungent. Sip white peony tea between courses of wok-fried Scottish lobster and Duke of Berkshire

CHINESE
FAMILY

pork with XO sauce, but only try the 15-course tasting menu if you have time and a big appetite. $ *Average main: £26* ⊠ *88 Worship St., The City* ☎ *020/3535–1888* ⊕ *www.hkklondon.com* ☽ *Closed Sun.* ⚴ *Reservations essential* Ⓜ *Liverpool St.* ✛ *2:G2.*

$$ ✕**The Modern Pantry.** It's around the world in 80 days at this popular
ECLECTIC two-story fusion food emporium on St. John's Square in Clerkenwell. Approach via the historic Jerusalem Passage, and kick off with a sugar-cured New Caledonian prawn omelet with green chilies, coriander, and Sri Lankan chili sambol, before moving on to slow-roasted Paddock Farm pork belly, Persian-spiced sweet potatoes, sour cherries, and *hijiki* relish. Ask the willing staff to decipher all the eclectic ingredients (such as Algerian *chermoula* marinade or Japanese *umeboshi* pickled plums) and look out for champion breakfasts and brunches, which are heavy with coconut waffles, English muffins, Rendang mince, and Urfa hash browns. $ *Average main: £18* ⊠ *47–48 St. John's Sq., Clerkenwell* ☎ *020/7553–9210* ⊕ *www.themodernpantry.co.uk* ☽ *Closed Mon. No dinner Sun.* ⚴ *Reservations essential* Ⓜ *Farringdon* ✛ *2:F3.*

$$ ✕**Moro.** Up from The City, you'll find Exmouth Market, a cluster of
MEDITERRANEAN cute indie boutiques, bookstores, vinyl shops, artisan bakeries, and
FAMILY more fine indie-spirited restaurants like this one. Lovingly nurtured for over a decade by husband-and-wife chefs Sam and Sam Clark, the menu includes a mélange of Spanish, Moroccan, and Moorish North African flavors. Flavor-packed tapas—like *babaganoush* (eggplant dip), Syrian lentils, and baby squid with harissa—compete with spiced meats, serrano ham, salt cod, and char-grilled offerings. Wood-fired sea bass with hispi cabbage, grilled lamb with aubergine, or sea bream with chickpea salad are among the standout mains. $ *Average main: £22* ⊠ *34–36 Exmouth Market, Clerkenwell* ☎ *020/7833–8336* ⊕ *www. moro.co.uk* ☽ *No dinner Sun.* ⚴ *Reservations essential* Ⓜ *Farringdon, Angel* ✛ *2:E3.*

$ ✕**Pitt Cue Co.** Everyone's gone bonkers for the Southern American BBQ
BARBECUE rare-breed Mangalitza pork-loin chops and bone marrow mash at this Broadgate trendsetter. Charred and flavor-packed oak- and ash-smoked offerings emerge from a blazing custom-built Grillworks wood grill. Lambs' hearts may come delicately sliced in a pool of viridian rosemary oil, but it's the fat-packed Cornish-reared Mangalitza pork chops, rack, or rib caps that really turn the dial. Look for the sucker-rich BBQ octopus, the blood cake, smoked scallops, or in-house baked malt bread slathered with beef drippings. Old school raisin-packed English lardy cake and house-churned ice cream make a fine finale. $ *Average main: £15* ⊠ *1 The Avenue, Devonshire Square, The City* ⊕ *www.pittcue. co.uk* ☽ *Closed weekends* Ⓜ *Liverpool Street* ✛ *2:G2.*

$ ✕**Simpson's Tavern.** The City of London's oldest tavern and chop house
BRITISH was founded in 1757 and is as every bit as raucous now as the day it
FAMILY opened. Approached via a cobbled Dickensian alley off Cornhill, it draws those who revel in the boarding school surroundings and are eager to down oodles of claret and English tavern-style grub—think potted shrimps, steak-and-kidney pie, grilled chump chops, and pots of stewed cheese. Desserts are schoolboy favorites like spotted dick and custard, and shared oak bench stalls, green cushions, and merry service

all add to the charm. $ *Average main: £9* ⊠ *Ball Court, 38½ Cornhill, The City* ☎ *020/7626–9985* ⊕ *www.simpsonstavern.co.uk* ⊘ *Closed weekends. No dinner* ⚶ *Reservations essential* Ⓜ *Bank* ✛ *2:G2.*

$$    ✕ **St. John.** Purists travel the globe for pioneering Brit-chef Fergus Henderson's nose-to-tail cuisine at this converted former smokehouse in Clerkenwell. Here Henderson uses all scraps of a carcass, and his waste-not, want-not chutzpah works. One appetizer is pig's skin and others like ox heart, rolled pig's spleen, or calves' brains and chicory are marginally less severe. Signatures like bone marrow and parsley salad, chitterlings with dandelion, or pheasant and pig's trotter pie appear stark on the plate, but arrive with aplomb. Finish with Eccles cakes and Lancashire cheese or half a dozen golden madeleines. $ *Average main: £19* ⊠ *26 St. John St., Clerkenwell* ☎ *020/7251–0848* ⊕ *www. stjohngroup.uk.com* ⊘ *No dinner Sun.* ⚶ *Reservations essential* Ⓜ *Farringdon, Barbican* ✛ *2:F4.*

MODERN BRITISH
FAMILY

$$    ✕ **Sweetings.** Established in 1889, little seems to have changed at this City time warp since the height of the British Empire. There are some things Sweetings doesn't do: dinner, reservations, coffee, or weekends. It does, mercifully, do seafood—and rather well. Not far from St. Paul's Cathedral, the restaurant is patronized by diners who down tankards of Black Velvet (Guinness and Champagne) and love to eat the potted shrimps, Dover sole, and skate wings with black butter sauce. West Mersea oysters are fresh and plump, and desserts like the baked jam roll are reliable. $ *Average main: £23* ⊠ *39 Queen Victoria St., The City* ☎ *020/7248–3062* ⊕ *www.sweetingsrestaurant.com* ⊘ *Closed weekends. No dinner* ⚶ *Reservations not accepted* Ⓜ *Mansion House* ✛ *2:H6.*

SEAFOOD

# EAST LONDON

An invasion of hipsters and foodies has transformed the once-bleak East End food scene into the city's most daring dining zone. Seek out new British breakout stars like Lyle's in Shoreditch or the Typing Room in Bethnal Green, or hunt down a nighttime food truck for a blast of the foodie underground.

$$    ✕ **Bistrotheque.** You'll need a GPS to find this East End fashionista headquarters located down an alley in Bethnal Green. Once inside, check out the striking loft dining space and bar in its postindustrial chic setting. Polished French and English dishes range from steak tartare and croque madame to cod and clams and Longhorn beef with red wine sauce. Be sure to catch the resident pianist at weekend brunch, camping up everything from Katy Perry to Girls Aloud on the baby grand. $ *Average main: £21* ⊠ *23–27 Wadeson St., Bethnal Green* ☎ *020/8983–7900* ⊕ *www.bistrotheque.com* ⚶ *Reservations essential* Ⓜ *Bethnal Green* ✛ *2:H1.*

MODERN
EUROPEAN

$    ✕ **E Pellicci.** It's all Cockney banter and full English breakfasts at this tiny 1900 family-run greasy spoon near the East End's Brick Lane and Columbia Road markets. It's a rowdy hole-in-the-wall for the greasy fry-ups Londoners still adore: eggs, bacon, sausages, baked beans, toast, tomatoes, mushrooms, black pudding, tea, and bubble-and-squeak

CAFÉ
FAMILY

(cabbage 'n' mash). Matriarch Mama Maria also rustles up Toscana spaghetti and lasagna, plus steamed sponge and bread pudding. Your arteries may clog up, but your wallet will survive, as everything's less than £8.20, but be aware it's cash only. $ *Average main: £8* ⊠ *332 Bethnal Green Rd., Bethnal Green* ☎ *020/7739–4873* ▬ *No credit cards* ☾ *Closed Sun.* ⚑ *Reservations not accepted* Ⓜ *Bethnal Green* ⊹ *2:H1.*

**$$** ✗ **Lyle's.** British chef and co-owner James Lowe forsakes sauces and sorcery at this stripped-back, Shoreditch-cool informal dining mecca. Über-stark but inventive local ingredients and dishes may include house-cured cod with radiant nasturtium flowers, or a combo of 24-hour megafresh Cornish Helford Estuary monkfish with wood sorel and pick-your-own East Sussex greengages. A firm slice of treacle tart comes with a neat blob of raw double cream, while all the top-notch sourdough bread, butter, charcuterie, pickles, and preserves are made in-house. Look for the Neal's Yard cheese plates (try Tymsboro and Stickleton), and marvel that wines by the glass start at £3.50. $ *Average main: £16* ⊠ *Tea Building, 56 Shoreditch High St., East End* ☎ *020/3011–5911* ⊕ *www.lyleslondon.com* ☾ *Closed Sun. and bank holiday Mon.* ⚑ *Reservations essential* Ⓜ *Shoreditch High St.* ⊹ *2:G1.*

MODERN BRITISH
**Fodor's**Choice
★

**$$** ✗ **Merchants Tavern.** The legend on the front of this Hoxton sleeper reads "Merchants of Good Fortune," and that sums up the exceptional smart-casual dining experience you'll encounter within. Seasonal, veg-focused left-field hits from France, Italy, and Britain emerge from the open kitchen inside the spacious dining salon and craft-beer bar, housed in a former Victorian warehouse and onetime apothecary. The rare-pink venison with braised red cabbage, Alsace bacon, and celeriac is unbelievably good, as are other peachy dishes like roast lamb with "forgotten" carrots, quail with foie gras, or wild partridge with sage polenta. Enjoy vanilla panna cotta with unstoned damsons, and don't forget about the £18 set lunch. $ *Average main: £19* ⊠ *38 Charlotte St., Hoxton* ☎ *0207/060–5335* ⊕ *www.merchantstavern.co.uk* ⚑ *Reservations essential* Ⓜ *Old St.* ⊹ *2:G1.*

FRENCH FUSION

**$$** ✗ **Rochelle Canteen.** You feel like quite the foodie insider once you finally track down the quirky Rochelle Canteen—it's set in a former bike shed at the Victorian-era Rochelle School. Ring the buzzer next to a blue door, go through the "Boys" entrance, and enter the long white canteen, which has an open kitchen and two long Formica tables, Ercol chairs, and Shaker coat pegs. Gloriously understated British fare ranges from deviled kidneys on toast to Yorkshire ham and parsley sauce. Bump along with the Frieze London art crowd, and enjoy guinea fowl with bacon or skate and capers, and finish with quince jelly or lemon posset. $ *Average main: £16* ⊠ *Rochelle School, Arnold Circus, Shoreditch* ☎ *020/7729–5677 for reservations only* ⊕ *www.arnoldandhenderson.com* ☾ *Closed weekends. No dinner* ⚑ *Reservations essential* Ⓜ *Liverpool St., Shoreditch High St.* ⊹ *2:G1.*

BRITISH
FAMILY

**$$** ✗ **Typing Room.** Star chef Lee Westcott attracts all of London's dining elite with his baroque natural dishes at this stupendious dining salon within the Town Hall Hotel in Bethnal Green. Watch Westcott in the open kitchen plate up fizzy dishes like raw, roasted, and deep-fried yeasted cauliflower with capers, raisins, and mint sauce; crinkly cod

MODERN BRITISH
**Fodor's**Choice
★

**14**

skins with smoked cod-roe cream; and smashes like duck, chicory, squash, chestnut, and plum sauce on the two-to-seven-course tasting menus. The brilliant wines are weighted towards natural and biodynamic. $ *Average main: £20* ⊠ *Town Hall Hotel, Patriot Sq., entrance on Cambridge Heath Rd., Bethnal Green* ☎ *020/7871–0461* ⊕ *www. typingroom.com* ⚄ *Reservations essential* Ⓜ *Bethnal Green* ✛ *2:H1.*

# SOUTH OF THE THAMES

First mentioned in 1276 and believed to have existed in Roman times, Borough Market in Southwark on the South Bank is a firm favorite with tourists, chefs, and foodies alike. Open Wednesday–Thursday 10–5, Friday 10–6, and Saturday 8–5, this Dickensian location under moody Victorian wrought-iron railway arches at London Bridge is packed with food lovers eager to pick up the finest and freshest fruit, vegetables, and grub in town. There are more than 130 stalls, plus a bunch of nearby pubs, bars, restaurants, and specialty shops. Ever more groovy new eateries are springing up in nearby Bermondsey Street, just south of The Shard.

**$$**
MODERN BRITISH
FAMILY

✕ **Anchor & Hope.** Exceptional Brit-focused fish and meat dishes at wallet-friendly prices fly out of the open kitchen at this permanently packed, no-reservations (apart for Sunday lunchtime) gastropub in Southwark. Pot-roast duck, braised pigs' cheeks, Swaledale steaks, guinea fowl pie, Arbroath smokies, and Orkney kippers keep the British flag flying and punch above their weight in terms of taste and tenderness. Mains are well priced at £9–£19, but bear in mind it's noisy, cramped, achingly informal, and always frightfully overcrowded. That said, the kitchen has smarts, and you'll find great feasting dishes to share—like the Sunday lunch seven-hour roasted shoulder of lamb or the carve-your-own whole roasted chicken that can easily feed three to four people. $ *Average main: £16* ⊠ *36 The Cut, Southwark* ☎ *020/7928–9898* ⊕ *www. anchorandhopepub.co.uk* ☉ *No dinner Sun.; no lunch Mon.* ⚄ *Reservations not accepted* Ⓜ *Waterloo, Southwark* ✛ *5:F2.*

**$$**
BISTRO
**Fodor's**Choice
★

✕ **Casse-Croûte.** French radio plays in the background, and a chubby Michelin Man perches benignly over the bar at this jaunty Parisian-style French bistro near The Shard. The daily changing blackboard offers a restricted three-option/course menu of exceptional Gallic bistro riffs, as well as classics. Sip Ricard pastis before lopping off two *oeufs à la coque* (boiled eggs with asparagus soldiers) or untangling your way through a blue cheese salad or French onion soup. The £5.50 desserts like Paris-Brest choux pastry and cream will instantly transport you back to the Left Bank. $ *Average main: £16* ⊠ *109 Bermondsey St., Bermondsey* ☎ *020/7407–2140* ⊕ *www.cassecroute.co.uk* ☉ *No dinner Sun.* ⚄ *Reservations essential* Ⓜ *London Bridge* ✛ *5:H2.*

**$$$**
MODERN FRENCH
FAMILY
**Fodor's**Choice
★

✕ **Chez Bruce.** Top-notch French and Mediterranean cuisine, faultless service, a winning wine list, and a straight-off-the-pistes glossy south-of-the-river Wandsworth neighborhood vibe make for one of London's all-star favorite restaurants. At this cozy, gimmick-free haunt overlooking Wandsworth Common, prepare for grown-up gastro wonders ranging from homemade charcuterie or offal to lighter, simply grilled fish dishes.

Pot-roast pigs' cheeks with polenta, roasted cod with truffle mash, and monkfish with scallops are all effortlessly conceived. Desserts like prune and Armagnac tart are packed with flavor, and the sommelier's a hoot. ⑤ *Average main: £27* ✉ *2 Bellevue Rd., Wandsworth Common, Battersea* ☎ *020/8672–0114* ⊕ *www.chezbruce.co.uk* ⚲ *Reservations essential* Ⓜ *Overland: Wandsworth Common* ✛ *4:E6.*

**$$**
TAPAS

✕ **José.** Spanish chef José Pizarro packs in diners at this tapas-and-sherry treasure trove on hot gastro-trail Bermondsey Street, just south of The Shard. With just 30 seats and no reservations, you'll be hard-pressed to find a spot after 6 pm, but it's worth the wait: the Spanish tapas dishes are superb. Quaff a glass of amontillado and keep those delicately handcrafted small plates coming; options include patatas bravas, croquetas, meatballs, pisto and crispy duck eggs, hake and aïoli, razor clams with chorizo, and ibérico pork–loin filets. Everything's impeccably sourced, from the peppery Marqués de Valdueza olive oil to the rare Manuel Maldonado chorizo. ⑤ *Average main: £18* ✉ *104 Bermondsey St., Southwark* ☎ *020/7403–4902* ⊕ *www.josetapasbar.com* ⚲ *Reservations not accepted* Ⓜ *Borough, London Bridge* ✛ *5:H2.*

**$$$**
FRENCH
FAMILY
**Fodor's** Choice
★

✕ **Le Pont de la Tour.** You'll find the winning combo of top-end French cuisine and smashing views of the River Thames, Tower Bridge, and the Tower of London at the storied Le Pont de la Tour in scrubbed-up Butler's Wharf. Dine out under awnings on the Thames-side terrace or otherwise sit by the window within the lavish art deco–inspired salon. Seared duck foie gras with caramelized black fig is set off with a touch of Madeira, while *recherché* roast Challans duck or herb-crusted rack of lamb with Provençal vegetables are both top draws. Service is first class, but prices can be high. ⑤ *Average main: £26* ✉ *36D Shad Thames, Bermondsey* ☎ *020/7403–8403* ⊕ *www.lepontdelatour.co.uk* ⚲ *Reservations essential* Ⓜ *London Bridge, Tower Hill* ✛ *2:H6.*

**$$**
MODERN BRITISH
FAMILY

✕ **Magdalen.** Not far from The Shard and the Tower and London Bridges, Magdalen is a self-assured beacon of class in an increasingly gastrocentric part of town. It specializes in gutsy but unpretentious modern British cuisine at keen prices; punchy surprises like fried calves' brains with gribiche, baked Somerset kid with butter beans, or blackberry-and-apple trifle are hardly going to break the bank. The dark bentwood chairs, chandeliers, and tea candles invite you to sit back with the short wine list and ponder whether to indulge in a feast of slow-baked rabbits with white beans or whole stuffed suckling pig instead. The two-course lunch (£16.50) is definitely worth indulging. ⑤ *Average main: £18* ✉ *152 Tooley St., Bermondsey* ☎ *020/7403–1342* ⊕ *www. magdalenrestaurant.co.uk* ⊗ *Closed Sun. No lunch Sat.* ⚲ *Reservations essential* Ⓜ *London Bridge* ✛ *5:H2.*

**$$$**
MODERN BRITISH

✕ **Restaurant Story.** British hotshot chef Tom Sellers storms the ramparts at this sell-out gastro-mecca, with his conceptual take on intensively flavored ingredient-led New British and New Nordic cuisine. Housed in a Scandinavian-inspired dining space, expect touches like edible nasturtium flowers or eel-mousse Oreos to kick things off. The real fun begins with a surprise beef-dripping candle that melts into a silver candle holder, which you mop up with bread throughout the meal. Genius dishes like puréed Désirée heritage potatoes with dandelion beurre blanc

**14**

or meadowsweet-pickled scallops with dill ash pop up throughout the three-, five-, or nine-course set menus. ⑤ *Average main: £28* ✉ *199 Tooley St., Bermondsey* ☎ *020/7183–2117* ⊕ *www.restaurantstory. co.uk* ⊘ *Closed Sun. and Mon.* ⚘ *Reservations essential* Ⓜ *London Bridge* ✛ *2:H6.*

## KENSINGTON, CHELSEA, KNIGHTSBRIDGE, AND BELGRAVIA

If you're fab, famous, wealthy, or preferably all three, chances are you'll be living—and dining—in one of these neighborhoods among London's world-class museums, royal parks, shops, hotels, monuments, fashion boutiques, and top restaurants. (Does the name of superchef Heston Blumenthal ring a bell?) In Chelsea, made famous in the swingin' '60s, restaurants range from bijou boîtes to exclusive little froufrou places ideal for gossip, an Aperol, and a no-carb bite on the go. Over in upscale Knightsbridge, you'll find Harrods and the high-end fashion boutiques of Sloane Street, plus a heap of platinum-class hotel-based restaurants. Come here for an amazing celebratory dining experience, but don't expect bargains (except at lunch). Nearby Kensington is a Victorian residential neighborhood with a wider range of restaurants, from French bistros to funky Persian hideaways.

### KENSINGTON

$$$

JAPANESE

✕ **Yashin.** At this top London sushi bar off Kensington High Street, you can watch Japanese head chef and co-founder Yasuhiro Mineno tease, slice, tweak, and blowtorch his way to the most awesome, fresh, funky, spunky, colorful and exquisite sushi, sashimi, salads, and carpaccio that you're likely to find this side of the East China Sea. Tofu-topped miso cappuccino comes in a Victorian cup and saucer, and softshell blue crab salad is a tangle of *mizuna* (Japanese greens). Delectable sushi spreads might mesmerize with ponzu-spiked salmon or Japanese sea bream with rice cracker dust, while the salmon *nigiri* set lunch is a smashing way to sample Yashin's below-the-radar brilliance. ⑤ *Average main: £25* ✉ *1A Argyll Rd., Kensington* ☎ *020/7938–1536* ⊕ *www.yashinsushi. com* ⚘ *Reservations essential* Ⓜ *High Street Kensington* ✛ *4:B1.*

### CHELSEA

$$$

MODERN BRITISH

FAMILY

Fodor's Choice

★

✕ **The Harwood Arms.** British game doesn't get much better than at this forest-floor and game lover's paradise (and London's only Michelin-star gastropub off Fulham Broadway). You'll find a catalog of awesome game like haunch of Berkshire roe deer with pickled mushrooms or Muggleswick grouse with potato and malt to keep you tickled. Tuck into game pie with Somerset cider jelly, Irish Sika deer with smoked bone marrow, or Herdwick lamb with rosemary curd in a relaxed 1840s pub setting. You'll find light openers like treacle-cured smoked salmon with spelt, as well as popular carve-your-own whole roasted lamb, pork, or beef joints for the table. ⑤ *Average main: £24* ✉ *27 Walham Grove, Chelsea* ☎ *020/7386–1847* ⊕ *www.harwoodarms.com* ⚘ *Reservations essential* Ⓜ *Fulham Broadway* ✛ *4:A5.*

$$

HUNAN

FAMILY

✕ **Hunan.** There's no menu at this quirky family-run Taiwanese stalwart situated a few blocks south of Sloane Square in Pimlico. Instead, diners simply state how spicy they like it, and sit back, relax, and chopstick their way through a succession of tasty tapas-size Hunanese, Hakka, Cantonese, and Japanese-inspired dishes to share. Using a blizzard of garlic, ginger, and fiery Szechuan chilies, the chef creates delicious dishes like Hunan water-fried dumplings, minced-pork broth with Chinese mushrooms, and pungent crab noodle soup. Chef Peng is highly thoughtful about what you might receive, the portions are generous, and the ongoing surprise is all part of the fun. $ *Average main: £23* ⊠ *51 Pimlico Rd., Pimlico, Chelsea* ☎ *020/7730–5712* ⊕ *www. hunanlondon.com* ☾ *Closed Sun.* ⚖ *Reservations essential* Ⓜ *Sloane Sq.* ✛ *4:G3.*

**$$$$** ✕ **Rasoi.** Some of London's finest contemporary Indian cuisine is found
**INDIAN** at this tony Victorian Chelsea townhouse decked out with Indian prints, masks, and carved wooden deities. The food exhibits godlike qualities of its own, with surprises like popcorn prawns, crab lollies with coconut soup, and wild mushroom rice with tomato ice cream, plus Bordeaux-infused lamb rogan josh and Darjeeling tea–soaked chicken. Grilled sea bass comes crusted in South Indian lentil-based gunpowder while the Punjabi chicken tikka is revealed from under a plume of smoke. Be sure to try the signature chocolate samosas, dubbed "Chocamosas." $ *Average main: £32* ⊠ *10 Lincoln St., Chelsea* ☎ *020/7225– 1881* ⊕ *www.rasoi-uk.com* ☾ *No lunch Sat.* ⚖ *Reservations essential* Ⓜ *Sloane Sq.* ✛ *4:F3.*

## KNIGHTSBRIDGE

**$$$** ✕ **Ametsa with Arzak Instruction.** At this modernist romp, lovers of all
**SPANISH** things Spain can bask in a fantasia of New Basque cuisine. Enjoy the
**FAMILY** passionate service and marvel at high-spec riffs on traditional Basque dishes, like slow-cooked hen's eggs flecked with paprika-rich chistorra sausage, wild ceps, and chorizo. Lobster is updated with a white cassava powder, and seared venison appears on a black plate with pickled red chilies and an electric green mint and sea buckthorn mojo. $ *Average main: £27* ⊠ *Halkin Hotel, 5 Halkin St., Knightsbridge* ☎ *020/7333– 1234* ⊕ *www.comohotels.com/thehalkin/dining/ametsa* ☾ *Closed Sun. No lunch Mon.* ⚖ *Reservations essential* Ⓜ *Hyde Park Corner, Knightsbridge* ✛ *4:G1.*

**$$** ✕ **Bar Boulud.** United States–based French superchef Daniel Boulud com-
**BRASSERIE** bines the best of French high-end brasserie fare with a dash of superior
**FAMILY** Yankee gourmet burgers and fries at this popular hangout in the Mandarin Oriental. Lilliputian-size platters of the most delicate Gilles Verot charcuterie, heartier coq au vin, or white pork sausages with truffle mash compete with palm-size Yankee, Frenchie, Piggie, or signature BB foie gras–beef burgers and fries in black onion or sesame-seed buns. The knockout grazing menu has something for everyone, and the professional but informal waitstaff give out a convivial vibe. Note the £17 two-course noon–7 prix-fixe deals. $ *Average main: £20* ⊠ *Mandarin Oriental Hyde Park, 66 Knightsbridge, Knightsbridge* ☎ *020/7201– 3899 for reservations only* ⊕ *www.barboulud.com/london* ⚖ *Reservations essential* Ⓜ *Knightsbridge* ✛ *4:F1.*

**$$$** ✕ **Brasserie Gustave.** Sleek French expats and inveterate Francophiles
**FRENCH** adore the triumphant procession of traditional Larousse-style classics found at this art deco–inspired South Kensington favorite. Six buttered

**14**

escargots à la Bourguignonnes come slathered in garlic and parsley sauce topped with a puff pastry snail, while deep green wild hedgerow garlic soup is adorned with crunchy frogs' legs. Try timeless treats like Barbary duck à l'orange, veal kidneys with three-mustard sauce, or achingly *bleu* beef tournedos Rossini with foie gras, truffles, and Madeira jus. For dessert, watch the mâitre d' theatrically flambé Cointreau and Cognac-rich crêpes Suzette at his trusty roving tableside stove. $ *Average main: £25* ✉ *4 Sydney St., South Kensington* ☎ *020/7352–1712* ⊕ *www.brasserie-gustave.com* ☾ *Closed Mon. No lunch Tues.* ⌲ *Reservations essential* Ⓜ *South Kensington* ✛ *4:E3.*

$$$$    ✕ **Dinner by Heston Blumenthal.** Splendidly revived old English dishes
BRITISH    executed with ultramodern precision is the schtick at Ashley Palmer-
FAMILY    Watts's award winner in the Mandarin Oriental (Palmer-Watts is a protégé of TV chef Heston Blumenthal, who's closely involved). As you take in views of Hyde Park, slice into a Meat Fruit appetizer (circa 1500), deceptively shaped like a mandarin but encasing the smoothest foie gras and chicken liver parfait you can imagine. A plate of Rice and Flesh (circa 1390) is a picture of yellow saffron rice with calves' tails, and grilled octopus Frumenty (circa 1390) is a lively dish of cracked wheat with lovage in a sea broth dating to the court of Richard II. Finish off with resplendent pineapple Tipsy cake (circa 1810), an homage to English spit-roasting from centuries past. $ *Average main: £34* ✉ *Mandarin Oriental Hyde Park, 66 Knightsbridge, Knightsbridge* ☎ *020/7201–3833* ⊕ *www.dinnerbyheston.com* ⌲ *Reservations essential* Ⓜ *Knightsbridge* ✛ *4:F1.*

$$$    ✕ **Koffmann's.** Set in the swish Berkeley Hotel, this is the last hurrah of
FRENCH    veteran French superchef Pierre Koffmann. Never paying heed to fads
FAMILY    or fashion, the clientele here enjoy such signatures as stuffed pig's trotters "Tante Claire" with sweetbreads and morels, or delicately seared scallops with a smudge of black squid ink. The culinary godfather to many of London's top chefs—from Gordon Ramsay to Tom Aikens—Gascon-born Koffmann showcases 35-odd years of experience and the best of regional Gascony cuisine in a cute, carpeted, and well-appointed basement setting. $ *Average main: £26* ✉ *The Berkeley, Wilton Pl., Knightsbridge* ☎ *020/7107–8844* ⊕ *www.the-berkeley.co.uk* ⌲ *Reservations essential* Ⓜ *Knightsbridge* ✛ *4:G1.*

$$$    ✕ **Mari Vanna.** All of London's Russian molls, dolls, and porcelain-
RUSSIAN    skinned babushkas squeeze into this White Russian fantasy dining salon in Knightsbridge, which overflows with a maximalist decor of vintage chandeliers, Tiffany lamps, tchotchkes, cheburashkas, and a Russian *pechka* stove. Snap into character with a horseradish vodka shot, then carb-up on pierogi sea bass savories, Siberian *pelmeni* (dumpling) soup, or smoked salmon blini. There's also tip-top borscht and creamy beef Stroganoff with wild mushrooms, and let's not forget the sweet crêpes with condensed milk. But it's the nostalgic dacha-like antebellum setting that makes you feel like you're participating in some kind of *Anna Karenina*–esque historical reenactment. $ *Average main: £28* ✉ *The Wellington Court, 116 Knightsbridge, Knightsbridge* ☎ *020/7225–3122* ⊕ *www.marivanna.ru/london* ⌲ *Reservations essential* Ⓜ *Knightsbridge* ✛ *4:F1.*

**$$** ✕ **Zuma.** An ever-fashionable informal Tokyo-style modern sushi joint
JAPANESE and hipsters' hangout, Zuma takes in a sake bar, robata grill, and open
FAMILY sushi counter—and attracts lots of beautiful people from the surround-
ing swanky neighborhood. Try fresh California maki rolls, tuna sushi,
sea bass sashimi, pork with yuzo, or the robata-grilled wagyu beef in a
hoba leaf. Enjoy the super polite service and be sure to grab the somme-
lier to guide you through the 40-odd varieties of rare sakes. ⑤ *Average
main: £22* ✉ *5 Raphael St., Knightsbridge* ☎ *020/7584–1010* ⊕ *www.
zumarestaurant.com* ⚓ *Reservations essential* Ⓜ *Knightsbridge* ✛ *4:F1.*

### BELGRAVIA

**$$$** ✕ **Pétrus.** A talented Gordon Ramsay team conducts a flawless dining
MODERN FRENCH experience at this haute cuisine honeypot. The dining salon may be a bit
FAMILY beige and dated, but between the impeccable food, assured sommelier,
and charming service, you've got a full-court gastro press. The food here
is all about technique, and it's impossible not to gasp at starters like Les
Landes duck foie gras with figs and bee pollen, or lobster ravioli with
creamed leaks and Champagne velouté. Bliss out on 25-day Caster-
bridge beef fillet with sticky Barolo sauce, and watch for surprises, like
the chocolate bomb that theatrically melts before your eyes. ⑤ *Average main: £29* ✉ *1 Kinnerton St., Belgravia* ☎ *020/7592–1609* ⊕ *www.
gordonramsay.com/petrus* ⚓ *Reservations essential* Ⓜ *Knightsbridge,
Hyde Park Corner* ✛ *4:G1.*

**14**

## NOTTING HILL AND BAYSWATER

Ever since Hugh Grant and Julia Roberts starred in *Notting Hill* and
put the area on the global map, Notting Hill's had a rep as London's
most glamorous neighborhood, with its myriad boutiques, chic cafés,
pâtisseries, restaurants, buzzy bars, and the famous Portobello Road
Market's collection of antiques shops, vintage-clothing stands, and food
stalls. Portobello is one of London's most popular street markets, so get
there early on Saturday morning (the market is open 8–6) to beat the
crowds. Peruse the antiques and vintage clothes stalls, and when you
want to eat, head to the north end where you'll find fresh fruit-and-veg
stalls, artisan bakeries, and rare Spanish olive and French cheese purveyors, plus numerous hot-food stalls peddling savory crêpes, gourmet
hamburgers, spicy German chicken rolls, paella, Moroccan kebabs,
and Malaysian noodles.

### NOTTING HILL

**$$$$** ✕ **E&O.** A long-standing Asian tapas supremo off Portobello Road street
MODERN ASIAN market, E&O offers a medley of blue-chip Chinese, Japanese, Vietnam-
FAMILY ese, and Thai dishes. All-star favorites include dim sum, sushi, sashimi,
and tempura, with a slew of low-carb and no-carb options. Don't skip
the lychee martinis in the hip, romantic bar before mooching over to the
moody monochrome dining room for miso black cod, snowcrab maki,
papaya salad, Thai rare beef, or lamb rendang; the sea bass sashimi
is achingly fresh. ⑤ *Average main: £32* ✉ *14 Blenheim Cres., Notting
Hill* ☎ *020/7229–5454* ⊕ *www.rickerrestaurants.com* ⚓ *Reservations
essential* Ⓜ *Ladbroke Grove, Westbourne Grove* ✛ *1:B1.*

**$$$$**
MODERN FRENCH
FAMILY
Fodor'sChoice
★

✕ **The Ledbury.** Aussie chef Brett Graham wins hearts, minds, and some serious global accolades at this no-dairy, no-carb modern French (with Pacific and British hints) dining landmark in deepest Notting Hill. You won't find a more inventive vegetable dish than Graham's ash-baked celeriac with hazelnut and wood sorrel, and it's impossible to best his pretty and complex mains like roasted quail with walnut cream, roe deer with bone marrow, or Cornish turbot with riesling, cockles, and sea lettuce. Besides his obsessive interest in all things British game, Graham's also famed for wicked desserts, so finish with thinly sliced figs with honey, olives, and sourdough ice cream. $ *Average main: £34* ✉ *127 Ledbury Rd., Notting Hill* ☎ *0207/7792–9090* ⊕ *www. theledbury.com* ⊘ *No lunch Mon. and Tues.* ⚖ *Reservations essential* Ⓜ *Westbourne Park, Ladbroke Grove* ✛ *1:A4.*

## BAYSWATER

**$**
MIDDLE EASTERN
FAMILY

✕ **Alounak.** Wonderful Persian dips, unleavened *taftoon* breads, steaming lamb bakes, and flame-grilled kebabs are found at this lantern-filled Iranian canteen beloved by hoards of local Middle Easterners. Lines form on Westbourne Grove for the hot pita and taftoon breads straight from the clay oven, and you may have to wait to get in. Once inside, try grilled eggplant purée with walnuts, feta, mint, and tarragon, the Alounak kebabs, skewered marinated lamb with rice and grilled tomatoes, or the *Zereshk polo*—pungent saffron chicken with sweet-and-sour Iranian forest berries. Enjoy the Persian black cardamom teas and sweets, and lime juice–and–pistachio *faloodeh* Persian sorbet, but know that the sour yogurt drinks are not to everyone's taste. $ *Average main: £12* ✉ *44 Westbourne Grove, Bayswater* ☎ *020/7229–4158* ⚖ *Reservations essential* Ⓜ *Queensway, Bayswater* ✛ *1:B4.*

**$$$**
BRASSERIE
FAMILY

✕ **Angelus.** Styled with swirly art nouveau mirrors and button-back red banquettes in a 200-year-old converted pub, Angelus has a reputation for unrivaled Parisian-style *brasserie de luxe* dishes: the duck's liver crème brûlée, egg cocotte, frogs' legs, saddle of lamb, or Grand Marnier soufflé are as good as they get. Classy all-day brunch and light bites like three-egg omelet and truffled brioche steak sandwiches are well conceived, and the French-focused wine list is top-notch. $ *Average main: £25* ✉ *4 Bathurst St., Hyde Park* ☎ *020/7402–0083* ⊕ *www.angelusrestaurant.co.uk* ⚖ *Reservations essential* Ⓜ *Lancaster Gate* ✛ *1:D4.*

**$**
MODERN BRITISH
FAMILY
Fodor'sChoice
★

✕ **Hereford Road.** A Bayswater favorite, Hereford Road is renowned for its pared-down, pomp-free, and ingredient-driven seasonal British fare. With an emphasis on well-sourced seasonal and regional British produce, many dishes are as unfussy as you'll find. Work your way through pure and uncluttered combos like steamed mussels with cider and thyme, lemon sole with sea dulse, or English rice pudding with strawberry jam. Note the £13.50–£15.50 set lunches are arguably the best weekday set lunch deals in town. $ *Average main: £14* ✉ *3 Hereford Rd., Bayswater* ☎ *020/7727–1144* ⊕ *www.herefordroad.org* ⚖ *Reservations essential* Ⓜ *Bayswater, Queensway* ✛ *1:B4.*

# REGENT'S PARK, HAMPSTEAD, AND ISLINGTON

Stucco-fronted Regent's Park and Islington attract a boho-chic media and high-brow artsy crowd who love the slightly rough-and-rowdy neighborhood restaurants like Lemonia or Oldroyd. Meanwhile, farther north in leafy Hampstead, it's all Dick Turpin 17th-century wood-beam coach houses and inns with roaring fires, house ales, and trouser-busting Sunday lunches.

## REGENT'S PARK

$ ✕ **Lemonia.** Primrose Hill's favorite Greek Cypriot, vine-decked, and
GREEK '80s-taverna-style Lemonia is large and light, and always packed
FAMILY with hoards of hungry families and hobo-chic locals. Besides an endless supply of Hellenic small-dish meze dips, hot breads, and starters, there are rustic mains like slow-baked *kleftiko* lamb in lemon, Greek yogurt–and–potato *moussaka*, and pleasing beef on the bone stewed in red wine. Expect friendly Greek service and hospitality, plus an airy atrium in the back. Generous spreads are £25.75, and bargain weekday set lunches are £12.50. ⑤ *Average main: £14* ⊠ *89 Regent's Park Rd., Regent's Park* ☎ *020/7586–7454* ☺ *No lunch Sat.; no dinner Sun.* ⌂ *Reservations essential* Ⓜ *Chalk Farm* ✛ *1:F1.*

14

## ISLINGTON

$ ✕ **Oldroyd.** Islington's finest squeeze into this tiny 40-seat neighborhood
ITALIAN bistro on Upper Street thanks to the groovy Italian food and warm and friendly service. Well-priced and ingredient-driven, the daily changing menu of seasonal small plates might wow with creamy Somerset Cardo cheese and grilled tardivo radicchio risotto, or simple confit duck leg with porcini and pearl barely. A tousled Parmesan-covered tower of fettuccine with oxtail ragù will please the whole table, while desserts like baked apple and Ameretti or hazelnut affogato are an appetizing £6. The short Italian-focused wine list starts at a handy £22 a bottle. ⑤ *Average main: £11* ⊠ *344 Upper St., Islington* ☎ *020/8617–9010* ⊕ *www.oldroydlondon.com* ⌂ *Reservations essential* Ⓜ *Angel* ✛ *2:F1.*

$ ✕ **Ottolenghi.** Captivating foodie window displays and a funky mod-
CAFÉ ern all-white interior characterize this flagship North African, Middle
FAMILY Eastern, and Mediterranean deli-bakery-café set in Islington's main Upper Street drag. Dig into exceptionally inventive, tasty, and healthy veg-centric dishes like roasted sweet potatoes with burnt eggplant and pomegranate, lamb cutlets with okra, Tunisian harissa-spiced chicken, or golden beetroot, red cabbage, and sour cream, along with cult Ottolenghi fresh salads, soups, flaky pastries, and artisanal cakes. Go home with a knockout chocolate meringue or a plum-and-quince tart, and pick up Ottolenghi's outstanding Israeli- and Palestinian-inspired cookbook, *Jerusalem,* on the way out. ⑤ *Average main: £13* ⊠ *287 Upper St., Islington* ☎ *020/7288–1454* ⊕ *www.ottolenghi.co.uk* Ⓜ *Angel* ✛ *2:F1.*

## THE THAMES UPSTREAM

These wealthy, leafy suburbs may be under the Heathrow flight path and follow the meandering course of the River Thames, but there's nothing sleepy about the neighborhood dining scene here, which is becoming more and more "West End" in style and substance by the day. One fanatical locavore maverick stands out: the bearded Mikael Jonsson, a self-taught Swedish obsessive genius, who knows his wild scallops from his foraged blueberries, and meals of staggering brilliance.

### CHISWICK

$$$
MODERN
EUROPEAN
Fodor's Choice
★

✕ **Hedone.** Only a loony or genius would serve an appetizer of half a Cévennes onion with a few pear shavings and beurre blanc, but luckily maverick Swedish chef Mikael Jonsson falls triumphantly in the latter camp at his 22-seat no-menu foodie haven in Chiswick. A former lawyer and food blogger, Jonsson's obsessive approach to the provenance of his largely British-sourced ingredients—often rare, wild, or foraged—means his daily changing dishes are some of the most intense and vivid around. Sit on stools and watch Jonsson in an open kitchen prepare ingredient-driven marvels like wild Dorset sea bass with pickled black radishes and hyssop oil, hand-caught Devon scallops with stuffed zucchini flower, or gloriously marbled 55-day-aged Darragh O'Shea Black Angus beef on the bone with juniper-smoked potatoes. $ *Average main: £27* ✉ *301–303 Chiswick High Rd., Chiswick* ☎ *020/8747–0377* ⊕ *www.hedonerestaurant.com* ☾ *Closed Sun. and Mon. No lunch Mon.–Wed.* ⚘ *Reservations essential* Ⓜ *Chiswick Park* ✛ *1:A2.*

# LONDON
# DINING AND
# LODGING ATLAS

**KEY**

☐ *Hotels*
■ *Restaurants*
■ *Restaurant in Hotel*
**U** **WESTMINSTER**
*Station*
*London Underground*
*National Rail Connection*

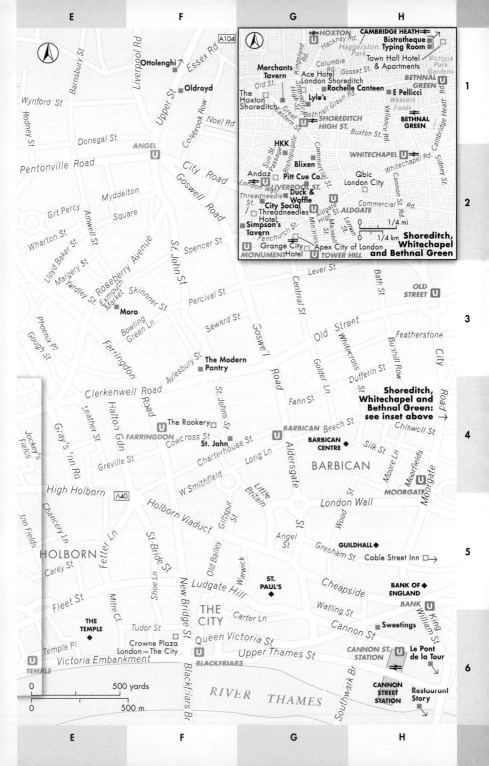

# Map 3

- Bloomsbury
- Covent Garden
- Soho

**A**　**B**　**C**　**D**

**1**

TELECOM TOWER ◆

Maple St

Jesmond Hotel □

The Ridgemount Hotel □

Howland St

Malet St

Tottenham Court Rd.

Huntley St

Torrington Pl

Chenies St

Ridgmount Gdns

Ridgmount St

Alfred Pl

Bloomsbury St

BLOOMSBURY

**2**

New Cavendish St

Great Portland St

Portland ■

Great Titchfield St

Cleveland St

Bonnie Gull Seafood Shack ■

Foley St

Charlotte St

Scala St

Tottenham St

Dabbous ■

Whitfield St

Store St

Bedford Square

Langham St

Riding House St.

Goodge St

Charlotte Street Hotel □

Berners St

Newman St

Windmill St

Percy St

Bayley St

The Riding House Café ■

Newman Arms ■

**3**

Regent St

Mortimer St.

Wells St

Berners St

Sanderson Hotel □

Rathbone Pl

Great Russell St

TOTTENHAM COURT ROAD Ⓤ

Margaret St

Eastcastle St

Berners Tavern ■
The London Edition

Oxford St.

**4**

A40 Ⓤ OXFORD CIRCUS

Blanchette ■

Grt Marlborough St

Poland St

Berwick St

Wardour St

Dean St

Greek St

Sutton Row

Soho Square

Greek St

Charing Cross Rd

Hanover

Hanover Square

The Soho Hotel □

Hazlitt's □

Frith St

10 Greek Street

Square

Little Social ■

Maddox St

Social Eating House ■

Broadwick St

Polpetto ■

Pollen Street Social ■

No. 5 Maddox Street □

BAO ■

Dean Street Townhouse ■
Dean Street Townhouse

Hoppers ■

Bar Italia ■

Goodman ■

Hibiscus ■

Andrew Edmunds ■

Burger & Lobster ■

Maison Bertaux ■

**5**

Regent St

Carnaby St

Lexington St

Old Compton St

Shaftesbury Premier London Piccadilly □

Conduit St

Savile Row

Flat Iron ■

SOHO

Spuntino ■

Shaftesbury Ave

Wardour St

Lisle St

Sartoria ■

Beak St

Bocca di Lupo ■

Rupert St

Leicester

Brewer St

Blacklock ■

The Palomar ■

**6**

New Bond St

Cecconi's ■

Burlington Gdns

Vigo St

Swallow St

Glasshouse St

PICCADILLY CIRCUS ◆

Ⓤ PICCADILLY CIRCUS

Coventry St

Haymarket

Whitcomb St

Orange St

Old Bond St

Park Chinois ■ ←

Piccadilly

Jermyn St

**A**　**B**　**C**　**D**

# WHERE TO STAY

Updated by
Jack Jewers

Queen Elizabeth hasn't invited you this time? No worries: staying at one of London's grande dame hotels is the next best thing to being a guest at the palace—and some say it's even better. Luckily there is no dearth of options where friendliness outdistances luxe; London has plenty of atmospheric places that won't cost a king's ransom.

That noted, until fairly recently it was extremely difficult to find a decent hotel in the center of town for less than £150 per night. Things have improved, thanks in part to the global recession, but also to a flurry of new midpriced hotels that have sprung up in the last few years. You'll still have to shop around for deals—never assume you'll be able to find somewhere good *and* cheap on short notice.

Of course, it's very different if money is no object. London has some of the very best and most luxurious hotels in the world. Freshly minted billionaires favor the rash of super-trendy hot spots like the Corinthia or ME London, while fashionistas gravitate toward Kit Kemp's super-stylish hotels like the Covent Garden and the Charlotte Street. But even these places have deals, and you can sometimes snag a bargain within reach of mere mortals, particularly in the off-season, or just be a spectator to all the glamour by visiting for afternoon tea, the most traditional of high-society treats.

Meanwhile, several midrange hotels have dropped their average prices in response to the choppy waters of the global economy, which has pulled some fantastic places, such as Hazlitt's, the Rookery, and Town Hall, back into the affordable category. There's also a clutch of new, stylish, and supercheap hotels that are a real step forward for the city. The downside is that these places tend to be a little out of the way, but that's often a price worth paying. Another attractive alternative includes hotels in the Premier and Millennium chains, which offer sleek, modern rooms, lots of up-to-date conveniences, and sales that frequently bring room prices well below £100 a night.

At the budget level, London has come a long way in the last couple of years, with a familiar catch: to find a good, reasonably priced B&B, you must be prepared to look outside the very center of town. This means that you have to weigh the city's notoriously high transport costs against any savings—but on the plus side, the Tube can shuttle you out to even some far-flung suburbs in less than 20 minutes. Prepare to be just a little adventurous with your London base and you will be rewarded by a collection of unique and interesting B&Bs and small boutiques, in the kinds of neighborhoods real Londoners live in—places like King Henry's Road, the Cable Street Inn, and the Church Street Hotel. If you're willing to fend for yourself, the city also has some great rental options.

But if you are interested in luxury, London is just the place. Although the image we love to harbor about Olde London Towne may be fast fading in the light of today's glittering city, when it comes time to rest your head, the old-fashioned clichés remain enticing. Choose one of London's heritage-rich hotels—Claridge's supplies perfect parlors; the Savoy has that river view—and you'll find that these fantasies can, and always will, be fulfilled.

**15**

# PLANNING

### NEED A RESERVATION?

Yes, hotel reservations are an absolute necessity when planning your trip to London, so book your room as far in advance as possible. The further in advance you can book, the better a deal you're likely to get. Just watch out if you change your mind—cancellation fees can be hefty. On the other hand, it is possible to find some amazing last-minute deals at mid- to high-range places, but this is a real gamble, as you could just as easily end up paying full rate. Fierce competition means properties undergo frequent improvements, so when booking inquire about any ongoing renovations that may interrupt your stay.

### CHECKING IN

Typical check-in and checkout times are 2 pm and 11 am, respectively. Many flights from North America arrive early in the morning, but having to wait six hours for a room after arriving jet-lagged at 8 am isn't the ideal way to start a vacation. Alert the hotel of your early arrival; large hotels can often make special early check-in arrangements, and almost all will look after your luggage in the meantime. Be prepared to drop your bags and strike out for a few hours. On the plus side, this can effectively give you a whole extra day for sightseeing.

### HOTEL QUALITY

Note that rooms can vary considerably in a single hotel. If you don't like the room you're given, ask to see another. Hotels often renovate room by room—you might find yourself allocated a dark, unrenovated room, whereas bright, newly decorated quarters await just down the hall. Be prepared for the fact that, while smoking is now banned in public areas, this doesn't apply to hotel rooms; be firm and ask to change if you're given a smoking room and didn't request one.

## BREAKFAST

Some hotels include breakfast in the price of the room. It ranges from a gourmet spread to what is known as the "full English" (one fried egg, two "bangers," or English-style sausage links, two thick slices of bacon, a grilled tomato, sautéed mushrooms or baked beans, and toast). In many budget hotels and B&Bs, this is the only hot breakfast available. Most expensive hotels (and the most imaginative small ones) may also offer pancakes, French toast, waffles, and omelets. Luckily, virtually all accommodations also offer packaged cereals, muffins, yogurt, and fresh fruit, so when the sausage-and-bacon brigade begins to wear you down, go continental.

## FACILITIES

Keep in mind that some facilities come with the room rate while others cost extra. So, when pricing accommodations, always ask what's included. Modern hotels usually have air-conditioning, but B&Bs and hotels in older buildings often do not, and it is generally not the norm in London. Wi-Fi is common, but don't assume it's free (large hotels in particular can charge outrageous fees). If you want a double room, specify whether you want a double bed or a twin (two single beds next to each other). *All hotels listed here have private bathrooms unless otherwise noted.*

## PRICES

If you're planning to visit in fall, winter, or early spring, start monitoring bargain rates online a few months before your trip and book whenever you see a good rate. Chains such as Hilton, Premier, and Millennium are known for their low-season sales during which prices can be as little as half the normal rate. And business-oriented hotels frequently have lower rates on weekends.

The exchange rate between the pound and the dollar is also unpredictable, so if it's looking good when you book, an advance-payment deal could end up saving you a decent amount of money. ■TIP➔ **The Visit London Accommodation Booking Service (☎ 020/7932–2020; ⊕ www. visitlondon.com) offers a best-price guarantee. Also try the clearing-house websites Late Rooms (⊕ www.laterooms.com), Booking (⊕ www. booking.com), and Last Minute (⊕ www.lastminute.com).**

| WHAT IT COSTS IN POUNDS | | | |
|---|---|---|---|
| $ | $$ | $$$ | $$$$ |
| Hotels | Under £116 | £116–£200 | £201–£300 | Over £300 |

Prices in the reviews are the lowest cost of a standard double room in high season, including 20% V.A.T.

# WHERE SHOULD I STAY?

| | Neighborhood Vibe | Pros | Cons |
|---|---|---|---|
| Westminster, St. James's, and Royal London | This historic section is home to major tourist attractions like Buckingham Palace. | Central area near tourist sites; easy Tube access; considered a safe area to stay. | Mostly expensive lodging options; few good restaurants and entertainment venues nearby. |
| Mayfair and Marylebone | Traditional, old money, a mixture of the business and financial set with fashionable shops. | In the heart of the action; some of London's best hotels are found here. | Pricey part of town; the city-that-never-sleeps buzz makes peace and quiet hard to come by. |
| Soho and Covent Garden | A tourist hub with endless entertainment—this is party central for young adults. | Buzzing area with plenty to see and do; late-night entertainment abounds; wonderful shopping district. | Perhaps London's busiest (and noisiest) district after dark; few budget hotels. |
| Bloomsbury and Holborn | Diverse area that is part bustling business center and part tranquil respite with tree-lined streets and parks. | Easy access to Tube, and 15 minutes to city center; major sights, like the British Museum in Bloomsbury. | Holborn has busy and noisy streets; the area around King's Cross can be sketchy—particularly at night. |
| The City | London's financial district, where most of the city's banks and businesses are headquartered. | Extremely central with easy transportation access and great hotel deals. | The City can be as quiet as a tomb on weekends—even the pubs close. |
| East London | Increasingly trendy area east of the city center, with a great arts scene. | Great for art lovers, shoppers, and business execs with meetings in Canary Wharf. | Still a transitional area; parts of Hoxton can be a bit dodgy at night; 20-minute Tube ride from central London. |
| South of the Thames | South of the river is a vibrant cultural hub, centered around the South Bank, the Globe, and the Royal National Theatre. | South of the River is London's unofficial cultural quarter, and walking distance from the West End theaters. | You don't have to go very far from the South Bank before you hit some of London's dodgiest neighborhoods. |
| Kensington, Chelsea, Knightsbridge, and Belgravia | These are some of London's most upscale neighborhoods and a hub of London's tourist universe. | Diverse hotel selection; great area for meandering urban walks; London's capital of high-end shopping. | Depending on where you are, the nearest Tube might be a hike; residential area might be too quiet for some. |
| Notting Hill and Bayswater | This is an upscale, trendy area favored by locals, with plenty of good hotels. | Hotel deals abound if you know where to look; gorgeous greenery in Hyde Park. | Choose the wrong place and you may end up in a flea pit; residential area may be quiet. |
| Regent's Park and Hampstead | A mix of arty, fashionable districts with a villagelike feel in other places. | Some of London's most fashionable neighborhoods; easy to fall in love with. | Some distance from center; lack of hotel options. |

15

# HOTEL REVIEWS

*Listed alphabetically by neighborhood. Use the coordinate (✢ 1:B2) at the end of each listing to locate a site on the corresponding map. To locate the property on a map, turn to the London Dining and Lodging Atlas at the end of the Where to Eat chapter. The first number after the symbol indicates the map number. Following that is the property's coordinate on the map grid.*

*Hotel reviews have been shortened. For full information, visit Fodors.com.*

## WESTMINSTER, ST. JAMES'S, AND ROYAL LONDON

### WESTMINSTER

**$$$$**
HOTEL
Fodor's Choice
★
**⊞ The Corinthia.** The London outpost of the exclusive Corinthia chain is design heaven-on-earth, with levels of service that make anyone feel like a VIP. **Pros:** so much luxury and elegance you'll feel like royalty; low rate guarantee means they'll match the price of a cheaper room of the same standard at another hotel. **Cons:** prices jump to the stratosphere once the least expensive rooms sell out; not many special offers. ⑤ *Rooms from: £510* ⊠ *Whitehall Pl., Westminster* ☎ *020/7930–8181* ⊕ *www.corinthia.com* ⇴ *294 rooms* ❙⊙❙ *Breakfast* Ⓜ *Embankment* ✢ *5:C1.*

**$$**
HOTEL
FAMILY
**⊞ DoubleTree by Hilton Hotel London Westminster.** Spectacular views of the river, Big Ben, and the London Eye fill the floor-to-ceiling windows in this rather stark, steel-and-glass building steps from the Tate Britain, and a plethora of techy perks await inside. **Pros:** amazing views; flat-screen TVs and other high-tech gadgetry; can be surprisingly affordable for the location. **Cons:** small bedrooms; tiny bathrooms; TV has to be operated through a computer (confusing if you're not used to it). ⑤ *Rooms from: £159* ⊠ *30 John Islip St., Westminster* ☎ *020/7630–1000* ⊕ *www.doubletreewestminsterhotel.com* ⇴ *444 rooms, 16 suites* ❙⊙❙ *Some meals* Ⓜ *Westminster, Pimlico* ✢ *5:C4.*

**$$$$**
HOTEL
**⊞ The Goring.** With Buckingham Palace just around the corner, this hotel, built in 1910 and now run by third-generation Gorings, has always been a favorite among discreet VIPs—including Kate Middleton's family on the night before her marriage to Prince William in 2011. **Pros:** elegant, spacious rooms; overlooks Buckingham Palace; great attention to detail. **Cons:** price is still too high for what you get; interiors a bit fussy. ⑤ *Rooms from: £362* ⊠ *15 Beeston Pl., Grosvenor Gardens, Westminster* ☎ *020/7396–9000* ⊕ *www.thegoring.com* ⇴ *69 rooms, 6 suites* ❙⊙❙ *Some meals* Ⓜ *Victoria* ✢ *5:A3.*

**$$$$**
HOTEL
Fodor's Choice
★
**⊞ Hotel 41.** With faultless service, sumptuous designer furnishings, and a sense of fun to boot, this impeccable hotel breathes new life into the cliché "thinks of everything," yet the epithet is really quite apt. **Pros:** impeccable service; beautiful and stylish; Buckingham Palace is on your doorstep. **Cons:** unusual design is not for everyone; expensive. ⑤ *Rooms from: £370* ⊠ *41 Buckingham Palace Rd., Westminster* ☎ *020/7300–0041* ⊕ *www.41hotel.com* ⇴ *26 rooms, 4 suites, 2 apartments* ❙⊙❙ *Breakfast* Ⓜ *Victoria* ✢ *5:A3.*

**$$** ⛣ **Lime Tree Hotel.** In a central neighborhood where hotels veer from
HOTEL wildly overpriced at one extreme to grimy boltholes at the other, the
Lime Tree gets the boutique style just about right—and at a surprisingly
reasonable cost for the neighborhood. **Pros:** lovely and helpful hosts;
great location; rooms are decent size. **Cons:** cheaper rooms are small;
some are up several flights of stairs and there's no elevator; two-night
minimum stay on weekends. Ⓢ *Rooms from: £175* ✉ *135–137 Ebury
St., Westminster* ☎ *020/7730–8191* ⊕ *www.limetreehotel.co.uk* ⇆ *25
rooms* ⦿ *Breakfast* Ⓜ *Victoria, Sloane Sq.* ✛ *4:H2.*

**$$** ⛣ **Sanctuary House Hotel.** This is a classic example of what the British
B&B/INN mean when they refer to an "inn"—a pub with bedrooms, albeit one of
better-than-average quality for London. **Pros:** cozy, authentic London
feel; friendly staff; "wow" location right in the heart of Westminster.
**Cons:** pub can be noisy (light sleepers should ask for a room as far
from the ground floor as possible). Ⓢ *Rooms from: £160* ✉ *33 Tothill
St., Westminster* ☎ *020/7799–4044* ⊕ *www.sanctuaryhousehotel.co.uk*
⇆ *34 rooms* ⦿ *Breakfast* Ⓜ *St. James's Park* ✛ *5:B2.*

**$$$** ⛣ **Windermere Hotel.** This sweet and rather elegant old hotel, on the
HOTEL premises of London's first B&B (1881), is a decent, well-situated option.
**Pros:** good location close to Victoria Station; free Wi-Fi; good amenities
for an old hotel of this size, including air conditioning and an elevator.
**Cons:** rooms and bathrooms are tiny. Ⓢ *Rooms from: £205* ✉ *142–144
Warwick Way, Westminster* ☎ *020/7834–5163* ⊕ *www.windermere-
hotel.co.uk* ⇆ *19 rooms* ⦿ *Breakfast* Ⓜ *Victoria* ✛ *5:A4.*

## ST. JAMES'S

**$$$** ⛣ **Dukes Hotel.** At this small, exclusive hotel in a discreet cul-de-sac,
HOTEL ample natural light brightens contemporary-style rooms. **Pros:** low-
key ambience; peaceful setting in a central location; excellent restaurant. **Cons:** maybe a bit too quiet for some; price is still rather high
for what's available. Ⓢ *Rooms from: £289* ✉ *35 St. James's Pl., St.
James's* ☎ *020/7941–4840, 800/381–4702 in U.S.* ⊕ *www.dukeshotel.
com* ⇆ *78 rooms, 12 suites* ⦿ *Breakfast* Ⓜ *Green Park* ✛ *5:A1.*

**$$$$** ⛣ **The Ritz.** If you're wondering if the *Downton Abbey*–style world of
HOTEL the old British upper class still exists, look no further than here: the Ritz
is as synonymous with London's high society and decadence today as
it was when it opened in 1906. **Pros:** historic luxury hotel; service at
every turn. **Cons:** snooty service; tediously old-fashioned dress code.
Ⓢ *Rooms from: £390* ✉ *150 Piccadilly, St. James's* ☎ *020/7493–8181*
⊕ *www.theritzlondon.com* ⇆ *136 rooms* ⦿ *Some meals* Ⓜ *Piccadilly
Circus* ✛ *5:A1.*

**$$$$** ⛣ **The Stafford London.** This is a rare find: a posh hotel that's equal parts
HOTEL elegance and friendliness, and located in one of the few peaceful spots
**Fodor$Choice** in the area, down a small lane behind Piccadilly. **Pros:** great staff; big,
★ luxurious rooms; quiet location. **Cons:** traditional style is not to all
tastes; perks in the more expensive rooms could be more generous
(free airport transfer, but one-way only; free clothes pressing, but only
one item per day). Ⓢ *Rooms from: £323* ✉ *16-18St. James's Pl., St.
James's* ☎ *020/7493–0111* ⊕ *www.thestaffordlondon.com* ⇆ *81 rooms*
⦿ *Breakfast* Ⓜ *Green Park* ✛ *5:A1.*

**15**

## MAYFAIR AND MARYLEBONE

### MAYFAIR

**$$$$** ⚅ **Athenaeum Hotel and Apartments.** This grand hotel overlooking Green
**HOTEL** Park offers plenty for the money: rooms are both comfortable and
lavishly decorated, with deeply comfortable Hypnos beds, plasma-
screen TVs, luxurious fabrics, and original contemporary artworks.
**Pros:** peaceful park views; handy for Buckingham Palace and Piccadilly;
great value for elegant setting. **Cons:** bathrooms are almost all small.
⑤ *Rooms from: £317* ✉ *116 Piccadilly, Mayfair* ☎ *020/7499–3464*
⊕ *www.athenaeumhotel.com* ⟳ *111 rooms, 46 suites and apartments*
†○| *Breakfast* Ⓜ *Green Park* ✛ *1:H6.*

**$$$$** ⚅ **Brown's Hotel.** Founded in 1837 by James Brown, Lord Byron's "gen-
**HOTEL** tleman's gentleman," this hotel occupying 11 Georgian townhouses
holds a treasured place in London society. **Pros:** elegant spaces; attentive service; good afternoon tea. **Cons:** even the most basic room is very
pricey. ⑤ *Rooms from: £360* ✉ *34 Albemarle St., Mayfair* ☎ *020/7493–*
*6020, 888/667–9477 in U.S.* ⊕ *www.roccofortehotels.com* ⟳ *88*
*rooms, 29 suites* †○| *Breakfast* Ⓜ *Green Park* ✛ *1:H5.*

**$$$$** ⚅ **The Cavendish.** Located next door to Fortnum and Mason (one of the
**HOTEL** most luxurious department stores in the world), it seems appropriate
**Fodor's**Choice that the Cavendish comes with a touch of Gilded Age history, a whiff of
★ historical scandal, and a pleasant air of joie de vivre. **Pros:** sophisticated
yet relaxed; great service; unbeatable location. **Cons:** guestrooms are
small; some street noise; rooms near the elevator can be particularly
noisy. ⑤ *Rooms from: £320* ✉ *81 Jermyn St., Mayfair* ☎ *020/7930–*
*2111* ⊕ *www.thecavendish-london.co.uk* ⟳ *230 rooms* †○| *Breakfast*
Ⓜ *Piccadilly* ✛ *5:B1.*

**$$$** ⚅ **Chesterfield Mayfair Hotel.** Deep in the heart of Mayfair, the former
**HOTEL** townhouse of the Earl of Chesterfield welcomes guests in wood-and-
leather public rooms that match the dark-wood furnishings in the bed-
rooms—small but like fashion magazine spreads, with bold designer
wallpaper or tones of fawn and gray. **Pros:** laid-back atmosphere; atten-
tive service; great afternoon tea. **Cons:** prices rise sharply if you don't get
the cheapest rooms; some rooms are tiny; restaurant is very expensive.
⑤ *Rooms from: £224* ✉ *35 Charles St., Mayfair* ☎ *020/7491–2622,*
*877/955–1515 in U.S.* ⊕ *www.chesterfieldmayfair.com* ⟳ *94 rooms,*
*13 suites* †○| *Breakfast* Ⓜ *Green Park* ✛ *1:H6.*

**$$$$** ⚅ **Claridge's.** The well-heeled have been meeting—and eating—at Clar-
**HOTEL** idge's for generations, and the tradition continues in the original art
**FAMILY** deco public spaces of this super-glamorous London institution. **Pros:**
**Fodor's**Choice see-and-be-seen dining and drinking; serious luxury everywhere—this
★ is an old-money hotel; comics, books, and DVDs to help keep kids
amused. **Cons:** better pack your designer wardrobe if you want to fit in
with the locals; all that luxury means an expensive price tag. ⑤ *Rooms*
*from: £480* ✉ *Brook St., Mayfair* ☎ *020/7629–8860, 866/599–6991*
*in U.S.* ⊕ *www.claridges.co.uk* ⟳ *136 rooms, 678 suites* †○| *Breakfast*
Ⓜ *Bond St.* ✛ *1:H4.*

$$$$
HOTEL
FAMILY
Fodor's Choice
★

**The Connaught.** A huge favorite of the "we wouldn't dream of staying anywhere else" monied set since its opening in 1917, the Connaught has many dazzlingly modern compliments to its famously historic delights. Pros: legendary hotel; great for star-spotting. Cons: history comes at a price; bathrooms are small. ⑤ *Rooms from: £540* ✉ *Carlos Pl., Mayfair* ☎ *020/7499–7070, 866/599–6991 in U.S.* ⊕ *www.the-connaught.co.uk* ⇱ *87 rooms, 34 suites* ⑂ *Breakfast* Ⓜ *Bond St.* ✛ *1:H5.*

$$$$
HOTEL

**The Dorchester.** Few hotels this opulent manage to be as personable as the Dorchester, which opened in 1939 and boasts a prime Park Lane location with unparalleled glamour; gold leaf and marble adorn the public spaces, and guest quarters are awash in English country house meets art deco style. Pros: historic luxury in 1930s building; lovely views of Hyde Park; top-notch star-spotting; excellent spa; Michelin-starred dining from Alain Ducasse. Cons: traditional look is not to all tastes; prices are sky-high; some rooms are disappointingly small. ⑤ *Rooms from: £580* ✉ *Park La., Mayfair* ☎ *020/7629–8888* ⊕ *www.thedorchester.com* ⇱ *195 rooms, 55 suites* ⑂ *Breakfast* Ⓜ *Marble Arch, Hyde Park Corner* ✛ *1:H6.*

$$$$
HOTEL

**Four Seasons Park Lane.** A racy departure for the Four Seasons, this hotel has an English clubhouse look with a dose of boudoir. Pros: highly elegant rooms; excellent spa; lovely location next to Hyde Park. Cons: not for strict traditionalists; haute design comes with high prices. ⑤ *Rooms from: £480* ✉ *Hamilton Pl., Park La., Mayfair* ☎ *020/7499–0888* ⊕ *www.fourseasons.com/london* ⇱ *147 rooms, 46 suites* ⑂ *Breakfast* Ⓜ *Hyde Park Corner* ✛ *1:H6.*

$$$$
HOTEL

**InterContinental London Park Lane.** Overlooking busy Hyde Park Corner and the grounds of Buckingham Palace (much to the Queen's chagrin, allegedly), this hotel's luxurious rooms are aimed at high-end business travelers. Pros: great location; feel-like-a-million-dollars service; good business facilities. Cons: no park views with standard rooms; prices sky-high in mid-summer. ⑤ *Rooms from: £450* ✉ *1 Hamilton Pl., Park La., Mayfair* ☎ *020/7409–3131* ⊕ *www.ihg.com/intercontinental/hotels/gb/en/london/lonhb/hoteldetail* ⇱ *447 rooms, 60 suites* ⑂ *Some meals* Ⓜ *Hyde Park Corner* ✛ *1:H6.*

$$$$
HOTEL
Fodor's Choice
★

**The Langham.** Hotel pedigrees don't come much greater than this one; built in 1865, the Langham was *the* original luxury hotel in the city, all but inventing the very image of what a great London hotel looked like. Pros: beautiful historic building; outstanding service; great restaurant and bar. Cons: price rises considerably once cheapest rooms sell out; bathrooms in basic rooms are somewhat utilitarian. ⑤ *Rooms from: £372* ✉ *1C Portland Pl., Mayfair* ☎ *020/7636–1000* ⊕ *www.langhamhotels.co.uk* ⇱ *331 rooms, 47 suites* ⑂ *Some meals* Ⓜ *Oxford Circus* ✛ *2:A4.*

$$$
RENTAL
FAMILY

**No. 5 Maddox Street.** Just five minutes' walk from Oxford Street, this is a great option for those who tire of traditional hotels: 12 luxury suites—some with balconies and working fireplaces—filled with everything you could ever need, including a handy kitchen. Pros: cozy and private; room service will deliver meals from local restaurants; guests have access to nearby health club. Cons: no elevator; no communal lobby can make you feel isolated; central location can (predictably) be

**15**

noisy. ⑤ *Rooms from: £266* ✉ *5 Maddox St., Mayfair* ☎ *020/7647–0200* ⊕ *www.living-rooms.co.uk/hotel/no5maddoxstreet* ⇨ *12 suites* ⫶○⫶ *No meals* Ⓜ *Oxford Circus* ✚ *3:A5.*

**$$$** ⊞ **Radisson Blu Edwardian Berkshire Hotel.** In a dangerously good loca-
**HOTEL** tion for shopaholics, with Oxford Street on the doorstep, the pleasant and well-run Radisson Berkshire offers a similar level of service to some of the more established hotels in the neighborhood, at a lower rate. **Pros:** great location; good restaurant; free Wi-Fi; worthwhile deals and promotions. **Cons:** walk-in rate is still quite expensive; small bed-rooms. ⑤ *Rooms from: £229* ✉ *350 Oxford St., Mayfair* ☎ *020/7629–7474, 0800/374–411 toll-free in U.K., 1800/333–3333 toll-free in U.S.* ⊕ *www.radissonblu-edwardian.com* ⇨ *145 rooms, 2 suites* ⫶○⫶ *Some meals* Ⓜ *Bond St., Oxford Circus* ✚ *1:H4.*

**$$$** ⊞ **Shaftesbury Premier London Piccadilly.** This hotel couldn't be better situ-
**HOTEL** ated for theater lovers; it's right in the famed West End district with three such venues within sight of the front door alone. **Pros:** unbeat-able location; some thoughtful extras. **Cons:** noise is unavoidable; you're paying for the location rather than the amenities, and it shows. ⑤ *Rooms from: £245* ✉ *65–73 Shaftesbury Ave., Mayfair* ☎ *020/898–1586, 877/898–1586 in U.S.* ⊕ *www.theshaftesbury.com* ⇨ *67 rooms* ⫶○⫶ *Breakfast* Ⓜ *Piccadilly Circus* ✚ *3:D5.*

**$$** ⊞ **22 York Street.** This lovely Georgian townhouse has a cozy, family
**B&B/INN** feel, with polished pine floors and fetching antiques decorating the homey, individually furnished guest rooms. **Pros:** live out your Lon-don townhouse fantasy; friendly hosts; nicely flexible check-in times; good location for shoppers. **Cons:** if you take away the great location, you're paying a lot for a B&B; not everyone enjoys socializing with strangers over breakfast. ⑤ *Rooms from: £150* ✉ *22 York St., Mayfair* ☎ *020/7224–2990* ⊕ *www.22yorkstreet.co.uk* ⇨ *10 rooms* ⫶○⫶ *Break-fast* Ⓜ *Baker St.* ✚ *1:G3.*

## MARYLEBONE

**$$$** ⊞ **Dorset Square Hotel.** This fashionable boutique hotel occupies a
**HOTEL** charming old townhouse in one of London's most upscale neighbor-
**Fodor's**Choice hoods. **Pros:** ideal location; lovely design; good afternoon tea. **Cons:**
★ some rooms are small; no bathtub in some rooms; fee for Wi-Fi. ⑤ *Rooms from: £246* ✉ *39 Dorset Sq., Marylebone* ☎ *020/7723–7874* ⊕ *www.firmdalehotels.com* ⇨ *35 rooms, 3 suites* ⫶○⫶ *Breakfast* Ⓜ *Baker St.* ✚ *1:F2.*

**$$$** ⊞ **Hyatt Regency London—The Churchill.** Even though it's one of London's
**HOTEL** largest hotels, the Churchill is always abuzz with guests smiling at the perfection they find here, including warmly personalized service and calmly alluring guest rooms. **Pros:** comfortable and stylish; efficient service; up to three can stay in one room. **Cons:** feels more geared to business than leisure travelers; lots of renovation. ⑤ *Rooms from: £240* ✉ *30 Portman Sq., Marylebone* ☎ *020/7486–5800* ⊕ *www.london. churchill.hyatt.com* ⇨ *389 rooms, 45 suites* ⫶○⫶ *Breakfast* Ⓜ *Marble Arch* ✚ *1:G4.*

**$$$** ⊞ **Park Plaza Sherlock Holmes Hotel.** Named in honor of the fictional
**HOTEL** detective who had his home on Baker Street, rooms here have a mas-culine edge with lots of earth tones and pinstripe sheets (along with

## BED-AND-BREAKFASTS

You can stay in small, homey B&Bs for an up-close-and-personal brush with city life (Parkwood Hotel; Arlington Avenue), or find yourself in what is really a modern guesthouse, where you never meet the owners (B&B Belgravia; The Main House). The main benefit of staying in a B&B is that the rate is usually lower than that of a hotel room of comparable quality, and you receive more personal service. However, the limitations may be off-putting for some. Although you can sometimes arrange for daily maid service, there's usually no restaurant, bar, or room service. Prices start at around £60 a night, and in that bracket the grimmer places are legion, so make your choice carefully. Prices usually (though not always) go up for more central neighborhoods and larger and more luxurious homes. Overall, however, it's a nice option, both for seasoned travelers who want a more authentic taste of London, and for those trying to travel well without busting their budgets.

**AirBnB.** This popular global network of private lets and small bed-and-breakfasts has several hundred London-based properties listed on its website. ⊠ *London* ⊕ *www.airbnb.co.uk.*

**15**

hypermodern bathrooms stocked with fluffy bathrobes). **Pros:** nicely decorated; international electrical outlets, including those that work with American equipment. **Cons:** have to walk through the bar to get to reception; not well soundproofed from the noisy street; total lack of Benedict Cumberbatch. ⑤ *Rooms from. £212* ⊠ *108 Baker St., Marylebone* ☎ *020/7486–6161* ⊕ *www.sherlockholmeshotel.com* ⟲ *99 rooms, 20 suites* ⎟◯⎟ *Breakfast* Ⓜ *Baker St.* ✛ *1:G3.*

**$$** 　 ⬚ **The Sumner.** You can feel yourself relaxing the minute you enter this
HOTEL 　elegant Georgian townhouse. **Pros:** excellent location for shopping; small enough that the staff know your name; attractive conservatory and garden. **Cons:** services are limited; high prices. ⑤ *Rooms from: £176* ⊠ *54 Upper Berkley St., Marble Arch, Marylebone* ☎ *020/7723–2244* ⊕ *www.thesumner.com* ⟲ *20 rooms* ⎟◯⎟ *Breakfast* Ⓜ *Marble Arch* ✛ *1:F4.*

# SOHO AND COVENT GARDEN

## SOHO

**$$$** 　 ⬚ **Dean Street Townhouse.** Discreet and unpretentious—and right in the
HOTEL 　heart of Soho—this oh-so-stylish place has a bohemian vibe and an
**Fodor's Choice** 　excellent modern British restaurant, hung with pieces by renowned
★ 　artists like Peter Blake and Tracy Emin. **Pros:** ultracool vibe; resembles an upper-class pied-à-terre. **Cons:** some rooms are extremely small; rooms at the front of the building can be noisy, especially on weekends. ⑤ *Rooms from: £220* ⊠ *69–71 Dean St., Soho* ☎ *020/7434–1775* ⊕ *www.deanstreettownhouse.com* ⟲ *39 rooms* ⎟◯⎟ *Breakfast* Ⓜ *Leicester Sq., Tottenham Court Rd.* ✛ *3:D5.*

**$$$** 　 ⬚ **Hazlitt's.** This disarmingly friendly place, full of personality, robust
HOTEL 　antiques, and claw-foot tubs, occupies three connected early 18th-century houses, one of which was the last home of essayist William

Hazlitt (1778–1830). **Pros:** great for lovers of art and antiques; historic atmosphere with lots of small sitting rooms and wooden staircases; truly beautiful and relaxed. **Cons:** no in-house restaurant; breakfast is £12 extra; no elevators. $ *Rooms from: £227* ✉ *6 Frith St., Soho* ☎ *020/7434–1771* ⊕ *www.hazlittshotel.com* ⮬ *20 rooms, 3 suites* ⦿| *No meals* Ⓜ *Tottenham Court Rd.* ✥ *3:D4.*

$$$
HOTEL
⬚ **The Soho Hotel.** This supertrendy hotel personifies Soho's enduring hipness with its artsy, urban chic vibe. **Pros:** small and sophisticated; excellent service; great restaurant. **Cons:** bar can be crowded and noisy on weeknights. $ *Rooms from: £300* ✉ *4 Richmond Mews, off Dean St., Soho* ☎ *020/7559–3000* ⊕ *www.firmdalehotels.com/hotels/london/ the-soho-hotel* ⮬ *91 rooms, 4 apartments* ⦿| *Some meals* Ⓜ *Tottenham Court Rd.* ✥ *3:C4.*

## COVENT GARDEN

$$$$
HOTEL
Fodor's Choice
★
⬚ **Covent Garden Hotel.** It's little wonder this is now the London home-away-from-home for off-duty celebrities, actors, and style mavens, with its Covent Garden location and guest rooms that are design-magazine stylish, using mix-and-match couture fabrics to stunning effect. **Pros:** great for star-spotting; supertrendy. **Cons:** you can feel you don't matter if you're not famous; location in Covent Garden can be a bit boisterous. $ *Rooms from: £372* ✉ *10 Monmouth St., Covent Garden* ☎ *020/7806–1000, 800/553–6674 in the U.S.* ⊕ *www.firmdalehotels. com/hotels/london/covent-garden-hotel* ⮬ *55 rooms, 3 suites* ⦿| *Some meals* Ⓜ *Covent Garden* ✥ *3:E4.*

$$$$
HOTEL
Fodor's Choice
★
⬚ **ME London.** A shiny fortress of luxury, the ME brings a splash of modern cool to a rather stuffy patch of the Strand. **Pros:** sleek and fashionable; full of high-tech comforts; excellent service; stunning views from rooftop bar. **Cons:** design can sometimes verge on form over function; very small closets and in-room storage areas. $ *Rooms from: £319* ✉ *336 The Strand, Covent Garden* ☎ *0808/234–1953* ⊕ *www.melia. com* ⮬ *141 rooms, 16 suites* ⦿| *Breakfast* Ⓜ *Covent Garden* ✥ *3:G5.*

$$$
HOTEL
⬚ **One Aldwych.** An Edwardian building, with an artsy lobby and understated blend of contemporary and classic, provides pure, modern luxury in a great location for theaters and shopping. **Pros:** understated luxury; ultracool atmosphere; good deals and special offers, including big advance booking discounts. **Cons:** all this luxury doesn't come cheap; fashionable ambience is not always relaxing. $ *Rooms from: £294* ✉ *1 Aldwych, Covent Garden* ☎ *020/7300–1000* ⊕ *www. onealdwych.co.uk* ⮬ *93 rooms, 12 suites* ⦿| *Breakfast* Ⓜ *Charing Cross, Covent Garden* ✥ *3:G5.*

$$$$
HOTEL
Fodor's Choice
★
⬚ **The Savoy.** One of London's most iconic hotels maintains its status at the top with winning attributes of impeccable service, stunning decor, and a desirable Covent Garden location. **Pros:** one of the top hotels in Europe; iconic pedigree; Thames-side location. **Cons:** everything comes with a price tag; street noise is surprisingly problematic, particularly on lower floors; right off the superbusy Strand. $ *Rooms from: £486* ✉ *The Strand, Covent Garden* ☎ *020/7836–4343, 800/257–7544 in the U.S.* ⊕ *www.fairmont.com/savoy-london* ⮬ *206 rooms, 62 suites* ⦿| *Breakfast* Ⓜ *Covent Garden, Charing Cross* ✥ *3:G6.*

## BLOOMSBURY, HOLBORN, AND FITZROVIA

### BLOOMSBURY

**$**
HOTEL
**Celtic Hotel.** This is a solid, dependable budget choice in an otherwise expensive district (close to the West End and British Museum), where you'll be hard-pressed to find a better price. **Pros:** free Wi-Fi; good location; bargain rates. **Cons:** no-frills approach means few extras; no elevator; not all rooms have private bathrooms. ⑤ *Rooms from: £85* ✉ *62 Guilford St., Bloomsbury* ☎ *020/7837–6737* ⊕ *www.stmargaretshotel. co.uk* ⟿ *35 rooms* ⑩ *Breakfast* Ⓜ *Russell Sq.* ✛ *3:F1.*

**$$$**
HOTEL
**Fodor's** Choice
★
**Charlotte Street Hotel.** Tradition and modern flair are fused together in this superstylish Soho retreat, a short walk from Oxford Street. **Pros:** elegant, luxurious; great attention to detail; decent chance at finding a good deal. **Cons:** the popular bar can be noisy; reservations essential for the restaurant. ⑤ *Rooms from: £270* ✉ *15 Charlotte St., Bloomsbury* ☎ *020/7806–2000, 800/553–6674 in the U.S.* ⊕ *www.firmdalehotels. com* ⟿ *46 rooms, 6 suites* ⑩ *Breakfast* Ⓜ *Goodge St.* ✛ *3:C2.*

**$**
HOTEL
**Grange Blooms Hotel.** In this white Georgian-townhouse hotel, just around the corner from the British Museum, rooms are not too tiny by London standards, and those in the back look out onto a leafy green garden. **Pros:** great location; overall good value; excellent rates if you book early through the website. **Cons:** guests can be bumped to sister hotel if fully booked; no air-conditioning; street noise in some rooms. ⑤ *Rooms from: £91* ✉ *7 Montague St., Bloomsbury* ☎ *020/7323– 1717, 800/2247–2643* ⊕ *www.grangehotels.com* ⟿ *26 rooms, 1 suite* ⑩ *Some meals* Ⓜ *Russell Sq.* ✛ *3:F2.*

**$$**
HOTEL
**Harlingford Hotel.** The most contemporary of the hotels around Bloomsbury's Cartwright Gardens offers sleek, quiet, and comfortable bedrooms and perfectly appointed public rooms. **Pros:** good location; friendly staff; private garden; wider breakfast choice than many small London hotels. **Cons:** rooms are small; no air-conditioning; no elevator. ⑤ *Rooms from: £124* ✉ *61–63 Cartwright Gardens, Bloomsbury* ☎ *020/7387–1551* ⊕ *www.harlingfordhotel.com* ⟿ *43 rooms* ⑩ *Breakfast* Ⓜ *Russell Sq.* ✛ *2:C3.*

**$**
B&B/INN
**Jesmond Hotel.** This friendly little hotel is great value given the location: a short walk from the British Museum in one direction, and Soho and Covent Garden in the other. **Pros:** great location; friendly staff; free Wi-Fi; 15% discount on stays of one week. **Cons:** some rooms are very small; nearly half have shared bathrooms. ⑤ *Rooms from: £90* ✉ *63 Gower St., Bloomsbury* ☎ *020/7636–3199* ⊕ *www.jesmondhotel.org. uk* ⟿ *15 rooms* ⑩ *Breakfast* Ⓜ *Goodge St., Euston Sq., Warren St., Russell Sq.* ✛ *3:C1.*

**$$**
HOTEL
**Megaro.** Directly across the street from St. Pancras International station (good Eurostar travelers), the snazzy, well-designed, modern rooms here surround guests with startlingly contemporary style and amenities that include powerful showers and espresso machines. **Pros:** comfortable beds; great location for Eurostar; short hop on Tube to city center. **Cons:** neighborhood isn't great; standard rooms are small; interiors may be a bit stark for some. ⑤ *Rooms from: £170* ✉ *Belgrove St., King's Cross* ☎ *020/7843–2222* ⊕ *www.hotelmegaro.co.uk* ⟿ *49 rooms* ⑩ *Breakfast* Ⓜ *Kings Cross, St. Pancras* ✛ *2:C2.*

**15**

**$**   ⊞ **The Ridgemount Hotel.** Mere blocks away from the British Museum
B&B/INN   and London's West End theaters, this handsomely fronted guesthouse
has clean, neat, and plainly decorated rooms at bargain rates. **Pros:**
good location for theaters and museum; helpful staff; family rooms
(accommodating up to five) are excellent value. **Cons:** decoration is
basic; no elevator; cheapest rooms have shared bathrooms. $ *Rooms
from: £86* ⊠ *65–67 Gower St., Bloomsbury* ☎ *020/7636–1141* ⊕ *www.
ridgemounthotel.co.uk* ↪ *32 rooms (15 with bath)* ⍥ *Breakfast*
Ⓜ *Goodge St.* ✢ *3:D1.*

**$$**   ⊞ **Rough Luxe.** Bloomsbury's most avant-garde guesthouse won't be
B&B/INN   for everyone, but this 19th-century building has been renovated with
an appealing mix of shabby chic and modern comfort. **Pros:** made
for art and design lovers; free Wi-Fi; very close to St. Pancras station.
**Cons:** design is not for everyone; many rooms are tiny; no restau-
rant or bar. $ *Rooms from: £169* ⊠ *1 Birkenhead St., Bloomsbury*
☎ *020/7837–5338* ⊕ *www.roughluxe.co.uk* ↪ *10 rooms* ⍥ *Breakfast*
Ⓜ *Kings Cross* ✢ *2:C2.*

**$$$**   ⊞ **Sanderson Hotel.** At this fashionable and surreal urban spa in a con-
HOTEL   verted 1950s textile factory, the lobby looks like a design museum;
bedrooms have sleigh beds and a mix of over-the-top Louis XV and
postmodern furnishings. **Pros:** popular with design mavens; your every
whim gratified; unique afternoon tea. **Cons:**"designer cool" can be
self-consciously hip; bar and restaurant are so exclusive it's hard to
get in; you need to book far in advance to get lower rates. $ *Rooms
from: £274* ⊠ *50 Berners St., Fitzrovia* ☎ *020/7300–1400* ⊕ *www.
sandersonlondon.com* ↪ *150 rooms* ⍥ *Breakfast* Ⓜ *Oxford Circus,
Tottenham Court Rd.* ✢ *3:B3.*

**$$$**   ⊞ **St. Pancras Renaissance.** This stunningly restored Victorian landmark—
HOTEL   replete with gingerbread turrets and castlelike ornaments—started as a
**Fodor's**Choice   love letter to the golden age of railways, and now it's one of London's
★   most sophisticated places to stay. **Pros:** unique and beautiful; faultless
service; close to the train station. **Cons:** very popular bar and restau-
rant; streets outside are busy 24/7. $ *Rooms from: £219* ⊠ *Euston Rd.,
King's Cross* ☎ *020/7841–3540* ⊕ *www.marriott.com* ↪ *207 rooms, 38
suites* ⍥ *Breakfast* Ⓜ *Kings Cross, St. Pancras. National Rail: Kings
Cross, St. Pancras* ✢ *2:C2.*

## HOLBORN

**$$$$**   ⊞ **Rosewood London.** So striking it was featured in the movie *Howards
HOTEL   End,* this landmark structure (built by the Pearl Assurance Company in
1914) now houses a beautiful hotel with a clubby atmosphere, subtly
elegant India Jane fabrics, and huge, comfortable beds. **Pros:** gorgeous,
romantic space; excellent restaurant; great spa; friendly service. **Cons:**
luxury comes at a price; area is a ghost town at night and on weekends.
$ *Rooms from: £410* ⊠ *252 High Holborn, Holborn* ☎ *020/7781–
8888, 888/767–3966 in U.S.* ⊕ *www.rosewoodhotels.com/en/london*
↪ *294 rooms, 12 suites* ⍥ *Some meals* Ⓜ *Holborn* ✢ *3:G3.*

**$$$**   ⊞ **SACO Holborn.** Down a quiet backstreet, a 10-minute walk from
RENTAL   the British Museum, these serviced apartments are spacious, modern,
and extremely well equipped, including a kitchen with dishwasher
and washing machine. **Pros:** more independence than hotels; pleasant

## LONDON CHAIN HOTEL PRIMER

Here's a quick rundown of some hotel chains worth considering:

**easyHotel:** One of the first chains to bring "pod hotels" to London, the easyHotel chain specializes in very cheap (less than £50 a night for a double) rooms that are clean, secure, and offer all the basics, but are teeny-tiny and have no free extras at all. ⊕ www.easyhotel.com.

**Grange Hotels:** This chain includes a mix of moderately priced hotels with neutral interior design, good service, and gadgets for business travelers. ⊕ www.grangehotels.com.

**Malmaison:** With lavish, elegant small hotels around the country, this upscale chain offers luxurious designer style, good restaurants, and trendy bars. ⊕ www.malmaison.com.

**Millennium:** Similar in style to Premier Inns, Millennium (and its other brand, Copthorne) hotels are targeted at both business and leisure travelers. They offer well-designed rooms with plenty of gadgets and have frequent sales ⊕ www.millenniumhotels.co.uk.

**myhotel:** A chain of pricey hotels with designer style and trendy bars. Myhotels offer reliable comfort and service, if you don't mind the price tag. ⊕ www.myhotels.com.

**Premier Inns:** This chain features medium-size, moderately priced hotels. They're known for their attractive look, and for frequent sales which keep prices low. ⊕ www.premierinn.com.

**15**

and spacious accommodations, on-site parking. **Cons:** exterior is dated; you must provide own bedding for baby cots. ⓢ *Rooms from: £255* ✉ *82 Lamb's Conduit St., Holborn* ☎ *0330/202–0505* ⊕ *www.sacoapartments.co.uk* ⤳ *30 apartments (studios, 1-, 2-, and 3-bed)* ⊚ *No meals* Ⓜ *Russell Sq.* ✛ *3:G1.*

### FITZROVIA

$$$$

HOTEL

Fodor's Choice

★

⊡ **The London Edition.** A solidly bohemian air permeates this handsome hotel in the heart of Fitzrovia, the second hotel in Ian Schrager's venture with Marriott. **Pros:** very trendy; great bars; beautifully designed bedrooms. **Cons:** rooms may feel small to some; lobby can get crowded with trendsetters descending upon the bars and nightclub. ⓢ *Rooms from: £312* ✉ *10 Berners St., Fitzrovia* ☎ *020/7781–0000* ⊕ *editionhotels.marriott.com/london* ⤳ *173 rooms* ⊚ *Breakfast* Ⓜ *Oxford Circus* ✛ *3:C3.*

## THE CITY

$$

HOTEL

⊡ **Apex City of London.** At this sleek, modern branch of the small Apex chain near the Tower of London, bedrooms are reasonably spacious, with contemporary color schemes, 40-inch flat screen TVs, and little sofas. **Pros:** great location; helpful staff; good advance booking discounts; free Wi-Fi. **Cons:** geared more to business than leisure travelers; price can rise sharply during busy times. ⓢ *Rooms from: £152* ✉ *1 Seething La., The City* ☎ *020/7702–2020* ⊕ *www.apexhotels.co.uk* ⤳ *130 rooms, 49 suites* ⊚ *Breakfast* Ⓜ *Tower Hill* ✛ *2:G2.*

$$ **⌐ Crowne Plaza London—The City.** Don't let the hotel's all-business
HOTEL   appearance put you off: it's a polished operation, with stylish minimal-
ist rooms, just steps from the Blackfriars Tube and train station in one
direction and bustling Fleet Street in the other. **Pros:** good rates avail-
able with advance booking; great location near the river and transport.
**Cons:** neighborhood is superbusy during the day and empty at night.
⑤ *Rooms from: £152* ⊠ *19 New Bridge St., The City* ☎ *0871/942–9190*
⊕ *www.cplondoncityhotel.co.uk* ➦ *203 rooms, 3 suites* ⵔⵔ *Breakfast*
Ⓜ *Blackfriars* ✛ *2:F6.*

$   **⌐ Grange City Hotel.** With an eye on business, this sleek City hotel has
HOTEL   everything the workaholic needs to feel right at home: chic bedrooms
subtly decorated, modern furnishings, plenty of space (by London stan-
dards), and more. **Pros:** good-size rooms; rates can drop considerably
on weekends; female-friendly rooms are great for lone female travelers.
**Cons:** a bit off the tourist track; some rooms overlook train platform;
prices can soar midweek; online discounts tend to not allow changes
or cancellation. ⑤ *Rooms from: £112* ⊠ *8–14 Cooper's Row, The City*
☎ *020/7863–3700* ⊕ *www.grangehotels.com* ➦ *307 rooms, 11 suites*
ⵔⵔ *Some meals* Ⓜ *Tower Hill, Aldgate, Monument* ✛ *2:G2.*

$$ **⌐ The Rookery.** An absolutely unique and beautiful 1725 townhouse,
HOTEL   the Rookery is the kind of place where you want to allow quality time
Fodor's Choice   to enjoy and soak up the atmosphere. **Pros:** helpful staff; free Wi-Fi;
★   good deals in the off-season. **Cons:** breakfast costs extra; Tube ride to
tourist sites. ⑤ *Rooms from: £175* ⊠ *12 Peter's La., at Cowcross St.,
The City* ☎ *020/7336–0931* ⊕ *www.rookeryhotel.com* ➦ *30 rooms, 3
suites* ⵔⵔ *No meals* Ⓜ *Farringdon* ✛ *2:F4.*

$$ **⌐ Threadneedles Hotel.** The elaborate building housing this grand hotel
HOTEL   in the financial district is a former bank, and the vast old banking
hall—beautifully adapted as the lobby, with luxurious marble and
mahogany panels—really sets the scene. **Pros:** lap of luxury; excellent
service. **Cons:** a bit stuffy for some tastes; can be at least three times
more expensive weekdays; neighborhood is quiet at night. ⑤ *Rooms
from: £161* ⊠ *5 Threadneedle St., The City* ☎ *020/7657–8080* ⊕ *www.
hotelthreadneedles.co.uk* ➦ *63 rooms, 6 suites* ⵔⵔ *Breakfast* Ⓜ *Bank*
✛ *2:G2.*

$$$ **⌐ The Zetter.** The five-story atrium, art deco staircase, and slick Euro-
HOTEL   pean restaurant hint at the delights to come in this converted ware-
Fodor's Choice   house—a breath of fresh air with its playful color schemes, elegant
★   wallpapers, and wonderful views of The City from the higher floors.
**Pros:** huge amounts of character; big rooms; free Wi-Fi; award-winning restaurant. **Cons:** rooms with good views cost more. ⑤ *Rooms
from: £231* ⊠ *86–88 Clerkenwell Rd., Clerkenwell* ☎ *020/7324–4444*
⊕ *www.thezetter.com* ➦ *59 rooms* ⵔⵔ *Breakfast* Ⓜ *Farringdon* ✛ *3:H1.*

## EAST LONDON

$$ **⌐ Ace Hotel London Shoreditch.** The first European outlet of the superhip
HOTEL   Ace hotel chain fits right into the scenery in achingly cool Shoreditch,
surrounded by galleries and on-trend boutiques every bit as style con-
scious as its own creatively minimalist interiors. **Pros:** extremely fash-
ionable; large and comfortable bedrooms; great bar. **Cons:** not everyone

will enjoy being surrounded by hipsters; street noise can be a problem; frustrating online booking system. ⑤ *Rooms from: £120* ✉ *100 Shoreditch High St., Shoreditch* ☎ *020/7613–9800* ⊕ *www.acehotel. com* ⤵ *258 rooms* ❍*I Breakfast* Ⓜ *Shoreditch High St.* ✢ *2:G1.*

**$$**
HOTEL
⊡ **Andaz.** Swanky and upscale, this hotel sports a modern, masculine design, and novel check-in procedure—instead of standing at a desk, guests sit in a lounge while a staff member with a tablet takes their information. **Pros:** nice attention to detail; no standing in line to check in; "healthy minibars" are stocked with nuts, fruit, and yogurt. **Cons:** sparse interior design is not for all; rates rise significantly for midweek stays. ⑤ *Rooms from: £181* ✉ *40 Liverpool St., East End* ☎ *020/7961– 1234, 800/492–8804 in U.S.* ⊕ *www.andaz.hyatt.com* ⤵ *267 rooms* ❍*I Breakfast* Ⓜ *Liverpool St.* ✢ *2:G2.*

**$$**
B&B/INN
**Fodor's Choice**
★
⊡ **Cable Street Inn.** Wonderful modern art lines the walls of this former Victorian pub a mile east of the Tower of London, which has been beautifully restored and converted into a modern B&B. **Pros:** true one-of-a-kind place; beautiful art; wonderful host; free Wi-Fi. **Cons:** 20-minute journey by DLR then Tube to the center; historic nature of the building makes it unsuitable for those with mobility problems. ⑤ *Rooms from: £130* ✉ *232 Cable St., East End* ☎ *020/7790– 4019* ⊕ *www.cablestreetinn.co.uk* ⤵ *3 rooms* ❍*I Breakfast* Ⓜ *DLR: Shadwell* ✢ *2:H5.*

**$$**
HOTEL
**Fodor's Choice**
★
⊡ **The Hoxton Shoreditch.** The design throughout this trendy East London lodging is contemporary—but not so modern as to be absurd—and in keeping with a claim to combine a country-lodge lifestyle with true urban living, a fire crackles in the lobby. **Pros:** cool vibe; neighborhood known for funky galleries and boutiques; huge weekend discounts; very hip restaurant. **Cons:** price skyrockets during the week; away from major tourist sights; cheapest rooms are called "shoeboxes" for a reason. ⑤ *Rooms from: £116* ✉ *81 Great Eastern St., East End* ☎ *020/7550–1000* ⊕ *www.hoxtonhotels.com* ⤵ *205 rooms* ❍*I Breakfast* Ⓜ *Shoreditch High St.* ✢ *2:G1.*

**$**
HOTEL
⊡ **Qbic London City.** A contrast to the super expensive business hotels that proliferate in this part of the East End on the edge of the City, the Qbic is a modern and surprisingly affordable option in a trendy corner of town. **Pros:** quirky, original vibe; great value for money; environmentally friendly. **Cons:** bit out of the way; not everyone will love the style; cheapest rooms have no windows. ⑤ *Rooms from: £75* ✉ *42 Adler St., East End* ⊕ *www.qbichotels.com* ⤵ *171 rooms* ❍*I Breakfast* Ⓜ *Aldgate East* ✢ *2:H2.*

**$$**
HOTEL
⊡ **Town Hall Hotel and Apartments.** An art deco town hall, abandoned in the early 1980s and turned into a chic hotel 30 years later, is now a lively and stylish place, with the best of the building's elegant original features intact. **Pros:** beautifully designed; lovely staff; big discounts on weekends. **Cons:** though touted as "cool" and "cutting edge," this is not a great part of town; a 15-minute Tube ride from Central London. ⑤ *Rooms from: £173* ✉ *Patriot Sq., Bethnal Green, East End* ☎ *020/7657–8080* ⊕ *www.townhallhotel.com* ⤵ *98 rooms, 86 suites* ❍*I Breakfast* Ⓜ *Bethnal Green* ✢ *2:H1.*

15

## SOUTH OF THE THAMES

$ **Church Street Hotel.** Like rays of sunshine in gritty South London,
HOTEL these rooms above a popular tapas restaurant are individually deco-
Fodor's Choice rated in rich, bold tones and authentic Central American touches like
★ elaborately painted crucifixes, tiles handmade in Guadalajara, and
homemade iron bed frames. **Pros:** unique and arty; great breakfasts;
lovely staff; closer to central London than it might appear. **Cons:** a
trendy but not great part of town (stay out of neighboring Elephant
and Castle); would suit adventurous young things more than families;
a mile from a Tube station (though bus connections are handier); some
rooms have shared bathrooms. $ *Rooms from: £90 ⊠ 29–33 Camber-
well Church St., Camberwell, South East* ☎ *020/7703–5984* ⊕ *www.
churchstreethotel.com* ↬ *31 rooms* ⦿ *Breakfast* Ⓜ *Oval St.* ✛ *5:H6.*

$$ **London Bridge Hotel.** Steps away from the London Bridge rail and Tube
HOTEL stations, and handy for the South Bank, this thoroughly modern, stylish
hotel is popular with business travelers, but leisure travelers find it just
as appealing. **Pros:** good location for visiting South Bank attractions;
free Wi-Fi; good deals available online in the off-season. **Cons:** small
bedrooms; prices rise by £100 or more midweek. $ *Rooms from: £168
⊠ 8–18 London Bridge St., Southwark* ☎ *020/7855–2200* ⊕ *www.
london-bridge-hotel.co.uk* ↬ *138 rooms, 3 apartments* ⦿ *Breakfast*
Ⓜ *London Bridge* ✛ *5:H1.*

$$$$ **London Marriott Hotel County Hall.** This grand hotel on the Thames
HOTEL enjoys perhaps the most iconic view in the city—right next door is
the London Eye, and directly across the Thames are the Houses of
Parliament and Big Ben. **Pros:** handy for South Bank arts scene, Lon-
don Eye, and Westminster; great gym; good weekend discounts. **Cons:**
interior design can be overdone for some tastes; rooms facing the river
cost extra; high summer midweek rates are just ridiculous. $ *Rooms
from: £311 ⊠ County Hall, Westminster Bridge Rd., South Bank*
☎ *020/7928–5200, 888/236–2427 in U.S.* ⊕ *www.marriott.com* ↬ *186
rooms, 14 suites* ⦿ *Breakfast* Ⓜ *Westminster, Waterloo. National Rail:
Waterloo* ✛ *5:D2.*

$ **Premier Travel Inn County Hall.** The small but nicely decorated rooms at
HOTEL this budget choice share the same County Hall complex as the fancier
FAMILY London Marriott Hotel County Hall, and though it has none of the
spectacular river views, and facilities are more basic, the selling point is
the same convenient location at a fraction of the price. **Pros:** fantastic
location for the South Bank; bargains to be had if you book in advance;
kids (sharing with adults) stay free. **Cons:** limited services; cookie-cutter
chain-hotel atmosphere; on a busy road. $ *Rooms from: £79 ⊠ Bel-
vedere Rd., South Bank* ☎ *0871/527–8648* ⊕ *www.premierinn.com*
↬ *313 rooms* ⦿ *Breakfast* Ⓜ *Westminster, Waterloo. National Rail:
Waterloo* ✛ *5:D2.*

# KENSINGTON, CHELSEA, KNIGHTSBRIDGE, AND BELGRAVIA

## KENSINGTON

**$$$**
**HOTEL**
🖼 **Ampersand.** A sense of style emanates from every surface of this sumptuous hotel in the heart of Kensington, and the playful, vintage vibe lends the property a refreshingly down-to-earth feel in a neighborhood that often feels cooler-than-thou. **Pros:** flawless design; great service; good restaurant. **Cons:** ground-floor rooms can be noisy. ⑤ *Rooms from: £216* ✉ *10 Harrington Rd., Kensington* ⊕ *www.ampersandhotel. com* ⤵ *106 rooms, 5 suites* ⦿⧵ *Breakfast* Ⓜ *Gloucester Rd.* ✛ *4:D2.*

**$$**
**HOTEL**
🖼 **Ashburn Hotel.** A short walk from Gloucester Road Tube station and within walking distance of Harrods and the Kensington museums, the Ashburn is one of the better "boutique" hotels in this part of town. **Pros:** friendly atmosphere; free Wi-Fi; turndown gift (different every night). **Cons:** summer prices sometimes hike the cost; some rooms on the small side. ⑤ *Rooms from: £149* ✉ *111 Cromwell Rd., Kensington* ☎ *020/7938–5930 for reservations, 020/7244–1999* ⊕ *www.ashburn-hotel.co.uk* ⤵ *55 rooms, 3 suites* ⦿⧵ *Breakfast* Ⓜ *Gloucester Rd.* ✛ *4:C2.*

**$$**
**HOTEL**
🖼 **The Cranley Hotel.** Old-fashioned British propriety is the overall feeling at this small, Victorian-townhouse hotel, where high ceilings, huge windows, and a pale, creamy color scheme flood the bedrooms with light. **Pros:** good-size rooms; attractively decorated; friendly staff; free evening nibbles are a nice touch. **Cons:** steep stairs into lobby; no restaurant; prices rise in mid-summer. ⑤ *Rooms from: £152* ✉ *10–12 Bina Gardens, South Kensington* ☎ *020/7373–0123* ⊕ *www. thecranley.com* ⤵ *29 rooms, 5 suites, 4 apartments* ⦿⧵ *Breakfast* Ⓜ *Gloucester Rd.* ✛ *4:C3.*

**$**
**HOTEL**
🖼 **easyHotel South Kensington.** London's original "pod hotel" has tiny rooms with a double bed, private shower room, and little else—each brightly decorated in the easyGroup's trademark orange and white (to match their budget airline easyJet). **Pros:** amazing rates; safe and decent enough space; good location. **Cons:** not for the claustrophobic—rooms are truly tiny and most have no windows; six floors and no elevator; basic as basic can be. ⑤ *Rooms from: £39* ✉ *14 Lexham Gardens, Kensington* ⊕ *www.easyhotel.com* ⤵ *34 rooms* ⦿⧵ *No meals* Ⓜ *Gloucester Rd.* ✛ *4:B2.*

**$$**
**HOTEL**
🖼 **The Gore Hotel.** Just down the road from the Albert Hall, this gorgeous, friendly hotel has a luxurious mixture of the comfortable and the extraordinary. **Pros:** gorgeously designed and spacious rooms; outstanding, attentive service; air-conditioning in all rooms. **Cons:** Wi-Fi is not free; bar can be noisy. ⑤ *Rooms from: £170* ✉ *190 Queen's Gate, Kensington* ☎ *020/7584–6601, 888/757–5587 in U.S* ⊕ *www. gorehotel.com* ⤵ *50 rooms* ⦿⧵ *Breakfast* Ⓜ *Gloucester Rd.* ✛ *4:D1.*

**$$**
**HOTEL**
🖼 **Kensington House Hotel.** A short stroll from High Street Kensington and Kensington Gardens, this refurbished 19th-century townhouse has streamlined, contemporary rooms with large windows letting in plenty of light and comfortable beds with luxurious fabrics and soft comforters. **Pros:** attractive design; relaxing setting; free Wi-Fi. **Cons:** rooms are small; bathrooms are minuscule. ⑤ *Rooms from: £168* ✉ *15–16 Prince of Wales Terr., Kensington* ☎ *020/7937–2345* ⊕ *www.kenhouse.com* ⤵ *39 rooms, 2 suites* ⦿⧵ *Breakfast* Ⓜ *High Street Kensington* ✛ *4:C1.*

**15**

**$$** ⊞ **London Marriott Kensington.** A big favorite for the business crowd,
HOTEL this pleasant, modern outpost of the Marriott megachain is just one of
several big-name hotels on busy Cromwell Road. **Pros:** friendly, efficient service; good neighborhood; one-minute Tube ride to Kensington
museums. **Cons:**"could be anywhere in the world" business ambience
feels impersonal; bedrooms are on the small side. ⑤ *Rooms from: £151*
✉ *147 Cromwell Rd., Kensington* ☎ *020/7973–1000* ⊕ *www.marriott.
com* ☞ *216 rooms* ⭐ *Some meals* Ⓜ *Earl's Ct., Gloucester Rd.* ✛ *4:B2.*

**$$$$** ⊞ **The Milestone Hotel.** This pair of intricately decorated Victorian
HOTEL townhouses overlooking Kensington Palace and Gardens is an inti-
Fodor's Choice mate, luxurious alternative to the city's more famous high-end hotels,
★ offering thoughtful hospitality and sumptuous, distinctive rooms full
of antiques. **Pros:** beautiful and elegant; big rooms, many with park
views; excellent location; good package deal includes tickets to Kens-
ington Palace and £50 in shopping vouchers. **Cons:** actual room rate
discounts are rare. ⑤ *Rooms from: £382* ✉ *1 Kensington Ct., Kensing-
ton* ☎ *020/7917–1000* ⊕ *www.milestonehotel.com* ☞ *44 rooms, 12
suites, 6 apartments* ⭐ *Breakfast* Ⓜ *High Street Kensington* ✛ *4:C1.*

**$$** ⊞ **Millennium Gloucester.** With a Tube station opposite and Kensington's
HOTEL many attractions nearby, this hotel is both convenient and alluring.
**Pros:** great location; elegant design; good deals available if you book in
advance. **Cons:** lighting in some bedrooms is a bit too subtle; bathrooms
are relatively small. ⑤ *Rooms from: £120* ✉ *4–18 Harrington Gardens,
Kensington* ☎ *020/7373–6030* ⊕ *www.millenniumhotels.co.uk* ☞ *610
rooms* ⭐ *Breakfast* Ⓜ *Gloucester Rd.* ✛ *4:C2.*

**$$** ⊞ **The Nadler Kensington.** Known as an "aparthotel," this creamy white
HOTEL Georgian townhouse offers a useful compromise between full-service
hotel and the freedom of self-catering in the form of comfortable rooms
with a stylish, modern look and tiny kitchenettes. **Pros:** great alterna-
tive to hotel; handy minikitchens; free Wi-Fi; 24-hour reception. **Cons:**
basic rooms are small; movies in entertainment system are pay-per-
view; 15-minute Tube ride to central London. ⑤ *Rooms from: £155*
✉ *25 Courtfield Gardens, South Kensington* ☎ *020/7244–2255* ⊕ *www.
thenadler.com* ☞ *65 rooms* ⭐ *No meals* Ⓜ *Earl's Ct.* ✛ *4:B3.*

**$$$** ⊞ **Number Sixteen.** Rooms at this lovely luxury guesthouse, just around
HOTEL the corner from the Victoria & Albert Museum, look like they come from
Fodor's Choice the pages of *Architectural Digest,* and the delightful garden is an added
★ bonus. **Pros:** just the right level of helpful service; interiors are gorgeous.
**Cons:** no restaurant; small elevator. ⑤ *Rooms from: £282* ✉ *16 Sumner
Pl., South Kensington* ☎ *020/7589–5232, 888/559–5508 in U.S.* ⊕ *www.
firmdale.com* ☞ *42 rooms* ⭐ *Breakfast* Ⓜ *South Kensington* ✛ *4:D2.*

**$$$** ⊞ **The Pelham Hotel.** One of the first and most stylish of London's famed
HOTEL "boutique" hotels, this still-chic choice is but a short stroll away from
the Natural History, Science, and Victoria & Albert museums. **Pros:**
great location for museum-hopping; soigné interior design; lovely staff.
**Cons:** taller guests will find themselves cursing the top-floor rooms with
sloping ceilings. ⑤ *Rooms from: £252* ✉ *15 Cromwell Pl., South Kens-
ington* ☎ *020/7589–8288, 888/757–5587 in U.S.* ⊕ *www.pelhamhotel.
co.uk* ☞ *47 rooms, 4 suites* ⭐ *Breakfast* Ⓜ *South Kensington* ✛ *4:D2.*

**$$** ⊞ **The Rockwell.** Despite being on the notoriously traffic-clogged Crom-
HOTEL well Road, this excellent little place is one of the best boutique hotels
in this part of London—and windows have good soundproofing. **Pros:**
large bedrooms; stylish surroundings; helpful staff. **Cons:** on a busy
road; 20-minute Tube ride to central London. ⑤ *Rooms from: £136*
⊠ *181 Cromwell Rd., South Kensington* ☎ *020/7244–2000* ⊕ *www.*
*therockwell.com* ⥱ *38 rooms, 2 suites* ⦿ *Breakfast* Ⓜ *Earl's Ct.* ✛ *4:B2.*

### CHELSEA

**$** ⊞ **myhotel chelsea.** Rooms at this small, chic charmer—tucked away
HOTEL down a side street in an upscale neighborhood—are bijou tiny but
sophisticated, with mauve satin throws atop crisp white down com-
forters. **Pros:** stylish rooms made for relaxation; good neighborhood.
**Cons:** tiny rooms; no restaurant. ⑤ *Rooms from: £93* ⊠ *35 Ixworth*
*Pl., Chelsea* ☎ *020/7225–7500* ⊕ *www.myhotels.com* ⥱ *45 rooms, 9*
*suites* ⦿ *Breakfast* Ⓜ *South Kensington* ✛ *4:E3.*

### KNIGHTSBRIDGE

**$$$** ⊞ **The Beaufort.** This gracious boutique hotel is a favorite entry in the
HOTEL little black books of many a visiting high-society *fashionista*—Har-
rods is the merest toss of a diamond from the front door. **Pros:** gorgeous interiors; friendly and professional staff; air-conditioning; free
Wi-Fi. **Cons:** standard doubles are much smaller than the price might
indicate. ⑤ *Rooms from: £250* ⊠ *33 Beaufort Gardens, Knightsbridge*
☎ *020/7584–5252* ⊕ *www.thebeaufort.co.uk* ⥱ *22 rooms, 7 suites*
⦿ *Breakfast* Ⓜ *Knightsbridge* ✛ *4:F1.*

**$$$$** ⊞ **The Berkeley.** Convenient for Knightsbridge shopping, the very elegant
HOTEL Berkeley is known for its renowned restaurants and luxuries that cul-
FAMILY minate—literally—in a splendid penthouse swimming pool. **Pros:** lavish
Fodor'sChoice and elegant; attentive service; prices aren't quite as stratospheric as some
★ high-end places. **Cons:** you'll need your best designer clothes to fit in.
⑤ *Rooms from: £360* ⊠ *Wilton Pl., Knightsbridge* ☎ *020/7235–6000,*
*800/637–2869 in U.S.* ⊕ *www.the-berkeley.co.uk* ⥱ *103 rooms, 55*
*suites* ⦿ *Breakfast* Ⓜ *Knightsbridge* ✛ *4:G1.*

**$$$** ⊞ **The Capital Hotel.** Nothing is ever too much at this elegant hotel that
HOTEL was formerly a private house; mattresses are handmade, sheets are
450-thread count, bathrooms are marble, and everything is done in
impeccable taste. **Pros:** beautiful space; handy for shopping at Harrods;
excellent restaurant. **Cons:** breakfast is expensive. ⑤ *Rooms from: £260*
⊠ *22–24 Basil St., Knightsbridge* ☎ *020/7589–5171, 800/926–3199*
*in U.S.* ⊕ *www.capitalhotel.co.uk* ⥱ *40 rooms, 9 suites* ⦿ *Breakfast*
Ⓜ *Knightsbridge* ✛ *4:F1.*

**$$$** ⊞ **Egerton House.** A sensationally soigné and chic space that feels like
HOTEL your own private London home, this hotel has some truly luxuriant
Fodor'sChoice design touches, including guest rooms lavishly decorated with rich
★ fabrics and a knockout white-on-gold dining room. **Pros:** lovely staff;
magnificent interiors; striking art. **Cons:** some style touches a little too
froufrou. ⑤ *Rooms from: £236* ⊠ *17–19 Egerton Terr., Knightsbridge*
☎ *020/7589–2412, 877/955–1515 in U.S.* ⊕ *www.redcarnationhotels.*
*com* ⥱ *23 rooms, 6 suites* ⦿ *Breakfast* Ⓜ *Knightsbridge, South Kens-*
*ington* ✛ *4:F2.*

15

# APARTMENT RENTALS & HOME EXCHANGES

## APARTMENT RENTALS

For a home base that's roomy enough for a family and that comes with cooking facilities, consider renting furnished "flats" (the British word for apartments).

## INTERNATIONAL AGENTS

**Hideaways International.** This company offers boutique hotels, tours, and cruises. ⊠ *767 Islington St., Portsmouth* ☎ *603/430–4433, 800/843–4433* ⊕ *www.hideaways.com.*

## LOCAL AGENTS

**The Apartment Service.** This agency specializes in executive apartments for business travelers, so prices are high, but so is the quality. ⊠ *5 Francis Grove, Wimbledon* ☎ *020/8944–1444* ⊕ *www.apartmentservice.com.*

**At Home in London.** Rooms in private homes in Knightsbridge, Kensington, Mayfair, Chelsea, and West London are handled by this agency. ⊠ *70 Black Lion La., Hammersmith* ☎ *020/8748–2701* ⊕ *www.athomeinlondon.co.uk.*

**The Bed and Breakfast Club.** Contact this company for delightful little London hideaways, in Kensington, Chelsea, and Knightsbridge, costing around £75–£125 per night with full English breakfasts. ⊠ *405 Kings Rd., Suite 192, Chelsea* ☎ *01243/370–692* ⊕ *www.thebedandbreakfastclub. co.uk* ☞ *There's a 2.5% fee for using a credit card; debit cards incur no fees. The full price of room must be paid in advance; check cancellation policies carefully.*

**Landmark Trust.** Specializing in unusual and historic buildings, this agency has London apartments starting at around £650 for a four-night (minimum) stay. ⊠ *Shottesbrooke, Maidenhead* ☎ *01628/825–925* ⊕ *www.landmarktrust.org.uk.*

## HOME EXCHANGES

If you would like to exchange your home for someone else's, join a home-exchange organization, which will send you its updated listings of available exchanges for a year.

**Intervac U.S.** It costs from $99 per year for a listing and online access with this company. ☎ *866/884–7567* ⊕ *us.intervac-homeexchange.com.*

---

**$$$$**
**HOTEL**
**Fodor'sChoice**
★

☷ **The Lanesborough.** Beautiful, traditional, and luxurious, the Lanesborough is like a gilded cocoon for the seriously wealthy that exudes a spectacular richness, from the design-magazine perfection of the bedrooms to the magnificent 19th-century antiques. **Pros:** beautiful and historic; great service; your wish is their command—there's even an in-house butler. **Cons:** prices are extraordinary; might be too fancy for some. ⑤ *Rooms from: £650* ⊠ *Hyde Park Corner, Knightsbridge* ☎ *020/7259–5599, 800/999–1828 in U.S.* ⊕ *www.lanesborough.com* ▭ *No credit cards* ⇌ *52 rooms, 43 suites* ☉ *Breakfast* Ⓜ *Hyde Park Corner* ✛ *4:H1.*

**$$$$**
**HOTEL**
**Fodor'sChoice**
★

☷ **Mandarin Oriental Hyde Park.** Built in 1880, the Mandarin Oriental welcomes you with one of the most exuberantly Victorian facades in town, then fast-forwards you to high-trend modern London, thanks to striking and luxurious guest rooms filled with high-tech gadgets. **Pros:** great shopping at your doorstep; amazing views of Hyde Park;

excellent service. **Cons:** nothing comes cheap; you must dress for dinner (and lunch and breakfast). *$ Rooms from: £468 ⊠ 66 Knightsbridge, Knightsbridge ☎ 020/7235–2000 ⊕ www.mandarinoriental.com/london ⟿ 177 rooms, 23 suites ⊙ Breakfast ⓜ Knightsbridge ✧ 4:F1.*

### BELGRAVIA

**$$**
HOTEL
Fodor'sChoice
★

⬚ **Artist Residence.** As packed with character and charm as they come, this artsy boutique hotel oozes bohemian sophistication. **Pros:** romantic and charming; close to Victoria Station; great staff. **Cons:** the wrong side of Victoria for most attractions; stairs to climb. *$ Rooms from: £166 ⊠ 52 Cambridge St., Belgravia ☎ 020/7931–8946 ⊕ www.artistresidencelondon.co.uk ⟿ 10 rooms ⊙ Breakfast ⓜ Victoria, Pimlico ✧ 5:A4.*

**$$**
B&B/INN

⬚ **B&B Belgravia.** At this modern guesthouse near Victoria Station, a clean, chic white color scheme, simple modern furniture, and a lounge where a fire crackles away in the winter are all geared to homey comforts. **Pros:** nice extras like free use of a laptop in hotel lounge; coffee and tea always available. **Cons:** rooms and bathrooms are small; can be noisy, especially on lower floors. *$ Rooms from: £140 ⊠ 64–66 Ebury St., Belgravia ☎ 020/7259–8570 ⊕ www.bb-belgravia.com ⟿ 17 rooms ⊙ Breakfast ⓜ Sloane Sq., Victoria ✧ 4:H2.*

**$$**
HOTEL

⬚ **The Luna Simone Hotel.** This delightful and friendly little family-run hotel, a short stroll from Buckingham Palace, is a real find for the price in central London. **Pros:** friendly and well run; family rooms are outstanding value; superb location. **Cons:** tiny bathrooms; thin walls; no elevator or air-conditioning. *$ Rooms from: £139 ⊠ 47–49 Belgrave Rd., Belgravia ☎ 020/7834–5897 ⊕ www.lunasimonehotel.com ⟿ 36 rooms ⊙ Breakfast ⓜ Pimlico, Victoria ✧ 5:A4.*

**$$**
RENTAL

⬚ **Studios@82.** A great little side operation from B&B Belgravia, these self-catering apartments present a fantastic value. **Pros:** great rates; lovely location; all the independence of self-catering. **Cons:** lots of stairs and no elevator; check-in is at B&B Belgravia, six doors down the street. *$ Rooms from: £130 ⊠ 82 Ebury St., Belgravia ☎ 020/7259–8570 ⊕ www.bb-belgravia.com ⟿ 9 apartments ⊙ Breakfast ⓜ Knightsbridge ✧ 4:H2.*

## NOTTING HILL AND BAYSWATER

### NOTTING HILL

**$$**
B&B/INN
Fodor'sChoice
★

⬚ **The Main House.** A stay in this delightfully welcoming B&B feels more like sleeping over at a friend's house than a stay in a hotel—albeit a particularly wealthy and well-connected friend. **Pros:** unique and unusual place; charming and helpful owners. **Cons:** three-night minimum stay is restrictive; few in-house services. *$ Rooms from: £120 ⊠ 6 Colvile Rd., Notting Hill ☎ 020/7221–9691 ⊕ www.themainhouse.com ⟿ 4 rooms ⊙ Breakfast ⓜ Notting Hill Gate ✧ 1:A4.*

**$**
B&B/INN

⬚ **Portobello Gold.** This no-frills B&B, in the heart of the Portobello Road antiques area above the pub and restaurant of the same name, offers comfortable guest rooms where double beds take up almost all the space. **Pros:** great Notting Hill location; pleasant staff; free Wi-Fi. **Cons:** tiny bedrooms; "wet rooms" replace proper bathrooms (be prepared to

15

shower by the sink); can be noisy. $ *Rooms from: £80* ⊠ *95–97 Portobello Rd., Notting Hill* ☎ *020/7460–4910* ⊕ *www.portobellogold.com* ⤣ *6 rooms, 1 apartment* ⫯⃝⫯ *Breakfast* Ⓜ *Notting Hill Gate* ✛ *1:A4.*

**$$**
**HOTEL**
⛉ **The Portobello Hotel.** One of London's quirkiest hotels, the little Portobello (formed from two adjoining Victorian houses) has attracted scores of celebrities to its small but stylish rooms over the years, and the decor reflects these hip credentials with joyous abandon. **Pros:** stylish and unique; celebrity vibe; guests have use of nearby gym and pool. **Cons:** all but the priciest rooms are quite small; may be too eccentric for some. $ *Rooms from: £195* ⊠ *22 Stanley Gardens, Notting Hill* ☎ *020/7727–2777* ⊕ *www.portobello-hotel.co.uk* ⊙ *Closed 10 days at Christmas* ⤣ *21 rooms* ⫯⃝⫯ *Breakfast* Ⓜ *Notting Hill Gate* ✛ *1:A5.*

## BAYSWATER

**$$**
**HOTEL**
⛉ **Colonnade.** Near a canal filled with colorful "narrowboats" in the Little Venice neighborhood, this lovely townhouse offers individually styled rooms, some of which are split-level; others have balconies filled with rich brocades, velvets, and antiques. **Pros:** beautifully decorated; unique and little-known part of London, five minutes from Paddington Station; free Wi-Fi. **Cons:** you have to go through shoddier parts of town to get here; rooms are small. $ *Rooms from: £116* ⊠ *2 Warrington Crescent, Bayswater* ☎ *020/7286–1052* ⊕ *www.colonnadehotel.co.uk* ⤣ *15 rooms, 28 suites* ⫯⃝⫯ *Breakfast* Ⓜ *Warwick Ave.* ✛ *1:C2.*

**$**
**HOTEL**
⛉ **London House Hotel.** Set in a row of white Georgian townhouses, this excellent budget option in hit-or-miss Bayswater is friendly, well run, and spotlessly clean. **Pros:** friendly and efficient; emphasis on value; good location. **Cons:** some public areas feel a bit too clinical; smallest rooms are tiny. $ *Rooms from: £76* ⊠ *81 Kensington Garden Sq., Bayswater* ☎ *020/7243–1810* ⊕ *www.londonhousehotels.com* ⤣ *100 rooms* ⫯⃝⫯ *Breakfast* Ⓜ *Queensway, Bayswater* ✛ *1:B4.*

**$**
**B&B/INN**
⛉ **Parkwood Hotel.** Just seconds from Hyde Park in one of London's swankiest enclaves (the Blairs live a few doors away), this sweet little guesthouse is an oasis of value, with warm and helpful hosts and bright guest rooms that are simply furnished with pastel color schemes and reproduction antique beds. **Pros:** lovely hosts; free Wi-Fi; hotel guarantees to match or beat rate of any other hotel of its class in the area. **Cons:** often booked up in advance; no elevator and no ground-floor bedrooms; front-facing rooms can be noisy. $ *Rooms from: £95* ⊠ *4 Stanhope Pl., Bayswater* ☎ *020/7402–2241* ⊕ *www.parkwoodhotel.com* ⤣ *18 rooms* ⫯⃝⫯ *Breakfast* Ⓜ *Marble Arch* ✛ *1:F4.*

**$$**
**RENTAL**
⛉ **Space Apart Hotel.** These studio apartments near Hyde Park are done in soothing tones of white and gray, with polished wood floors and attractive modern kitchenettes equipped with all you need to make small meals. **Pros:** especially good value; the larger suites have space for four people; handy location. **Cons:** no in-house restaurant or bar; two-night minimum stay. $ *Rooms from: £140* ⊠ *32–37 Kensington Gardens Sq., Bayswater* ☎ *020/7908–1340* ⊕ *www.aparthotel-london.co.uk* ⤣ *30 rooms* ⫯⃝⫯ *No meals* Ⓜ *Bayswater* ✛ *1:B4.*

**$$**
**RENTAL**
⛉ **Vancouver Studios.** This pleasant aparthotel, in a converted Victorian townhouse, is full of quirky design flourishes, from flock wallpaper in the sitting room to a suit of armor at the top of the stairs. **Pros:** more

## LODGING ALTERNATIVES

**London School of Economics Vacations.** London School of Economics Vacations starts at around £75 for a double with shared bathroom, or £95 for a double with private bathroom. ⊠ *Passfield Hall, 1–7 Endsleigh Pl., Bloomsbury* ☎ *020/7955-7676* ⊕ *www.lsevacations.co.uk* ⊟ *No credit cards* ⦿ *No meals.*

**University College London.** University College London opens up its accommodations mid-June–mid-September (for two-night minimum stays). ⊠ *Residence Manager, Campbell House, 5–10 Taviton St.* ☎ *020/7837-6704* ⊕ *www.ucl.ac.uk/residences* ⦿ *No meals.*

space than most traditional hotel rooms; unique and pleasantly designed little apartments. **Cons:** a bit out of the way. ⑤ *Rooms from: £149* ⊠ *30 Prince's Sq., Bayswater* ☎ *020/7243-1270* ⊕ *www.vancouverstudios. co.uk* 🛏 *45 studios* ⦿ *No meals* Ⓜ *Bayswater, Queensway* ✛ *1:B4.*

**15**

## REGENT'S PARK AND HAMPSTEAD

### HAMPSTEAD

$
B&B/INN

🖥 **Glenlyn Guest House.** An excellent option for travelers who don't mind being a long Tube ride away from the action, this converted Victorian townhouse offers a high standard of accommodation a few miles north of Hampstead. **Pros:** comfortable and friendly; you get more for your money than you would in central London; five-minute walk to Tube station. **Cons:** you have to factor in the cost and inconvenience of a half-hour Tube ride to central London; no restaurant. ⑤ *Rooms from: £90* ⊠ *6 Woodside Park Rd., Hampstead* ☎ *020/8445-0440* ⊕ *www. glenlynhotel.com* 🛏 *27 rooms, 2 apartments* ⦿ *Breakfast* Ⓜ *Woodside Park* ✛ *1:D1.*

$
HOTEL
Fodor's Choice
★

🖥 **The Hide.** This cozy, chic little hideaway is exceptional value for money and exceeds virtually anything you could hope to find in central London for the price; the downside is that the half-hour Tube ride to and from town can be exhausting after a long day of sightseeing. **Pros:** excellent value; great service; free Wi-Fi; close to Tube station. **Cons:** far from the center; somewhat dull neighborhood. ⑤ *Rooms from: £105* ⊠ *230 Hendon Way, Hendon, Hampstead* ☎ *020/8203-1670* ⊕ *www.thehidelondon.com* 🛏 *22 rooms* ⦿ *Breakfast* Ⓜ *Hendon Central* ✛ *1:H1.*

$
B&B/INN

🖥 **La Gaffe.** The name of this simple B&B (located above an Italian restaurant) means "the mistake" in Italian, and is also the punchline to the unlikely tale of how the original husband-and-wife proprietors met in the 1950s—but it also rather neatly chimes with the Cockney term "gaff," meaning a simple, cozy residence. **Pros:** unusual place with a cheerful atmosphere; great price. **Cons:** few services; no elevator; outside city center. ⑤ *Rooms from: £105* ⊠ *107–111 Heath St., Hampstead* ☎ *020/7435-8965* ⊕ *www.lagaffe.co.uk* 🛏 *18 rooms, 3 suites* ⦿ *Breakfast* Ⓜ *Hampstead* ✛ *1:D1.*

### ISLINGTON

$

B&B/INN

⌂ **Arlington Avenue.** A find like this in London is as rare as hen's teeth: an immaculate, friendly, Georgian-townhouse B&B, full of character, not too far from the city center, *and* at a rock-bottom rate. **Pros:** genuinely stylish and comfortable; friendly hosts; quiet street; cheap as you'll ever hope to find for a place this nice in London. **Cons:** really more of a private house with guest rooms than a B&B, which isn't to everyone's taste; shared guest bathroom; 20-minute commute into city center. ⑤ *Rooms from: £65* ⊠ *Arlington Ave., Islington* ☎ *07711/265–183* ⊕ *www.arlingtonavenue.co.uk* ⟳ *2 rooms* ⦿ *Breakfast* Ⓜ *Angel, Essex Rd.* ✛ *2:D1.*

### PRIMROSE HILL

$$

B&B/INN

Fodor's Choice

★

⌂ **30 King Henry's Road.** Floor-to-ceiling books and a wealth of art decorate this lovely little B&B in Primrose Hill, the perennially trendy "village" neighborhood north of Regent's Park. **Pros:** unique, homey atmosphere; lovely hosts; great neighborhood. **Cons:** no extras; not very central; smaller rooms share a bathroom. ⑤ *Rooms from: £140* ⊠ *30 King Henry's Rd., Primrose Hill* ☎ *020/7483–2871* ⟳ *5 rooms* ⦿ *Breakfast* Ⓜ *Chalk Farm* ✛ *1:G1.*

# PUBS AND
# NIGHTLIFE

Updated by Jo Caird

There isn't a London nightlife scene—there is a multitude of them. As long as there are crowds for obscure teenage rock bands, Dickensian-style pubs, comedy cabarets, and "bodysonic" dance nights, someone will create clubs and venues for them in London. The result? London has become a veritable utopia for excitement junkies, culture fiends, and those who—simply put—like to party.

Nearly everyone who visits London these days is mesmerized by the city's energy, which reveals itself in layers. Whether you prefer rhythm and blues with fine French food, the gritty guitar-riff music of Camden Town, the boutique beers of East London, a pint and a gourmet pizza at a local gastropub, or swanky cocktails and sushi at London's sexiest lair, London is sure to feed your fancy.

# PLANNING

### GETTING AROUND
There are currently plans for Tube lines serving central London (see ⊕ www.tfl.gov.uk for details) to run all night on Friday and Saturday starting in late 2016, making getting home after a night out cheaper and easier than ever before. The rest of the network stops running around 12:30 am Monday–Saturday and midnight on Sunday. Night buses are largely safe and reliable but far slower than taxis, as you'd expect. The best place to hail a black taxi is at the front door of one of the major hotels; or find a licensed local minicab firm on the Transport for London website. Avoid unlicensed taxis that tout for business around closing time.

### LIQUOR AND SMOKING LAWS
Laws now allow London drinking establishments to extend their opening hours beyond the traditional 11 pm closing, and smoking is banned. Most pubs and bars still close by midnight or a few short hours later.

### CAN I TAKE MY KIDS TO THE PUB?

As pubs increasingly emphasize what's coming out of the kitchen alongside what's flowing from the tap, bringing the kids is more of an option. The law dictates that children 14–17 may enter a pub but are not permitted to purchase or drink alcohol, and children under 14 are not permitted in the bar area of a pub unless the pub has a "children's certificate" and the kids are accompanied by an adult. Some pubs have a section set aside for families, especially during the day, but many don't allow children in the evening.

### WHAT TO WEAR

As a general rule, you won't see too many people in the upscale London nightspots wearing jeans and sneakers. People are more likely to dress down for an evening in the pub.

### FIND OUT WHAT'S PLAYING WHERE

Because today's cool spot is often tomorrow's forgotten or closed venue, check the weekly listings in the *Evening Standard* (⊕ *www.standard. co.uk*) and especially *Time Out* (⊕ *www.timeout.com/london*). Other websites to consult are ⊕ *www.londontown.com,* ⊕ *www.allinlondon. co.uk,* and ⊕ *www.viewlondon.co.uk.* Although most clubs are frequented by those under 30, there are plenty of others that are popular with patrons of all ages and types. One particularly useful website for clubs and club nights is ⊕ *www.residentadvisor.net.*

Door and bar staff are hawkish about underage drinking, so take photo ID with you on a night out.

# PUBS

Pubs are where Londoners go to hang out, see and be seen, act out the drama of life, and, for some, drink themselves into varying degrees of oblivion. The pub is still a vital part of London life, though many of the traditions of the pub experience are evolving. There are few better places to meet Londoners in their local habitat. There are somewhere around 4,000 pubs in London; some are dark and woody, others plain and functional, a few still have original Victorian etched glass, Edwardian panels, and art nouveau carvings.

Not long ago, before the smoking ban, pubs tended to be smoky, male-dominated places with a couple of ubiquitous beers on tap and the only available food a packet of salt-and-vinegar-flavor crisps (potato chips). All that has changed. Gastropub fever swept through London around the turn of the 21st century and at many places, char-grills are installed in the kitchen and inventive pub grub is on the menu. A new wave of enthusiasm for craft beers is now having a similar effect on the liquid offerings.

The big decision is what to drink. The beer of choice among Britons has traditionally been **"bitter,"** lightly fermented, with an amber color, and getting its bitterness from hops. It's usually served at cellar temperature (that is, cooler than room temperature but neither chilled, nor, as common misconception would have it, warm). **Real ales,** served from wooden kegs and made without chilling, filtering, or pasteurization, are flatter than other bitters and are enjoying a renaissance. Many small London breweries have sprung up in recent years, and bottled designer and American beers can be found in most bars across London. **Stouts,** like Guinness, are a meal in themselves and something of an acquired taste—they have a dark, caramel-infused flavor and look like thickened flat Coke with a frothy top. Chilled **lagers,** most familiar to American drinkers, are light in color and carbonated. ■ **TIP→ The most commonly served lagers in Britain are from continental Europe.**

Many English pubs are owned by chains such as Mitchells and Butlers, Punch Taverns, or Samuel Smith, and are tenanted, meaning that they are run on a sort of franchise basis. Most are not obviously branded and retain at least some independence. Independently owned pubs, sometimes called "free houses," tend to offer a more extensive selection of beer. Other potations available include apple-based **ciders,** ranging from sweet to dry and from alcoholic to very alcoholic (Irish cider, served over ice, is now also ubiquitous), and **shandies,** a mix of beer and lemonade. Friendly pubs will usually be happy to give you a taste of the brew of your choice before you order.

*The list below offers a few pubs selected for interesting beer, historical interest, a pleasant garden, music, or good food, but you might just as happily adopt your own temporary "local."*

**16**

## MAYFAIR

The pubs in this central London neighborhood tend to be as upscale as the people that frequent them, but you'll also find plenty of informal establishments with a lot of character.

**Audley.** Big, smart, old-school, and a little brash, the Audley makes up in friendly atmosphere what it lacks in charm. There's a good selection of beer on tap, and it's far enough away from the tourist hot spots that, on the right day, it can feel like a village pub. ✉ *41–43 Mount St., Mayfair* ☎ *020/7499–1843* ⊕ *www.taylor-walker.co.uk/pub/audley-mayfair/c3003* Ⓜ *Bond St., Green Park.*

**Punch Bowl.** In a quiet corner of Mayfair, the cozy little Punch Bowl has a worn wood floor and well spoken staff. The pub dates to 1750 and the interior remains steadfastly old-fashioned, with a painting of Churchill, candles, polished dark wood, and engraved windows. Try the place's own ale, made specially in Scotland by Caledonian. A dining area at the rear buzzes at lunchtime with locals who come for the upscale English pub food, and there's a fancier restaurant upstairs. ✉ *41 Farm St., Mayfair* ☎ *020/7493–6841* ⊕ *www.punchbowllondon.com* Ⓜ *Green Park, Bond St.*

## SOHO AND COVENT GARDEN

Traditional British "boozers" stand side-by-side with informal continental-style drinking dens in this buzzing central neighborhood. Drop by for a late drink and you may find yourself rubbing shoulders with musicians and actors from the West End's many theaters.

### SOHO

**Dog and Duck.** A beautiful example of a late 19th-century London pub, the Dog and Duck has a well-preserved interior furnished with tiles, mirrors, and polished wood, though it's often so packed that it's hard to get a good look. There's a good selection of real ales at the bar, and a restaurant serving standard pub dishes upstairs. ✉ *18 Bateman St., Soho* ☎ *020/7494–0697* ⊕ *www.nicholsonspubs.co.uk* Ⓜ *Tottenham Court Rd.*

**French House.** In the pub where the French Resistance convened during World War II, Soho hipsters and eccentrics now rub shoulders with theater people and the literati—more than shoulders, actually, because this tiny, tricolor-waving, photo-lined pub is almost always packed. In the French style, beer is served in half-pints only. If you're around on July 14, come and join in the rapturous Bastille Day celebrations. ✉ *49 Dean St., Soho* ☎ *020/7437–2477* ⊕ *www.frenchhousesoho.com* Ⓜ *Leicester Sq., Tottenham Court Rd.*

### COVENT GARDEN

**Harp.** This is the sort of friendly little local you might find on some out-of-the-way backstreet, except that it's right in the middle of town, between Trafalgar Square and Covent Garden. As a result, the Harp can get crowded, especially because it was named British pub of the year by the Campaign for Real Ale in 2011, but the squeeze is worth it for the excellent beer and cider (there are usually 10 carefully chosen ales, often including a London microbrew, plus 10 ciders and perries) and a no-frills menu of high-quality British sausages, cooked behind the bar. ✉ *47 Chandos Pl., Covent Garden* ☎ *020/7836–0291* ⊕ *www.harpcoventgarden.com* Ⓜ *Charing Cross.*

**Lamb & Flag.** This refreshingly ungentrified 17th-century pub was once known as the Bucket of Blood because the upstairs room was used as a ring for bare-knuckle boxing. Now it's a friendly (and bloodless) place, serving food and real ale. It's on the edge of Covent Garden, up a hidden alley off Garrick Street. ✉ *33 Rose St., Covent Garden* ☎ *020/7497–9504* ⊕ *www.lambandflagcoventgarden.co.uk* Ⓜ *Covent Garden.*

## BLOOMSBURY, HOLBORN, AND FITZROVIA

The gorgeous pubs in this literary neighborhood attract tourists in the daytime and huge crowds of after-work drinkers in the early evening. They tend to quiet down as the night advances, making this area a great spot for a relaxing evening out.

### BLOOMSBURY

**The Lamb.** Charles Dickens and his contemporaries drank here, but today's enthusiastic clientele make sure this intimate and eternally popular pub avoids the pitfalls of feeling too old-timey. For private chats at the bar, you can close a delicate etched-glass "snob screen" to the bar staff, opening it only when you fancy another pint. ✉ *94 Lamb's Conduit St., Bloomsbury* ☎ *020/7405–0713* ⊕ *www.youngs. co.uk* Ⓜ *Russell Sq.*

**Museum Tavern.** Across the street from the British Museum, this friendly and classy Victorian pub makes an ideal resting place after the rigors of the culture trail. Karl Marx unwound here after a hard day in the Library. He could have spent his *Kapital* on any of around 15 well-kept beers available on tap. ⊠ *49 Great Russell St., Bloomsbury* ☎ *020/7242–8987* ⊕ *www.taylor-walker.co.uk* Ⓜ *Tottenham Court Rd., Holborn.*

**The Queen's Larder.** The royal associated with this tiny pub is Queen Charlotte, who is said to have stored food here for her "mad" husband, George III, when he was being treated nearby. The interior preserves its antique feel, with dark wood and old posters, and in the evenings fills up quickly with office workers and students. In good weather, you might prefer to grab one of the seats outdoors. ⊠ *1 Queen's Sq., Bloomsbury* ☎ *020/7837–5627* ⊕ *www.queenslarder.co.uk* Ⓜ *Russell Sq.*

## HOLBORN

**Holborn Whippet.** An impressive number of craft beers are served from unmarked taps set into a brick column behind the bar in this new-breed London pub. Names of the brews are all chalked onto boards, while empty barrels outside testify to the popularity of the best; lunch and supper are served daily. It's popular, especially when nearby offices empty out in early evening, with punters spilling out onto ornate, pedestrian-only Sicilian Avenue. Inside, it's a deliberately plain affair, with little to detract from the liquid experience. ⊠ *25-29 Sicilian Ave., Holborn* ☎ *020/3137–9937* ⊕ *www.holbornwhippet.com* Ⓜ *Holborn.*

Fodor'sChoice ★ **Princess Louise.** This fine, popular pub is an exquisite museum piece of a Victorian interior, with glazed tiles and intricately engraved glass screens that divide the bar area into cozy little annexes. It's not all show, either. There's a good selection of excellent-value Yorkshire real ales from Samuel Smith's brewery. ⊠ *208 High Holborn, Holborn* ☎ *020/7405–8816* ⊕ *www.princesslouisepub.co.uk* Ⓜ *Holborn.*

## FITZROVIA

**The Green Man.** This bright and friendly pub is a great refueling stop for Oxford Street shoppers. Cider is the specialty, with 10 varieties on tap, plus bottled beers from around the world. Board games, tasty pub food, and Sunday roasts make it the sort of place you'll find hard to leave. ⊠ *36 Riding House St., Fitzrovia* ☎ *020/7580–9087* ⊕ *www.thegreenmanw1.co.uk* Ⓜ *Goodge St., Oxford Circus.*

**Newman Arms.** This tiny pub, here since 1730, is a no-nonsense affair, but there's a certain cosy charm to its flagstone floor, polished wood panelling and corner seating area. A handful of craft ales are available on tap, lots more in bottles, and the wine list is impressive, thanks to the presence of the well-regarded upstairs dining room. ⊠ *23 Rathbone St., Fitzrovia* ☎ *020/3643–6285* ⊕ *www.newmanarmspub.com* Ⓜ *Goodge St., Tottenham Court Rd.*

16

## WHAT'S IN A NAME?

Pictorial signs traditionally helped illiterate customers identify establishments. The practice goes back to Roman times, with tavernas hanging vines outside to advertise the fact that they sold wine. The naming of pub and inns was widespread by the 12th century, and in 1393 King Richard II made it law for all pubs to display a sign, in order to make it easier for the official ale-taster to find the establishments he needed to visit.

The most common pub names offer an illustrated guide to Britain's past, with various monarchs, legends and eras referenced in the colorful signs swinging above the doors of drinking dens all over the country. The Red Lion, for example, one of the most common pub names in use today, dates to the time when King James VI of Scotland became James I of the united kingdoms of England and Scotland and ordered that the heraldic lion of Scotland be displayed on all important buildings. Other pub names highlight the importance of specific events (the Trafalgar), mythical figures (Robin Hood), and technological advances (the Railway).

In "pub cricket," a game traditionally played on long car journeys in the United Kingdom, players take turns at "bat." For each pub passed, the batter gets a score corresponding to the number of legs possessed by any beings that are part of the pub's name. For instance, passing the Swan gets you two points, because swans have two legs. The batter continues to accrue points until he or she is "batted out" by passing a pub with "head" or "arms" in its name (the Queen's Head, for example). The next player then takes over and the game continues until the end of the journey, when whoever has the highest score is declared the winner.

## CLERKENWELL AND THE CITY

Workers from The City's many finance firms pour into the neighborhood's pubs at the end of the day, but by 8 pm the party is pretty much over and you'll have no trouble finding a place to sit. It's always worth ducking down a side street, as this is where some of the area's most interesting establishments can be found.

### CLERKENWELL

**Craft Beer Co.** With 37 beers on tap and 250 more in bottles (one brewed exclusively for the Craft Beer Company), the main problem here is knowing where to start. Luckily, friendly and knowledgeable staff are happy to advise or give tasters—or why not sign up for a guided tasting session? A huge chandelier and a mirrored ceiling lend antique charm to the interior, and a smattering of tourists and beer pilgrims break up the crowds of Leather Lane workers and locals. ⊠ *82 Leather La., Clerkenwell* ☎ *020/7404–7049* ⊕ *www.thecraftbeerco.com* Ⓜ *Chancery La.*

Fodor's Choice
★ **Jerusalem Tavern.** Owned by the well-respected St. Peter's Brewery in Suffolk, the Jerusalem Tavern is one-of-a-kind: small, and endearingly eccentric. Ancient Delft-style tiles meld with wood and concrete in a converted watchmaker and jeweler's shop dating back to the 18th

century. The beer, both bottled and on tap, is some of the best available anywhere in London. It's loved by Londoners and is often busy, especially after work. ✉ *55 Britton St., Clerkenwell* ☎ *020/7490–4281* ⊕ *www.stpetersbrewery.co.uk/london-pub* Ⓜ *Farringdon.*

## THE CITY

**The Blackfriar.** A step from Blackfriars Tube station, this spectacular pub has an Arts and Crafts interior that is entertainingly, satirically ecclesiastical, with inlaid mother-of-pearl, wood carvings, stained glass, and marble pillars all over the place. Under finely lettered temperance tracts on view just below the reliefs of monks, fairies, and friars, there is a nice group of ales on tap from independent brewers. The 20th-century poet Sir John Betjeman once led a successful campaign to save the pub from demolition. ✉ *174 Queen Victoria St., The City* ☎ *020/7236–5474* ⊕ *www.nicholsonspubs.co.uk/theblackfriarblackfriarslondon* Ⓜ *Blackfriars.*

**Viaduct Tavern.** Queen Victoria opened the nearby Holborn Viaduct in 1869, and this eponymous pub honored the road bridge by serving its first pint the same year. Much of the Victorian decoration is still extant, with gorgeous paintings (depicting the statues on the viaduct), carved wood, and engraved glass. The tavern has a haunted reputation, which stems from its proximity to the former Newgate Prison and its gallows. What are said to be former debtors' prison cells in the basement can be seen with a free tour when staff aren't busy with customers. There are usually three or four ales on tap; lunch is also served. ✉ *126 Newgate St., The City* ☎ *020/7600 1863* ⊕ *www.viaducttavern.co.uk* ⊘ *Closed weekends* Ⓜ *St. Paul's.*

**Ye Olde Cheshire Cheese.** Yes, this extremely historic pub (it dates to 1667, the year after the Great Fire of London) is full of tourists, but it deserves a visit for its sawdust-covered floors, low wood-beam ceilings, and the 14th-century crypt of Whitefriars' monastery under the cellar bar. This was the most regular of Dr. Johnson's and Dickens's many locals. Food is served. ✉ *145 Fleet St., The City* ☎ *020/7353–6170* ⊘ *Closed Sun. from 4* Ⓜ *Blackfriars.*

**Ye Olde Mitre.** Hidden off the side of 8 Hatton Gardens, this cozy pub's roots go back to 1546, though it was rebuilt around 1782. Originally built for the staff of the Bishop of Ely, whose London residence was next door, it remained officially part of Cambridgeshire until the 20th century. It's a friendly little labyrinthine place, with a fireplace, well-kept ales, wooden beams, and traditional bar snacks. ✉ *1 Ely Ct., The City* ☎ *020/7405–4751* ⊕ *www.yeoldemitreholburn.co.uk* ⊘ *Closed weekends* Ⓜ *Chancery La.*

**Ye Olde Watling.** This busy corner pub has been rebuilt at least three times since 1666. One of its incarnations was as the drawing office for Sir Christopher Wren, who used it while building nearby St. Paul's Cathedral. The ground floor is a laid-back pub, while upstairs houses an atmospheric restaurant, complete with wooden beams and trestle tables, with a basic English pub menu. ✉ *29 Watling St., The City* ☎ *020/7248–8935* ⊕ *www.nicholsonspubs.co.uk/yeoldewatlingwatlingstreetlondon* Ⓜ *Mansion House.*

**16**

# EAST LONDON

East London is better known these days for its bars and clubs than for its pubs, but in historic neighborhoods such as Spitalfields and Wapping there's a cozy old drinking den around practically every corner.

**Prospect of Whitby.** Named after a ship, this is one of London's oldest riverside pubs, dating to around 1520. Once upon a time it was called the Devil's Tavern because of the lowlifes—thieves and smugglers—who congregated here. Ornamented with pewter ware and nautical objects, this much-loved "boozer" has a terrace with views of the Thames, from where boat trips often point it out. ⊠ *57 Wapping Wall, East End* ☎ *020/7481–1095* ⊕ *www.taylor-walker.co.uk* Ⓜ *Wapping. DLR: Shadwell.*

# SOUTH OF THE THAMES

Head to the area around Borough Market—one of London's oldest neighborhoods—for lively historic pubs where locals and tourists jostle for craft ales and gourmet snacks.

**Anchor & Hope.** One of London's most popular gastropubs, the Anchor & Hope doesn't take reservations (except for the three-course prix-fixe Sunday lunch that begins at 12:30 pm). Would-be diners snake around the red-wall, wood-floor pub, kept happy by some good real ales and a fine wine list as they wait for at least 45 minutes for a table; get there by 6 pm, and you're in with a chance of being seated right away. The excellent, meaty food is old-fashioned English—for instance, salt cod, tripe, and chips (fries)—with a few modern twists. ⊠ *36 The Cut, South Bank* ☎ *020/7928–9898* ⊕ *www.anchorandhopepub.co.uk* Ⓜ *Southwark.*

**The George Inn.** Shakespeare drank in this Southwark pub, and Dickens featured the place in his writing. Now owned by the National Trust, the George has a cobblestone courtyard; inside several small, low-ceilinged rooms lead to a so-so restaurant and the cozy Parliament Bar. ⊠ *77 Borough High St., South Bank* ☎ *020/7407–2056* ⊕ *www.george-southwark.co.uk* Ⓜ *London Bridge.*

**Market Porter.** Opposite the foodie treasures of Borough Market, this atmospheric pub opens at 6 am (weekdays) for the stallholders, and always seems busy. Remarkably, the place manages to remain relaxed, with helpful staff and happy customers spilling out onto the road right through the year. The wide selection of real ales is lovingly tended (and you'll find an astonishing number of pump badges and beer mats covering the ceiling and walls). The pub was used as a set for one of the Harry Potter movies. ⊠ *9 Stoney St., Borough* ☎ *020/7407–2495* ⊕ *www.markettaverns.co.uk* Ⓜ *London Bridge.*

**The Mayflower.** This atmospheric 17th-century riverside inn (rebuilt in the following century) has exposed beams and a terrace near the onetime berth of the famous ship on which the Pilgrims sailed to what became the American colonies. The pub has a heated jetty where customers can sit outside; alternatively, opt to enjoy the wood-beam interiors, although this can get quite packed with sightseers. ⊠ *117 Rotherhithe St., South East* ☎ *020/7237–4088* ⊕ *www.themayflowerrotherhithe. com* Ⓜ *Overground: Rotherhithe.*

## GREENWICH

FAMILY  **Cutty Sark.** Take a break from Greenwich's cultural and historical attractions at this spacious riverside pub, which dates back to the late 1700s. Mismatched furniture give the large rooms a homey feel, while the wood-burning stove keeps things cozy. There's outdoor seating, too, with fantastic views of the Thames. A classic pub menu includes several tasty sharing platters, and the beer list features tipples from local London breweries. ✉ *4–6 Ballast Quay, Greenwich* ☎ *020/8858–3146* ⊕ *www.cuttysarkse10.co.uk* Ⓜ *DLR: Cutty Sark. South Eastern Railway: Maze Hill.*

## CHELSEA AND BELGRAVIA

Pubs in this upscale central west neighborhood range from classy modern affairs with impressive wine lists and sharing platters to tiny local institutions guaranteed to make you feel like you've stepped back in time.

### CHELSEA

FAMILY  **The Anglesea Arms.** This traditional, family-friendly pub has a large terrace out front that's just ideal for resting your weary feet after a shopping spree on the King's Road or a culture-packed afternoon at the museums of South Kensington. A menu of pub-grub classics, plus fancier dishes like fresh fish or shoulder of lamb, is available both in the bar and in the more refined dining room upstairs. You'll find six lovingly tended ales on tap, and a wine list with a largely French focus. ✉ *15 Selwood Terr., Chelsea* ☎ *020/7373–7960* ⊕ *www.metropolitanpubcompany. com* Ⓜ *South Kensington.*

**The Antelope.** Just around the corner from chic Sloane Square is the perfect spot to grab an unpretentious pint. Wood paneling and comfy seating create a snug environment, and there's a more genteel dining room upstairs. ✉ *22 Eaton Terr., Chelsea* ☎ *020/7824–8512* ⊕ *www. antelope-eaton-terrace.co.uk* Ⓜ *Sloane Sq.*

### BELGRAVIA

Fodor's Choice  **The Nag's Head.** The landlord of this idiosyncratic little mews pub in
★  Belgravia runs a tight ship, and no cellphones are allowed. The lovingly collected artifacts (including antique penny arcade games) that decorate every inch of the place, high-quality beer, and old-fashioned pub grub should provide more than enough distraction. ✉ *53 Kinnerton St., Belgravia* ☎ *020/7235–1135* Ⓜ *Knightsbridge, Hyde Park Corner.*

## NOTTING HILL

The line between pub and bar is frequently blurred in this trendy area on the west side of the capital, with the emphasis on good—often haute—food, sleek style, and extensive wine lists.

**The Cow.** Crowds head to this chic mix of fun, haute food and friendly, retro style for Guinness and oysters, either enjoying them in the unpretentious downstairs bar or the more formal restaurant upstairs. The pub food is all excellent, though pricey, with lots of seafood and steaks. The

**16**

atmosphere's always warm, welcoming, and buzzing. ⊠ *89 Westbourne Park Rd., Notting Hill* ☎ *020/7221–0021* ⊕ *www.thecowlondon.co.uk* Ⓜ *Royal Oak, Westbourne Park.*

## REGENT'S PARK AND HAMPSTEAD

London's villagelike northern neighborhoods—Hampstead, Highgate, and Primrose Hill, to name a few—all boast fantastic local boozers where you can easily while away an afternoon. Camden Town has more of a buzz to it and attracts a younger crowd.

### HAMPSTEAD

**The Holly Bush.** A short walk up the hill from Hampstead Tube station, the friendly Holly Bush was a country pub before London spread this far north. It retains something of a rural feel, with stripped wooden floors and an open fire, and is an intimate place to enjoy great ales and organic and free-range pub food. Try the homemade pork scratchings (crispy rinds) and pickled eggs, and don't miss the hot cider in the wintertime ⊠ *22 Holly Mount, Hampstead* ☎ *020/7435–2892* ⊕ *www. hollybushhampstead.co.uk* Ⓜ *Hampstead.*

**Spaniards Inn.** Ideal as a refueling point when you're on a hike in Hampstead Heath, this historic, country-style, oak-beam pub has a gorgeous garden—the scene of the tea party in Dickens's *Pickwick Papers*. Dick Turpin, the highwayman, frequented the inn before Dickens's time, and Shelley, Keats, and Byron hung out here as well. The place is extremely popular, especially on Sunday, when Londoners roll in. It's canine-friendly, too—there's even a dog wash in the garden. ⊠ *Spaniards Rd., Hampstead* ☎ *020/8731–8406* ⊕ *www.thespaniardshampstead.co.uk* Ⓜ *Hampstead.*

### HIGHGATE

FAMILY **The Bull and Last.** A luxurious menu featuring dishes like roast venison and handmade ricotta and black cabbage ravioli makes this large corner pub a must for visitors to Parliament Hill (aka Kite Hill), the area of Hampstead Heath just across the road. It's a good idea to make a reservation, particularly on Sunday, when the roasts attract punters from far and wide. Or in the summertime (April–September) order a hamper and have a picnic with London spreading out beneath you and kites flying overhead. ⊠ *168 Highgate Rd., Highgate* ☎ *020/7267–3641* ⊕ *www.thebullandlast.co.uk* Ⓜ *Tufnell Park; Overground: Gospel Oak.*

## THE THAMES UPSTREAM

A pint in a riverside pub is a London must, and the capital's western reaches offer some truly picturesque drinking opportunities. Pick a traditional establishment and you'll feel like you've ventured far from the Big Smoke.

### RICHMOND

**Roebuck.** Perched on top of Richmond Hill, the Roebuck has perhaps the best view of any pub in London. The most sought-after seats are the benches found directly across the road, which look out over the Thames as it winds its way into the countryside below. Friendly and surprisingly unpretentious, given its lofty surrounds, it is well worth the long climb up the hill from the center of Richmond. ⊠ *130 Richmond Hill, Richmond* ☎ *020/8948–2329* ⊕ *www.taylor-walker.co.uk* Ⓜ *National Rail: Richmond.*

### HAMMERSMITH

**Blue Anchor.** This unaltered Georgian pub has been seen in the movie *Sliding Doors* and was the site where *The Planets* composer Gustav Holst wrote his *Hammersmith Suite.* Sit out by the river, or shelter inside with a good ale. ⊠ *13 Lower Mall, Hammersmith* ☎ *020/8748–5774* ⊕ *www.blueanchorlondon.com* Ⓜ *Hammersmith.*

**Dove Inn.** Read the list of famous ex-regulars, from Charles II and Nell Gwyn to Ernest Hemingway, as you wait for a beer at this smart, comely, and popular 16th-century riverside pub. If—as is often the case—the Dove is too full, stroll upstream along the bank to the Old Ship or the Blue Anchor. ⊠ *19 Upper Mall, Hammersmith* ☎ *020/8748–9474* ⊕ *www.dovehammersmith.co.uk* Ⓜ *Hammersmith.*

# NIGHTLIFE

**16**

The pace with which London bars and clubs go in and out of fashion is mind-boggling. New trends, likewise, emerge all time. In one somewhat recent development, the dreaded velvet rope has been usurped by the doorbell-ringing mystique of members-only drinking clubs. Some of the city's most talked-about nightlife spots these days are those attached to some of the best restaurants and hotels—no wonder, when you consider the increased popularity of London cuisine in international circles. Moreover, the gay scene in London is still going strong. One constant of the nightlife here is variety. The understated glamour of north London's Primrose Hill, which makes movie stars feel so at ease, might be considered dull by the übertrendy club goers of London's East End. Likewise, the price of a pint in Chelsea would be considered blasphemous by the musicians and poets of multicultural Peckham.

Whatever your pleasure, however your whim turns come evening, chances are you'll find what you're looking for in London's ever-changing arena of activity and invention.

## WESTMINSTER, ST. JAMES'S, AND ROYAL LONDON

Elegant drinking holes catering to London's political and social elites abound in these central neighborhoods. Streets that are thronged with tourists and workers by day quiet down by evening, leaving the area to its few residents and a handful of sophisticated drinkers and diners.

### WESTMINSTER

#### BARS

**Cinnamon Club.** In the basement of what was once the Old Westminster Library, the Club Bar of this contemporary Indian restaurant (the curries are superb) has Bollywood scenes projected onto the glass back wall, Asian-theme cocktails (mango mojitos, "Delhi mules"), delicious bar snacks, and a clientele that includes fashionable young politicos.

Upstairs, the Library Bar also serves cocktails through the day. ✉ *The Old Westminster Library, 30-32 Great Smith St., Westminster* ☎ *020/7222-2555* ⊕ *www.cinnamonclub.com* Ⓜ *St James's, Westminster.*

**Fodor's Choice**
★ **Gordon's Wine Bar.** Nab a rickety table in the atmospheric, vaulted interior of what claims to be the oldest wine bar in London, or fight for standing room in the long pedestrian-only alley that runs alongside it. Either way, the mood is always cheery as a diverse crowd sips on more than 60 different wines, ports, and sherries. Tempting cheese and meat plates are great for sharing. ✉ *47 Villiers St., Westminster* ☎ *020/7930-1408* ⊕ *www.gordonswinebar.com* Ⓜ *Charing Cross, Embankment.*

## JAZZ AND BLUES

Jazz in London is highly eclectic. You can expect anything from danceable, smooth tunes played at a supper club to groovy New Orleans–style blues to exotic world-beat rhythms, which can be heard at some of the less central venues throughout the capital. London hosts the **London Jazz Festival** (⊕ *www.efglondonjazzfestival.org.uk*) in November, which showcases top and emerging artists in experimental jazz. The **Ealing Jazz Festival** (⊕ *www.ealing.gov.uk*), at the end of July, claims to be the biggest free jazz event in Europe.

**The Mint Leaf Bar.** The renowned long bar is stocked with more than 500 spirits and serves more than 1,000 well-prepared cocktails. Nibbles and light snacks with an Indian twist are available, and if you're up for some more substantial spicy food, there's also a full restaurant. A sister bar and restaurant is in Angel Court in The City. ✉ *Suffolk Pl., Haymarket* ☎ *020/7930-9020* ⊕ *www.mintleaflondon.com* Ⓜ *Piccadilly Circus, Charing Cross.*

## ST. JAMES'S

### BARS

**Fodor's Choice**
★ **American Bar.** Festooned with a chin-dropping array of club ties, signed celebrity photographs, sporting mementos, and baseball caps, this sensational hotel cocktail bar has superb martinis. The name dates from the 1930s, when hotel bars in London started to cater to growing numbers of Americans crossing the Atlantic in ocean liners, but it wasn't until the 1970s, when a customer left a small carved wooden eagle, that the collection of paraphernalia was started. ✉ *Stafford Hotel, 16–18 St. James's Pl., St. James's* ☎ *020/7493-0111* ⊕ *www.thestaffordhotel.co.uk* Ⓜ *Green Park.*

# MAYFAIR

Bars in this upscale central neighborhood—many of which can be found within luxury hotels—attract a polished crowd. Cocktails, fine wines, and rare aged spirits are the tipples of choice.

### BARS

**Claridge's Bar.** This elegant Mayfair meeting place remains unpretentious even when it brims with beautiful people. The bar has an art deco heritage made hip by the sophisticated touch of designer David Collins. A

## THE GAY SCENE

Gay nightlife is as busy as it is in New York or Los Angeles. Soho's the traditional hub, and "Voho," the previously unfashionable Vauxhall, south of the river, is one upstart area for gay London (though the vibe here can be pretty hardcore).

Clubs in London cater to almost every desire, whether that be the suited-up Tommy Hilfiger–look–alike scene, dingy dives for cruising, flamboyant drag shows, lesbian tea dances, or themed fetish nights.

There's also a cornucopia of queer theater and performance art that runs throughout the year. Whatever your tastes, you'll be able to satisfy them with a night on the town in London.

Choices are admittedly much better for men than women; although many of the gay clubs are female-friendly, those catering strictly to lesbians are rare.

The British Film Institute puts on BFI Flare: London LGBT Film Festival (⊕ www.bfi.org.uk/flare) in late March and early April every year.

Pride London in June (an annual event that encompasses a parade, sports, art, comedy, theater, music, cabaret, and dance) welcomes anyone and everyone, and claimed around 800,000 participants in 2014. This extravagant 30,000-strong pageant spirals its way through London's streets, with major events taking place in Trafalgar Square and Leicester Square, and culminates in Victoria Embankment with ticketed parties continuing on afterward. See ⊕ www.prideinlondon.org for details.

For up-to-date listings, consult *QX Magazine* (⊕ www.qxmagazine.com) or *Boyz* (⊕ www.boyz.co.uk).

### BARS, CAFÉS, AND PUBS
Most bars in London are gay-friendly, though there are a number of cafés and pubs that are particularly known as gay hangouts after-hours. The latest serve drinks until 3 am (11 pm on Sunday).

### CLUBS
Many of London's best gay dance clubs can be found on particular nights in mixed clubs like Fabric.

**16**

library of rare Champagnes and brandies as well as a delicious choice of traditional and exotic cocktails—try the Flapper or the Black Pearl—will occupy your taste buds. Request a glass of vintage Cristal in the darkly moody Fumoir. ✉ *55 Brook St., Mayfair* ☎ *020/7629–8860* ⊕ *www.claridges.co.uk* Ⓜ *Bond St.*

**Oscar Wilde Bar at Hotel Café Royal.** Sit where Oscar Wilde once sat in this beautifully restored bar and tea room at the luxurious Hotel Café Royal. Established in 1865, the Grill Room (as it was known until recently) was the place where Wilde met Lord Alfred Douglas, and over the years it has hosted everyone from Mick Jagger and Elizabeth Taylor to Kanye West and Kate Moss. The bar has a very fine Champagne list—including some delicious Champagne cocktails—but for the really "Wilde," it's got to be absinthe. On Friday and Saturday nights, the gold-leaf ceiling and mirrored walls ring with the sultry sounds of Black Cat Cabaret's Salon des Artistes; tickets are available with or without dinner. An indulgent afternoon tea is served daily on the hour noon–5.

✉ *Hotel Café Royal, 68 Regent St., Piccadilly Circus* ☎ *020/7406–3333 for bar, 020/7284–4700 for cabaret bookings* ⊕ *www.hotelcaferoyal. com* ✉ *Free; cabaret from £30* Ⓜ *Piccadilly Circus.*

Fodor'sChoice   **Sketch.** One seat never looks like the next at this downright extraordi-
★   nary collection of esoteric living-room bars. The exclusive Parlour, a pâtisserie during the day, exudes plenty of rarefied charm; the intimate East Bar at the back is reminiscent of a sci-fi film set; and in the Glade it's permanently sunset in a forest. The restrooms are surely London's quirkiest. ✉ *9 Conduit St., Mayfair* ☎ *020/7659–4500* ⊕ *www.sketch. london* Ⓜ *Oxford Circus.*

## SOHO AND COVENT GARDEN

The center of town is famous for its vibrant gay scene, atmospheric music, cabaret venues, and acclaimed comedy clubs. In Covent Garden, recent bar openings have also brought in some new buzz.

### SOHO

#### BARS

**Bar Américain.** The art deco interior of this underground bar just north of Piccadilly Circus is so opulent and glamorous that you'd be forgiven for thinking it had been here since the 1930s. In fact it's a relatively new arrival and has been a hit since it opened in 2012, along with the brasserie, café, and cabaret bar that share the premises. The cocktails aren't quite as imaginative or accomplished as they might be, but the surroundings make up for what the drinks don't deliver. ✉ *20 Sherwood St., Soho* ☎ *020/7734–4888* ⊕ *www.brasseriezedel.com* Ⓜ *Piccadilly Circus.*

**The Blind Pig.** Chances are you won't have heard of half the ingredients on the cocktail menu at this dark and sultry bar above Jason Atherton's casual restaurant, Social Dining House, but the sense of mystery only adds to the experience. So, too, do the antique mirrored ceilings, the delectable small plates (for instance, macaroni and cheese with shaved mushroom, and black pepper prawn crackers), and the knowledge that you've nabbed a seat at one of the coolest spots in Soho. ✉ *58 Poland St., Soho* ☎ *020/7993–3251* ⊕ *www.socialeatinghouse.com* Ⓜ *Oxford Circus, Tottenham Court Rd.*

**Le Beaujolais.** Around 60 lovingly selected French wines are available here, and you can snack on olives, charcuterie, and homemade croques monsieur while staying snug and warm under a bottle-laden ceiling as a funky blues soundtrack plays. The romantic, shabby-around-the-edges feel and authentic French insouciance may come as a surprise in the heart of tourist-centric London. ✉ *25 Litchfield St., Soho* ☎ *020/7836– 2955* ⊕ *www.lebeaujolais.london* Ⓜ *Leicester Sq.*

#### COMEDY

**Comedy Store.** Before heading off to prime time, some of the United Kingdom's funniest stand-ups cut their teeth here, at what's considered the birthplace of alternative comedy. Comedy Store Players, a team with six comedians doing improvisation with audience suggestions, entertain on Wednesday and Sunday; the Cutting Edge steps in every

Tuesday; and Thursday, Friday, and Saturday have the best stand-up acts. There's also a bar with food. You must be over 18 to enter. ✉ *1A Oxendon St., Soho* 🕾 *0844/871–7699 for tickets and booking* ⊕ *www. thecomedystore.co.uk* ✆ *£14–£26.50* Ⓜ *Piccadilly Circus, Leicester Sq.*

### GAY AND LESBIAN

**Fodor's Choice**
★

**Friendly Society.** An unremarkable-looking door in a Soho alleyway leads down some dingy steps into one of the most fun joints in the neighborhood. Hopping with activity almost any night of the week, the place is known for its welcoming atmosphere to everyone, gay or straight. The interior alone—including garden gnome stools and a ceiling covered in Barbie dolls and disco balls—is enough to lift the spirits. ✉ *79 Wardour St., Soho* 🕾 *020/7434–3804* Ⓜ *Leicester Sq.*

**Ku Bar.** A deliciously camp vibe, toned bar staff, and a friendly atmosphere make this one of Soho's most popular gay bars. The crowd is mostly male, but women are very welcome. Head to the quieter upstairs lounge bar for a more laid-back mood, or dance the night away at Ku Klub in the basement. There's a second branch around the corner on Frith Street. ✉ *30 Lisle St., Soho* 🕾 *020/7437–4303* ⊕ *www.ku-bar. co.uk* Ⓜ *Leicester Sq.*

**The Shadow Lounge.** This fabulous little lounge and dance club glitters with twinkling fiber-optics after an extensive makeover. It has a serious A-list celebrity factor, with the glamorous London glitterati camping out in the snug booths around the dance floor. Members are given priority to enter when the place gets full, especially on weekends, so show up early, book onto the guest list online, or prepare to wait in line. ✉ *5–7 Brewer St., Soho* 🕾 *020/7317–9270* ⊕ *www.theshadowlounge.co.uk* ✆ *£5–£15* Ⓜ *Leicester Sq.*

**She.** This basement club, part of the popular Ku group of gay venues, is a recent arrival on the Soho scene. It welcomes a mostly young lesbian crowd for informal cocktails early in the evening followed by dancing—of the pop and house variety—later on. The vibe is fun and friendly, especially on the last Thursday of each month, when She hosts London's only drag-king open-mic night. ✉ *23A Old Compton St., Soho* 🕾 *020/7437–4303* ⊕ *www.she-soho.com* ✆ *£3 Fri. and Sat. after 9 pm; otherwise free* Ⓜ *Leicester Sq., Piccadilly Circus.*

**The Yard.** A corridor of kitsch leads to a surprisingly laid-back bar and spacious terrace at The Yard. This oasis of calm in the middle of Soho attracts a mixed, friendly crowd. ✉ *57 Rupert St., Soho* 🕾 *020/7437–2652* ⊕ *www.yardbar.co.uk* Ⓜ *Piccadilly Circus.*

### ECLECTIC MUSIC

**100 Club.** Since this small club opened in 1942, many of the greats have played here, from Glenn Miller and Louis Armstrong to the Who and the Sex Pistols. Saved from closure in 2010 by a campaign led by Sir Paul McCartney, the space now reverberates to jazz, '60s R&B, and northern soul. ✉ *100 Oxford St., Soho* ⊕ *www.the100club.co.uk* ✆ *£7–£20* Ⓜ *Oxford Circus, Tottenham Court Rd.*

**16**

### JAZZ AND BLUES

**Ain't Nothin' but . . . The Blues Bar.** This sweaty, fun place does exactly what its name suggests. Local musicians, as well as some notable names, squeeze onto the tiny stage and there's good bar food of the chili-and-gumbo variety. Most weekday nights there's no cover. ⊠ *20 Kingly St., Soho* ☎ *020/7287–0514* ⊕ *www.aintnothinbut.co.uk* ⊠ *£5 Fri. and Sat. after 8:30 pm; otherwise free* Ⓜ *Oxford Circus.*

**Fodor's Choice** **Pizza Express Jazz Club Soho.** One of the United Kingdom's most ubiquitous pizza chains also runs a leading Soho jazz venue. The dimly lighted restaurant hosts top-quality international jazz acts every night, with food available in the downstairs venue (as opposed to the upstairs restaurant) around 90 minutes before stage time. The Italian-style thin-crust pizzas are about what you'd expect from a major chain. ⊠ *10 Dean St., Soho* ☎ *0845/602–7017 for club, 020/7437–9595 for restaurant* ⊕ *www.pizzaexpresslive.com* ⊠ *£15–£35* Ⓜ *Tottenham Court Rd.*

**Fodor's Choice** **Ronnie Scott's.** This legendary jazz club has attracted big names since the 1960s. It's usually crowded and hot, but the food and service are much better than they used to be. The mood can't be beat, even since the sad departure of the eponymous founder and saxophonist. Shows take place every night, with additional late gigs on Friday and Saturday. Reservations are recommended ⊠ *47 Frith St., Soho* ☎ *020/7439–0747* ⊕ *www.ronniescotts.co.uk* ⊠ *£25–£42.50* Ⓜ *Leicester Sq.*

## COVENT GARDEN

### BARS

**Bedford and Strand.** The wine bar enjoyed something of a renaissance in the first decade of the 21st century in London, and this is one of the best of a new generation. You'll find it down below the streets of Covent Garden, with dark wood and hanging shades; the wine list is short but well chosen, the service faultless, and the bistro food created with plenty of care. ⊠ *1A Bedford St., Charing Cross* ☎ *020/7836–3033* ⊕ *www. bedford-strand.com* ☉ *Closed Sun.* Ⓜ *Charing Cross.*

**Earlham Street Clubhouse.** Reasonably priced cocktails and superthin-crust pizzas are the order of the day at this vaulted basement bar in Covent Garden. A fun atmosphere reigns in the main bar area, where the style is "college kids do speakeasy," according to the manager. Nooks and crannies abound for those more in the mood for a quiet drink. ⊠ *35 Earlham St., Covent Garden* ☎ *020/7240–5142* ⊕ *www. esclubhouse.com* Ⓜ *Covent Garden.*

**Terroirs.** Specializing in "natural wines" (organic and sustainably produced with minimal added ingredients), Terroirs has an unusually careful selection of 200 wines from small French and Italian winemakers. These are served, along with delicious, relatively simple dishes—charcuterie, tapas, and more substantial French-inspired dishes—at a bar and tables surrounded by whitewashed walls and wooden floors. ⊠ *5 William St., Covent Garden* ☎ *020/7036–0660* ⊕ *www.terroirswinebar. com* Ⓜ *Charing Cross.*

### GAY AND LESBIAN

Fodor'sChoice **Heaven.** With the best light show on any London dance floor, Heaven
★ is unpretentious, loud, and huge, with a labyrinth of rooms, bars, and
live-music parlors. Friday and Saturday nights there's a comedy night
(7–10 pm; £13–£19). Check in advance about live performances—they
can take place any night of the week. If you go to just one gay club in
London, Heaven should be it. ⊠ *The Arches, Villiers St., Covent Garden*
☎ *020/7930–2020* ⊕ *www.heavennightclub-london.com* ✉ *£3–£12*
Ⓜ *Charing Cross, Embankment.*

## BLOOMSBURY, FITZROVIA, AND ISLINGTON

The ongoing redevelopment of the area around King's Cross St. Pancras station has invigorated Bloomsbury's nightlife scene. Fitzrovia,
meanwhile, manages to blend sophistication, informality, and a certain
edginess that's not found elsewhere in the center of town.

### BLOOMSBURY

#### BARS

**Big Chill House.** King's Cross has changed almost beyond recognition in
recent years, thanks to the wonders of culture-focused neighborhood
regeneration. What used to be an area you avoided or hurried through
has become a major destination, particularly on the food front. That
said, this fun bar, which occupies a big old Victorian pub, has been a
draw since long before the area started smartening up its act. It's at its
best on Friday and Saturday night (over 21s only), when DJs keep the
party going until late, and when the spacious outdoor terrace buzzes
with life. ⊠ *257–59 Pentonville Rd., King's Cross* ☎ *020/7427–2540*
⊕ *www.wearebigchill.com* ✉ *Free* Ⓜ *King's Cross St. Pancras.*

**Booking Office.** Taking full advantage of the soaring Victorian redbrick
vaults and arches of the restored St. Pancras Renaissance Hotel, Book-
ing Office is closer in feel to a cathedral than a traditional station bar.
Seasonal cocktails using traditional English ingredients are high on
flavor and low on mixers, and there's also a restaurant and live music
Thursday–Saturday. ⊠ *St. Pancras Renaissance Hotel, Euston Rd.,
King's Cross* ☎ *020/7841–3566* ⊕ *www.bookingofficerestaurant.com*
Ⓜ *King's Cross St. Pancras.*

#### COMEDY

Fodor'sChoice **Invisible Dot.** Tucked away in a King's Cross back street, this small venue
★ (the first purpose-built comedy club to open in the capital for aeons) is
a hotbed of alternative comedy talent. Big names in stand-up, including Tim Key and Josie Long, perform alongside sketch groups like
Sheeps and character comics like Joseph Morpurgo. Show days and
times vary, but each week brings a mix of established and upcoming
acts, with a longer mixed bill of new and old on Saturday night (at
8 pm). ⊠ *2 Northdown St., King's Cross* ☎ *020/7424–8918* ⊕ *www.
theinvisibledot.com* ✉ *£6–£12* Ⓜ *King's Cross.*

**16**

## FITZROVIA

### BARS

**Artesian.** They don't take reservations at this jewel box of a cocktail bar at the Langham Hotel, but you can order a drink while you wait for a mirror-top table surrounded by some of the most beautiful people in London. The cocktails—innovative creations involving ingredients like sandalwood and Japanese salt seasoning—are pricey, but service is top notch, making this a nightlife experience that's hard to fault. After 6 pm it's for ages 18 and over only. ⊠ *1C Portland Pl., Fitzrovia* ☎ *020/7636–1000* ⊕ *www.artesian-bar.co.uk* Ⓜ *Oxford Circus, Goodge St.*

**The London Edition bars.** Visitors to the London Edition hotel are spoiled for choice when it comes to bars. High ceilings, eclectic artwork, and innovative cocktails can be found at the all-day Berners Tavern and in the Lobby Bar, which opens in the evening. You'll need a reservation to get into the cozy Punch Room, but the bar's reinventions of traditional (and communal) punches and the exemplary service are worth the extra effort. On the weekend there's dancing until late in the more informal Basement (guest list only; visit ⊕ *www.basementldn.com* for the current lineup). ⊠ *10 Berners St., Fitzrovia* ☎ *020/7908–7979* ⊕ *www.edition-hotels.marriott.com/london* Ⓜ *Tottenham Court Rd., Oxford Circus.*

## ISLINGTON

Exmouth Market and Upper Street are the main nightlife hot spots in this neighborhood just north and east of central London. The fun, informal bars in Islington make it a reliable choice for going out.

### BARS

**69 Colebrooke Row.** This elegant faux speakeasy must be London's tiniest cocktail lounge. Book one of the handful of tables or a seat at the diminutive bar to sample perfectly made twists on classic cocktails, like the panettone bellini, which uses a purée of the sweet Italian bread instead of peach. Staff are immaculate but approachable. ⊠ *69 Colebrooke Row, Islington* ☎ *07540/528–593* ⊕ *www.69colebrookerow. com* Ⓜ *Angel.*

### ECLECTIC MUSIC

**Union Chapel.** The beauty of this sublime old chapel and its impressive multicultural not-for-profit programming make this spot one of London's best musical venues, especially for acoustic shows. Performers have included Björk, Beck, and Goldfrapp, although now you're more likely to hear lower-key alternative country, world music, and jazz, alongside poetry and literary events, film screenings, and stand-up comedy gigs. ⊠ *Compton Terr., Islington* ☎ *020/7226–1686 for venue (no box office; ticket sales numbers vary with each event)* ⊕ *www. unionchapel.org.uk* ☑ *Free–£35* Ⓜ *Highbury & Islington.*

---

# CLERKENWELL AND THE CITY

### BARS

**Café Kick.** This homey continental-style café-bar is open all day for meals, snacks, coffee, and cocktails. It's famous for its foosball tables, which give the place a fun, informal environment. Deals are available on "cocktails of the month" and house beers during happy hour

(4–7). You can reserve foosball tables in advance. There's a branch in Shoreditch. ⊠ *43 Exmouth Market, Clerkenwell* ☎ *020/7837–8077* ⊕ *www.cafekick.co.uk* Ⓜ *Angel.*

### DANCE CLUBS

**Fabric.** This sprawling subterranean club opposite Smithfield Meat Market is a firm fixture on the London scene and is regularly voted as one of the top clubs in the world. "FabricLive" hosts drum 'n' bass, dubstep, and hip-hop crews and live acts on Friday; international big-name DJs play slow, sexy bass lines and cutting-edge music on Saturday. The devastating sound system ensures that bass riffs vibrate through your entire body. Get there early to avoid a lengthy line-up and don't wear a suit. Expect a mainly young crowd. ⊠ *77A Charterhouse St., The City* ☎ *020/7336–8898* ⊕ *www.fabriclondon.com* ⊠ *£14–£22 (discounts after 3 or 4 am)* Ⓜ *Farringdon.*

## EAST LONDON

East London's bar scene is ever evolving, with the trendy crowd constantly pushing farther east in search of the next big thing. Shoreditch has bars and clubs to suit nearly all tastes these days, while Dalston, the neighborhood to its north, attracts a younger clientele.

### BARS

**Birthdays.** Dalston is probably London's hippest neighborhood for nightlife right now. This stark, industrial bar near the top of the main drag is as hot as it gets. Join the youngish crowd for craft beers and high-end burgers. There's a club in the basement that hosts DJs and live gigs. ⊠ *33–35 Stoke Newington Rd., Dalston* ☎ *020/7923–1680* ⊕ *www.birthdaysdalston.com* ⊠ *Bar free, club £5–£12.50* Ⓜ *Overground: Dalston Kingsland, Dalston Junction.*

**Book Club.** Light and friendly, the Book Club tops off a dose of Shoreditch's fashionable industrial chic with a dollop of culture. White tiles, bare brick walls, and big black-and-white photos set the tone, and there's a separate room for table tennis. Breakfast is served weekday mornings, a full lunch menu is offered through the week, and a modern menu of cocktails accompanies music, book launches, and workshops in the evenings. It's best avoided on weekend evenings, when it heaves with a raucous crowd. ⊠ *100–106 Leonard St., Shoreditch* ☎ *020/7684–8618* ⊕ *www.wearetbc.com* Ⓜ *Old St. Overground: Shoreditch High St.*

**Crate Bar and Pizzeria.** Canalside craft beer and pizza at the busiest of a handful of grown-up bars in this übertrendy area of East London. Rub shoulders with the locals—the community still has its share of artists who made their way east following rent hikes in Shoreditch—as well as visitors who come for late-night raves in the area's many warehouses. There's a warm atmosphere inside, with quirky upcycled interior design and DJs playing on weekend evenings. The beer comes from the on-site brewery, while thin-crust pizzas emerge from the open kitchen. ⊠ *Unit 7, Queens Yard, Hackney* ☎ *07834/275–687* ⊕ *www.cratebrewery.com* Ⓜ *Overground: Hackney Wick.*

16

**Fodor's Choice**  **White Lyan.** Cocktail making has been turned into an exact science at
★   this stark Hoxton bar, with everything made in-house and all ice, per-
ishables, and visible liquor brands outlawed to ensure that drinks turn
out perfectly every time (they're chilled ahead of time). It's fascinating to watch the bartenders at work over their digital scales (they're
more exact than spirit measures), using eye-droppers and spritzing
bottles to add precise quantities of unusual ingredients like blueberry
vinegar or lager syrup. It sounds pretentious but manages not to be,
and the results are delicious. Over 21s only. ⊠ *153–155 Hoxton St.,
Hoxton* ☏ *020/3011–1153* ⊕ *www.whitelyan.com* Ⓜ *Old St. Overground: Hoxton.*

### DANCE CLUBS

**Cargo.** Housed under a series of old railroad arches, this spacious brick-
wall bar, restaurant, dance floor, and live-music venue pulls a young,
international crowd with its hip vibe and diverse selection of music.
Long tables bring people together, as does the food, which draws on
global influences and is served tapas-style. Drinks are expensive. There's
a Banksy in the garden. ⊠ *83 Rivington St., Shoreditch* ☏ *020/7739–
3440* ⊕ *www.cargo-london.com* ▣ *Free–£20* Ⓜ *Old St.*

**Fodor's Choice**  **Cafe Oto.** A relaxed café by day, and London's leading venue for experi-
★   mental music by night, Cafe Oto is a Dalston institution. Its programming of free jazz, avant-garde electronica, and much more is enough
of a draw that it regularly sells out, with music fans steaming up the
windows and spilling out onto the pavement and road outside to smoke
in the breaks. Healthy Japanese food is served in the daytime, before
customers are kicked out at 5:30 pm to make way for sound checks. It's
open as a bar (no cover) on nights when no concerts are taking place.
⊠ *18–22 Ashwin St., Dalston* ⊕ *www.cafeoto.co.uk* ▣ *Café free, concerts free–£30* Ⓜ *Overground: Dalston Junction.*

**XOYO.** Big international DJs regularly play this cool Shoreditch spot
that's on a small side street off the main drag. The interior is industrial
chic, with some banquet seating in the relaxed upstairs room and a
downstairs that's a bit more hardcore. A youngish crowd dances the
night away on the weekend, while weeknight live gigs attract a more
diverse bunch. ⊠ *32–37 Cowper St., Shoreditch* ☏ *020/7354–9993*
⊕ *www.xoyo.co.uk* ▣ *Club nights £12.50–£20; gig ticket prices vary*
Ⓜ *Old St.*

## SOUTH OF THE THAMES

Recent years have seen an explosion in South London nightlife, including the gentrification of Brixton, the artistic colonization of Peckham,
and the continuing popularity of Vauxhall's gay clubs.

### BARS

**Aqua Shard.** This classy bar on level 31 of the Shard, London's new
skyscraper and the tallest building in Western Europe, is worth a visit
for the phenomenal views alone. The cocktail list is pretty special,
too—big on fruit purées and unusual bitters. No reservations are
taken in the bar, so be prepared to wait during busy periods. ⊠ *The*

*Shard, 31 St. Thomas St., Level 31, London Bridge* ☎ *020/3011–1256* ⊕ *www.aquashard.co.uk* Ⓜ *London Bridge.*

Fodor'sChoice ★ **Bussey Building.** This multilevel warehouse (officially called the CLF Art Café) is the epicenter of nightlife and culture in Peckham, attracting an edgy and young crowd. Have a chilled-out drink at Rye Wax, the record store–café bar in the basement; catch a theater performance, indie movie, or comedy gig on levels two through four, or dance the night away as big-name DJs and live acts work their magic. Expect an eclectic mix of soul, hip-hop, dubstep, house, and electronica, plus an "anything goes" vibe that keeps this one of the best places to party in South London. ✉ *133 Rye La., South East* ☎ *020/7732–5275* ⊕ *www. clfartcafe.org* 🎫 *Free–£15* Ⓜ *Overground: Peckham Rye.*

**The Dogstar.** This popular South London hangout was here years before Brixton's hipster renaissance and is still going strong today. The vibe is unpretentious, with top-name DJs playing cutting-edge sounds Thursday–Saturday in the main bar, comedy and cabaret upstairs, and pizza available until late. ✉ *389 Coldharbour La., Brixton* ☎ *020/7733–7515* ⊕ *www.dogstarbrixton.com* 🎫 *£5 Fri. and Sat. after 10 pm, otherwise free* Ⓜ *Brixton.*

Fodor'sChoice ★ **Three Eight Four.** Epitomizing a new breed of Brixton bar, Three Eight Four mixes up inventive cocktails. The menu changes seasonally but always involves boutique spirits and unusual mixing techniques—try the Nightshade, for example, which comes with a pipette that you use to add the final ingredient (crème de cassis) yourself. Bare lightbulbs and brick walls seem to be the style of choice for lots of cool London bars these days, but this place manages it with particular panache. A delectable selection of small dishes is also available. ✉ *384 Coldharbour La., Brixton* ☎ *020/3417–7309* ⊕ *www.threeeightfour.com* Ⓜ *Brixton.*

### DANCE CLUBS

**Ministry of Sound.** This is more of an industry than a club, with its own record label, online radio station, and international DJs. Though it's too much a part of the establishment these days to be at the forefront of cool, the stripped-down warehouse-style club has a super sound system and still pulls in the world's most legendary names in dance. There are chill-out rooms, four bars, four dance floors, and a spacious smoking area with its own snack bar. ✉ *103 Gaunt St., Borough* ☎ *0870/060–0010* ⊕ *www.ministryofsound.com* 🎫 *£15–£25* Ⓜ *Elephant & Castle.*

### ECLECTIC MUSIC

Fodor'sChoice ★ **O2 Academy Brixton.** This legendary Brixton venue has seen it all—mods and rockers, hippies and punks—and it remains one of the city's top indie and rock venues. Despite a capacity for almost 5,000, this refurbished Victorian hall with original art deco fixtures retains a clublike charm; it has plenty of bars and upstairs seating. ✉ *211 Stockwell Rd., Brixton* ☎ *0844/477–2000 for box office* ⊕ *www.o2academybrixton. co.uk* 🎫 *£15–£50* Ⓜ *Brixton.*

**16**

## KENSINGTON, CHELSEA, AND KNIGHTSBRIDGE

The pages of society magazines are full of photographs of gorgeous young people dancing the night away at clubs—many of which are members only—in these famously swanky neighborhoods. Dress up and be prepared to splurge.

### KENSINGTON
#### PIANO BARS/LOUNGES

**Piano Kensington.** Grab a cocktail at the tiny bar and fight your way in to grab a prime spot around the piano for a night of riotous fun at this compact Kensington joint. The talented pianists that play here six nights a week somehow know every song requested by this surprisingly diverse crowd, and it's clear they're having a great time too. Table bookings recommended. ⊠ *106 Kensington High St., Kensington* ☎ *020/7938–4664* ⊕ *www.pianokensington.com* Ⓜ *High St. Kensington.*

### CHELSEA
#### JAZZ AND BLUES

**606 Club.** This Chelsea jazz club has been doing things speakeasy-style since long before it became a nightlife trend in London. Buzz the door and you'll find a basement venue showcasing mainstream and contemporary jazz by well-known U.K.-based musicians. You must eat a meal in order to consume alcohol, so allow for an extra £30. Reservations are advisable. Lunchtime jazz takes place on select Sundays; call ahead. ⊠ *90 Lots Rd., Chelsea* ☎ *020/7352–5953* ⊕ *www.606club. co.uk* 🎫 *£10–£12 music charge added to bill* Ⓜ *Fulham Broadway. Overground: Imperial Wharf.*

### KNIGHTSBRIDGE
#### BARS

**The Blue Bar at the Berkeley Hotel.** With low-slung dusty-blue walls, this hotel bar is ever so slightly sexy. Immaculate service, an excellent seasonal cocktail list and a trendy David Collins design make this an ideal spot for a romantic tête-à-tête, complete with jazzy music in the background. ⊠ *Wilton Pl., Knightsbridge* ☎ *020/7235–6000* ⊕ *www.theberkeley.co.uk* Ⓜ *Knightsbridge, Hyde Park Corner.*

## NOTTING HILL

The focus is more on bars than clubs in this West London neighborhood, although late-night fun is on offer at a few notable exceptions. In general, you can expect a young, moneyed crowd making this their first stop on a wild night out elsewhere.

### BARS

**Beach Blanket Babylon.** In a Georgian house close to Portobello Market, this always-packed bar is distinguishable by its eclectic indoor-outdoor spaces with Gaudí-esque curves and snug corner spaces—like a fairy-tale grotto or a medieval dungeon. A sister restaurant-bar-gallery offers a slightly more modern take on similar themes in an ex-warehouse in Shoreditch (⊠ *19–23 Bethnal Green Rd.* ☎ *020/7749–3540*). ⊠ *45 Ledbury Rd., Notting Hill* ☎ *020/7229–2907* ⊕ *www.beachblanket. co.uk* Ⓜ *Notting Hill Gate.*

**Electric Diner.** A huge selection of bottled beers and quirky twists on classic cocktails (Courvoisier, mint, and champagne anyone?) are the attractions at this bar and diner next to Notting Hill's famed Electric Cinema. Run by the people behind the members-only Soho House, the place exudes the same mixture of posh and cool, but is open to anyone and everyone. Sit in the window and watch the world go by along Portobello Road, or opt for one of the luxury takes on classic diner fare at a table in the moody, vaulted interior. ⊠ *191 Portobello Rd., Notting Hill* ☎ *020/7908–9696* ⊕ *www.electricdiner.com* Ⓜ *Ladbroke Grove.*

### DANCE CLUBS

**Notting Hill Arts Club.** Rock stars like Liam Gallagher and Courtney Love have been seen at this small basement club-bar. What the place lacks in looks it makes up for in mood, and an alternative crowd swills beer to eclectic music that spans Asian underground, hip-hop, Latin-inspired funk, deep house, and jazzy grooves. ⊠ *21 Notting Hill Gate, Notting Hill* ☎ *020/7460–4459* ⊕ *www.nottinghillartsclub.com* ✉ *Free–£8* Ⓜ *Notting Hill Gate.*

# REGENT'S PARK AND HAMPSTEAD

**16**

Camden Town boasts a handful of dance clubs, but it's this north London neighborhood's music venues that are the big draw for most. Every genre is covered, from folk and pop, to jazz and world music, with interesting gigs taking place every night of the week.

## REGENT'S PARK

### COMEDY AND CABARET

**Canal Café Theatre.** Famous comics and cabaret stars perform every night of the week in this intimate, canalside venue. The long-running News-Revue is a topical song-and-sketch show performed Thursday–Sunday. ⊠ *Bridge House, Delamere Terr., Little Venice* ☎ *020/7289–6054* ⊕ *www.canalcafetheatre.com* ✉ *Free–£15* Ⓜ *Warwick Ave., Royal Oak, Paddington.*

### DANCE CLUBS

**KOKO.** This Victorian theater has seen acts from Charlie Chaplin to Madonna, and genres from punk to rave. Furnished with lush reds that make it not unlike a cockney Moulin Rouge, this is still one of London's most stunning venues. Sounds of live indie rock, cabaret, funky house, and club classics keep the big dance floor moving, even when it's not heaving. ⊠ *1A Camden High St., Camden Town* ☎ *0870/432–5527* ⊕ *www.koko.uk.com* ✉ *£5–£30* Ⓜ *Mornington Crescent.*

### ECLECTIC MUSIC

**Roundhouse.** This former steam-engine repair shed hosts some of the most atmospheric medium-scale rock and pop gigs in the capital, plus a varied program of circus, theater, dance, and the occasional art installation. There's a good restaurant on the first floor, and in the summer the terrace bar is transformed into an "urban beach," complete with sand. ⊠ *Chalk Farm Rd., Camden* ☎ *030/0678–9222* ⊕ *www.roundhouse. org.uk* ✉ *£5–£40* Ⓜ *Chalk Farm.*

### JAZZ AND BLUES

**Jazz Café.** A palace of cool in bohemian Camden, this remains an essential hangout for fans of both the mainstream end of the jazz repertoire and hip-hop, funk, world music, and Latin fusion. It's also the unlikely venue for "I Love the 80s Vs I Love the 90s" on Saturday night. Book ahead if you want a prime table in the balcony restaurant overlooking the stage. ⊠ *5 Parkway, Camden Town* ☎ *020/7485–6834 for venue info, 0844/847–2514 for tickets (Ticketmaster)* ⊕ *www. thejazzcafelondon.com* ⊡ *£6–£35* Ⓜ *Camden Town.*

### ROCK

**Barfly Club.** At one of the finest small clubs in the capital, punk, indie guitar, and new metal rock attract a nonmainstream crowd. Weekend club nights upstairs host DJs (and live bands) who rock the decks. ⊠ *49 Chalk Farm Rd., Camden Town* ☎ *020/7424–0800 for venue, 0844/847–2424 for tickets* ⊕ *www.mamacolive.com/thebarfly* ⊡ *Free– £11* Ⓜ *Chalk Farm.*

**Dublin Castle.** Run by the same family for nearly three decades, the Dublin Castle has hosted almost every British rock group you care to name, from Madness to Coldplay. With four bands on the bill almost every night, and DJs taking over afterward on Friday and weekends, there's something for most tastes at this legendary venue. ⊠ *94 Parkway, Camden Town* ☎ *020/7485–1773* ⊕ *www.thedublincastle.com* ⊡ *£4–£8* Ⓜ *Camden Town.*

# PERFORMING ARTS

Updated by
Jo Caird

"All the world's a stage," said Shakespeare, immortal words heard for the first time right here in London. And whether you prefer your theater, music, and art classical or modern, or as contemporary twists on time-honored classics, you'll find that London's vibrant cultural scene more than holds its own on the world stage.

Divas sing original-language librettos at the Royal Opera House, Shakespeare's plays are brought to life at the reconstructed Globe Theatre, and challenging new writing is produced at the Royal Court. Whether you feel like basking in the lighthearted extravagance of a West End musical or taking in the next shark-in-formaldehyde at the White Cube gallery, the choice is yours.

There are international theater festivals, innovative music festivals, and critically acclaimed seasons of postmodern dance. Short trip or long, you'll find the cultural scene in London is ever-changing, ever-expanding, and ever-exciting.

No matter where you head, London's art and performing arts scenes have been setting global trends for decades—and when you count Shakespearean theater and Handel oratorios, for centuries. Fringe theater, classical ballet, participatory chorales: you name it, London probably did it first and often does it best.

# PLANNING

### TOP THEATER TIPS

**Behind the pillars.** Many theaters and concert halls sell discounted seats with restricted views.

**Matinees.** Afternoon performances are almost always better value than evening ones.

**Previews.** Tickets to shows are usually less expensive in the first few weeks of their run, before the critics have had their say.

**Monday.** Most movie theaters and some theaters, including the Royal Court, have a reduced-price ticketing policy on Monday.

**Standing.** Shakespeare's Globe Theatre and the BBC Proms are the two most prominent places where remaining upright saves you money.

### FIND OUT WHAT'S PLAYING WHERE

To find out what's showing now, the free weekly magazine *Time Out* (issued every Tuesday outside major stations and around the city; also online at ⊕ *www.timeout.com*) is invaluable.

The free *Evening Standard* carries listings, many of which are also available online at ⊕ *www.standard.co.uk*. *Metro,* London's other widely available free newspaper, is also worth checking out, as are many Sunday papers, and the Saturday *Independent, Guardian,* and *Times*.

The website ⊕ *www.whatsonstage.com* is an invaluable resource for theater listings.

There are hundreds of small private galleries all over London with interesting work by famous and emerging artists. The bimonthly free pamphlet "new exhibitions of contemporary art" (⊕ *www.newexhibitions. com*), available at most galleries, lists and maps nearly 200 art spaces in London.

# PERFORMING ARTS REVIEWS

**17**

## ST. JAMES'S AND WESTMINSTER

Wander the streets of this chic central London neighborhood—home to aristocrats in the 17th century—and you'll discover small commercial galleries, fine-art auction houses, and antiques dealers mixed in among the high-end tailors and gentlemen's clubs.

### ART GALLERIES

**Institute of Contemporary Arts.** Housed in an elegant John Nash–designed Regency terrace, the ICA's two galleries have changing exhibitions of contemporary visual art. The ICA also programs performances, underground and vintage movies, talks, and photography, and there's an excellent arts bookstore, a cafeteria, and a funky bar. ⊠ *The Mall, St. James's* ☎ *020/7930–3647* ⊕ *www.ica.org.uk* ▨ *Free* ◷ *Tues.–Sun. 11–11. Galleries Sun.–Tues. 11–6, Thurs. 11–9* Ⓜ *Charing Cross, Piccadilly Circus.*

**White Cube.** The English role in the exploding contemporary art scene has been major, thanks in good portion to Jay Joplin's influential gallery, which has regularly moved around London since 1993. This striking modern concrete structure was the first freestanding building to be built in the area for 30 years when it opened in 2006. It is home base for an array of British artists who have won the Turner Prize, including Damien Hirst, Tracey Emin, and Gary Hume. ⊠ *25–26 Mason's Yard, St. James's* ☎ *020/7930–5373* ⊕ *www.whitecube.com* ▨ *Free* ◷ *Tues.–Sat. 10–6* Ⓜ *Green Park, Piccadilly Circus.*

Random Dance Company performs at Sadler's Wells.

### CLASSICAL MUSIC

**St. James's Church.** The organ was brought here in 1691 after fire destroyed its former home, the Palace of Whitehall. St. James's holds regular classical music concerts and free lunchtime recitals Monday, Wednesday, and Friday at 1:10 pm (free but donation of £3.50 suggested). ⊠ *197 Piccadilly, St. James's* ☎ *020/7381–0441* ⊕ *www.sjp.org.uk* 🎟 *Free, but £3.50 donation suggested* Ⓜ *Piccadilly Circus, Green Park*.

**St. John's Smith Square.** This baroque church behind Westminster Abbey offers chamber music and organ recitals as well as orchestral concerts. There are three or four lunchtime recitals a month. ⊠ *Smith Sq., Westminster* ☎ *020/7222–1061* ⊕ *www.sjss.org.uk* 🎟 *£10* Ⓜ *Westminster*.

**St. Martin-in-the-Fields Concerts.** Popular lunchtime concerts are held in this lovely 1726 church, as are regular evening concerts. Stop for a snack at the Café in the Crypt. ⊠ *Trafalgar Sq., Westminster* ☎ *020/7766–1100* ⊕ *www.stmartin-in-the-fields.org* 🎟 *£3.50 donation suggested* Ⓜ *Charing Cross*.

## MAYFAIR AND MARYLEBONE

The historic center of the London art world, Mayfair has a thriving gallery scene that has undergone a renaissance in recent years. With East End gallerists relocating to central London and a number of top international galleries opening new premises here, there's a real buzz about the place. Directly north of Mayfair, Marylebone has more of a village atmosphere, with a few choice galleries and arts institutions dotted around.

## DANCE: LONDON TODAY

Dance fans in London can enjoy the classicism of the world-renowned Royal Ballet, as well as innovative works by several contemporary dance companies—including Rambert Dance Company and Matthew Bourne's New Adventures—and scores of independent choreographers. The English National Ballet and visiting international companies perform at the Coliseum and at Sadler's Wells, which also hosts various other ballet companies and dance troupes. Encompassing the refurbished Royal Festival Hall, the Southbank Centre has a seriously good contemporary dance program that hosts top international companies and important U.K. choreographers, as well as multicultural offerings, such as Japanese *butoh*, Indian classical, and hip-hop. The Place and the Lilian Baylis Theatre at Sadler's Wells are where you'll find the most daring, cutting-edge performances.

Check ⊕ *www.londondance.com* for current performances and fringe venues.

**Dance Umbrella.** The biggest annual event is Dance Umbrella, a 15-day festival in October that hosts international and British-based artists at venues across the city. ⊠ *London* ☎ *020/7257–9384* ⊕ *www.danceumbrella.co.uk* ⊠ *Free.*

## MAYFAIR
### ART GALLERIES

**David Zwirner.** This is just one of several influential New York gallerists to open a London space in Mayfair in recent years, a trend that has revitalized an area that's been losing ground to edgier neighborhoods like Bethnal Green. Zwirner's roster contains the likes of Bridget Riley and Jeff Koons, and modern masters such as Piet Mondrian are exhibited in this grand converted townhouse, too. ⊠ *24 Grafton St., Mayfair* ☎ *020/3538–3165* ⊕ *www.davidzwirner.com* ⊠ *Free* ◷ *Closed Sun.* Ⓜ *Green Park.*

**Marlborough Fine Art.** This veteran of the Mayfair art scene has been presenting exhibitions by masters old and new since it was founded in 1946. You'll find work by great living artists like Paula Rego and Frank Auerbach in the main first floor space, plus exhibitions of graphic works from a whole host of starry names. The recently opened contemporary gallery on the second floor shows a younger generation of artists from the U.K. and abroad. ⊠ *6 Albermarle St., Mayfair* ☎ *020/7629–5161* ⊕ *www.marlboroughfineart.com* ⊠ *Free* ◷ *Closed Sun.* Ⓜ *Green Park, Piccadilly Circus.*

## MARYLEBONE
### ART GALLERIES

**Lisson.** Owner Nicholas Logsdail represents about 50 blue-chip artists, including the minimalist Sol LeWitt and performance artist Marina Abramović, at one of the most respected galleries in London. The gallery is most associated with New Object sculptors like Anish Kapoor and Richard Deacon, many of whom have won the Turner Prize. A branch down the road at 27 Bell Street features work by up-and-coming artists.

17

The Royal Opera House, one of the world's greatest opera houses and home to the Royal Ballet, offers regular tours of the auditorium and backstage.

⊠ *52 Bell St., Marylebone* ☎ *020/7724–2739* ⊕ *www.lissongallery.com* ⌨ *Free* ⊘ *Weekdays 10–6, Sat. 11–5* Ⓜ *Edgware Rd., Marylebone.*

### CLASSICAL MUSIC

FAMILY
Fodor'sChoice
★

**Wigmore Hall.** Hear chamber music and song recitals (including concerts for toddlers) in this charming hall with near-perfect acoustics. Don't miss the Sunday morning concerts (at 11:30 am). ⊠ *36 Wigmore St., Marylebone* ☎ *020/7935–2141* ⊕ *www.wigmore-hall.org.uk* Ⓜ *Bond St.*

## SOHO AND COVENT GARDEN

London's hip center has it all, from multiplexes playing the biggest blockbuster movies to niche contemporary art galleries tucked away in back streets, and from world-famous opera houses to sultry cabaret joints.

### SOHO

### ART GALLERIES

Fodor'sChoice
★

**Photographer's Gallery.** Britain's first and foremost photography gallery programs cutting-edge and provocative exhibitions. The prestigious Deutsche Börse Photography Prize is exhibited and awarded here annually. The gallery also has a print sales room, a bookstore, and a café-bar—a great spot to escape the bustle of nearby Oxford Street. ⊠ *16–18 Ramillies St., Soho* ☎ *020/7087–9300* ⊕ *www.thephotographersgallery. org.uk* ⌨ *Free daily 10–noon; prices vary for exhibitions* ⊘ *Mon.–Wed. 10–6, Thurs. 9:30–8, Fri. and Sat. 10–6, Sun. 11–6* Ⓜ *Oxford Circus.*

## TOP FIVE FOR THE ARTS

**Stand with the "plebs" in Shakespeare's Globe Theatre.** There are seats, but to really experience theater Shakespeare-style, you should stand in the yard with the stage at eye level (plus, it's a bargain at £5).

**Visit the latest grand art installation in the Turbine Hall at Tate Modern.** The enormity of the central space regularly inspires striking work.

**Catch a world-class performance at the BBC Proms.** There's a surprisingly down-to-earth atmosphere among the elated company at these great concerts.

**Enjoy a night at the BFI Southbank.** Mingle with the real aficionados at screenings of foreign, classic, and experimental films.

**Watch a Hollywood star in a West End production.** Film stars often come to London to boost their artistic credibility in small-scale theaters.

**Riflemaker.** Inside the oldest public building in the West End (a Georgian-era rifle maker's workshop), this hip but accessible gallery exhibits ambitious works by emerging artists, as well as shining a light on established figures who haven't gotten the recognition they deserve. Names on the roster include Judy Chicago, Josephine King, and William S. Burroughs. ⊠ *79 Beak St., Soho* ☎ *020/7439–0000* ⊕ *www.riflemaker.org* ⊒ *Free* ⊙ *Weekdays 11–7, Sat. noon–6* Ⓜ *Piccadilly Circus, Oxford Circus.*

**Sadie Coles HQ.** This light-filled art space overlooking busy Regent Street marked a major expansion for respected British gallerist Sadie Coles when it opened in fall 2013. You'll find the work of important British and international artists such as Sarah Lucas and Wilhelm Sasnal. ⊠ *62 Kingly St., Soho* ☎ *020/7493–8611* ⊕ *www.sadiecoles.com* ⊙ *Tues.–Sat. 11–6.*

### FILM

**Curzon Soho.** This popular, comfortable movie theater runs a vibrant and artsy program of mixed repertoire and mainstream films, with a good calendar of director talks and other events, too. The bar is great for a quiet drink, even when Soho is crawling with people. There are further Curzon branches in Mayfair, Bloomsbury, Victoria, Chelsea, Wimbledon, and Richmond. ⊠ *99 Shaftesbury Ave., Soho* ☎ *0330/500–1331* ⊕ *www.curzoncinemas.com* Ⓜ *Piccadilly Circus, Leicester Sq.*

FAMILY **Prince Charles Cinema.** This repertory movie theater right off Leicester Square offers a chance to catch up with independent features, documentaries, and even blockbusters you may have missed. A second screen upstairs shows newer movies at more usual West End prices. This is where the "sing-along screening" took off; come in character and warble along to *The Sound of Music, Grease, The Rocky Horror Picture Show,* and more. ⊠ *7 Leicester Pl., Soho* ☎ *020/7494–3654* ⊕ *www.princecharlescinema.com* ⊒ *£8 (£4 if you purchase a £10 annual membership)* Ⓜ *Leicester Sq., Piccadilly Circus.*

**17**

## THEATER: LONDON TODAY

In London, the play really *is* the thing—from long-running popular musicals like *Mamma Mia!* to a groundbreaking reworking of Pinter, imaginative physical theater from an experimental company like Complicite, a lavish Disney spectacle, or a small fringe production above a pub. West End glitz and glamour continue to pull in the audiences, and so do the more innovative productions.

In London the words "radical" and "quality," or "classical" and "experimental," are not mutually exclusive. The Royal Shakespeare Company (⊕ *www.rsc.org.uk*) and the National Theatre (⊕ *www. nationaltheatre.org.uk*) often stage contemporary versions of the classics. The Almeida, Donmar Warehouse, Royal Court Theatre, Young Vic, and Old Vic attract famous actors and have excellent reputations for new writing and innovative theatrical approaches. These are the venues where you'll see an original production before it becomes a hit in the West End or on Broadway (and at a fraction of the cost).

The London theater scene remains vibrant throughout the summer months. Open-air productions of Shakespeare are particularly well served, whether in the faithful reconstruction of the Elizabethan Globe Theatre or under the stars in Regent's Park's Open Air Theatre. Theater festivals such as **LIFT** (the London International Festival of Theatre ⊕ *www.liftfestival.com*) and the **London International Mime Festival** (⊕ *www.mimelondon. com*) provide the chance to see international and cutting-edge companies throughout the year.

Theatergoing isn't cheap. Tickets less than £15 are a rarity, although designated productions at the National Theatre offer seats at this price. At commercial theaters, you should expect to pay from £20 for a seat in the upper balcony to at least £40 for a good one in the stalls (orchestra) or dress circle (mezzanine). However, last-minute returns available on the night of the performance may yield some good deals. Tickets may be booked through ticket agents, at individual theater box offices in person or online, or over the phone by credit card. Be sure to inquire about any extra fees; prices can vary enormously, but agents are legally obliged to reveal the face value of the ticket if you ask. All the larger hotels offer theater bookings, but they tack on a hefty service charge.

**Ticketmaster** (⊕ *www.ticketmaster. co.uk*) sells tickets for a number of different theaters, although they do charge a booking fee. For discount tickets, **Society of London Theatre** (⊕ *www.tkts.co.uk*) operates TKTS, a half-price ticket booth on the south side of Leicester Square, and sells the best available seats to performances at about 30 theaters. It's open Monday–Saturday 10–7, Sunday 11–4:30; there's a £3 service charge (included in the price; major credit cards are accepted).

■TIP→ Be very wary of ticket touts (scalpers) and unscrupulous ticket agents outside theaters and working the line at TKTS.

**THEATER**

Fodor's Choice ★ **Soho Theatre.** This sleek theater in the heart of Soho is devoted to fostering new work and is a prolific presenter of plays by emerging writers, comedy performances, cabaret shows, and other entertainment. The bar is always buzzing. ✉ *21 Dean St., Soho* ☎ *020/7478–0100* ⊕ *www. sohotheatre.com* Ⓜ *Tottenham Court Rd.*

## COVENT GARDEN

**DANCE**

**The London Coliseum.** Ballet troupes (the top dance company to perform here is the English National Ballet) are booked into the spectacular Coliseum during the summer and at Christmas, and any time when the resident English National Opera is not in town. The Edwardian baroque theater is known for its magnificent auditorium and a glass dome; tours offer fascinating insights into the architecture and history of the building. ✉ *St. Martin's La., Covent Garden* ☎ *020/7845–9300* ⊕ *www.eno.org* Ⓜ *Leicester Sq., Charing Cross.*

Fodor's Choice ★ **Royal Opera House.** The renowned Royal Ballet performs classical and contemporary repertoire in this spectacular theater, where the interior may be Victorian but the stagecraft behind the red velvet curtain is state-of-the-art. Backstage tours and auditorium tours book up several weeks in advance, so check the schedule before you travel. ✉ *Bow St., Covent Garden* ☎ *020/7304–4000* ⊕ *www.roh.org.uk* ✉ *Performances £3–£235, backstage tours £12, auditorium tours £9.50* ⊙ *Backstage tours (75 mins) Mon.–Sat. 10:30–2:30; auditorium tours (45 mins) at 4 pm (days vary)* Ⓜ *Covent Garden.*

**OPERA**

**The London Coliseum.** A veritable architectural extravaganza of Edwardian exoticism, the baroque-style theater has a magnificent auditorium and a rooftop glass dome with a bar and great views. As one of the city's most venerable theaters, the Coliseum functions mainly as the home of the English National Opera which continues to produce innovative opera, sung in English, for lower prices than the Royal Opera House. During opera's off-season, the house hosts the English National Ballet (*www.ballet.org.uk*). Guided tours are on alternate Saturdays at 11 am, plus the occasional Thursday and Friday, when productions are scheduled). ✉ *St. Martin's La., Covent Garden* ☎ *020/7845–9300 box office, 020/7836–0111 inquiries* ⊕ *www.eno.org* ✉ *Guided tours £10* Ⓜ *Leicester Sq.*

Fodor's Choice ★ **Royal Opera House.** Along with Milan's La Scala, New York's Metropolitan, and the Palais Garnier in Paris, this is one of the world's greatest opera houses. The resident troupe has mounted spectacular productions in the past, though recent productions have tended toward more contemporary operas. Whatever the style of the performance, the extravagant theater—also home to the famed Royal Ballet—delivers a full dose of opulence. The box office opens at 10 am, but lines for same-day tickets for popular productions start forming as early as 7 am. If you wish to see the hall but are not able to procure a ticket, you can join a backstage tour or one of the less frequent tours of the auditorium. ✉ *Bow St., Covent Garden* ☎ *020/7304–4000* ⊕ *www.*

**17**

The giants of modern art are on display at South Bank's Tate Modern, one of the largest modern art galleries in the world and housed in a former power station.

*roh.org.uk* ✉ *Performances £4–£250, backstage tour £12; auditorium tour £9.50* ⊘ *Public areas generally 10–3, backstage tours Mon.–Sat. 10:30–2:30 (check in advance), auditorium tours at 4 pm (days vary)* Ⓜ *Covent Garden.*

### THEATER

**Donmar Warehouse.** Hollywood stars often perform in this not-for-profit theater in diverse and daring new works, bold interpretations of the classics, and small-scale musicals. Nicole Kidman, Gwyneth Paltrow, and Ewan McGregor have all been featured. ✉ *41 Earlham St., Seven Dials, Covent Garden* ☎ *0844/871–7624* ⊕ *www.donmarwarehouse. com* Ⓜ *Covent Garden.*

## BLOOMSBURY AND HOLBORN

Once the heart of fashionable literary London, there's still an air of refinement about this neighborhood. A handful of small theaters with links to the colleges with campuses in the area create a vibrant small-scale performance scene with theater, dance, and stand-up comedy.

### CLASSICAL MUSIC

**Kings Place.** This airy concert venue opened in 2008. The cultural jewel in the huge new developments near the Eurostar terminal in King's Cross, it is the permanent home of the London Sinfonietta and the Orchestra of the Age of Enlightenment. It offers week-long programs by musicians in a range of genres and a hugely varied cultural calendar of jazz, comedy, folk, and political and literary lectures, plus two gallery

## CONTEMPORARY ART: LONDON TODAY

In the 21st century, the focus of the city's art scene has shifted from the past to the future. Helped by the prominence of Tate Modern, London's contemporary art scene has never been so high profile. In publicly funded exhibition spaces like the Barbican Gallery, the Hayward Gallery, the Institute of Contemporary Arts, and the Serpentine Galleries, London now has a modern art environment on par with that of Bilbao and New York. The so-called Young British Artists (YBAs, although no longer that young) Damien Hirst, Tracey Emin, and others are firmly planted in the public imagination. The celebrity status of British artists has a lot to do with the annual Turner Prize, which always stirs up controversy in the media during the display of the work, usually at Tate Britain.

Depending on who you talk to, the Saatchi Gallery is considered to be either the savior of contemporary art or the wardrobe of the emperor's new clothes. After a couple of moves it is now ensconced in the former Duke of York's barracks off Chelsea's King's Road.

The South Bank's Tate Modern may house the giants of modern art, but East London is where the innovative action is. There are dozens of galleries in the fashionable spaces around Old Street, and the truly hip have already moved even farther afield, to areas such as Bethnal Green, to the east, and Peckham, to the south. The Whitechapel Art Gallery and Jay Jopling's influential White Cube, with branches in Bermondsey and St. James's, remain essential parts of the new art establishment and continue to show exciting work by emerging British artists.

On the first Thursday of every month, more than 130 museums and galleries in East London stay open late and host talks, workshops, and other events (more information at ⊕ www.firstthursdays.co.uk).

**17**

spaces. ⊠ *90 York Way, King's Cross* ☎ *020/7520–1490 for box office, 020/7520–1440 for inquiries* ⊕ *www.kingsplace.co.uk* Ⓜ *King's Cross.*

### DANCE

**Peacock Theatre.** Sadler's Wells's West End annex, this modernist theater near the London School of Economics (which uses it as a lecture hall during the day) focuses on younger companies and shows in popular dance genres like flamenco, tango, and hip-hop. ⊠ *Portugal St., Holborn* ☎ *020 /7863–8222 for box office* ⊕ *www.peacocktheatre.com* Ⓜ *Holborn.*

**The Place.** The Robin Howard Dance Theatre at The Place is London's only theater dedicated to contemporary dance, and with tickets often under £20 (performances by student dancers, for example, cost just £10) it's good value, too. The "Resolution!" festival in January and February is the United Kingdom's biggest platform event for new choreographers. ⊠ *17 Duke's Rd., Bloomsbury* ☎ *020/7121–1100* ⊕ *www.theplace.org.uk* Ⓜ *Euston.*

# ISLINGTON

Close to central London, yet with its own unique atmosphere, this neighborhood is home to a handful of renowned theaters and music venues that make the short journey northeast well worth the effort.

### ART GALLERIES

**Victoria Miro Gallery.** This large, important commercial gallery, in a former furniture factory, has exhibited some of the biggest names on the British contemporary art scene: Grayson Perry, the Chapman Brothers, and Peter Doig, to name a few. Some exhibitions spill out into the gallery's own garden. It also brings in exciting talent from abroad. There's another branch in Mayfair. ⊠ *16 Wharf Rd., Islington* ☎ *020/7336–8109* ⊕ *www.victoria-miro.com* ⊠ *Free* ⊙ *Tues.–Sat. 10–6, Mon. by appointment only* Ⓜ *Old St., Angel.*

### DANCE

FAMILY

Fodor'sChoice

★

**Sadler's Wells.** This gleaming building opened in 1998, the seventh on the site in its 300-year history. Head here to see performances by leading classical and contemporary dance companies. The Random Dance Company is in residence, and the little Lilian Baylis Theatre hosts avant-garde work. ⊠ *Rosebery Ave., Islington* ☎ *020 /7863–8000* ⊕ *www. sadlerswells.com* Ⓜ *Angel.*

### THEATER

**Almeida Theatre.** This Off West End venue, helmed by director Rupert Goold, premiers excellent new plays and exciting twists on the classics, often featuring high-profile actors. There's a good café and a licensed bar that serves "sharing dishes," as well as tasty main courses. ⊠ *Almeida St., Islington* ☎ *020/7359–4404* ⊕ *www.almeida.co.uk* Ⓜ *Angel, Highbury & Islington.*

FAMILY

**Little Angel Theatre.** Innovative puppetry performances for children and adults have been taking place in this adorable former temperance hall since 1961. The theater runs a number of festivals a year, including the biennial Suspense festival, with puppetry for adults. ⊠ *14 Dagmar Passage, Islington* ☎ *020/7226–1787* ⊕ *www.littleangeltheatre.com* Ⓜ *Angel, Highbury & Islington.*

# THE CITY

It may seem at first glance like the denizens of London's financial center are far too busy to take time out for culture, but if you look a little closer you'll see that arts events are taking place all over, courtesy of a number of acclaimed annual festivals. Art exhibits in empty offices and chamber performances in historic churches are regular occurrences.

### PERFORMING ARTS CENTERS

FAMILY

**Barbican Centre.** Opened in 1982, the Barbican is an enormous Brutalist concrete maze that Londoners either love or hate—but its importance to the cultural life of the capital is beyond dispute. At the largest performing arts center in Europe, you could listen to Elgar, see 1960s photography, and catch German animation with live accompaniment, all in one day. The main theater, known for its acoustics, is most famous as the home of the London Symphony Orchestra. The Barbican is also a frequent host to the BBC Symphony Orchestra. ⊠ *Silk St., The City* ☎ *020/7638–8891* ⊕ *www.barbican.org.uk* 🎫 *Ticket prices vary, with some free events* ⊙ *Mon.–Sat. 9 am–11 pm, Sun. 10 am–11 pm* Ⓜ *Barbican.*

## EAST LONDON

Artists and other creative types, no longer able to afford central London rents, have been making their way eastward for years. It began in Shoreditch, but as rents increased there, too, neighborhoods farther and farther out have taken on these new residents. Go gallery hopping in Vyner Street in Bethnal Green or catch a hip band in action at one of Shoreditch's myriad music venues.

### PERFORMING ARTS CENTERS

Fodor's Choice

★

**Wilton's.** Arguably London's most atmospheric cultural space, Wilton's has been entertaining the crowds since 1743, first as an alehouse, then as a music hall. It now hosts gigs, talks, theater performances, movie screenings (often with live scores), and swing-dance evenings. The cozy Mahogany Bar, the oldest part of the building, serves a good range of quality local ales, along with typical pub food. There's a cocktail bar upstairs, in what was once the artists' green room. ⊠ *Graces Alley, East End* ☎ *020/7702–2789* ⊕ *www.wiltons.org.uk* Ⓜ *Aldgate East, Tower Hill.*

### THEATER

FAMILY **Hackney Empire.** The history of this treasure of a theater is drama in its own right. Charlie Chaplin is said to have appeared here during its days as a thriving variety theater and music hall in the early 1900s. It now hosts traditional family entertainment and variety shows, opera, music, musical theater, dance, and drama, often with a multicultural slant. Its annual Christmas pantomime show is legendary. ⊠ *291 Mare St., Hackney* ☎ *020/8985–2424* ⊕ *www.hackneyempire.co.uk* Ⓜ *Overground: Hackney Central.*

## SOUTH OF THE THAMES

The South Bank and its easterly near neighbor Bankside together make up one of the richest areas in London when it comes to arts and entertainment. Whether you want to watch a play, hear a concert, or see an art exhibit, you won't have to wander far to find something top class. Venture a little farther into South London, and you'll be rewarded with a sprinkling of fringe theaters that act as incubators for the capital's mainstream theater scene.

### FILM

FAMILY **BFI London IMAX Cinema.** The British Film Institute's glazed drum-shaped IMAX theater (now, confusingly, operated by Odeon) has the largest screen in the United Kingdom (approximately 75 feet wide and the height of five double-decker buses). It shows state-of-the-art 2-D and 3-D films. ⊠ *1 Charlie Chaplin Walk, South Bank* ☎ *0330/333–7878* ⊕ *www.bfi.org.uk/imax* Ⓜ *Waterloo.*

17

## FILM: LONDON TODAY

There are many wonderful movie theaters in London and several that are committed to nonmainstream and repertory cinema, in particular the excellent Curzon cinemas and the British Film Institute. The **BFI London Film Festival** (⊕ *www.bfi.org.uk/lff*) brings hundreds of films made by masters of world cinema to London each October, accompanied by often sold-out talks and other events. The smaller, avantgarde **Raindance Film Festival** (⊕ *www.raindance.co.uk*) highlights independent filmmaking, September into October.

Open-air screenings of new releases and classic movies take place throughout the summer months at atmospheric locations including Somerset House, and the 19th-century Brompton Cemetery (⊕ *www.whereisthenomad.com*).

West End movie theaters continue to do good business. Most of the major houses, such as the Odeon Leicester Square and the Empire, are in the Leicester Square–Piccadilly Circus area, where tickets average £15. Monday screenings and matinees are often cheaper, around £8–£12, and there are also smaller crowds.

Check out *Time Out*, one of the London papers, or ⊕ *www.viewlondon.co.uk* for listings.

FAMILY **BFI Southbank.** With the best repertory programming in London, the three movie theaters and studio here are effectively a national film center run by the British Film Institute. More than 1,000 titles are screened each year, with art-house, foreign, silent, overlooked, classic, noir, and short films favored over recent Hollywood blockbusters. The center also has a gallery, bookshop, and "mediatheque" where visitors can watch film and television from the National Archive for free (closed Monday). This is one of the venues for the BFI London Film Festival; throughout the year there are minifestivals, seminars, and guest speakers. Benugo Bar & Kitchen, toward the back of the building, is a great secret spot for a drink. ⊠ *Belvedere Rd., South Bank* ☎ *020/7928–3232* ⊕ *www.bfi.org.uk* Ⓜ *Waterloo.*

### PERFORMING ARTS CENTERS

FAMILY **Southbank Centre.** The Royal Festival Hall is one of London's best spaces for large-scale choral and orchestral works and is home to the Philharmonia and London Philharmonic orchestras. The Queen Elizabeth Hall is a popular venue for top-tier soloists, and the Purcell Room is known for chamber music recitals—although both are closed for refurbishment until fall 2017 (with chamber concerts taking place at St. John's Smith Square during this period). Free family and adult events take place in foyer spaces around the complex. Southbank hosts everything from the London International Mime festival to large-scale dance performances, plus highly regarded pop, rock and jazz acts. Also part of the complex (but also closed for refurbishment) is the **Hayward Gallery,** a landmark 1960s building and one of London's best contemporary art venues. ⊠ *Belvedere Rd., South Bank* ☎ *020/7960–4200,* ⊕ *www.southbankcentre.co.uk* Ⓜ *Waterloo, Embankment.*

London's Royal Opera House is also home to the Royal Ballet and an in-house orchestra.

### THEATER

Fodor's Choice ★ **BAC.** Battersea Arts Centre has a reputation for producing innovative new work, as well as hosting top alternative stand-up comics. Performances take place in quirky spaces all over this atmospheric former town hall. Check out Scratch events, low-tech theater where the audience provides feedback on works-in-progress. Entry for Scratch events is pay-what-you-can (minimum £1). There's also a fun bar that serves good food. ⊠ *176 Lavender Hill, Battersea* ☎ *020/7223–2223* ⊕ *www. bac.org.uk* Ⓜ *National Rail: Clapham Junction.*

FAMILY
Fodor's Choice ★ **National Theatre.** When this theater designed by Sir Denys Lasdun opened in 1976, Londoners weren't all so keen on the low-slung Brutalist block. Prince Charles described it as "a clever way of building a nuclear power station in the middle of London without anyone objecting." But whatever its merits or demerits, the National Theatre's interior spaces are worth a visit. Interspersed with the three theaters—the 1,150-seat Olivier, the 890-seat Lyttelton, and the 450-seat Dorfman—is a multilayered foyer with exhibitions, bars, restaurants, and free entertainment. Musicals, classics, and plays are performed by top-flight professionals. Backstage tours lasting 75 minutes are available (call to check times). The Clore Learning Centre offers courses and events on all aspects of theater making, and you can watch staff at work in the backstage workshops from the Sherling High-Level Walkway. The Temporary Theatre, a 225-seat space made of eye-catching red wood that occupies the terrace in front of the NT, will be hosting emerging companies and more avant-garde work until it's dismantled in spring 2017. ⊠ *Belvedere Rd., South Bank* ☎ *020/7452–3000*

## CLASSICAL MUSIC: LONDON TODAY

Whether it's a concert by pianist Lang Lang or a Mozart requiem by candlelight, it's possible to hear first-rate musicians in world-class venues almost every day of the year. The London Symphony Orchestra is in residence at the Barbican Centre, although other top orchestras—including the Philharmonia and the Royal Philharmonic—also perform here. The Barbican also hosts chamber-music concerts, with celebrated orchestras such as the City of London Sinfonia. Kings Place has a varied calendar of musical events. The Southbank Centre also has a varied and impressive international music season. Full houses are rare, so even at the biggest concert halls you should be able to get a ticket for £12. If you can't book in advance, arrive at the hall an hour before the performance for a chance at returns.

■TIP➔ Lunchtime concerts take place all over the city in smaller concert halls, arts-center foyers, and churches; they usually cost less than £5 or are free. St. John's Smith Square and St. Martin-in-the-Fields are popular locations. Performances usually begin about 1 pm and last one hour.

Classical-music festivals include the stimulating avant-garde **Meltdown** (⊕ *meltdown.southbankcentre.co.uk*), curated each year by a prominent musician—David Byrne in 2015 and Guy Garvey in 2016—at the Southbank Centre in June; the **Spitalfields Festival** (⊕ *www.spitalfieldsfestival.org.uk*), a program of recitals held in beautiful, historic East End churches in June and December; and the **City of London Festival** (⊕ *www.colf.org*), held in the Square Mile for a month in summer. A great British tradition since 1895, the **Henry Wood Promenade Concerts** (⊕ *www.bbc.co.uk/proms*), better known as the "Proms," run eight weeks, July–September, at the Royal Albert Hall and Cadogan Hall. Despite its numerous high-quality concerts, it's renowned for its (atypical) last night: a very patriotic display of singing "Land of Hope and Glory," Union Jack–waving, and general madness. For regular Proms, tickets run £5–£95, with hundreds of standing tickets for £5 available at the hall on the night of the concert.

■TIP➔ The last night is broadcast in Hyde Park on a jumbo screen, but even here a seat on the grass requires a paid ticket that costs around £40.

⊕ *www.nationaltheatre.org.uk* ▨ Tour £9 ⊘ Lobby Mon.–Sat. 9:30 am–11 pm, selected Sun. noon–6 Ⓜ Waterloo.

**The Old Vic.** In 2015 Matthew Warchus, the director behind *Matilda the Musical*, took over as artistic director at this grand old theater, the former haunting grounds of such stage legends as John Gielgud, Vivien Leigh, Peter O'Toole, Richard Burton, and Judi Dench. The venue had suffered decades of financial duress before being brought under the ownership of a dedicated trust headed by its previous artistic director, actor Kevin Spacey. It's now in great shape, secure for the future and producing some of the best theater in London. ⊠ *The Cut, Southwark* ☏ *0844/871–7628* ⊕ *www.oldvictheatre.com* Ⓜ Waterloo, Southwark.

**Shakespeare's Globe Theatre.** *See full listing in Chapter 8: South of the Thames.*

**Southwark Playhouse.** This impressive little theater, in what was once a car showroom, produces award-winning new musicals and gritty drama for a fraction of the cost of the West End. The bar-café is good too, which is fortunate—the surrounding area is something of a culinary no-man's-land. ✉ *77–85 Newington Causeway, Borough* ☏ *020/7407–0234* ⊕ *www.southwarkplayhouse.co.uk* Ⓜ *Borough, Elephant & Castle.*

FAMILY
Fodor's Choice
★
**Unicorn Theatre.** Dedicated to innovative work for young audiences, this modern theater hosts plays, musicals, and interactive theater for everyone from toddlers on up. Inclusivity is a major focus, with performances for those with visual and hearing and other impairments taking place regularly. ✉ *147 Tooley St., Borough* ☏ *020/7645–0560* ⊕ *www. unicorntheatre.com* Ⓜ *London Bridge.*

Fodor's Choice
★
**Young Vic.** In its home near Waterloo, big names perform alongside young talent, often in daring, innovative productions of classic plays that appeal to a more diverse audience than is traditionally found in London theaters. Good food is served all day at the bustling bar. ✉ *66 The Cut, Waterloo, South Bank* ☏ *020/7922–2922* ⊕ *www.youngvic. org* Ⓜ *Southwark, Waterloo.*

# KENSINGTON AND CHELSEA

17

These refined neighborhoods just west of central London have a wide variety of galleries and performance spaces, with several located within the area's large public green spaces.

## KENSINGTON

### CLASSICAL MUSIC

**Cadogan Hall.** Once a church, this spacious venue is home to the Royal Philharmonic Orchestra, and the English Chamber Orchestra performs here regularly. The hall also hosts a wide range of choral and chamber concerts, plus the occasional folk, rock, and world-music gig. ✉ *5 Sloane Terr., Kensington* ☏ *020/7730–4500* ⊕ *www.cadoganhall.com* Ⓜ *Sloane Sq.*

Fodor's Choice
★
**Royal Albert Hall.** Opened in 1871, this splendid iron-and-glass-domed auditorium hosts everything from pop and classical headliners to Cirque du Soleil, awards ceremonies, and sumo wrestling championships, but is best known for the annual July–September BBC Promenade Concerts. Bargain-price standing-room (or promenading or sitting-on-the-floor) tickets for "the Proms" are sold on the night of the concert. The circular 5,272-seat auditorium has a terra-cotta exterior surmounted by a mosaic frieze depicting figures engaged in cultural pursuits. The hall is open most days for daytime guided tours (£12.25) and Tuesday–Sunday for afternoon tea (£23.46–£33.66). ✉ *Kensington Gore, Kensington* ☏ *0845/401–5034* ⊕ *www.royalalberthall.com* Ⓜ *South Kensington.*

## OPERA: LONDON TODAY

The two key players in London's opera scene are the internationally renowned Royal Opera House and the more innovative English National Opera (ENO), which presents English-language productions at the London Coliseum. Only the Theatre Royal, Drury Lane, has a longer theatrical history than the Royal Opera House—the third theater to be built on the site since 1732.

Despite occasional performances by the likes of Ben Folds, the Royal Opera House struggles to shrug off its reputation for stuffiness. Ticket prices can rise to £250, though some are less than £10.

In summer, the increasingly adventurous Opera Holland Park presents the usual warhorses alongside some obscure works under a canopy in leafy Holland Park. Tête à Tête, an irreverent festival of new work, takes place in venues across King's Cross in summer, too.

International touring companies often perform at Sadler's Wells, the Barbican, the Southbank Centre, and Wigmore Hall, so check the weekly listings for details.

### CHELSEA
#### THEATER
**Royal Court Theatre.** Britain's undisputed epicenter of new theatrical works, the Court continues to produce gritty British and international drama. Don't miss the best deal in town: four 10p standing tickets go on sale one hour before each performance, and £10 tickets are available on Monday. ⊠ *Sloane Sq., Chelsea* ☎ *020/7565–5000* ⊕ *www.royalcourttheatre.com* Ⓜ *Sloane Sq.*

## NOTTING HILL

This cosmopolitan West London neighborhood, shown to advantage in the 1999 film of the same name, is best known for the Notting Hill Carnival, a lively music-focused street festival that takes over the wider area on the final weekend of August each year. There's a year-round culture scene, too, catering mainly to the neighborhood's trendy young professionals.

#### FILM
FAMILY **The Electric Cinema.** This refurbished Portobello Road art house screens mainstream and international movies. The emphasis is on comfort, with leather sofas for two, armchairs, coffee tables for your wine and appetizers, and even double beds in the front row. The Electric also has another movie theater in east London on Redchurch Street, with sofas and wine coolers. ⊠ *191 Portobello Rd., Notting Hill* ☎ *020/7908–9696* ⊕ *www.electriccinema.co.uk* ▣ *£15.50–£22.50* Ⓜ *Ladbroke Grove, Notting Hill Gate.*

#### OPERA
FAMILY **Opera Holland Park.** In summer, well-loved operas and imaginative productions of lesser-known works are presented under a spectacular canopy against the remains of Holland House, one of the first great houses

built in Kensington. The company has successfully branched out into opera for families in recent years, too. Ticket prices run £17–£70, with 1,000 tickets offered free to young people ages 7–18 every season. Tickets go on general sale in April (earlier for members). ✉ *Holland Park, Kensington High St., Kensington* ☎ *0300/999–1000 for box office (opens Apr.), 020/7361–3570 for inquiries* ⊕ *www.operahollandpark. com* Ⓜ *High Street Kensington, Holland Park.*

## REGENT'S PARK AND HAMPSTEAD

Leafy north London has long been a stomping ground for the capital's cultural elite—stroll through Primrose Hill and you're practically guaranteed to spot a film star or musician—but there's diversity here, too. Camden Town is justifiably famous for its indie music scene, while respected fringe theaters in Swiss Cottage and Kilburn don't shy away from major topics.

### REGENT'S PARK

#### THEATER

FAMILY

Fodor's Choice

★

**Open Air Theatre.** On a warm summer evening, open-air theater in the pastoral Regent's Park is hard to beat. Enjoy a supper before the performance, a bite during the intermission on the lawn, or drinks in the bar. The only downside is that warm summer nights in London are not always reliable—a raincoat is advisable. ✉ *Inner Circle, Regent's Park* ☎ *0844/826–4242* ⊕ *www.openairtheatre.com* Ⓜ *Baker St., Regent's Park.*

### HAMPSTEAD

#### FILM

FAMILY

**Everyman Cinema.** Kick off your shoes, curl up on the large comfy sofas, and have tapas and champagne brought to you in front of classic, foreign, cutting-edge, and Hollywood titles. This venue also screens the Metropolitan Opera live from New York, and is a popular place for Hampstead denizens to bring their kids. Other branches around London also tend to offer a movie experience a cut above average. ✉ *5 Holly Bush Vale, Hampstead* ☎ *0871/906–9060* ⊕ *www.everymancinema. com* Ⓜ *Hampstead.*

#### THEATER

FAMILY

**Tricycle Theatre.** Committed to representing the cultural diversity of its community, the Tricycle shows the best in black, Irish, Jewish, Asian, and South African drama, and also promotes new work. There is a movie theater, too: expect top-quality new European and international cinema, including films from the United States, occasionally screened at film festivals the theater organizes. Discounted movie tickets are available on Monday. ✉ *269 Kilburn High Rd., Kilburn* ☎ *020/7328–1000 for box office* ⊕ *www.tricycle.co.uk* Ⓜ *Kilburn.*

17

# SHOPPING

Updated by
Ellin Stein

The keyword of London shopping has always been "individuality," whether expressed in the superb custom tailoring of Savile Row, the nonconformist punk roots of quintessential British designer Vivienne Westwood, or the unique small stores that purvey their ownerss private passions, be they paper theaters, toy soldiers, or buttons. This tradition is under threat from the influx of chains—global luxury, domestic mid-market, and international youth—but the distinctively British mix of quality and originality, tradition, and character remains.

You can try on underwear fit for a queen at Her Majesty's lingerie supplier, track down a leather-bound Brontë classic at an antiquarian bookseller, or find a bargain antique on Portobello Road. Whether you're just browsing—there's nothing like the size, variety, and sheer theater of London's street markets to stimulate the acquisitive instinct—or on a fashion-seeking mission, London shopping offers something for all tastes and budgets.

Although it's impossible to pin down one particular look that defines the city, London style tends to fall into two camps: one is the quirky, individualistic, somewhat romantic look exemplified by homegrown designers like Matthew Williamson, Vivienne Westwood, and Lulu Guinness; the other reflects Britain's celebrated tradition of classic knitwear and suiting, with labels like Jaeger, Pringle, and Brora, while Oswald Boateng, Paul Smith, and Richard James take tradition and give it a very modern twist. Traditional bespoke men's tailoring can be found in the upscale gentlemen's shops of Jermyn Street and Savile Row—there's no better place in the city to buy custom-made shirts and suits—while the handbags at Mulberry, Asprey, and Anya Hindmarch are pure classic quality. If your budget can't stretch that far, no problem; the city's chain stores like Topshop, Zara, and H&M, aimed at the younger end of the market, are excellent places to pick up designs copied straight from the catwalk at a fraction of the price, while mid-market chains like Reiss, Jigsaw, and L.K. Bennett offer smart design and better quality for the more sophisticated shopper.

If there's anything that unites London's designers, it's a commitment to creativity and originality, underpinned by a strong sense of heritage. This combination of posh and rock 'n' roll sensibilities turns up in everyone from Terence Conran, who revolutionized product and houseware design in the '60s (and is still going strong), to Alexander McQueen, who combined the Punk aesthetic with the rigor of couture. You'll see it in fanciful millinery creations by Philip Treacy and Stephen Jones, and in the work of imaginative shoemakers Nicholas Kirkwood, United Nude, and Terry de Havilland—and it keeps going, right through to current hot designers Erdem, Christopher Kane, and Christopher Bailey, the latter responsible for making traditional label Burberry relevant again.

One reason for London's design supremacy is the strength of local fashion college Central St. Martin's, whose graduates include Conran, Kane, McQueen, his successor at his eponymous label—and designer of the Duchess of Cambridge's wedding dress—Sarah Burton, and Stella McCartney's equally acclaimed successor at Céline, Phoebe Philo.

To find the McQueens, McCartneys, and Baileys of tomorrow, head for the independent boutiques of the East End and Bermondsey. If anything, London is even better known for its vibrant street fashion than for its high-end designers. Stock up from the stalls at Portobello, Camden, and Spitalfields markets.

Aside from bankrupting yourself, the only problem you may encounter is exhaustion. London's shopping districts are spread out over the city, so do as savvy locals do: plan your excursion with military precision, taking in only one or two areas in a day, and stopping for lunch with a glass of wine or for a pint at a pub.

**18**

# PLANNING

### OPENING HOURS
Most shops are open from about 9:30 or 10 am to 6 or 6:30 pm. Larger department stores generally stay open until 7 or even as late as 9. Because shop hours, particularly for the smaller shops, vary, it's a good idea to phone or check websites ahead. Stores that have late shopping—and not all do—are usually open until 7 or 8 pm on Thursday only. On Sunday, many shops open between 11 am and noon and close at 5 or 6 pm. Most stores are open on Sunday in December for the Christmas season.

### WATCH YOUR LANGUAGE
Locals like to say that Brits and Americans are separated by a common language. Here are a few confusing terms to watch for when out and about in the shops:

**Pants** means underwear. Every other type of long-legged bottoms (except jeans) are called **trousers**. Also in the underwear category is the **vest**

**REGENT'S PARK**

**BLOOMSBURY**
antiquarian books and Lamb's Conduit Street

**EAST LONDON**
edgy young designers

**MARYLEBONE**
small shops in village-like setting

**NOTTING HILL**
antiques, vintage clothing, and smart boutiques

**OXFORD CIRCUS**
global flagships, department stores, and funky shops off Carnaby

**SOHO**
vinyl abounds on Berwick Street

BAYSWATER

**COVENT GARDEN**
shoes galore around Seven Dials

**MAYFAIR**
catwalk names on Bond St., trad tailors on Savile Row

HYDE PARK

**ST JAMES'S**
traditional specialists, from hatters to shirtmakers

**KNIGHTSBRIDGE**
luxe labels and, of course, Harrods

BELGRAVIA

WESTMINSTER

LAMBETH

**CHELSEA**
the Kings Rd. spans fashion to furniture

VICTORIA

1/2 mile
1/2 km

(undershirt in the United States); if you are looking for a vest, ask for a **waistcoat**.

**Knickers** are ladies' underwear. If you want pantyhose, ask for **tights**.

**Jumper** means sweater—unless it's a cardigan, in which case it may be shortened to **cardie**. If you ask for a **sweater**, you may be offered a sweatshirt.

Men use **braces** to hold up their trousers; in England **suspenders** is another word for garters.

If you want some Adidas- or Nike-type athletic shoes, ask for **trainers**, not sneakers.

Don't ask for a **pocketbook** or a **purse** if you mean a handbag—the former will be incomprehensible, and the latter will produce a coin purse. Ask for a **fanny pack** and it will produce a laugh—"fanny" means something altogether different in the United Kingdom, so ask for a "bum-bag."

Nightgowns are usually abbreviated to **nighties** and bathrobes may be **dressing gowns**.

### A WORD ABOUT SERVICE

American standards of customer service are rare in London—you may find attentive customer service at old-school, traditional names and some independent stores, but salespeople elsewhere can seem abrupt or indifferent.

# SHOPPING REVIEWS

## ST. JAMES'S

18

### ACCESSORIES

**Fodor's** Choice ★ **Lock & Co. Hatters.** Need a silk top hat, a flat-weave Panama, or a traditional tweed flat cap? Or, for ladies, an occasion hat? James Lock of St. James's has been providing hats from this wood-paneled shop since 1676 for customers ranging from Admiral Lord Nelson, Oscar Wilde, and Frank Sinatra to, more recently, Robert Downey Jr., Guy Ritchie, and Kate Middleton, as well as trendsetting musicians and models. ⊠ 6 *St. James's St., St. James's* ☎ *020/7930–8874* ⊕ *www.lockhatters.co.uk* ☾ *Closed Sun.* Ⓜ *Green Park.*

**Fodor's** Choice ★ **Swaine Adeney Brigg.** Providing practical supplies for country pursuits since 1750, Swaine Adeney Brigg carries beautifully crafted umbrellas, walking sticks, and hip flasks, or ingenious combinations, such as the umbrella with a slim tipple-holding flask secreted inside the stem. The same level of quality and craftsmanship applies to the store's leather goods, which include attaché cases (you can buy the "Q Branch" model that James Bond carried in *From Russia with Love*) and wallets. You'll find scarves, caps, and the Herbert Johnson "Poet Hat," the iconic headgear (stocked since 1890) worn by Harrison Ford in every Indiana Jones film. ⊠ *7 Piccadilly Arcade, St. James's* ☎ *020/7409–7277* ⊕ *www.swaineadeney.co.uk* ☾ *Closed Sun., except by appointment* Ⓜ *Green Park.*

## Know Your Shopping Personality

"Where is the best place to shop in London?" There are thousands of shops in the city, and dozens of neighborhoods worth shopping in. Start by identifying your shopping personality to narrow your choices for a successful outing.

**Easygoing.** If you want to pop in and out of a variety of shops, as well as avoid the crowds around Oxford Street, head to King's Road in Chelsea. You'll find department store Peter Jones, plus Marks & Spencer and plenty of chains and trendy boutiques. Another safe bet is High Street Kensington for the usual big chains, in addition to some smaller ones less oriented toward disposable fashion, such as Cos, Karen Millen, and Oliver Bonas.

**Eclectic.** If you are looking for well-crafted, original items, start at Liberty on Regent Street, then head to Marylebone to the north, or the warren of cobblestone streets lined with independent shops off Carnaby Street, immediately to the south.

**Fashionista.** When only the top designers will do, start at the designer boutiques along Sloane Street in Knightsbridge before hopping on Bus 19 to Green Park. From there you can cover Bond Street (both Old and New) finishing at Fenwick, or veer off onto Conduit Street, designer-heavy Bruton Street, or, at the northwest end of Berkeley Square, ultrachic Mount Street. If you still have time and energy, check out South Molton Street opposite Bond Street Tube or St. Christopher's Place across Oxford Street.

**Funky and Avant-Garde.** For cutting-edge fashion and housewares, head to the East End neighborhoods. Start at Columbia Road in Hoxton, with its charming specialty shops (and the Sunday flower market), then wander through Shoreditch, Spitalfields, and Bethnal Green, where you'll find stores filled with one-of-a-kind designs. There's also lots here to appeal to vintage hunters.

**Whirlwind.** If you're after a one-stop-shopping experience, head to one of the big department stores. Selfridges and Fenwick are near the Bond Street Tube station, Liberty is near Oxford Circus Tube station, while Harvey Nichols and Harrods share the Knightsbridge Tube station.

### ANTIQUES AND COLLECTIBLES

**The Armoury of St. James's.** The fine toy soldiers representing all eras and military models in stock here are collectors' items. Painted and mounted knights only 6 inches high can cost up to £1,200 (although figures start at a mere £7.50 for a toy soldier). Besides lead and tin soldiers, the shop has regimental brooches, historic orders and medals, and military antiques. ⊠ *17 Piccadilly Arcade, St. James's* ☎ *020/7493–5082* ⊕ *www.armoury.co.uk* ☉ *Closed Sun.* Ⓜ *Piccadilly Circus.*

### BEAUTY

**Floris.** What did Queen Victoria, Mary Shelley, and Marilyn Monroe have in common? They all used products from Floris, one of the most beautiful shops in London, with gleaming glass-and-Spanish-mahogany showcases salvaged from the Great Exhibition of 1851. In addition to scents for both men and women, Floris has been making its own shaving products (plus combs, brushes, and fragrances) since 1739, reflecting its origins as a barbershop. Other gift possibilities include goose-down powder puffs, a famous rose-scented mouthwash, and beautifully packaged soaps and bath essences. There's another branch in Belgravia. ⊠ *89 Jermyn St., St. James's* ☎ *0845/702–3239* ⊕ *www.florislondon. com* Ⓜ *Piccadilly Circus, Green Park.*

## BOOKS

**Fodor's Choice** ★

**Hatchards.** This is the United Kingdom's oldest bookshop, open since 1797 and beloved by writers themselves—customers have included Oscar Wilde, Rudyard Kipling, and Lord Byron. Despite its wood-paneled, "gentleman's library" atmosphere, and eclectic selection of books, Hatchards is owned by the large Waterstone's chain. Nevertheless, the shop still retains its period charm, aided by the staff's old-fashioned helpfulness and expertise. Look for the substantial number of books signed by notable contemporary authors on the well-stocked shelves. There's another branch in the St. Pancras International train station. ⊠ *187 Piccadilly, St. James's* ☎ *020/7439–9921* ⊕ *www.hatchards. co.uk* Ⓜ *Piccadilly Circus.*

## FOOD

**Fodor's Choice** ★

**Berry Bros. & Rudd.** Nothing matches Berry Bros. & Rudd for rare offerings and a unique shopping experience. A family-run wine business since 1698 (Lord Byron was a customer), BBR stores more than 4,000 vintage bottles and casks in vaulted cellars that are more than 300 years old. The in-house wine school offers educational tasting sessions, while the dedicated whiskey room also has an excellent selection. The shop has a quirky charm and the staff are extremely knowledgeable—and not snooty if you're on a budget. ⊠ *3 St. James's St., St. James's* ☎ *800/280–2440* ⊕ *www.bbr.com* ☉ *Closed Sun.* Ⓜ *Green Park.*

**18**

**Fodor's Choice** ★

**Fortnum & Mason.** Although F&M is jokingly known as "the Queen's grocer" and the impeccably mannered staff still wear traditional tailcoats, its celebrated food hall stocks gifts for all budgets, including irresistibly packaged luxury foods stamped with the gold "By Appointment" crest for under £5. Try the teas, preserves (including the unusual rose-petal jelly), condiments, or Gentleman's Relish (anchovy paste). The store's famous hampers are always a welcome gift. The gleaming food hall spans two floors and incorporates a sleek wine bar, with the rest of the store devoted to upscale housewares, men's and women's accessories and toiletries, a dedicated candle room, a jewelry department featuring exclusive designs by breakthrough talent, and clothing and toys for children. If you start to flag, take a break in the tea salon, the cafe offering tastes of the Food Hall, the new contemporary 45 Jermyn St. restaurant where you can find decadent treats like a float with sarsaparilla syrup and rum over gingerbread cream, an equally indulgent ice-cream parlour—or a treatment in the Bamford spa. There's another branch at St. Pancras International train station. ⊠ *181 Piccadilly, St. James's* ☎ *020/7734–8040* ⊕ *www.fortnumandmason.com* Ⓜ *Green Park, Piccadilly Circus.*

## LONDON SHOPPING STEALS AND DEALS

Even at the best of times, London has never been known as a budget shopping destination, and when the pound is strong prices can seem stratospheric. However, whatever the exchange rate, there are still bargains to be had as long as you know where, and when, to look. To get the maximum mileage out of your cash, visit during the widespread biannual sales, which kick off in late June and just after Christmas, and last about a month.

Fashion insiders attend the many sales held throughout the year, from big warehouse clearances, such as the London Designer (⊕ www.thelondondesignersale. co.uk) and Designer Sales UK (⊕ www.designersales.co.uk), to individual designers' sample sales—check out *Time Out* (⊕ www. timeout.com) for information and to register for updates. London outlets, such as Browns Labels for Less, Paul Smith Sale Shop, and the Joseph Sale Shop on King's Road offer year-round designer bargains. If time permits, travel outside London to Bicester Village (pronounced "Bister") (⊕ www. bicestervillage.com), a luxury outlet mall in Oxfordshire. It's completely worth the nearly one-hour train journey (direct service from London Marylebone station, from £12 one-way), if only for the opportunity to score an item from such highly coveted British brands as Alexander McQueen, Temperley, Mulberry, Burberry, and Aquascutum, as well as other top labels.

If you're not fussy about labels, there are even more choices, including Primark.

### MEN'S CLOTHING

**Turnbull & Asser.** The Jermyn Street store sells luxurious jackets, cashmere sweaters, suits, ties, pajamas, ready-to-wear shirts, and accessories perfect for the billionaire who has everything. The brand is best known for its superb custom-made shirts—worn by Prince Charles, Woody Allen, and every filmic James Bond, to name a few. These can be ordered at the nearby Bury Street branch. At least 15 separate measurements are taken, and the cloth, woven to the company's specifications, comes in 1,000 different patterns—the cottons feel as good as silk. The first order must be for a minimum of six shirts, which start at £195 each. There's another branch in The City. ⊠ *71–72 Jermyn St., St. James's* ☎ *020/7808–3000* ⊕ *www.turnbullandasser.com* ⊘ *Closed Sun.* Ⓜ *Green Park.*

### SHOES

**Loake Shoemakers.** Long established in England's Midlands and a provider of boots to the British armed forces in both world wars, this family-run firm specializes in classic handcrafted men's shoes. Whether you're after brogues, loafers, or deck shoes, the staff will take the time to ensure you have the right fit. In terms of quality and service, Loakes represents real value for money, though they definitely aren't inexpensive. There's another branch on Bow Street in The City. ⊠ *8–10 Princes Arcade, off Jermyn St., St. James's* ☎ *020/7734–8643* ⊕ *www.loake. co.uk* ⊘ *Closed Sun.* Ⓜ *Piccadilly.*

**SPECIALTY STORES**

**Geo F. Trumper.** If you don't have the time for an old-fashioned hot-towel shave at this "traditional gentlemen's barbers" established in 1875, pick up a razor, a shaving brush, or other mens' grooming accessory to take home for yourself or as a gift. The Extract of Limes is a popular, zingy aftershave, and the Coconut Oil Hard Shaving Soap, which comes in a hand-turned wooden bowl, is a classic. There is also a store at 9 Curzon Street in Mayfair. ✉ *1 Duke of York St., St. James's* ☎ *020/7734–6553* ⊕ *www.trumpers.com* ⊗ *Closed Sun.* Ⓜ *Piccadilly Circus.*

# MAYFAIR AND MARYLEBONE

## MAYFAIR
### ACCESSORIES

**Lulu Guinness.** Famous for her amusing, imaginatively themed bags (think the satin "bucket" topped with roses or the elaborately beaded red "lips" clutch), Guinness also showcases vintage-inspired luggage and beauty accessories in this frilly little shop, which is just as whimsical as her designs. There are other branches in Covent Garden and The City. ✉ *42 Burlington Arcade, Belgravia* ☎ *020/7491–9252* ⊕ *www.luluguinness.com* Ⓜ *Piccadilly Circus.*

**Mulberry.** Staying true to its rural Somerset roots, this luxury goods company epitomizes *le style anglais,* a sophisticated take on the earth tones and practicality of English country style. Best known for highly desirable luxury handbags—such as the Alexa, the Cara Delevingne, and Bayswater models—the company also produces gorgeous leather accessories, from wallets to luggage, as well as shoes and clothing for men and women. Aside from the New Bond Street flagship, there are branches in Knightsbridge, Covent Garden, and the Westfield Centres, along with Mulberry concessions in most of the major department stores. The small store on St. Christopher's Place in Marylebone stocks accessories only. ✉ *50 New Bond St., Mayfair* ☎ *020/7491–3900* ⊕ *www.mulberry.com* Ⓜ *Bond St.*

**William & Son.** William Asprey, scion of a jewelry dynasty, sells his carefully chosen, British-made luxury goods using a friendlier and less formal approach. You'll find all sorts of items here that you didn't know you needed, like silver-tipped retractable pencils, lizard-skin passport holders, crocodile backgammon sets, or a silver piggy bank. The jewelry is tasteful and subtle rather than knock-your-eyes-out, and the store will also do custom work. ✉ *34–36 Bruton St., Mayfair* ☎ *020/7493–8385* ⊕ *www.williamandson.com* ⊗ *Closed Sun.* Ⓜ *Bond St.*

### ANTIQUES

**Grays Antique Market.** There are approximately 200 dealers here, specializing in everything from Bakelite items to Mughal art. The majority focus on jewelry, ranging from contemporary to antique. Bargains are not out of the question, and proper pedigrees are guaranteed. Go on a weekday for the most choice; not all stalls are open on Saturday. Also try Grays in Davies Mews around the corner: stalls there sell less expensive merchandise, including antique dolls at Glenda's and excellent vintage

18

Those who want the best and have the budget to afford it head to Mayfair and St. James's.

clothing at Vintage Modes. ✉ *58 Davies St., Mayfair* ☎ *020/7629–7034* ⊕ *www.graysantiques.com* 🕐 *Closed Sun.* Ⓜ *Bond St.*

## BOOKS AND STATIONERY

**Heywood Hill.** Open since 1936, Heywood Hill is considered by some to be the best small bookstore in the English-speaking world—John Le Carré, who set a scene in *Tinker Tailor Soldier Spy* here, is a long-standing customer. Here's where you can pick up a leather-bound volume on architecture, gardening, natural history, and topography—just some of the topics in which the antiquarian collection specializes. The contemporary selection emphasizes literature, history, biography, travel, architecture, and children's books, and the knowledgeable staff are happy to provide advice. During World War I, author Nancy Mitford helped keep the bookstore going. Today, the 12th Duke of Devonshire, a descendant of her brother-in-law, the 11th Duke, is the owner. ✉ *10 Curzon St., Mayfair* ☎ *020/7629–0647* ⊕ *www.heywoodhill.com* 🕐 *Closed Sun.* Ⓜ *Green Park.*

**Maggs Bros. Ltd.** How could any book lover resist a shop with such a Dickensian name? Maggs has been selling rare books and manuscripts since 1853 and is one of the world's oldest and largest such dealers (they also deal in autographs). The staff are expert enough to advise important collectors, but friendly and helpful to all interested visitors. Far from being fussy, the store includes a "counterculture" section with works on subversion, extremism, punk, the occult, and more. Moved out of its longtime location on Berkeley Square, the shop is now temporarily relocated on Curzon Street until its new, larger premises nearby are ready, expected to be toward the end of 2016. ✉ *46 Curzon St., Mayfair* ☎ *020/7493–7160* ⊕ *www.maggs.com* ⊘ *Closed Sun.* Ⓜ *Green Park.*

**Smythson of Bond Street.** No hostess of any standing would consider having a leather-bound guest book made by anyone besides this elegant stationer, and the shop's social stationery and distinctive diaries with their pale-blue pages are the epitome of British good taste. These, along with other made-in-Britain leather goods including a small line of handbags, backpacks, purses, can be personalized. You'll find branches in Chelsea, Notting Hill, and The City, plus concessions in leading department stores. ✉ *40 New Bond St., Mayfair* ☎ *020/7629–8558* ⊕ *www. smythson.com* Ⓜ *Bond St., Oxford Circus.*

**Waterstone's.** At this megabookshop (Europe's largest, with over eight miles of bookshelves) in a former art deco department store near Piccadilly Circus, browse through your latest purchase or admire the view with a glass of wine or a snack at the 5th View Bar and Food (open until 9). Waterstone's is the country's leading book chain, and they've pulled out all the stops to make their flagship as comfortable and welcoming as a bookstore can be. There are several smaller branches throughout the city. ✉ *203–206 Piccadilly, Mayfair* ☎ *0207/851–2400* ⊕ *www. waterstones.com* Ⓜ *Piccadilly Circus.*

### CLOTHING

**Alexander McQueen.** Since McQueen's untimely death in 2010, his right-hand woman Sarah Burton has been at the helm, receiving raves for continuing his tradition of theatrical, darkly romantic, and beautifully cut clothes incorporating corsetry, lace, embroidery, and hourglass silhouettes, all of which were exemplified in Burton's celebrated wedding dress for Kate Middleton. Can't afford a gala gown? Go home with a skull-print scarf. ✉ *4–5 Old Bond St., Mayfair* ☎ *020/7355–0088* ⊕ *www.alexandermcqueen.com* Ⓜ *Bond St.*

**Belstaff.** For years the purveyors of Britain's coolest motorcycle leathers, Belstaff has expanded into dresses, skirts, and handbags, as well as knitwear, boots, tops, and trousers for both men and women. All the items reflect the brand's functional but unconventional heritage (previous customers include Lawrence of Arabia, Amelia Earhart, and Che Guevara) but now, under new Italian ownership, with added fashion flair. Outerwear in general and leather jackets in particular remain a strength. There's another branch in Spitalfields. ✉ *135–137 New Bond St., Mayfair* ☎ *020/7495–5897* ⊕ *www.belstaff.co.uk* Ⓜ *Bond St.*

**Browns.** This shop—actually a collection of small shops—was a pioneer designer boutique in the 1970s and continues to talent-spot the newest and best around. You may find the windows showcasing the work of top graduates from this year's student shows or displaying well-established international luxury designers such as Givenchy, Valentino, or St. Laurent. The men's store at No. 23 has a similar designer selection, while Browns Focus at No. 24 showcases emerging and edgier designers like Hussain Chalayan, J.W. Andersen, and Christopher Kane, as well as denim lines. There is a smaller boutique on Sloane Street, too. If you're about to go down the aisle, check out the two bridal boutiques, one at 12 Hinde Street, which stocks various designers, and another at 59

**18**

Brook Street, devoted to Vera Wang gowns exclusive to Browns in the United Kingdom. ⊠ *24–27 S. Molton St., Mayfair* ☎ *020/7514–0016* ⊕ *www.brownsfashion.com* ⊙ *Closed Sun.* Ⓜ *Bond St.*

**Burberry.** Known for its trademark tartan, this company has cultivated an edgy, high-fashion image in recent years, with designs like fetish-y boots and sexy leather jackets perfect for any catwalk. The raincoats are still a classic buy, along with plaid scarves in every color imaginable and handbags. If you're up for a trek, there's a huge factory outlet in Hackney on Chatham Place that has clothes and accessories for men, women, and children at half price or less. There are also branches in Mayfair, Knightsbridge, and Covent Garden, in addition to this spectacular flagship store. ⊠ *121 Regent St., Mayfair* ☎ *020/7806–8904* ⊕ *uk.burberry.com* Ⓜ *Piccadilly Circus.*

Fodor's Choice
★
**Fenwick.** A manageably sized department store, Fenwick is a welcome haven of affordability in a shopping area where stratospheric prices are the norm. The store is particularly strong on accessories (notably lingerie, wraps, and hats), cosmetics, perfumes, and chic, wearable fashion by both big names and more niche designers such as Issa, Goat, and Theory. There are also three small spas (Chantecaille, Clarins, and Pure Massage), various beauty services (including a Blinc brow bar), and two restaurants, plus a men's department in the basement. ⊠ *163 New Bond St., Mayfair* ☎ *020/7629–9161* ⊕ *www.fenwick.co.uk* Ⓜ *Bond St.*

**Isabel Marant London.** The first London store from Marant, a favorite of French fashion editors, this airy skylit space is full of her signature skinny jeans, slouchy knits, wedge sneakers, and rock-chick miniskirts, all exuding Left Bank boho cool. ⊠ *29 Bruton St., Mayfair* ☎ *020/7499–7887* ⊕ *www.isabelmarant.com* ⊙ *Closed Sun.* Ⓜ *Bond St.*

**Stella McCartney.** It's not easy emerging from the shadow of a Beatle father, but Stella McCartney has become a major force in fashion in her own right. Her signature jumpsuits and tuxedo pantsuits embody her design philosophy, combining minimalist tailoring with femininity, and sophistication with ease of wear. Her love of functionality and clean lines has led to her branching off into lingerie, accessories, and sportswear, designing a line for Adidas and dressing Team GB for the London Olympics. A vegetarian like her parents, she refuses to use fur or leather, making her a favorite with similarly minded fashionistas. There's another boutique in South Kensington. ⊠ *30 Bruton St., Mayfair* ☎ *020/7518–3100* ⊕ *www.stellamccartney.com* ⊙ *Closed Sun.* Ⓜ *Bond St.*

**Vivienne Westwood.** From beginnings as the most shocking and outré designer around, Westwood (now Dame Vivienne) has become a standard-bearer for high-style British couture. At the Chelsea boutique where she first sold the lavish corseted ball gowns, dandyfied nipped-waist jackets, and tartan-meets-punk daywear that formed the core of her signature look, you can still buy ready-to-wear—mainly items from the more casual Anglomania diffusion line and the exclusive Worlds End label, which draws from her archives. The small Davies Street boutique sells only the more expensive Gold Label and Couture collections (plus bridal), while the flagship Conduit Street store carries all of the above. ✉ *44 Conduit St., Mayfair* ☎ *020/7439–1109* ⊕ *www. viviennewestwood.co.uk* Ⓜ *Oxford Circus.*

## DEPARTMENT STORES

**Thomas Goode.** This spacious luxury housewares shop has been at the same smart Mayfair address since 1845. The china, silver, crystal, and linen, whether from the store's own line or from luxury brands like Christofle and Puiforcat, are simply the best that money can buy, a legacy of its original customer base of international royals and heads of state. The store still holds two royal warrants, but anyone who can afford it can commission their own bespoke set of china. If such luxury is beyond you, visit anyway for the shop's small museum of plates, either antique or designed for royalty, including some created for Princess Diana's wedding. ✉ *19 South Audley St., Mayfair* ☎ *020/7499– 2823* ⊕ *www.thomasgoode.co.uk* ⊗ *Closed Sun.* Ⓜ *Green Park.*

## FOOD

**Charbonnel et Walker.** Established in 1875, this master chocolatier's Mayfair shop specializes in traditional handmade chocolates (rose-petal creams and champagne truffles, for example) and has been creating these beautifully packaged, high-quality candies from long before most of today's fashionable brands appeared. Their drinking chocolate—coarsely grated fine chocolate in a tin—is worth carrying home in a suitcase. ✉ *One The Royal Arcade, 28 Old Bond St., Mayfair* ☎ *020/7491–0939* ⊕ *www.charbonnel.co.uk* Ⓜ *Green Park.*

## JEWELRY

**Asprey.** Refurbished a decade ago by architect Norman Foster and interior designer David Mlinaric (some 155 years after Asprey first moved in), this "global flagship" store displays exquisite jewelry—as well as silver and leather goods, watches, china, and crystal—in a discreet, very British setting that oozes quality, expensive good taste, and hushed comfort. If you're in the market for an immaculate 1930s cigarette case, a silver cocktail shaker, a pair of pavé diamond and sapphire earrings, or a ladylike handbag, you won't be disappointed. And, for the really well-heeled, there's a custom jewelry service available as well. ✉ *167 New Bond St., Mayfair* ☎ *020/7493–6767* ⊕ *www.asprey.com* ⊗ *Closed Sun.* Ⓜ *Green Park.*

**Garrard.** The oldest jewelry house in the world, Garrard has been in business since 1735. Between 1843 and 2007, the company was responsible for the upkeep of the Crown Jewels in the Tower of London and for creating several royal crowns (you can see some on display in the Tower). Today the focus is on precious gems in simple, classic settings, along with silver accessories. Although some collections are definitely contemporary (with items like minimalist hoop earrings or two-finger rings), many of the designs are traditional and impressive—which will be handy should you be in the market for an old-school diamond tiara. There's another branch in South Kensington. ✉ *24 Albemarle St., Mayfair* ☎ *207/518–1070* ⊕ *www.garrard.com* ⊗ *Closed Sun.* Ⓜ *Green Park.*

18

## MEN'S CLOTHING

**Alfred Dunhill.** For more than 100 years, Dunhill has been synonymous with the most luxurious and sophisticated men's goods, including accessories, briefcases, and superbly tailored clothes. This Georgian mansion, their flagship, also features a barbershop, men's spa, humidor, cellar bar, courtyard restaurant, and bespoke services, where you can order custom-fitted menswear or unique versions of the brand's celebrated leather goods. The smaller, original St. James's shop has been on Jermyn Street since 1906. ⊠ *2 Davies St., Mayfair* ☏ *020/7853–4440* ⊕ *www. dunhill.com* ⊘ *Closed Sun.* Ⓜ *Bond St.*

**Gieves and Hawkes.** One of the grand men's tailoring houses of Savile Row, this company made its name outfitting British royals who served as officers in the armed forces. The company still supplies custom-made military uniforms, as well as beautifully tailored civilian wear. Prices for a bespoke suit start around £3,800, but you can find ready-made designs from around £600, while a new line of casualwear has several items under £200. There's also a branch in The City. ⊠ *1 Savile Row, Mayfair* ☏ *020/7432–6403* ⊕ *www.gievesandhawkes.com* Ⓜ *Piccadilly Circus.*

**Ozwald Boateng.** The dapper menswear by Ozwald Boateng (pronounced "Bwa-teng") combines contemporary funky style with traditional Savile Row quality. His made-to-measure suits have been worn by the likes of Jamie Foxx, Mick Jagger, and Laurence Fishburne, who appreciate the sharp cuts, luxurious fabrics, and occasionally vibrant colors (even the more conservative choices have jacket linings in bright silk). ⊠ *30 Savile Row, Mayfair* ☏ *020/7437–2030* ⊕ *www.ozwaldboateng.co.uk* ⊘ *Closed Sun.* Ⓜ *Piccadilly Circus.*

## SHOES

**Nicholas Kirkwood.** Kirkwood is one of Britain's most fashionable shoe designers, and this is his first retail boutique. You won't be able to hike in his imaginative, elegant, sky-high stilettos (be warned: prices are similarly high), but you will be able to make quite an entrance. There are also more wearable styles that are equally flattering and gorgeous. Be sure to check out Kirkwood's attractive collaborations with designers like Peter Pilotto and Erdem. ⊠ *5 Mount St., Mayfair* ☏ *020/7499–5781* ⊕ *www.nicholaskirkwood.com* ⊘ *Closed Sun.* Ⓜ *Green Park.*

**Rupert Sanderson.** Designed in London and made in Italy, Sanderson's elegant shoes have been a huge hit in fashion circles. Red-carpet-ready high heels as worn by celebs including Claire Danes, Nicole Kidman, and Sandra Bullock, bright colors, tough motorcycle boots, and a penchant for peep toes are signature elements. The high prices reflect the impeccable craftsmanship. ⊠ *19 Bruton Pl., Mayfair* ☏ *0207/491–2260* ⊕ *www.rupertsanderson.com* ⊘ *Closed Sun.* Ⓜ *Bond St., Green Park.*

## MARYLEBONE
## ANTIQUES

**Alfie's Antique Market.** This four-story, bohemian-chic labyrinth is London's largest indoor antiques market, housing more than 75 dealers specializing in art, lighting, glassware, textiles, jewelry, furniture, and collectibles, with a particular strength in vintage clothing and

20th-century design. Come here to pick up vintage (1900–70) clothing, accessories, and luggage from Tin Tin Collectables, antique and vintage glassware and vases at Robinson Antiques, or a spectacular mid-20th-century Italian lighting fixture at Vincenzo Caffarrella. The atmosphere may be funky but the prices are not. There's also a rooftop café with free Wi-Fi if you need a coffee break. In addition to the market, this end of Church Street is lined with excellent antiques shops. ⊠ *13–25 Church St., Marylebone* ☎ *020/7723–6066* ⊕ *www.alfiesantiques.com* ⊗ *Closed Sun. and Mon.* Ⓜ *Marylebone.*

### BOOKS

**Daunt Books.** An independent bookstore chain (there are additional branches in Belsize Park, Chelsea, Hampstead, Holland Park, and Cheapside), Daunt favors a thoughtful selection of contemporary and classic fiction and nonfiction. The striking Marylebone branch is an original Edwardian bookstore, where a dramatic room with a long oak-paneled gallery under lofty skylights houses the noted travel section, which includes not only guidebooks but also related literature and poetry. The Hampstead branch is strong on children's books. ⊠ *83 Marylebone High St., Marylebone* ☎ *020/7224–2295* ⊕ *www. dauntbooks.co.uk* Ⓜ *Baker St.*

### CLOTHING

**Matches Fashion.** The rising British designers featured in this carefully curated boutique include Christopher Kane, Erdem, and J.W. Anderson, as well as more-established figures like McCartney and McQueen and international labels such as Isabel Marant, Balenciaga, Balmain, Valentino, Saint Laurent, Marni, and Chloe. There's also an equally stylish menswear department, plus jewelry, lingerie, and accessories. Other branches can be found in Notting Hill and southwest London. ⊠ *87 Marylebone High St., Marylebone* ☎ *020/7487–5400* ⊕ *www. matchesfashion.com* Ⓜ *Regent's Park, Baker St.*

**Reiss.** With an in-house design team whose experience includes stints at Gucci and Calvin Klein and customers like Beyoncé and the Duchess of Cambridge, who wore a Reiss dress for her official engagement picture, this reliable chain brings luxury standards of tailoring and details to mass-market women's and menswear. The sleek and contemporary style doesn't come cheap, but does offer value for money. There are branches in Knightsbridge, The City, Covent Garden, Chelsea, Hampstead, Islington, Soho, Kensington, and basically all over London. ⊠ *10 Barrett St., Marylebone* ☎ *020/7486–6557* ⊕ *www.reiss. com* Ⓜ *Oxford St.*

**Fodor's Choice**
★ **So Tiny London.** This small store has loads of imaginative gifts for babies and young children, such as distinctive onesies and T-shirts emblazoned with Union Jacks, "Darth Vader Is My Father," logos of rock bands like Pink Floyd, Motörhead, the Rolling Stones, and even "Baby Gaga." You'll also find pretty dresses with an English Rose print, dinosaur costumes for dress-up, Jellycat plush toys (favorites of royal babies William and Charlotte), and child-friendly joke items like rubber chickens. ⊠ *64 Great Titchfield St., Marylebone* ☎ *020/7636–2501* ⊕ *www. sotinylondon.com* Ⓜ *Oxford Circus.*

18

### DEPARTMENT STORES

**Marks & Spencer.** You'd be hard-pressed to find a Brit who doesn't have something in the closet from Marks & Spencer (or M&S, as it's popularly known). This major chain is famed for its classic, dependable clothing for men, women, and children—affordable cashmere and lambswool sweaters are particularly good buys—and occasionally scores a fashion hit. The food department at M&S is consistently good, especially for frozen food, and a great place to pick up a sandwich or premade salad on the go (look for M&S Simply Food stores all over town). The flagship branch at Marble Arch and the Pantheon location at 173 Oxford Street have extensive fashion departments. ⊠ *458 Oxford St., Marylebone* ☎ *020/7935–7954* ⊕ *www.marksandspencer. com* Ⓜ *Marble Arch.*

Fodor'sChoice   **Selfridges.** This giant, bustling store (the second largest in the United
★   Kingdom after Harrods) gives Harvey Nichols a run for its money as London's most fashionable department store. Packed to the rafters with clothes ranging from midprice lines to the latest catwalk names, the store continues to break ground with its innovative retail schemes, especially the ground-floor Wonder Room (for extravagant jewelry and luxury gifts), the self-contained Louis Vuitton "townhouse," a dedicated Denim Studio, an array of pop-up shops, and the Concept Store, used for a rotating series of themed displays There are so many zones that merge into one another—from youth-oriented Miss Selfridge to audio equipment to the large, comprehensive cosmetics department—that you practically need a map. Don't miss the Shoe Galleries, the world's largest shoe department, which is filled with more than 5,000 pairs from 120 brands, displayed like works of art under spotlights. Take a break with a glass of wine at the rooftop restaurant or pick up some tea in the Food Hall as a gift. At the Everyman movie theater in the basement, you can watch first-run art-house movies. ⊠ *400 Oxford St., Marylebone* ☎ *0800/123400* ⊕ *www.selfridges.com* Ⓜ *Bond St.*

### JEWELRY

**Kabiri.** A carefully curated array of exciting contemporary jewelry by emerging and established designers from around the world is packed into this small shop. There is something to suit most budgets and tastes, from flamboyant statement pieces to subtle, minimalist adornment. Look out for British talent Bam B, among many others. ⊠ *37 Marylebone High St., Marylebone* ☎ *020/7317–2150* ⊕ *www.kabiri. co.uk* Ⓜ *Baker St.*

### SPECIALTY STORES

Fodor'sChoice   **The Button Queen.** Extremely specialized shops like this one once helped
★   make London so distinctive, but now they are in danger of disappearing. The Button Queen began life as a market stall in the 1950s, and now it has amassed a vast selection of buttons, from antique to modern, encompassing an array of styles and prices. You can also have a set made using fabric you supply. ⊠ *76 Marylebone La., Marylebone* ☎ *020/7935–1505* ⊕ *www.thebuttonqueen.co.uk* ✆ *Closed Sun.* Ⓜ *Oxford Circus.*

# SOHO AND COVENT GARDEN

## SOHO

### ACCESSORIES

Fodor's Choice ★ **Peckham Rye.** On the small cobblestone streets leading off Carnaby Street you'll find little specialty shops like the family-run Peckham Rye, which sells heritage-style men's accessories: handmade silk and twill ties, bow ties, and scarves, all using traditional patterns drawn from the archives going back to 1799. More Ralph Lauren than Ralph Lauren, the socks, striped shirts, and handkerchiefs attract modern-day dandies like Mark Ronson and David Beckham. Bespoke tailoring for men is also offered. ✉ *11 Newburgh St., Soho* ☎ *0207/734–5181* ⊕ *www.peckhamrye.com* Ⓜ *Oxford St.*

### BOOKS

Fodor's Choice ★ **Foyles.** Founded in 1903 by the Foyle brothers after they failed the Civil Service exam, this family-owned bookstore is in a 1930s art deco building, once the home of the renowned art college Central Saint Martins. Foyles carries more than 200,000 titles on its 4 miles of bookshelves. One of London's best sources for textbooks and the United Kingdom's largest retailer of foreign language titles, Foyles also stocks everything from popular fiction to military history, sheet music, medical tomes, graphic novels, and handsome illustrated fine arts books. It also offers the store-within-a-store Ray's Jazz (one of London's better outlets for music) and a cool café. Foyles has branches in the Southbank Centre, Waterloo station, and the Westfield shopping center in Stratford. ✉ *107 Charing Cross Rd., Soho* ☎ *020/7437–5660* ⊕ *www.foyles.co.uk* Ⓜ *Tottenham Court Rd.*

### CLOTHING

**Other.** Aimed at men and women in search of stylish cool, this independent boutique stocks its own brand of entirely made-in-England clothing, as well as accessories, housewares, books, and clothing from other carefully selected, high-end cult brands such as Boboutic, Christopher Lemaire, and Peter Jensen. The look is understated, slightly geeky, and totally contemporary. ✉ *21 Kingly St., Soho* ☎ *020/7734–6846* ⊕ *www.other-shop.com* Ⓜ *Oxford Circus.*

**Primark.** Primark's huge, two-story flagship is fantastic for low-cost, trendy clothing (there are other branches in Hammersmith and Kilburn). But keep in mind, you get what you pay for: some of the fabrics and finishes reflect the store's budget prices, and its labor practices have drawn criticism. This is the home of fast, youthful, disposable fashion, so don't expect attentive service or classic styling and you won't be disappointed. ✉ *499–517 Oxford St., Soho* ☎ *020/7495–0420* ⊕ *www.primark.co.uk* Ⓜ *Marble Arch.*

**Wolsey.** Specializing in men's knitwear since 1755, Wolsey now sells rugged but stylish outerwear, sweaters, shirts, hats, scarves, socks, T-shirts, sweatshirts, and underwear (the undies of choice for polar explorers Roald Amundsen, Captain Robert Scott, and Ernest Shackleton). The company also supplied woollen garments to British troops in 1914. It's not all heritage, though; they also make hoodies, while the premium 1775 collection has slimmer, more directional styles. The

18

interior reflects this blend of the traditional and the contemporary, with exposed brick walls, brushed steel beams, and photographs of expeditions the brand has outfitted. There's another branch in Covent Garden. ⊠ *83A Brewer St., Soho* ☎ *020/7434–4257* ⊕ *www.wolsey. com* Ⓜ *Piccadilly Circus.*

## DEPARTMENT STORES

**Fodor's**Choice
★ **Liberty.** The wonderful black-and-white mock-Tudor facade, created from the timbers of two Royal Navy ships, reflects this store's origins in the late-19th-century Arts and Crafts movement. Leading designers were recruited to create the classic art nouveau Liberty prints that are still a centerpiece of the brand, gracing everything from cushions and silk kimonos to embossed leather bags and photo albums. Inside, Liberty is a labyrinth of nooks and crannies stuffed with thoughtfully chosen merchandise, including niche beauty, perfume, footwear, and housewares lines. Clothes for both men and women focus on high quality and high fashion, with labels like Alexander Wang and Roland Mouret. The store regularly commissions new prints from contemporary designers, and sells both these and its classic patterns by the yard. If you're not so handy with a needle, an interior design service will create soft furnishings for you. There's also a florist, a hair salon, a traditional men's barber, beauty treatment rooms, and a foot spa, ⊠ *Regent St., Soho* ☎ *020/7734–1234* ⊕ *www.liberty.co.uk* Ⓜ *Oxford Circus.*

## FOOD

**Fodor's**Choice
★ **The Vintage House.** If whiskey is more to your taste than wine, visit the Vintage House, which has the country's largest selection of single malts (more than 1,300), including many rare bottles and some exclusive to the shop. You'll also find more than 100 tequilas as well as Cuban cigars. The shop is open until 11 pm (10 pm on Sunday). ⊠ *42 Old Compton St., Soho* ☎ *020/7437–2592* ⊕ *www.vintagehouse.london* Ⓜ *Leicester Sq.*

## SHOES

**Irregular Choice.** If you want to blend in with the crowd, these shoes are not for you. But if you like footwear that is fun and flattering (not to mention reasonably priced), head for Irregular Choice. Styles tend toward Louis XIV–like court shoes ornamented with ribbon ties or silk flowers; pumps in interesting patterns ranging from polka dots to houndstooth, as well as bejeweled flats, leopard-print boots, red patent leather stilettos, and even a Star Wars-inspired line. Best of all, many have round toes and supportive heels, proving that comfortable doesn't have to be dull. There's another branch near Camden Market. ⊠ *35 Carnaby St., Soho* ☎ *020/7494–4811* ⊕ *www.irregularchoice.com* Ⓜ *Oxford Circus.*

## TOYS

FAMILY **Hamleys.** When British children visit London, Hamleys is at the top of their agenda. This institution—the oldest toy store in the world—has six floors of the latest dolls, soft toys, video games, and technological devices, plus such old-fashioned pleasures as train sets, drum kits, and magic tricks. They stock every must-have on the preteen shopping list, although some parents may find the offerings to be overly commercialized (it's heavy on movie and TV tie-ins). Hamleys is a mad-house at Christmastime, but the Santa's grotto is one of the best in town. There's a smaller branch in St. Pancras International train station. ⊠ *188–196 Regent St., Soho* ☎ *0871/704–1977* ⊕ *www.hamleys.com* Ⓜ *Oxford Circus, Piccadilly Circus.*

## COVENT GARDEN
### BOOKS AND PRINTS
**Grosvenor Prints.** London's largest collection of 17th- to early-20th-century prints emphasizes views of the city and architecture as well as sporting and decorative motifs. The selection is eclectic, with prices ranging from £5 to the thousands. ⊠ *19 Shelton St., Covent Garden* ☎ *020/7836–1979* ⊕ *www.grosvenorprints.com* ☽ *Closed Sun.* Ⓜ *Covent Garden, Leicester Sq.*

**Fodor's Choice**
★ **Stanfords.** When it comes to encyclopedic coverage, there is simply no better travel shop on the planet. At this site for more than 100 years, Stanfords is packed with a comprehensive selection of travel books and travel accessories, including ordinance surveys, cycle route maps, travel adaptors, globes, replicas of antique maps, mosquito nets, and more. Even the floor is decorated with giant maps. Whether you're planning a day trip to Surrey or an adventure to the South Pole, this should be your first stop. ⊠ *12–14 Long Acre, Covent Garden* ☎ *020/7836–1321* ⊕ *www.stanfords.co.uk* Ⓜ *Covent Garden.*

### CLOTHING
**Paul Smith.** British classics with an irreverent twist define Paul Smith's collections for women, men, and children. Beautifully tailored suits for men and women take hallmarks of traditional British style and turn them on their heads with humor and color, combining exceptional fabrics with flamboyant linings or unusual detailing. Gift ideas abound—wallets, scarves, diaries, spectacles, even a soccer ball—all in Smith's signature rainbow stripes. There are several branches throughout London, in Notting Hill, Soho, Canary Wharf, and Borough Market, plus a Mayfair shop that includes vintage furniture and a shoes-and-accessories shop on Marylebone High Street. ⊠ *40–44 Floral St., Covent Garden* ☎ *020/7379–7133* ⊕ *www.paulsmith.co.uk* Ⓜ *Covent Garden.*

**Tabio.** For everything hosiery—knee socks, ankle socks, leggings, leg warmers, pantyhose, tights—this is the place. Patterns range from simple and elegant to lively and attention-getting and come in a wide assortment of weights, but all are functional without being boring. There's another branch on King's Road in Chelsea. ⊠ *66 Neal St., Covent Garden* ☎ *020/7836–3713* ⊕ *www.tabio.com* Ⓜ *Covent Garden.*

### HOUSEHOLD
**Cath Kidston.** If you love chintz and colorful patterns, you'll love Cath Kidston's bright feminine signature look. Textiles bearing ginghams, polka dots, and lots of big, blooming roses appear on everything in sight, from ceramics and bed linens to fine china, stationery, and doggie beds. There are clothing and nightwear lines for women and children, along with handbags, totes, and cosmetic bags. Branches can be found throughout the city, including in Marylebone, Chelsea, Notting Hill, St. Pancras International train station, and a flagship store

**18**

## BRING A BIT OF ENGLAND HOME

To avoid panic-buying a bulk pack of Cadbury chocolate at Heathrow, it's wise to plan your gift purchasing with care.

For a well-chosen, eclectic selection, unique department store Liberty is hard to beat. Here you'll find everything from exquisite Miller Harris fragrances by British perfumer Lyn Harris to small leather goods embossed with the famous Liberty prints.

Fortnum & Mason has equally carefully curated, though perhaps more sedate, offerings, such as leather-covered hip flasks and model boats with Union Jack sails.

The big attraction here is the world-famous food hall, which carries cookies, teas, and unusual condiments. A. Gold is another source of British-made treats.

Looking for a gift for the hard-to-shop-for man in your life? Consider some traditional shaving cream from Geo. F. Trumper.

The museum shops are also bursting with original gift ideas, from art books and posters at Tate Modern or the Fashion Museum to double-decker bus models and Tube-map mouse pads at the London Transport Museum, in Covent Garden.

on Piccadilly. ⊠ *28–32 Shelton St., Covent Garden* ☎ *020/7836–4803* ⊕ *www.cathkidston.co.uk* Ⓜ *Covent Garden.*

### MARKETS

**Covent Garden.** Covent Garden actually comprises three markets. Forty stalls selling handcrafted jewelry, clothes, ceramics, antiques, curios, and other unique items are in the covered area, which was originally designed by Inigo Jones and is known as the Apple Market. The Jubilee Market, in Jubilee Hall toward Southampton Street, tends toward the more pedestrian (kitschy T-shirts, unremarkable household goods, and the like) Tuesday–Friday, but has vintage collectibles on Monday and worthwhile handmade goods on weekends. A "Real Food" market on Thursday offers artisanal street food, while the East Colonnade market has stalls with specialty items that include handmade soaps and magic tricks, as well as housewares, jewelry, and accessories. Covent Garden is something of a tourist magnet, and the prices can be high, but don't miss the magicians, musicians, and escape artists who perform in the open-air piazza. Covent Garden has started aiming for a more sophisticated image with the opening of upscale restaurants and chains in the surrounding arcades (including the world's largest Apple Store) and boutiques for brands like Chanel beauty, agnès b, Dior beauty, Mulberry, Kate Spade, and Jo Malone. Even noted celebrity haunt The Ivy has a branch there now. ⊠ *The Piazza, off Wellington St., Covent Garden* ⊕ *www.coventgardenlondonuk.com* ☉ Ⓜ *Covent Garden.*

### SHOES

Fodor'sChoice ★ **United Nude.** Cocreated by famed architect Rem Koolhaas (who also designed this Covent Garden flagship store) and Galahad Clark (of the Clarks' shoes dynasty), this brand sells distinctive, futuristic designs that use up-to-the-minute techniques such as carbon-fiber heels and injection-molded soles. The shoes' edginess doesn't stop them from being flattering and surprisingly comfortable. ✉ *13 Floral St., Covent Garden* ☎ *0207/240–7106* ⊕ *www.unitednude.com* Ⓜ *Covent Garden.*

### TOYS

FAMILY

Fodor'sChoice

★

**Benjamin Pollock's Toyshop.** This landmark shop still carries on the tradition of its founder, who sold miniature theater stages made from richly detailed paper from the late 19th century until his death in 1937. Among his admirers was Robert Louis Stevenson, who wrote, "If you love art, folly, or the bright eyes of children, speed to Pollock's." Today the antique model theaters are expensive, but there are plenty of magical reproductions for less than £10. There's also an extensive selection of new but nostalgic puppets, marionettes, teddy bears, spinning tops, jack-in-the-boxes, and similar traditional children's toys from the days before batteries were required (or even possible). ✉ *44 The Market Bldg., Covent Garden* ☎ *020/7379–7866* ⊕ *www.pollocks-coventgarden.co.uk* Ⓜ *Covent Garden.*

## BLOOMSBURY, HOLBORN, ISLINGTON, AND FITZROVIA

### BLOOMSBURY

#### ACCESSORIES

Fodor'sChoice

★

**James Smith & Sons Ltd.** This has to be the world's ultimate umbrella shop, and a must for anyone interested in real Victorian London. The family-owned shop has been in this location on a corner of New Oxford Street since 1857 and sells every kind of umbrella, cane, and walking stick imaginable (including some containing a small flask or a corkscrew). The interior is unchanged since the 19th century; you will feel as if you have stepped back in time. Umbrellas range from about £60 for a folding umbrella to more than £250 for a classic man's umbrella with a carved animal-head handle. If the umbrella prices are too steep, James Smith also sells smaller accessories and handmade wooden bowls. ✉ *Hazelwood House, 53 New Oxford St., Bloomsbury* ☎ *020/7836–4731* ⊕ *www.james-smith.co.uk* ۞ *Closed Sun.* Ⓜ *Tottenham Court Rd., Holborn.*

#### BOOKS

**Gay's the Word.** Open since 1979, this is London's leading gay and lesbian bookshop. Thousands of titles, from literature and thoughtful nonfiction to erotica and prodiversity children's books, fill the shelves. The shop is a well-loved fixture on the scene (it features prominently in the 2014 movie *Pride*) and often hosts discussion groups, readings, and other events. ✉ *66 Marchmont St., Bloomsbury* ☎ *020/7278–7654* ⊕ *www.gaystheword.co.uk* Ⓜ *Russell Sq.*

Fodor'sChoice

★

**Persephone Books.** A must for all lovers of fiction and nonfiction by women, Persephone is a gem of a bookshop specializing in their own reprints of mostly neglected 20th-century works from predominately female writers. Exquisitely decorated endpapers make these books perfect gifts for your bibliophile friends. ✉ *59 Lamb's Conduit St., Bloomsbury* ☎ *020/7242–9292* ⊕ *www.persephonebooks.co.uk* ۞ *Closed Sun.* Ⓜ *Russell Sq., Holborn.*

**18**

### SPECIALTY STORES

**Blade Rubber.** This unique shop near the British Museum specializes in rubber stamps, with everything from businesslike "Paid" stamps to *Alice in Wonderland* characters, Egyptian gods, VW Beetles, flying saucers, and more. Get a custom-made personal stamp—a great gift for a young person—or bring back stamps of British icons like a double-decker bus, the Tower of London, or a bust of Shakespeare as souvenirs. It also carries scrapbooking materials and offers scrapbooking classes on Saturday. ⊠ *12 Bury Pl., Bloomsbury* ☎ *020/7831–4123* ⊕ *www.bladerubber.co.uk* Ⓜ *Holborn.*

## HOLBORN

### ANTIQUES

**London Silver Vaults.** Originally built in 1876 as basement strong rooms to securely store household valuables like jewelry, silver, and documents, this extraordinary space has been converted to house stalls for more than 30 silver dealers. Products range from 16th-century to contemporary pieces (with everything in between), and from the spectacularly over-the-top costing thousands to smaller items—like teaspoons, candlesticks, or a set of Victorian cake forks—at £25. Most of the silver merchants actually trade out of the room-size, underground vaults. ⊠ *53–64 Chancery La., Holborn* ☎ *020/7242–3844* ⊕ *www.silvervaultslondon.com* ⊗ *Closed Sun.* Ⓜ *Chancery La.*

## ISLINGTON

### HOUSEHOLD

Fodor'sChoice ★ **TwentyTwentyOne.** A must for lovers of modernist design. Among the huge selection of 20th-century classics here are a chaise lounge from Le Corbusier as well as pieces from Noguchi, Aalto, Prouvé, Saarinen, and the husband-and-wife team Robin and Lucienne Day, in the form of both originals and licensed reissues, along with contemporary pieces from modern masters like Tom Dixon, Thomas Heatherwick, and Marc Newson. The kids' line is particularly cool, with items like a classic elephant sculpture/toy from another married design team, Charles and Ray Eames. Small accessories like tote bags and cushions will easily fit into your luggage. There's another branch in Clerkenwell. ⊠ *274–275 Upper St., Islington* ☎ *020/7288–1996* ⊕ *www.twentytwentyone.com* Ⓜ *Highbury & Islington.*

## FITZROVIA

### CLOTHING

**Topshop.** A hot spot for straight-from-the-runway affordable fashion, Topshop is destination shopping for teenagers and fashion editors alike. Clothes and accessories are geared to the youthful end of the market, although women who are young at heart and girlish of figure can find plenty of wearable items here. However, you will need a high tolerance for loud music and busy dressing rooms. The store also features collections designed by a rotating roster of high-end designers, as well as offering its own premium designer line called Topshop Unique. The amount of stock at this flagship store is vast, but a clear layout helps make it navigable. Keep an eye out for pop-up extras like free minimakeovers, a blow-dry bar, or nail art from Wah Nails. Topman brings the same fast-fashion approach to clothing for men. If the crowds become too much, head to one of the smaller Topshops in Kensington High Street, Knightsbridge, Victoria, Marble Arch, The City, or Holborn. ✉ *36–38 Great Castle St., Fitzrovia* ☎ *0844/848–7487* ⊕ *www. topshop.com* Ⓜ *Oxford Circus.*

## CAMDEN
### MARKETS

**The Camden Markets.** Grouped around two locks on the Regent's Canal, Camden Lock Market proper began in the early 1970s, when weekend stalls sold the output of nearby craft workshops. It later expanded to four markets: Camden, Camden Lock, The Stables, and Camden Lock Village. For many years, the markets have hosted more than 1,000 stalls offering a spectacular array of merchandise: vintage and new clothes, antiques and junk, rare vinyl, ceramics, Indian bedspreads, fetishwear, obscure band memorabilia, and toys.

The outdoor Camden Market on Camden High Street mainly sells cheap jeans, secondhand clothes, and tacky pop-culture paraphernalia; it's best to head to Camden Lock Market for crafts and the Stables Market for furniture. The Stables Market has expanded into the so-called Catacombs, which are Victorian brick arches, and now has more than 700 shops and stalls. Camden Lock Village is currently closed, while being turned into a mixed-use retail and residential development. Though much of the merchandise is targeted at young, aging hippies, street-fashion aficionados, and anyone with a taste for alternative culture—Goths are particularly well catered to—will also find plenty that appeals. This shopping experience is best suited to those who don't mind large crowds and a boisterous atmosphere, especially on weekends. Camden Market, Camden Lock Market, and Stables Market are open daily (10–6). All four markets are earmarked for redevelopment, so their focus is likely to change—enjoy the scrappy, bohemian atmosphere while you can. ✉ *Camden High St. to Chalk Farm Rd., Camden Town* ⊕ *www.camdenlockmarket.com* Ⓜ *Camden Town, Chalk Farm.*

## EAST LONDON

### ACCESSORIES

**Fodor's Choice**
★
**Bernstock Speirs.** Here since 1982, Paul Bernstock and Thelma Speirs have put a quirky, fashionable spin on traditional hats for men and women, with street-smart trilbies, whimsical rabbit-ear baseball caps, and knitted beanies that feature unusual colors and detailing (like veils, for instance). ✉ *234 Brick La., Spitalfields* ☎ *020/7739–7385* ⊕ *www. bernstockspeirs.com* Ⓜ *Overground: Shoreditch High St.*

### CLOTHING

**Absolute Vintage.** This is a warehouse of all sorts of handpicked items from the 1930s through the 1980s, but the specialty here is shoes and bags. The shop has the largest collection of vintage shoes in the United Kingdom—more than 1,000 pairs—and, best of all, prices are reasonable. There's another branch on Commercial Street. ✉ *15 Hanbury St., Spitalfields* ☎ *020/7274–3883* ⊕ *www.absolutevintage.co.uk* Ⓜ *Overground: Shoreditch High St.*

18

**Beyond Retro.** The more than 10,000 vintage items for men and women here—from cowboy boots to bowling shirts to prom dresses—include the largest collection of American retro in the United Kingdom. There's another outpost in Dalston and one in Soho. ⊠ *110–112 Cheshire St., Spitalfields* ☏ *020/7297–9001* ⊕ *www.beyondretro.com* Ⓜ *Whitechapel. Overground: Shoreditch High St.*

Fodor's Choice **Hostem.** Drawing style-conscious customers from nearby tech start-ups,
★ Hostem is for the man who wants to be well dressed without looking like he's trying too hard, with a mixture of casual luxury, street wear, and fashion-forward edge. You'll find established names like Raf Simons, Dries van Noten, and Rick Owens as well as newcomers like Geoffrey B. Small. The womenswear area offers pieces by designers like Commes des Garçons and Yohji Yamamoto. There's also a bespoke service for clothing and men's shoes. It's achingly hip, so expect lots of black. ⊠ *41–43 Redchurch St., Shoreditch* ☏ *020/7739–9733* ⊕ *www. hostem.co.uk* Ⓜ *Overground: Shoreditch High St.*

**The Laden Showroom.** Sienna Miller and Victoria Beckham are among the celebs who regularly check out emerging talent at this East End showroom for new designers, a must for anyone looking for an alternative to mass-produced generic fashion. The store retails the work of more than 50 independent labels, some selling unique, one-off items—so you're likely to find a look that's both affordable and original. ⊠ *The Rib Man, 103 Brick La., Spitalfields* ☏ *020/7247–2431* ⊕ *www.laden. co.uk* Ⓜ *Overground: Shoreditch High St.*

**Rokit.** Here's where to find the perfect outfit for a Mad Men party. Magazine and music stylists love these two premises along Brick Lane that carry everything from handbags and ball gowns to jeans, military garb, and Western wear. The ever-changing stock spans the 1920s to the 1990s. There are also branches in Camden and Covent Garden. ⊠ *101 and 107 Brick La., Spitalfields* ☏ *020/7375–3864* ⊕ *www.rokit.co.uk* Ⓜ *Overground: Shoreditch High St.*

Fodor's Choice **Sunspel.** This British firm has been making fine men's underwear since
★ the mid-19th century and it's still their specialty, along with luxury basics. Prince Charles is a real-life customer and James Bond a cinematic one (he wore their shorts in *Thunderball* and polo shirt in *Quantum of Solace*). They also carry elegant, minimalist T-shirts, sweaters, and sweats for women. There are other branches in Marylebone, Notting Hill, St. James's, and Soho. ⊠ *7 Redchurch St., Shoreditch* ☏ *020/7739–9729* ⊕ *www.sunspel.com* Ⓜ *Overground: Shoreditch High St.*

## FOOD

Fodor's Choice **A. Gold.** All of the traditional or retro foodstuffs here—such as jars of
★ locally produced honey, relish, or even gin—are British-made and make excellent and portable presents. Also available in this re-creation of a village shop are stylish gift baskets and old-fashioned picnic hampers, as well as freshly made take-out sandwiches (like honey roast ham with cheddar and apple chutney), salads, homemade cakes, and hot daily specials. ⊠ *42 Brushfield St., Spitalfields* ☏ *020/7247–2487* ⊕ *www. agoldshop.com* Ⓜ *Overground: Shoreditch High St.*

### HOUSEHOLD GOODS

**Fodor's Choice** ★ **Labour & Wait.** Although mundane items like colanders and clothespins may not sound like ideal souvenirs, this shop (selling both new and vintage items) will make you reconsider. The owners are on a mission to revive retro, functional British household goods, such as enamel kitchenware, genuine feather dusters, bread bins, aluminum dustpans, and traditional Welsh blankets. ⊠ *85 Redchurch St., Shoreditch* ☎ *020/7729–6253* ⊕ *www.labourandwait.co.uk* Ⓜ *Overground: Shoreditch High St.*

### MARKETS

**Brick Lane.** The noisy center of the Bangladeshi community is a hubbub of buying and selling on Sunday. Stalls have food, hardware, household and electrical goods, books, bikes, shoes, clothes, spices, and traditional saris. At least some of the CDs and DVDs are pirated, and the bargain iron may not have a plug, so check carefully. Shoppers nevertheless flock to the market to enjoy the buzz, sample curries and Bangladeshi sweets, or indulge in salt beef on a bagel at Beigel Bake—London's 24-hour bagel bakery, a survivor of the neighborhood's Jewish past. Brick Lane's activity spills over into nearby Petticoat Lane Market, where there are similar goods but less atmosphere. ⊠ *Shoreditch* ⊕ *www.visitbricklane.org* ⊘ *Closed Mon.–Sat.* Ⓜ *Aldgate East. Overground: Shoreditch High St.*

**Fodor's Choice** ★ **Columbia Road Flower Market.** London's premier flower market is about as pretty and photogenic as they come, with more than 50 stalls selling flowers, shrubs, bulbs, and trees—everything from bedding plants to 10-foot banana trees—as well as garden tools, pots, and accessories at competitive prices. The stallholders' patter is part of the fun. It's on Sunday only, and it's all over by 2 pm. Columbia Road itself is lined with interesting independent shops purveying art, fashion, furnishings, and jewelry, and the local cafés are superb. ⊠ *Columbia Rd., Hoxton* ⊕ *www.columbiaroad.info* ⊘ *Closed Mon.–Sat.* Ⓜ *Old St. Overground: Hoxton.*

**Old Spitalfields Market.** Once the East End's wholesale fruit and vegetable market and now restored to its original splendor, this fine example of a Victorian market hall is at the center of the area's gentrified revival. The original building is largely occupied by shops (including trendy shoe retailers like Author, Camper, and Dr. Martens), with traders' stalls in the courtyard. A modern shopping precinct under a Norman Foster–designed glass canopy adjoins the old building and holds many more traders' stalls. You may have to wade through a certain number of stalls selling cheap imports to find the good stuff, which includes crafts, vintage and new clothing, handmade rugs, jewelry, hand-carved toy trains, unique baby clothes, rare vinyl, and cakes. Thursday is particularly good for antiques; Friday for fashion, art, and a biweekly record fair; and Saturday for produce and handmade crafts. The food outlets (mostly small, upscale chains but some indies as well) sell Spanish tapas, Thai satays, and many other dishes from all over. ⊠ *16 Horner Sq., Brushfield St., Spitalfields* ☎ *020/7375–2963* ⊕ *www.oldspitalfieldsmarket. com* Ⓜ *Liverpool St. Overground: Shoreditch High St.*

**18**

### MUSIC

**Rough Trade East.** Although many London record stores are struggling, this veteran indie-music specialist in the Old Truman Brewery seems to have gotten the formula right. The spacious surroundings are as much a hangout as a shop, complete with a stage for live gigs, a café, and Internet access. There's another branch on Portobello Road in Notting Hill. ✉ *Dray Walk, Old Truman Brewery, 91 Brick La., Spitalfields* ☎ *020/7392–7788* ⊕ *www.roughtrade.com* Ⓜ *Liverpool St. Overground: Shoreditch High St.*

## SOUTH OF THE THAMES

### ART

**Oxo Tower Wharf.** The artisans creating fashion, jewelry, home accessories, textiles, prints and photographs, furniture, and other design items have to pass rigorous selection procedures to set up in these prime riverside studios, where they make, display, and sell their work. The Oxo Tower Restaurant & Brasserie on the top floor is expensive, but with its fantastic view of London, it's worth popping up for a drink. There's also a public terrace where you can take in the view. ✉ *Oxo Tower Wharf, Bargehouse St., South Bank* ☎ *020/7021–1686 24-hr info* ⊕ *www.coinstreet.org* ☉ *Closed Mon.* Ⓜ *Waterloo.*

### MARKETS

Fodor's Choice  **Borough Market.** There's been a market in Borough since Roman times.
★  This latest incarnation, spread under the arches and railroad tracks leading to London Bridge station, is where some of the city's best food sellers set up stalls. Fresh coffees, gorgeous cheeses, olives, and baked goods complement the organically farmed meats, fresh fish, fruits, and vegetables.

Don't make any other lunch plans for the day; this is where celebrity chef Jamie Oliver's scallop man cooks them up fresh at Shell Seekers, and The Ginger Pig's rare-breed sausages sizzle on grills, while for the sweets lover there are chocolates, preserves, and Whirld's artisanal confectionery, as well as 18 restaurants and cafés, most above average. The Market Hall hosts workshops, tastings, and demonstrations, and also acts as a greenhouse (even hops are grown here).

Seven of the original Borough Market traders, including the celebrated Kappacasein Swiss raclette stand that serves heaping plates of melted Ogleshield cheese, have established a separate market on nearby Maltby Street. This opens on Saturday morning at 9 am. ✉ *8 Southwark St., Borough* ☎ *020/7402–1002* ⊕ *www.boroughmarket.org.uk* ☉ *Closed Sun.–Tues.* Ⓜ *London Bridge.*

## KENSINGTON, CHELSEA, KNIGHTSBRIDGE, AND BELGRAVIA

### KENSINGTON

#### CLOTHING

FAMILY  **Marie-Chantal.** If you love beautiful, tasteful, and somewhat formal clothing for babies and children, head to this boutique created by Princess Marie-Chantal of Greece. As you'd imagine, the look is elegant and the prices are high. Materials used include silk, linen, and Liberty prints. There's another branch in Notting Hill. ✉ *148 Walton St., South Kensington* ☎ *020/7838–1111* ⊕ *www.mariechantal.co.uk* ⊙ *Closed weekends* Ⓜ *South Kensington.*

**Orsini Vintage London.** High-end vintage fashion from the 1930s to 1980s is the trademark at this tiny but desirable boutique, which sells big designer names like Pucci, Hermès, Chanel, and Alaïa at bargain prices. There's also an in-house line of made-to-measure dresses based on Vogue patterns from the same period, as well as accessories, furs, and even bridalwear. ✉ *76 Earl's Court Rd., Kensington* ☎ *020/7937–2903* ⊕ *www.orsinivintage.co.uk* Ⓜ *Earl's Court, High St. Kensington.*

## HOUSEHOLD GOODS

**The Conran Shop.** This is the brainchild of Sir Terence Conran, who has been a major influence on British taste since he opened Habitat in the 1960s. Although he is no longer associated with Habitat, his Conran Shops remain bastions of similarly clean, unfussy modernist design. Housewares from furniture to lighting, stemware, and textiles—both handmade and mass-produced, by famous names and emerging designers—are housed in a building that is a modernist landmark in its own right. Both the flagship store and the branch on Marylebone High Street are bursting with great gift ideas. ✉ *Michelin House, 81 Fulham Rd., South Kensington* ☎ *020/7589–7401* ⊕ *www.conranshop.co.uk* Ⓜ *South Kensington.*

**Mint.** Owner Lina Kanafani has scoured the globe to curate an eclectic mix of conceptual statement furniture, art, ceramics, glassware, and home accessories. Mint also showcases avant-garde works by an international selection of up-and-coming designers and sells plenty of limited edition and one-off pieces. If you don't want to ship a couch home, consider a miniature flower vase or a handmade ceramic pitcher. ✉ *2 North Terr., at Alexander Sq., South Kensington* ☎ *020/7225–2228* ⊕ *www.mintshop.co.uk* ⊙ *Closed Sun.* Ⓜ *South Kensington.*

**Skandium.** Largely thanks to its thrillers and chefs, Scandinavia is having a moment in Britain. Skandium brings together many of the region's top designers of furniture, lighting, rugs, and housewares under one roof. Designers include giants of Scandinavian Modernism like Artek, Aalto, Saarinen, and Georg Jensen, as well as non-Scandinavian modernists, such as Ron Arad. Clean lines and stripped-down, unfussy elegance abound (although the Moomins make an appearance on ceramics). There's another branch in Marylebone. ✉ *245–249 Brompton Rd., South Kensington* ☎ *020/7584–2066* ⊕ *www.skandium.com* ⊙ *Closed Sun.* Ⓜ *South Kensington.*

## JEWELRY

**Butler & Wilson.** Specialists in bold costume jewelry and affordable glamor, Butler & Wilson have added semiprecious stones to their foundation diamanté, colored rhinestone, and crystal collections. Flamboyant skull brooches or dainty floral earrings make perfect gifts. There's another branch on South Moulton Street in Mayfair. ✉ *189 Fulham Rd., South Kensington* ☎ *020/7352–3045* ⊕ *www.butlerandwilson. co.uk* Ⓜ *South Kensington.*

18

## CHELSEA
### ACCESSORIES

**Anya Hindmarch.** Exquisite leather bags and personalized, printed canvas totes are what made Hindmarch famous. Here you'll find her complete collection of bags and shoes. You can also order a custom piece like the "Be A Bag," a tote bag imprinted with your chosen photo. There are also branches around the corner on Pont Street, in Mayfair, in Hackney, and in Notting Hill. ✉ *157–158 Sloane St., Chelsea* ☎ *020/7730–0961* ⊕ *www.anyahindmarch.com* Ⓜ *Sloane Sq., Knightsbridge.*

**The Shop at Bluebird.** The brainchild of the couple behind popular womenswear brand Jigsaw, this 10,000-square-foot space in the old Bluebird garage brings together men's and women's fashion from of-the-moment designers like J.W. Anderson, Alexander Wang, Isabel Marant, and Victoria Beckham as well as numerous hip denim lines from J Brand to Acne. There's also furniture, collectibles, designer tech accessories, and music—all chosen for style and originality. It's worth visiting for the displays alone, which change regularly, although the funky ceiling-light installation of more than 1,000 bulbs seems to be a constant feature. After browsing, unwind with a treatment at the on-site spa or join the ladies who lunch at the restaurant in the same complex. It's a good 20-minute walk from the nearest Tube station at Sloane Square, so catch Bus No. 11 or 22 along King's Road. ✉ *350 King's Rd., Chelsea* ☎ *020/7351–3873* ⊕ *www.theshopatbluebird.com* Ⓜ *Sloane Sq.*

### BOOKS

**John Sandoe (Books) Ltd.** This atmospheric warren that crams some 25,000 titles into an 18th-century building off King's Road is the antithesis of a soulless chain bookstore—no surprise it has attracted equally idiosyncratic customers like Tom Stoppard and Keith Richards. Staff members are wonderfully knowledgeable (don't try to figure out how the stock is organized without their help), and there are a lot of them per customer. If a book isn't in stock, they will try to find it for you, even if it is out of print. ✉ *10 Blacklands Terr., Chelsea* ☎ *020/7589–9473* ⊕ *www.johnsandoe.com* Ⓜ *Sloane Sq.*

### CLOTHING

**Brora.** The knitwear is cozy, but the style is cool in this contemporary Scottish cashmere emporium for men, women, and kids. There are dressed-up camisoles, sweaters and cardigans, and adorable baby ensembles, as well as noncashmere items such as picnic blankets and scarves. Other branches are in Notting Hill, Marylebone, Islington, Covent Garden, and Sloane Square. ✉ *344 King's Rd., Chelsea* ☎ *020/7352–3697* ⊕ *www.brora.co.uk* Ⓜ *Sloane Sq.*

**Hackett.** If J. Crew isn't preppy enough for you, try Hackett, with branches in Covent Garden, Spitalfields, St. James's, Soho, Mayfair, and The City. Originally a posh thrift shop recycling cricket flannels, hunting pinks, Oxford brogues, and other staples of a British gentleman's wardrobe, Hackett now creates its own line and has become a genuine—and very good—men's outfitter. The look is traditional and classic best buys include polo shirts, corduroys, and striped scarves. There's also a boys' line for the junior man-about-town. ⊠ *137–138 Sloane St., Chelsea* ☎ *020/7730–3331* ⊕ *www.hackett.com* Ⓜ *Sloane Sq.*

**Jigsaw.** Jigsaw specializes in clothes that are classic yet trendy, elegant without being dull. The style is epitomized by the Duchess of Cambridge, who, as Kate Middleton before her marriage, was a buyer for the company. The quality of fabrics and detailing belie the reasonable prices, and the cuts are kind to the womanly figure. Although there are numerous branches across London, no two stores are the same. Preteens have their own line, Jigsaw Junior. ⊠ *The Chapel, 6 Duke of York Sq., Chelsea* ☎ *020/730–4404* ⊕ *www.jigsaw-online.com* Ⓜ *Sloane Sq.*

### DEPARTMENT STORES

Fodor's Choice
★

**Peter Jones.** A beloved local institution since it opened in 1937—the poet John Betjeman remarked that come the end of the world he would like to be in the haberdashery department of Peter Jones, "because nothing bad could ever happen there"—this tasteful department store is the traditional default wedding-list option of Kensington & Chelsea brides. The selection of bed and bath linens (many provided by John Lewis, the store's parent company), flatware, ceramics, and glassware is outstanding, with offerings at all price points. There's also an extensive and eclectic beauty department, as well as kitchenware and appliances, tech stuff, a florist, clothing, shoes, and accessories for the whole family, and pretty much everything else you can think of, along with a restaurant and a Clarins spa. ⊠ *Sloane Sq., Chelsea* ☎ *020/7730–3434* ⊕ *www. johnlewis.com* Ⓜ *Sloane Sq.*

### FOOD

**L'Artisan du Chocolat.** Praised by top chefs Gordon Ramsay and Heston Blumenthal, L'Artisan raises chocolate to an art form. "Couture" chocolates are infused with fruits, nuts, and spices (including such exotic flavorings as Szechuan pepper and tobacco). This is one of the few chocolate shops in the world that makes liquid salted caramels. There are also branches in Notting Hill and Borough Market. ⊠ *89 Lower Sloane St., Chelsea* ☎ *0845/270–6996* ⊕ *www.artisanduchocolat.co.uk* Ⓜ *Sloane Sq.*

### SHOES

Fodor's Choice
★

**Manolo Blahnik.** Blink and you'll miss the discreet sign that marks fashionista footwear central. Blahnik, the man who single-handedly managed to revive the sexy stiletto, has been trading out of this small shop on a Chelsea side street since 1973. It's a must for shoe lovers with generous budgets. If you decide to wear your new Manolos, hop on Bus No. 11 or 22 or grab a cab—the nearest Tube station is about a 20-minute totter away. ⊠ *49–51 Old Church St., Chelsea* ☎ *020/7352–8622* ⊕ *www.manoloblahnik.com* ⊙ *Closed Sun.* Ⓜ *Sloane Sq., South Kensington.*

### SPECIALTY STORES

**Green & Stone Art Materials.** This fabulous cave of artists' materials, papers, art books, easels, and mannequins is one of the longest-established shops on King's Road. It began life in 1927 as part of the Chenil Gallery, run by a distinguished group that included the artist Augustus John and the playwright George Bernard Shaw. At the current location

**18**

since 1934, the shop also has a framing service, antique paint boxes, and craft supplies. Francis Bacon and David Hockney have been among their clients. ⊠ *259 King's Rd., Chelsea* ☎ *020/7352–0837* ⊕ *www. greenandstone.com* Ⓜ *Sloane Sq.*

## KNIGHTSBRIDGE

### CLOTHING

**Egg.** Tucked away in a residential mews, this spartan shop in a former Victorian dairy is the brainchild of Maureen Doherty, once Issey Miyake's assistant. More than half the minimalist, unstructured styles for men and women in natural fabrics such as silk, cashmere, and antique cotton are handmade. Garments may be casually hung on hooks or folded on wooden tables, but the price tags are anything but unassuming. The clientele includes the likes of Donna Karan and photographer Bruce Weber. Unusual ceramics and jewelry are also on display. ⊠ *36 Kinnerton St., Knightsbridge* ☎ *020/7235–9315* ⊕ *www. eggtrading.com* ☉ *Closed Sun.* Ⓜ *Knightsbridge.*

FAMILY **Rachel Riley.** Specializing in traditional English style for boys and girls, Riley's luxurious, vintage-inspired collection includes classics like duffel coats and hand-smocked floral dresses. Mothers who love the Riley look (including the Duchess of Cambridge, who has put Prince George in Riley clothes) can pick up coordinating outfits for themselves here or at the Marylebone High Street location. ⊠ *14 Pont St., Knightsbridge* ☎ *020/7259–5969* ⊕ *www.rachelriley.co.uk* ☉ *Closed Sun.* Ⓜ *Knightsbridge.*

**Rigby & Peller.** Lovers of luxury lingerie shop here for brands like Prima Donna and Aubade, as well as R&P's own line. If the right fit eludes you, the made-to-measure service starts at around £300. Many of London's most affluent women shop here, not only because this is the Queen's favored underwear supplier but also because the quality is excellent and the service impeccably knowledgeable while being much friendlier than you might expect. There are also branches in Mayfair, Chelsea, St. John's Wood, and The City. ⊠ *2 Hans Rd., Knightsbridge* ☎ *020/7225–4760* ⊕ *www.rigbyandpeller.com* Ⓜ *Knightsbridge.*

### DEPARTMENT STORES

**Harrods.** With an encyclopedic assortment of luxury brands, this Knightsbridge institution, now owned by the Qatar Investment Authority, has more than 300 departments and 30 eating and drinking options, all spread over 1 million square feet on a 4½-acre site. Now populated more by window-shopping tourists and superrich visitors from abroad than by the bling-averse natives, Harrods is best approached as the world's largest, most upscale and expensive mall. Focus on the spectacular food halls, the huge ground-floor perfumery and jewelry departments, the excellent Urban Retreat spa, and Shoe Heaven, Europe's biggest shoe department. The new Superbrands area houses haute couture from top international designers like Dior, Fendi, Prada, Valentino, Chanel, and more, while the children's department has a mini-me version for the toddler who wouldn't be seen in anything less than Burberry, Baby Dior, Chloé for Kids, Armani Junior, Moncler, and similar designer togs. Be prepared to brave the crowds, especially on weekends.

✉ *87–135 Brompton Rd., Knightsbridge* ☎ *020/7730–1234* ⊕ *www. harrods.com* Ⓜ *Knightsbridge.*

**Harvey Nichols.** While visiting tourists flock to Harrods, fashionistas shop at Harvey Nichols, aka "Harvey Nicks." The womenswear and accessories departments are outstanding, featuring top designers like Alexander McQueen, 3.1 Phillip Lim, Lanvin, Louboutin, and just about every fashionable name you can think of. The furniture and housewares are equally gorgeous (and pricey), although they become somewhat more affordable during the biannual sales in January and July. The Fifth Floor bar is the place to see and be seen, but if you're in search of food, the same floor also has a café, a tapas-style Japanese restaurant, a branch of Burger & Lobster, or sushi-to-go from Yo! Sushi. To keep you looking as box-fresh as your purchases, there's also a Beyond MediSpa, an Elemis spa, and a hair salon, plus nail and brow bars. ✉ *109–125 Knightsbridge, Knightsbridge* ☎ *020/7235–5000* ⊕ *www.harveynichols.com* Ⓜ *Knightsbridge.*

### BELGRAVIA

#### ACCESSORIES

**Fodor's** Choice
★

**Philip Treacy.** Magnificent hats by Treacy are annual showstoppers on Ladies Day at the Royal Ascot races and regularly grace the glossy magazines' society pages. Part Mad Hatter, part Cecil Beaton, Treacy's creations always guarantee a grand entrance and are favorites with both Hollywood and actual royalty. In addition to the extravagant, haute couture hats handmade in the atelier, ready-to-wear hats are also for sale, as are some bags. ✉ *69 Elizabeth St., Belgravia* ☎ *020/7730–3992* ⊕ *www.philiptreacy.co.uk* ⊗ *Closed Sun.* Ⓜ *Sloane Sq.*

#### SPECIALTY STORES

**Mungo & Maud.** If you don't want to leave London without buying something for your pet, pick up a well-designed coat, leash, blanket, bowl, toy, or comfortable bed that will make your dog the snazziest pooch in town (some collars are hand-stitched). Cats are also catered to with baskets, suede collars, and catnip toys. Even owners get a nod with luxurious merino throws (soon to be covered in pet hair) and a leather poop pouch. There's also a branch in Notting Hill. ✉ *79 Elizabeth St., Belgravia* ☎ *020/7022–1207* ⊕ *www.mungoandmaud.com* ⊗ *Closed Sun.* Ⓜ *Sloane Sq.*

## NOTTING HILL

#### BOOKS

**Fodor's** Choice
★

**Books for Cooks.** It may seem odd to describe a bookshop as delicious-smelling, but the aromas wafting out of the tiny test kitchen—which serves daily-changing lunch dishes drawn from recipes in the 8,000 cookbooks on the shelves, as well as cakes and culinary experiments—will whet your appetite even before you've opened one of the books. Just about every world cuisine is represented, along with a complete lineup of works by celebrity chefs. Before you come to London, visit the shop's website to sign up for a cooking class. ✉ *4 Blenheim Crescent, Notting Hill* ☎ *020/7221–1992* ⊕ *www.booksforcooks.com* ⊗ *Closed Sun. and Mon.* Ⓜ *Notting Hill Gate, Ladbroke Grove.*

**18**

## CLOTHING

**Aimé.** French-Cambodian sisters Val and Vanda Heng-Vong launched this shop to showcase the best of French clothing and designer house-wares. Expect to find cult French labels like Isabel Marant and A.P.C. as well as a couple of Italian brands like Forte Forte, along with house-wares and a well-chosen collection of ceramics. Petit Aimé, next door, sells children's clothing. There's also a Shoreditch branch. ⊠ *32 Ledbury Rd., Notting Hill* ☎ *020/7221–7070* ⊕ *www.aimelondon.com* ⊗ *Closed Sun.* Ⓜ *Notting Hill Gate.*

FAMILY **Caramel Baby & Child.** Here you'll find adorable yet unfussy clothes for children six months and up: handcrafted Peruvian alpaca cardigans in sherbet colors, floral cotton dresses for girls; check shirts and earth-tone tees for boys; comfortable pants in twill, corduroy, and cotton for both; and merino cashmere sweaters for extremely fashionable babies, plus shoes and accessories. Caramel also sells a small selec-tion of children's books and traditional toys, as well as decorative-functional items like mobiles and child-friendly chairs and stools. Prices are no bargain, but the quality is superb. On Monday, Tuesday, and Saturday the shop offers a hair salon for little customers. There are also branches in South Kensington and Soho. ⊠ *77 Ledbury Rd., Notting Hill* ☎ *020/7727–0906* ⊕ *www.caramel-shop.co.uk* Ⓜ *West-bourne Park, Notting Hill Gate.*

**The Cross.** One of the first "lifestyle boutiques" and still one of the best, this West London favorite carries fashion by in-the-know favorites like Vanessa Bruno, Velvet, Forte Forte, Dosa, and more, plus accessories, jewelry, housewares, and kids' clothes. The emphasis is on feminine and quirky boho chic. ⊠ *141 Portland Rd., Notting Hill* ☎ *020/7727–6760* ⊕ *www.thecrossshop.co.uk* ⊗ *Closed Sun.* Ⓜ *Holland Park.*

**Jack Wills.** Heritage and country sports-inspired styles have a fresh, sexy edge here. This means crowds of lithe young things who don't mind the pumping music while browsing for slim-line Fair Isle sweat-ers, fitted plaid shirts, little black dresses, and short floral sundresses for the girls, plus sweatshirts, blazers, skinny cords, and rugby shirts for the boys. The store also carries Union Jack carry-on bags, bobble hats galore, knitted jackets for hot-water bottles, and other traditional-with-irony items. Other branches are in Covent Garden, Soho, and Bat-tersea. ⊠ *184 Portobello Rd., Notting Hill* ☎ *020/7792–8690* ⊕ *www. jackwills.com* Ⓜ *Ladbroke Grove.*

**Rellik.** Now in the modernist landmark known as the Trellick Tower and favored by the likes of Kate Moss, Rellik began as a stall in the Portobello Market. Vintage hunters looking to splurge can find a selec-tion of YSL, Dior, Pierre Cardin, and Ossie Clark as well as items from lesser-known designers. ⊠ *Trellick Tower, 8 Golborne Rd., Notting Hill* ☎ *020/8962–0089* ⊕ *www.relliklondon.co.uk* ⊗ *Closed Sun. and Mon.* Ⓜ *Westbourne Park.*

## MARKETS

**Portobello Market.** Still considered the best all-round market in town by many fans, and certainly the most famous, Portobello Market stretches almost 2 miles, from fashionable Notting Hill to the lively cultural melting pot of North Kensington, changing character as it goes.

The southern end, starting at Chepstow Villas and going to Elgin Crescent, is lined with shops and stalls, and, on Saturday, arcades selling antiques, silver, and bric-a-brac. The middle, from Elgin Crescent to Talbot, is devoted to fruit and vegetables, interspersed with excellent hot food stalls. On Friday and Saturday, the area between Talbot Road and the elevated highway (called the Westway) becomes more of a flea market, specializing in new household and mass-produced goods sold at a discount. North of the Westway up to Goldborne Road are more stalls selling even cheaper secondhand household goods and bric-a-brac. Scattered throughout but mostly concentrated under the Westway are clothing stalls selling vintage pieces and items from emerging designers, custom T-shirts, and supercool baby clothes, plus jewelry. New and established designers are also found in the boutiques of the Portobello Green Arcade.

Some say Portobello Road has become a tourist trap, but if you acknowledge that it's a circus and get into the spirit, it's a lot of fun. Perhaps you won't find many bargains, but this is such a fascinating part of town that just hanging out is a good enough excuse to come. There are some food and flower stalls throughout the week (try the Hummingbird Bakery for delicious cupcakes), but Saturday is when the market in full swing. Serious shoppers avoid the crowds and go on Friday morning. Bring cash—several vendors don't take credit cards—but also be sure to keep an eye on it. ⊠ *Portobello Rd., Notting Hill* ⊕ *www. portobelloroad.co.uk* ⊙ *Closed Sun.* Ⓜ *Notting Hill Gate.*

## MUSIC

**Music & Video Exchange.** This store is a music collector's treasure trove, with a constantly changing stock refreshed by customers selling and exchanging as well as buying. The ground floor focuses on rock, pop, indie, and punk, both mainstream and obscure, in a variety of formats ranging from vinyl to CD, cassette, and even minidisk. Don't miss the classical music in the basement and the soul, jazz, house, techno, reggae, and more upstairs. Movie fans will find a wide variety of Blu-ray and DVD box sets, as well as bargain classic and cult films. Keep an eye out for rarities—including first pressings and one-offs—in all departments. There are also branches in Soho and Greenwich. A similar comics and books exchange is at No. 14 on nearby Pembridge Road (also a destination for vintage clothing for men [No. 34] and women [Nos. 32 and 20], accessories [No. 30] and retro bric-a-brac [No. 28]). ⊠ *38 Notting Hill Gate, Notting Hill* ☎ *020/7243–8573* ⊕ *www.mgeshops. com* Ⓜ *Notting Hill Gate.*

## SHOES

**Emma Hope.** The signature look of the footwear here is elegant and ladylike, with pointed toes and kitten heels, often ornamented with bows, lace, crystals, or exquisite embroidery (such craftsmanship doesn't come cheap, unfortunately). Ballet flats and sneakers in velvet or animal prints provide glamor without sacrificing comfort. Small but perfectly formed handbags, as well as shoes and accessories for men, are stocked both here and in the Sloane Square branch. ⊠ *207 Westbourne Grove, Notting Hill* ☎ *020/7313–7490* ⊕ *www.emmahope. com* Ⓜ *Notting Hill Gate.*

## REGENT'S PARK AND HAMPSTEAD

### GIFTS

**Susan Wainwright.** If you're looking for an alternative to the cheesy and the mass-produced, this eclectic shop packs loads of distinctive, stylish, affordable gifts into a small space. There are handsome gloves and fake fur accessories, handmade silver jewelry, tweed travel blankets, cashmere shawls, leather handbags, comfortable yet attractive robes and pyjamas, natural fiber baby and children's clothes and accessories, retro toys, sophisticated stationery, artisanal creams and lotions, flasks and leather goods for him, and more. ⊠ *31 South End Rd., Hampstead* ☎ *020/7431–4337* Ⓜ *Overground: Hampstead Heath.*

### HOUSEHOLD GOODS

**Graham & Green.** Combining style with practicality and an added whimsical twist, this delightful interiors shop carries faux fur and mohair throws, elegant lamps and lampshades, embroidered cushions, felt animal rugs for children, Venetian glass doorknobs, folding deck chairs (as found in the Royal Parks), shabby-chic sofas, and even a pedal-powered kiddie car that's a replica of a classic Bugatti. There's another branch in Notting Hill. ⊠ *164 Regent's Park Rd., Primrose Hill* ☎ *020/7586–2960* ⊕ *www.grahamandgreen.co.uk* Ⓜ *Chalk Farm.*

### SHOES

**Spice.** Touring London requires a lot of walking, so if your feet are crying out for mercy, stop in at this long-established boutique that specializes in spiffy but comfortable shoes and boots for men and women from brands like Camper, Audley, Chie Mihara, and their own Spice line. There's another branch in Islington. ⊠ *162 Regent's Park Rd., Primrose Hill* ☎ *020/7722–2478* ⊕ *www.spiceshu.co.uk* Ⓜ *Chalk Farm.*

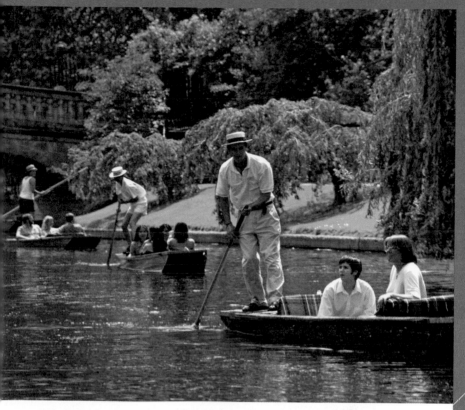

# SIDE TRIPS FROM LONDON

Updated by
Kate Hughes
and Jack
Jewers

Londoners are undeniably lucky. Few urban populations enjoy such glorious—and easily accessible—options for day-tripping. Even if you have only one day to spare, head out of the city. A train ride past hills dotted with sheep, a stroll through a medieval town, or a visit to one of England's great castles could make you feel as though you've added another week to your vacation.

Not only is England extremely compact, but its train and bus networks, although somewhat inefficient and expensive compared with their European counterparts, are extensive and easily booked (though pricing structures can be confusing), making "a brilliant day out" an easy thing to accomplish.

Although you can do the Warner Bros. Harry Potter Studio Tour in a day, many of the towns near London would make for a frenzied day trip. And in summer, heavy crowds make it difficult to sightsee in a relaxed manner, so consider staying for a day or two instead. You'd then have time to explore a different England—one with quiet country pubs, tree-lined lanes, and neat fields. No matter where you go, lodging reservations are a good idea June–September, when foreign visitors saturate the English countryside.

# PLANNING

### GETTING AROUND

Normally the towns near London are best reached by train. Bus travel costs less, but can take twice as long. Wherever you're going, plan ahead: check the latest timetables before you set off, and try to get an early start. ⇨ *Also see Travel Smart London.*

### STATION TIPS

You can reach any of London's main-line train stations by Tube. London's bus stations can be confusing for the uninitiated, so here's a quick breakdown:

**KEY**

Ferry Lines

## Side Trips from London

houses Cambridge University's computer laboratory) in this growing city—dominated culturally and architecturally by its famous university, whose students make up around one fifth of the city's 109,000 inhabitants, and beautified by parks, gardens and the quietly flowing River Cam. One quintessential Cambridge pursuit is punting on the Cam (one occupant propelling the narrow, square-end, flat-bottom boat with a long pole), followed by a stroll along the Backs, the left bank of the river fringed by St. John's, Trinity, Clare, King's, and Queens' colleges, and by Trinity Hall.

### VISITING THE COLLEGES

College visits are certainly a highlight of a Cambridge tour, but remember that the colleges are private residences and workplaces, even when school isn't in session. Each is an independent entity within the university; some are closed to the public, but at others you can see the chapels, dining rooms (called halls), and sometimes the libraries, too. Some colleges charge a fee for the privilege of nosing around. All are closed during exams (usually mid-April–late June), and the opening hours often vary. Additionally, all are subject to closure at short notice (especially King's); check the websites in advance. For details about visiting specific colleges not listed here, contact Cambridge University.

**Green Line Coach Station** is on Bulleid Way, in front of the Colonnades Shopping Centre on Buckingham Palace Road; it's the departure point for most Green Line and Megabus services.

**Victoria Bus Station** is where many of the local London bus services arrive and depart, and is directly outside the main exits of the train and Tube stations.

**Victoria Coach Station** is on Buckingham Palace Road: it's a five-minute walk from Victoria Tube station. This is where to go for coach departures; arrivals are at a different location, a short walk from here.

| TO GET TO . . . | | |
| --- | --- | --- |
| | Take the Train From . . . | Take the Bus From . . . |
| Cambridge | King's Cross (45–90 minutes, every 10 or 20 minutes); Liverpool St. (80 minutes, every 30 minutes) | Victoria Coach (about 3 hours, every 60–90 minutes) |
| Oxford | Paddington (55–110 minutes, every 3–20 minutes) | Victoria Coach (100 minutes, every half hour) or Oxford Tube, Buckingham Palace Rd. (100 minutes, every 12–20 minutes) |
| Stratford-upon-Avon | Marylebone (2–2½ hours, every 2 hours); or Euston (1½ hours, every 20 or 40 minutes or hourly) | Victoria Coach (3 hours 25 minutes, about 3 times daily) |
| Warner Bros. Harry Potter Studio Tour | Euston Station (20 minutes) to Watford, then shuttle bus to attraction | Watford (15 minutes, every 20 minutes), after taking London train from Euston. |
| Windsor | Paddington (25–50 minutes, every 5–30 minutes) or Waterloo (1 hour 5 minutes, every half hour) | Green Line Coach, Victoria (1 hour 5 minutes, hourly) |

**19**

# CAMBRIDGE

*60 miles northeast of London.*

With the spires of its university buildings framed by towering trees and expansive meadows, its medieval streets and passages enhanced by gardens and riverbanks, the city of Cambridge is among the loveliest in England. The city predates the Roman occupation of Britain, but there's confusion over exactly how the university was founded. The most widely accepted story is that it was established in 1209 by a pair of scholars from Oxford, who left their university in protest over the wrongful execution of a colleague for murder.

This university town may be beautiful, but it's no museum. Even when the students are on vacation, there's a cultural and intellectual buzz here. Well-preserved medieval buildings sit cheek-by-jowl with the latest in modern architecture (for example, the William Gates building, which

## TOURS

**City Sightseeing.** This company operates open-top bus tours of Cambridge, including the Backs, colleges, and Botanic Gardens. Tours can be joined at marked bus stops in the city. Ask the tourist office about additional tours. ⊠ *Cambridge Train Station, Station Rd.* ☎ *01223/433250* ⊕ *www.city-sightseeing.com* ⊠ *From £14.*

**Visit Cambridge.** Walking tours, as well as others, are led by an official Blue Badge guide. The two-hour tours leave from the tourist information center at Peas Hill. Hours vary according to the tour, with the earliest leaving at 11 am and the latest at 1 or 2 pm. ⊠ *Peas Hill* ☎ *0871/226–8006* ⊕ *www.visitcambridge.org/official-tours* ⊠ *From £18.50.*

## ESSENTIALS

**Visitor Information Cambridge University.** ☎ *01223/337733* ⊕ *www.cam.ac.uk.*

# EXPLORING

## TOP ATTRACTIONS

**Fodor's**Choice
★

**Fitzwilliam Museum.** In a Classical Revival building renowned for its grand Corinthian portico, this museum, founded by the 7th Viscount Fitzwilliam of Merrion in 1816, has one of Britain's most outstanding collections of art and antiquities. Highlights include two large Titians, an extensive collection of French impressionist paintings, and many works by Matisse and Picasso. The opulent interior displays these treasures to marvelous effect, from Egyptian pieces like inch-high figurines and painted coffins to sculptures from the Chinese Han dynasty of the 3rd century BC. Other collections of note here include a fine assortment of medieval illuminated manuscripts and a fascinating room full of armor and muskets. ⊠ *Trumpington St.* ☎ *01223/332900* ⊕ *www.fitzmuseum.cam.ac.uk* ⊠ *Free* ⊙ *Tues.–Sat. 10–5, Sun. noon–5.*

**King's College.** Founded in 1441 by Henry VI, King's College has a magnificent late-15th-century chapel that is its most famous landmark. Other notable architecture includes the neo-Gothic Porters' Lodge, facing King's Parade, which was a comparatively recent addition in the 1830s, and the classical Gibbs building. ■TIP➔ **Head down to the river, from where the panorama of college and chapel is one of the university's most photographed views.** Past students of King's College include the novelist E.M. Forster, the economist John Maynard Keynes, and the World War I poet Rupert Brooke. ⊠ *King's Parade* ☎ *01223/331212* ⊕ *www.kings.cam.ac.uk* ⊠ *£8, includes chapel* ⊙ *During term: Mon. 9:45–3:30, Tues.–Fri. 9:30–3:30, Sat. 9:30–3:15, Sun. 1:15–2:30. Out of term: Mon. 9:45–4:30, Tues.–Sun. 9:30–4:30.*

**Fodor's**Choice
★

**King's College Chapel.** Based on Sainte-Chapelle, the 13th-century royal chapel in Paris, this house of worship is perhaps the most glorious flowering of Perpendicular Gothic in Britain. Henry VI, the king after whom the college is named, oversaw the work. From the outside, the most prominent features are the massive flying buttresses and the fingerlike spires that line the length of the building. Inside, the most obvious impression is of great space—the chapel was once described as "the noblest barn in Europe"—and of light flooding in from its huge

**19**

windows. The brilliantly colored bosses (carved panels at the intersections of the roof ribs) are particularly intense although hard to see without binoculars. An exhibition in the chantries, or side chapels, explains more about the chapel's construction. Behind the altar is *The Adoration of the Magi*, an enormous painting by Peter Paul Rubens. ■ **TIP**➜ The chapel, unlike the rest of King's College, stays open during exam periods. Every Christmas Eve, a festival of carols is sung by the chapel's famous choir. It's broadcast on national television and considered a quintessential part of the traditional English Christmas. To compete for the small number of tickets available, join the line at the college's main entrance early—doors open at 7 am. ⊠ *King's Parade* 🕾 *01223/331212* ⊕ *www.kings.cam.ac.uk* ⛭ *£8, includes college and grounds* ☉ *During term: Mon. 9:45–3:30, Tues.–Fri. 9:30–3:30, Sat. 9:30–3:15, Sun. 9:45–4:30. Out of term: Mon. 9:45–5:30, Tues.–Sun. 9:30–4:30. Sometimes closed for events; call ahead to confirm.*

**Fodor's Choice** **Polar Museum.** Beautifully designed, this museum at Cambridge University's Scott Polar Research Institute chronicles the history of polar ★ exploration. There's a particular emphasis on the British expeditions of the 20th century, including the ill-fated attempt by Robert Falcon Scott to be the first to reach the South Pole in 1912. Norwegian explorer Roald Amundsen reached the pole first; Scott and his men perished on the return journey, but their story became legendary. There are also collections devoted to the science of modern polar exploration; the indigenous people of northern Canada, Greenland, and Alaska; and frequently changing art installations. ⊠ *Scott Polar Research Institute, Lensfield Rd.* 🕾 *01223/336540* ⊕ *www.spri.cam.ac.uk/museum* ⛭ *Free* ☉ *Tues.–Sat. 10–4. Closed Sat. of holiday weekends.*

## WORTH NOTING

**Emmanuel College.** The master hand of architect Sir Christopher Wren (1632–1723) is evident throughout much of Cambridge, particularly at Emmanuel, built on the site of a Dominican friary, where he designed the chapel and colonnade. A stained-glass window in the chapel has a likeness of John Harvard, founder of Harvard University, who studied here. The college, founded in 1584, was an early center of Puritan learning; a number of the Pilgrims were Emmanuel alumni, and they remembered their alma mater in naming Cambridge, Massachusetts. ⊠ *St. Andrew's St.* 🕾 *01223/334200* ⊕ *www.emma.cam.ac.uk* ⛭ *Free* ☉ *Daily 9–6. Closed during exam period.*

**Queens' College.** One of the most eye-catching colleges, Queens' is named after Margaret, wife of Henry VI, and Elizabeth, wife of Edward IV. Founded in 1448, the college is tucked away on Queens' Lane, next to the wide lawns that lead down from King's College to the Backs. The secluded "cloister court" looks untouched since its completion in the 1540s. Queens' masterpiece is the **Mathematical Bridge,** the original version of which is said to have been built without any fastenings. The current bridge (1902) is securely bolted. The college is closed to visitors late May–late June. ⊠ *Queens' La.* 🕾 *01223/335511* ⊕ *www.quns. cam.ac.uk* ⛭ *£3* ☉ *Daily 10–4:30. Closed during exam study periods, certain wks Apr.–July; call to confirm.*

**Trinity College.** Founded in 1546 by Henry VIII, Trinity replaced a 14th-century educational foundation and is the largest college in either Cambridge or Oxford, with nearly 700 undergraduates. In the 17th-century great court, with its massive gatehouse, is **Great Tom,** a giant clock that strikes each hour with high and low notes. The college's greatest masterpiece is Sir Christopher Wren's **library,** colonnaded and seemingly constructed with as much light as stone. Among the things you can see here is A. A. Milne's handwritten manuscript of *The House at Pooh Corner.* Trinity alumni include Sir Isaac Newton, William Thackeray, Lord Byron, Lord Tennyson, and 31 Nobel Prize winners. ⊠ *St. John's St.* ☎ *01223/338400* ⊕ *www.trin.cam.ac.uk* ⛩ *£2* ⊙ *College and chapel daily 10–4, except exam period and event days. Wren Library weekdays noon–2, Sat. during term 10:30–12:30. Great Court daily 10–4:30.*

## WHERE TO EAT

$$   ✕ **Loch Fyne.** Part of a Scottish chain that harvests its own oysters, this
SEAFOOD   airy, casual place across from the Fitzwilliam Museum is deservedly popular. The seafood is fresh and well prepared, served in a traditional setting with a modern ambience. Try the Bradan Rost smoked salmon if it's on the menu; it's flavored with Scotch whisky. The restaurant is also open for breakfast. Ⓢ *Average main: £17* ⊠ *37 Trumpington St.* ☎ *01223/362433* ⊕ *www.lochfyne-restaurants.com.*

$$$$   ✕ **Midsummer House.** Beside the River Cam on the edge of Midsummer
FRENCH   Common, this gray-brick building holds a two–Michelin star restaurant
**Fodor**ŚChoice   with a comfortable conservatory and a handful of tables under fruit
★   trees in a lush, secluded garden. Fixed-price menus for lunch and dinner (three to five courses) present innovative French and Mediterranean-influenced dishes. Choices might include roasted sea bass or venison with blue cheese and sloe berries. Ⓢ *Average main: £48* ⊠ *Midsummer Common* ☎ *01223/369299* ⊕ *www.midsummerhouse.co.uk* ⊙ *Closed Sun. and Mon. No lunch Tues.*

$$$   ✕ **River Bar Steakhouse & Grill.** Across the river from Magdalene College,
MODERN BRITISH   this popular waterfront bar and grill serves delicious steaks and burgers, plus specialties such as lobster mac and cheese, and roast chicken with a bourbon barbecue glaze. Light lunches are served in the afternoon, and the evening cocktail list is small but elegant. Try the French 75 (gin with lemon juice, sugar, and sparkling wine). Ⓢ *Average main: £20* ⊠ *Quayside, Thompsons La., off Bridge St.* ☎ *01223/307030* ⊕ *www. riverbarsteakhouse.com* ⌖ *Reservations essential.*

# OXFORD

*55 miles northwest of London.*

With arguably the most famous university in the world, Oxford has been a center of learning since 1167, with only the Sorbonne preceding it. It doesn't take more than a day or two to explore its winding medieval streets, photograph its ivy-covered stone buildings and ancient churches and libraries, and even take a punt down one of its placid waterways. The town center is compact and walkable, and at its heart is Oxford University. Alumni of this prestigious institution include 48 Nobel Prize winners, 26 British prime ministers (including David Cameron), and 28 foreign presidents (including Bill Clinton), along with poets, authors, and artists such as Percy Bysshe Shelley, Oscar Wilde, and W. H. Auden.

Oxford is northwest of London, at the junction of the rivers Thames and Cherwell. The city is more interesting and more cosmopolitan than Cambridge, and although it's also bigger, its suburbs aren't remotely interesting to visitors. The interest is all at the center, where the old town curls around the grand stone buildings, great restaurants, and historic pubs. Victorian writer Matthew Arnold described Oxford's "dreaming spires," a phrase that has become famous. Students rush past on the way to exams, clad with antiquarian style in their requisite mortar caps, flowing dark gowns, stiff collars, and crisp white bow ties.
■ TIP➜ Watch your back when crossing roads, as bikes are everywhere.

### VISITING THE COLLEGES

You can explore the town's major sights in a day, but it takes more than a day to spend an hour in each of the key museums and absorb the college scene. Some colleges are open only in the afternoons during university terms. When undergraduates are in residence, access is often restricted to the chapels, dining rooms, and libraries, and you're requested to refrain from picnicking in the quadrangles. All are closed certain days during exams, usually mid-April–late June.

### TOURS

**City Sightseeing.** This company runs hop-on, hop-off bus tours with 19 stops around Oxford. Your ticket, purchased from the driver, is good for 24 hours. ☎ 01865/790522 ⊕ *www.citysightseeingoxford. com* ✉ *From £14.*

**Oxford Tourist Information Centre.** You can find information here on the many guided walks of the city. The best way of gaining access to the collegiate buildings is to take the two-hour university and city tour, which leaves the Tourist Information Centre at 10:45 and 1 daily, plus at 2 on Saturday. You can book in advance. ✉ *15–16 Broad St.* ☎ *01865/252200* ⊕ *www.visitoxfordandoxfordshire.com* ✉ *From £9.*

# EXPLORING

## TOP ATTRACTIONS

Fodor's Choice ★ **Ashmolean Museum.** Britain's oldest public museum displays its rich and varied collections from the Neolithic to the present day over five floors. Innovative and spacious galleries on the theme of "Crossing Cultures, Crossing Time" explore connections between the priceless Greek, Roman, and Indian artifacts, as well as the Egyptian and Chinese objects, all of which are among the best in the country. In regards to the superb art collection, not to be missed are drawings by Raphael, the shell-encrusted mantle of Powhatan (father of Pocahontas), the lantern belonging to Guy Fawkes, and the Alfred Jewel, set in gold, which dates to the reign of King Alfred the Great (ruled 871–899). There's too much to see in one visit, but the free admission makes

Radcliffe Camera, an unmissable circular library at Oxford University

return trips easy. The rooftop Ashmolean Dining Room is a good spot for refreshments. ⊠ *Beaumont St.* ☎ *01865/278002* ⊕ *www.ashmolean. org* ⊠ *Free* ☉ *Tues.–Sun. and bank holiday Mon. 10–5.*

**Fodor's** Choice
★
**Magdalen College.** Founded in 1458, with a handsome main quadrangle and a supremely monastic air, Magdalen (pronounced "*maud*-lin") is one of the most impressive of Oxford's colleges and attracts its most artistic students. Alumni include such diverse people as P. G. Wodehouse, Oscar Wilde, and John Betjeman. The school's large, square tower is a famous local landmark. ■**TIP→ To enhance your visit, take a stroll around the Deer Park and along Addison's Walk; then have tea in the Old Kitchen, which overlooks the river.** ⊠ *High St.* ☎ *01865/276000* ⊕ *www.magd.ox.ac.uk* ⊠ *£5* ☉ *July–Sept., daily noon–7 or dusk; Oct.– June, daily 1–6 or dusk.*

**19**

FAMILY
**Fodor's** Choice
★
**Pitt Rivers Museum.** More than half a million intriguing archaeological and anthropological items from around the globe, based on the collection bequeathed by Lieutenant-General Augustus Henry Lane Fox Pitt Rivers in 1884, are crammed into a multitude of glass cases and drawers. Labels are handwritten, and items are organized thematically rather than geographically, an eccentric approach that's surprisingly thought-provoking. Give yourself plenty of time to wander through the displays of shrunken heads, Hawaiian feather cloaks, and fearsome masks. Children will have a field day, as they use flashlights to explore the farthest corners and spot the world's smallest dolly. ⊠ *S. Parks Rd.* ☎ *01865/270927* ⊕ *www.prm.ox.ac.uk* ⊠ *Free (suggested donation £3)* ☉ *Mon. noon–4:30, Tues.–Sun. and bank holiday Mon. 10–4:30.*

## WORTH NOTING

**Christ Church.** Built in 1546, the college of Christ Church is referred to by its members as "The House." This is the site of Oxford's largest quadrangle, Tom Quad, named after the huge bell (6¼ tons) that hangs in the Sir Christopher Wren–designed gate tower and rings 101 times at five past nine every evening in honor of the original number of Christ Church scholars. The vaulted, 800-year-old chapel in one corner has been Oxford's cathedral since the time of Henry VIII. The college's medieval dining hall contains portraits of many famous alumni, including 13 of Britain's prime ministers, but you'll recognize it from its recurring role in the Harry Potter movies (although they didn't actually film here, the room was painstakingly re-created in a film studio). ■TIP→ Plan carefully, as the dining hall is only open weekdays 10:30–11:40 and 2:30–4:30, weekends 2:30–4:30. Lewis Carroll, author of *Alice in Wonderland,* was a teacher of mathematics here for many years; a shop opposite the meadows on St. Aldate's sells Alice paraphernalia. ⊠ *St. Aldate's* ☎ *01865/276492* ⊕ *www.chch.ox.ac.uk* ✆ *£8 (£9 in July and Aug.)* ⊙ *Mon.–Sat. 10–5, Sun. 2–5; last admission 45 mins before closing. Sometimes closed for events; call to confirm.*

**Radcliffe Camera and Bodleian Library.** A vast library, the domed Radcliffe Camera is Oxford's most spectacular building, built in 1737–49 by James Gibbs in Italian Baroque style. It's usually surrounded by tourists with cameras trained at its golden-stone walls. The Camera contains part of the Bodleian Library's enormous collection, begun in 1602 and one of six "copyright libraries" in the United Kingdom. Like the Library of Congress in the United States, this means it must by law contain a copy of every book printed in Great Britain. The shelves are therefore very crowded—the collection grows by about 5,000 items a week. It also contains valuable treasures such as a Gutenberg Bible and a Shakespeare First Folio. Tours reveal the magnificent Duke Humfrey's Library, which was the original chained library, completed in 1488 (the ancient tomes are dusted once a decade). Guides can show you the spots used for Hogwarts School in the Harry Potter films. ■TIP→ Arrive early to secure tickets for the two to six daily tours. The 10:30 am tour can be prebooked, as can the extended tours on Wednesday and Saturday; otherwise tours are first-come, first-served. Audio tours, the only ones open to kids under 11, don't require reservations. Call ahead to confirm times, as tours don't run on days when private events are booked at the library. ⊠ *Broad St.* ☎ *01865/287400* ⊕ *www.bodleian. ox.ac.uk* ✆ *Audio tour £2.50, minitour £5, standard tour £7, extended tour £13* ⊙ *Bodleian and Divinity School weekdays 9–5, Sat. 9–4:30, Sun. 11–5; sometimes closed for events, call to confirm.*

**St. John's College.** One of Oxford's most attractive campuses, St. John's has seven quiet quadrangles surrounded by elaborately carved buildings. You enter the first through a low wooden door. This college dates to 1555, when Sir Thomas White, a merchant, founded it. His heart is buried in the chapel (it's a tradition for students to curse as they walk over it). The Canterbury Quad represented the first example of Italian Renaissance architecture in Oxford, and the Front Quad includes the buildings of the old St. Bernard's Monastery. ✉ *St. Giles* ☎ *01865/277300* ⊕ *www.sjc.ox.ac.uk* 🎫 *Free* ☉ *Daily 1–5 or dusk.*

**University Church of St. Mary the Virgin.** Seven hundred years' worth of funeral monuments crowd this galleried and spacious church, including the alter-step tombstone of Amy Robsart, the wife of Robert Dudley, Elizabeth I's favorite. One pillar marks the site where Thomas Cranmer, author of the *Anglican Book of Common Prayer,* was brought to trial and executed for heresy by Queen Mary I (Cranmer had been a key player in the Protestant reforms). The top of the 14th-century tower has a panoramic view of the city's skyline—it's worth the 127 steps. The Vaults and Garden Café, part of the church accessible from Radcliffe Square, serves breakfasts and cream teas as well as good lunches. ✉ *High St.* ☎ *01865/279111* ⊕ *www.university-church.ox.ac. uk* 🎫 *Church free, tower £4* ☉ *Sept.–June, daily 9–5; July–Aug., daily 9–6; last admission 30 mins before closing.*

## WHERE TO EAT

**$$** ✕ **Brasserie Blanc.** Raymond Blanc's sophisticated brasserie in the Jeri-
FRENCH cho neighborhood is the more affordable chain restaurant cousin of Le Manoir aux Quat'Saisons in Great Milton. Wood floors, pale walls, and large windows keep the restaurant open and airy. The changing menu always lists innovative adaptations of bourgeois French fare, sometimes with Mediterranean or Asian influences. Try the cod fillet marinated in lemon or the chicken served with mousseline potato. There's a good selection of steaks as well. The £12 fixed-price lunch is a good value, and kids have their own menu. ⑤ *Average main: £16* ✉ *71–72 Walton St.* ☎ *01865/510999* ⊕ *www.brasserieblanc.com.*

**$** ✕ **Jamie's Italian.** One of Chef Jamie Oliver's missions is to re-create the
ITALIAN best rustic Italian fare all over the country, and it's no different at this big and buzzing eatery. There's a diverse range of starters, pastas, and mains like truffle tagliatelle with Parmesan and nutmeg or British lamb lollipops with toasted nuts and lemon yogurt. Desserts are light and refreshing—tutti frutti lemon meringue pie and granola crumble, for example—and the lively crowd appreciates it all. ⑤ *Average main: £14* ✉ *24–26 George St.* ☎ *01865/838383* ⊕ *www.jamieoliver.com.*

**19**

# STRATFORD-UPON-AVON

*104 miles north of London.*

Stratford-upon-Avon has become adept at accommodating the hordes of people who stream in for a glimpse of William Shakespeare's world. Filled with distinctive, Tudor half-timber buildings, this is certainly a handsome town, and the Royal Shakespeare Theatre is a don't-miss for those who want to see Shakespeare performed in England. But the town can feel, at times, like a literary amusement park, so if you're not a fan of the Bard, you may want to explore elsewhere.

Stratford-upon-Avon honors Shakespeare's birthday with an annual procession.

## TOURS AND TICKETS

**City Sightseeing.** Hop-on, hop-off guided tours of Stratford are run by City Sightseeing, and you can combine the tour (about an hour with no stops) with entry to either three or five Shakespeare houses. ☎ 01789/412680 ⊕ www.city-sightseeing.com ✆ From £12.50.

**Shakespeare Birthplace Trust.** The main places of Shakespearean interest (Anne Hathaway's Cottage, Hall's Croft, Mary Arden's House, New Place and Nash's House, Shakespeare's Birthplace, and Shakespeare's Grave) are run by the Shakespeare Birthplace Trust. Buy a money-saving combination ticket to five properties for £26.25, or pay separate entry fees if you're visiting only one or two. Family tickets are an option, too. Advance booking online gives you a 10% discount and tickets are valid for a year. ☎ 01789/204016 ⊕ www.shakespeare.org.uk.

**Stratford Town Walk.** This walking tour runs year-round and also offers ghost-themed walks and cruises. ☎ 0785/576–0377, 01789/292478 ⊕ www.stratfordtownwalk.co.uk ✆ From £5 ⊗ Weekdays at 11, weekends at 11 and 2.

## ESSENTIALS

**Visitor Information Stratford-upon-Avon Tourist Information Centre.** ✉ Bridgefoot ☎ 01789/264293 ⊕ www.discover-stratford.com.

# EXPLORING

**Hall's Croft.** One of the finest surviving Jacobean (early 17th-century) townhouses, this impressive residence has a delightful walled garden. Hall's Croft was the home of Shakespeare's elder daughter, Susanna, and her husband, Dr. John Hall, a wealthy physician who, by prescribing an herbal cure for scurvy, was well ahead of his time. One room is furnished as a medical dispensary of the period, and throughout the building are fine examples of heavy oak Jacobean furniture, including a child's high chair and some 17th-century portraits. The café serves light lunches and afternoon teas. ⊠ *Old Town* ☎ *01789/292107* ⊕ *www. shakespeare.org.uk* ✉ *£17.50, includes admission to Shakespeare's Birthplace, New Place and Nash's House, and Shakespeare's Grave* ⊙ *Mid-Mar.–Oct., daily 10–5; Nov.–mid-Mar., daily 11–4.*

**Holy Trinity Church.** The burial place of William Shakespeare, this 13th-century church sits on the banks of the Avon with a graceful avenue of lime trees framing its entrance. Shakespeare's final resting place is in the chancel, rebuilt in 1465–91 in the late Perpendicular style. He was buried here not because he was a famed poet but because he was a lay rector of Stratford, owning a portion of the township tithes. On the north wall of the sanctuary, over the altar steps, is the famous marble bust created by Gerard Jansen in 1623 and thought to be a true likeness of Shakespeare. The bust offers a more human, even humorous, perspective when viewed from the side. Also in the chancel are the graves of Shakespeare's wife, Anne; his daughter, Susanna; his son-in-law, John Hall; and his granddaughter's husband, Thomas Nash. Nearby, the Parish Register is displayed, containing Shakespeare's baptismal entry (1564) and his burial notice (1616). ⊠ *Trinity St.* ☎ *01789/266316* ⊕ *www.stratford-upon-avon.org* ✉ *£3 for Shakespeare's Grave* ⊙ *Mar. and Oct., Mon.–Sat. 9–5, Sun. 12:30–5; Apr.–Sept., Mon.–Sat. 8:30–6, Sun. 12:30–5; Nov.–Feb., Mon.–Sat. 9–4, Sun. 12:30–5; last admission 20 mins before closing.*

**New Place and Nash's House.** Originally built in 1483 "of brike and tymber" for a lord mayor of London, **New Place** was Stratford's grandest piece of real estate when Shakespeare bought it in 1597 for £60. Along with a celebrated mulberry tree, revered for being planted by Shakespeare himself, the house was torn down in 1759 by the Reverend Francis Gastrell, who was angry at the hordes of Shakespeare-related sightseers. This in turn provoked the wrath of the local inhabitants, who drove him out of town. Now imaginatively reinterpreted to mark the 400th anniversary of Shakespeare's death in 1616, it shows the footprint of the original house and focuses on a deep, illuminated pool. Next door is **Nash's House,** the residence of Thomas Nash, who married Shakespeare's last direct descendant, his granddaughter Elizabeth Hall; it holds finds from recent excavations of the area. The grounds contain a restored Elizabethan knot garden and a fine display of cloud topiary. The site is currently closed for a massive restoration project, with a projected reopening of July 2016. Check the website for further details. ⊠ *Chapel St.* ☎ *01789/292325* ⊕ *www.shakespeare.org. uk* ✉ *£17.50, includes admission to Shakespeare's Birthplace, Hall's*

**19**

*Croft, and Shakespeare's Grave* ⊘ *Mid-Mar.–Oct., daily 10–5; Nov.–mid-Mar., daily 11–4.*

Fodor's Choice   **Royal Shakespeare Company.** One of the finest repertory troupes in the
★   world and long the backbone of the country's theatrical life, the company performs plays year-round in Stratford and at venues around Britain. The stunning Royal Shakespeare Theatre, home of the RSC, has a thrust stage based on the original Globe Theater in London. The Swan Theatre, part of the theater complex and also built in the style of Shakespeare's Globe, stages plays by Shakespeare and contemporaries such as Christopher Marlowe and Ben Jonson, as well as works by contemporary playwrights. Prices run £5–£50. ■ TIP➔ Seats book up fast, but day-of-performance and returned tickets are sometimes available. ✉ *Waterside* ☎ *0844/800–1110 for tickets* ⊕ *www.rsc.org.uk.*

Fodor's Choice   **Shakespeare's Birthplace.** A half-timber house typical of its time, the play-
★   wright's birthplace is a much-visited shrine that has been altered and restored since he lived here. Passing through the modern visitor center, you are immersed in the world of Shakespeare through an exhibition that displays the First Folio, deeds to his properties, what is thought to be his signet ring, busts, and other memorabilia. The house itself is across the garden from the visitor center. Colorful wall decorations and the furnishings reflect comfortable, middle-class Elizabethan domestic life. Shakespeare's father, John, a glove maker and wool dealer, purchased the house; a reconstructed workshop shows the tools of the glover's trade. Mark Twain and Charles Dickens were both pilgrims here, and you can see the signatures of Thomas Carlyle and Walter Scott scratched into Shakespeare's windowpanes. In the garden, actors present excerpts from the plays. There's also a café and bookshop on the grounds. ✉ *Henley St.* ☎ *01789/201822* ⊕ *www.shakespeare.org.uk* 🎫 *£17.50, includes entry to Hall's Croft, Nash's House and New Place, and Shakespeare's Grave* ⊘ *Mid-Mar.–June, Sept., and Oct., daily 9–5; July and Aug., daily 9–6; Nov.–mid-Mar., daily 10–4.*

## AROUND STRATFORD

Two additional stops on the Shakespeare trail are just outside Stratford; also nearby is spectacular Warwick Castle.

Fodor's Choice   **Anne Hathaway's Cottage and Gardens.** The most picturesque of the Shake-
★   speare Trust properties, on the western outskirts of Stratford, is the family home of the woman Shakespeare married in 1582. The "cottage," actually a substantial Tudor farmhouse, has latticed windows and a grand thatch roof. Inside is period furniture, including the settle where Shakespeare reputedly conducted his courtship, and a rare carved Elizabethan bed; outside is a garden planted in lush Edwardian style with herbs and flowers. A stroll through the adjacent orchard takes you to willow cabins where you can listen to sonnets and view sculptures with Shakespearean themes, while the nearby arboretum has trees, shrubs, and roses mentioned in Shakespeare's works. ■ TIP➔ The best way to get here is on foot, especially in late spring when the apple trees are in blossom. The signed path runs from Evesham Place (an extension of Grove Road) opposite Chestnut Walk. Pick up a leaflet with a map

from the tourist office; the walk takes a good half hour. ⊠ *Cottage La., Shottery* ☎ *01789/295517* ⊕ *www.shakespeare.org.uk* 🏷️*£10.25; Five House Pass £26.25, includes Hall's Croft, Mary Arden's Farm, New Place and Nash's House, Shakespeare's Birthplace, and Shakespeare's Grave* ⊗ *Mid-Mar.–Oct., daily 9–5; Nov.–mid-Mar., daily 10–4.*

FAMILY **Mary Arden's Farm.** A working farm, where food is grown using methods common in the 16th century, is the main attraction at Mary Arden's House (the childhood home of Shakespeare's mother) and Palmer's Farm. This bucolic stop is great for kids, who can try their hand at basket weaving and gardening, listen as the farmers explain their work in the fields, and watch the cooks prepare food in the Tudor farmhouse kitchen—it all brings the past to life. There are crafts exhibits, a café, and a garden. The site is 3 miles northwest of Stratford; you need to walk or drive here, or else go with a tour. ⊠ *Off A3400, Wilmcote* ☎ *01789/293455* ⊕ *www.shakespeare.org.uk* 🏷️*£13.25; Five House Pass £26.25, includes Anne Hathaway's Cottage and Gardens, Hall's Croft, Mary Arden's Farm, Nash's House and New Place, Shakespeare's Birthplace, and Shakespeare's Grave* ⊗ *Mid-Mar.–Oct., daily 10–5.*

FAMILY
Fodor's Choice
★

**Warwick Castle.** The vast bulk of this medieval castle rests on a cliff overlooking the Avon, "the fairest monument of ancient and chivalrous splendor which yet remains uninjured by time," to use the words of Sir Walter Scott. Today the company that runs the Madame Tussauds wax museums owns the castle, and the exhibits and diversions can occupy a full day. Warwick is a great castle experience for kids, and although it's pricey, there are family rates. Warwick's two soaring towers, bristling with battlements, can be seen for miles: the 147-foot-high Caesar's Tower, built in 1356, and the 128-foot-high Guy's Tower, built in 1380. The castle's most powerful commander was Richard Neville, Earl of Warwick, known during the 15th-century Wars of the Roses as the Kingmaker. Warwick Castle's monumental walls enclose an impressive armory of medieval weapons, as well as state rooms with historic furnishings and paintings by Peter Paul Rubens, Anthony van Dyck, and other old masters. Twelve rooms are devoted to an imaginative wax exhibit, *A Royal Weekend Party—1898*. Other exhibits display the sights and sounds of a great medieval household as it prepares for an important battle and of a princess's fairy-tale wedding. At the Mill and Engine House, you can see the turning water mill and the engines used to generate electricity early in the 20th century. In the spooky dungeon exhibit, you can wander by wax re-creations of decaying bodies, chanting monks, witches, executions, and "the labyrinth of lost souls"—a modern mirror maze. Elsewhere, a working trebuchet (a kind of catapult), falconry displays, and rat-throwing (stuffed, not live) games add to the atmosphere. Below the castle, strutting peacocks patrol the 60 acres of grounds elegantly landscaped by Capability Brown in the 18th century. ■ **TIP→ Arrive early to beat the crowds. If you book online, you save 20% on ticket prices.** Lavish medieval banquets (extra charge) and special events, including festivals, jousting tournaments, and a Christmas market, take place throughout the year, and plenty of food stalls serve lunches. For the ultimate castle experience, you can "glamp" (glamorously camp) in a medieval tent or stay in your own luxury suite

**19**

in Ceasar's Tower. ✉ *Castle La. off Mill St., Warwick* ☎ *01926/495421, 0871/265–2000 for info (24 hrs), 01926/406–660 for accommodations* ⊕ *www.warwick-castle.com* 🖃 *£30.20 castle and dungeon, £25.20 castle only; parking £6* ⊙ *Late July and Aug., daily 10–6; mid-Sept.–mid-July, daily 10–5; last admission 30 mins before closing.*

## WHERE TO EAT

$    ✕ **The Black Swan/The Dirty Duck.** The only pub in Britain to be licensed
BRITISH   under two names (the more informal one came courtesy of American
**Fodor's**Choice   GIs who were stationed here during World War II), this is one of Strat-
★   ford's most celebrated pubs—it's attracted actors since the 18th-century thespian David Garrick's days. A little veranda overlooks the theaters and the river here. Along with your pint of bitter, you can choose from the extensive menu of baked potatoes, steaks, burgers, and grills; there are also good-value set menus. Few people come here for the food (although you will need to book ahead for dinner): the real attraction is the ambience and your fellow customers. $ *Average main: £8* ✉ *Waterside* ☎ *01789/297312* ⊕ *www.oldenglishinns.co.uk.*

$    ✕ **Opposition.** Hearty, warming meals are offered at this informal,
MODERN BRITISH   family-style restaurant in a 16th-century building on the main dining street near the theaters. The English and international dishes—chicken roasted with banana and served with curry sauce and basmati rice, for instance—win praise from the locals. There's a good range of light and vegetarian options and fixed-price menus as well. Make reservations a month ahead in summer. $ *Average main: £14* ✉ *13 Sheep St.* ☎ *01789/269980* ⊕ *www.theoppo.co.uk* ⊙ *Closed Sun.*

# WARNER BROS. HARRY POTTER STUDIO TOUR

*20 miles northwest of London.*

Popular and family-friendly, the Warner Bros. Harry Potter Studio Tour has sets and props from the successful films, and plenty of engaging interactive diversions for all ages. The train and a special shuttle bus from Watford get you here.

## EXPLORING

FAMILY   **Warner Bros. Harry Potter Studio Tour.** Muggles, take note: this spectacular
**Fodor's**Choice   attraction just outside Watford gives you a good three hours of the mag-
★   ical world of Harry Potter. From the Great Hall of Hogwarts—faithfully restored—to magical props beautifully displayed in a vast studio space, each section of this attraction showcases the real sets, props, and special effects used in the eight movies. Visitors enter the Great Hall, a fitting stage for costumes from each Hogwarts house. You can admire the intricacies of the huge Hogwarts Castle model, ride a broomstick, try butterbeer, explore Platform 9¾, or just take refuge in the comforting confines of Dumbledore's office. The new Hogwarts Express section—in a faithfully reproduced King's Cross Station—allows you to walk through the actual steam train and see what it's like to ride with Harry and the

gang. Tickets, pegged to a 30-minute arrival time slot, must be pre-booked online. The studio tour is a 20-minute drive from St. Albans. You can also get here by taking a 20-minute train ride from London's Euston Station to Watford Junction (then a 15-minute shuttle-bus ride). Via car from London, use M1 and M25—parking is free. ⊠ *Studio Tour Dr., Leavesden* ☎ *0845/084-0900* ⊕ *www.wbstudiotour.co.uk* ☎ *£35* ⊙ *Daily hrs vary, generally 10–8 in summer months; last tour slot 2½–3½ hrs before closing. Call or check website to confirm hrs.*

# WINDSOR CASTLE

*21 miles west of London.*

The tall turrets of Windsor Castle, one of the homes of the Royal Family, can be seen for miles around. The grand stone building is the star attraction in this quiet town with some remaining medieval elements—although Eton College, England's most famous public school, is also just a lovely walk away across the Thames.

### ESSENTIALS

**Visitor Information Royal Windsor Information Centre.** ⊠ *Old Booking Hall, Windsor Royal Station, Thames St.* ☎ *01753/743900, 01753/743907 for accommodations* ⊕ *www.windsor.gov.uk.*

## EXPLORING

**19**

**Fodor's Choice** **Eton College.** Signs warn drivers of "Boys Crossing" as you approach
★ the splendid Tudor-style buildings of Eton College, the distinguished boarding school for boys ages 13–18 founded in 1440 by King Henry VI. It's all terrifically photogenic—during the college semester students still dress in pin-stripe trousers, swallow-tail coats, and stiff collars. Rivaling St. George's at Windsor in terms of size, the Gothic **Chapel** contains superb 15th-century grisaille wall paintings juxtaposed with modern stained glass by John Piper. Beyond the cloisters are the school's playing fields where, according to the Duke of Wellington, the Battle of Waterloo was really won, since so many of his officers had learned discipline and strategy during their school days. Among the country's prime ministers to be educated here is David Cameron. The **Museum of Eton Life** has displays on the school's history and vignettes of school life. The school gives public tours, although as of this writing they were suspended due to construction. They are set to resume again by early 2016, but call ahead for more information. ⊠ *Brewhouse Yard, Eton* ☎ *01753/370100* ⊕ *www.etoncollege.com*

**Fodor's Choice** **Windsor Castle.** From William the Conqueror to Queen Victoria, the
★ kings and queens of England added towers and wings to this brooding,
imposing castle, visible for miles and now the largest inhabited castle
in the world. Despite the multiplicity of hands involved in its design,
the palace manages to have a unity of style and character. The most
impressive view of Windsor Castle is from the A332 road, coming into
town from the south. Admission includes an audio guide and, if you
wish, a guided tour of the castle precincts. Entrance lines can be long in
season, and you're likely to spend at least half a day here, so come early.

William the Conqueror began work on the castle in the 11th century,
and Edward III modified and extended it in the mid-1300s. One of
Edward's largest contributions was the enormous and distinctive **Round
Tower.** Later, between 1824 and 1837, George IV transformed the still
essentially medieval castle into the fortified royal palace you see today.
Most of England's kings and queens have demonstrated their undying
attachment to the castle, the only royal residence in continuous use by
the Royal Family since the Middle Ages.

As you enter the castle, **Henry VIII's gateway** leads uphill into the wide
castle precincts, where you're free to wander. Across from the entrance
is the exquisite **St. George's Chapel** (closed Sunday). Here lie 10 of
the kings of England, including Henry VI, Charles I, and Henry VIII
(Jane Seymour is the only one of his six wives buried here). One of the
noblest buildings in England, the chapel was built in the Perpendicular
style popular in the 15th and 16th centuries, with elegant stained-glass
windows; a high, vaulted ceiling; and intricately carved choir stalls.
The colorful heraldic banners of the Knights of the Garter—the oldest
British Order of Chivalry, founded by Edward III in 1348—hang in the
choir. The ceremony in which the knights are installed as members of
the order has been held here with much pageantry for more than five
centuries. The elaborate **Albert Memorial Chapel** was created by Queen
Victoria in memory of her husband.

The **North Terrace** provides especially good views across the Thames
to Eton College, perhaps the most famous of Britain's exclusive public
schools (confusingly, "public schools" in Britain are highly traditional,
top-tier private schools). From the terrace, you enter the **State Apartments,** which are open to the public most days. On display to the left of
the entrance to the State Apartments in Windsor Castle, **Queen Mary's
Dolls' House** is a perfect miniature Georgian palace-within-a-palace,
created in 1923. Electric lights glow, the doors all have tiny keys, and
a miniature library holds Lilliputian-size books written especially for
the young queen by famous authors of the 1920s. Five cars, including
a Daimler and Rolls-Royce, stand at the ready. In the adjacent corridor are exquisite French couturier–designed costumes made for the
two Jumeau dolls presented to the Princesses Elizabeth and Margaret
by France in 1938.

Although a fire in 1992 gutted some of the State Apartments, hardly
any works of art were lost. Phenomenal repair work brought to new life
the **Grand Reception Room,** the **Green and Crimson Drawing Rooms,**
and the **State and Octagonal Dining Rooms.** A green oak hammer-beam

(a short horizontal beam that projects from the tops of walls for support) roof looms magnificently over the 600-year-old **St. George's Hall,** where the Queen gives state banquets. The State Apartments contain priceless furniture, including a magnificent Louis XVI bed and Gobelin tapestries; carvings by Grinling Gibbons; and paintings by Canaletto, Rubens, Van Dyck, Holbein, Dürer, and Bruegel. The tour's high points are the **Throne Room** and the **Waterloo Chamber,** where Sir Thomas Lawrence's portraits of Napoléon's victorious foes line the walls. You can also see arms and armor—look for Henry VIII's ample suit. A visit October–March also includes the Semi-State rooms, the private apartments of George IV, resplendent with gilded ceilings.

To see the castle come magnificently alive, check out the Changing the Guard, which takes place daily at 11 am April–July, and on alternate days at the same time August–March. Confirm the exact schedule before traveling to Windsor. ⊠ *Castle Hill* ☎ *020/7766–7304 for tickets, 01753/831118 for recorded info* ⊕ *www.royalcollection.org.uk* ⌨ *£19.50 for Precincts, State Apartments, Gallery, St. George's Chapel, and Queen Mary's Dolls' House; £10.50 when State Apartments are closed* ⊙ *Mar.–Oct., daily 9:45–5:15; Nov.–Feb., daily 9:45–4:15; last admission 1 hr 15 mins before closing.*

**Fodor's** Choice **Windsor Great Park.** The remains of an ancient royal hunting forest, this
★ park stretches for some 5,000 acres south of Windsor Castle. Much of it is open to the public and can be explored by car or on foot. Its chief attractions are clustered around the southeastern section, known (or at least marketed) as the **Royal Landscape.** These include **Virginia Water,** a 2-mile-long lake that forms the park's main geographical focal point. More than anything, however, the Royal Landscape is defined by its two beautiful gardens. **Valley Gardens,** located on the north shore of Virginia Water, is particularly vibrant in April and May, when the dazzling multicolored azaleas are in full bloom.

If you're feeling fit, the romantic **Long Walk** is one of England's most photographed footpaths—the 3-mile-long route, designed by Charles II, starts in the Great Park and leads all the way to Windsor Castle.

Divided from the Great Park by the busy A308 highway, the smaller **Windsor Home Park,** on the eastern side of Windsor Castle, is the private property of the Royal Family. It contains **Frogmore House,** a lavish royal residence. Completed in 1684, Frogmore was bought by George III as a gift for his wife, Queen Charlotte. The sprawling white mansion later became a beloved retreat of Queen Victoria. Today it's mainly used for official functions, but you can visit by guided tour (£9.80) on a handful of days in July and August; see ⊕ *www.royalcollection. org.uk,* or call *020/7766–7321* for more information. ⊠ *Entrances on A329, A332, B383, and Wick La.* ☎ *01784/435544* ⊕ *www.windsor. gov.uk/things-to-do/windsor-great-park-p236491* ⌨ *Free; Saville Garden £9.75 Mar.–Nov., free Dec.–Feb.* ⊙ *Daily dawn–dusk. Last admission 30 min before closing.*

**19**

## WHERE TO EAT

**$$$$**  **✕ Fat Duck.** One of the top restaurants in the country, and ranked by
MODERN BRITISH  many food writers among the best in the world, this extraordinary
Fodor's Choice  place packs in fans of hypercreative, hyperexpensive cuisine. "Culi-
★  nary alchemist" Heston Blumenthal is famed for bizarre taste combinations—scrambled-egg-and-bacon ice cream, for example—and his
laboratorylike kitchen, where this advocate of molecular gastronomy
creates his dishes. There's just one sitting per night, which is just as well,
as the 14-course tasting menu takes around 4½ hours to get through. It's
impossible to say exactly where the culinary flights of fancy may take
you. A tray of oak moss with truffle toast is brought to life with liquid
nitrogen, poured like gravy (it smells like a forest after a rainstorm); at
one point you're given headphones, which play the sounds of the sea
from conch shells, while you munch edible sand and seaweed. It's as
much theater as it is food, and the very definition of "not for everyone."
However, those with a taste for adventure (and deep pockets) find it
a magical experience. The Fat Duck is a discreet building in the small
village of Bray; look for the duck-inspired implements hanging outside.
You must reserve a table two months in advance, and the booking process is strict; call or see the website for details. ⑤ *Average main: £225*
✉ *High St., Bray-on-Thames* ☎ *01628/580333* ⊕ *www.fatduck.co.uk*
⊘ *Closed Sun. and Mon.* ⌘ *Reservations essential.*

**$**  **✕ Two Brewers.** Locals congregate in a pair of low-ceiling rooms at this
BRITISH  tiny 17th-century establishment by the gates of Windsor Great Park.
Those under 18 aren't allowed inside the pub (although they can be
served at a few outdoor tables), but adults will find a suitable collection of wine, espresso, and local beer, plus an excellent menu with
such dishes as sausages with mash and pea gravy, fish cakes, and a
good selection of hot and cold sandwiches. On Sunday the pub serves
a traditional, hearty lunchtime roast. ⑤ *Average main: £15* ✉ *34 Park
St.* ☎ *01753/855426* ⊕ *www.twobrewerswindsor.co.uk* ⊘ *No dinner
Fri.–Sun.* ⌘ *Reservations essential.*

# UNDERSTANDING LONDON

**LONDON AT-A-GLANCE**

**ENGLISH VOCABULARY**

**BOOKS AND MOVIES**

# LONDON AT-A-GLANCE

## FAST FACTS

**Type of government:** Representative democracy. In 1999 the Greater London Authority Act reestablished a single local governing body for the Greater London area, consisting of an elected mayor and the 25-member London Assembly. Elections, first held in 2000, take place every four years.

**Population:** Inner city 3 million, Greater London 7.7 million

**Population density:** 12,331 people per square mile

**Median age:** 38.4

**Infant mortality rate:** 5 per 1,000 births

**Language:** English. More than 300 languages are spoken in London. All city government documents are translated into Arabic, Bengali, Chinese, Greek, Gujurati, Hindi, Punjabi, Turkish, Urdu, and Vietnamese.

**Ethnic and racial groups:** White British 70%, White Irish 3%, Other White 9%, Indian 6%, Bangladeshi 2%, Pakistani 2%, other Asian 2%, Black African 6%, Black Caribbean 5%, Chinese 1%, Other 3%.

**Religion:** Christian 58%, nonaffiliated 15%, Muslim 8%, Hindu 4%, Jewish 2%, Sikh 1%, other religion 1%, Buddhist 0.8%.

*When a man is tired of London, he is tired of life; for there is in London all that life can afford.*

*—Samuel Johnson*

## GEOGRAPHY AND ENVIRONMENT

**Latitude:** 51° N (same as Calgary, Canada; Kiev, Ukraine; Prague, Czech Republic)

**Longitude:** 0° (same as Accra, Ghana). A brass line in the ground in Greenwich marks the prime meridian (0° longitude).

**Elevation:** 49 feet

**Land area:** City, 67 square miles; metro area, 625 square miles

**Terrain:** River plain, rolling hills, and parkland

**Natural hazards:** Drought in warmer summers, minor localized flooding of the Thames caused by surge tides from the North Atlantic

**Environmental issues:** The city has been improving its air quality, but up to 1,600 people die each year from health problems related to London's polluted air. Only half of London's rivers and canals received passing grades for water quality from 1999 through 2001. More than £12 million ($22 million) is spent annually to ensure the city's food safety.

*I'm leaving because the weather is too good. I hate London when it's not raining.*

*—Groucho Marx*

## ECONOMY

**Workforce:** 3.8 million; financial/real estate 28%, health care 10%, manufacturing 4%, education 7%, construction 5%, public administration 5%

**Unemployment:** 7.2%

**Major industries:** The arts, banking, government, insurance, tourism

*London: a nation, not a city.*

*—Benjamin Disraeli, Lothair*

# ENGLISH VOCABULARY

You and a Londoner may speak the same language, but some phrases definitely get lost in translation once they cross the Atlantic.

| BRITISH ENGLISH | ENGLISH |
| --- | --- |

## BASIC TERMS AND EVERYDAY ITEMS

| | |
| --- | --- |
| bill | check |
| flat | apartment |
| holiday | vacation |
| lift | elevator |
| nappy | diaper |
| note | bill (currency) |
| plaster | Band-Aid |
| queue | line |
| row | argument |
| rubbish | trash |
| tin | can |
| toilet/loo/WC | bathroom |

## CLOTHING

| | |
| --- | --- |
| braces | suspenders |
| bum bag | fanny pack |
| dressing gown | robe |
| jumper | sweater |
| pants/knickers | underpants/briefs |
| rucksack | backpack |
| suspender | garter |
| tights | pantyhose |
| trainers | sneakers |
| trousers | pants |
| vest | undershirt |
| waistcoat | vest |

## TRANSPORTATION

| | |
| --- | --- |
| bonnet | hood |
| boot | trunk |

| BRITISH ENGLISH | ENGLISH |
| --- | --- |
| coach | bus (long-distance) |
| pavement | sidewalk |
| petrol | gas |
| pram | baby carriage |
| puncture | flat |
| windscreen | windshield |

## FOOD

| | |
| --- | --- |
| aubergine | eggplant |
| banger | sausage |
| biscuit | cookie |
| chips | fries |
| courgette | zucchini |
| crisps | potato chips |
| jam | jelly |
| main course (or main) | entrée |
| pudding | dessert |
| rocket | arugula |
| starter | appetizer |
| sweet | candy |
| tea | early dinner |

## SLANG

| | |
| --- | --- |
| all right | hi there |
| cheers | thank you |
| chuffed | pleased |
| fit | attractive |
| geezer | dude |
| guv'nor, gaffer | boss |
| hard | tough |
| mate | buddy |
| sound | good |
| Ta | thank you |

# BOOKS AND MOVIES

## London in Books

London has been the focus of countless books and essays. For sonorous eloquence, you still must reach back more than half a century to Henry James's *English Hours* and Virginia Woolf's *The London Scene*. Today most suggested reading lists begin with V. S. Pritchett's *London Perceived* and H. V. Morton's *In Search of London*, both decades old. Four more-up-to-date books with a general compass are Peter Ackroyd's *Thames* and his anecdotal *London: The Biography*, which traces the city's growth from the Druids to the 21st century; John Russell's *London*, a sumptuously illustrated art book; and Christopher Hibbert's *In London: The Biography of a City*. Stephen Inwood's *A History of London* explores the city from its Roman roots to its swinging '60s heyday. Piet Schreuders's *The Beatles' London* follows the footsteps of the Fab Four.

That noted, there are books galore on the various facets of the city. *The Art and Architecture of London*, by Ann Saunders, is fairly comprehensive. *Inside London: Discovering the Classic Interiors of London*, by Joe Friedman and Peter Aprahamian, has magnificent color photographs of hidden and overlooked shops, clubs, and townhouses. For a wonderful take on the golden age of the city's regal mansions, see Christopher Simon Sykes's *Private Palaces: Life in the Great London Houses*. For various other aspects of the city, consult Mervyn Blatch's helpful *A Guide to London's Churches*, Andrew Crowe's *The Parks and Woodlands of London*, Sheila Fairfield's *The Streets of London*, Ann Saunders's *Regent's Park*, Ian Norrie's *Hampstead, Highgate Village, and Kenwood*, and Suzanne Ebel's *A Guide to London's Riverside: Hampton Court to Greenwich*. For keen walkers, there are two books by Andrew Duncan: *Secret London* and *Walking Village London*. *City Secrets: London*, edited by Robert Kahn, is a handsome book of anecdotes from London writers,

artists, and historians about their favorite places in the city. For the last word on just about every subject, see *The London Encyclopaedia*, edited by Ben Weinreb and Christopher Hibbert. HarperCollins's *London Photographic Atlas* has a plethora of bird's-eye images of the capital. For an alternative view of the city, it would be hard to better Iain Sinclair's witty and intelligent *London Orbital: A Walk Around the M25* in which he scrutinizes the history, mythology, and politics of London from the viewpoint of its ugly ring road. Sinclair is also the editor of *London: City of Disappearances*, an anthology exploring what has vanished.

Of course, the history and spirit of the city are also to be found in celebrations of great authors, British heroes, and architects. Peter Ackroyd's massive *Dickens* elucidates how the great author shaped today's view of the city; Martin Gilbert's magisterial, multivolume *Churchill* traces the city through some of its greatest trials; J. Mansbridge's *John Nash* details the London buildings of this great architect. Liza Picard evokes mid-18th-century London in *Dr. Johnson's London*. For musical theater buffs, Mike Leigh's *Gilbert and Sullivan's London* takes a romantic look at the two artists' lives and times in the capital's grand theaters and wild nightspots. *Rodinsky's Room*, by Rachel Lichtenstein and Iain Sinclair, is a fascinating exploration of East End Jewish London and the mysterious disappearance of one of its occupants.

Maureen Waller's *1700: Scenes from London Life* is a fascinating look at the daily life of Londoners in the 18th century. Nineteenth-century London—the city of Queen Victoria, Tennyson, and Dickens—comes alive through *Mayhew's London*, a massive study of the London poor by Henry Mayhew, and Gustave Doré's *London*, an unforgettable series of engravings of the city (often reprinted in modern editions) that detail its horrifying slums and grand avenues. When it comes to fiction, of course, Dickens's immortal works top the list. Stay-at-home detectives have long walked the streets of London, thanks to great mysteries by Dorothy L. Sayers, Agatha Christie, Ngaio Marsh, and Antonia Fraser. Cops and bad guys wind their way around 1960s London in Jake Arnott's pulp fiction books, *The Long Firm* and *He Kills Coppers*. Martin Amis's *London Fields* tracks a murder mystery through West London. For so-called "tart noir," pick up anything by Stella Duffy. Marie Belloc-Lowndes's *The Lodger* is a fictional account of London's most deadly villain, Jack the Ripper. Victorian London was never so salacious as in Sarah Waters's story of a young girl who travels the theaters as a singer, the Soho squares as a male prostitute, and the East End as a communist in *Tipping the Velvet*. Late-20th-century London, with its diverse ethnic makeup, is the star of Zadie Smith's famed novel *White Teeth*. The vibrancy and cultural diversity of London's East End come to life in Monica Ali's *Brick Lane*.

## London in Film

Many films—from *Waterloo Bridge* and *Georgy Girl* to *Secrets and Lies* and *Notting Hill*—have used London as their setting. The great musicals Walt Disney's *Mary Poppins*, George Cukor's *My Fair Lady*, and Sir Carol Reed's *Oliver!* evoke the Hollywood soundstage version of London.

Children of all ages enjoy Stephen Herek's *101 Dalmatians*, with Glenn Close as fashion-savvy Cruella de Vil. King's Cross Station in London was shot to cinematic fame by the movie version of J.K. Rowling's *Harry Potter and the Philosopher's Stone*. Look for cameos by the city in all other Harry Potter films.

The swinging '60s are loosely portrayed in M. Jay Roach's *Austin Powers: International Man of Mystery*, full of references to British slang and some great opening scenes in London. For a truer picture of the '60s in London, Michelangelo Antonioni weaves a mystery plot around the world of a London fashion photographer in *Blow-Up*. British gangster films came into their own with Guy Ritchie's amusing tales of London thieves in *Lock, Stock, and Two Smoking Barrels*, filmed almost entirely in London, and the follow-up *Snatch*. More sobering portraits of London criminal life include Neil Jordan's *Mona Lisa*, Paul McGuigan's *Gangster No. 1*, and John Mackenzie's *The Long Good Friday*. Of course, the original tough guy is 007, and his best exploits in London are featured in the introductory chase scene in *The World Is Not Enough*.

Sir Arthur Conan Doyle knew the potential of London as a chilling setting, and John Landis's *An American Werewolf in London* and Hitchcock's *The 39 Steps* and *The Man Who Knew Too Much* exploit the Gothic and sinister qualities of the city. For a fascinating look at Renaissance London, watch John Madden's *Shakespeare in Love*. Dickensian London is indelibly depicted in David Lean's *Oliver Twist*.

Some modern-day romantic comedies that use London as a backdrop are Peter Howitt's *Sliding Doors* with Gwyneth Paltrow and the screen adaptations of Helen Fielding's *Bridget Jones's Diary* (and its sequel), starring Renée Zellweger, Hugh Grant, and Colin Firth. Glossy London is depicted in Woody Allen's *Match Point*, bohemian London in David Kane's *This Year's Love*, gritty London in Shane Meadow's *Somers Town*, and post-zombie London in Danny Boyle's *28 Days Later*, while Patrick Kellior's *London* offers a uniquely informed, idiosyncratic view of the city.

# TRAVEL SMART
# LONDON

# GETTING HERE AND AROUND

Central London and its surrounding districts are divided into 32 boroughs (33, counting the City of London). More useful for finding your way around, however, are the subdivisions of London into postal districts. The first one or two letters give the location: N means north, NW means northwest, and so on. Don't expect the numbering to be logical, however. You won't, for example, find W2 next to W3. The general rule is that the lower numbers, such as W1 or SW1, are closest to Buckingham Palace, but it is not consistent—SE17 is closer to the city center than E4, for example.

## ▌ AIR TRAVEL

Flying time to London is about 6½ hours from New York, 7½ hours from Chicago, 11 hours from San Francisco, and 21½ hours from Sydney.

For flights out of London, the general rule is that you should be at the airport at least one hour before your scheduled departure time for domestic flights and two hours before international flights for off-peak travel.

**Airline Security Issues Transportation Security Administration.** ☎ 866/289-9673 ⊕ www.tsa.gov.

### AIRPORTS

Most international flights to London arrive at either Heathrow Airport (LHR), 15 miles west of London, or at Gatwick Airport (LGW), 27 miles south of the capital. Most flights from the United States go to Heathrow, which is divided into five terminals, with Terminals 3–5 handling transatlantic flights. Gatwick is London's second gateway. It has grown from a European airport into an airport that also serves dozens of U.S. destinations. A third airport, Stansted (STN), is 35 miles northeast of the city; it handles European and domestic traffic. Three smaller airports, Luton (LTN), 30 miles

north of town, Southend (SEN), 40 miles to the east, and business-oriented London City (in East London E16) mainly handle flights to Europe.

**Airport Information Gatwick Airport.** ☎ 0844/892-0322 ⊕ www.gatwickairport. com. **Heathrow Airport.** ☎ 0844/335-1801 ⊕ www.heathrow.com. **London City Airport.** ☎ 020/7646-0088 ⊕ www.londoncityairport. com. **Luton Airport.** ☎ 01582/405-100 ⊕ www.london-luton.co.uk. **Southend Airport.** ☎ 01702/538-500 ⊕ www.southendairport. com. **Stansted Airport.** ☎ 0844/355-1803 ⊕ www.stanstedairport.com.

### GROUND TRANSPORTATION

London has excellent if pricey bus and train connections between its airports and central London. If you're arriving at Heathrow, you can pick up a map and fare schedule at the Transport for London (TfL) Information Centre, in the Underground station serving Terminals 1–3. Train service can be quick, but the downside (for trains from all airports) is that you must get yourself and your luggage to the train via a series of escalators and connecting trams. Airport link buses (generally National Express airport buses) may ease the luggage factor and drop you closer to central hotels, but they're subject to London traffic, which can be horrendous and make the trip drag on for hours. Taxis can be more convenient than buses, but beware that prices can go through the roof. Airport Travel Line has additional transfer information and takes advance booking for transfers between airports and into London.

| FROM HEATHROW TO CENTRAL LONDON | | |
|---|---|---|
| TRAVEL MODE | TIME | COST |
| Taxi | 1 hour+ | £50–£70 (depending on traffic) |
| Heathrow Express Train | 15 minutes | £21.50 (£35 round-trip), £29.50 for first class |
| Underground | 50 minutes | £5.70 one-way (less with Oyster card) |
| National Express Bus | 1 hour | From £6 one-way |

**Heathrow by Bus:** National Express buses take one hour to reach the city center (Victoria) and cost from £6 one-way and £11 round-trip (book online for best prices). The National Express Hotel Hoppa service runs from all airports to 27 hotels near the airport (from £4.50). SkyShuttle offers a shared minibus service between Heathrow and any London hotel. The N9 night bus runs to Aldwych every 20 minutes midnight–5 am; it takes just over an hour and costs £1.50 (you need to pay with an Oyster card or a contactless debit/credit card). Please note: the N9 doesn't stop at Terminal 4; take Bus Nos. 490 or 482 to Terminal 5 and catch it there.

**Heathrow by Tube and Train:** The cheap, direct route into London is via the Piccadilly line of the Underground (London's extensive subway system, or "Tube"). Trains normally run every four to eight minutes from all terminals from early morning until just before midnight. The 50-minute trip into central London costs £5.70 one-way and connects with other central Tube lines. The Heathrow Express train is comfortable and convenient, if costly, speeding into London's Paddington station in 15 minutes. Standard one-way tickets cost £21.50 (£35 round-trip) and £29.50 for first class. Book ahead (online is the cheapest option; at a counter/kiosk

# NAVIGATING LONDON

London is a confusing city to navigate, even for people who've visited it a few times. Its streets are arranged in medieval patterns that no longer make much sense, meaning that you can't always use logic to find your way around. A good map is essential, and public transportation can be a lifesaver: buses will take you magically from point A to point B, and the Tube is often the quickest way to reach your destination. Here are some basic tips to help you find your way around.

■ Although free tourist maps can be handy, they're usually quite basic and include only major streets. If you're going to be doing lots of wandering around, buy the pocket-size map book *London A–Z*, which is sold in bookstores and Tube and train stations throughout the city. Its detailed maps are invaluable.

■ To find your way, look for tall landmarks near where you are headed: the London Eye, for example, or the cross atop St. Paul's Cathedral—or the most obvious of all, Big Ben.

■ If you get properly lost, the best people to ask are the Londoners hustling by you; they know the area like nobody else. The worst people to ask are the people working in souvenir kiosks and street vendors handing out the local *Evening Standard* newspaper; they're famously rude and unhelpful to lost tourists.

■ The tourist hubs of Soho, Covent Garden, Leicester Square, and Trafalgar Square are separated from one another by only a few blocks. Taking the Tube from one to another actually takes longer than walking.

■ On the other hand, when you're lost, the Tube is often the shortest distance between two points. Don't hesitate to use it.

less so), as tickets are more expensive to buy on board. There's daily service 5:10 am–11:40 pm, with departures usually every 15 minutes. The Heathrow Connect service leaves from Paddington station and makes five local stops before arriving at Terminals 1, 3, and 5. It takes 25 minutes, only a little more time than the Express, although trains are less frequent (two an hour in peak times). One-way tickets are £10.10.

**Heathrow by Taxi:** This is an expensive and time-consuming option. The city's congestion charge (£11.50) may be added to the bill if your hotel is in the charging zone; you run the risk of getting stuck in traffic; and if you take a taxi from the stand, the price will be even more expensive (whereas a minicab booked ahead is a set price). The trip can take more than an hour and can cost in the region of £60, depending on time of day.

**Gatwick by Bus:** An hourly bus service runs from Gatwick's north and south terminals to London's Victoria station, with stops at Hooley, Coulsdon, Mitcham, Streatham, Stockwell, and Pimlico. The journey takes upward of 90 minutes (depending on time of day) and costs from £8 one-way. The easyBus service runs to West London (Earl's Court) or Waterloo from as little as £2 if booked in advance; the later the ticket is booked online, the higher the price (up to £11 on board).

**Gatwick by Train:** The fast, nonstop Gatwick Express leaves for Victoria station every 15 minutes 4:35 am–1:35 am. The 30-minute trip costs £19.90 one-way, and £34.90 round-trip, though cheaper tickets are available online. The Thameslink Great Northern rail company runs nonexpress services that are cheaper; Thameslink trains run regularly throughout the day to St. Pancras International, London Bridge, and Blackfriars stations; departures are every 15 minutes (hourly during the night), and the journey takes 45–55 minutes. Tickets are from £7.90 one-way to St. Pancras International. FlyBy service to Victoria (£11 single) is

not express, taking almost an hour, and the fare applies only on trains operated by Southern Trains.

**Stansted by Bus:** Hourly service on National Express Airport bus A6 (24 hours a day) to Victoria Coach station costs from £12 one-way, £19 round-trip, and takes about 1 hour 45 minutes. Stops include Golders Green, Finchley Road, St. John's Wood, Baker Street, Marble Arch, and Hyde Park Corner. The easyBus service to Victoria via Baker Street costs from £2 one-way, but book early and online for best prices.

**Stansted by Train:** The Stansted Express to Liverpool Street station (with a stop at Tottenham Hale) runs daily every 15 minutes, 5:30 am–12:30 am. The 50-minute trip costs £19 one-way, £32 round-trip, if booked online. Tickets cost more when purchased on board.

**Luton by Bus and Train:** An airport shuttle runs from Luton Airport to the nearby Luton Airport Parkway station, from which you can take a train or bus into London (this shuttle is free if you have bought a rail ticket in advance; otherwise it's £1.60 one-way). From there, the Thameslink Great Northern train service runs to St. Pancras, Farringdon, Blackfriars, and London Bridge. The journey takes about 30 minutes. Trains leave every 10 minutes or so during the day, and hourly during the night. Single tickets cost from £12.40 one-way, if booked in advance. The Green Line 757 bus service from Luton to Victoria station runs three times an hour, takes about 90 minutes, and costs from £10 one-way, if booked in advance.

### TRANSFERS BETWEEN AIRPORTS

Allow at least two to three hours for an inter-airport transfer. The cheapest option—but most complicated—is public transportation: from Gatwick to Stansted, for instance, you can catch the nonexpress commuter train from Gatwick to Victoria station, take the Tube to Liverpool Street station, then catch the train to Stansted from there. To get from Heathrow to

Gatwick by public transportation, take the Tube to King's Cross, then change to the Victoria line, get to Victoria station, and then take the commuter train to Gatwick.

The National Express airport bus is the most direct option. Between Gatwick and Heathrow, buses pick up passengers every 15–20 minutes 5:35 am–midnight from both airports. The trip takes around 75 minutes, and the fare is from £20 one-way, but it's advisable to book tickets in advance. National Express buses between Stansted and Gatwick depart every 30–45 minutes and can take 3–4½ hours, depending on traffic. The adult one-way fare is from £20. Some airlines may offer shuttle services as well—check with your travel agent in advance of your journey.

**Contacts easyBus.** ⊕ www.easybus.co.uk. **Gatwick Express.** ☎ 0345/850–1530 ⊕ www.gatwickexpress.com. **Heathrow Express.** ☎ 0345/600–1515 ⊕ www.heathrowexpress.com. **National Express.** ☎ 0871/781–8181 ⊕ www.nationalexpress.com. **SkyShuttle.** ☎ 0845/481–0960 ⊕ www.skyshuttle.co.uk. **Stansted Express.** ☎ 0345/600–7245 ⊕ www.stanstedexpress.com. **Thameslink Great Northern.** ☎ 0345/026–4700 ⊕ www.thameslinkrailway.com.

**Transfer Information Airport Travel Line.** ☎ 0871/200–2233 ⊕ www.travelline.co.uk.

## FLIGHTS

British Airways is the national flagship carrier and offers mostly nonstop flights from more than 20 U.S. cities to Heathrow and Gatwick airports, along with flights to Manchester, Birmingham, and Glasgow. It also offers flights to New York from London City Airport near Docklands.

**Airline Contacts American Airlines.** ☎ 207/660–2300, 0844/369–9899 in London ⊕ www.aa.com. **British Airways.** ☎ 800/247–9297 in U.S., 0844/493–0787 in U.K. ⊕ www.britishairways.com. **Delta Airlines.** ☎ 800/241–4141 for international reservations, 020/7660–0767 in U.K. ⊕ www.delta.com. **United Airlines.** ☎ 800/864–8331 for international reservations, 0845/607–6760 in U.K. ⊕ www.united.com. **Virgin Atlantic.** ☎ 800/862–8621 in U.S., 0344/209–7777 in U.K. ⊕ www.virgin-atlantic.com.

## ∎ BIKE TRAVEL

London's mayor, Boris Johnson, is a real cycling enthusiast and keen to make the capital more bike-friendly. A 24-hour bike-rental program called Santander Cycles enables Londoners to pick up a "Boris bike" at one of more than 700 docking stations and return it at another. The first 30 minutes are free, then it's £2 for every 30-minute period thereafter. There is also a £2-per-day access charge. Fees are payable online, by phone, or at docking stations, by credit or debit cards only—cash is not accepted. To sign up, a user goes to the TfL (Transport for London) website and then receives a bike key in the mail, so this very popular system is really only practical for locals, not most tourists.

## ∎ BUS TRAVEL

### ARRIVING AND DEPARTING

National Express is the biggest British long-distance bus operator and the nearest equivalent to Greyhound. It's not as fast as traveling by train, but it's comfortable (with bathrooms on board). Services depart mainly from Victoria Coach station, a well-signposted short walk behind the Victoria mainline train station. The departures point is on the corner of Buckingham Palace Road; this is also the main information point. The arrivals point is opposite, at Elizabeth Bridge. National Express buses travel to all large and mid-size cities in southern England and the midlands. Scotland and the north are not as well served. The station is extremely busy around holidays and weekends. Arrive at least 30 minutes before departure so you can find the correct exit gate. Smoking is not permitted on board.

Another bus company, Megabus, offers cross-country fares for as little as £1 per person. The company's single- and double-decker buses serve an extensive array of cities across Great Britain with a cheerful budget attitude. In London, buses for all destinations depart from the Green Line bus stand at Victoria station. Megabus does not accommodate wheelchairs, and the company strictly limits luggage to one piece per person checked, and one piece of hand luggage.

Green Line serves the counties surrounding London, as well as airports. Bus stops (there's no central bus station) are on Buckingham Palace Road, between the Victoria train station and Victoria Coach station.

Tickets on many long-distance routes are cheaper if purchased in advance, and traveling midweek costs less than over weekends and at holiday periods.

## GETTING AROUND LONDON

Private, as opposed to municipal, buses are known as coaches. Although London is famous for its double-decker buses, the old beloved rattletrap Routemasters, with the jump-on, jump-off back platforms, now only serve a single "heritage" route (No. 15)—from Trafalgar Square down Fleet Street and on to St. Paul's Cathedral. That said, modernized Routemaster buses have taken to the streets on other routes.

Bus stops are clearly indicated; signs at bus stops feature a red TfL symbol on a plain white background. You must flag the bus down at some stops. Each numbered route is listed on the main stop, and buses have a large number on the front with their end destination. Not all buses run the full route at all times; check with the driver to be sure. You can pick up a free bus guide at a TfL Travel Information Centre (at Euston, Liverpool Street, Piccadilly Circus, King's Cross, and Victoria Tube stations; and at Heathrow Airport).

Buses are a good way of seeing the town, particularly if you plan to hop on and off to cover many sights, but don't take a bus if you're in a hurry, as traffic can really slow them down. To get off, press the red "Stop" buttons mounted on poles near the doors. You will usually see a "Bus Stopping" sign light up. Expect to get sardined during rush hour, 8–9:30 am and 4:30–6:30 pm.

Night buses, denoted by an "N" before their route numbers, run midnight–5 am on a more restricted route than day buses. However, some night-bus routes should be approached with caution, and the top deck avoided (the danger is that muggings are most likely to occur there, since it's farthest from both the exit doors and the drivers). All night buses run by request stop, so flag them down if you're waiting, or push the button if you want to alight.

All London buses are now cash-free, which means you must buy your ticket *before* you board the bus. Ticket machines are located at most bus stops, but they can be the most expensive option: tickets bought here cost £2.50 for all journeys, as opposed to £1.50 if you pay by prepaid Oyster card or "contactless" payment card. Visitor Oyster cards cost £3, but must be purchased either before you arrive or at London's Standsted airport. Normal Oyster cards, which cost £5, are available from ticket desks at all major airports or at any Tube station and are transferable if you have money left over. Contactless cards are meant to be the future of London travel: you touch a compatible debit or credit card on a bus or Tube-station's reader, and the fare is automatically debited from your bank account.

One alternative is to buy a one- or seven-day Travelcard, which is good for both Tube and bus travel. Travelcards can be bought at Tube stations, travel information centers, and some newsagents. However, note that seven-day Travelcards bought in London *must be loaded onto an Oyster card*. Although using a Travelcard may save you some money, it might be easier to just add additional money to your Oyster card as needed, since there are machines at all Tube stations and at lots of London newsagents. A seven-day paper Travelcard can only be purchased in advance, online. However you buy your ticket, just make sure you have one: traveling without a valid ticket makes you liable for a significant fine (£80). Buses are supposed to swing by most stops every five or six minutes, but in reality you often end up waiting a bit longer, although those in the city center are quite reliable.

**Long-Distance Bus Contacts easyBus.** ⊕ *www.easybus.co.uk.* **Green Line.** ☎ *0344/801–7261* ⊕ *www.greenline.co.uk.* **Megabus.** ☎ *0900/160–0900* ⊕ *www.megabus.com.* **National Express.** ☎ *0871/781–8181* ⊕ *www.nationalexpress.com.*

**Bus Information Transport for London.** ☎ *0343/222–1234* ⊕ *www.tfl.gov.uk.* **Victoria Coach Station.** ✉ *164 Buckingham Palace Rd., Victoria* ☎ *0343/222–1234* Ⓜ *Victoria.*

## ■ CAR TRAVEL

The best advice on driving in London is this: don't. London's streets are a winding mass of chaos, made worse by one way roads. Parking is also restrictive and expensive, and traffic is tediously slow at most times of the day; during rush hours (8–9:30 am and 4:30–6:30 pm) it often grinds to a standstill, particularly on Friday, when everyone wants to leave town. Avoid city-center shopping areas, including the roads feeding Oxford Street, Kensington, and Knightsbridge. Other main roads into the city center are also busy, such as King's Cross and Euston in the north. Watch out also for cyclists and motorcycle couriers, who weave between cars and pedestrians that seem to come out of nowhere, and you may get a heavy fine for straying into a bus lane during its operating hours—check the signs.

If you are staying in London for the duration of your trip, there's virtually no reason to rent a car, because the city and its suburbs are widely covered by public transportation. However, you may want a car for day trips to castles or stately homes out in the countryside. Consider renting your car in a medium-size town in the area where you'll be traveling, and then journeying there by train and picking up the car once you arrive. Rental rates are generally reasonable, and insurance costs are lower than in comparable U.S. cities. Rates generally begin at £20 per day for a small economy car (such as a subcompact General Motors Vauxhall Corsa, or Renault Clio), usually with manual transmission. Air-conditioning and unlimited mileage generally come with the larger-size automatic cars.

In London your U.S. driver's license is acceptable (as long as you are over 23 years old, with no driving convictions). If you have a driver's license from a country other than the United States, it may not be recognized in the United Kingdom. An International Driver's Permit is a good idea no matter what; it's available from the American (AAA) or Canadian (CAA) Automobile Association and, in the United Kingdom, from the Automobile Association (AA) or Royal Automobile Club (RAC). International permits are universally recognized, and having one may save you a problem with the local authorities.

Remember that Britain drives on the left, and the rest of Europe on the right. Therefore, you may want to leave your right-side rental in Britain and pick up a left-side rental if you cross the Channel.

### CONGESTION CHARGE

Designed to reduce traffic through central London, a congestion charge has been instituted. Vehicles (with some exemptions) entering central London on weekdays 7 am–6 pm (excluding public holidays) have to pay £11.50 per day; it can be paid up to 90 days in advance, or on the day of travel, or on the following "charging day," when the fee goes up to £14. Day-, month-, and yearlong passes are available on the Congestion Charging page of the Transport for London website, at gas stations, parking lots (car parks), by mail, by phone, and by SMS text message. One day's payment is good for all access into the charging zone on that day. Traffic signs designate the entrance to congestion areas, and cameras read car license plates and send the information to a database. Drivers who don't pay the congestion charge by midnight of the next charging day following the day of driving are penalized £130, which is reduced to £65 if paid within 14 days.

**Information Congestion Charge Customer Service.** ☏ *0343/222–2222 in U.K. only, 020/7649–9122* ⊕ *www.cclondon.com.* **Transport for London.** ☏ *0343/222–1234* ⊕ *www.tfl.gov.uk.*

## GASOLINE

Gasoline (petrol) is sold in liters and is expensive (at this writing about £1.10 per liter—around $6.15 per gallon). Unleaded petrol, denoted by green pump lines, is predominant. Premium and Super Premium are the two varieties, and most cars run on regular Premium. Supermarket pumps usually offer the best value. You won't find many service stations in the center of town; these are generally on main, multilane trunk roads out of the center. Service is self-serve, except in small villages, where gas stations are likely to be closed on Sunday and late evening. Most stations accept major credit cards.

## PARKING

During the day—and probably at all times—it's safest to believe that you can park nowhere except at a meter, in a pay-and-display bay, or in a garage; otherwise, you run the risk of an expensive ticket, plus possibly even more expensive clamping and towing fees (some boroughs are clamp-free). Restrictions are indicated by the "No Waiting" parking signpost on the sidewalk (these restrictions vary from street to street), and restricted areas include single yellow lines or double yellow lines, and Residents' Parking bays. Parking at a bus stop is prohibited; parking in bus lanes, restricted. On Red Routes, indicated by red lines, you are not allowed to park or even stop. It's illegal to park on the sidewalk, across entrances, or on white zigzag lines approaching a pedestrian crossing.

Meters have an insatiable hunger in the inner city—a 20p coin may buy just three minutes—and some will permit only a maximum two-hour stay. Meters take 20p and £1 coins, pay-and-display machines 10p, 20p, 50p, £1, and £2 coins. Some take payment by credit card. In some parts of central London, meters have been almost entirely replaced by pay-and-display machines that require payment by cell phone. You will need to set up an account to do this (⊕ *www.westminster.gov.uk*). Meter parking is free after 6:30 or 8:30 in the evening, on Sunday, and on holidays; always check the sign. In the evening, after restrictions end, meter bays are free. After meters are free, you can also park on single yellow lines—but not double yellow lines. In the daytime, take advantage of the many NCP parking lots in the center of town (from about £9 per hour, up to six hours).

**Information NCP.** ☏ *0345/050–7080* ⊕ *www.ncp.co.uk.*

## ROADSIDE EMERGENCIES

If your car is stolen, you're in a car accident, or your car breaks down and there's nobody around to help you, contact the police by dialing 999.

The general procedure for a breakdown is the following: position the red hazard triangle (which should be in the trunk of the car) a few paces away from the rear of the car. Leave the hazard warning lights on. Along highways (motorways), emergency roadside telephone booths are positioned at intervals within walking distance. Contact the car-rental company or an auto club. The main auto clubs in the United Kingdom are the Automobile Association (AA) and the RAC. If you're a member of the American Automobile Association (AAA), check your membership details before you depart for Britain; under a reciprocal agreement, roadside assistance in the United Kingdom should cost you nothing. You can join and receive roadside assistance from the AA on the spot, but the charge is higher (around £95) than a simple membership fee.

**Emergency Services American Automobile Association.** ☎ *800/564-6222* ⊕ *www.aaa.com.* **Automobile Association.** ☎ *0800/085-2721, 161/333-0004 from outside U.K., 0800/887-766 for emergency roadside assistance from mobile phones* ⊕ *www.theaa.com.* **Royal Automobile Club.** ☎ *0800/828-282 for emergency roadside assistance, 0333/159-1111 for membership inquiries* ⊕ *www.rac.co.uk.*

### RULES OF THE ROAD

London is a mass of narrow, one-way roads and narrow, two-way streets no bigger than the one-way roads. If you must risk life and limb and drive in London, note that the speed limit is either 20 or 30 mph—unless you see the large 40 mph signs found only in the suburbs. Speed bumps are sprinkled about with abandon in case you forget. Speed is strictly controlled and cameras, mounted on occasional lampposts, photograph speeders for ticketing.

Medium-size circular intersections are often designed as "roundabouts" (marked by signs in which three curved arrows form a circle). On these, cars travel left in a circle and incoming cars must yield to those already on their way around from the right. Make sure you're in the correct lane when approaching a roundabout—this will make leaving the roundabout at your desired exit easier. Stay in the left lane if you wish to go left, the middle lane for going straight ahead, and the right-hand lane for turning right. Signal when about to leave the roundabout.

Jaywalking is not illegal in London and everybody does it, despite the fact that striped crossings with blinking yellow lights mounted on poles at either end—called "zebra crossings"—give pedestrians the right-of-way to cross. Cars should treat zebra crossings like stop signs if a pedestrian is waiting to cross or already starting to cross. It's illegal to pass another vehicle at a zebra crossing.

At other crossings (including intersections) pedestrians must yield to traffic, but they do have the right-of-way over traffic turning left at controlled crossings—if they have the nerve.

Traffic lights sometimes have arrows directing left or right turns; try to catch a glimpse of the road markings in time, and don't get into the turn lane if you mean to go straight ahead. Turning on a red light is not permitted. Signs at the beginning and end of designated bus lanes give the time restrictions for use (usually during peak hours); if you're caught driving on bus lanes during restricted hours, you will be fined. By law, seat belts must be worn in the front and back seats. Drink-driving laws are strictly enforced, and it's safest to avoid alcohol altogether if you'll be driving. The legal limit is 80 milligrams of alcohol per 100 milliliters of blood, which roughly translated means two units of alcohol—two small glasses of wine, one pint of beer, or one glass of whiskey.

## ■ DLR: DOCKLANDS LIGHT RAILWAY

For reaching destinations in East London, the quiet, driverless Docklands Light Railway (DLR) is a good alternative, with interesting views of the area.

The DLR connects with the Tube network at Bank and Tower Hill stations as well as at Canary Wharf. It goes to London City Airport, the Docklands financial district, and Greenwich, running 5:30 am–12:30 am Monday–Saturday, 7 am–11:30 pm Sunday. The DLR takes Oyster cards and Travelcards, and fares are the same as those on the Tube.

**Information Transport for London.** ☎ *0343/222-1234* ⊕ *www.tfl.gov.uk.*

## ■ RIVER BUS

One legacy of the 2012 Olympics was a new push to develop river travel as part of London's overall public transportation system. The service, operated by Thames

Clippers, now stops at 10 piers between London Eye/Waterloo and Greenwich, with peak-time extensions to Putney in the west and Woolwich Arsenal in the east. The Waterloo–Woolwich commuter service runs 6:30 am–11 pm on weekdays, 9:30 am–midnight on weekends (peak-time frequency: every 20 minutes). Tickets are £7.50, with a one-third discount for Travelcard holders and a 15% discount for Oyster card holders. When there are events at the O2 (North Greenwich Arena), a half-hourly express service runs to and from Waterloo starting three hours before the event. Thames Clippers also operate the special Tate to Tate Boat, a 15-minute trip between Tate Modern and Tate Britain that costs £7.50. Boats run every 40 minutes, usually 10–4:30 on weekdays and 9–7 on weekends. A River Roamer ticket (£17.35 per day) offers unlimited river travel after 9 am.

**Contacts Thames Clippers.**
⊕ *www.thamesclippers.com.*

# ▌TAXI

Universally known as "black cabs" (even though many of them now come in other colors), the traditional big black London taxicabs are as much a part of the city's streetscape as red double-decker buses, and for good reason: the unique, spacious taxis easily hold five people, plus luggage. To earn a taxi license, drivers must undergo intensive training on the history and geography of London. The course, and all that the drivers have learned in it, is known simply as "the Knowledge." There's almost nothing your taxi driver won't know about the city. Partly because of lobbying efforts by the black cab industry, companies such as Uber have yet to make significant inroads into the London market, although the battle is ongoing.

Hotels and main tourist areas have cabstands (just take the first in line), but you can also flag one down from the roadside. If the orange "For Hire" sign on the top is lighted, the taxi is available. Cab drivers sometimes cruise at night with their signs unlighted so that they can choose their passengers and avoid those they think might cause trouble. If you see an unlighted, passengerless cab, hail it: you might be lucky.

Fares start at £2.40 and charge by the minute—a journey of a mile (which might take 6–13 minutes) will cost £5.60–£8.80 (the fare goes up 10 pm–6 am—a system designed to persuade more taxi drivers to work at night). A surcharge of £2 is applied to a telephone booking. At Christmas and New Year, there is an additional surcharge of £4. You may, but do not have to, tip taxi drivers 10% of the tab. Usually passengers round up to the nearest pound.

Minicabs, which operate out of small, curbside offices throughout the city, are generally cheaper than black cabs, but are less reliable and less trustworthy. These are usually unmarked passenger cars, and their drivers are often not native Londoners, and do not have to take or pass "the Knowledge" test. Still, Londoners use them in droves because they are plentiful and cheap. If you choose to use them, do not ever take an unlicensed cab: anyone who curb-crawls looking for customers is likely to be unlicensed. Unlicensed cabs have been associated with many crimes and can be dangerous. All cab companies with proper dispatch offices are likely to be licensed. Look for a small purple version of the Underground logo on the front or rear window with "private hire" written across it.

There are plenty of trustworthy and licensed minicab firms. For London-wide service try Lady's and Gent's Mini Cabs, or Addison Lee, which uses comfortable minivans but requires that you know the full postal code for both your pickup location and your destination. When using a minicab, always ask the price in advance when you phone for the car, then verify with the driver before the journey begins.

**Black Cabs Dial-a-Cab.** ☏ *020/7253–5000 for cash bookings, 020/7426–3420 for credit/ debit card bookings* ⊕ *www.dialacab.co.uk.*
**Radio Taxis.** ☏ *020/7272–0272* ⊕ *www.radiotaxis.co.uk.*

**Minicabs Addison Lee.** ☏ *020/7407–9000* ⊕ *www.addisonlee.com.* **Lady's and Gent's MiniCabs.** ☏ *020/8348 0000* ⊕ *www.ladysandgentsminicabs.com.*

# ❚ TRAIN TRAVEL

The National Rail Enquiries website is the clearinghouse for information on train times and fares as well as the main place for booking rail journeys around Britain—and the earlier the better. Tickets bought two to three weeks in advance can cost a quarter of the price of tickets bought on the day of travel. However, journeys within commuting distance of city centers are sold at unvarying set prices, and those can be purchased on the day you expect to make your journey without any financial penalty. You may also be able to purchase a PlusBus ticket, which adds unlimited bus travel at your destination. Note that, in busy city centers such as London, all travel costs more during morning rush hour. You can purchase tickets online, by phone, or at any train station in the United Kingdom. Check the website or call the National Rail Enquiries line to get details of the train company responsible for your journey and have them give you a breakdown of available ticket prices. Regardless of which train company is involved, many discount passes are available, such as the 16–25 Railcard (for which you must be under 26 and provide a passport-size photo), the Senior Railcard, and the Family & Friends Travelcard, which can be bought from most mainline stations. But if you intend to make several long-distance rail journeys, it can be a good idea to invest in a BritRail Pass, available to non-U.K. residents (which you must buy before you leave home).

You can get a BritRail Pass valid for London and the surrounding counties, for England, for Scotland, or for all of Britain. Discounts (usually 20%–25%) are offered if you're between 16 and 25, over 60, traveling as a family or a group, or accompanied by a British citizen. The pass includes discounts on the Heathrow Express and Eurostar. BritRail Passes come in two basic varieties. The Consecutive Pass allows travel on consecutive days, and the FlexiPass allows a number of travel days within a set period of time. The cost (in U.S. dollars) of a BritRail Consecutive Pass adult ticket for 8 days is $402 standard and $598 first-class; for 15 days, $598 and $884; and for 22 days, $748 and $1,123. The cost of a BritRail FlexiPass adult ticket for 4 days' travel within one month is $346 standard and $502 first-class; for 8 days' travel within one month, $495 and $738; and for 15 days' travel within one month, $745 and $1,103. Prices drop by about 20% for off-peak travel passes November–February.

Most long-distance trains have refreshment carriages, called buffet cars. Most trains these days also have "quiet cars" where the use of cell phones and music devices is banned. Smoking is forbidden in all railcars.

Generally speaking, rail travel in the United Kingdom is expensive and the ticketing system unnecessarily convoluted: for instance, a round-trip ticket to Bath from London can cost more than £150 per person at peak times, although for an off-peak ticket purchased far enough in advance, that price can drop to £20 or even less. It's best to avoid the frantic business commuter rush (before 9:30 am and 4:30 pm–7 pm). Credit cards are accepted for train fares paid in person, by phone, and online.

Delays are not uncommon, but they're rarely long. You almost always have to go to the station to find out if there's going to be one (because delays tend to happen at the last minute). Luckily, most stations have coffee shops, restaurants, and pubs where you can cool your heels while you wait for the train to get rolling. National Rail Enquiries provides an up-to-date state-of-the-railroads schedule.

Most of the time, first-class train travel in England isn't particularly first class. Some train companies don't offer at-seat service, so you still have to get up and go to the buffet car for food or drinks. First class is generally booked by business travelers on expense accounts because crying babies and noisy families are quite rare in first class and quite common in standard class.

Short of flying, taking the Eurostar train through the Channel Tunnel is the fastest way to reach the continent: it's 2 hours 15 minutes from London's St. Pancras International station to Paris's Gare du Nord. You can also go from St. Pancras to Midi station in Brussels in around two hours. If purchased in advance, round-trip tickets from London to Belgium or France cost from as little as £69, especially if you travel in the very early or very late hours of the day. If you want to bring your car over to France (ask the rental company if this is permitted), you can use the Eurotunnel Shuttle, which takes 35 minutes from Folkestone to Calais, plus at least 30 minutes to check in. The Belgian border is just a short drive northeast of Calais.

**Information BritRail Travel.** ☎ 866/938–7245 in U.S. and Canada ⊕ www.britrail.com. **Eurostar.** ☎ 03432/186–186, 1233/617–575 outside U.K. ⊕ www.eurostar.com. **National Rail Enquiries.** ☎ 0345/748–4950 ⊕ www.nationalrail.co.uk.

**Channel Tunnel Car Transport Eurotunnel.** ☎ 0844/335–3535 in U.K., +33/3–21–00–20–61 from outside Europe ⊕ www.eurotunnel.com.

# ▌ UNDERGROUND TRAVEL: THE TUBE

London's extensive Underground train system (Tube) has color-coded routes, clear signage, and many connections. Trains run out into the suburbs, and all stations are marked with the London Underground circular symbol. (Do not be confused by similar-looking signs reading "subway," which is British for "pedestrian underpass.") Trains are all one class; smoking isn't allowed on board or in the stations. There is also an Overground network serving the farther reaches of Inner London. These now accept Oyster cards.

Some lines have multiple branches (Central, District, Northern, Metropolitan, and Piccadilly), so be sure to note which branch is needed for your particular destination. Do this by noting the end destination on the lighted sign on the platform, which also tells you how long you'll have to wait until the train arrives. Compare that with the end destination of the branch you want. When the two match, that's your train.

London is divided into six concentric zones (ask at Underground ticket booths for a map and booklet, which give details of the ticket options), so be sure to buy a ticket for the correct zone or you may be liable for an on-the-spot fine of £80. Don't panic if you do forget to buy a ticket for the right zone: just tell a station attendant that you need to buy an "extension" to your ticket. Although you're meant to do that in advance, if you're an out-of-towner, they generally don't give you a hard time.

For one-way fares paid in cash, a flat £4.80 price per journey now applies across all central zones (1–2), whether you're traveling one stop or 12 stops. If you're planning several trips in one day, it's much cheaper to buy a visitor Oyster card. The off-peak Oyster-card fare for Zones 1–2, for example, is £2.30. One-day travelcards used to be good value for money but now, costing from £12 per card, they're a less attractive option. The more zones included in your travel, the more the Travelcard will cost. For example, Kew is Zone 4, and Heathrow is Zone 6. If you're going to be in town for several days, buy a seven-day Travelcard (£32.10 for Zones 1–2, £58.60 for Zones 1–6).

Children 11–15 can travel at discounted rates on the Tube and free on buses and trams with an Oyster photocard (order at least four weeks before date of travel), while children under 11 travel free on the Tube if accompanied by an adult or with an Oyster photocard and on buses at all times. Young people 16–18 and students over 18 get discounted Tube fares with an Oyster photocard.

Oyster cards are "smart cards" that can be charged with a cash value and then used for discounted travel throughout the city. A Visitor Oyster card, which you must buy before arriving in the United Kingdom, costs £3. Normal Oyster cards cost £5. Each time you take the Tube or bus, you place the blue card on the yellow readers at the entrance and the amount of your fare is deducted. Passengers using Oyster cards pay lower rates. Oyster-card Tube fares start at £1.70 and go up depending on the number of zones you're covering, the time of day, and whether you're traveling into Zone 1. You can open an Oyster account online or pick up an Oyster card at any London Underground station, and then prepay any amount you wish for your expected travel while in the city. Using an Oyster card, bus fares are £1.50 instead of £2.50. If you make numerous journeys in a single day, your Oyster card deductions will always be capped: at £6.40 for travel in Zones 1–2 and £7.50 for Zones 1–3.

However, although Oyster cards sound like the way of the future, they will soon be a thing of the past. Moves are underway to gradually phase out Oyster cards and to encourage passengers to move to a system of direct payments using their bank debit or credit cards instead. In practice, this will mean swiping a "contactless" bank card instead of your Oyster card at ticket barriers.

Now slated for summer 2016 (almost a year behind schedule), Tube trains will run for 24 hours a day on weekends on five major lines: Piccadilly, Victoria, Northern, Central, and Jubilee—that is,

if transportation chiefs can finally reach agreement with the powerful train drivers' union. On all other lines the usual timetable still applies, with trains running from just after 5 am Monday–Saturday, and with the last services leaving central London between midnight and 12:30 am. On Sunday, trains start an hour later and finish about an hour earlier. The frequency of trains depends on the route and the time of day, but normally you should not have to wait more than 10 minutes in central areas.

There are TfL Travel Information Centres at the following Tube stations: Euston and Liverpool Street (7:30 am–7 pm), Piccadilly Circus (9:30 am–4 pm), King's Cross (8 am–6 pm), Victoria (7:30 am–10 pm), Paddington (8 am–6 pm), Gatwick Airport, North Terminal (8 am–4 pm), and at Heathrow Airport (in Terminals 1–3) 7:30 am–10:30 pm.

Important note: As with the Metro system in Paris—and unlike the subway system in New York City—you need to have your ticket (Oyster card, Travelcard, or regular ticket) handy in order to exit the turnstiles of the Tube system, not just to enter them.

**Information Transport for London.**
☎ *0343/222-1234* ⊕ *www.tfl.gov.uk.*

# ESSENTIALS

## ▌BUSINESS SERVICES AND FACILITIES

There are several Color Company outlets and Mail Boxes Etc. locations in London to handle your photocopying, next-day mail, and packaging needs. Check their websites for more locations.

**Contacts The Color Company** (*FedEx Kinko's*). ✉ *1 Curzon St., Mayfair* ☎ *0800/939–493* ⊕ *www.color.co.uk* Ⓜ *Green Park.* **Mail Boxes Etc.** ✉ *19–21 Crawford St., Marylebone* ☎ *020/7224–2666* ⊕ *www.mailboxes-etc.co.uk* Ⓜ *Marylebone.*

## ▌COMMUNICATIONS

### INTERNET

If you're traveling with a laptop, carry a spare battery and adapter: new batteries and replacement adapters are expensive. If you do need to replace them, head to Tottenham Court Road (W1), which is lined with computer specialists. For Apple computers, Micro Anvika is a good chain for parts and batteries, and the Apple Stores on Regent Street off Oxford Street and in the Covent Garden Piazza do repairs. John Lewis department store and Selfridges, on Oxford Street (W1), also carry a limited range of computer supplies.

In London, free Wi-Fi is increasingly available in hotels, pubs, coffee shops—even certain branches of McDonald's—and broadband coverage is widespread; generally speaking, the pricier the hotel, the more likely you are to find Wi-Fi there, though it is not usually included in rates.

**Contacts My Hot Spots.** ⊕ *www.myhotspots.co.uk.*

### PHONES

The good news is that you can now make a direct-dial telephone call from virtually any point on Earth. The bad news? You can't always do so cheaply. Calling from a hotel is almost always the most expensive option; hotels usually add huge surcharges to all calls, particularly international ones. Calling cards usually keep costs to a minimum, but only if you purchase them locally. And then there are cell phones, which are also likely to be cheaper than calling from your hotel.

The minimum charge from a public phone is upwards of 60p for a two-minute call. To make cheap calls it's a good idea to pick up an international phone card, available from newsstands, which can be used from residential, hotel, and public pay phones. With these, you can call the United States for as little as 5p per minute.

To dial from the United States or Canada, first dial 011, then Great Britain's country code, 44. Continue with the local area code, dropping the initial "0." The code for London is 020 (so from abroad you'd dial 20), followed by a 7 for numbers in central London, or an 8 for numbers in the Greater London area. Freephone (toll-free) numbers start with 0800 or 0808; low-cost national information numbers start with 0345, 0343, or 0844.

A word of warning: 0900 numbers are *not* toll-free numbers; in fact, numbers beginning with this prefix are "premium rate" numbers, and it costs extra to call them. The amount varies and is usually relatively small when dialed from within the country but can be excessive when dialed from outside the United Kingdom.

### CALLING WITHIN BRITAIN

There are three types of phones: those that accept (1) only coins, (2) only British Telecom (BT) phone cards, or (3) BT phone cards and credit cards, although with the advent of cells, it's increasingly difficult to find any type of public phone, especially in London.

The coin-operated phones are of the push-button variety; the workings of coin-operated telephones vary, but there are usually instructions on each unit. Most take 10p, 20p, 50p, £1, and £2 coins. Insert the coins *before* dialing (the minimum charge is 60p). If you hear a repeated single tone after dialing, the line is busy; a continual tone means the number is unobtainable (or that you have dialed the wrong—or no—prefix). The indicator panel shows you how much money is left; add more whenever you like. If there is no answer, replace the receiver and your money will be returned.

There are several different directory-assistance providers. For information anywhere in Britain, try dialing 118–888 (59p per call, then £1.29 per minute); you'll need to know the town and the street (or at least the neighborhood) of the person or organization for which you're requesting information. For the operator, dial 100.

You don't have to dial London's central area code (020) if you are calling inside London itself—just the eight-digit telephone number. However, you do need to use it if you're dialing a 0207 (Inner London) number from a 0208 (Outer London) number, and vice versa.

For long-distance calls within Britain, dial the area code (which begins with 01), followed by the number. The area-code prefix is used only when you are dialing from outside the destination. In provincial areas, the dialing codes for nearby towns are often posted in the booth.

### CALLING OUTSIDE BRITAIN
For assistance with international calls, dial 155.

To make an international call from London, dial 00, followed by the country code and the local number.

The United States country code is 1.

**Access Codes AT&T Direct.** ☎ *0800/890–011 in U.K.,. MCI.* ☎ *0800/279–5088 in U.K., 800/888-8000 for U.S. and other areas.* **Sprint International Access.** ☎ *0808/234–6616 in U.K.*

### CALLING CARDS
Public card phones operate either with cash or with special cards that you can buy from post offices or newsstands.

Ideal for longer calls, they are composed of units of 10p, and come in values of £5, £10, and more. To use a card phone, lift the receiver, insert your card, and dial the number. An indicator panel shows the number of units used. At the end of your call, the card will be returned. Where credit cards are taken, slide the card through, as indicated.

### CELL PHONES
If you have a multiband phone (Britain uses different frequencies from those used in the United States) and your service provider uses the world-standard GSM network (as do T-Mobile, AT&T, and Verizon), you can probably use your phone abroad. Roaming fees can be steep, however: 99¢ per minute is considered reasonable. And overseas you normally pay the toll charges for incoming calls. It's almost always cheaper to send a text message than to make a call, since text messages have a very low set fee (often less than 5¢).

If you just want to make local calls, consider buying a new SIM card (note that your provider may have to unlock your phone for you to use a different SIM card) and a prepaid service plan in London. You'll then have a local number and can make local calls at local rates. If your trip is extensive, you could also simply buy a new cell phone in your destination, as the initial cost will be offset over time.

■ TIP→ If you travel internationally frequently, save one of your old cell phones or buy a cheap one online; ask your cell phone company to unlock it for you, and take it with you as a travel phone, buying a new SIM card with pay-as-you-go service in each destination.

Any cell phone can be used in Britain if it's tri-band/GSM. Travelers should ask their cell phone company if their phone is tri-band and what network it uses, and make sure it is activated for international calling before leaving their home country.

You can rent a cell phone from most car-rental agencies in London. Some upscale hotels now provide loaner cell phones to their guests. Beware, however, of the per-minute rates charged, as these can be shockingly high.

**Contacts Cellular Abroad.** ☎ *800/287–5072 in U.S., 310/862–7100 international, 800/3623–3333 in U.K.* ⊕ *www.cellularabroad. com.* **Mobal.** ☎ *888/888–9162 in U.S., 01543/426–999 in U.K.* ⊕ *www.mobal.com.* **Planet Fone.** ☎ *888/988–4777* ⊕ *www. planetfone.com.*

# ▌ CUSTOMS AND DUTIES

You're always allowed to bring goods of a certain value back home without having to pay any duty or import tax. But there's a limit on the amount of tobacco and liquor you can bring back duty-free, and some countries have separate limits for perfumes; for exact figures, check with your customs department. The values of so-called "duty-free" goods are included in these amounts. When you shop abroad, save all your receipts, as customs inspectors may ask to see them as well as the items you purchased. If the total value of your goods is more than the duty-free limit, you'll have to pay a tax (most often a flat percentage) on the value of everything beyond that limit.

There are two levels of duty-free allowance for entering Britain: one for goods bought outside the European Union (EU) and the other for goods bought within the EU.

Of goods bought outside the EU you may import the following duty-free: 200 cigarettes or 100 cigarillos or 50 cigars or 250 grams of tobacco; 4 liters of still wine and 16 liters of beer and, in addition, either 1 liter of alcohol over 22% by volume (most spirits), or 2 liters of alcohol under 22% by volume (fortified or sparkling wine or liqueurs).

Of goods bought within the EU, you should not exceed the following (unless you can prove they are for personal use): 800 cigarettes, 400 cigarillos, 200 cigars, or 1 kilo of tobacco, plus 10 liters of spirits, 20 liters of fortified wine such as port or sherry, 90 liters of wine, or 110 liters of beer.

Pets (dogs and cats) can be brought into the United Kingdom from the United States without six months' quarantine, provided that the animal meets all the PETS (Pet Travel Scheme) requirements, including microchipping and vaccination. Other pets have to undergo a lengthy quarantine, and penalties for breaking this law are severe and strictly enforced.

Fresh meats, vegetables, plants, and dairy products may be imported from within the EU. Controlled drugs, switchblades (aka flick knives), obscene material, counterfeit or pirated goods, and self-defense sprays may not be brought into the United Kingdom; firearms (both real and imitation) and ammunition, as well as souvenirs made from endangered plants or animals, are barred except with relevant permits.

**Information HM Revenue and Customs.** ✉ *Glasgow* ☎ *0300/200–3700* ⊕ *www.hmrc.gov.uk.* **U.S. Customs and Border Protection.** ⊕ *www.cbp.gov.*

# ▌ ELECTRICITY

The electrical current in London is 220–240 volts (coming into line with the rest of Europe at 230 volts), 50 cycles alternating current (AC); wall outlets take three-pin plugs, and shaver sockets take two round, oversize prongs. For converters, adapters, and advice, stop in one of the many STA Travel shops around London or at Nomad Travel.

Consider making a small investment in a universal adapter, which has several types of plugs in one lightweight, compact unit. Most laptops and cell phone chargers are dual voltage (i.e., they operate equally well on 110 and 220 volts), and thus require only an adapter. These days the same is true of small appliances such as hair dryers. Always check labels and manufacturer instructions to be sure. Don't use 110-volt outlets marked "For Shavers Only" for high-wattage appliances such as hair dryers.

**Contacts Nomad Travel.** ⊠ *11 S. Moulton St., Mayfair* ☎ *0134/155–5061* ⊕ *www. nomadtravel.co.uk.* **Walkabout Travel Gear.** ⊕ *www.walkabouttravelgear.com.*

# ∎ EMERGENCIES

London is a relatively safe city, though crime does happen (more so than in New York City), especially in areas of built-up public project housing or in tourist meccas. If you need to report a theft or an attack, head to the nearest police station (listed in the Yellow Pages or the local directory) or dial 999 for police, fire, or ambulance (be prepared to give the telephone number you're calling from). National Health Service hospitals give free round-the-clock treatment in Accident and Emergency sections, where waits can be up to four hours, depending on the severity of your ailment or injury. If you are admitted to hospital for treatment, or referred to a hospital by a General Practitioner, as a non-EU foreign visitor you will be expected to pay for any treatment you receive before you leave the country. Prescriptions are valid only if made out by doctors registered in the United Kingdom. All branches of Boots are dispensing pharmacies.

**Doctors and Dentists Dental Emergency Care Service.** ☎ *020/8748–9365* ⊕ *www.24hour-emergencydentist.co.uk.* **Medical Express Clinic.** ⊠ *117A Harley St., Marylebone* ☎ *020/7499–1991,* ⊕ *www. medicalexpressclinic.co.uk* Ⓜ *Regent's Park.* **UCL Eastman Dental Hospital.** ⊠ *256 Gray's Inn Rd., King's Cross* ☎ *020/3456–7899* ⊕ *www.uclh.nhs.uk* Ⓜ *Russell Sq., King's Cross St. Pancras.*

**Foreign Embassies U.S. Embassy.** ⊠ *24 Grosvenor Sq., Mayfair* ☎ *020/7499–9000* ⊕ *www.usembassy.org.uk* Ⓜ *Marble Arch, Bond St.*

**General Emergency Contacts Ambulance, fire, police.** ☎ *999 in U.K. only, 112 pan-European.*

**Hospitals and Clinics Charing Cross Hospital.** ⊠ *Fulham Palace Rd., Fulham* ☎ *020/3311–1234* ⊕ *www.imperial.nhs. uk/charingcross* Ⓜ *Hammersmith.* **Royal Free Hospital.** ⊠ *Pond St., Hampstead* ☎ *020/7794–0500* ⊕ *www.royalfree.nhs. uk* Ⓜ *Belsize Park.* **St. Thomas's Hospital.** ⊠ *Westminster Bridge Rd., Lambeth* ☎ *020/7188–7188* ⊕ *www.guysandstthomas. nhs.uk* Ⓜ *Westminster.* **University College Hospital.** ⊠ *235 Euston Rd., Bloomsbury* ☎ *020/3456–7890* ⊕ *www.uclh.nhs.uk* Ⓜ *Euston Sq., Warren St.*

**Hotlines Samaritans.** ☎ *116–123 Freephone* ⊕ *www.samaritans.org.*

**Pharmacies Boots.** ⊠ *44–46 Regent St., Piccadilly Circus* ☎ *020/7734–6126* ⊕ *www.boots.com* Ⓜ *Piccadilly Circus.*

# ∎ HOLIDAYS

Standard holidays are New Year's Day, Good Friday, Easter Monday, May Day (first Monday in May), spring and summer bank holidays (last Monday in May and August, respectively), Christmas, and Boxing Day (December 26). On Christmas Eve and New Year's Eve, some shops, restaurants, and businesses close early. Some museums and tourist attractions may close for at least a week around Christmas, or operate on restricted hours—call to verify.

# ∎ MAIL

Stamps can be bought from post offices (generally open weekdays 9–5:30, Saturday 9–noon), from stamp machines outside post offices, and from some newsagents and newsstands. Mailboxes are known as post or letter boxes and are painted bright red; large tubular ones are set on the edge of sidewalks, whereas smaller boxes are set into post-office walls. Allow seven days for a letter to reach the

United States. Check the Yellow Pages for a complete list of branches, though you cannot reach individual offices by phone.

Airmail letters up to 10 grams (0.35 ounce) to North America, Australia, and New Zealand cost £1. Letters under 9.4 inches by 6.4 inches within Britain are from 63p for first class, 54p for second class. Large letters (larger than 9.4 inches by 6.4 inches, smaller than 13.8 inches by 9.8 inches) cost from 95p first class, 74p second class within the United Kingdom, depending on weight. Airmail is assessed by weight alone.

If you're uncertain where you'll be staying, you can have mail sent to you at the London Main Post Office, c/o poste restante. The post office will hold international mail for one month.

**Contact Post Office.** ☎ *0345/611–2970* ⊕ *www.postoffice.co.uk.*

**Main Branch London Main Post Office.** ✉ *24–28 William IV St., Charing Cross* ⊕ *www.postoffice.co.uk* Ⓜ *Charing Cross.*

## SHIPPING PACKAGES

Most department stores and retail outlets can ship your goods home. You should check your insurance for coverage of possible damage. Private delivery companies such as DHL, FedEx, and Parcelforce offer two-day delivery service to the United States, but you'll pay a considerable amount for the privilege.

**Express Services DHL.** ☎ *0844/248–0844* ⊕ *www.dhl.com.* **FedEx.** ☎ *0345/600–0068* ⊕ *www.fedex.com.* **Parcelforce.** ☎ *0344/800–4466* ⊕ *www.parcelforce.com.*

# ▋ MONEY

London is one of the most expensive cities in the world: getting around is expensive, eating can be pricey, travel costs are steep, and hotels aren't cheap. However, for every yin there's a yang, and travelers do get a break in other places: most museums are free, for example, and Oyster cards help cut the price of travel.

## ATMS AND BANKS

Your own bank will probably charge a fee for using ATMs abroad; the foreign bank you use may also charge a fee. Nevertheless, you'll usually get a better rate of exchange at an ATM than you will at a currency-exchange office or even when changing money in a bank. And extracting funds as you need them is a safer option than carrying around a large amount of cash.

■TIP→ PIN numbers with more than four digits are not recognized at ATMs in many countries. If yours has five or more, remember to change it before you leave.

Credit cards or debit cards (also known as check cards) will get you cash advances at ATMs, which are widely available in London. To make sure that your Cirrus or Plus card (to cite just two of the leading names) works in European ATMs, have your bank reset it to use a four-digit PIN number before your departure.

## CREDIT CARDS

■TIP→ Remember to inform your credit-card company before you travel, especially if you're going abroad and don't travel internationally very often. Otherwise, the credit-card company might put a hold on your card owing to unusual activity—not a good thing halfway through your trip. Record all your credit-card numbers—as well as the phone numbers to call if your cards are lost or stolen—in a safe place, so you're prepared should something go wrong. MasterCard and Visa have general numbers you can call (collect if you're abroad) if your card is lost, but you're better off calling the number of your issuing bank, because MasterCard and Visa usually just transfer you to your bank; your bank's number is usually printed on your card.

If you plan to use your credit card for cash advances, you'll need to apply for a PIN at least two weeks before your trip. Although it's usually cheaper (and safer) to use a credit card abroad for large purchases (so you can cancel payments or be reimbursed if there's a problem), note that some credit-card companies *and* the banks that issue them add substantial percentages to all foreign transactions, whether they're in a foreign currency or not. Check on these fees before leaving home, so there won't be any surprises when you get the bill.

■ TIP→ Before you charge something, ask the merchant whether he or she plans to do a dynamic currency conversion (DCC). In such a transaction the credit-card processor (the shop, restaurant or hotel, not Visa or MasterCard) converts the currency and charges you in dollars. In most cases, you'll pay the merchant a 3% fee for this service in addition to any credit-card company and issuing-bank foreign-transaction surcharges.

Dynamic currency conversion programs are becoming increasingly widespread. Merchants who participate in them are supposed to ask whether you want to be charged in dollars or the local currency, but they don't always do so. And even if they do offer you a choice, they may well avoid mentioning the additional surcharges. The good news is that you *do* have a choice. And if this practice really gets your goat, you can avoid it entirely thanks to American Express; with its cards, DCC simply isn't an option.

Credit cards are accepted virtually everywhere in London.

**Reporting Lost Cards American Express.** ☎ *800/528–4800 in U.S., 0800/917–8047 in U.K.* ⊕ *www.americanexpress.com.* **Diners Club.** ☎ *800/234–6377 in U.S., 514/877–1577 collect from abroad* ⊕ *www.dinersclub. com.* **MasterCard.** ☎ *800/627–8372 in U.S., 0800/964–767 in U.K.* ⊕ *www.mastercard.com.* **Visa.** ☎ *800/847–2911 in U.S., 020/7795–5777 in U.K.* ⊕ *www.visa.com.*

### CURRENCY AND EXCHANGE

The unit of currency in Great Britain is the pound sterling (£), divided into 100 pence (p). Bills (called notes) come in denominations of £50, £20, £10, and £5; coins are for £2, £1 (100p), 50p, 20p, 10p, 5p, 2p, and 1p. At this writing, the exchange rate was about Australian $2.14, Canadian $2.03, New Zealand $2.33, U.S. $1.52, and €1.41 to the pound (also known as quid).

Even if a currency-exchange booth has a sign promising no commission, rest assured that there's some kind of huge, hidden fee. (Oh . . . that's right. The sign didn't say no *fee*.) And as for rates, you're almost always better off getting foreign currency at an ATM or exchanging money at a bank or post office.

■ TIP→ Banks never have every foreign currency on hand, and it may take as long as a week to order. If you're planning to exchange funds before leaving home, don't wait until the last minute.

## ▌PACKING

London's weather is unpredictable. It can be cool, damp, and overcast, even in summer, but the odd summer day can be uncomfortably hot, as not many public venues, theaters, or the Tube are air-conditioned. In general, you'll need a heavy coat for winter and light clothes for summer, along with a lightweight coat or jacket. Always pack a small umbrella that you can easily carry around with you. Pack as you would for any American city: jackets and ties for expensive restaurants and nightspots, casual clothes elsewhere. Jeans are popular in London and are perfectly acceptable for sightseeing and informal dining. Sports jackets are popular with men. In five-star hotels, men can expect to be asked to wear a jacket and tie in the restaurant and bar, and women might feel out of place unless they're in smart clothes. Otherwise, for women, ordinary dress is acceptable just about everywhere.

## ▌PASSPORTS AND VISAS

U.S. citizens need only a valid passport to enter Great Britain for stays of up to six months. If you're within six months of your passport's expiration date, renew it before you leave—nearly extinct passports are not strictly banned, but they make immigration officials anxious, and may cause you problems.

## PASSPORTS

It's always surprising how few Americans have passports—only 35% at this writing. This number is expected to grow now that it is impossible to reenter the United States from trips to neighboring Canada or Mexico without one. Remember this: a passport verifies both your identity and nationality—a great reason to have one.

U.S. passports are valid for 10 years. You must apply in person if you're getting a passport for the first time; if your previous passport was lost, stolen, or damaged; or if your previous passport has expired and was issued more than 15 years ago or when you were under 16. All children under 18 must appear in person to apply for or renew a passport. Both parents must accompany any child under 14 (or send a notarized statement with their permission) and provide proof of their relationship to the child.

There are 24 regional passport offices, as well as 7,000 passport acceptance facilities in post offices, public libraries, and other governmental offices. If you're renewing a passport, you can do so by mail. Forms are available at passport acceptance facilities and online.

The cost to apply for a new passport is $140 for adults, $95 for children under 16; renewals are $140. There is an additional "execution fee" of $25. Allow six weeks for processing, both for first-time passports and renewals. For an expediting fee of $60 you can reduce this time to about two weeks. If your trip is less than two weeks away, you can get a passport even more rapidly by going to a passport office with the necessary documentation. Private expediters can get things done in as little as 48 hours, but charge hefty fees for their services.

■TIP➔ Before your trip, make two copies of your passport's data page (one for someone at home and another for you to carry separately). Or scan the page and email it to someone at home and/or yourself.

## VISAS

A visa is essentially formal permission to enter a country. Visas allow countries to keep track of you and other visitors—and generate revenue (from application fees). You *always* need a visa to enter a foreign country; however, many countries routinely issue tourist visas on arrival, particularly to U.S. citizens. When your passport is stamped or scanned in the immigration line, you're actually being issued a visa. Sometimes you have to stand in a separate line and pay a small fee to get your stamp before going through immigration, but you can still do this at the airport on arrival. Getting a visa isn't always that easy. Some countries require that you arrange for one in advance of your trip. There's usually—but not always—a fee involved, and said fee may be nominal ($10 or less) or substantial ($100 or more).

If you must apply for a visa in advance, you can usually do it in person or by mail. When you apply by mail, you send your passport to a designated consulate, where your passport will be examined and the visa issued. Expediters—usually the same ones who handle expedited passport applications—can do all the work of obtaining your visa for you; however, there's always an additional cost (often more than $50 per visa).

Most visas limit you to a single trip—basically during the actual dates of your planned vacation. Other visas allow you to visit as many times as you wish for a specific period of time. Remember that requirements change, sometimes at the drop of a hat, and the burden is on you to make sure that you have the appropriate visas. Otherwise, you'll be turned away at the airport or, worse, deported after you arrive in the country. No company or travel insurer gives refunds if your travel plans are disrupted because you didn't have the correct visa.

**U.S. Passport Information**
**U.S. Department of State.** ☎ 877/487-2778 ⊕ travel.state.gov/passport.

**U.S. Passport and Visa Expediters A. Briggs Passport & Visa Expeditors.** ☎ 800/806-0581 ⊕ www.abriggs.com. **American Passport Express.** ☎ 800/455-5166 ⊕ www.americanpassport.com. **Travel Document Systems.** ☎ 800/874-5100, 202/638-3800 ⊕ www.traveldocs.com. **Travel the World Visas.** ☎ 866/886-8472 ⊕ www.world-visa.com.

## ▮ SAFETY

The rules for safety in London are the same as in New York City or any big metropolis. If you're carrying a considerable amount of cash and do not have a safe in your hotel room, it's a good idea to keep it in something like a money belt, but don't get cash out of it in public. Keep a small amount of cash for immediate purchases in your pocket or purse.

Beyond that, use common sense. In central London, nobody will raise an eyebrow at tourists studying maps on street corners, and don't hesitate to ask for directions. However, outside of the center, exercise general caution about the neighborhoods you walk in: if they don't look safe, take a cab. After midnight, outside of the center, take cabs rather than wait for a night bus. Although London has plenty of so-called minicabs—normal cars driven by self-employed drivers in a cab service—don't ever get into an unmarked car that pulls up offering you "cab service." Take a licensed minicab only from a cab office, or, preferably, a normal London "black cab," which you flag down on the street.

If you carry a purse, keep a firm grip on it (or even disguise it in a local shopping bag). Store only enough money in the purse to cover casual spending. Distribute the rest of your cash and any valuables among deep front pockets, inside jacket or vest pockets, and a concealed money pouch. Never leave your bag beside your chair or hanging from the back of your chair. Be careful with backpacks, as pickpockets can unzip them on the Tube, or even as you're traveling up an escalator.

**Advisories U.S. Department of State.** ⊕ travel.state.gov.

## ▮ TAXES

Departure taxes are divided into two bands. The Band A tax on a per-person Economy fare is £13; Band B, for everything else, is £71. The fee is subject to government tax increases.

The British sales tax (V.A.T., value-added tax) is 20%. The tax is almost always included in quoted prices in shops, hotels, and restaurants.

Most travelers can get a V.A.T. refund by either the Retail Export or the more cumbersome Direct Export method. Many, but not all, large stores provide these services, but only if you request them; they will handle the paperwork. For the Retail Export method, you must ask the store for Form VAT 407 when making a purchase (you must have identification—passports are best). Some retailers will refund the amount on the spot, but others will use a refund company or the refund booth at the point when you leave the country. For the latter, have the form stamped like any customs form by U.K. customs officials when you leave the country, or, if you're visiting several European Union countries, when you leave the EU. After you're through passport control, take the form to a refund-service counter for an on-the-spot refund (which is usually the quickest and easiest option), or mail it to the address on the form (or the envelope with it) after you arrive home. You receive the total refund stated on the form (the retailer or refund company may deduct a handling fee), but the processing time can be long, especially if you request a credit-card adjustment. This may be preferable to a check, however, as U.S. banks will charge a fee for depositing a check in a foreign currency.

With the Direct Export method, the goods are shipped directly to your home. You must have a Form VAT 407 certified by customs, the police, or a notary public when you get home and then send it back to the store, which will refund your money. For inquiries, contact Her Majesty's Revenue & Customs office.

Global Blue (formerly, Global Refund) is a worldwide service with 270,000 affiliated stores and more than 200 Refund Offices. Its refund form, called a Tax Free Check, is the most common across the European continent. The service issues refunds in the form of cash, check, or credit-card adjustment.

**V.A.T. Refunds Global Blue.** ☎ 866/706–6090 in U.S., 800/32–111–111 in U.K. ⊕ www.globalblue.com. **Her Majesty's Revenue & Customs.** ☎ 0300/200–3700 within U.K., 292/050–1261 from outside U.K. ⊕ www.hmrc.gov.uk/vat.

# ∎ TIME

London is five hours ahead of New York City at most times of the year. In other words, when it's 3 pm in New York (or noon in Los Angeles), it's 8 pm in London. Note that Great Britain and most European countries also move their clocks ahead for the one-hour differential when daylight saving time goes into effect (although they make the changeover several weeks after the United States).

**Time Zones Timeanddate.com.** ⊕ www.timeanddate.com/worldclock.

# ∎ TIPPING

Tipping is done in Britain just as in the United States, but at a lower level. Tipping less than you would back home in restaurants—and not tipping at all in pubs—is not only accepted, but standard. Do not tip movie or theater ushers,

elevator operators, or bar staff in pubs—although you can always offer to buy the latter a drink.

| TIPPING GUIDELINES FOR LONDON | |
|---|---|
| Bartender | In cocktail bars, if you see a tip plate, it's fine to leave £1–£2. For table service, tip 10% of the cost of the bill. However, the gratuity is often included in the check at more expensive bars. |
| Bellhop | £1 per bag, depending on the level of the hotel. |
| Hotel Concierge | £5 or more, if a service is performed for you. |
| Hotel Doorman | £1 for hailing taxis or for carrying bags to check-in desk. |
| Hotel Maid | It's extremely rare for hotel maids to be tipped; £1–£2 would be generous. |
| Porter at Airport or Train Station | £1 per bag |
| Skycap at Airport | £1–£3 per bag |
| Taxi Driver | Optional 10%–12%, perhaps a little more for a short ride. |
| Tour Guide | Tipping optional; £1–£2 would be generous. |
| Waiter | 10%–15%, with 15% being the norm at high-end restaurants; nothing additional if a service charge is added to the bill. |
| Other | Restroom attendants in expensive restaurants expect some small change (50p or so). Tip coat-check personnel £1 unless there is a fee (then nothing). Hairdresser and barbers get 10%–15%. |

# ∎ TOURS

## BIKE TOURS

Whether you join the Santander Cycles hire scheme or just, per usual, get one from a rental shop, remember that London is still a busy metropolis: unless you're familiar with riding in London traffic, the best way to see it on two wheels is probably to contact one of the excellent cycle-tour companies.

**Santander Cycles.** ☎ *0343/222–6666 within U.K., 208/216–6666 from outside U.K.* ⊕ *www.tfl.gov.uk/modes/ cycling/santander-cycles.*

**Tour Operators Cycle Tours of London.** ☎ *07788/994430* ⊕ *www.biketoursoflondon. com.* **Fat Tire Bike Tours.** ☎ *07882/338779* ⊕ *www.fattirebiketours.com.* **London Bicycle Tour Company.** ☎ *020/7928–6838* ⊕ *www.londonbicycle.com.*

## BOAT TOURS
Year-round, but more frequently April–October, boats cruise the Thames, offering a different view of the London skyline. Most leave from Westminster Pier, Charing Cross Pier, and Tower Pier. Downstream routes go to the Tower of London, Greenwich, and the Thames Barrier via Canary Wharf. Upstream destinations include Kew, Richmond, and Hampton Court (mainly in summer). Most of the launches seat between 100 and 250 passengers, have a public-address system, and provide a running commentary on passing points of interest. Some include musical entertainment. Depending on the destination, river trips may last from one to four hours.

Details on all other operators are available as a PDF from Transport for London's River Services page ⊕ *www.tfl.gov.uk.*

**River Cruise Operators Bateaux London.** ☎ *020/7695–1800* ⊕ *www.bateauxlondon. com.* **London Duck Tours.** ☎ *020/7928–3132* ⊕ *www..londonducktours.co.uk.* **Thames Cruises.** ☎ *020/7928–9009* ⊕ *www. thamescruises.com.* **Thames River Boats.** ☎ *020/7930–2062* ⊕ *www.wpsa.co.uk.* **Thames River Services.** ☎ *020/7930–4097* ⊕ *www.thamesriverservices.co.uk.*

## BUS, COACH, AND TAXI TOURS
Guided sightseeing tours from the top of double-decker buses, which are open-top in summer, are a good introduction to the city, as they cover all the main central sights. A number of companies run daily bus tours that depart (usually 8:30–9 am) from central points. In hop-on, hop-off fashion, you may board or alight at any of the numerous stops to view the sights, and reboard on the next bus. Most companies offer this hop-on, hop-off feature but others, such as Best Value, remain guided tours in traditional coach buses. Tickets can be bought from the driver and are good all day. Prices vary according to the type of tour. For that more personal touch, try out a guided tour in a taxi.

**Bus Tour Operators Best Value Tours.** ☎ *0870/803–1316* ⊕ *www.bestvaluetours. co.uk.* **Big Bus Tours.** ☎ *020/7808–6753* ⊕ *www.bigbustours.com.* **Black Taxi Tour of London.** ☎ *020/7935–9363* ⊕ *www. blacktaxitours.co.uk.* **Golden Tours.** ☎ *020/7630–2028 in U.K., 800/509–2507 in U.S.* ⊕ *www.goldentours.co.uk.* **Original London Sightseeing Tour.** ☎ *020/8877–1722* ⊕ *www.theoriginaltour.com.* **Premium Tours.** ☎ *020/7713–1311, 800/250–5775 in U.S.* ⊕ *www.premiumtours.co.uk.*

## CANAL TOURS
The tranquil side of London can be found on narrow boats that cruise the city's two canals, the Grand Union and Regent's Canal; most vessels operate on the latter, which runs between Little Venice in the west (nearest Tube: Warwick Avenue on the Bakerloo line) and Camden Lock (about 200 yards north of Camden Town Tube station). Fares start at about £9 for 1½-hour round-trip cruises.

**Canal Tour Operators Canal Cruises.** ☎ *020/8440–8962* ⊕ *www.londoncanalcruises. com.* **Jason's Trip.** ⊕ *www.jasons.co.uk.* **London Waterbus Company.** ☎ *020/7482–2550* ⊕ *www.londonwaterbus.co.uk.*

## EXCURSIONS
Evan Evans, Green Line, and National Express all offer day excursions by bus to places within easy reach of London, such as Hampton Court, Oxford, Stratford-upon-Avon, and Bath.

**Tour Operators Evan Evans.**
☎ *020/7950–1777, 866/382–6868 in U.S.*
⊕ *www.evanevanstours.co.uk.*

## WALKING TOURS

One of the best ways to get to know London is on foot, and there are many guided and themed walking tours available. For more options, pick up a copy of *Time Out* magazine and check the weekly listings for upcoming one-off tours.

**Walking Tour Operators**
**Blood and Tears Walk.** ☎ *07905/746–733*
⊕ *www.shockinglondon.com.* **Blue Badge.**
☎ *020/7403–1115* ⊕ *www.britainsbestguides.*
*org.* **Context London.** ☎ *020/3514–1780,*
*800/691–6036 in U.S.* ⊕ *www.contexttravel.*
*com/city/london.* **London Walks.** ☎ *020/7624–*
*3978* ⊕ *www.walks.com.* **Richard Jones's**
**London Walking Tours.** ☎ *020/8530–8443*
⊕ *www.londondiscoverytours.co.uk.* **Shake-**
**speare City Walk.** ☎ *07905/746733*
⊕ *www.shakespeareguide.com.*

# ▌ VISITOR INFORMATION

You can get good information at the Travel Information Centre near the Eurostar arrivals area at St. Pancras International train station and at Victoria and Liverpool Street stations. These are helpful if you're looking for brochures for London sights, or if something's gone horribly wrong with your hotel reservation—if, for example, you don't have one—as they have a useful reservations service. The Victoria station center, opposite Platform 8, is open Monday–Saturday 7:30 am–8 pm, Sunday 8:30 am–7 pm; the St. Pancras center daily 8 am–6 pm; Liverpool Street weekdays 7:30 am–7 pm, weekends 8 am–6 pm, Euston station (opposite Platform 10) daily 8 am–7 pm, Paddington station (opposite Platform 1) daily 8 am–6 pm. The one at Piccadilly Circus Tube station is open daily 9:30 am–4 pm. The Travel Information Centre at Heathrow is open daily 7:30 am–8:30 pm, and at Gatwick Airport (North Terminal) daily 8 am–4 pm. There are also London Tourist Information Centres in Greenwich and some other Outer London locations.

**Official Websites:** ⊕ *www.visitbritain.com*
⊕ *www.visitlondon.com*

**Other Websites:** ⊕ *www.londontown.com*
⊕ *www.standard.co.uk* ⊕ *www.bbc.co.uk*

**Entertainment Information:**
⊕ *www.timeout.com/london*
⊕ *www.officiallondontehatre.co.uk*

# INDEX

## PHOTO CREDITS

# NOTES

# NOTES

# NOTES

# NOTES

# NOTES

# NOTES

# ABOUT OUR WRITERS

**Jo Caird** is a travel and arts journalist who writes on theater, visual arts, film, literature, and food and drink, as well as cycling and scuba diving. Her travel stories, city guides, and arts features appear regularly in the *Guardian,* the *Independent,* the *Sunday Telegraph,* the *Economist, Condé Nast Traveler,* and *World of Interiors.* Born and raised in London, Caird has an endless fascination for the city, and is delighted to write about it whenever the opportunity arises. For this edition, she updated the Pubs and Nightlife; Performing Arts; East London; and Soho and Covent Garden chapters. Follow her on Twitter (⊕ *www.twitter.com/jocaird*) or visit her website (⊕ *www.jocaird.com*).

Writer and editor **Kate Hughes** studied classical literature in Liverpool and also has a master's degree in garden history, so she feels qualified to pass judgment on matters both urban and rural. She is responsible for Stratford-upon-Avon and various Thames Valley side trips in *Fodor's London,* and also updates parts of *Fodor's England.*

**Jack Jewers** updated the Where to Stay chapter, along with the neighborhood chapters on Greenwich; The Thames Upstream; Westminster, St. James's and Royal London; and The City. A resident of London and its penumbra since public transport was cheap, Jack knows slightly more than is healthy about the city's secret underground world of abandoned train lines, mysterious tunnels, and other things hidden below the streets. When he isn't writing guidebooks, he makes independent films.

**James O'Neill** loves London and—as his work updating our chapters on Mayfair and Marylebone; Bloomsbury and Holborn; Notting Hill and Bayswater; and Travel Smart for this edition proves—loves rediscovering it,

too. Although originally from Ireland, he's lived in London for almost 20 years—and still loves it just as much now as he did back then. He has written extensively for TV (BBC and Channel 4), the stage, and the page. He is currently finishing his debut novel, which is set in—where else?—London.

**Ellin Stein** has written for publications on both sides of the Atlantic, including the *New York Times,* the *Times* (London), the *Guardian,* the *Telegraph,* and *InStyle,* for whom she was European correspondent. Her book *That's Not Funny, That's Sick: The National Lampoon and the Comedy Insurgents Who Captured the Mainstream,* was published by W. W. Norton & Co. in 2013. Originally from Manhattan, she has lived in London for two decades. For this edition, she updated our chapters on Kensington, Chelsea, Knightsbridge, and Belgravia; South of the Thames; Regent's Park and Hampstead; and Shopping.

London restaurant maven **Alex Wijeratna** is permanently blown away by the capital's rocket-fueled restaurant scene. From locavore heroes and street-food gourmet democrats, to global gastro-panjandrums, Alex tickles out the best joints that restaurant-mad London has to offer. With his first full Fodor's guidebook out last year (*Around London with Kids*), Alex has written for the *Times* (London), the *Guardian,* the *Independent,* the *Daily Mail,* the *Daily Express,* and the *Face.* For this edition, he updated the Where to Eat and Experience London chapters.